EUROPE'S
BUSINESS
CITIES

The Economist
BUSINESS
TRAVELLER'S
GUIDES

EUROPE'S
BUSINESS
CITIES

The
Economist
Books

PRENTICE HALL

NEW YORK

Guidebook information is notoriously subject to being outdated by changes to telephone numbers and opening hours, and by fluctuating hotel and restaurant standards. While every care has been taken in the preparation of this guide, the publishers cannot accept any liability for any consequence arising from the use of information contained herein.
Where opinion is expressed it is that of the author and does not necessarily coincide with the editorial views of The Economist Newspaper.
The publishers welcome corrections and suggestions from business travellers; please write to The Editor, *The Economist Guides*, Axe and Bottle Court, 70 Newcomen Street, London SE1 1YT, United Kingdom.

Series Editor Stephen Brough
Assistant Series Editor Brigid Avison
Editors Moira Johnston, Isla MacLean, Stephen Dobell
Designer Alistair Plumb
Editorial Assistants Karen Eves, Bettina Whilems
Design Assistants Alison Leggate, Jenny Sadler

Contributors Nic Allen, John Ardagh, Norman Bartlett, Susie Boulton, Christopher Catling, Nicholas Denton, Peter Graham, Chris Gill, Ray Granger, Vicky Hayward, Michael Leapman, Sheila Mackay, Angus McGeoch, Vivienne Menkes-Ivry, Nicholas Monson, Jeremy Round, Frances Roxburgh, Andrew Shaw, Gillian Thomas, Roger Thornham

This edition published in the United States and Canada in 1989 by Prentice Hall Trade Division
A division of Simon & Schuster Inc.
15 Columbus Circle
New York, New York 10023

Library of Congress Cataloging-in-Publication Data
The Economist business traveller's guides. Europe's business cities.
"The Economist publications."
ISBN 0-13-291972-9: $19.95
1. Europe—Description and travel—1971—Guide-books.
2. Business travel—Europe—Guide-books. 3. Europe—Commerce—Handbooks. manuals, etc.
I. Economist (London, England)
D909.E26 1989
914.04'558—dc20 89-16170CIP

Maps by Lovell Johns, Oxford and Oxford Illustrators, Oxford
Typeset by Tradespools Ltd, Frome, England
Printed in Italy by Graphicom

Contents

Symbols and abbreviations

Hotel and restaurant prices
Prices are denoted by symbols which correspond approximately to the following actual prices at the time of going to press.

Hotel prices are for a standard single room, including tax and service. *Restaurant prices* are for a typical meal, including half a bottle of wine, coffee and service.

AUSTRIA
Hotels

S	up to Sch1,100
S/	Sch1,100–1,800
S//	Sch1,800–2,700
S///	Sch2,700–3,400
S////	over Sch3,400

Restaurants

S	up to Sch400
S/	Sch400–600
S//	Sch600–850
S///	Sch850–1,200
S////	over Sch1,200

BELGIUM
Hotels

B	up to Bfr2,500
B/	Bfr2,500–4,000
B//	Bfr4,000–5,500
B///	Bfr5,500–7,000
B////	over Bfr7,000

Restaurants

B	up to Bfr500
B/	Bfr500–1,500
B//	Bfr1,500–2,500
B///	Bfr2,500–3,500
B////	over Bfr3,500

DENMARK
Hotels

K	up to Dkr800
K/	Dkr800–1,100
K//	Dkr1,100–1,400
K///	Dkr1,400–1,700
K////	over Dkr1,700

Restaurants

K	up to Dkr420
K/	Dkr420–500
K//	Dkr500–600
K///	Dkr600–700
K////	over Dkr700

FINLAND
Hotels

M	up to Fmk420
M/	Fmk420–500
M//	Fmk500–650
M///	Fmk650–820
M////	over Fmk820

Restaurants

M	up to Fmk250
M/	Fmk250–375
M//	Fmk375–450
M///	Fmk450–520
M////	over Fmk520

FRANCE
Hotels

F	up to F250
F/	F250–400
F//	F400–600
F///	F600–900
F////	F900–1,200
F/////	over F1,200

Restaurants

F	up to F180
F/	F180–230
F//	F230–300
F///	F300–400
F////	F400–500
F/////	over F500

GERMANY
Hotels

DM /	up to DM75
DM //	DM75–150
DM ///	DM150–200
DM ////	DM200–275
DM /////	over DM275

Restaurants

DM /	up to DM45
DM //	DM45–70
DM ///	DM70–90
DM ////	DM90–120
DM /////	over DM120

GREECE
Hotels

D	up to Dr9,500
D/	Dr9,500–14,000
D//	Dr14,000–19,000
D///	Dr19,000–23,000
D////	over Dr23,000

Restaurants

D	up to Dr2,750
D/	Dr2,750–3,750
D//	Dr3,750–4,750
D///	Dr4,750–5,750
D////	over Dr5,750

Credit card abbreviations

AE	American Express
DC	Diners Club
MC	Access/ MasterCard
V	Visa

IRELAND

Hotels

P⃞	up to I£60
P⃞/	I£60–75
P⃞//	I£75–90
P⃞///	I£90–110
P⃞////	over I£110

Restaurants

P⃞	up to I£18
P⃞/	I£18–25
P⃞//	I£25–35
P⃞///	I£35–45
P⃞////	over I£45

NORWAY

Hotels

K⃞	up to Nkr650
K⃞/	Nkr650–850
K⃞//	Nkr850–1,000
K⃞///	Nkr1,000–1,150
K⃞////	over Nkr1,150

Restaurants

K⃞	up to Nkr200
K⃞/	Nkr200–300
K⃞//	Nkr300–400
K⃞///	Nkr400–500
K⃞////	over Nkr500

SWEDEN

Hotels

K⃞	up to Skr900
K⃞/	Skr900–1,100
K⃞//	Skr1,100–1,300
K⃞///	Skr1,300–1,500
K⃞////	over Skr1,500

Restaurants

K⃞	up to Skr420
K⃞/	Skr420–500
K⃞//	Skr500–650
K⃞///	Skr650–820
K⃞////	over Skr820

ITALY

Hotels

L⃞	up to L90,000
L⃞/	L90,000–130,000
L⃞//	L130,000–170,000
L⃞///	L170,000–220,000
L⃞////	L220,000–300,000
L⃞/////	over L300,000

Restaurants

L⃞	up to L30,000
L⃞/	L30–50,000
L⃞//	L50–70,000
L⃞///	L70–90,000
L⃞////	L90–110,000
L⃞/////	over L110,000

PORTUGAL

Hotels

E⃞	up to Esc12,000
E⃞/	Esc12,000–15,000
E⃞//	Esc15,000–20,000
E⃞///	Esc20,000–25,000
E⃞////	over Esc25,000

Restaurants

E⃞	up to Esc4,500
E⃞/	Esc4,500–5,000
E⃞//	Esc5,000–5,500
E⃞///	Esc5,500–6,000
E⃞////	over Esc6,000

SWITZERLAND

Hotels

SF⃞	up to Swfr125
SF⃞/	Swfr125–200
SF⃞//	Swfr200–275
SF⃞///	Swfr275–350
SF⃞////	over Swfr350

Restaurants

SF⃞	up to Swfr88
SF⃞/	Swfr88–98
SF⃞//	Swfr98–108
SF⃞///	Swfr108–118
SF⃞////	over Swfr118

THE NETHERLANDS

Hotels

G⃞	up to G100
G⃞/	G100–200
G⃞//	G200–300
G⃞///	G300–400
G⃞////	over G400

Restaurants

G⃞	up to G90
G⃞/	G90–110
G⃞//	G110–130
G⃞///	G130–175
G⃞////	over G175

SPAIN

Hotels

P⃞	up to Pta9,000
P⃞/	Pta9,000–14,000
P⃞//	Pta14,000–19,000
P⃞///	Pta19,000–30,000
P⃞////	over Pta30,000

Restaurants

P⃞	up to Pta4,000
P⃞/	Pta4,000–5,000
P⃞//	Pta5,000–6,000
P⃞///	Pta6,000–7,500
P⃞////	over Pta7,500

UNITED KINGDOM

Hotels

£⃞	up to £50
£⃞/	£50–70
£⃞//	£70–100
£⃞///	£100–130
£⃞////	£130–160
£⃞/////	over £160

Restaurants

£⃞	up to £18
£⃞/	£18–25
£⃞//	£25–35
£⃞///	£35–45
£⃞////	over £45

AUSTRIA

The Austrian economy experienced a period of high growth in the 1960s and early 1970s, then contracted in the wake of rising oil prices and a fall in export demand. Expansionist policies failed to reverse the trend; growth remained sluggish; unemployment rose; and the budget deficit and foreign debt burden increased. The economy picked up in the late 1980s, however, helped by increased export and domestic demand.

Services (including tourism and banking) account for over 55% of GDP, while industry (including mining and utilities) accounts for over 30%. Manufacturing involves traditional industries such as iron and steel production, glass, timber processing and paper-making, and modern industries such as machinery, vehicles, electrical engineering and chemical production. The fastest growing industries are electronics and specialty chemicals. Although the agriculture sector is small, production meets most food needs.

The state plays a major role in the economy, particularly in heavy industry such as textiles, steel and machinery. In the postwar years a quarter of manufacturing industry was nationalized and benefited from generous government support. But these industries suffered persistent losses due to a drop in output and productivity, and declining markets. Since the mid-1980s the nationalized industries have been going through a period of restructuring. The huge state holding company ÖIAG has been reorganized and opened to domestic and foreign capital.

Austria was an importer of raw materials and exporter of manufactured goods, but it has become a net importer of manufactures, machinery, transport equipment, and chemicals. Fuels and energy account for 5–10% of imports. The trade balance is regularly in deficit, but it is largely offset by a surplus on invisibles. West Germany accounts for over 30% of Austria's exports and over 40% of its imports, the EC as a whole for about 60% of all exports and imports.

Geography Much of Austria is alpine with densely wooded mountains and hills cut by river valleys. The only lowland areas are the Vienna basin and the valley of the Danube.
Climate In the lowlands average monthly temperatures are 1–20°C (34–68°F); above 3,000 metres (9,800 ft) they drop to -11–2°C (12–36°F).
Population 7.5m.
Government The federal republic consists of 9 provinces, each with its own assembly and government. The federal assembly has a 183-member national council elected every 4 years by proportional representation and a 63-member federal council elected by the provincial assemblies. The chancellor is usually the leader of the largest party in the national council. The federal president is directly elected for 6 years.
Currency Schilling (Sch).
Time 1hr ahead of GMT; end Mar–end Sep, 2hrs ahead of GMT.
Dialling codes Austria's IDD code is 43. Omit the initial 0 from the city code when dialing from abroad. To make an international call from Austria, dial 00 (with a few exceptions) before dialling the relevant country code.
Public holidays Jan 1, Jan 6, Easter Mon, May 1, Ascension Day, Whit Mon, Corpus Christi, Aug 15, Oct 26, Nov 1, Dec 8, Dec 25, Dec 26.

VIENNA (Wien)
City code ☎ 01

The old capital of the Austro-Hungarian Empire is home to 1.5m people, about 20% of Austria's population. It lies close to the Danube (Donau), just 40kms/25 miles from the Iron Curtain, farther east than Prague and closer to West Germany than to western Austria. It is both the capital and a federal province, the site of Parliament, the supreme courts and stock exchange, and the headquarters of most of Austria's major companies and banks. Vienna is one of Europe's great cultural centres: most great Romantic composers were born, lived or died here, and the Habsburg emperors amassed fabulous collections of works of art. The University, founded in 1365, claims to be the oldest in the German-speaking world. There are several scientific research institutes here, including the International Institute for Applied Systems Analysis.

Vienna has sought a new international role since World War II and has become a centre for major conferences. It has the 3rd branch of the UN after New York and Geneva with the headquarters of the International Atomic Energy Agency and the UN Industrial Development Organization.

The city is an important link between the capitalist West and Communist East, especially in establishing banking relations. Some 500 firms with East European representatives and many East European companies have offices here. The Vienna International Fair and other exhibitions are significant showcases for East-West trade. A joint World Fair with Budapest is planned for 1995.

Vienna's industry, trade and services contribute about 30% of Austria's GNP. The principal industries are engineering, the manufacture of chemicals, vehicles, metals (especially precision instruments) and electrical goods, and the processing of foodstuffs, drink and tobacco. The big industrial groups, Montana and Constantia, are based here. The state holding company ÖIAG controls nationalized concerns like Austria Metall, Steyr-Daimler-Puch and Österreichische Mineralölverwaltung which runs the Schwechat oil refinery and petrochemicals subsidiary. High subsidies and few strikes have attracted many multinationals including Grundig, Philips, Siemens, General Motors and Unilever.

Arriving

Most business travellers fly to Vienna, which is linked by scheduled flights with capitals all around the world and European business cities. Vienna is easily accessible by road and rail from Prague, Budapest and West Germany via Linz and Salzburg.

Schwechat airport
Schwechat handles 4.5m passengers a year. The arrivals area is spacious, stylish and well-organized, The departure floor is more crowded.

Facilities on both floors include banks and bureaux de change (open daily from around 6am to 11pm); tourist information and accomodation offices (open daily, 9–10, winter; 9–11, Jun–Sep), bars and upmarket shops. Le Gourmet restaurant has an excellent reputation (reservations ☎ 7770-2827). Useful services include a VIP and business centre with a press conference area and meeting rooms (reservations ☎ 7770-3300) and InterPax lounges with business facilities (members and airline VIP guests only ☎ 7770-3407). Freight inquiries ☎ 7770-2142 (import) 7770-2188 (export). Passenger inquiries ☎ 7770-2231.

Nearby hotel Novotel Wien Airport, A-1300, Schwechat ☎ 776666 Ⓣⓧ 1115666, fax 773239 ● AE DC MC V, with conference rooms, parking, restaurant and pool.

City link The airport is 19kms/12 miles southeast of the centre, a 20–30min drive. A taxi or limousine is the best method of getting into town, but the bus service to the air terminal (on the entrance level of the Hilton International Hotel) is only marginally slower.

Taxi The normal charge is Sch300 (Sch110 more for fares from central Vienna to the airport).

Limousine Airport Service Mazur ☎ 7770-2901.

Car rental Arac, Avis, Budget Car, Denzel, Hertz, InterCity and InterRent have offices in arrivals. A car is useful only outside the centre.

Bus There is a service to the Hilton every 20–30mins and in the evening to coincide with flights (fare Sch50). Reservations for shuttle buses to hotels (fare Sch180 per person) should be made in advance with your airline; on arrival go to the Mazur offices ☎ 7770-2901.

Railway stations

Vienna's railway stations are outside the centre and badly served by public transport; it is usually necessary to take a cab to your hotel. Information ☎ 1717.

Westbahnhof is the main terminal for trains arriving from most parts of Europe and from Salzburg. It is well-organized and modern; facilities include a bureau de change (open daily, 7am–10pm), 24hr post office, shops (open until 11pm) and travel agencies (for hotel reservations).

Südbahnhof provides mainly local services, plus motorail and some trains from Italy and Budapest. Bureau de change (open daily, 6.30am–10pm), travel agencies (for hotel reservations).

Getting around

It takes less than 30mins to walk across the city centre, and some streets around the Stefansdom are closed to traffic. Taxis are most useful for trips on or beyond the Ring. Blocks of 4 tickets or a 72hr pass (*Netzkarte*) from tourist information offices, tobacconists and Transit Authority ticket windows are useful on public transport.

Taxis Pick up a cab from one of the main squares or call *Radio taxis* ☎ 3130 or 4369 (additional Sch10). Drivers know districts by number, rather than name. A 5–10% tip is normal.

Limousines Austrian Chauffeur Limousines ☎ 5133841, *Jet-Car* ☎ 789966, *Frutschnigg* ☎ 223140.

Driving Parking vouchers are required for "Blue Zones" (most daytime parking in the centre); these are sold at Transit Authority windows at *U-Bahn* stations, tobacconists and some banks. Rental firms include ARAC ☎ 5971675, *Avis* ☎ 5873595, *Hertz* ☎ 7131596. But avoid driving in Vienna if possible.

Walking Orientation is easy in the centre, and street crime is rare.

Bus and tram Red minibuses run a circular route in the inner city; trams circle the Ring and beyond.

Subway The *U-Bahn* has three colour-coded routes, with a 4th under construction. The network is extensive and the service efficient.

Train Commuter and rapid transit routes and stations (*S-Bahn*) are marked on local transport maps and connect with the subway system.

Area by area

The city districts (*Bezirke*) are numbered 1–23. The centre is bounded, except on the northeast, by the Ringstrasse, known as "The Ring," a continuous boulevard that changes its name eight times. Most business headquarters, the banks and the stock exchange, major tourist sights, the Opera, the finest shops and nearly all the best hotels and restaurants are within this area, the

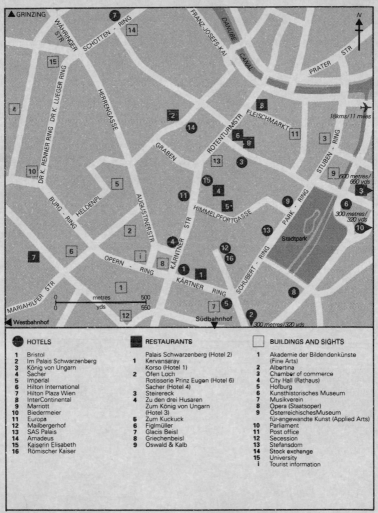

HOTELS

1	Bristol
2	Im Palais Schwarzenberg
3	König von Ungarn
4	Sacher
5	Imperial
6	Hilton International
7	Hilton Plaza Wien
8	InterContinental
9	Marriott
10	Biedermeier
11	Europa
12	Mailbergerhof
13	SAS Palais
14	Amadeus
15	Kaiserin Elisabeth
16	Römischer Kaiser

RESTAURANTS

1	Palais Schwarzenberg (Hotel 2)
	Kervansaray
	Korso (Hotel 1)
2	Ofen Loch
	Rotisserie Prinz Eugen (Hotel 6)
	Sacher (Hotel 4)
3	Steirereck
4	Zu den drei Husaren
	Zum König von Ungarn (Hotel 3)
5	Zum Kuckuck
6	Figlmüller
7	Glacis Beisl
8	Griechenbeisl
9	Oswald & Kalb

BUILDINGS AND SIGHTS

1	Akademie der Bildendenkünste (Fine Arts)
2	Albertina
3	Chamber of commerce
4	City Hall (Rathaus)
5	Hofburg
6	Kunsthistorisches Museum
7	Musikverein
8	Opera (Staatsoper)
9	ÖsterreichischesMuseum für-angewandte Kunst (Applied Arts)
10	Parliament
11	Post office
12	Secession
13	Stefansdom
14	Stock exchange
15	University
i	Tourist information

1st district. On the Ring are Parliament and City Hall.

The 3rd and 4th districts, to the west, are the most elegant residential areas, with many embassies. The 8th district, Josefstadt, and the 13th, Hietzing (near Schönbrunn), are solidly respectable. The 19th district in the north (Nussdorf, Döbling, Grinzing and Neustift am Walde) is more rural on the edge of the Vienna Woods (Wienerwald). Northeast of the Danube is the UN complex, UNO-City, a 15min taxi ride from the centre.

The suburbs Industry around Vienna is to the east (General Motors at Aspern) and southeast near Schwechat (oil refineries and breweries). To the south are industrialized Wienerberg and Liesing, the shopping centre of Vösendorf and Baden, a spa and commuter town.

Hotels

Vienna's imperial past established a legacy of grand old hotels in which service and standards are high and which today are well-equipped. Modern chain hotels like the Hilton, InterContinental and the Hilton Plaza Wien are used for OPEC, UN and other international conferences and have extensive business and fitness facilities. Viennese business associates may be daunted if you stay at the extremely grand Imperial or even at the Palais Schwarzenberg; the Bristol and Sacher are safer.

Facilities include IDD telephones, TVs, 24hr room, valet and laundry services, currency exchange and concierge. It is advisable to make reservations well in advance from May to October and during holiday periods. The district number of each hotel is given by the second and third digits in the zip code.

Bristol ⑤////
A-1010, Kärntner-Ring 1 ☎ *515161-0* ⸋ *112474 fax 51516-550* • *Imperial Hotels* • AE DC MC V • *141 rooms, 11 suites, 2 restaurants, 1 bar*
Opposite the Opera, the Bristol is favoured by business people and diplomats; it is less ostentatious than the Imperial, but offers the same impeccable service. The executive floor has a club-like lounge and bedrooms with working areas. Bedrooms are traditional but light (quieter on Mahlerstrasse) and public rooms are grandly *fin-de-siècle* with several splendid function rooms. The Korso offers a suitable atmosphere for business lunches (see *Restaurants*). The concierge is reputed to get the best opera tickets. Fitness centre, sauna • business centre, 7 meeting rooms (capacity up to 120).

Im Palais Schwarzenberg ⑤////
A-1030, Schwarzenbergpl 9 ☎ *784515* ⸋ *136124 fax 784714* • AE DC MC V • *34 rooms, 4 suites, 1 restaurant, 1 bar*
The price for staying in a baroque palace surrounded by its own park is inevitably high, especially as there are no single rooms. This is a friendly and comfortable hotel, with the atmosphere of a grand country house. Bedrooms are individually decorated and calm, the most charming overlooking the park. Meals are served on the terrace and adjoining Red Salon (see *Restaurants*) and the small *Kaminzimmer*. The spectacular

ceremonial halls are prestigious venues for conferences and banquets. Limousine • pool, tennis • 8 meeting rooms (capacity up to 300).

König von Ungarn ⑤//
A-1010, Schulerstr 10 ☎ *526520-0* ⸋ *116240 fax 526520-8* • DC MC V • *32 rooms including 7 apartments, 1 restaurant, 1 bar*
This pleasing, centrally located and moderately priced mansion is a place for the discerning. The König von Ungarn is warm and welcoming, with comfortable and quiet (if quite small) bedrooms, and gleaming, well-lit bathrooms. The winter bar and restaurant (see *Restaurants*) are under separate management.

Sacher ⑤//
A-1015, Philharmonikerstr 4 ☎ *51456* ⸋ *112520 fax 51457-810* • AE DC MC V • *122 rooms, 4 suites, 3 restaurants, 1 bar*
Vienna's classic *belle époque* hotel, wartime headquarters of the British, is still in private ownership and resolutely traditional. It attracts opera stars, ball-goers, VIPs and tourists as well as business people. The imperial decor of brocade, gilt and crystal has been preserved, but continuous improvements and renovations are made. The small Blaue Bar and the café – serving the famous *Sachertorte* – are favourite meeting places (see also *Restaurants*). Airport limousine • 9 meeting rooms (capacity up to 120).

OTHER HOTELS

Imperial $\boxed{S}////$ *A-1015, Kärnter-Ring 16* ☎ *50110* ⊺ˣ *112630 fax 50110-410* • *AE DC MC V*. One of the most aristocratic hotels in the world, used by VIPs. Business travellers may feel out of place.

For modern amenities, including business and sports facilities:

Hilton International $\boxed{S}//$ *A-1030, Am Stadtpark* ☎ *752652-0* ⊺ˣ *136799 fax 752652-20* • *AE DC MC V*.

Hilton Plaza Wien $\boxed{S}//$ *A-1010, Schottenring 11* ☎ *31390-0* ⊺ˣ *135859 fax 31390-160* • *AE DC MC V*.

InterContinental $\boxed{S}//$ *A-1037, Johannesgasse 28* ☎ *71122* ⊺ˣ *131235 fax 7133389* • *AE DC MC V*.

Marriott $\boxed{S}//$ *A-1010, Parkring 12A* ☎ *51518-0* ⊺ˣ *112249 fax 51518-6736* • *AE DC MC V*.

More personal and generally less expensive business-oriented hotels:

Biedermeier $\boxed{S}/$ *A-1030, Landstrasser Hauptstr 28* ☎ *755575* ⊺ˣ *111039 fax 755575-503* • *AE DC MC V*. Large, efficient and pleasant.

Europa $\boxed{S}/$ *A-1015, Neuer Markt 3* ☎ *51594-0* ⊺ˣ *112292 fax 5138138* • *AE DC MC V*. Modern hotel overlooking Kärntner Strasse, with conference facilities.

Mailbergerhof $\boxed{S}/$ *A-1010, Annagasse 7* ☎ *5120641-0* ⊺ˣ *13828* • *AE DC V*. Small hotel in old mansion, with apartments.

SAS Palais $\boxed{S}//$ *A-1010, Parkring/ Weihburggasse 32* ☎ *515170* ⊺ˣ *136127 fax 5122216* • *AE DC MC V*. Well-equipped modern hotel in fine palace. Excellent restaurant, business centre, sauna and solarium.

Small, traditional hotels with some atmosphere and lower prices:

Amadeus $\boxed{S}$ *A-1010, Wildpretmarkt 5* ☎ *638738* ⊺ˣ *111102 fax 63873838* • *AE DC V*.

Kaiserin Elisabeth $\boxed{S}/$ *A-1010, Weihburggasse 3* ☎ *51526-0* ⊺ˣ *112422 fax 51526-7* • *AE DC MC V*.

Römischer Kaiser $\boxed{S}/$ *A-1 010, Annagasse 16* ☎ *5127751-0* ⊺ˣ *113696 fax 5127751-13* • *AE DC MC V*.

Hotel and restaurant price guide
For the meanings of the hotel and restaurant price symbols, see pages 6 and 7.

Restaurants

Vienna's grand hotels provide a formal setting for business entertaining. The modern hotels, notably the Hilton and InterContinental (Vier Jahreszeiten restaurant), compete successfully with restaurants on the gastronomic front. Reservations are usually essential. Typical Viennese recipes are goulasch (often served as a soup), *Wiener Schnitzel* and *Tafelspitz* (boiled beef, traditional at lunch time). Lighter cuisine, *Neue Wiener Kuche*, has adapted traditional Viennese dishes to modern tastes.

Im Palais Schwarzenberg $\boxed{S}//$
Hotel im Palais Schwarzenberg
☎ *784515-600* • *AE DC MC V* • *jacket and tie*
The Viennese come to the Palais Schwarzenberg for expense-account or celebratory meals, either in the formal Red or Blue Salons (with adjacent small conference room) or on the chic terrace overlooking the park. The food is Viennese and international; the wine list includes some *raritäten*.

Kervansaray $\boxed{S}//$
Mahlerstr 9 ☎ *5128843* • *Hummerbar D only: closed Sun* • *AE DC MC V* • *D reservations essential*
The Kervansaray has several dining-rooms. Downstairs Turkish and international food are served in quite formal but unpretentious surroundings; suitable for a working lunch. Upstairs is the more elegant and busy Hummerbar, frequented by the chic Opera crowd. Fresh fish

from the Bosphorus is imaginatively prepared and is probably the best in town. Dinner in the Hummerbar is the greater gastronomic experience. Be careful when you reserve to specify where you want to eat.

Korso S//
Bristol Hotel, Mahlerstr 2 ☎ 51516-546 • closed Sat L • AE DC MC V • tie
The Korso is the place for a proper business lunch. The decor and faultless service are conducive to concentration. Reinhard Gerer's creative interpretation of the rich Viennese diet is superb, and the wine is outstanding. For complete privacy reserve the smaller dining room. In the evenings there are fewer politicians, more personalities, and a pianist.

Ofen Loch S
Kurrentgasse 8 ☎ 5338844 • closed Sun, Aug • no credit cards
This typically Austrian restaurant, with pretty murals and waitresses in dirndl skirts, is favoured by the Viennese. Local dishes are well-prepared and can be superb. For a meal with business colleagues ask for a table away from the bar. Summer lunches on the terrace outside are particularly pleasant.

Rotisserie Prinz Eugen S//
Hilton Hotel ☎ 752652-355 • AE DC MC V • suit and tie • summer reservations essential
The Hilton must be one of the ugliest of the breed, but its restaurant is civilized. The Rotisserie has a well-founded reputation for excellent food, inspired by the tradition of Prinz Eugen's baroque banquets and realized by some 60 cooks, and a vast range of wines. Pianist in the evenings.

Sacher S//
Hotel Sacher ☎ 51456-846 • AE DC MC V • jacket and tie
The quality of the service and food at the Sacher may have declined, but the *Tafelspitz* is still to be

recommended and the atmosphere is well suited to a business lunch; politicians are seen here daily. The *Rote Bar*, resplendent in red brocade, is small and ideal for dining after the Opera. The "hunting" and "fishing" rooms of the *Stockl* upstairs are tailormade for a confidential *tête-à-tête* (reserve, several days ahead).

Steirereck S////
Rasumofskygasse 2, Ecke Weissgerberlände ☎ 7133168 • closed Sat & Sun • AE
This is considered by many the best restaurant in Vienna, if not Austria. The luxurious, pseudo-classical surroundings and the outstanding, inventive cooking of Helmut Österreicher are eminently suitable for impressing those at the top (the Chancellor is a regular customer). Ask the *patron*, or sommelier Adolf Schmid, to show you the fabulous wine cellar (90% Austrian but with Château Yquem 1921, Sch15,000), the superb cheese, the cigar trolleys and the cognac card.

Zu den drei Husaren S/////
Weihburggasse 4 ☎ 5121092 • D only; closed mid-Jul–mid-Aug • AE DC MC V • jacket and tie
Opinions are divided on this classic Viennese restaurant. Brocade *banquettes*, velvet-buttoned chairs, chandeliers, antique furniture, tapestries and paintings create an old-fashioned atmosphere. The food is not always worthy of the scene, but the *hors d'oeuvre* trolleys are prodigious. Old Viennese families still dine here, as do tourists in droves, and it may be rather fussy for some tastes. For a business meal, request a table in the library.

Zum König von Ungarn S//
König von Ungarn Hotel ☎ 525319 • closed Sat • no credit cards • L reservations essential
Like the hotel (same owner, different management), the restaurant of the König von Ungarn is unpretentious but civilized. The vaulted dining

room is both elegant and welcoming, formal and relaxed. Tables are quite well spaced, with one up a small flight of stairs more private than the rest. Good for a business lunch. Dinner is candlelit and less crowded, with taped classical music.

Zum Kuckuck $\boxed{S}$/
Himmelpfortgasse 15 ☎ *5128470* •
closed Sun & Mon • AE DC MC V
This unpretentious restaurant attracts a discerning clientele, though you should not expect total privacy. Food is traditional French and Austrian with a *nouvelle* touch, and service is formal but friendly. The *menu dégustation* is a good choice for dinner and the *petit menu* ideal for lunch. The wine list is wide-ranging. Under the same ownership is *Steinerne Eule* ☎ 932250 in the 7th district.

OTHER RESTAURANTS
Figlmüller, Wollzeile 5 ☎ 526177, is a noisy, popular and very Austrian tavern, serving giant but excellent Wiener Schnitzel. The Viennese enjoy *Glacis Beisl*, Messepl 1 (7th district) ☎ 9307374, a good place for an informal business meal. *Griechenbeisl*, Fleischmarkt 11 ☎ 5331977, is quaint but more touristy. *Oswald & Kalb*, Bäckerstr 14 ☎ 5121371, is an old-fashioned *beisel* (local pub or bistro), founded by left-wing intellectuals and frequented by media folk, politicians and artists (always crowded).

Out of town
In the environs, particularly the Wienerwald, wine from local vineyards is sold by growers in taverns called *Heurige*, each distinguished by a pine branch above the door, accompanied by buffet food. The best include *Zum Martin Sepp* ☎ 323333, at Grinzing, 6kms/3.8 miles, and *Zimmermann* ☎ 441207, at Neustift am Walde, 7kms/4 miles.
　　Römischer Kaiser ☎ 441104, also at Neustift am Walde, has a lovely position with a garden and beautiful views of Vienna. *La Tour* ☎ 864763

at Perchtoldsdorf (10kms/6 miles) has earned a Michelin rosette.

Bars and cafés
The famous Viennese coffeehouses are very much part of the social scene and can be suitable for an informal business meeting. Most serve lunch and early evening snacks. Useful for a business rendezvous is the *Café Central*, a former retreat of the literary, now used by civil servants, in the Gothic Palais Ferstel in Herrengasse. *Café Landtmann*, Karl-Renner-Ring 4, is popular with politicians. For off-duty cakes and coffee, *Demel*, in Kohlmarkt, is the most famous of all and disputes the recipe for the original *Sachertorte* with the Sacher Hotel. *Hawelka*, Dorotheergasse 6, is smoky and very relaxed, and the *Braunerhof*, Stallburggasse 2, is typically Balkan.
　　The hotel bar most used for business encounters is the *Klimt Bar* at the Hilton. The Viennese quite often meet over breakfast, and the Marriott is a good choice.

Entertainment
Vienna's wide-ranging cultural scene is covered in *Monatsprogramm* and other tourist office publications. Concerts and operas are a major part of the social scene and of the whole experience of visiting Vienna (except in Jul–Aug); most Viennese are very knowledgeable. Annual events include the Carnival (Jan and Feb; formal balls), the Viennale Film Festival (Mar) and the Festival of Vienna (theatre and concerts; May and Jun).
　　The *Bundestheaterkassen*, Goethegasse 1 ☎ 51444, is the central box office for the state operas and theatres. *Lienerbrünn*, Augustinerstr 1 ☎ 5330961, is a ticket agency near the opera. Written applications for the Vienna Boys' Choir and Spanish Riding School are accepted months in advance (write c/o A-1010, Hofburg).
Opera The Vienna State Opera (*Staatsoper*), on the Opernring, is one of the best in the world and the chief

evening venue for Viennese high society. Men often wear black tie. The *Volksoper*, Währinger Str 78 ☎ 51444, shows operettas.

Music The main concert venues are the *Konzerthaus*, Lothringerstr 20 ☎ 721211, the *Musikverein*, Dumbrastr 3 (box office ☎ 5058190), home of the Vienna Philharmonic, and *Bösendorfer*, Graf Starhemberger Gasse 14 ☎ 656651.

Theatre The magnificent *Burgtheater* ☎ 51444, on the Ring, the *Akademietheater* ☎ 51444, Lisztstr 1, and the *Theater in der Josefstadt*, Josefstädterstr 26 ☎ 425127, are worth a visit if your German is good. Otherwise try the *English Theatre*, Josefsgasse 12 ☎ 421260, or *International Theatre*, Porzellangasse 8 ☎ 316272. Musicals are staged at the *Theater an der Wien*, Linke Wienzeile 6 ☎ 58830-310.

Cinema Burg Kino, Opernring 19, shows undubbed English-language films, *Top Kino*, Rahlgasse 1, cult and avant-garde movies.

Nightclubs and casinos The *Eden Bar*, Liliengasse 2 ☎ 5127450, is a classic nightclub. The *Casino Wien*, Palais Esterhazy, Kärntner Str 41 ☎ 5124836, is open daily from 4pm.

Spanish Riding School Tickets (very hard to get) and information from ticket and travel agencies. You can wait at Josefsplatz for the weekday morning training sessions.

Vienna Boys' Choir sing mass in the chapel of the Hofburg most Sundays at 9.30am; tickets, when available (mostly in the off-season), from agencies or from the box office the preceding Friday after 5pm.

Shopping

Most shops are open Mon–Fri, 8 or 9–6 (some break for lunch), and Sat until noon. Pedestrianized Kärntner Strasse is the main shopping street, but Graben and the streets leading to the Hofburg have some of the most exclusive shops, including the best art and antique dealers.

Porcelain, leather goods, cakes and chocolates, records and traditional Austrian clothing are the best things to buy here.

Department store Steffl, Kärntner Str 19.

Fashion For lodens, dirndls and knitwear visit *Loden Plankl* on Michaelerplatz.

Gifts The *Sacher Confiserie* (next to Sacher Hotel) and *Imperial Café* will send Sachertorte anywhere in the world. *Altmann & Kühne*, Graben 30, and *Demel* in Kohlmarkt both sell beautifully packaged confectionery.

Glass Lobmeyr, Kärntner Str 26.

Porcelain Augarten, Stock-im-Eisen Pl 3–4.

Sightseeing

The most richly rewarding Viennese sights are the palaces and collections of the Habsburgs, notably the Kunsthistorisches Museum, and small specialized museums. The tourist board publishes a *Museums* leaflet in English. The most impressive church is the baroque *Karlskirche*. Wandering around the streets of old Vienna near the Stefansdom will reveal many of its architectural charms.

Belvedere Palace The twin pavilions of Prinz Eugen's baroque mansion contain the Austrian Gallery: medieval to baroque art in the Lower Belvedere and 19th and 20thC art (including famous works by Klimt and Schiele) in the Upper Belvedere (superb views). *Prinz-Eugen-Str 1. Open Tue–Sun, 10–4.*

Hofburg The state rooms and private apartments of the imperial winter palace may be visited on guided tours. The treasury (entered from the Schweizerhof), the chapel and ornate library are also worth seeing, and there are specialist museums in the Neue Berg. *State rooms open Mon–Sat, 8.30–4; Sun, 8.30–12.30; other parts of the Hofburg have different hours.*

Kunsthistorisches Museum One of the world's greatest museums. The Italian and Flemish sections are particularly fine, with masterpieces by Titian, Pieter Brueghel the Elder and Rubens; and rich collections of

otices of nearest

pl 3 ☎ 317601.

gs, A-1060,
70226 (agency
ss and foreign
e Aussenhandel
uptstr 55–57
Trade and
licensing

ndeskammer
ft,
rkehr)
r 63
er of
er, A-1010,
) (Vienna

band
5335218
ciation);
Industrieller
☎ 71135

WFF,
☎ 4350463
Fund).
A-1041   for
ria: Facts
mbassies

eitung has   ions
country.
the
d and   itted
a   ian
rian   day
Spanish   nube

ourist
435974;
                              (tennis,
160813.

e held
ion,
a-Wien
teams.

ping fit

e are sports facilities at the hotels
ol (fitness centre), Hiltons
rnational (pool, fitness centre) and
a Wien (fitness centre) (see
els); the Marriott and Palais
warzenberg have pools. *City Club
nna*, Vösendorf, Parkallee 2
693535, run by the Club
editerranée, has golf, tennis, pools
d a fitness centre beside the hotel.
itness centres Club Alvarez,
Hietzinger Hauptstr 29 ☎ 826500;
Vienna International Fitness Centre
☎ 5873710; *Zimmermann* ☎ 9393990
(several branches); *Heilquelle Oberlaan*,
Kurbadstr 14 ☎ 681611 (pools,
tennis and squash courts, about
15mins from centre).
Squash Fit & Fun, Landstrasser
Hauptstr 2A ☎ 736165.
Skiing The nearest major resort is
fashionable and popular Kitzbühel (a
5hr drive), but there are runs in the
Vienna Woods and at Semmering.
Tennis Floridsdorfer Tennis Club,
Lorettopl 5 ☎ 381283 (16 courts;
season ticket or by the hour), 21st
district. Or *Vereinigte Tennisanlagen* in
the Prater Park ☎ 2181811.

Local resources
Business services
The hotels Bristol, both Hiltons and
SAS Palais have business centres.
There are copy shops all over town.
*Photocopying and printing Österr.
Kopier-Drive-in*, Taubstummengasse
13 ☎ 5053165, or Reichsratstr 5
☎ 424687 (open Sat). *Color Copy
Center*, Hintere Zollamsstr 3
☎ 7133680.
*Secretarial Dolmetschcenter Irene
Voigt*, Hilton Hotel ☎ 754226.
Translation The Translating and
Interpreting Institute of Vienna
University ☎ 317273 will advise on
translators for specific needs.

Communications
Local delivery Taxis will deliver
packets locally (ask for *Botendienst*,
messenger). *Arge Funk* ☎ 765577,
City Express ☎ 333192, *Funk-Trans*
☎ 59909, *Quick Trans* ☎ 333139.

Long-distance delivery DHL ☎ 71161
or 736551 (or 7770-3621 at the
airport); *Federal Express* ☎ 1711.
Post office Central Post office:
Fleischmarkt 19 open 24hrs. The post
offices at the main railway stations are
also open 24hrs.
Telex and fax *Offentliche
Fernschreibstelle*, Borseplatz 1
☎ 533 6319.

Conference/exhibition centres
For conference organization contact
Interconvention ☎ 2369640 ⊤Ⓧ 111803
fax 2369648, *Mondial Congress*
☎ 501550 ⊤Ⓧ 132597, *Vienna
Convention Bureau* ☎ 431608
⊤Ⓧ 134653 fax 433292. The main
venues are: *Austria Center Vienna*,
Wagramer Str 23 ☎ 26310 (5kms/3
miles from the centre, adjacent to the
UN buildings; capacity up to 4,200);
Wiener Kongresszentrum, Hofburg,
Heldenplatz ☎ 5873666 (in the
Hofburg palace, capacity up to
3,000); *Sofiensäle*, Marxergasse 17
☎ 722198 and *Konferenz-Zentrum
Laxenburg*, Schlosspl 1 ☎ (2236)
71521 (16kms/10 miles south, former
Habsburg hunting lodge, capacity up
to 350). Locations for trade fairs
include *Wiener Messepalast*, Messepl 1
☎ 931524 ⊤Ⓧ 133491, and
Kongresszentrum Messegelände
☎ 262561 ⊤Ⓧ 136294. The most
prestigious venues are in former
palaces: *Palais Ferstel* ☎ 633763,
Palais Palffy ☎ 5125681, *Palais
Pallavicini* ☎ 5122538 and *Palais
Schwarzenberg* ☎ 784515.

Emergencies
Bureaux de change The air terminal
exchange office at the Hilton is open
daily, 8–12.30, 2–6. Travel agencies
are open shop hours for currency
exchange. Normal bank hours are
Mon–Fri, 8–3 (Thu, 8–5.30).
Hospitals *Allgemeines Krankenhaus*,
Alser Strasse 4 ☎ 4800. Medical
information for foreign patients,
Weihburggasse 10–12 ☎ 51501-0
(51501-238 for dental emergencies).
Emergency doctor after 7pm and
weekends ☎ 141.

Pharmacies display n
ones open or ☎ 1550.
Police Deutschmeiste
Emergency ☎ 133.

Government offices
Wiener Betriebsansiedlu
Windmühlgasse 26 ☎
for promotion of busin
investment); *Zentralstel*
u. Zoll, Landstrasse Ha
☎ 7256410 (Ministry of
Industry, export/import
office).

Information sources
Business information B
der gewerblichen Wirtscha
(*Bundessektion Fremdenve*
A-1045, Wiedner Haupts
☎ 50105 (Federal chamb
commerce); *Handelskamm*
Stubenring 8–10 ☎ 5145
chamber of commerce);
Österreichischer Kongressve
A-1010, Judenplatz 3–4 ☎
(Austrian Convention Ass
Vereinigung Österreichischer
A-1031, Schwarzenbergpl 4
(Association of Austrian
Industrialists); *Wiener
Wirtschaftsforderungsfond w*
A-1082, Ebendorfer Str 2 ☎
(Vienna Business Promotion

The *Federal Press Service*
Ballhauspl 2, publishes *Aus*
and Figures, available from
abroad.
Local media Neue Kronen-Z
the widest circulation in the
Also published in Vienna are
Kurier, *Die Presse der Standa*
Wiener Zeitung. Radio Austri
International broadcasts Aust
news in English, French and
from 8.05 to 8.15am.
Tourist information Vienna
Board, Kinderspitalgasse 5 ☎
tourist information office in
Opernpassage, open 9–7 ☎ 4

Thank-yous
Chocolates See *Shopping*.
Florist Sädtler ☎ 5874219.

BELGIUM

With growth rates exceeding 2% a year towards the end of the 1980s, the Belgian economy is showing signs of recovering from the serious difficulites it encountered in the early part of the decade.

Endowed with few mineral or energy resources but capitalizing on its geographical position, Belgium has built up a large industrial sector based on processing imported raw materials for re-export. Industry currently, contributes around 25% to GDP. Its percentage share has fallen in recent years, reflecting a decline in the older industries (particularly mining and steel) as well as a rapid expansion of service industries, encouraged by the importance of Brussels as a centre for international institutions. Manufacturing output has registered a slow but steady recovery since 1983 due to the growth of newer industries (such as light engineering, chemicals and food processing) and an upturn in export demand. But the contrasting performance of the traditional industries, most of which are located in French-speaking Wallonia in the south, and the newer industries, most of which are located in Dutch-speaking Flanders in the north, threatens to exacerbate long-standing divisions between the country's two main communities. Agriculture and fishing are small, but important sectors.

Economic growth in the late 1980s has been primarily export-led. Exports and imports of goods and services are each equivalent to more than 70% of GDP. External trade figures (which include those for Luxembourg) show that the visible trade balance moved into surplus in 1986 after several years in deficit. The main exports are machinery and transport equipment (including motor vehicles), chemicals, metals, food products, textiles and clothing, precious stones and jewellery. Raw materials and semi-manufactures for industry account for well over half of imports. These include machinery and transport equipment, chemicals and fossil fuels. Belgium is also a net importer of food and agricultural products. Most external trade is conducted with EC countries, particularly West Germany, France and the Netherlands.

Geography Most of Belgium is fertile lowland, except for the wooded plateau and foothills of the Ardennes in the east. Much of the coastal region has been reclaimed from the sea and is protected by dykes.
Climate The climate is temperate, with warm summers and mild winters.
Population 9.8m.
Government Belgium is a parliamentary monarchy. The parliament consists of the chamber of representatives (the lower house), with 212 members elected for 4 years and the senate (upper house), with 184 members (106 directly elected, plus 50 from the provincial councils, 25 co-optees and the heir to the throne).
Currency Belgian franc (BFr).
Time 1hr ahead of GMT; end Mar–end Sep, 2hrs ahead of GMT.
Dialling codes Belgium's IDD code is 32. Omit the initial 0 from the city code when dialling from abroad. To make an international call from Belgium, dial 00 before dialling the relevant country code.
Public holidays Jan 1, Easter Mon, May 1, Ascension, Whit Mon, Jul 21, Aug 15, Nov 1, Nov 11, Dec 25.

BRUSSELS (Bruxelles)

City code ☎ 02

About 80% of visitors to Brussels come on business, and most directly or indirectly because of the city's importance in the EC as home of the Commission and meeting place of the Council of Ministers as well as prospective sole base of the European Parliament (which has traditionally moved between Brussels and Strasbourg). Since 1967 Brussels has also been the headquarters of NATO. Other inter-governmental and private organizations have followed, turning this small capital of a small kingdom into a European metropolis and international conference centre.

Out of a population of 1m, about a quarter is foreign. Most are immigrant workers from North Africa and Turkey or European civil servants, but there are also hundreds of foreign diplomats, journalists, translators, lawyers, consultants and other professionals. Many multinational companies have chosen Brussels as their main European base, and the city is also a financial centre, with the headquarters of Euro-Clear, the largest international clearing-house, as well as many foreign banks.

The main Belgian industrial holding companies have their headquarters in Brussels, but there is no heavy industry in the city. Other major Belgian companies with headquarters here are Petrofina, GB-Inno-BM (the largest retailer), Sabena, Solvay and UCB (chemicals). High-technology and scientific research are being encouraged.

The Belgians themselves are stolidly bourgeois and family-oriented, and their capital remains at heart a respectable provincial town. Brussels is officially bilingual but, although most *Bruxellois* are French-speaking, the city is in Flanders. The problem is as much political as cultural, and generates friction between the Flemish and French communities as well as much dual-language bureaucracy. For the foreign visitor a happy side-effect is that in some places you will find the locals more helpful if you speak English than French.

Arriving

Brussels has good road connections with Amsterdam (200kms/125 miles), Paris (300kms/190 miles) and Frankfurt (400kms/250 miles). The European rail network also covers these and other cities. Trains from Amsterdam, Paris, Cologne and Luxembourg all take about 2hrs 30mins. There are fast trains all over Belgium (Brussels to Antwerp 34mins, to Ostend 1hr 15mins, and to Liège 1hr). Visitors from the UK can use the rail/sea routes via Ostend or Zeebrugge (journey time from London 6hrs), but there are frequent flights from Gatwick, Heathrow and London City airport and most prefer to fly. Those travelling between Strasbourg and Brussels often find a car more convenient than the half-day train trip or flying (flights are fully booked during the monthly sessions of the European Parliament and are quite often grounded at Strasbourg in winter owing to bad weather).

Brussels airport
All major international airlines serve Brussels, linking it with over 90 cities in the world. The domestic network is limited and little used. The airport is well-organized, but there can be long lines for immigration. Allow 20–30mins to clear the airport. Facilities include a post office (Mon–Fri, 9–5), telegram and telex office (7am–10pm), telephone office (Mon–Fri, 9–12, 2–5; Sat, 8–12, 12.30–4) and banks open between 7.15am and 10pm. There is

an excellent duty-free shopping arcade. In the arrivals hall the "Best of Belgium" desk ☎ 725 10 88 gives information and video presentation of export products. Passenger inquiries ☎ 720 71 67 (Sabena and most airlines); ☎ 723 03 11 for other airlines, including British Airways, Lufthansa and PanAm. Brussels Airport Services ☎ 722 31 24 will arrange to meet passengers or assist with transfers. Freight inquiries ☎ 720 59 80.

Nearby hotels The nearest hotel is the new *Sheraton*, Aéroport Bruxelles-National, 1930 Zaventem ☎ 725 10 00 TX 27085 fax 725 11 55. Also within easy reach: *Novotel*, 1 Olmenstraat, 1920 Diegem ☎ 720 58 30 TX 26751 fax 721 39 58, 2kms/1 mile from the airport, with its own shuttle service; *Sofitel*, 15 Bessenveldstraat, 1920 Diegem ☎ 720 60 50 TX 26595, which has a pool and fitness centre.

City link The airport is 12kms/7.5 miles northeast of the city centre. Most people take taxis into town and there are often lines waiting for them outside the arrivals hall. The train is cheap, but uncomfortable; it is worth buying a first-class ticket.

Taxi Airport-based cabs are expensive (the journey into Brussels can cost around Bfr1,000). To avoid exorbitant rates telephone for a radio taxi (Taxis Verts ☎ 347 47 47 or others listed under *Getting around*). Or copy the locals and pick up a cab from outside the departures hall.

Limousines Brussels Limousine Service ☎ 216 19 01.

Car rental Major firms have desks at the airport. Hours vary, and it is advisable to phone in advance. A car is useful for trips outside Brussels and parking in town is fairly easy.

Bus Between 8.30pm and 11pm there is a bus service to the Gare Centrale. (Sabena also runs buses to Antwerp, Ghent, Liège and Maastricht.)

Train There is a half-hourly service to the Gare du Nord (15mins) and the Gare Centrale (18mins), between 6.15 and 11.46pm.

Railway stations
Most trains stop at all three main stations, which are only a few minutes apart. However, airport trains only use the Gare du Nord and the Gare Centrale. General inquiries ☎ 219 26 40 or 218 60 50.

None of the stations is pleasant to use: the Gare Centrale is old and shabby; the others, both in tawdry districts, are modern and unattractive. All stations are connected to the subway system and taxis are on hand.

Gare du Midi Brussels' most important station with numerous EuroCity and InterCity services, including all high-speed trains to Paris. The station is being extended.

Gare Centrale The central – but not the main – station is located 200 metres/220yds from the Grand-Place. Some international trains do not stop here.

Gare du Nord The most efficient and best-equipped station to use. Most high-speed trains to Paris leave from here (but it serves fewer destinations than the Gare du Midi).

Getting around
Public transport is quite efficient and easy to use. A single ticket is valid for one hour on bus, tram or subway. Tickets can be bought in multiples of 5 or 10 and there is a 24hr tourist ticket.

Taxis are usually available on the street. Radio cabs ATR ☎ 647 22 22; *Autolux* ☎ 512 31 23; *Taxis Oranges* ☎ 513 62 00; or *Taxis Verts* ☎ 511 22 44. Tips are not necessary; leave small change.

Limousines Brussels Limousine Service ☎ 216 19 01.

Driving Driving in Brussels presents few problems, although traffic is on the increase. Street signs are in both French and Flemish. Trams have priority over cars. Parking is fairly easy, except on the streets around the Commission. It is worth renting a car for visits to factories outside Brussels: *Avis* ☎ 537 12 80 has desks at several hotels.

Walking Brussels is fairly spread out, so walking is seldom a practical way to get around. It is generally safe, but avoid the parks at night and beware of pickpockets in the stations and in and around Rue des Bouchers.

Bus and tram The network is comprehensive and integrated with the subway system: lines 3 and 5 of the "Pré-métro" are tram services, but indicated on subway maps.

Subway The Métro system is useful and straightforward: line 1 runs west to east (Schuman is the stop for the European Commission); line 2 runs around the city centre from the northwest (Simonis) via the Gare du Nord to the Gare du Midi. Arts-Loi is the junction between the two lines. Métro stations are indicated by a white "M" on a blue background.

Train There is a rail link between the Gare du Nord and the Gare du Midi, via the Gare Centrale.

Area by area

At the heart of old Brussels is the beautiful Grand-Place. Nearby business districts are around the Bourse and along Rue Royale (with the Cité Administrative). Place Rogier, near the Gare du Nord, is also a commercial area. Overlooking the Parc de Bruxelles is the imposing Palais de la Nation (the Belgian Parliament); to the south lies the elegant, aristocratic Sablon district, with the Royal Palace and museums and the neo-classical Palais de Justice (Law Courts).

The headquarters of the European Commission and the important commercial area of Avenue Louise lie just to the east of the inner ring, a few minutes' drive from the Gare Centrale or the Grand-Place. Ixelles is an expensive residential district.

The suburbs

Residential and commercial areas within the outer ring road barely count as suburbs in the strictest sense; all are within a 15min drive of NATO (at Evere, near the airport), the European Commission and satellite buildings, and the multinational companies in Chaussée de la Hulpe and Boulevard de Woluwé, as well as central Brussels. Suburbs to the west have a mainly Flemish population.

Foreign residents choose districts like Woluwé-St-Lambert, Woluwé-St-Pierre and Kraainem. Tervuren is traditionally popular with the British, while wealthy American expatriates favour Waterloo. The villas of Uccle are inhabited by "old money" Brussels families.

Old industry is concentrated mainly to the north of Brussels, beyond the Heysel district (trade fairs) and Laeken (Royal Palace).

Hotels

Brussels has a fair range of business hotels, and both quality and quantity will increase as the momentum for the single market gathers force. A new SAS Palais and a Sofitel should be open in 1990.

Facilities standard to major hotels include a concierge, currency exchange and valet/laundry service. All hotels given full entries have IDD, minibars and television in the bedrooms, and, except for the Pullman Astoria, 24hr room service and parking. Reasonable amounts of typing, photocopying, fax and telex can usually be done in-house: a few larger hotels have secretarial staff for guests.

Amigo   🅱///
1–3 rue de l'Amigo, 1000 ☎ *511 59 10*
🆇 *21618 fax 513 52 77* • *AE DC MC V* • *183 rooms, 11 suites, 1 restaurant, 1 bar*

This well-established hotel close to the Grand-Place remains a favourite, especially with bankers and those who appreciate tradition. The stone-flagged entrance hall, the solid

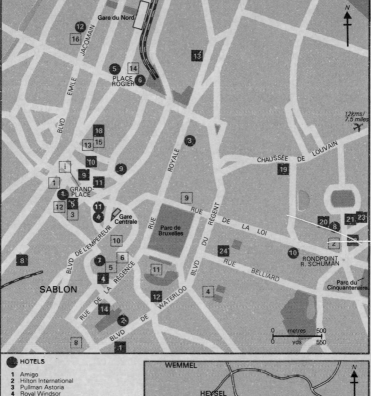

Gare du Nord

PLACE ROGIER

GRAND PLACE

Gare Centrale

Parc de Bruxelles

SABLON

CHAUSSÉE DE LOUVAIN

RONDPOINT R. SCHUMAN

Parc du Cinquantenaire

BLVD EMILE JACQMAIN

RUE ROYALE

RUE DE LA LOI

RUE DE LA RÉGENCE

BLVD DE WATERLOO

BLVD DE L'EMPEREUR

RUE BELLIARD

RUE DU RÉGENT

12kms/ 7.5 miles

| 0 | metres | 500 |
| 0 | yds | 550 |

HOTELS

1 Amigo
2 Hilton International
3 Pullman Astoria
4 Royal Windsor
5 Sheraton
6 Albert Premier
7 Alfa Sablon
8 Archimède
9 Arenberg
10 Brussels Europa
11 Novotel
12 President World Trade Center
13 Ramada
14 Stephanie

RESTAURANTS

1 Adrienne
2 Bruneau
3 Claude Dupont
4 Ecailler du Palais Royal
5 La Maison du Boeuf (Hotel 2)
   La Maison du Cygne
6 L'Orangeraie
7 Villa Lorraine
8 Comme Chez Soi
9 Aux Armes de Bruxelles
10 Chez Léon
11 Taverne du Passage
12 Bernard
13 de Ultieme Hallucinatie
14 Au Duc d'Arenberg
15 La Cravache d'Or
16 L'Armagnac
17 La Porte des Indes
18 Samurai
19 Fujiyama
20 Takesushi
21 Villa de Bruselas
22 Barbanera
23 L'Atelier
24 Chez Callans

WEMMEL

HEYSEL

LAEKEN

GANSHOREN

EVERE

WOLUWE-ST-LAMBERT

WOLUWE-ST-PIERRE

IXELLES

UCCLE

Bois de la Cambre

RING ROAD

AV. LOUISE

| 0 | kms | 3.0 |
| 0 | miles | 1.8 |

BUILDINGS AND SIGHTS

1 Bourse
2 EC Commission/Berlaimont
3 Hôtel de Ville
4 Ministry of Economic Affairs
5 Musée d'Art Ancien
6 Musée d'Art Moderne
7 NATO
8 Palais de Justice (Law Courts)
9 Palais de la Nation (Parliament)
10 Palais des Congrès
11 Palais du Roi
12 Police
13 Post Office
14 Rogier centre
15 Théâtre Royal de la Monnaie
16 World Trade Center
i Tourist information

Flemish oak furniture, the tapestries, pictures and rugs create an atmosphere not found elsewhere. Bedrooms are spacious and old-fashioned; half overlook the Gothic Town Hall. There are some fine function rooms and *petits salons* for meetings, but the restaurant has been struggling to maintain the reputation of this hotel in the face of new competition. 5 meeting rooms (capacity up to 100).

Hilton International *B*////
38 blvd de Waterloo, 1000
☎ *513 88 77* ☒ *22744 fax 513 72 33 • AE DC MC V • 347 rooms, 22 suites, 3 restaurants, 1 bar*
The high-rise Hilton has a good location close to Avenue Louise and the Palais de Justice, and the back overlooks the Parc d'Egmont. It is frequently used for conferences. Standard rooms are spacious; there are few singles. Corner rooms are the biggest. The four self-contained executive floors are favoured for their fine views, calm atmosphere and for the security and service; rooms here are not significantly more expensive than de luxe rooms below. The conservatory-style Café d'Egmont is popular for buffet lunches and there is also a roof restaurant, but the best place for a business meal is the Maison du Boeuf (see *Restaurants*). Hairdresser, newsstand, shops • sauna, solarium, jacuzzi • secretarial service, 9 meeting rooms (capacity up to 500).

Pullman Astoria *B*///
103 rue Royale, 1000 ☎ *217 62 90* ☒ *25040 fax 217 11 50 • AE DC MC V • 123 rooms, 12 suites, 1 restaurant, 1 bar*
Since being taken over by Pullman in 1987, the Astoria, which dates from the turn of the century, has regained some of its former glory. The ornate foyer and ballroom, the Louis XVI-style Palais Royal restaurant, and the Pullman Bar, with fixtures and furnishings from the Golden Arrow train, are redolent of the *belle époque*.

Bedrooms are old-fashioned and surprisingly quiet for such a central location. 8 meeting rooms (capacity up to 250).

Royal Windsor *B*////
5 rue Duquesnoy, 1000 ☎ *511 42 15* ☒ *62905 fax 511 60 04 • AE DC MC V • 290 rooms, 10 suites, 1 restaurant, 1 bar*
The Royal Windsor is being luxuriously refurbished and looks set to occupy the top spot in the Brussels hotel hierarchy, with suitably high prices. It now has light oak panelling in the public areas and bedrooms, and bathrooms are to be re-done in marble. But there is a certain anonymity in the air and the bedrooms, while tastefully decorated and well-equipped, are rather cramped. The hotel is geared to business and conference needs, and the restaurant, Les Quatre Saisons, maintains a high standard. In addition to the elegant Waterloo bar in the lobby there is an English-style "pub" and dancing in The Crocodile Club. Business centre, 4 meeting rooms (capacity up to 320).

Sheraton *B*////
3 pl Rogier, 1210 ☎ *219 34 00* ☒ *26887 fax 218 66 18 • AE DC MC V • 483 rooms, 40 suites, 2 restaurants, 1 bar*
The biggest hotel in Brussels, part of the Manhattan Center complex of offices and ministries. The atmosphere and decor are typical of this luxury chain. Service is efficient if sometimes stretched: there are always several conferences going on. The main restaurant, Les Comtes de Flandres, is a good place for a leisurely business lunch. Bedrooms are spacious and plain, with good-quality walnut custom-built furnishings but fairly small tiled bathrooms; those in the Sheraton Towers (separate check-in) are more luxurious. The suites on the top four floors are suitable for meetings. There is also a nonsmoking floor. The rather dark Rendez-vous Bar has the

atmosphere of a gentlemen's club.
Shops • pool, sauna and fitness room
• 15 meeting rooms (capacity up to
1,000).

OTHER HOTELS

Albert Premier *B* *20 pl Rogier,*
1210 ☎ *217 21 25* Ⓣ *27111*
fax 217 93 31 • *AE DC MC V.* Totally
refurbished in an old shell: stylish
contemporary decor and sensible
prices.

Alfa Sablon *B*// *2–4 rue de la*
Paille, 1000 ☎ *513 60 40* Ⓣ *21248*
fax 511 81 41 • *AE DC MC V.*
A spruce small hotel in the smart
Sablon district.

Archimède *B*// *22–24 rue*
Archimède, 1040 ☎ *231 09 09*
Ⓣ *20420 fax 230 33 71* • *AE DC*
MC V. A sound cheaper choice for
those with Commission business.
Contemporary decor is odd but
cheerful; well-equipped bedrooms.

Arenberg *B*// *15 rue d'Assaut,*
1000 ☎ *511 07 70* Ⓣ *25660*
fax 514 19 76 • *City Hotels* • *AE DC*
MC V. Well-run, reasonably priced,
central hotel with modern comforts.

Brussels Europa *B*/// *107 rue de la*
Loi, 1040 ☎ *230 13 33* Ⓣ *25121*
fax 230 36 82 • *Forum Hotels* • *AE*
DC MC V. Convenient for the EC;
otherwise valued chiefly for its two
restaurants and fitness centre.

Novotel *B*/// *120 rue Marché-aux-*
Herbes, 1000 ☎ *514 33 33* Ⓣ *20377*
fax 511 77 23 • *AE DC MC V.* A new
hotel in a Flemish-style building
between the Gare Centrale and the
Grand-Place.

**President World Trade
Center** *B*/// *180 blvd E.*
Jacqmain, 1210 ☎ *217 20 20*
Ⓣ *21066 fax 218 84 02* • *AE DC*
MC V. Calm, luxurious new hotel in a
desolate area near the Gare du Nord.
Sauna, gym, jacuzzi. Shuttle service
to centre and European Commission.

Ramada *B*// *38 chaussée de*
Charleroi, 1060 ☎ *539 30 00*
Ⓣ *25539* • *AE DC MC V.* Luxury
chain hotel near Avenue Louise, with
its own limousine service.

Stephanie *B*// *91–93 ave Louise,*
1050 ☎ *539 02 40* Ⓣ *25558*
fax 538 03 07 • *Copthorne Hotels* •
AE DC MC V. Completely redesigned
hotel with very big bedrooms and a
pool. Popular for longer stays.

Hotel price guide
For the meanings of the hotel
price symbols, see *Symbols and
abbreviations* on pages 6 and 7.

Clubs

There are several establishment clubs:
the *Cercle du Parc, Cercle Gaulois,
Cercle des Nations* and *Club de
Bruxelles*, all private membership
places. The *Château Ste-Anne* can be
rented for functions. ˙

Restaurants

Brussels is one of the great gastronomic cities of Europe, with some 1,500
restaurants. Although the top restaurants rely on expense-account business, some of the best are accessible to fairly modest budgets if you
choose a fixed-price menu. All restaurants are busiest on Friday and
Saturday nights when advance reservations are advisable if not essential.
One of the top gourmet restaurants gets fully booked as much as three
months in advance for weekends.

Adrienne *B*//
*Ave de La Toison d'Or (entrance 1A rue
Crespel)* ☎ *511 93 39* • *AE DC MC V*
This airy first-floor restaurant
opposite the Hilton is always packed
at lunchtime. The reason for its
success is the splendid *buffet à
volonté*; appetizing, fresh food at a
fixed price, which includes desserts
(an extra *plat au choix* can also be
ordered). There are more impressive
places to take guests, but Adrienne's,

with its informal service, semi-rustic decor and summer terrace is a happy choice for a light lunch with colleagues or for those on their own.

Bruneau _B_////
73 ave Broustin ☎ _427 69 78_ • _closed Tue D, Wed_ • _AE DC MC V_ • _jacket and tie_
This modest redbrick townhouse in the northern suburb of Ganshoren has acquired a third Michelin rosette for its exquisite, inventive _nouvelle cuisine_. Those reserving far enough in advance may be able to choose between the lovely panelled dining room in Louis XVI-style or a lighter room overlooking the garden, also in immaculate taste, which can be taken for private meals. There is an extremely luxurious private dining room and _salon_ on the first floor used by VIPs. Bruneau is a place for a really special night out, or an important, and prolonged, business lunch.

Claude Dupont _B_////
46 ave Vital Riethuisen ☎ _427 54 50_ • _closed Mon & Tue_ • _AE DC MC V_ • _jacket and tie preferred_
The nearby Bruneau may have eclipsed Dupont as the gourmet's favourite, but this remains a classic temple of fine cooking. Over the years Claude Dupont has won many major gastronomic awards, and he continues to do so. The dining room is small but comfortable: a good ambience for business entertaining. There is also a private room for up to 22 people.

Ecailler du Palais Royal _B_////
18 rue Bodenbroek ☎ _512 87 51_ • _closed Sun, Aug, nat hols_ • _AE DC MC V_
Until recently, this was one of the last bastions of the Belgian establishment, a stone's throw from the Royal Palace in aristocratic Sablon. The great pride of the Ecailler – meaning oyster bar – is that no meat enters its doors: there is a wide choice of fresh fish and _fruits de mer_, with a daily special. The wine list is also excellent. Behind the

mullioned windows, the decor is as resolutely traditional (and masculine) as the regular clientele. It is more spacious and comfortable upstairs but many people prefer to be downstairs.

La Maison du Boeuf _B_//
Hilton Hotel ☎ _513 88 77_ • _AE DC MC V_
The clientele at the Hilton's prime restaurant is mainly from nearby offices, notably those of the Ministry of Foreign Affairs in the Palais d'Egmont, whose gardens it overlooks. Well-spaced tables, unfussy decor and dependable service make it a good choice for a business meal without distractions. The US beef, the weekly market menus and the wine list are entirely reliable. The adjacent book-lined Bibliothèque provides a suitable atmosphere for a private working lunch.

La Maison du Cygne _B_////
2 rue Charles Buls ☎ _511 82 44_ • _closed Sat L, Sun_ • _AE DC MC V_ • _jacket and tie_
Prominently located on the beautiful Grand-Place, but beyond the pocket of the average tourist, this classic restaurant retains an exclusive, establishment aura. The panelled, beamed dining room upstairs, hung with oil paintings, overlooks the square but is quiet. Downstairs is the Ommegang, with a slightly cosier, club atmosphere, and a separate bar area with leather sofas. In both parts of the house traditional French cuisine is served.

L'Orangeraie _B_//
81 ave Winston Churchill ☎ _345 71 47_ • _closed Sat L, Sun, late Jul to mid Aug_ • _AE DC MC V_
An appealing new restaurant in the Uccle district, not far from Avenue Louise. The formula is neat: downstairs a chic oyster bar, offering light fish dishes (or meat from the trolley), upstairs an altogether grander dining room, with gracious period features and fabulous flower arrangements, where guests linger

over the *menu dégustation* or choose from the seasonally-adjusted *carte*. Wines are well chosen and reasonably priced. Downstairs, they are available by the glass – unusual in Brussels.

Villa Lorraine *B*////
75 ave du Vivier d'Oie ☎ *374 31 63 • closed Sun, Aug •* AE DC MC V *• jacket and tie*
Just outside the city limits, but only a 15min drive from the centre, the Villa Lorraine has long been famous for its woodland setting and excellent food. Even in winter the elegant inner rooms are less popular than the charming terrace room (specify when reserving). But the private *petits salons*, for 16 to 40 guests, are ideal for confidential meetings. There is also a separate bar. The set lunch menu is highly recommended; the *menu dégustation* is more suitable for the evening. A shorter wine list, with judicious selections from the main list, is offered with the fixed-price menus.

OTHER RESTAURANTS

No guide to eating in Brussels would be complete without mention of *Comme Chez Soi*, 23 pl Rouppe ☎ 512 29 21, a place of gastronomic pilgrimage but too cramped for a business discussion and impossible to get into without several weeks' notice.

The touristy, but typical, area of L'Ilôt Sacré is a good place for less formal business meals or an evening off-duty; favourites include the traditional *Aux Armes de Bruxelles*, 13 rue des Bouchers ☎ 511 55 50, and *Chez Léon*, 18 rue des Bouchers ☎ 511 14 15, famous for its mussels (but no reservations). The most upmarket is the *Taverne du Passage*, 30 galerie de la Reine ☎ 512 37 32, open late and with an excellent wine list. Central restaurants used for business lunches include *Bernard*, 93 rue de Namur ☎ 512 88 21 (entrance through the grocers' shop), and the Flemish *De Ultieme Hallucinatie*, 316 rue Royale ☎ 277 60 66, famous for its Art Nouveau interior. *Au Duc*

d'Arenberg, 9 pl du Petit Sablon ☎ 511 14 75, is a chic restaurant in the Sablon district; in the Ixelles area the very formal *La Cravache d'Or*, 10 pl A. Leemans ☎ 538 37 46, is used by Belgian business people, and has a reasonably-priced "business lunch." *L'Armagnac*, 591 chaussée de Waterloo ☎ 345 92 79, is appreciated locally for its rich cuisine from southwest France and pleasant atmosphere.

Exotic foreign restaurants are very popular, especially with the resident international community. They include *La Porte des Indes*, 455 ave Louise ☎ 647 86 51 (Indian), and *Samurai* 28 rue Fossé-aux-Loups ☎ 217 56 39, *Fujiyama*, 55 rue Willems ☎ 230 12 56, and *Takesushi*, 21 blvd Charlemagne ☎ 230 56 27 (all Japanese).

The European Commission and Parliament offices have their own restaurant "scene." One of the most prestigious places is the new *Villa de Bruselas*, 65–67 rue Archimède ☎ 735 60 90, offering expensive Spanish food in very comfortable surroundings, but with a *tapas* bar in the basement. *Barbanera*, 69 rue Archimède ☎ 736 14 50, is favoured for its garden and terrace, and *L'Atelier*, 28 rue Franklin ☎ 734 91 40, has rooms for private meals. EC commissioners and senior functionaries take their guests to *Chez Callans*, 73 rue du Commerce ☎ 512 08 42. A bit further out, but within easy driving distance of the Rondpoint Schuman, is the *Trois Couleurs*, 453 ave de Tervuren ☎ 770 33 21, a country *auberge*. Also a short drive from the centre is *L'Oasis*, 9 pl Marie-José (in the Boondael area). It has a summer terrace, discreet service, and a quiet atmosphere.

Restaurant price guide
For the meanings of the restaurant price symbols, see *Symbols and abbreviations* on pages 6 and 7.

Out of town
There are several well-known restaurants in the suburbs just beyond the outer ring. These include *De Bijgaarden* ☎ 466 44 85 at Groot-Bijgaarden and *Eddie van Maele* ☎ 460 61 45 at Wemmel; and three on the edge of the Fôret de Soignes: *Aloyse Kloos* ☎ 657 37 37, an *auberge* offering high-class Luxembourgeois food and wine; nearby *Romeyer* ☎ 657 05 81 at Groenendaal, famous for experimental cooking; and luxurious *Barbizon* ☎ 657 04 62 at Jesus-Eik. Slightly farther afield are *Hostellerie Bellemolen* ☎ 66 62 38, in a romantic restored mill at Essene, and the *Tréfle à Quatre* ☎ 654 07 98, in the beautiful Château du Lac Hotel at Genval.

Bars and cafés
Local residents meet for a beer at typical bistros such as *Au Roi d'Espagne* on the Grand-Place, but formal business discussions are usually held in offices or over a meal. The club-like *Rendez-vous Bar* of the Sheraton, the *Waterloo Bar* of the Royal Windsor, and the Hilton lobby are safe places to meet.

Entertainment
The Bulletin (see *Local media*) has a good "What's On" section, revised weekly. *A Key to Brussels*, free in most hotels, has a "Brussels this Month" section. The Festival of Flanders (opera, dance, music) takes place from August to early October; information ☎ 737 31 11.
Ticket agencies Tourist Information Brussels on the Grand-Place will reserve seats for opera, ballet, theatre and concerts.
Opera, theatre, dance Opera standards in Brussels are now high, thanks to the patronage of the international community. The *Théâtre Royal de la Monnaie*, pl de la Monnaie ☎ 218 12 11 or 218 12 02, is the main venue; the *Cirque Royal*, 81 rue de l'Enseignement ☎ 218 20 15, is also used. The Brussels-based Ballet Béjart makes only occasional appearances. There are numerous theatres, but almost all plays are in French or Dutch.
Music The main venue for classical music is the *Palais des Beaux-Arts*, 23 rue Ravenstein ☎ 512 50 45. There are classical concerts at the *Pullman Astoria* on Sun mornings ☎ 513 09 65.
Cinema The latest films can often be seen in the original version. The *Kinepolis* at the Bruparck leisure centre, 1 blvd du Centenaire, is the largest cinema complex in Europe.
Nightclubs The *Crocodile Club*, 7 rue Duquesnoy ☎ 511 42 15 (in the Royal Windsor Hotel), is a cosmopolitan disco.

Shopping
Smart shopping areas include the top end of Avenue Louise and Boulevard de Waterloo for designer boutiques, and Place du Grand Sablon for antiques shops and interior designers. The Galeries St-Hubert (Galerie de la Reine and Galerie du Roi) are the oldest and grandest of the many shopping arcades. Best buys are chocolates (see *Thank-yous*), Val St-Lambert crystal and high-quality carpets. If purchasing an expensive item, it is worth asking for a *ristourne* (discount).
Carpets CBRS, 431 blvd Emile Bockstael.
Department stores Inno at Cité 2, 111 rue Neuve.
Fashion Olivier Strelli, 72 ave Louise, is the best-known Belgian designer.
Gifts Crystal from *Jadoul*, 17 ave Louise, or leather accessories from *Delvaux*, 31 galerie de la Reine.
Street markets There is an antiques market on Place du Grand Sablon on Sat and Sun.

Sightseeing
The chief glory of Brussels is the *Grand-Place*, with its Gothic *Town Hall* and guilds in unique Flemish baroque style. The *Maison du Roi* houses a museum of the history of the

city. Nearby, in Rue de L'Etuve, is the tiny statue of *Mannekin Pis*, the adopted symbol of the city. The 18thC architecture of the *Sablon* (Royal Brussels) area should also be seen. The *Atomium*, an iron crystal molecule magnified 165bn times, is a curious landmark to the north of the city.

Musée d'Art Ancien Fine national and European collection, with rooms devoted to masterpieces by Brueghel and Rubens. *3 rue de la Régence. Open Tue–Sun, 10–12, 1–5.*

Musée d'Art Moderne Mainly Belgian artists. *1 pl Royale. Open Tue–Sun, 10–1, 2–5.*

Musée d'Ixelles Belgian and French Impressionist paintings. *71 rue J. van Volsem, Ixelles. Open Tue–Fri, 1–7.30; Sat & Sun, 10–5.*

Musée Horta Home of the great Art Nouveau architect, Victor Horta. *25 rue Américaine, Ixelles. Open Tue–Sun, 2–5.30.*

Musées Royaux d'Art et d'Histoire Antiquities, Oriental and Islamic art (open even dates); European sculpture and decorative arts (open odd dates). *10 parc du Cinquantenaire. Open Tue–Fri, 9.30–12.30, 1.30–4.45; Sat & Sun, 10–4.45.*

Guided tours
Guided tours are organized by ARAU, 37 rue H. Maus ☎ 513 47 61, and *De Boeck*, 8 rue de la Colline ☎ 513 77 44 (2–3hrs). Guided walks are arranged by the *Artistic Heritage Association*, 20 rue aux Laines ☎ 512 34 21.

Out of town
The fine medieval cities of Bruges and Ghent are less than 1hr away by train: Bruges, with more charm and concentrated cultural interest than Brussels, merits a weekend's stay. The countryside of the Ardennes is also worth exploring. *Panorama Tours* ☎ 513 61 54 and *De Boeck* ☎ 513 77 44 offer day trips by coach. Waterloo is nearby, to the south, and De Boeck runs a "Battlefields of World War I" tour.

Sport and fitness
Football is the most popular sport. Anderlecht, the top local team, play at the *Heysel stadium*, 135 ave du Marathon ☎ 478 93 00, also the venue for international matches.

Fitness centres California Gym, 280–300 chaussée d'Ixelles ☎ 640 93 44; *European Athletic City*, 25A ave Winston Churchill ☎ 345 30 77; *Winner's*, 13 rue Borneels ☎ 230 47 02 (squash and sauna).

Golf Royal Golf Club de Belgique, Château de Ravenstein, ave de Tervuren ☎ 767 58 01.

Jogging In the Parc de Bruxelles or the Forêt de Soignes.

Riding Centre Equestre de la Cambre, 872 chaussée de Waterloo ☎ 375 34 08.

Squash Fort Jaco Squash Club, 1333 chaussée de Waterloo ☎ 375 39 08.

Swimming Municipal pools (such as *Poseidon*, ave des Vaillants ☎ 771 66 55, at Woluwé-St-Lambert) are excellent. The pool at the Stephanie Hotel is open to nonresidents.

Tennis There are many tennis clubs; most will allow nonmembers to reserve courts. Try *Davis Tennis Club*, 26 F. Landrainstraat, Wezembeek-Oppem ☎ 731 77 07, or *Wimbledon Club*, 220 chaussée de Waterloo ☎ 358 35 23.

Local resources
Business services
Numerous firms offer help: consult "Office Services for Firms" in the *Pages d'Or*, or try *Burotel*, 507 rue de la Presse ☎ 217 83 60.

Photocopying and printing Brussels City Copy, 37 blvd du Jardin Botanique ☎ 218 51 80 (open Mon–Sat, will deliver); *Color Copy*, 150 ave Firmin Lecharlier ☎ 425 49 91. After hours use *L'Etoile*, 144 blvd Adolphe Max ☎ 219 05 67 (open 8am–midnight), or the *General Store*, 276 chaussée de Boondael, Ixelles ☎ 647 34 07 (7pm–3am).

Secretarial BCF (Business Communication Facilities), 375/382 ave Louise ☎ 647 05 67; ACTE, 304 ave Louise ☎ 640 24 85.

Translation *Berlitz*, 36 ave des Arts
☎ 513 92 74 (technical and general);
Mendez, 8 ave F. Roosevelt ☎ 647 27
00 (general translation and printing).

Communications
Local delivery *Les Scooters Bruxellois*
☎ 537 98 27.
Long-distance delivery DHL ☎ 720
96 60; *Federal Express* ☎ 722 77 77;
Halbart Express ☎ 735 91 16.
Post office The Gare du Midi post
office, 48A ave Fonsny (24hrs).
Telex and fax There is a public telex
office at 17 blvd de l'Impératrice
☎ 513 44 90 (near Gare Centrale),
open until 11pm. The *International
Press Centre*, 1 blvd Charlemagne
☎ 230 62 15, has a post office with
telex facilities for the use of
journalists.

Conference/exhibition centres
The *Palais des Congrès*, 3 Coudenberg
1000 ☎ 513 41 30, and the *Brussels
International Conference Centre*,
(capacity up to 1,200), Parc des
Expositions ☎ 478 48 60, are the
main conference centres. The Hilton
and Sheraton hotels have excellent
facilities for company conferences.
The *Expo Rogier Centre*, 32A rue du
Progrès ☎ 218 50 91, is used mainly
for exhibitions.

Emergencies
Bureaux de change The bureaux de
change at the main stations are open
in the evenings (Nord and Midi until
11) and at weekends. *Eurogold*, 30–32
rue de la Bourse ☎ 513 74 10, and
Paul Laloy, rue de la Montagne
☎ 511 92 17, are open on Sat (Paul
Laloy also Sun, 11–1, Jun–Sep).
Some banks also open on Sat
mornings.
Hospitals *Cliniques Universitaires St
Luc*, 10 ave Hippocrate ☎ 764 11 11;
Institut Medical Edith Cavell, 32 rue
E. Cavell ☎ 348 41 11. Emergency
dental treatment ☎ 426 10 26.
Pharmacies have lists in their
windows of those on late duty.

Police ☎ 101. There is a police
station on the Grand-Place.

Government offices
Ministry of Economic Affairs,
23 sq de Meeûs, 1000 ☎ 512 66 90
(investment opportunities and
regulations), 233 61 11 (patents and
trademarks) or 513 96 40 (trade fairs);
OBCE (Belgian Foreign Trade Office),
World Trade Center, 162 blvd Emile
Jacqmain, 1000 ☎ 219 44 50,
provides commercial information and
help with contacts.

Information sources
Business information *Chambre de
Commerce de Bruxelles*, 500 ave
Louise, 1050 ☎ 648 50 02; EC
COMMISSION, 200 rue de la Loi,
1048 ☎ 235 11 11; INBEL, 3 rue
Montoyer, 1040 ☎ 512 66 68 (Belgian
Institute for Information and
Documentation); ORI *data base*, 25/12
pl de l'Université, B-1348 Ottignies-
Louvain-la-Neuve ☎ (010) 47 67 11
(commercial, financial and legal
profiles of all Belgian companies);
Union des Entreprises de Bruxelles:
UEB, 75 rue Botanique, 1030 ☎ 219
32 23 (Brussels Business Federation
with export promotion service).
Local media The principal daily
newspapers are *Le Soir* and the Dutch
language *De Standaard* (catholic
independent). The main economic
dailies are *L'Echo de la Bourse* and *De
Financieel Ekonomische*; *Trends/
Tendances* is an economic weekly,
with separate French and Flemish
versions. *The Bulletin* is an excellent
news weekly with a monthly business
supplement for subscribers only.
Tourist information Offices at 61 rue
du Marché-aux-Herbes ☎ 512 30 30
and at the Town Hall ☎ 513 89 40.

Thank-yous
Chocolates *Corné Toison d'Or*,
24–26 galerie du Roi ☎ 512 49 84;
Mary, 180 rue Royale ☎ 217 45 00.
Florist *Kuipers*, 93 rue du Marché-
aux-Herbes ☎ 513 02 91.

DENMARK

Denmark is one of the wealthiest members of the EC; in terms of income per head, it ranks well above France, West Germany and the UK. But it approaches the 1990s with its economy in trouble (after strong growth in the period 1982–86), recurrent balance of payments problems and heavy debt burden, and high inflation and unemployment. The government has responded by tightening economic policies and providing incentives for exporters. Hopes for the future rest on improvements in export performance and development of offshore oil and gas reserves.

The industrial sector (manufacturing and mining) accounts for 20% of GDP and 70% of exports. Industrial production has increased rapidly since Denmark joined the EC in 1973. Most manufacturing is based on the processing of agricultural produce and timber, and on light industry such as chemicals, electronics, metal production, engineering and shipbuilding. Manufacturing is almost wholly under private ownership and small firms predominate; only about 80 companies employ more than 500 people. The main industrial concentrations are around Copenhagen, Odense, Århus and Alborg-Norresundby. The service sector, which grew rapidly in the 1970s, now represents over 50% of GDP.

The agricultural sector is also important, although less so since World War II. Today it accounts for 5% of GDP and 20–25% of total exports. The main activities are livestock production (pigmeat, beef, veal, poultry and dairy produce), flower-growing and vegetable production. Over 60% of agricultural output is exported. Although the world's third largest fish exporter, the Danish fishing industry has been hit by rising fuel costs, falling prices, overcapacity and falling fishing stocks.

About 70% of Danish exports are manufactured goods (mainly in the high-technology sectors). Other exports include meat and meat products, dairy produce, fish and chemicals. Denmark is dependent on imports for capital goods and raw materials (including oil). About 45% of Denmark's external trade is with fellow members of the EC, principally West Germany and the UK. The balance of trade has for some years shown a considerable deficit.

Geography Denmark consists of the Jutland Peninsula, which connects Denmark with the European mainland, and a total of 483 low-lying islands, of which 97 are inhabited and the rest are mostly reefs or sandbanks.
Climate Mild and equable, the climate is moderated by the North Atlantic drift.
Population 5.1m.
Government Denmark is a constitutional monarchy. The single chamber legislature, the Folketing, has 179 members elected for 4 years by proportional representation.
Currency Danish krone (DKr).
Time 1hr ahead of GMT; end Mar–end Sep, 2hrs ahead of GMT.
Dialling codes Denmark's IDD dialling code is 45. The city codes are incorporated into the 8-digit subscriber's number. To make an international call from Denmark, dial 009 before dialling the relevant country code.
Public holidays Jan 1, Maundy Thu, Good Fri, Easter Mon, 4th Fri after Good Fri, Ascension Day, Jun 5, Whit Mon, Dec 25, Dec 26.

COPENHAGEN (København) *City code* ☏ *included in numbers*

The Danish capital is on the island of Zealand at the extreme east of the country. Although its metropolitan area is home to about 1.35m, it also includes villages, unspoiled coast and countryside.

Founded as a port, Copenhagen no longer has important working docks. Fifty per cent of the city's manufacturing sector has moved out of the centre in the last decade, and there has also been a population exodus. However, the city remains the country's financial, administrative and service hub, home to the stock exchange, major banks and insurance companies, as well as publishing and printing, advertising and PR, architects and designers; and tourism is important.

Factories near Copenhagen process food, assemble high-tech equipment and make garments and furniture. The big names with international reputations include: Carlsberg in Frederiksberg, Tuborg in Hellerup, the head offices of øK (East Asiatic Company) and A.P. Møller (shipbuilding), Holmegård glass, Bang & Olufsen and Georg Jensen.

Arriving

Copenhagen is the gateway to Scandinavia. There are daily flights from all the European capitals as well as direct from the USA, Canada, Australia and Japan.

Copenhagen International airport
Completely renovated in 1987, this airport is one of Europe's best. Separate terminals, linked by a shuttle that departs every 15mins, handle international and domestic flights.

Numerous daily flights are operated by SAS to the Danish cities of Billund, Esbjerg, Karup, Aalborg, Århus, Odense and Bornholm (duration 40–60 mins); reservations ☏ 33 15 52 66, business class ☏ 33 13 62 77.

The terminals are spotless and spacious, and waiting is rare. A marble and glass arcade contains shops for china, glass, clothing and jewellery, books, flowers, food and duty-frees as well as restaurants.

Other facilities include banking, hotel reservations, a post office and car rental services, all open 6.30am–10.30pm. Several airlines provide lounges for business and first-class travellers; the SAS Scanorama Lounge has office space, a conference room and business services. Airport information ☏ 31 54 17 01, freight inquiries ☏ 32 52 25 11.

Nearby hotels SAS *Globetrotter*, Engvej 171, DK-2300 ☏ 31 55 14 33 ⊠ 31222 fax 55 81 45 ● AE DC MC V. Well-equipped modern hotel, 3mins from the airport and near the Bella Center exhibition complex. *Sara Dan*, Kastruplundsgade 15, DK-2770 Kastrup ☏ 31 51 14 00 ⊠ 31111 fax 31 51 37 01. Minutes from the airport, comfortable and well-equipped.

City link The airport is 9kms/5 miles southwest of the city centre and a 15–20min drive.

Taxis wait outside the terminal; fare to the city centre about Dkr75.

Limousine service is available from hotels if ordered when rooms are reserved. Those staying at SAS hotels can check in at the airport.

Car rental is recommended only for journeys outside the city. All the main firms have desks at the airport.

Bus Luxury SAS buses leave every 15mins for the city terminal beside the central railway station, 5.45am–11.10pm, fare Dkr24. Tickets from the driver. Journey time 20–30mins.

Railway station
Hovedbanegården is a splendid, monumental building with a

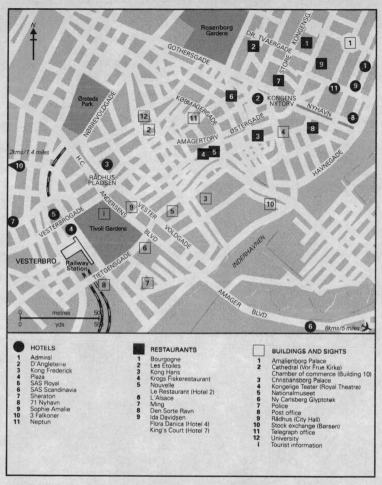

HOTELS
1 Admiral
2 D'Angleterre
3 Kong Frederick
4 Plaza
5 SAS Royal
6 SAS Scandinavia
7 Sheraton
8 71 Nyhavn
9 Sophie Amalie
10 3 Falkoner
11 Neptun

RESTAURANTS
1 Bourgogne
2 Les Étoiles
3 Kong Hans
4 Krogs Fiskerestaurant
5 Nouvelle
Le Restaurant (Hotel 2)
6 L'Alsace
7 Ming
8 Den Sorte Ravn
9 Ida Davidsen
Flora Danica (Hotel 4)
King's Court (Hotel 7)

BUILDINGS AND SIGHTS
1 Amalienborg Palace
2 Cathedral (Vor Frue Kirke)
Chamber of commerce (Building 10)
3 Christiansborg Palace
4 Kongelige Teater (Royal Theatre)
5 Nationalmuseet
6 Ny Carlsberg Glyptotek
7 Police
8 Post office
9 Rådhus (City Hall)
10 Stock exchange (Børsen)
11 Telegraph office
12 University
i Tourist information

restaurant, bank (open summer, 6.45am–10pm; winter, 7–9), post office, supermarket (open late and on Sunday) and small shops. An accommodation bureau is open daily, summer, 9–midnight; winter, Mon–Fri, 9–5; Sat, 9–noon. Inquiries ☎ 33 14 17 01.

Fast, hourly (6am–9pm) express trains link Copenhagen with the main Danish cities, including Esbjerg, Århus and Aalborg, involving a 1hr ferry crossing. Seats should be reserved through a travel agency or at the station ☎ 33 14 88 00. A rail bridge and tunnel to the mainland are due for completion 1992/3.

Getting around
Downtown Copenhagen is best covered on foot.
Taxis are plentiful (often Mercedes). They will stop if hailed in the street and wait outside hotels, in main streets and squares. Vacant cabs display a green illuminated *FRI* sign. Most drivers speak English and know the city well. A typical cross-town

journey costs Dkr30; tipping is not expected. Radio cabs: *Autolux* ☎ 33 11 22 21; *Radio Codan Bilen* ☎ 31 35 30 01.

Limousines Alterna Limousine Service ☎ 31 34 85 00 (24hrs); *Copenhagen Limousine Service* ☎ 31 31 12 34.

Driving Most hotels provide garages; street parking at meters is limited to one hour, and public parking facilities are often full. Hotels usually give residents discounted rates on car rentals. *InterRent* ☎ 33 11 62 00 undercuts competitors; *Avis* ☎ 33 15 22 99; *Budget* ☎ 33 13 39 00; *Europcar* ☎ 31 24 66 77; *Hertz* ☎ 33 12 77 00.

Walking Distances are short, major roads have pedestrian crossings and the centre is traffic-free; signs are in English as well as Danish. Bicycles are a hazard, particularly in summer.

Bus and subway The integrated public transport system extends for 40kms/25 miles around the city. Tickets, valid for 2hrs (*grundbillet*), and a Copenhagen card, valid for 3 days and giving free entry to many museums, are sold at stations or by bus drivers. They should be cancelled in machines on buses or on station platforms.

Trains There are frequent services (s-trains) to the suburbs (5am–midnight), twice-hourly services north to Helsingør and 3–6 times hourly west to Roskilde.

Ferries Highspeed hydrofoils link Copenhagen to the Swedish port of Malmö (40mins), for onward train connections to Stockholm (7hrs) and Oslo (9hrs 30mins), and to Helsingborg (50mins). Information and reservations ☎ 33 12 80 88.

Area by area

Copenhagen is very small and compact. Its heart is the island now occupied by the Christiansborg Palace, site of the Folketing (Parliament) and housing the Supreme Court, royal state rooms and reception rooms of the ministries.

The Børsen (stock exchange) is on the eastern edge of this small island, a building with a landmark spire of four entwined dragons' tails. This faces the financial district where the fortress-like Danmarks Nationalbank is located, along with the head offices of major public banks such as Handelsbanken and Den Danske Bank as well as ØK, the East Asiatic Company, and other long-established insurance and trading firms.

A more recent business sector has grown up north of the railway station. Here, the city's few high-rise office blocks stand beside the Tivoli Gardens to the east and the Vesterbro district to the west, home to many of the city's immigrants (mainly from Turkey, Yugoslavia and Pakistan) and its red-light district. The new Scala complex containing restaurants, shops and cinemas opened early in 1989 just opposite the Tivoli Gardens.

The administrative centre of the city is Rådhuspladsen, the neo-Gothic, red-brick City Hall. Going north towards the University is a shopping district of upmarket boutiques. The "Latin Quarter" around the University and the early 19thC Cathedral is full of antiquarian bookshops and student cafés.

The principal shopping street, which is traffic-free, known as Strøget but comprising five separate streets, runs west to east from Rådhuspladsen to Kongens Nytorv. The most picturesque streets and buildings lie south of it, especially in the old port, Nyhavn which was gentrified in the 1960s. Now many wealthy residents live in the wooded north of the city, which is also the embassy district, in Lyngby and as far out as Hillerød. The defunct port of Copenhagen, which extends for some 40kms/25 miles of waterfront, is north of Nyhavn. Some of the older warehouses are now apartments. Wooded Vallø Storskov, to the south of the city, is another desirable residential district.

Light industrial factories (food processing, electronics, shoes and garment manufacture) are around the port and southwestern suburbs.

Hotels

Copenhagen's hotels are of a very high standard and expensive. The SAS Royal or Scandinavia are the best-equipped for business travellers; D'Angleterre is the most prestigious hotel. From May to September, the high tourist season, reservations are essential. Standard facilities, unless otherwise stated, are 24hr room service and IDD telephones, minibars and TVs, with a choice of videos.

Admiral K/
Toldbodgade 24–28, DK-1253 K
☎ *33 11 82 82* TX *15941*
fax 33 32 55 42 • AE MC V •
362 rooms, 4 suites, 1 restaurant,
1 bar
In the charming Admiral, converted from an old waterfront warehouse, many rooms have massive timber beams and views onto the dock for ferries bound for Norway and Sweden. A well-appointed hotel used by business travellers and local firms for seminars and receptions. Parking, newsstand, shops • sauna, solarium • 10 meeting rooms (capacity to 230).

D'Angleterre K////
Kongens Nytorv 34, DK-1050 K
☎ *33 12 00 95* TX *15877*
fax 33 12 11 18 • Royal Classic • AE
DC MC V • 102 rooms, 28 suites,
2 restaurants, 1 bar
Copenhagen's most luxurious hotel and the first choice for royalty, heads of state and leading industrialists. D'Angleterre faces the Royal Theatre and the financial sector of the city and is near the shops in Østergade. Dating from 1755, it was completely renovated in 1987. The public lounges and restaurants are palatial, the spacious bedrooms comfortably furnished in a more contemporary style. Many have large desks and armchairs and are suitable for meetings. The main restaurant is one of the city's finest (see *Restaurants*).

Credit card abbreviations

AE	American Express
DC	Diners Club
MC	Access/MasterCard
V	Visa

Service is polished and friendly. Room service 7am–10.30pm. Parking, hairdresser, shops • secretarial and word processing services, ballroom, 8 other meeting rooms (capacity up to 600).

Kong Frederick K//
Vester Voldgade 25, DK-1552 V
☎ *33 12 59 02* TX *19702*
fax 33 93 59 01 • Royal Classic • AE
DC MC V • 97 rooms, 13 suites,
2 restaurants, 1 bar
Famous guests, their names inscribed in brass in the reception hall, range from the Swedish King Carl XVI Gustav to the rock band Dire Straits. Wood panelling, log fires in winter and heavy furnishings create an old-world atmosphere, and the Queen's Garden restaurant, with its fountains and glass roof, is very pleasant in summer. Room service 7am–11pm. Valet parking • 4 banquet and meeting rooms (capacity up to 100).

Plaza K//
Bernstorffsgade 4, DK-1577 V
☎ *33 14 92 62* TX *15330*
fax 33 93 93 62 • Royal Classic •
AE DC MC V • 87 rooms, 6 suites,
1 restaurant, 1 bar
This congenial hotel, in a late-19thC building near the central railway station and the Tivoli Gardens, is comfortable and civilized and attracts a loyal clientele of European business travellers and affluent tourists. The large bedrooms are traditionally furnished, and the book-lined Library Bar is a good place to meet before lunch or dinner in the Flora Danica (see *Restaurants*). Room service 7am–11pm. Valet parking • 2 meeting rooms (capacity up to 60).

SAS **Royal** 𝐊////
Hammerichsgade 1, DK-1611 v
☎ *33 14 14 12* ⊠ *27155*
fax 33 14 14 21 • *AE DC MC V* •
257 rooms, 9 suites, 2 restaurants,
2 bars
The atmosphere of SAS's flagship hotel
in Copenhagen is luxurious and
comfortable. It has useful business
facilities. The main dining room
opened in 1987, and there is a
nightclub, the Fellini. Royal Club
rooms (more expensive) at the top of
this tower block have good working
space. Parking • fitness centre, sauna,
solarium • offices and computers, 9
meeting rooms with a/v facilities
(capacity up to 250).

SAS **Scandinavia** 𝐊////
Amager Blvd 70, DK-2300 s
☎ *33 11 23 24* ⊠ *31330*
fax 33 57 01 93 • *AE DC MC V* •
498 rooms, 45 suites, 2 restaurants,
1 bar
Copenhagen's largest hotel is a 15min
walk from the city centre and near
the Bella Center, a conference
complex. Designed for the conference
trade, it has comprehensive business
facilities. This is a busy, well-
organized hotel with modern decor.
The Top of the Town restaurant,
with panoramic views, is suitable for
entertaining. Nightclub, nonsmoking
rooms, shops, parking • pool, fitness

Hotel and restaurant price guide
For the meanings of the hotel and
restaurant price symbols, see
pages 6 and 7.

---

centre, sauna, • 14 meeting rooms
with a/v and simultaneous translation
facilities (capacity up to 800).

Sheraton 𝐊//
Vester Søgade 6, DK-1601 v
☎ *33 14 35 35* ⊠ *27450*
fax 33 32 12 23 • *AE DC MC V* •
436 rooms, 31 suites, 2 restaurants,
2 bars
A large, modern high-rise hotel on
the edge of the city centre, the
Sheraton is dependable and efficient
and has a convenient restaurant, the
King's Court (see *Restaurants*).
Nightclub, shops, parking • fitness
room, sauna • secretarial, word
processing and translation services,
11 meeting rooms (capacity up
to 400).

OTHER HOTELS
71 Nyhavn 𝐊// *Nyhavn 71,*
DK-1051 κ ☎ *33 11 85 85* ⊠ *27558*
fax 33 93 15 85 • *Romantic* • *AE DC*
MC V. A converted warehouse,
intimate and popular with tourists.
Sophie Amalie 𝐊 *Sankt Annae*
Plads 21, DK-1250 κ ☎ *33 13 34 00*
⊠ *15815 fax 33 32 55 42* • *AE DC*
MC V. A pleasant hotel with few
facilities. No restaurant.
3 Falkoner 𝐊// *Falkoner Allé 9,*
Frederiksberg, DK-2000 ☎ *31 19 80 01*
⊠ *15550 fax 31 87 11 91* • *Best*
Western • *AE DC MC V*. A conference
hotel, out of the centre.
Neptun 𝐊 *Sankt Annae Plads 18*
DK-1250-κ ☎ *33 13 89 00* ⊠ *19554*
fax 33 14 12 50 • *AE DC MC V*.
Pleasant small hotel with a good
restaurant.

Restaurants

Copenhagen has many first-class restaurants, but most are small, and advance reservations are necessary. Prices are high, but many offer several
more reasonable special dishes, often fish and game. Danes tend to drink
beer on its own, or as an accompaniment to the traditional fiery Aquavit,
rather than wine. Restaurants are often closed on Sunday.

Bourgogne 𝐊//
Dronningens Tvaergade 2
☎ *33 14 80 66* • *closed Sat & Sun*

• *AE DC MC V*
Deep in the cellars of a 200-year-old
former palace, this restaurant attracts

art dealers from the nearby auction rooms of Sotheby's, Christie's and others. The walls are appropriately decorated with antiques, the tables well separated to allow discreet conversation. The food is *nouvelle* in style, and the wine list is suitably distinguished.

Les Etoiles *K/*
Dronningens Tvaergade 43
☎ *33 15 05 54* • *closed Sat L, Sun* • *AE DC MC V*
Unpromisingly situated in a modern housing block, this is a fine restaurant with a young and dedicated staff. Embassy officials, art dealers and wine merchants come here because it is near, others for the high quality of the food – always fresh and original. A *menu dégustation* can be ordered a day in advance.

Kong Hans *K/////*
Vingåardsstraede 6 ☎ *33 11 68 68* • *closed Sun, 4 weeks Jul–Aug* • *AE DC MC V*
The short menu reveals little of the excellence of the food at this cellar restaurant. It has a loyal following for the combination of Italian and French cooking. Private room available.

Krogs Fiskerestaurant *K///*
Gammel Strand 38 ☎ *33 15 89 15* • *closed Sun* • *AE DC MC V*
A venerable institution in a row of 18thC canalside houses, Krogs traditional fish restaurant stands close to the site of the old fish market. Members of Parliament from Christiansborg Castle across the canal eat here occasionally, but lawyers and civil servants are the regulars. The service is respectful, and the green walls and sea paintings are very appropriate. The menu concentrates on fresh fish, oysters and lobster, but includes beef, veal and game.

Nouvelle *K/*
Gammel Strand 34 ☎ *33 13 50 18* • *closed Sun* • *AE DC MC V*
This chic restaurant with grey and white decor is just two doors away

from the long-established Krogs Fiskerestaurant. It attracts the PR, design and advertising folk who have begun to move into this quarter of the city, but underlying the apparent modernity is a respect for traditional excellence. Superb fish and game and fine wines.

Le Restaurant *K////*
Hotel d'Angleterre ☎ *33 12 00 95* • *AE DC MC V* • *tie preferred*
Le Restaurant provides everything for the grand occasion. The classical French cuisine and Danish variants, old-fashioned service and elegant ambience combine to make this the choice of senior politicians, bankers and industrialists as well as foreign visitors looking to impress. The frequently changed menu offers the best of the season's fresh products. The celebrated house special is *canard à la presse*.

OTHER RESTAURANTS
Copenhagen's restaurants cater mainly for hungry tourists, enticing them with open sandwiches and, in the hotels, *smørrebrød* lunch. But for the less formal business occasions try *L'Alsace*, Pistolstraede ☎ 33 14 57 43, not far from Kongens Nytorv in a recently restored street; *Ming*, Kongens Nytorv 2 ☎ 33 93 16 90, for its Chinese dishes based on local fish with salads; and *Den Sorte Ravn*, Nyhavn 14 ☎ 33 13 12 33, in the cellar of an 18thC residence, which offers the freshest fish presented with flair. *Ida Davidsen*, Store Kongensgade 70 ☎ 33 91 36 55, is popular with business people for lunch and for its excellent *smørrebrød*.

Several hotel restaurants have a loyal following in business circles. The Plaza's *Flora Danica* ☎ 33 14 92 62 specializes in Danish dishes and provides a quiet background for relaxed conversation. The *King's Court*, Sheraton Hotel ☎ 33 14 35 35, is convenient in west Copenhagen, where the choice of places to eat is limited.

Out of town

Some 15kms/10 miles north of Copenhagen in Holte, the 500-year-old *Søllerød Krø* ☎ 42 80 25 05 is a good choice for entertaining important clients. There are several rooms for private parties and a courtyard for summer dining. Chef Michel Michaud bases his French-style dishes on the local produce, using wild game, mushrooms and berries in season and fresh fish all the year round.

Bars and cafés

Many of Copenhagen's numerous bars spill outside in summer; in winter their dim lighting and wood panelling have charm. They may have live music in the evening and serve a light meal. Hotel bars where you can meet for discussions are the *Libary Bar* at the Plaza Hotel, the comfortable *Queen's Pub* at the Kong Frederick and *Le Bar* at the Hotel d'Angleterre.

Wine bars are popular, especially the long-established *Victoria Bodega*, Gammeltorv 26, and, with theartregoers, smart *Vinstue Bernikow*, just off Østergade at Kristen Bernikows Gade 29, and *Hviids Vinstue*, Kongens Nytorv 19, which also serves beer. The bars along Nyhavn, formerly the preserve of sailors, are changing as the area develops into a tourist attraction.

Café Victor, Ny Østergade 8, is the haunt of the young, affluent and fashionable, and *La Brasserie*, Kongens Nytorv 34, is equally chic.

Entertainment

Copenhagen This Week lists events and sources for tickets.

Theatre, dance and opera Kongelige Teater (Royal Theatre), Kongens Nytorv (information ☎ 33 15 22 20), is Denmark's national theatre, and nightly (except Sun) between September and June offers drama (mainly in Danish), opera or ballet by the highly regarded national companies. The famous *Royal Ballet* stages classical and modern works; box office ☎ 33 14 10 02.

English-language plays, usually by overseas companies, are produced at the *Mermaid Theatre*, Sankt Peder Straede 27 ☎ 33 11 43 03.

Music The *Danish Radio Symphony Orchestra and Choir* perform most Thursdays and Fridays at the *Radio House Concert Hall*, Julius Thomsensgade, and the *Light Symphony Orchestra* at weekends. Ticket agents include ARTE ☎ 31 10 16 22 or *Wilhelm Hansen* ☎ 33 15 54 57.

The Royal Danish Orchestra and the resident *Tivoli Symphony Orchestra* give concerts at the *Tivoli Concert Hall*, Tivoli Gardens (entrance, Tietgensgade), also the venue for overseas guest orchestras and performers box office ☎ 33 15 10 12 or 33 15 00 01.

Copenhagen hosts a major jazz festival every summer and regards itself as the European jazz capital. Leading international jazz bands play (Tue–Thu), and rock and folk is performed (Fri–Mon) at *Montmartre*, Nørregade 41 ☎ 33 13 69 66. *The Three Musketeers*, Nikolaj Plads 25 ☎ 33 11 25 07, is a nightclub and concert hall, offering traditional jazz nightly except Sundays.

Cinema See Friday's *I Byen* (*In Town*) supplement of the *Politiken* newspaper. Films are generally shown in their original languages, with Danish subtitles. For recent releases, check *ABC Cinema*, *Cinema 1-8*, the *Palladium* and *Tivoli Bio*, all on or near Rådhaus Pladsen.

Nightclubs Fellini in the SAS Hotel Royal is the best for mildly *risqué* entertainment. *After 8*, SAS Hotel Scandinavia, and *King's Court* at the Sheraton Hotel are select nightclubs.

Discotheques are generally for the under-30s but *Woodstock*, Vestergade 10 ☎ 33 11 20 71, attracts a wider age group with its relatively low sound level. The affluent and sophisticated go to *Club Privé*, Ny Østergade 14 ☎ 33 13 75 20, *On the Rox*, Pilestraede 12–14, or *Penthouse Club* at the Sheraton. Striptease clubs cater mainly for tourists.

Shopping

Denmark has a high rate of value added tax (MOMS); enquire at stores about tax concessions.

Shops are usually open Mon–Thu, 9.30–5.30; Fri, 9.30–7; Sat, 9–2. A few, mainly selling food, are open weekend afternoons in summer.

The main shopping area is the pedestrianized Strøget in the city centre extending from Rådhuspladsen to the east. Most upmarket outlets are in Østergade, the end nearest Kongens Nytorv; the side streets, such as Ny Østergade, are lined with boutiques and other small shops. The Latin Quarter, around the University, has many antique stores and new and antiquarian bookshops.

Copenhagen has much to offer in what is locally known as "kitchen to tableware." Danish designers still produce objects with functional and elegant outlines. *Georg Jensen* is as famous for his stainless steel and silver cutlery and elegant coffee pots (Østergade 44) as he is for his jewellery (Østergade 40).

Other silversmiths inlude: *Hans Hansen*, Amagertorv 16, *Peter Hertz*, Købmagergade 34, and a recent designer whose work has found favour with the Danish royal family, *A. Dragsted*, Bredgade 17.

The Royal Copenhagen Porcelain shop exhibits its hand-painted figurines and dinner services at Amagertorv 6. *Bing & Grøndahl*, next door, is also known for the quality of its tableware. The two best-known glassmakers are *Rosenthal*, with their shop at Frederiksberggade 21, and *Holmegård* at Østergade 15.

The products of all these companies can be seen at *Illum*, Østergade 52; numerous departments display the best of Scandinavian design, including furs, children's toys, crystal, textiles and furnishings.

Sightseeing

Copenhagen is a flourishing tourist city with excellent museums, historic buildings, an old port and the famous Tivoli Gardens.

Historic sailing ships are now moored in the dock that divides picturesque Nyhavn into the so-called "decent-side," lined with 18thC gentlemen's houses, and the north side, where the inns, once the domain of drunken sailors and prostitutes, are now modern restaurants.

The famous *Little Mermaid* is along *Langelinie Promenade* on the site of the former free port. The wistful bronze figure, made by Edvard Eriksen in 1913, is one of several statues and monuments along the popular Promenade and in the adjoining park.

Amalienborg Palace Royal residence (1749–60) considered one of the finest rococo buildings in Europe. Changing of the guard daily at noon. *Amaliegade. Not open to the public.*

Christiansborg Palace Seat of Parliament and built in the early 20th century. The royal reception rooms and 12thC remains of the first castle are open to the public. *Christiansborg Slotsplads. Open Tue–Sun, 9.30–4 (Jun–Aug); Sun–Fri, 9.30–4 (Sep–May).*

Nationalmuseet Viking relics and household objects from Denmark's peat bogs excellently displayed. *Frederiksholms Kanal. Open Tue–Sun, 10–4 (mid-Jun–mid-Sep); Tue–Fri, 11–3; Sat & Sun, 12–4 (mid-Sep–mid-Jun).*

Ny Carlsberg Glyptotek Founded by Carlsberg beer magnate, Carl Jacobsen, and containing work by Degas, Gauguin, Rodin and French Impressionists. *Dantes Plads. Open Tue–Sun, 10–4 (May–Aug); Tue–Sat, 12–3; Sun, 10–4 (Sep–Apr).*

Rosenborg Slot Early 17thC Renaissance-style palace, containing the Danish crown jewels, fine furniture and royal memorabilia; surrounded by a pleasant park. *Øster Voldgade 4. Open daily, 10–4 (Apr–Sep); 11–3 (Oct); Tue, Fri, Sun, 11–1 (Nov–Mar).*

Statens Museum for Kunst Works by Danish artists as well as by Munch, Matisse and others. *Sølvgade 48. Open Tue–Sat, 10–3; Wed, 10–5.*

Tivoli Gardens Huge amusement park (open Apr–Sep) in gardens, with many fountains, flowers, lights and excellent open-air concerts. *Vesterbrogade. Open daily, 10am–midnight (May–Sep).*

Guided tours
The Copenhagen tourist information office ☎ 33 11 13 25 organizes coach and walking tours, factory visits (breweries and porcelain) and motor boat excursions. *Copenhagen Air Taxi* ☎ 42 39 11 14 offers aerial tours (1hr) for up to three people.

Out of town
At *Roskilde*, 20kms/12 miles west, are five Viking ships, discovered intact in the nearby fjord: *Viking Ship Museum*; open daily, 9–5 (Apr & May, Sep & Oct); 9–7 (Jun–Aug); 10–4 (Nov–Mar). The *Cathedral*, built in the 12th century, has been the burial place of Danish monarchs ever since.

The route to Roskilde shows off the tidy Danish countryside, and cruise ships call at museums where there are recreated ancient villages, such as the one at Lejre.

Inside the castle of *Helsingør* (Elsinore), built 1637, are 15C remains. Performances of *Hamlet* are given in the Great Hall in summer, and the castle is open Apr–Oct.

Spectator sports
The Copenhagen Sports Centre ☎ 31 42 68 60 provides information on sports Mon–Fri, 8–4; most are listed in *Copenhagen This Week*. Horse-racing is held at *Klampenborg*, Klampenborgvej ☎ 31 63 78 98 on Sat (Apr–Dec), trotting at Charlottenlund, Traverbanevej ☎ 31 63 11 00. Weekend soccer matches take place at *Idraetsparken*, off Østerbrogade, north of the city centre.

Keeping fit
Fitness centres The best hotel facilities are at the SAS *Hotels Royal* and *Scandinavia*. The new *Scala*

centre, Axeltorv 2, contains a fitness centre and pool ☎ 33 15 12 15.
Golf Those with membership cards from their own clubs can play at *Københavns Golfklub*, Dyrehaven 2, Lyngby ☎ 31 63 04 83, in Jaegersborg Deer Park (10kms/6 miles north), and at the equally rural *Rungsted Golfklub*, Vestre Stationsvej 6, Rungsted Kyst ☎ 42 86 34 44 (24kms/13 miles north). Information available from *Dansk Golf Union* ☎ 33 13 12 21.
Squash Copenhagen Squash Club, Vester Søgade ☎ 33 11 86 38.
Swimming Frederiksberg Baths Helgesvej 29 ☎ 31 34 40 02, or go to the island of Bornholm in summer.
Tennis Københavns Boldklub ☎ 31 71 41 80 or 31 30 23 00.

Local resources
Business services
Hotels will organize most facilities.
Photocopying and printing *Prontaprint*, Skindergarde 41 ☎ 33 93 99 90; *A-1 Service*, Rebaek Søpark 3 ☎ 33 47 45 47; at many bookshops and post offices.
Secretarial Danish Management Group, Tagensvej ☎ 31 85 90 70; *Scandinavian Executive Office Service*, Studiestraede 38 ☎ 33 32 25 25; *Scheidegger Management International*, Gammel Kongevej 135 ☎ 31 21 11 51.
Translation CS *Translators*, Gothersgade 115 ☎ 33 12 03 33; *Sprogkonsulenterne*, Admiralgade 22 ☎ 33 11 02 33.

Communications
Local delivery Taxa Ringbilen ☎ 31 35 35 35 (taxi-operator).
Long-distance delivery DHL, Ringager 2 ☎ 43 43 07 43 or, within Scandinavia, the post office's *International Express Service*.
Post offices Main office: Tietgensgade 37, open Mon–Fri, 9–7; Sat, 9–1 ☎ 33 14 62 98. The post office at the central railway station is open Mon–Fri, 9–9; Sat, 9–6; Sun, 10–4 for letters and express packages.
Telex and fax at hotels, post offices or the main telegraph office,

Købmagergade 37. For sending telegrams by phone ☎ 0022.

Conference/exhibiiton centres
The Danish Convention Bureau, Skindergade 29, DK-1159 K ☎ 33 32 86 01, provides comprehensive advice.

International conferences and trade fairs, such as those on travel and tourism, business, data and robots, are held at *Bella Center*, Center Blvd, Copenhagen s ☎ 31 51 88 11. It has 40,000 sq metres/432,00 sq ft of space, capacity for up to 4,200, parking, cinemas, restaurants and banqueting facilities.

Central hotels with conference facilities include the SAS *Scandinavia*, SAS *Royal*, *D'Angleterre* and *Sheraton* (see *Hotels*).

Private firms offering convention/exhibition services are DIS *Congress Service* ☎ 31 71 22 44, *Spadille Congress Service* ☎ 42 20 24 96, and *Interpreters Secretariat* ☎ 33 32 25 25.

Emergencies
Bureaux de change Banking hours are Mon–Fri, 9.30–4; Thu 9.30–6. Outside these hours, exchange facilities at the central railway station are open daily, 7–9 (Oct–Apr); 6.45–10 (Apr–Sep) and at the airport daily, 6.30–8.30. Red cash dispensers, *Kontanten*, throughout the city take Visa and Eurocheque. American Express, Amagertorv 18, has a cash machine.
Hospitals Doctor on call 24hrs ☎ 33 12 00 41 (fee about Dkr300 in cash). For an ambulance ☎ 000. *Kommunehospitalet*, Øster Farimagsgade 5; *Rigshospitalet*, Blegdamovej 9; *Frederiksberg Hospital*, Nordre Fansanvej 57; *Bispebjerg Hospital*, Bispebjerg Bakke 23. Emergency dental service at *Tandlaegevagten*, Oslo Plads 14 (no telephone) weekdays, 8am–9.30pm; weekends and holidays, 10–noon; fees payable in cash.

Pharmacy Steno Apotek, Vesterbrogade 6c ☎ 33 14 82 66 (open 24hrs). A doctor's prescription is often needed for medicines sold over the counter in the rest of Europe or the USA.
Police Emergency ☎ 000. Police headquarters (*Politigarden*) ☎ 33 14 14 48 (24hrs). *Polititornet* (central railway station) ☎ 33 15 38 01. Lost property, Carl Jacobsensvej 20 ☎ 31 16 14 06.

Government offices
Danish Ministry of Foreign Affairs, Asiatisk Plads 2 ☎ 33 92 00 00.

Information sources
Business information Danish Chamber of commerce, Børsen, Børsgade ☎ 33 91 23 23; *Federation of Danish Industries*, H.C. Andersens Blvd 18 ☎ 33 15 22 33; *Association of Commercial Agents of Denmark*, Børsen, Børsgade ☎ 33 14 49 41; *Chamber of Danish Trades and Crafts*, Amaliegade 15 ☎ 33 12 36 76; *Danish Agricultural Council*, Axeltorv 3 ☎ 33 14 56 72.
Local media The radio station Denmark 1 on 91.8MLZ carries news in English Mon–Sat, 8.10am. The Danish-language newspapers *Politiken*, *Børsen* and *Information* cover business and economic affairs.

Major foreign newspapers and magazines are available on publication day.
Tourist information Danish Tourist Board, H.C. Andersens Blvd 22 ☎ 33 11 13 25, open Mon–Fri, 9–6; Sat, 9–2; Sun, 9–1 (May–Sep); Mon–Fri, 9–5; Sat, 9–12 (Oct–Apr).

Thank-yous
Chocolates Agnete, Bredgade 25 ☎ 33 13 23 75, and *Alida Marstrand*, Bredgade 14 ☎ 33 15 13 63.
Florist Erik Bering, Købmagergade 7 ☎ 33 15 26 11.
Wine Otto Svenson & Co, Dronnigens Tvaergade 7 ☎ 33 14 04 82.

FINLAND

Unlike most European countries, Finland experienced a period of sustained economic growth in the 1980s due to an upturn in demand for its exports and high investment; growth was well above the OECD European average, and by the late 1980s per capita income was among the highest in the world.

Finland's economy is dominated by two manufacturing industries, in terms of both employment and output; the timber and associated industries (producing pulp, paper, furniture and other by-products) and the metal and engineering industries (producing, for example, machinery for the paper industry). Other expanding areas include chemicals, electronics and shipbuilding.

The basis of Finland's prosperity has been its performance as a trading nation; exports and imports of goods and services account for about 30% of GDP. The timber and associated industries have been the mainstay of export trade: in 1986, 80% of output was sold abroad, accounting for 40% of Finland's export earnings and representing 10% of world trade. However, in recent years the value of timber-related exports has fallen slightly as those of metal/engineering products and chemicals have grown. Given its limited natural resources, Finland must import most of its requirements; in 1987, about 60% of imports were raw materials and semi-manufactures.

Most foreign trade is covered by free trade agreements, 20% is with other EFTA members and 40% with EC countries. Finland's relationship with Eastern Europe is unique; it has had a free trade agreement with Comecon countries since 1974 and its special arrangement with the Soviet Union (whereby only the balance of goods is paid for in cash) shielded it from recession in the early 1980s. More recently, the value of trade with the Soviet Union has declined; however, growing West European demand has more than compensated.

Geography One-third of Finland lies within the Arctic Circle. The country is low-lying, apart from the mountains in the northwest. More than half is forested, roughly a third is marshy and a tenth is lakeland.
Climate In the far north temperatures drop as low as -30°C (-22°F) but rise as high as 27°C (81°F) in summer. In the south the extremes are less marked.
Population 4.9m.
Government Finland has been a republic since 1917. The president is elected every 6 years by a college of 301 electors chosen by popular vote. The single chamber legislature, the Eduskunta, has 200 members elected by proportional representation for a maximum term of 4 years. Coalition and minority governments are the rule. The average life expectancy of a government is less than one year.
Currency Markka (FMk).
Time 2hrs ahead of GMT; end Mar–end Sep, 3hrs ahead of GMT.
Dialling codes Finland's IDD code is 358. Omit the initial 9 from the city code when dialling from abroad. To make an international call from Finland, dial 990 before dialling the relevant country code.
Public holidays Jan 1, Jan 6, Good Fri, Easter Mon, May 1, Ascension, Whit weekend, Jun 21, Nov 1, Dec 6, Dec 25, Dec 26.

HELSINKI
City code ☎ 90

Helsinki has been the capital of Finland since 1812 when, under Russian Tsarist rule, the city was laid out in imitation of St Petersburg (Leningrad), then the capital of Russia. Relations between the two countries have been friendly, especially since World War II.

The capital, with a population of under 500,000, is Finland's centre of administration, finance, culture and retailing and the headquarters of the leading banks and the state-owned and semi-private corporations that control activities in a wide range of areas – such as Outokumpu (mining), Metsä-Serla (paper and timber products), Finnair, Kemira (chemicals and fertilizers), Valmet (engineering) and Neste (state oil importing and refining). Joint ventures with the Soviet Union are increasingly ambitious (for example, the project for a new highway through the Baltic States and Moscow to Turkey); and Helsinki is now a springboard for Western companies to enter the Soviet market in partnership with Finnish concerns. Helsinki's industry is small-scale, run by private enterprise and concentrated in the nearby satellite towns of Espoo and Vantaa, to which there is a population drift from the rest of the Finland.

Arriving

Helsinki is well served by flights from the rest of Europe and from the other Scandinavian capitals in particular. There are also direct flights from New York, Tokyo and Beijing but most visitors arrive via Frankfurt, London or Copenhagen. Silja and Viking Lines operate overnight luxury ferries from Stockholm, and there is a service from Lübeck.

Helsinki-Vantaa airport

This small airport has a restaurant, banks (open daily, 6.30–11), post office, hotel reservations desk, shops and duty-free shops.

Finnair flies to the 15 largest towns in Finland (average flight time 30–45mins); inquiries ☎ 818800. Airport inquiries ☎ 81851. For freight services, contact airlines.

Nearby hotel Airport Rantasipi, Takamaantie 4, 01510 Vantaa ☎ 87051 Ⓣ 121812 fax 822846 • AE DC MC V. A large modern hotel 3kms/2 miles from the airport with a shuttle bus service to the city. Rooms are large and comfortable. Nightclub, shop, pool, 16 meeting rooms (capacity up to 250).

City link The airport is 12kms/8 miles north of the city centre. The option is taxi or airport bus.

Taxi The rank is in front of the terminal. In the evenings and at weekends you may have to wait. The journey to the centre takes 20mins; the fare is around Fmk80.

Car rental Major firms have desks at the airport.

Bus The Finnair bus leaves at 15min intervals from 5.45am to midnight, (fare Fmk13) calling at the city terminal, next to the InterContinental and Hesperia hotels, and the central railway station.

Railway station

The monumental central station was designed in the 1920s by Eliel Saarinen. Facilities include a bank, post office, photocopying, shops, restaurants and supermarkets (open till 10pm and on Sundays) and taxi-ranks outside. Modern express trains run between main towns and north to the Arctic Circle; reservations are advisable. Inquiries ☎ 659411.

Getting around

Central Helsinki is small enough to get around on foot, but the city extends over a wide area, and a car or taxi is useful if you want to visit industrial Vantaa or Espoo.

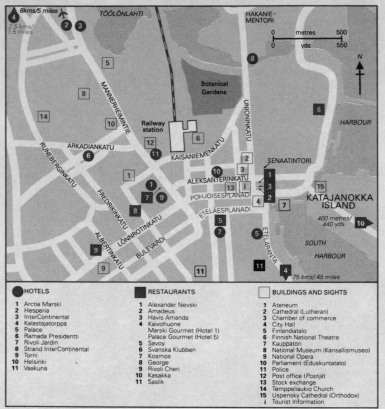

HOTELS

1 Arctia Marski
2 Hesperia
3 InterContinental
4 Kalastajatorppa
5 Palace
6 Ramada Presidentti
7 Rivoli Jardin
8 Strand InterContinental
9 Torni
10 Helsinki
11 Vaakuna

RESTAURANTS

1 Alexander Nevski
2 Amadeus
3 Havis Amanda
4 Kaivohuone
  Marski Gourmet (Hotel 1)
  Palace Gourmet (Hotel 5)
5 Savoy
6 Svanska Klubben
7 Kosmos
8 George
9 Rivoli Cheri
10 Kasakka
11 Saslik

BUILDINGS AND SIGHTS

1 Ateneum
2 Cathedral (Lutheran)
3 Chamber of commerce
4 City Hall
5 Finlandiatalo
6 Finnish National Theatre
7 Kauppatori
8 National Museum (Kansallismuseo)
9 National Opera
10 Parliament (Eduskuntatalo)
11 Police
12 Post office (Postijk)
13 Stock exchange
14 Temppeliaukio Church
15 Uspensky Cathedral (Orthodox)
i Tourist Information

Taxis Cabs can be picked up outside major hotels, the central station and in principal streets. They are not cheap; an average cross-town journey costs Fmk45. Have your destination written down; Finnish pronunciation defies most visitors. Taxis operate within defined areas; see the phone book under *Taxi*; central district ☎ 600044, 600366 or 600811; advance reservations ☎ 1824. Leave small change as a tip.

Limousines *International Limousine Service* ☎ 744577.

Driving Traffic is never very heavy. Streets are well signposted in Finnish and Swedish, but meter parking is difficult to find and the time limit of 1hr is strictly enforced. Multistoried parking is available in the centre (Fmk80 per day), and most hotels have garages. *Avis* ☎ 822600, *Europcar* ☎ 717211, *Hertz* ☎ 6221100.

Walking is easy in summer, but in winter the roads are icy.

Bus, tram, subway and train The transport system is integrated, but the subway is under construction and goes only to Itäkeskus. A day ticket allows unlimited use of the system, and 1hr tickets can be bought on the bus, at stations or newsstands. The benefits of a Helsinki Card (valid for up to 3 days) include free entrance to museums.

Area by area

Helsinki is small, clean, efficient and (in summer) green. It is built on a peninsula in the Bay of Finland. Downtown consists of a dozen blocks north of Pohjoisesplanadi and Eteläesplanadi, known as the North and South Esplanades, or the "Esplanadi." Either side of this avenue lie company headquarters, the principal banks and interior design and fashion boutiques. The stock exchange lies just off it, entered from Fabianinkatu.

One block north is the main shopping street, Aleksanterinkatu, with department stores and the new upmarket Senaatti-Center. Nearby, Senaatintori (Senate Square) is a 19thC assemblage so like Peter the Great's Leningrad that it has been used as a substitute by Western film directors. On the square are the Cathedral and Suomen Pankki (Bank of Finland), the Government Palace and the University.

On the North Esplanade are the City Hall and Presidential Palace. They face Kauppatori (Market Square), waterfront site of the market. In the natural harbour sheltered by the mainland and the island of Katajanokka is the ferry terminal known as the Eteläsatama, or South Harbour. The commercial ports are north of this island and around the southern perimeter of the mainland. There are proposals to relocate the docks and develop the waterfronts for offices and housing. Construction of a business centre around the Hakaniementori dock is under way.

The town has developed to the north along the Mannerheimintie avenue at the southern end of which are the railway station, the bus station, the main post office and the new Forum shopping centre. A little farther north are the red granite Parliament (Eduskuntatalo), the National Museum, the Finlandiatalo concert and convention centre, used in 1975 for the signing of the Human Rights Accords, and the Olympiastadion used in 1952.

Rapid postwar population increase has led to expansion mainly in new self-contained suburban cities, such as Espoo, Helsinki's "silicon valley," to the northwest, and, near the airport, the residential district of Vantaa which is also a distribution centre and an assembly site for a variety of goods from cars to instruments.

Hotels
The best hotels are the small and luxurious Rivoli Jardin, the InterContinental, the Hesperia and the Strand InterContinental.

Reservations are always advisable at least two weeks in advance. All hotels offer parking, currency exchange and rooms with TV, IDD telephones and minibars. Discounts may be available at weekends.

Arctia Marski *M* //
Mannerheimintie 10, 00100 ☎ *68061*
TX *121240 fax 642377* • *AE DC MC V*
• *157 rooms, 6 suites, 2 restaurants, 2 bars*
This central hotel is relatively small and convenient, and the service is attentive. Its chief attractions are the Gourmet (see *Restaurants*) and the popular nightclub, the Fizz Bar, which in the Cold War years was used as a retreat by Soviet and US eavesdropping intelligence agents. Nonsmoking rooms, sauna • 6 meeting rooms (capacity up to 600).

Hesperia *M* ///
Mannerheimintie 50, 00260 ☎ *43101*
TX *122117 fax 4310995* • *Sokos* • *AE DC MC V* • *379 rooms, 4 suites, 3 restaurants, 3 bars*
The Hesperia was used by signatories to the 1975 Helsinki Human Rights Accords. Refurbishment in 1986 was to a higher standard in the bedrooms than in the public areas, but the ordinary singles are small; opt for the de luxe version if you need working space. The smart French and Russian dining rooms are suitable for entertaining. Guests include conference delegates and tourists. The

Finlandia Congress Hall is nearby, and the town centre is a 15min walk by Töölönlahti Bay or a 5min cab ride. Nonsmoking rooms, nightclub, shop, hairdresser • pool, fitness centre, sauna, solarium • secretarial services, 12 meeting rooms (capacity up to 450).

InterContinental M////
Mannerheimintie 46, 00260 ☎ 40551 ℡ 122159 fax 4055255 • AE DC MC V • 555 rooms, 15 suites, 3 restaurants, 2 bars
This modern hotel, next to the Hesperia, is one of the largest in Scandinavia. The decor is gold and red and the furniture reproduction antique. American business travellers and visiting politicians and ministers figure prominently among the guests. The best rooms have views of the tree-fringed Töölönlahti Bay. The Brasserie is suitable for a serious working lunch, and the Baltic Bar is lively in the evening. Shops • pool, saunas • business centre with offices to rent, translation, secretarial and courier services, ballroom (capacity up to 700), 6 other meeting rooms with a/v equipment (capacity up to 100).

Kalastajatorppa M/////
Kalastajatorpantie 1, 00330 ☎ 488011 ℡ 121571 fax 4581668 • AE DC MC V • 235 rooms, 8 suites, 3 restaurants, 3 bars
A few minutes' drive north of the town centre, this luxurious modern hotel is set in a park along a private beach. Ronald Reagan and George Schultz have stayed here. Conference and sports facilities are excellent, and the Red Room nightclub is popular. Nonsmoking rooms • 2 indoor pools, fishing • 14 meeting rooms (capacity up to 550).

Palace M////
Eteläranta 10, 00130 ☎ 171114 ℡ 121570 fax 654786 • AE DC MC V • 53 rooms, 6 suites, 4 restaurants, 1 bar
The Palace is popular with British and other European visitors who find

that the service in this welcoming, small hotel is very helpful. The restaurants include the upmarket Italian La Vista and the Gourmet, which attracts members of government and the business community (see *Restaurants*). Nonsmoking rooms, hairdresser • sauna • ballroom, 9 meeting rooms (capacity up to 100).

Ramada Presidentti M////
Eteläinen rautatiekatu 4, 00100 ☎ 6911 ℡ 121953 fax 6947886 • AE DC MC V • 495 rooms, 5 suites, 3 restaurants, 1 bar
The busy and central Ramada has its own airport shuttle bus and offers free use of the sauna and pool 7–10am. It is also a popular conference venue for local firms. Nonsmoking rooms, shop, nightclub • 10 meeting rooms, a/v and simultaneous translation facilities (capacity up to 400).

Rivoli Jardin M//
Kasarmikatu 40, 00130 ☎ 177880 ℡ 125881 fax 656988 • AE DC MC V • 53 rooms, 1 suite, 1 bar
The small Rivoli Jardin is set in its own quiet courtyard in the heart of the business district area. Its spacious rooms have been furnished with Art Deco touches, the bathrooms are luxurious and the atmosphere is welcoming. No restaurant. Sauna, solarium • 1 meeting room (capacity up to 20).

Strand InterContinental M////
John Stenbergin ranta 4, 00530 ☎ 39351 ℡ 126202 fax 761362 • AE DC MC V • 175 rooms, 10 suites, 2 restaurants, 1 bar
Opened in January 1989 and slightly north of the commercial centre, this is the best of the large city hotels. Many rooms have harbour views, as does the top-floor restaurant. Aimed at business visitors and the conference trade. Nonsmoking rooms, gift shop • pool, sauna • secretarial and word processing services, 8 meeting rooms (capacity up to 300).

Torni M//
Yrjönkatu 26, 00100 ☎ *131131*
TX *125153 fax 1311361* • *Sokos* • AE
DC MC V • *155 rooms, 18 suites,*
2 restaurants, 2 bars
The Torni is a curious mixture of the
old world and the new. Built in the
1950s, it has stained-glass windows in
the public areas and massive
decorative ceramic stoves in the

Hotel and restaurant price guide
For the meanings of the hotel and
restaurant price symbols, see
Symbols and abbreviations on pages
6 and 7.

---

spacious suites, all of which add
character. Popular with prominent
Finns and overseas travellers who
appreciate its quirkiness. Saunas • 4
meeting rooms (capacity up to 40).

OTHER HOTELS
Helsinki M/ *Hallituskatu 12,*
00100 ☎ *171401* TX *121022*
fax 176014 • *Sokos* • AE DC MC V.
Small, central hotel with spacious
rooms.
Vaakuna M// *Asema-aukio 2,*
00100 ☎ *131181* TX *121381*
fax 13118234 • *Sokos* • AE DC MC V.
An efficient business hotel opposite
the station, with a highly regarded
restaurant.

Restaurants

The Alexander Nevski is arguably Helsinki's most fashionable restaurant
though it is widely accepted that the Gourmet in the Palace Hotel serves
the best food. Lunch, the main business meal, is a leisurely affair between noon and 3. All wines and spirits are expensive and many Finns
still prefer mineral water or beer. Advance reservations are essential.

Alexander Nevski M//
Pohjoisesplanadi 17 ☎ *639610* • *closed*
Sun • AE DC MC V
Diplomats, stockbrokers and
government officials come here for
Russian Imperial cuisine served with
style. The lavish decor, velvet drapes,
chandeliers and stained-glass windows
emblazoned with the double-headed
Romanov eagle match the richness of
the food, which includes genuine old
favourites, such as borscht, sturgeon
and blini with caviar. Some, rather
sweet, Russian wines, but mostly
European.

Amadeus M/
Sofiankatu 4 ☎ *626676* • *closed Sat L,*
Sun • AE DC MC V
Close to the City Hall and the
beautiful ice-white Lutheran
Cathedral, Amadeus is a smart
modern restaurant, decorated with
Impressionist art posters, and
frequented by bankers, government
employees and academics. The menu
includes assorted fish roes, reindeer
tongue, wild duck and grouse.

Havis Amanda M/
Unioninkatu 23 ☎ *666882* • *closed*
Sun • AE DC MC V
Next door to Alexander Nevski and
patronized by the same mix of
executives and politicians, this is
Helsinki's premier fish restaurant.
The chefs concentrate on unusual
combinations, rich soups and sauces
based on fresh herbs.

Kaivohuone M/
Kaivopuisto ☎ *177881* • *closed Sun,*
Mon, L in winter • AE DC MC V
The old Pump Room in Kaivopuisto
Park was founded in 1837 as a place
of public entertainment and still
contains a popular nightclub. Head
chef Juha Niemiö's French-style
cooking uses traditional Finnish
ingredients, such as reindeer, grouse
and fish.

Marski Gourmet M
Arctia Marski Hotel ☎ *68061* • AE DC
MC V • *smart dress*
Bankers and company directors come
here because of the excellent cooking

and civilized atmosphere. There is an extensive range of seafood dishes, and the special dessert is cheese pancakes with arctic berries.

Palace Gourmet *M/////*
Palace Hotel ☎ *171114 • closed Sat, Sun, July • AE DC MC V • jackets for D*
The Palace Gourmet is Helsinki's foremost restaurant, and its reputation has been earned by the inventive preparation of carefully chosen ingredients such as reindeer, wild mushrooms, willow grouse and pike-perch. Outstanding wine list.

Savoy *M/*
Eteläesplanadi 14 ☎ *176571 • closed Sat & Sun • AE DC MC V*
The Savoy draws its clientele from the surrounding banks, ministries, embassies and head offices. *Nouvelle cuisine* is a recent innovation; most customers prefer traditional dishes, such as salmon and herring smoked on the premises, and beef served with goose liver sausages.

Svenska Klubben *M//*
Maurinkatu 6 ☎ *628706 • AE DC MC V*
The wood-panelled walls and antiques of this "establishment" restaurant are reminiscent of past grandeur, and the menu is strong on traditional game dishes. Private rooms are available.

OTHER RESTAURANTS
Kosmos, Kalevankatu 3 ☎ 607603, cultivates an artistic and Bohemian image, and the menu offers everything from a smoked eel sandwich to Châteaubriand; a good choice for a quick working lunch. Nearby, *George*, Kalevankatu 17 ☎ 647662, is small and serves wild duck, grilled salmon or seasonal shellfish. *Rivoli Cheri*, Albertinkatu 38 ☎ 643455, is strong on romantic atmosphere and French-style cuisine.
Of several restaurants offering traditional dishes from different regions of the USSR, the best are *Kasakka*, Meritullinkatu 13 ☎ 662288, and *Saslik*, Neitsytpolku 12 ☎ 170544.

Bars and cafés
Social drinking is uncommon, and the few bars outside hotels cater mainly to foreigners, but *The Angleterre*, Fredrikinkatu 17, is frequented by both residents and visitors. *Kaarle XII*, by the Rivoli Jardin Hotel at Kasarmikatu 40, is informal, and *O'Malley's*, Yrjönkatu 26, an Irish-style pub, popular with Americans.

Entertainment
The free listings magazine *Helsinki This Week* is in English, German and Swedish. For tickets for opera, concerts, theatre and films ☎ 643043.
Theatre The *Finnish National Theatre* is near the central railway station ☎ 171826, and the *Helsinki City Theatre* sometimes performs modern ballet; Eläintarhantie 5 ☎ 717644. In summer, the open-air *Peacock Theatre*, in Linnanmäki amusement park, has variety shows with international stars; tickets from *Lippupalvelu*, Mannerheimintie 5 ☎ 643043.
Opera The *National Opera*, Bulevardi 23–27 ☎ 129255, also stages ballet.
Music Concerts at the *Finlandia Hall* (Finlandiatalo), Karamzininkatu 4 ☎ 409611, are given by the *Helsinki Philarmonic Orchestra*, the *Finnish Radio Symphony Orchestra* and guest orchestras and conductors.
Cinema All films have original sound tracks with Finnish subtitles. Art films are shown at *Diana* ☎ 646655 and new releases at *Arena* ☎ 7531113.
Nightlife Hotels offer the best night-time hotspots, especially the *Kalastajatorppa, Hesperia, InterContinental, Fizz* (Hotel Arctia Marski) and *Sky Bar* at the Vaakuna. *Fanny and Alexander*, Pitkänsillanranta 3, is a smart disco.

Shopping
Most shops are open Mon–Fri, 9–5; Sat, 9–2; department stores, Mon–Fri, 9–8; Sat, 9–4. The stores, below the railway station are open on Sundays, as are other shops in the tourist season. Prices in Helsinki are high; inquire about tax-free concessions.

The department stores along the main shopping streets of Kaisaniemenkatu and Aleksanterinkatu include *Stockmann* (upmarket), *Sokos* and the trendier *Pukeva*. The most exclusive shops are on Pohjoisesplanadi or in the Senaatti-Center, Aleksanterinkatu 28. Typically Finnish items are furs, glass and jewellery. Farmed arctic fox and mink are available at *Osman Ali*, Yrjönkatu 8, or *Furella*, Bulevardi 14. For more exotic furs and designer products, try *Grunstein Boutique*, Senaatti-Center (entrance, Unioninkatu 27), *Furlyx*, Tehtaankatu 12, and *Tarja Niskanen*, Pohjoisesplanadi 33.

Finnish glass by Iittala and Nuutajärvi and porcelain by Arabia and Pentik are sold on Pohjoisesplanadi, where the fabric designers, *Marimekko* and *Vuokko*, and the craft and jewellery shop *Aarikka* have outlets.

Jewellers noted for contemporary designs are *Kalevala-Koru*, Unioninkatu 25, and *Björn Weckström*, Unioninkatu 30.

Sightseeing

The elegant neo-classical *Senaatintori* is the heart of Helsinki. Nearby *Kauppatori* is a lively market for fruits, flowers and live fish.

Ateneum (Ateneumintaidemuseo) National art gallery containing 18th–20thC Finnish art and works by Van Gogh, Gauguin and Modigliani. *Kansakoulukatu 3. Open Mon–Sat, 9–5; Wed, 9–8; Sun, 11–5.*

National Museum (Kansallismuseo) Impressive ethnographic collection of the Finno-Ugric people and the fishermen/hunters of the northern Lapp, Eskimo and Indian regions. *Mannerheimintie 34. Open Mon–Sat, 11–4 (Tue, 6–9); Sun, 11–4.*

Seurasaari Island Open-air museum of Finnish rural life and architecture. *Open Jun–Aug, daily, 11.30–5.30; May & Sep, Mon–Fri, 9.30–3; Sat & Sun, 11.30–5.*

Temppeliaukio Church Striking architectural monument, built inside a huge granite rock, completed 1969, with a waterfall cascading beside the altar. *Lutherinkatu. Open Mon–Sat, 10–8; Sun, 12–1.30, 4–5.30, 7–8.*

Uspensky Cathedral (Uspenskin Katedraali). Red brick 19thC Russian Orthodox cathedral, with onion-shaped domes and uncluttered interior with *iconostasis. Katajanokka. Open Wed, 2–6; Thu, 9–1.*

Guided tours Tourist office ☎ 174088 for boat trips, including a visit to the 18thC Suomenlinna Fortress.

Out of town

Porvoo, 50kms/31 miles south of Helsinki, is one of Finland's oldest towns, with a 15thC cathedral and colourful wooden houses. Those with spare time should consider a two-day excursion to Leningrad, for which visas are not needed (details from *Finland Travel Bureau* ☎ 18261).

Spectator sports

Racing and trotting at the *Vermo* racetrack to the north (train to Mäkkylä station) are popular. In summer, major events are held at the *Olympiastadion*, Paavo Nurmentie ☎ 440363. Tickets for all sporting events from *Lippupalvelu*, Mannerheimintie 5 ☎ 643043.

Keeping fit

Fitness centres The best-equipped are the *Nautilus Sports Center* ☎ 6946836 and the *World Class Fitness Center* ☎ 788360.

Golf At *Talinkartano* (Tali Manor) 7kms/4 miles from the centre ☎ 550235.

Squash Squash Club ☎ 642493.

Swimming at the Olympiastadion.

Tennis Helsinki Tennisstadion ☎ 556271 or *Sports Information* ☎ 1581.

Local resources

Business services

Hotels provide photocopying, fax and telex services and will arrange for secretaries and translators. Offices and conference rooms for rent plus usual services from *Helsinki Business*

Center, Salomonkatu 17A ☎ 6947711, or *Business Center Finland*, Melkonkatu 16A ☎ 670344.
Photocopying and printing Copycorner ☎ 2885888, *Multiprint* ☎ 642032.
Secretarial Clerical Oy, Aleksanterinkatu 19A ☎ 177770.
Translation Lisa Vermeer ☎ 781508.

Communications
Local deliveries Lähettipojat ☎ 7013122.
Long-distance delivery DHL Läkkisepänkuja 3 ☎ 799877.
Post office Main office (*Postijk*): Mannerheimintie 11, open 24hrs.
Telex and fax At all post offices.

Conference/exhibition centres
The ultramodern *Finlandiatalo* has 2 auditoriums, 2 halls (capacity up to 600 and 250) and meeting rooms (capacity from 20 to 100). Inquiries Karamzininkatu 4, 00100 ☎ 40241 ⊠ 123424 fax 446259. *Helsingin Messukeskus* (Helsinki Fair Centre), Rautatieläisenkatu 3, POB 21, 00521 ☎ 15091 ⊠ 121119 fax 142358 (one stop north from the central railway station), is used for international trade and public fairs (fur, fashion, business equipment, transport): 2 halls (capacity up to 4,000 and 13,000), 3 meeting rooms.
   The *Dipoli Congress Centre* Otaniemi, 02150, Espoo, ☎ 435811 ⊠ 121642 fax 462349, 9kms/5 miles to the west of the town centre, accommodates 4,000 in its 4 halls. Nearby the *Dipoli Hotel* has excellent sports facilities ☎ 461811.

Emergencies
Bureaux de change Banks open Mon–Fri, 9.15–4.15. Those at the central railway station and airport open every day and for longer hours.
Hospitals Standards are excellent; free treatment from *Meilahden sairaala* (Helsinki University Central Hospital), Haartmaninkatu 2 ☎ 4711. Emergency aid at *Töölönsairaala*, Töölönkatu 40 ☎ 40261. Ambulance ☎ 006. Private treatment available at

Diakonissalaitos (Deaconess Medical Centre), Alppikatu 2 ☎ 77501.
Dental treatment (not free) at *Hammaslääkärit* (Dental Clinic), Aleksanterinkatu 21 ☎ 176486; or *Oral, Dental and Medical Clinic*, Erottajankatu 5 ☎ 664011.
Pharmacy Yliopiston Apteekki at Mannerheimintie 96 is open 24hrs.
Police Emergency ☎ 000. The headquarters is outside the city at Olavinkatu 1 ☎ 6940633. The most central city station is at Pieni Robertinkatu 1–3 ☎ 1891.

Government offices
Ministry of Foreign Affairs, Ritarikatu 2B, *Department of Trade*, Laivastokuja 3 ☎ 134151; *Ministry of Trade and Industry, Foreign Investments Office*, Aleksanterinkatu 15 ☎ 1601.

Information sources
Business information Keskuskauppakamari (Central chamber of commerce), international trade department, Fabianinkatu 14B ☎ 650133. *Helsinki chamber of commerce*, Kalevankatu 12 ☎ 644601.
Local media The best paper for business coverage is the *Helsingin Sanomat*. *Radio Finland* broadcasts world news summaries Mon–Fri in English, French and German during the day on 558khz and 103.7Mhz. *Radio Ore* 91.1Mhz, carries BBC World Service News Mon–Fri, 7, 11 and 3.
Tourist information The Helsinki city tourist office, Pohjoisesplanadi ☎ 1693757, is open Mon–Fri, 8.30–4. The Finnish tourist board, Unioninkatu 26 ☎ 144511 or 174631, is open Mon–Fri, 9–1, 2–3.30.

Thank-yous
Chocolates Oona and Oliver Senaati-Center, Aleksanterinkatu 28.
Florists It is traditional to take flowers for your hostess or host. *Lisa Ward*, Eteläranta 14 ☎ 628878, and *Dan Ward*, Eteläesplanadi 22 ☎ 640721.
Wines and spirits are sold only from state-run stores called *Alko*.

FRANCE

The French economy achieved one of the highest postwar growth rates in real terms in the West, averaging nearly 6% a year in the 1960s and early 1970s, and just over 3% a year in the period 1973–79. Then growth rates fell below the average for major industrial countries, as industry became uncompetitive, export demand fell and oil prices rose. By the late 1980s the economy began to recover, helped by rising exports and industrial investment. Even so, high levels of unemployment and inflation, and trade deficits are recurrent problems.

The economy is fairly well diversified. France is the largest food producer in the EC and is among the leading exporters of fresh and processed food in the world. Agriculture's share of GDP has remained at about 4% for many years, but this does not reflect its importance as a source of export revenue and employment. Mineral and energy resources are relatively few. Manufacturing industry has expanded rapidly since the end of World War II although its relative share of GDP has declined in recent years as the service sector has grown. Today services account for more than 60% of GDP.

The 1980s have seen a reduction in the government's traditional interventionist role in the economy. Even the Socialist government has adopted a more market-oriented approach since economic recession in 1983 – liberalizing trade, removing price controls and reducing state subsidies to industry. Nevertheless the French economy remains planned to a degree, with a long-term strategy for further industrial restructuring, growth in export and fixed capital investment and development of new technologies.

Industrial activity has been concentrated in the Paris region, the Nord-Pas-de-Calais region, Lorraine and Alsace, the Upper Rhône region (around Lyon and St Etienne) and the southwest (around Bordeaux and Toulouse), but more recently has spread to the major ports of Marseille, Le Havre and Dunkerque and to the lower Seine valley. The main areas of production are heavy engineering, mechanical engineering, chemicals, electrical and electronic goods, and food processing.

After stagnating in the early 1980s, industrial output began to pick up as a result of rationalization, which has boosted productivity and cut unit labour costs. The fastest growing sectors are the newer industries such as telecommunications and computer software services. France has a nuclear power programme, a high-speed passenger train (train de grande vitesse) and a telephone service that are among the most advanced in the world. It is also the EC's leader in aeronautics, satellites and space research. Despite the overall growth in industrial output, some of the older industries – notably coal mining, textiles, steel manufacture and shipbuilding – have continued to suffer heavy losses.

About 60% of external trade is with other EC countries, principally West Germany and Italy. France is among the top five exporters in the world, but the visible trade balance has been in deficit since 1978 because import demand has risen while export demand, until recently, has weakened. The main exports are capital equipment, agricultural produce and foodstuffs, chemicals, non-durable consumer goods, motor vehicles and other transport equipment. The main imports are capital equipment, non-durable consumer goods, chemicals, agricultural produce and foodstuffs, energy products, steel and other metals, and household electrical goods.

Geography France is divided almost equally between uplands and lowlands. Its mountain ranges, the Alps and the Jura in the east and Pyrennees in the southwest, form natural frontiers. There are also four main hilly ranges: the Massif Central and Massif Armoricain in the centre, the Vosges in the northeast and the Ardennes on the border with Belgium. The most important lowland areas are the Paris basin in the north, the Aquitaine basin in the southwest and the southeastern area around the Rhône. The Rhône, the Rhein, the Seine, the Loire and the Garonne river systems have played a major part in France's economic development.

Climate The geographical diversity of the country produces marked local variations of climate. In general, the north has milder weather than the rest of the contry but has more rain; the south has a typically Mediterranean climate, with long hot summers and dry winters; the west tends to have wet springs and autumns; and the centre and upland areas have a continental climate.

Population 55.2m.

Government The Republic of France's head of state and chief executive is the president, who is elected for 7 years by a simple majority in a 2-round election. He appoints the prime minister, and on the latter's recommendation, the rest of the council of ministers.

The parliament has two chambers. The Assemblée Nationale consists of 577 deputies elected for 5 years. The electoral system has varied over the years; the current system is on the basis of single-member constituencies. The Sénat consists of 318 senators elected for 9 years by a college of

local councillors and members of the Assemblée Nationale. Its influence is limited.

The French Republic is divided into 96 départements, each of which has an elected assembly that has considerable autonomy over matters of finance, welfare and social services. The départements are grouped into 22 regions, which have had directly elected assemblies since 1982 that have control over local finance and matters of adult education and some aspects of culture, tourism and industrial development. Local government is further subdivided into 36,500 communes, which are in charge of their own town planning, building and enviornment.

Currency The unit of currency is the French franc (F), which is divided into 100 centimes.

France has been a member of the European Monetary System (EMS) since it was introduced in 1979. The franc is allowed to fluctuate by up to 2.25% against other currencies participating in the exchange rate mechanism.

Time France is on Central European Time, which is 1hr ahead of GMT. Summer time is in force from the end of Mar to the end of Sep; clocks are put forward, and France is then 2hrs ahead of GMT.

Dialling codes France's IDD code is 33. The city codes are incorporated into the 8-digit subscriber's number. To make an international call from France, dial 19 before dialling the relevant country code.

Public holidays Jan 1, Easter Mon, May 1, May 8, Ascension, Whit Mon, Jul 14, Aug 15, Nov 1, Nov 11, Dec 25.

PARIS

City code ☎ included within numbers

Paris lies on the river Seine, encircling the Ile de la Cité where its life began, in a fertile basin of northeastern France. By tradition, Paris has always had greater political and cultural importance, as capital of a great empire and generator of ideas and artistic creativity, than as a centre of trade and finance. Since 1945, however, France's cultural influence has declined, and it is in industry and technology that the country has made most progress. The capital of this highly centralized nation has seized the opportunity to develop rapidly as a modern focus of business.

In world financial markets, Paris still does not play as strong a role as might be expected. Although the Bourse has been expanding and modernizing, it is still old-fashioned and only one-fifth the size of the London Stock Exchange. However, as a business centre Paris has been surging ahead. Several major convention centres have been built, notably the Palais des Congrès, and during the last decade Paris has been one of the world's most popular cities for international business conferences, staging well over 200 a year. Several multinationals such as IBM have their European headquarters in Paris, which is also the base for leading French groups such as Elf-Aquitaine, Saint-Gobain and Thomson. New highrise business districts have been built, notably at La Défense, which lies to the west of the city, and at Quai de Bercy, which is east of the centre.

Industrially the city's importance is on the wane, but Paris still dominates most of French life. Nearly all the financial institutions and decision-making centres are based in Paris, including the state credit bodies and the main banks, and almost all the larger French firms have their head offices there. The recent decentralization policy has given a little more political and financial autonomy to the regions, but these moves are unlikely to reduce the importance of Paris as a business centre.

The business style of the capital is faster and tougher than is normal in the more easy-going provinces. If the French have a reputation in some quarters for arrogance, impatience and brusqueness, it is certainly the Parisians who have earned it. But they are industrious, competitive, quick to seize on new ideas and techniques, and more international in their outlook than provincials.

As its role changes, Paris continues to grow. The population of Greater Paris has almost doubled since 1945, and is now around 10.3m, although only 2.7m of these live within the city proper. The life of the city is vigorous, and its mood confident. People in business may worry about weakness in the French economy, but they are convinced that Paris is the most go-ahead of cities as well as the most beautiful. Certainly the government-led campaign to smarten up the capital has been highly successful. It is now very clean and more elegant than ever; and its new architectural showpieces, with their wide variety of styles, often highly controversial, are more striking than in any other European city.

Arriving

Paris has two large international airports, Roissy/Charles-de-Gaulle and Orly. It is also the hub of the country's excellent rail network, offering efficient services to all major national and international destinations. In addition, most of the country's autoroutes radiate from the capital.

Roissy/Charles-de-Gaulle airport

France's premier airport has two terminals, *Aérogare 1* and *Aérogare 2* (which has two separate sections, known as terminals 2A and 2B). As a general rule, Air France flies to Aérogare 2, using terminal 2A for intercontinental flights and some European destinations (particularly Italian cities) and terminal 2B for most European destinations; Aérogare 1 is mostly used by non-French airlines. Free shuttle buses link the terminals.

The futuristic design of the airport caused much comment when new and is enjoyed by some. Others find it confusing, even irritating. Be prepared for delays in collecting baggage and for long lines at passport control and the bureaux de change. Customs clearance, however, is usually fairly fast. Allow 45mins to clear the airport.

Facilities include those you would expect of a major international airport: restaurants, bars, snackbars, bureaux de change, telephones, post offices, hairdressers, photocopying, information desks, rail inquiry office. A special *2A Service* ☎ 48 62 22 90 rents out meeting rooms and will provide secretarial assistance and other business services.

Flight information inquiries ☎ 48 62 22 80; recorded information on the day's Air France flights ☎ 43 20 12 55 (arrivals) and 43 20 13 55 (departures); general inquiries ☎ 48 62 12 12; freight inquiries ☎ 48 62 20 00.

Nearby hotels Arcade ☎ 48 62 49 49 ⓉⓍ 212989 fax 43 20 14 55 and *Sofitel* ☎ 48 62 23 23 ⓉⓍ 230166

fax 48 62 78 49 are both at the airport. Close by are *Ibis*, ave de la Raperie ☎ 34 29 34 34 ⓉⓍ 699083 fax 34 29 34 19; *Holiday Inn*, 1 allée du Verger ☎ 34 29 30 00 ⓉⓍ 605143 fax 34 29 90 52; *Patio*, 54 ave des Nations ☎ 48 63 26 10 ⓉⓍ 232735 fax 48 63 28 01.

City link Charles-de-Gaulle is 25km/16 miles north of Paris, at Roissy-en-France. There are bus and rail links with Paris and with Orly airport, but a taxi is the most convenient way to travel.

Taxi Licensed cabs are available outside each terminal and usually plentiful, so you seldom have to wait long. Journeys are metered, and there is a special tariff as far as the Boulevard Périphérique, after which normal city rates apply. Check that the driver adjusts the meter rate when entering Paris, and beware of "cowboy" drivers in unlicensed cabs who charge exorbitant rates. The journey to central Paris takes 35–50min, depending on the traffic. Congestion is very severe during rush hours, especially on Friday evenings.

Bus Air France buses leave for Porte Maillot air terminal at 12min intervals between 6am and 11pm from gate 34 on the arrivals floor in Aérogare 1, gates A5 in terminal 2A and B6 in terminal 2B. The air terminal has a bureau de change, tourist information and hotel reservations desk, restaurant and shops. Porte Maillot terminal is also close to the Palais des Congrès. The local 350 bus service leaves every 15–20mins for the Gare du Nord (journey time about 50mins), 5.30–11.50pm. The 351 service leaves every 30mins for Place de la Nation (journey time about 40mins), 6am–12pm. Departures from boutiques floor in Aérogare 1 and gates A5 and B6 in terminals 2A and 2B.

Train A free shuttle bus leaves from gate 30 on arrivals level in Aérogare 1, and gates A5 and B6 in terminals 2A and 2B between 5.30am and 11.30pm, for Roissy-Rail station, from where trains run at 15min intervals to the Gare du Nord and other stations on the B line of the express Métro. Journey time to the Gare du Nord is 30mins. Highly efficient and worth considering if you are travelling light.

Car rental Not recommended for those whose business is only in Paris, but convenient for the suburbs and provinces. All the leading companies have offices in each Aérogare.

Orly airport
Orly has two terminals: *Orly-Sud*, used by Air France and many foreign airlines; and *Orly-Ouest*, used for internal flights by Air Inter and small private French companies.

Facilities Both terminals have bars, restaurants, snackbars, banks, telephones, photocopying facilities, hairdressers, post offices, information offices and *2A Service* (see Charles-de-Gaulle airport) ☎ 49 75 12 33; Orly-Sud also has a bureau de change open 6.30am–11.30pm.

Flight information ☎ 49 75 15 15; general inquiries ☎ 48 84 52 52.

Nearby hotels Altéa ☎ 46 87 23 37 TX 204345 fax 46 87 71 92 and *Hilton International Orly* ☎ 46 87 33 88 TX 250621 fax 49 78 06 75 are both at the airport and accept all or most major credit cards. Not far away are the *Holiday Inn* ☎ 46 87 26 66 TX 204679 fax 45 60 91 25 and *Videotel Paris Orly* ☎ 45 60 52 52 TX 261004 fax 49 78 06 25.

City link Orly is 16km/10 miles south of Paris. It is simplest to take a cab into the city.

Taxi Cabs wait outside both terminal exits; the journey rarely takes more than 45mins.

Bus Air France buses depart for Les Invalides air terminal (which has similar facilities to the Porte Maillot terminal) at 12min intervals from gate E at Orly-Sud and gate E on arrivals floor at Orly-Ouest between 5.50am and 11.30pm; additional buses meet flights landing after 11pm. Passengers may alight at the Porte d'Orléans, at Montparnasse and at Duroc Métro station on request and on the return

journey may board at the Gare Montparnasse rail station. Inquiries ☎ 43 23 87 75.

Train/Métro Trains run from Orly-Rail station (free shuttle bus) at 15min intervals (30min after 8pm) to the Gare d'Austerlitz and other stops on line C of the RER. Journey time to the Gare d'Austerlitz 35mins.

Car rental Major firms have offices at Orly.

Railway stations
Paris has six main rail termini, all of them on the Métro (subway). All offer a wide range of services: bars and restaurants, refreshment stands selling tray meals and snacks, newsstands and information points (not always manned). Porters are rarely available but trolleys can usually be found at the automatic counters. (You need a Fr10 coin for the refundable deposit.) All stations have taxi ranks (there is a supplementary pick-up charge) and many operate a taxi reservations service. Baggage may be sent from all stations, on production of a ticket, to any destination in France or the rest of Europe.

Passenger inquiries ☎ 45 82 50 50; reservations ☎ 45 65 60 60.

Gare d'Austerlitz For arrivals from the southwest; from Bordeaux and Toulouse and from Spain via Orléans, Tours, Poitiers and Angoulême.

Gare de l'Est For arrivals from the east; from Nancy and Strasbourg and from Switzerland and Germany.

Gare de Lyon For arrivals from the southeast including the TGV (high-speed train) service, and from Switzerland and Italy.

Gare Montparnasse For arrivals from western France, especially Brittany.

Gare du Nord For arrivals from the north, including the Channel ports, where trains connect with ferries and hovercrafts from Britain; also services from Belgium, Holland and the Scandinavian countries.

Gare Saint-Lazare For arrivals from Normandy and boat trains from Dieppe.

Getting around

Paris is small by international capital standards and you may well be able to walk to many destinations. The public transport system (called RATP), is also excellent, with the various methods of transport fully integrated. The same RATP tickets are used on buses, the subway and the RER and are best bought in blocks of ten (*carnets*) at stations or tobacconists'. Driving is not recommended. The streets are like race tracks when not congested; Parisian drivers are not patient; and parking is very difficult.

A booklet called *Plan de Paris par arrondissement* is widely available and has good maps of each district or *arrondissement*, with subway stations clearly marked, and separate bus maps of each bus route. Fatter editions also include maps of inner suburbs. RATP information ☎ 43 46 14 14.

Taxis These are often hard to find in Paris, especially during rush hours and in wet weather, and drivers are not always willing to pick up passengers in the street. There are plenty of taxi stands, recognized by blue and white TAXI signs. Journeys starting from stands at stations and airports are generally subject to a surcharge. Fares are metered and different rates apply in three separate zones (inner city, inner suburbs and outer suburbs). They are higher in the evenings and on Sundays and public holidays. Extra charges are made for baggage. Few drivers will take more than three passengers at a time. It is standard practice to add a 10–15% tip. Beware of unlicensed taxis: they are often uninsured and charge steep fares. Telephone numbers of taxi ranks can be found in the Yellow Pages but are not always answered.

Walking Central Paris is fairly safe for walking at most times, but beware of muggers and pickpockets in the main tourist areas (especially around the Champs-Elysées, the Opéra, Montmartre, Place Saint-Michel, Les Halles and, late at night, the Beaubourg). The Bois de Boulogne should be avoided after dark.

Buses move faster in Paris than in many capital cities, thanks to a good network of bus lanes, though the evening rush hour (roughly 6.30–7.30) causes delays. They are a pleasant way of getting about central Paris and are relatively easy to use. Clear route maps are posted up at bus stops and inside buses. Most services operate at frequent intervals, but not at all after about 8.30pm or on Sundays and public holidays. You pay as you enter; short journeys require one RATP ticket, longer ones two or more. Route maps indicate the number of tickets needed.

Subway The Paris Métropolitain or Métro offers an efficient service between approximately 5.15am and 1.15am every day. Trains run at 90-second intervals during the daytime on most lines and only slightly less frequently at night (till about 1.15am). As the system is shallow, platforms are quickly reached, so it is often worth taking the Métro even for very short journeys. It is generally clean (no smoking is now the rule in all carriages) and safe, with police patrols deterring would-be muggers. Métro lines are known by the names of the stations at either end of the routes; thus the central east–west line is called Vincennes–Neuilly.

There is only one fare in each class (each train has a first-class carriage), and a variety of bargain tickets is on offer, such as the one-day ticket valid on all forms of public transport.

Express Métro The three lines (called A, B and C) of the Réseau Express Régional (RER) are slotted into the ordinary Métro system and offer a very fast method of getting across Paris or out to the suburbs and nearby towns such as Versailles. Within the city limits use ordinary RATP tickets; for longer journeys use ticket machines inside RER stations.

Driving It is rarely sensible to drive in a capital city. Paris is no exception, but all the main car rental firms have offices.

Area by area

There is a sharp physical and political division in Paris, more than in most important capital cities, between the city and its suburbs. The former, the Ville de Paris, with its own local government and a population of 2.7m, is circumscribed by two concentric ring roads, the Boulevard Extérieur and a multilane highway, the Boulevard Périphérique, which can be very congested during rush hours. Outside lie the suburbs, each also with its own mayor and council, adding up to a conurbation with a population of around 9m.

Most places of interest and centres of business are within the Ville de Paris, oval in shape and divided roughly in two by the curving Seine. Traditionally the southern part, known as the Left Bank (*Rive Gauche*) has been a byword for the city's intellectual life, while the Right Bank (*Rive Droite*) has been more opulent and commercial. But modern development has blurred these distinctions, and the major public buildings such as ministries, museums and palaces have always been dispersed fairly evenly on either side of the river. The business life of the city, too, is today somewhat scattered, without the clearly defined sectors to be found in London or New York. Some big banks and finance houses are close to the Bourse (stock exchange) in the old heart of the city; but many modern offices are in the smart Champs-Elysées area, or out at La Défense, the new high-rise complex in the western suburbs, or spread about elsewhere. There is no single powerful financial focus in the manner of Wall Street or the City of London.

The older parts of central Paris, on both banks, consist of a dense network of narrow streets dissected by the broad boulevards dating from the redevelopment of the city in the 1860s. And today there is still a sharp contrast between these stately tree-lined avenues and the congested older quarters. It is the broad area astride the Seine, from the Eiffel Tower to Notre-Dame, that gives the most sweeping sense of space and grandiose urban planning; here mighty buildings stand back majestically from the river's banks – the Eiffel Tower, Trocadéro, Grand Palais, Invalides, Palais Bourbon, Louvre, Palais de Justice and others.

The Ville de Paris is divided into 20 *arrondissements*: these are postal districts numbering 75001 to 75020 (the last two digits indicate the *arrondissement*), but also administrative units each with its own *mairie*, and they spiral out from the centre to the edge. Each has its own personality, and Parisians will often say that they live in, say, the *seizième* (16e) or work in the *cinquième* (5e). Some older quarters of the city also have names, Montparnasse for example, and these mostly straddle the *arrondissements*.

The Champs-Elysées and the 16e

The smartest parts of the Right Bank are the 8e and 16e arr, along its western stretch. The 8e is partly residential but mainly an upmarket business area, home of the fashion and advertising industries and of many leading banks and hotels – even though its main thoroughfare, the Champs-Elysées, has itself moved downmarket and is today lined with fast-food eating places and split-screen cinemas as well as tourist cafés, travel agencies and car showrooms. Farther east, around the Madeleine church and the wide Place de la Concorde, is a highly fashionable area of boutiques, grand hotels and equally grand public buildings: here along the chic Rue du Faubourg Saint-Honoré lie the British and American Embassies and the presidential Palais de l'Elysée, while (just inside the 1er arr) the Ritz Hotel faces the graceful 17thC Place Vendôme, and the elegantly arcaded Rue de Rivoli skirts the Tuileries Gardens. Over to the west, the large 16e arr has long been the city's principal high-class residential quarter. Its late-19thC and early-

20thC apartment blocks are the homes of leading establishment figures; some, if they can afford it, join the oil sheikhs in the stately Avenue Foch, dubbed "millionaires' row." The 17e is also residential in a more modest way; at Porte Maillot is the city's main convention centre, the imposing new Palais des Congrès. The adjacent Bois de Boulogne, much the largest of Paris parks, is part of the 16e.

The Right Bank The 1er, 2e, 3e and 4e arr include the old heart of the city. Today this is a dense area of narrow commercial streets, much of it run-down and given over to small-scale commerce; but some parts are being redeveloped, and the area does contain several major buildings. Beside the river stands the vast Palais du Louvre which houses the Ministry of Finance as well as France's leading museum; close by are the Palais Royal and the Comédie Française theatre. Les Halles, to the east, was the site of the city's congested central food market until this was transferred to the suburbs in 1969; today Les Halles has been remodelled as a traffic-free shopping and leisure zone (it has a small park, a library, theatres and a sports centre) and it is full of lively activity. A short walk to the east, across Boulevard de Sébastopol, leads to the huge modernistic Pompidou arts centre, focus of a pedestrian zone (Beaubourg) that is usually full of street entertainers and is now becoming increasingly commercialized. Nearby, facing the river, is the Hôtel de Ville, and directly north Le Marais, a famous historic quarter of elegant 16th–18thC mansions, now beautifully restored. Some are museums, such as the Carnavalet, but many are fashionable private houses: some well-known people live here, especially in and around the lovely Place des Vosges. The Rue des Rosiers area is a traditional Jewish quarter, with synagogues and kosher food shops. To the south lie the two famous

islands in the Seine that were the kernel of Vieux Paris: the Ile de la Cité contains Notre-Dame, Sainte-Chapelle, the Palais de Justice and the Préfecture de Police, while the quiet and charming little Ile Saint-Louis, with its riverside walk and small park, has long been a fashionable place to live.

Northwest of Les Halles, the Bourse and the Banque de France are a focus for banking and insurance activity. Farther west stands the majestic Opéra, close to the two large department stores, the Galeries Lafayette and Au Printemps. Eastward from here sweeps a rather tawdry main avenue, known in the plural as Les Grands Boulevards because it keeps changing its name before it finally reaches the big Place de la République, gateway to the eastern working-class Paris. One of the streets it crosses is Rue Saint-Denis, whose northern part, in the 2e, is a major red-light district.

The Left Bank The central area towards the river comprises the 5e, 6e and 7e arr and it becomes steadily more bourgeois as it goes westward. The 5e, crowned by the Panthéon mausoleum, is the essence of the Latin Quarter, and the Sorbonne and other university buildings are here. This is a picturesque area of cheap student bistros, art movie houses and small apartments where many teachers and writers live. To the west, across Boulevard Saint-Michel ("Boul Mich"), the 6e is also a major centre of intellectual activity, but more prosperous: many bourgeois families live in the old streets around the Jardin du Luxembourg, while Saint-Germain-des-Prés with its bookshops, art galleries, trendy cafés and outdoor markets is well trodden by tourists seeking the "real" Paris. Many leading publishing houses are located here. Montparnasse, to the south, dominated by its much-criticized 200-metre/650-ft skyscraper, is today a lively entertainment area but has largely lost its artistic cachet of prewar years. The Faubourg Saint-

Germain, forming the eastern part of the 7e, is the area where aristocrats lived in the pre-1914 period described by Marcel Proust. Today it is given over mainly to ministries and other public buildings including the Assemblée Nationale (Palais Bourbon) overlooking the Seine and Place de la Concorde. This is France's main governmental district. West of Les Invalides, the quiet streets around the Eiffel Tower and Ecole Militaire are where many of the well-off live. To the east, the refurbished Gare d'Orsay, now a museum, is by the river opposite the Tuileries.

The outer arrondissements These are mostly of lesser interest. The 13e, 14e and 15e arr, sizable districts to the south, used to be largely working-class; but now, under pressure of rising land prices, they have become more middle-class as workers move out to suburban dormitories. Along the fringe of the 14e is the Cité Universitaire, a cluster of student hostels, and on the edge of the 15e, at the Porte de Versailles, is the main Paris exhibition centre. On the north side of central Paris, the mainly working-class 18e contains the picturesque hilltop "village" of Montmartre, as besieged by tourists as ever, and, lower down, the seedy *boîtes* and bars of the Place Pigalle area. The 9e is largely commercial and petit bourgeois, like the 10e, where the Gares du Nord and de L'Est are. The 11e, running down to the Place de la Bastille, is a zone of old workshops and workers' flats; the 12e is much the same, except for the imposing new business quarter which is springing up along the Quai de Bercy (the Ministry of Finance is due eventually to move there from the Louvre). The pleasant Bois de Vincennes is attached to the 12e. Lastly, the 19e and 20e have kept their old working-class character – except where there is a preponderance of immigrants.

The suburbs

The better residential suburbs lie out to the west where the prevailing winds bring a less polluted air. Much the smartest are Neuilly and Le Vésinet, home of many senior business people. Others, such as Saint-Cloud, Garches and Ville-d'Avray, lie farther out, stretching to Versailles and beyond, filling up the old fields and woodlands with smart new villas owned by young professionals.

Just west of Neuilly is La Défense with its 25 imposing skyscrapers, a new and highly impressive business complex that was built to provide an overspill for the crowded Champs-Elysées area: many big firms such as Esso, IBM and Saint-Gobain have their head offices at La Défense, where 40,000 people work. To the north, east and south of Paris, the inner suburbs are mainly working-class: these areas have often been dubbed the "Paris Red Belt," though not so many of them today remain Communist strongholds. Farther out, the suburbs have extended greatly since the war, as the conurbation has almost doubled in size. "New towns" were built somewhat at random in the 1960s, the best known being Sarcelles to the north, with a population of 40,000 which now includes a high proportion of immigrants. In more recent years five large "new towns" with pleasant architecture have been developed within 32km/20 miles of the city centre – Cergy-Pontoise to the northwest, Marne-la-Vallée to the east, Melun-Sénart and Evry to the southeast, Saint-Quentin-en-Yvelines to the southwest – and they have been attracting new light industry. Of older heavy industry, very little remains within the Ville de Paris, but there is plenty in the suburbs, led by the motor industries at Billancourt (Renault), Aulnay-les-Bois (Citroën) and Poissy (Talbot). Finally, the biggest new project in the Paris region today is the building of a Disneyland, the first in Europe, east of the city at Marne-la-Vallée: due to open in 1992, it will create some 30,000 permanent new jobs.

FRANCE

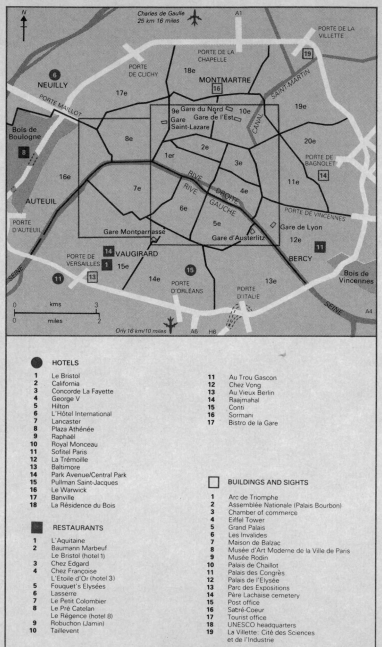

HOTELS

1	Le Bristol
2	California
3	Concorde La Fayette
4	George V
5	Hilton
6	L'Hôtel International
7	Lancaster
8	Plaza Athénée
9	Raphaël
10	Royal Monceau
11	Sofitel Paris
12	La Trémoille
13	Baltimore
14	Park Avenue/Central Park
15	Pullman Saint-Jacques
16	Le Warwick
17	Banville
18	La Résidence du Bois

11	Au Trou Gascon
12	Chez Vong
13	Au Vieux Berlin
14	Raajmahal
15	Conti
16	Sormani
17	Bistro de la Gare

RESTAURANTS

1	L'Aquitaine
2	Baumann Marbeuf
	Le Bristol (hotel 1)
3	Chez Edgard
4	Chez Françoise
	L'Étoile d'Or (hotel 3)
5	Fouquet's Elysées
6	Lasserre
7	Le Petit Colombier
8	Le Pré Catelan
	Le Régence (hotel 8)
9	Robuchon (Jamin)
10	Taillevent

BUILDINGS AND SIGHTS

1	Arc de Triomphe
2	Assemblée Nationale (Palais Bourbon)
3	Chamber of commerce
4	Eiffel Tower
5	Grand Palais
6	Les Invalides
7	Maison de Balzac
8	Musée d'Art Moderne de la Ville de Paris
9	Musée Rodin
10	Palais de Chaillot
11	Palais des Congrès
12	Palais de l'Elysée
13	Parc des Expositions
14	Père Lachaise cemetery
15	Post office
16	Sacré-Coeur
17	Tourist office
18	UNESCO headquarters
19	La Villette: Cité des Sciences et de l'Industrie

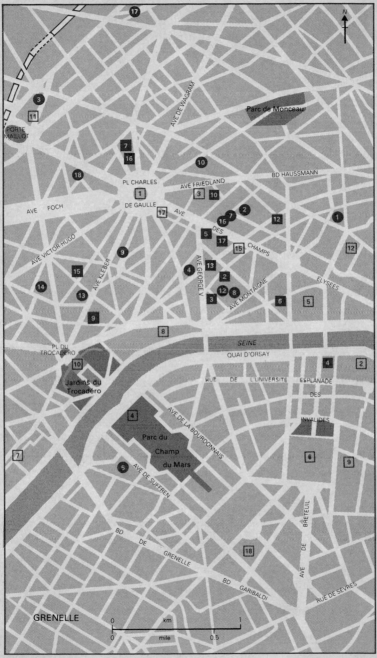

PORTE
MAILLOT

③

⑪

Parc de Monceau

⑰

AVE DE WAGRAM

⑦
◼16

⑩

PL CHARLES

AVE FRIEDLAND

BD HAUSSMANN

⑱

AVE FOCH

①
DE GAULLE

◻3 ⑩

⑰ AVE

②

⑫

①

AVE VICTOR-HUGO

⑨

◼5

◼16 ⑦

◻17 ◻15

DES

CHAMPS

⑫

◼15

④ ◻13

②

◼14

⑬
AVE KLEBER

AVE GEORGE V

◻3

◼12 ⑧

⑥

ELYSEES

◻5

◼9

⑧

AVE MONTAIGNE

PL DU
TROCADERO

⑩

SEINE

QUAI D'ORSAY

◻4 ◻2

Jardins du
Trocadero

RUE DE L'UNIVERSITE

ESPLANADE

DES

④

AVE DE LA BOURDONNAIS

INVALIDES

◻7

Parc du
Champ
du Mars

◻6 ◻9

⑤

AVE DE SUFFREN

AVE DE BRETEUIL

BD DE

GRENELLE

◻18

BD GARIBALDI

RUE DE SEVRES

GRENELLE

0   km   1

0   mile   0.5

FRANCE

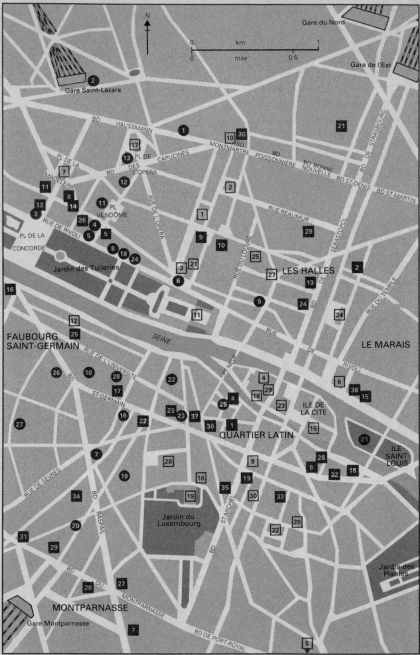

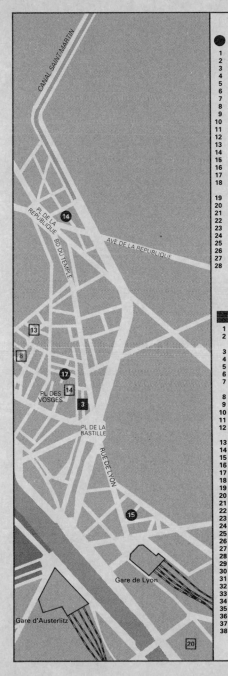

	HOTELS		BUILDINGS AND SIGHTS
1	Ambassador Concorde	1	Bibliothèque Nationale
2	Concorde Saint-Lazare	2	Bourse
3	Crillon	3	Comédie Française
4	France et Choiseul	4	Conciergerie
5	InterContinental	5	Gobelins tapestry factory
6	Louvre	6	Hôtel de Ville
7	Lutétia	7	La Madeleine
8	Meurice	8	Musée Carnavalet
9	Novotel Paris Les Halles	9	Musée de Cluny
10	Pont Royal	10	Musée Grévin
11	Ritz	11	Musée du Louvre
12	Westminster	12	Musée d'Orsay
13	Le Grand Hôtel	13	Musée Picasso (Hôtel Salé)
14	Holiday Inn	14	Musée Victor Hugo
15	Modern Hôtel Lyon	15	Notre-Dame
16	Pas-de-Calais	16	Odéon
17	Pavillon de la Reine	17	Opéra
18	Résidence Saint-James et Albany	18	Palais de Justice
		19	Palais du Luxembourg (Sénat)
19	Abbaye Saint-Germain	20	Palais Omnisports Bercy
20	Aramis Saint-Germain	21	Palais Royal
21	Deux-Iles	22	Panthéon
22	L'Hôtel	23	Police
23	La Louisiane	24	Pompidou centre (Beaubourg)
24	Montana Tuileries	25	Post office
25	Relais Christine	26	Saint-Étienne-du-Mont
26	Saint-Simon	27	Saint-Eustache
27	Suede	28	Saint-Sulpice
28	Université	29	Sainte-Chapelle
		30	La Sorbonne

	RESTAURANTS
1	Allard
2	L'Ambassade d'Auvergne
	Les Ambassadeurs (hotel 3)
3	Bofinger
4	Jacques Cagna
5	Carré des Feuillants
6	Dodin-Bouffant
7	Le Duc
	L'Espadon (hotel 11)
8	Goumard
9	Le Grand Vefour
10	Louis XIV
11	Lucas-Carton
12	Maxim's
	Le Paris (hotel 7)
13	Pharamond
14	Prunier Madeleine
15	Au Quai des Ormes
16	Au Quai d'Orsay
17	Le Relais Saint-Germain
18	La Tour d'Argent
19	Le Balzar
20	La Coupole
21	Flo
22	Lipp
23	Le Muniche
24	Joe Allen
25	Tan Dinh
26	Kinugawa
27	Dominique
28	Atelier Maitre Albert
29	Bistro de la Gare
30	Chartier
31	Chez Joséphine
32	Chez Toutoune
33	La Coupe-Chou
34	La Marlotte
35	Polidor
36	Le Procope
37	Orestias
38	e Trumilou

Hotels

Paris has more classic luxury "palace" hotels than in other large city in the world. The top ones are the Bristol, Crillon, George V, Plaza Athénée, Ritz and Meurice, where period decor and Parisian elegance go hand in hand with courteous old-style service and modern comfort. Their relative formality may not suit all tastes, and their range of specific business services is usually limited. The few modern hotels in the same top class may lack charm, but they tend to be better equipped for business needs.

Even the new hotels will often lack many of the facilities that a global traveller may expect. Very few have swimming pools or private parking, while health and business centres are only just beginning to appear. Services that are standard in the modern hotels are television and minibars in all rooms, IDD telephones, room service, currency exchange and assistance with travel and theatre reservations.

Prices in the smart hotels are about average by world standards. Paris also has scores of medium-priced places suitable for business visitors on a limited budget. For those who dislike large hotels, and would prefer a much smaller place of character and charm, even at the expense of some amenities, Paris is well provided with very attractive smaller hotels, and a selection of these is given on pages 70 and 71. Many of these have no restaurant. These small hotels are very popular and reservations need to be made well ahead. The larger ones are less often full, except for the periods of the major trade shows and conventions in spring and autumn. If you have to make a last-minute reservation, you can find help at the tourist offices.

Most of the better hotels are very central, in the 1er or 8e arr, close to the main business areas. Some other good ones are on the Left Bank, such as the Lutétia and the Hilton, or near the Palais des Congrès. A few, such as the Holiday Inn, are in eastern central Paris and yet others out on the periphery.

Best classic luxury palaces Le Bristol • Crillon • George V • Lancaster • Lutétia • Meurice • Plaza Athénée • Ritz • Royal Monceau.
Best modern hotels Concorde La Fayette • Hilton • L'Hôtel International.
Best small hotels of charm Abbaye Saint-Germain • Deux-Iles • L'Hôtel • Résidence du Bois • Saint-Simon.
Best for keeping fit Le Bristol • Royal Monceau • Sofitel.

Ambassador Concorde *F*///// *16 bd Haussmann, 9e* ☎ *42 46 92 63* ⊠ *650912 fax 40 22 08 74* • *AE DC MC V* • *305 rooms, 6 suites,*

1 restaurant, 1 bar
This "palace" built in 1927 is being sympathetically renovated by its new owners, the Concorde group. It has no great charm but is conveniently placed and efficient. Large, well modernized bedrooms, huge foyer and plenty of services. Limited parking. Hairdresser, gift shop • 8 meeting rooms (capacity up to 150).

Le Bristol *F*///// *112 rue du Faubourg St-Honoré, 8e* ☎ *42 66 91 45* ⊠ *280961 fax 42 66 68 68* • *AE DC MC V* • *156 rooms, 44 suites, 2 restaurants, 1 bar*
Leading politicians and diplomats use this excellent hotel, conveniently near

to the Elysée Palace. The Bristol is one of the three or four finest hotels in Paris, luxurious in a restrained and classic style, with service to match and with lovely marble bathrooms. It is also one of the few top Paris hotels to have a swimming-pool. The piano bar carries echoes of prewar days, and the Bristol restaurant is superb (see *Restaurants*). 24hr room service, hairdresser, garage • rooftop pool, sauna • 7 meeting rooms (capacity up to 180).

California *F* ////
16 rue de Berri, 8e ☎ *43 59 93 00*
Ⓣ *644634 fax 45 61 03 62 • Hôtels et Résidences du Roy • AE DC MC V • 177 rooms, 3 suites; no restaurant*
This top-class hotel off the Champs-Elysées has a pleasant patio and spacious bedrooms with Louis XVI style furniture but modern comforts. 1 meeting room (capacity up to 30).

Concorde La Fayette *F* ////
3 pl du Général-Koenig, 17e
☎ *47 58 12 84* Ⓣ *650905*
fax 47 57 53 21 • AE DC MC V • 963 rooms, 27 suites, 3 restaurants, 2 bars
The city's second largest hotel at Porte Maillot makes an excellent venue for the business visitor. Not only is it in the same block as the air terminal and Palais des Congrès, sharing many facilities, but it has recently opened an executive "Top Club." Here, by paying a little more, the guest has a bedroom with various extra touches, including video programmes, as well as the use of a private lounge-clubroom with free drinks, newspapers, and polyglot hostesses providing advice and secretarial help. Service is personal and courteous; bedrooms are all well equipped, many with splendid views over western Paris. Amenities include a lively jazz bar, a panoramic top-floor bar and good cuisine in the Etoile d'Or (see *Restaurants*). 24hr room service, parking • golf practice area, jogging track • 7 meeting rooms in hotel (capacity up to 150), others in Palais des Congrès.

Concorde Saint-Lazare *F* ////
108 rue St-Lazare, 8e ☎ *42 94 22 22*
Ⓣ *650442 fax 42 93 01 20 • AE DC MC V • 324 rooms, 2 restaurants, 1 bar*
This huge old "palace" was built in 1889 to serve visitors arriving at the adjacent Saint-Lazare rail terminus. Today its clientele consists mostly of Japanese and European tour groups coming by air, as well as French provincial businessmen. A recent facelift has modernized the spacious bedrooms but retained the period charm of the public rooms – notably the huge foyer with its high glass roof, marble galleries and many Art Nouveau flourishes. Its sophisticated bar opens late; the restaurant serves regional dishes. 24hr room service, hairdresser, duty-free boutique, gift shop • 9 meeting rooms (capacity up to 180).

Crillon *F* /////
10 pl de la Concorde, 8e
☎ *42 65 24 24* Ⓣ *290204*
fax 47 42 72 10 • Concorde • AE DC MC V • 149 rooms, 40 suites, 2 restaurants, 2 bars
This is the only one of the city's classic luxury "palaces" to remain in French ownership. The 18thC decor is luxurious, with marble pillars and gilt-framed mirrors; the atmosphere discreet, as befits its very select clientele. Service is studiously attentive; the bedrooms facing Place de la Concorde are double-glazed, but those facing the formal inner courtyard are quieter. The banqueting rooms and the Ambassadeurs restaurant are excellent (see *Restaurants*), and the famous bar has been elegantly restyled. 24hr room service, shop, limited parking • 6 meeting rooms (capacity up to 70).

France et Choiseul *F* ///
239 rue St-Honoré, 1er ☎ *42 61 54 60*
Ⓣ *680959 fax 40 20 96 32 • Ladbroke • AE DC MC V • 100 rooms, 20 suites, 1 brasserie/bar*
This classic hotel in a fashionable area, close to the Tuileries, has recently been renovated by its new

British owners. Its large open-plan bar/foyer has attractive decor in pale blue and gold, soft music plays, and there is a pretty courtyard for drinks. Snacks and light meals are served in the bar. Bedrooms are modern but not large; all have electric trouser-presses, rare in Paris. 5 meeting rooms (capacity up to 250).

George V F/////
31 ave George V, 8e ☎ *47 23 54 00*
Ⓣ𝕏 *650082/290776 fax 47 20 40 00* •
THF • *AE DC MC V* • *288 rooms, 63 suites, 2 restaurants, 1 bar*
The George V has a quieter and more sedate atmosphere than its flamboyant stablemate around the corner, the Plaza Athénée. Its appeal is less to the showy star than to the serious tycoon, but its mainly 18thC decor is even more magnificent, and there are Flemish tapestries, sculptures and paintings, including a Renoir. Recent renovation has enhanced this splendour while adding to the modern comforts and amenities. Rooms have videos, and some have balconies facing the pleasant patio with its red parasols; the stylish restaurant, Les Princes, also looks onto this. The tearoom and bar are two of the smartest venues in town. 24hr room service, hairdresser, massage, florist, gift shop • 7 meeting rooms (capacity up to 600).

Hilton F/////
18 ave de Suffren, 15e ☎ *42 73 92 00*
Ⓣ𝕏 *200955 fax 47 83 62 66* • *AE DC MC V* • *455 rooms, 28 suites, 2 restaurants, 2 bars*
The Hilton group has allowed its luxurious French showpiece to have a truly "Parisian" style that is all its own. The swift and polished service is up to the highest American standards, but there is little else about it that seems American; of the guests, about 25% are from the USA and over 50% European. The atmosphere is lively, informal and cosmopolitan, and the bedrooms are both attractive and well planned, many facing the nearby Eiffel Tower.

La Terrasse is an animated brasserie and coffeeshop; Le Western, the sole concession to American taste, serves Texan-style food. The range of business and other amenities is excellent. 24hr room service, Air France reservation desk, hairdresser, shops, garage • 3 meeting rooms (capacity up to 1,300).

InterContinental F/////
3 rue Castiglione, 1er ☎ *42 60 37 80*
Ⓣ𝕏 *220114 fax 42 61 14 03* • *AE DC MC V* • *380 rooms, 70 suites, 1 restaurant, 2 bars*
This palatial *belle époque* masterpiece close to Place Vendôme celebrated its centenary in 1978 and has recently been renovated. Bedrooms now have every modern comfort (some top-floor ones have fine views over the Tuileries Gardens, some suites have jacuzzis), and the ornate salons have been refurbished. The patio, with its flowers and fountain, is a fashionable place in summer for a business meal. Service is impeccable. 8 meeting rooms (capacity up to 1,000).

L'Hôtel International F///
58 bd Victor-Hugo, 92200 Neuilly
☎ *47 58 11 00* Ⓣ𝕏 *610971 fax 47 56 75 52* • *Tollman-Hundley*
•*AE DC MC V* • *330 rooms, 3 suites, 2 restaurants, 1 bar*
Built by the Club Méditerranée and now American-owned, this bright and breezy ultramodern hotel is convenient for La Défense or the Palais des Congrès. It offers members a wide range of facilities at its new "Business Club," with newspapers, free drinks, photocopying, Minitel and hostesses. A garden and piano bar are added attractions, while Le Club has bequeathed its formula of lavish buffet meals with unlimited wine. 24hr information desk, gift shop, garage • 5 meeting rooms.

Lancaster F/////
7 rue de Berri, 8e ☎ *43 59 90 43*
Ⓣ𝕏 *640991 fax 42 89 22 71* • *Savoy* •
AE DC MC V • *59 rooms, 8 suites, 1 restaurant, 1 bar*

The small but luxurious Lancaster, in a side street just off the busy Champs-Elysées, wears something of an upper-class English air, owing to its discreet and personal service. But the period decor and furnishings are Parisian, and many of the guests are publicity-shy American stage and screen stars who relish the quiet and privacy. Business people too enjoy the private atmosphere of the bar, and the flower- and statue-filled patio where meals are served in summer. 24hr room service • 4 meeting rooms (capacity up to 25).

Louvre *F*|||||
Pl André Malraux, 1er ☎ *42 61 56 01*
Ⓣ*x* *220412 fax 42 60 02 90* • *Concorde*
• *AE DC MC V* • *198 rooms, 5 suites,*
1 restaurant, 1 bar
Located just a few steps from the Palais Royal and the Louvre, this is a classic hotel with very well equipped bedrooms (all have Minitels). It has a highly cosmopolitan, mainly business clientele, but it was not always so: Camille Pissarro painted his famous *Avenue de l'Opéra* from a upper room when he stayed here in 1898. Today this can be rented as a suite. 24hr room service, gift shop, garage • 6 meeting rooms (capacity up to 200).

Lutétia *F*|||||
45 bd Raspail, 6e ☎ *45 44 38 10*
Ⓣ*x* *270424 fax 45 44 50 50* • *Concorde*
• *AE DC MC V* • *272 rooms, 20 suites,*
1 restaurant, 1 bar
The largest of the Left Bank's traditional hotels was built in 1910 and has long been a fashionable place. It is much admired for the Art Deco elegance of its public rooms and bedrooms, which have all been recently refurbished in gentle pastel colours; and today the large conservatory-style bar, the brasserie and the main restaurant, Le Paris (see *Restaurants*) are all much frequented by business people. The salons are well equipped with video and other amenities. 24hr room service • 12 meeting rooms (capacity up to 1,000).

Meurice *F*|||||
228 rue de Rivoli, 1er ☎ *42 60 38 60*
Ⓣ*x* *230673 fax 40 15 92 31* • *CIGA* •
AE DC MC V • *151 rooms, 36 suites,*
1 restaurant, 1 bar
Queen Victoria and other monarchs have stayed at the Meurice, oldest of the city's luxury "palaces," built in 1816. The present owners have brought in renovation (such as pink marble bathrooms) without spoiling the majestic decor of tapestries, great chandeliers and gilded panelling. The atmosphere might be a little too prim and sedate for some tastes, but the old-style service is impeccable and there is high-quality decor and equipment in all bedrooms, some of which overlook the Tuileries. The main restaurant is elegant but has no view. 24hr room service • 6 meeting rooms (capacity up to 250).

Novotel Paris Les Halles *F*|||
8 pl Marguerite-de-Navarre, 1er
☎ *42 21 31 31* Ⓣ*x* *216389*
fax 40 26 05 79 • *AE DC MC V* •
271 rooms, 14 suites, 1 restaurant,
1 bar
Pleasantly situated beside the brand-new park of Les Halles, this equally new chain hotel has functional but comfortable rooms and a spacious open-plan layout with cheerful decor. A good range of facilities includes satellite TV. Gift shop, newsstand • 5 meeting rooms (capacity up to 150).

Plaza Athénée *F*|||||
25 ave Montaigne, 8e ☎ *47 23 78 33*
Ⓣ*x* *650092 fax 47 20 20 70* • *THF* •
AE DC MC V • *179 rooms, 42 suites,*
2 restaurants, 1 bar, 1 tearoom
At the ultra-glamorous Plaza movie stars mingle with wealthy tourists of the more flamboyant kind, many of them South American. It's a place where people go to be seen, in the stylish gallery/tearoom beloved of Dietrich, the somewhat vulgar bar, the Régence restaurant (see *Restaurants*) and the Relais grillroom, a fashionable place for after-theatre suppers. Despite the razmatazz the

business guest is not forgotten but the accent is more on luxury. 24hr room service, beauty parlour, massage, hairdresser • 4 meeting rooms (capacity up to 180).

Pont Royal *F*////
7 rue de Montalembert, 7e
☎ *45 44 38 27* Ⓣ *270113*
fax 45 44 92 07 • *AE DC MC V* • *73 rooms, 5 suites, 1 restaurant, 1 bar*
Next to Gallimard the publishers on the left Bank, the Pont Royal has a literary pedigree, with William Faulkner and Ernest Hemingway among former guests, but it also offers solid comfort at less than top prices. The decor lacks charm, and rooms are small, but service is most efficient, and the meeting room by the small garden is especially attractive. The restaurant, Les Antiquaires, and the rather gloomy but well heated basement bar are still popular with literati. 5 meeting rooms (capacity up to 50).

Raphaël *F*////
17 ave Kléber, 16e ☎ *45 02 16 00*
Ⓣ *610356 fax 45 01 21 50* • *AE DC MC V* • *52 rooms, 36 suites, 1 restaurant, 1 bar*
Conveniently close to L'Etoile, the Raphaël is for those who want a marble-floored period-style, discreet luxury hotel; its clientele regularly includes senior business people as well as international film stars. In the bar and foyer, the dark panelling, Oriental tapestries and large oil paintings create an ambience that some may find snug, others a little heavy. The restaurant, too, is a bit dull. But there is a terrace overlooking all Paris, the bedrooms are elegant and well equipped, and service is efficient. 24hr room service • 5 meeting rooms (capacity up to 50).

Ritz *F*/////
15 pl Vendôme, 1er ☎ *42 60 38 30*
Ⓣ *220262 fax 42 86 00 91* • *AE DC MC V* • *142 rooms, 45 suites, 1 restaurant, 3 bars*

The most expensive hotel in Paris and arguably the most famous in the world, the Ritz numbers Proust, Churchill, Chaplin and Garbo among former guests. Today it is owned by the Al-Fayed family, who also own Harrods in London, and many of its visitors are Arab royalty. Indeed, the hotel has something of the hushed air of a royal palace, with long silent corridors and exquisite art treasures. But the facilities are modern and the service superb and unobtrusive. The famous bars, the lovely inner garden and the restaurant, L'Espadon (see *Restaurants*), are all ideal for discreet top-level talks. Hairdresser, florist, shops • health centre with sauna and massage • 3 meeting rooms (capacity up to 120).

Royal Monceau *F*/////
37 ave Hoche, 8e ☎ *45 61 98 00*
Ⓣ *650361 fax 45 63 28 93* • *CIGA* • *AE DC MC V* • *219 rooms, 35 suites, 3 restaurants, 2 bars*
This delightful Italian-owned luxury hotel caters well to the discerning senior business executive. In a quiet location near the Parc Monceau, it has well-equipped, elegant bedrooms and public rooms, a "business club" and good restaurants: Il Carpaccio, high-class Italian; Le Jardin, where sumptuous buffet-breakfasts are served in a pleasant garden setting; and a diet restaurant. Service could perhaps be more friendly. Limited parking. 24hr room service, beauty salon, hairdresser • health club with saunas, jacuzzi, small pool • 8 meeting rooms (capacity up to 300).

Sofitel Paris *F*///
8–12 rue Louis-Armand, 15e
☎ *40 60 30 30* Ⓣ *200432*
fax 45 57 04 22 • *AE DC MC V* • *635 rooms, 3 suites, 2 restaurants, 2 bars*
This huge modern chain hotel is handy for the Héliport and the Porte de Versailles exhibition centre, to which transport is provided. Rooms are smallish and the atmosphere not exactly personal, but the service is

deft and facilities include a well-equipped business centre and 15 rooms that are designed for daytime use as offices. Jazz club, piano bar. 24hr room service, gift shops, garage • rooftop pool, jacuzzi, fitness centre • 42 meeting rooms (capacity up to 1,000).

La Trémoille *F* ///// 14 rue de la Trémoille, 8e ☎ 47 23 34 20 ⊤X 640344 fax 40 70 01 08 • THF • AE DC MC V • 98 rooms, 13 suites, 1 restaurant, 1 bar
Just off the Champs-Elysées, a British-owned hotel of dignified Parisian elegance, popular with businessmen seeking high standards of comfort and service in unpretentious surroundings. The new penthouse suites are superb, and other rooms have pleasant balconies and luxurious bathrooms. The bar and restaurant are small but chic.

Westminster *F* ///// 13 rue de la Paix, 2e ☎ 42 61 57 46 ⊤X 680035 fax 42 60 30 66 • Warwick • AE DC MC V • 84 rooms, 18 suites, 1 restaurant, 1 bar
Recent renovation has transformed this hitherto rather dull hotel near the Opéra into yet another stylish Parisian "palace." Some bedrooms are in period style, some more modern; many have marble bathrooms and videos. Friendly service; intimate piano bar and restaurant. Limited parking. Jeweller's • 4 meeting rooms (capacity up to 50).

OTHER HOTELS
Baltimore *F* ///// 88 bis ave Kléber, 16e ☎ 45 53 83 33 ⊤X 611591 fax 45 53 94 84 • Cidotel • AE DC MC V. Comfortable, well renovated hotel of medium size, with an excellent restaurant, L'Estournel.
Le Grand Hôtel *F* ///// 2 rue Scribe, 9e ☎ 42 68 12 13 ⊤X 220875 fax 42 66 12 51 • InterContinental • AE DC MC V. A large and fairly luxurious hotel by the Opéra, with

lavish Second Empire decor. Fitness centre, sauna.
Holiday Inn *F* //// 10 pl de la République, 11e ☎ 43 55 44 34 ⊤X 210651 fax 47 00 32 34 • AE DC MC V. In eastern Paris, an old hotel, recently renovated, with pleasant patio and brasserie. Limited pay parking.
Modern Hôtel Lyon *F* / 3 rue Parrot, 12e ☎ 43 43 41 52 ⊤X 230369 • AE MC V. A useful small hotel near the Gare de Lyon, well modernized. No restaurant.
Park Avenue and **Central Park** *F* //// 55 ave Raymond-Poincaré, 16e ☎ 45 53 44 60 ⊤X 643862 fax 47 27 53 04 • Cidotel • AE DC MC V. Two brand-new functional hotels built around the same inner courtyard. Garage.
Pas-de-Calais *F* //// 59 rue de Saints-Pères, 6e ☎ 45 48 78 74 ⊤X 270476 fax 45 44 94 57 • MC V. A quiet, comfortable little Left Bank address. Some rooms overlook a pretty courtyard. No restaurant.
Pavillon de la Reine *F* //// 28 pl des Vosges, 3e ☎ 42 77 96 40 ⊤X 216160 fax 42 77 63 06 • AE DC MC V. An old building on a lovely square, recently converted into a smart little hotel. Garage. No restaurant or bar.
Pullman Saint-Jacques *F* //// 17 bd St-Jacques, 14e ☎ 45 89 89 80 ⊤X 270740 fax 45 88 43 93 • AE DC MC V. Gigantic and functional, with many facilities and small but comfortable bedrooms. Convenient for Orly airport. Garage.
Résidence Saint-James et Albany *F* ///// 202 rue de Rivoli, 1er ☎ 42 60 31 60 ⊤X 213031 fax 40 15 92 21 • AE DC MC V. A classic hotel, now attractively modernized, with very quiet rooms, many of them studios with kitchenettes. Limited parking.
Le Warwick *F* ///// 5 rue de Berri, 8e ☎ 45 63 14 11 ⊤X 642295 fax 45 63 75 81 • AE DC MC V. Very modern, just off the Champs-Elysées but quiet. Bedrooms are large, and some suites have roof-terraces.

Small hotels of quality and character

Paris has a remarkable range of charming small hotels, some cheap, others less so. Quiet and intimate, comfortable and stylish, they offer personal service but often lack amenities such as 24hr room service, air conditioning, telex or fax

Abbaye Saint-Germain *F*///
10 rue Cassette, 6e ☎ *45 44 38 11* •
45 rooms, 1 bar
A former 17thC monastery in a small street near Saint-Germain-des-Prés is now an elegant little hotel. Bedrooms are fairly small but well furnished, with modern marble bathrooms. Business contacts could be entertained in the bar or the flagged courtyard. Service is friendly and efficient. Reservations should be made well in advance.

Aramis Saint-Germain *F*//
124 rue de Rennes, 6e ☎ *45 48 03 75*
Ⓣ *205098* • *Best Western* • *AE DC MC V* • *42 rooms, 1 bar*
This very modern and efficient little place was recently opened by a graduate of the renowned Lausanne Hotel School. Its location, on a busy shopping street in Montparnasse, is noisy, but rooms have double glazing and air conditioning. Bedrooms are on the small side, but bathrooms are well equipped, some with jacuzzis. The neat breakfast room and cocktail bar is suitable for business talks • 2 meeting rooms (capacity up to 40).

Banville *F*///
166 bd Berthier, 17e ☎ *42 67 70 16*
Ⓣ *643025* • *AE MC V* • *40 rooms.*
Claiming to be the cheapest three-star hotel in Paris, the Banville has few special amenities but is run in a pleasant and personal way by very friendly people. Its large foyer is elegant, its bedrooms comfortable and prettily decorated, with modern

marble bathrooms. The residential 17e lacks charm, but is convenient for the air terminal and Palais des Congrès. 24hr room service.

Deux-Iles *F*///
59 rue St-Louis-en-l'Ile, 4e
☎ *43 26 13 35 fax 43 29 60 25* •
17 rooms, 1 bar
This elegantly converted 17thC house in the narrow main street of the city's smaller and quieter island retains much of the charm of Vieux Paris. The atmosphere is warm and friendly, and the intimate cellar bar with its log fire and deep sofas is just the place for a quiet chat, as is the little patio. Bedrooms are small, but are furnished with pretty Provençal fabrics.

L'Hôtel *F*/////
13 rue des Beaux-Arts, 6e
☎ *43 25 27 22* Ⓣ *270870*
fax 43 25 64 81 • *AE DC MC V* • *22 rooms, 3 suites, 1 restaurant, 1 bar*
When Oscar Wilde died here, broke, in 1900, this 18thC town house was a disreputable little place; now it is the most stylish and fashionable (and expensive) of the city's smaller hotels. Celebrity guests enjoy its intimacy and privacy and relish the plushy boudoir-like decor, with velvet and antiques in all rooms, pink Venetian marble in the bathrooms, and odd touches like the metal sculpture of a sheep in the very smart bar. Most rooms are quite small, except for the splendid penthouse suites with their balconies and rooftop views. You can apply for the room (and bed!) where Wilde died, or Mistinguett's room with her own Art Nouveau furniture. Reservations need to be made well in advance.

La Louisiane *F*/
60 rue de Seine, 6e ☎ *43 29 59 30* •
AE DC MC V • *80 rooms; no bar*
Another Left Bank hotel with literary associations, this one, unlike

L'Hôtel, has remained cheap and downmarket: it is recommended only for a businessman on a tight budget or nostalgically seeking communion with the great days when the likes of Sartre, Hemingway and Cyril Connolly used to stay here. Today it still has a cosmopolitan feel but absolutely no frills: rooms are plain but well modernized, with respectable plumbing, and they are protected by double glazing from the colourful Buci street market below.

Montana Tuileries *F//*
12 rue St-Roch, 1er ☎ *42 60 35 10*
TX *214404* ● *AE DC MC V* ● *25 rooms, 1 bar*
With its large well modernized rooms and air of friendly efficiency, this is a useful address for those wanting to avoid the generally high prices of the smart and central Tuileries area. 24hr room service.

Relais Christine *F////*
3 rue Christine, 6e ☎ *43 26 71 80*
TX *202606 fax 43 26 89 38* ● *AE DC MC V* ● *39 rooms, 12 duplexes*
A 16thC abbey in a narrow street near Saint-Germain-des-Prés has been recently converted into a small luxury hotel where breakfast is served in the former chapel in the basement. Rooms vary in size but are all furnished with antiques and pleasantly decorated; best are the penthouse suites, noisiest those by the lift, quietest those facing the pretty courtyard. 24hr room service, garage ● 1 meeting room.

La Résidence du Bois *F////*
16 rue Chalgrin, 16e ☎ *45 00 50 59*
● *Relais et Châteaux* ● *16 rooms, 3 suites, 1 bar*
A Third Empire mansion in a quiet residential street near L'Etoile has been transformed into one of the best small hotels in Paris, infinitely restful and run by friendly and helpful people. The compact bar, cheerfully decorated with murals,

and the pretty walled garden with its creepers and canopies are ideal for quiet and relaxed business discussions after a day in the city. Spacious bedrooms are furnished with silks and satins in gentle colours. Service is efficient. No restaurant, but simple meals are served to residents.

Saint-Simon *F///*
14 rue St-Simon 7e ☎ *45 48 35 66*
TX *203277 fax 45 48 68 25* ●
29 rooms, 5 suites, no bar
The tiny cobbled forecourt with its shrubs and trelliswork gives a rural air to this delightful 17thC house in a quiet Faubourg Saint-Germain street: a select hotel owned and run by a Swedish couple who have filled it with antiques. The elegant little bar and salons in the basement have tiled floors, old beams and rough stone walls with little alcoves. Some rooms have balconies.

Suède *F///*
31 rue Vaneau, 7e ☎ *47 05 00 08*
TX *200596* ● *AE MC V* ● *40 rooms, 1 suite, 1 bar*
The upper back bedrooms of this discreet and rather formal Faubourg Saint-Germain hotel overlook the leafy gardens of the Prime Minister's office and residence, the Hôtel Matignon. Service is efficient and the place is quiet and comfortable, with a large lounge and a patio where business talks can be held. Light refreshments are available till 10pm.

Université *F///*
22 rue de l'Université, 7e
☎ *42 61 09 39* TX *260717*
fax 46 64 00 80 ● *27 rooms, 1 suite; no bar*
Another 17thC town house on the Left Bank converted into an intimate and attractive hotel, stylishly decorated with antiques and tapestries. Rooms have safes and plenty of modern comforts. Delightful courtyard.

Restaurants

Paris certainly has more great restaurants than any other city on earth. Today as ever the quality of the cuisine is paramount, and most of the places considered suitable for high-level business entertaining will have really distinguished food: if your guests are French, the venue should be selected with this in mind.

Many of the best gourmet restaurants are in the smart hotels, such as the Bristol or Crillon. Others are run by famous *patron*/chefs, such as Alain Senderens, who at Lucas-Carton offers elegant surroundings and first-rate service as well as fine food: in Paris at least, if not in the provinces, it is rare to find top-level cuisine in a humble setting. The cooking, whether classical or *nouvelle* or a mix of the two, is almost always French: foreign restaurants seldom make the top grade and are not much used for business purposes. Most of the best restaurants are in the smarter central districts – the 1er, 6e, 7e, 8e and 16e *arrondissements* – though a few lie scattered elsewhere.

Lunch is the main business meal, while dinners are more likely to be social. Lunch appointments are for 1pm or a little later, dinners never before 8pm: Parisians often like to dine late. It is always advisable to make a reservation ahead in a serious restaurant, but this is less essential for the larger brasseries or for dinner in a hotel. Business eating is almost always *à la carte*, and expensive: but most of the top restaurants also offer interesting set menus at somewhat lower prices, and it would not be thought amiss to point these out to your guests, since the chef will be putting most effort into the day's "specials."

Some useful selections
For fine food in elegant surroundings
Les Ambassadeurs • Le Bristol • Carré des Feuillants • L'Espadon • Le Grand Vefour • Lasserre • Lucas-Carton • Le Pré Catelan • Robuchon • Taillevent • La Tour d'Argent.
For eating outdoors L'Aquitaine • L'Espadon • Le Pré Catelan • Le Régence.
Open very late All brasseries • Baumann Marbeuf • Chez Edgard • Fouquet's Elysées.

Allard *F*///
41 rue St-André-des-Arts, 6e
☎ *43 26 48 23* • *closed Sat, Sun, Aug, Dec 23–Jan 3* • *AE DC MC V*
The most famous bistro in Paris has confounded the pessimists by retaining its traditional character in spite of the death of André Allard in 1983 and the recent retirement of

Madame. All is as before: the sawdust on the floor, the zinc-topped bar, the worn furniture, the waiters in long cotton smocks, the noisy and cosmopolitan clientele. The food is still variable too, but much of it is excellent, notably the duck and the *turbot beurre blanc*, and portions are generous.

L'Ambassade d'Auvergne *F*/
22 rue du Grenier-St-Lazare, 3e
☎ *42 72 31 22* • *MC V*
At this friendly "embassy" of Auvergnat tradition, the decor is carefully rustic, with great hams hanging from the ceiling, but the seating is comfortable. The hearty peasant cuisine includes *pot-au-feu*, *boudin* with chestnuts and other local dishes served in generous portions, and the aromatic cheeses come from the *patron's* family farm in the Auvergne country side.

Les Ambassadeurs [F]/////
Hôtel Crillon ☎ *42 65 24 24* • *AE DC MC V* • *jacket and tie*
The formal 18thC elegance of the Crillon's main dining room makes an ideal setting for a really special meal with important guests. Service is smooth and discreet in the grand manner, and the unfussy cooking is excellent. The lunchtime set menu offers good value. On fine days meals are served in the hotel's attractive courtyard.

L'Aquitaine [F]///
54 rue Dantzig, 15e ☎ *48 28 67 38* • *closed Sun & Mon* • *AE DC MC V*
The friendly yet sophisticated Aquitaine is owned and run by Christiane Massia. Service is gentle and courteous, decor beguiling, with pretty table-lamps, beamed ceiling and unusual murals. The upstairs room is best, leading onto an elegant paved terrace where meals are served under parasols in fine weather. Mme Massia provides light and original variations on the cuisine of her native Landes (in Aquitaine), with the accent on fish, duck and *foie gras*. An excellent place for lunchtime work or evening pleasure, out of the way but worth the trek.

Baumann Marbeuf [F]/
15 rue Marbeuf, 8e ☎ *47 20 11 11* • *AE DC MC V* • *smart dress*
Until well past midnight Parisians crowd this lively Alsatian citadel of good *choucroute*, which is offered in various forms, with *pot-au-feu*, duck or even fish, as well as more classically with pork. Good meat dishes, too, and a fine selection of Alsatian wines and fruit spirits. Eye-catching glass and marble decor. Fine for a working lunch.

Bofinger [F]//
5 rue de la Bastille, 4e ☎ *42 72 87 82* • *AE DC MC V* • *smart dress*
Allegedly the city's oldest brasserie, Bofinger is famous for its exuberant high-ceilinged Art Nouveau decor and its draught beer. The food is brasserie-style but there are some more modern dishes from the *nouvelle cuisine* repertoire. A pleasant place for a relaxed meal with colleagues near the Place de la Bastille and the Marais. It also has various private rooms seating up to a hundred and a good-value fixed menu.

Le Bristol [F]/////
Hôtel Le Bristol ☎ *42 66 91 45* • *AE DC MC V* • *jacket required*
Shirts without ties in summer, and more than a dash of *nouvelle cuisine*, are about the only concessions to modernity permitted by the Bristol's two superlative restaurants, much patronized by the upper echelons of international business, politics and the rich. Here all is grace and elegance in the grandest classical tradition. In winter you dine in a noble oval hall, with oak panelling and a superb Gobelin tapestry; in summer, in a lovely light room open to the garden. Meals are generous and very good, punctuated by all the right appetizers, sorbets and petits-fours; some find that the service, by battalions of waiters, is almost too perfect and deferential. The set menus are good value.

Jacques Cagna [F]/////
14 rue des Grands-Augustins, 6e ☎ *43 26 49 39* • *closed Sat (exc twice a month), Sun, Aug, last week Dec* • *AE DC MC V* • *jacket and tie preferred*
Tucked away in a narrow street in Vieux Paris, Cagna's establishment in an attractive town mansion is quiet at lunch time and is a pleasant place for a business lunch, with its 16thC beams, salmon-coloured walls and Flemish still-lifes. In the evenings it is very popular and reservations are essential. Cagna's cuisine is personal and imaginative, and the menu includes at least one recipe borrowed from his mother as well as unusual seafood dishes such as *coquilles Saint-Jacques au jus de truffe*. There are good value set menus and an interesting wine list.

Carré des Feuillants [F]////
14 rue Castiglione, 1er ☎ *42 86 82 82*
• *closed Sat L, Sun, weekends in Jul &*
Aug • *AE DC MC V* • *jacket and tie*
preferred
Opened in 1986, in a 17thC house
near the Tuileries, this newcomer to
the ranks of top Paris restaurants is
owned and run by a brilliant and
ambitious young chef from Gascony,
Alain Dutournier. His business and
diplomatic clientele is glossy; so is his
fancy modern decor, in an intimate
setting of small connecting rooms.
His cuisine is inventive and delicious,
drawing on the traditions and the
produce of his native southwest.
Good value fixed-price business
lunch.

Chez Edgard [F]///
4 rue Marbeuf, 8e ☎ *47 20 51 15* •
closed Sun • *AE DC MC V*
This is one of the best-known middle-
price restaurants in Paris, a regular
rendezvous for politicians of all
parties (even Communist leaders) as
well as film and media people. It is
typically Parisian, always crowded at
lunch time (but quieter at night),
with brisk service and good
traditional food. Very fresh shellfish;
wines at reasonable prices.

Chez Françoise [F]/
Aérogare des Invalides, esplanade des
Invalides, 7e ☎ *47 05 49 03* • *closed*
Sun D, 2 weeks in Aug • *AE DC V*
Tucked discreetly away beneath the
Invalides air terminal, Chez Françoise
is frequented, especially at lunch time
(when reservations are essential), by
diplomats and politicians from the
nearby Quai d'Orsay and the
Chambre des Députés. The sober
decor of wood panelling and classical
white linen in the main dining room
is offset by a trellis effect in the
smaller front area, with cane chairs
and plants. The classical cuisine, with
particularly good fish, is served by
discreet and experienced waiters. The
"business menu" is available in the
evenings as well as at lunch time, and
the wine list reasonably priced.

Dodin-Bouffant [F]///
Pl Maubert-Mutualité/25 rue Frédéric-
Sauton, 5e ☎ *43 25 25 14* • *closed*
Sun, Aug, Christmas and New Year
period • *DC MC V*
A long-standing Left Bank restaurant
with a faithful local and international
clientele. Excellent fish and shellfish
(from the restaurant's own tanks)
feature prominently on the menu and
the game is to be recommended,
when in season. Like the long wine
list, the lunchtime fixed-price menu
offers good value. Reservations are
advisable at all times and essential on
summer evenings when the pretty
terrace outside is very popular (last
orders at 1am). A lively after-theatre
crowd frequents both upstairs and
downstairs dining rooms in winter.
The upper floor has a private room
for up to 50.

Le Duc [F]////
243 bd Raspail, 14e ☎ *43 20 96 30* •
closed Sat, Sun & Mon • *no credit*
cards
Appropriately for a restaurant
specializing in fish and shellfish, the
decor is all mahogany and brass,
suggesting the dining room of a
luxury yacht. The Minchelli brothers,
who long ago rejected rich sauces and
are now seen as precursors of *nouvelle*
cuisine, rely entirely on using the
freshest food and the simplest
preparation. If, because of storms, no
fresh fish is available, the restaurant
does not open. The approach is
purist; the results, like the wines, are
well worth the price.

L'Espadon [F]////
Hôtel Ritz ☎ *42 60 38 30* • *AE DC*
MC V • *jacket and tie in winter*
The Ritz's restaurant is surprisingly
small and intimate, and its period
decor and furnishings have a
charmingly feminine flavour, evoking
Madame de Pompadour herself. In
fact, you are likely to find Arab oil
sheikhs, American tycoons or Parisian
singing stars, whether indoors or out
in the formal garden. Service is old-
fashioned and masterly, and the

equally superb cooking tends towards the traditional.

L'Etoile d'Or   *F////*
Hôtel Concorde La Fayette
☎ *47 58 12 84* • *AE DC MC V* •
jacket and tie
That this gigantic and somewhat functional modern hotel should sport so elegant and ambitious a restaurant is a sign that its business customers tend to appreciate true quality. Joël Renty's cooking is inventive without being fussy, the service is stylish and the seating spacious. There is live piano music in the evenings. The set menus are good value.

Fouquet's Elysées   *F////*
99 ave des Champs-Elysées, 8e
☎ *47 23 70 60* • *closed (1st floor)*
Sat, Sun, Aug • *AE DC MC V* • *jacket and tie*
Fouquet's remains an oasis of chic and grandeur among all the fast-food places and the car showrooms. Pagnol and Simenon were habitués, and Fouquet's has retained its literary cachet; many well-known faces can still be spotted. The upper restaurant is rather grand; the luxurious ground-floor brasserie with its elegant glass-fronted terrace is cheaper and more entertaining. The food is defiantly traditional, the service is courteous and the set menu good value.

Goumard   *F////*
17 rue Duphot, 1er ☎ *42 60 36 07* •
closed Sun, 1 week Aug, Dec 21–Jan 4 • *AE DC MC V* • *smart dress*
This elegant little restaurant near the Madeleine makes an ideal business venue. The two smallish dining rooms are discreet and comfortable, the decor of blue and yellow tiles is pretty, and the service by waiters in naval-style uniform is impeccable. Excellent fish and shellfish dishes.

Le Grand Vefour   *F/////*
17 rue de Beaujolais, 1er
☎ *42 96 56 27* • *closed Sat L, Sun, Aug* • *AE DC MC V* • *jacket and tie*
This famous old showpiece of Vieux

Paris stands tucked away down an arcade at the north end of the Palais Royal. It belonged for many years to the great *patron*/chef Raymond Oliver, but is now run by the charming Mme Ruggieri, who has carefully restored its majestic early 19thC decor. Here the rich and famous come to enjoy some of the best cooking in Paris prepared by reputed chef Jean-Claude Llonheur, mainly classical dishes but with many *nouvelle* additions. Distinguished Bordeaux wines, outstanding service and a good value set menu.

Lasserre   *F/////*
17 ave Franklin-Roosevelt, 8e
☎ *43 59 53 43 or 43 59 67 45* • *closed Mon L, Sun, Aug* • *no credit cards* • *jacket and tie*
The rituals of *haute cuisine* in fine surroundings are fully maintained at this classic establishment, still warmly in favour with a discerning international clientele. Impeccable waiters serve the food onto gold-rimmed plates, and at night the roof opens up to reveal the stars. The cuisine has lost its top ratings in the French guides, for this rich cooking is now out of fashion: but the older generation of gourmets remain delighted with it.

Louis XIV   *F////*
1 bis place des Victoires, 1er
☎ *40 26 20 81* • *closed Sat, Sun, Aug* • *MC V*
This lively traditional bistro near the Bourse is a good place for an unpretentious lunch with business colleagues in the area: it is used a lot by executives and journalists working nearby. Friendly service, a terrace out on the square for fine days, and very reliable Lyonnais cooking.

Credit card abbreviations	
AE	American Express
DC	Diners Club
MC	Access/MasterCard
V	Visa

Lucas-Carton F|||||
9 pl de la Madeleine, 8e
☎ *42 65 22 90 • closed Sat, Sun, Aug,
Dec 23–Jan 4 • DC MC V • jacket and
tie D*
Alain Senderens, most celebrated of
Parisian practitioners of *nouvelle
cuisine*, has taken over the venerable
Lucas-Carton. He has kept the
magnificent *belle époque* decor with
red velvet banquettes and Art
Nouveau woodwork, and has added
his own individual style of cooking,
enticing fashionable diners back to a
place whose glory had begun to fade.
The duck is excellent; the food,
generally, which includes a *menu
dégustation*, is as good as anywhere in
Paris and the wine list matches the
food.

Maxim's F|||||
3 rue Royale, 8e ☎ *42 65 27 94 • AE
DC MC V • jacket and tie; Fri D
evening dress*
With its gleaming mirrors and
chandeliers, its orchestra playing
waltzes in the evenings, its famous
private rooms and its glamorous
history, Maxim's remains the epitome
of "La Vie Parisienne." Nowadays
the crowds come as much for the
history as for the food, although that
is better than some like to make out.
The rosettes and the gourmets have
mostly gone, it is true, but perhaps
both were misplaced in a restaurant
catering to hundreds both at lunch
time and for dinner. For all its visual
splendour, Maxim's was regarded in
earlier days simply as the best
brasserie in the world. It must have
been easier then, but Maxim's is still
a Parisian institution.

Le Paris F|||
Hôtel Lutétia, 23 rue de Sèvres, 6e
☎ *45 48 74 34 • closed Sun, Mon,
Aug • AE DC MC V • jacket and tie
preferred*
Like the rest of the hotel, this
intimate and luxurious little
restaurant has recently been restored
to its original 1920s' splendour. Here
under the chandeliers, senior

politicians and publishers, for
instance, come to enjoy the inventive
and subtle cooking of Jacky Fréon.
Excellent set menu at lunch.

Le Petit Colombier F|||
42 rue des Acacias, 17e ☎ *43 80 28 54
• closed Sat, Sun L, first 2 weeks Aug
• MC V*
Useful either for a business lunch or
an intimate dinner, this snug little
place not far from Porte Maillot and
the Palais des Congrès, with its old-
fashioned woodwork, has something
of the atmosphere of a provincial
auberge. Service is friendly, if
sometimes slow, and Bernard
Fournier's excellent cooking brings
modern touches to such classics as
navarin d'agneau. Good set menu.

Pharamond F||
24 rue de la Grande-Truanderie, 1er
☎ *42 33 06 72 • closed Mon L, Sun,
mid-Jul–mid-Aug • AE DC MC V*
A noble survivor of the rebuilding of
the Les Halles quarter, this fine old
timbered building serves some of the
best Norman food in town, at
moderate prices and amid a splendid
Art Nouveau decor of mirrors and
ceramic tiles. Business and other
customers come to enjoy dishes such
as tripe or scallops in cider, served
classically or with modern variations.
For a real taste of Normandy, try the
ciders and the calvados.

Le Pré Catelan F|||||
*Route de Suresnes, Bois de Boulogne,
16e* ☎ *45 24 55 58 • Sun D, Mon,
2 weeks Feb • DC MC V*
This palatial building dating from
1901 in the leafy setting of the Bois
de Boulogne has various salons which
are much in demand for smart
receptions. It is run by the celebrated
patissier Gaston Lenôtre, whose food
is exquisite. In summer you can eat
in the flowery garden; for winter,
there is an indoor winter garden and
an elegantly snug dining room with a
welcoming open fire. Le Pré Catelan
is an ideal place for high-level
entertaining.

Prunier Madeleine *F*/////
9 rue Duphot, 1er ☎ *42 60 36 04*
● *AE DC MC V*
A rather tired old seafood restaurant
was recently revived by a change of
ownership and some redecoration.
The very young chef, Marc Singer,
serves an interesting mixture of
exciting new dishes and the old-
established Prunier standard recipes.
There are private rooms, useful for
discreet occasions, the smallest
intimate and charming, the largest
holding up to 60 for the grander
occasions. There have been reports
that the service can be brusque and
intimidating.

Au Quai des Ormes *F*/////
72 quai de l'Hôtel-de-Ville, 4e
☎ *42 74 72 22* ● *closed Sat, Sun* ●
MC V ● *smart dress*
This spacious and discreetly elegant
restaurant offers a fine view of the Ile
Saint-Louis from the small upper
terrace. It is much used at lunch time
by a business clientele (a private room
holding 30 people is available), who
appreciate the reliable *nouvelle cuisine*,
with its emphasis on fish, the rather
grand but not pompous service and
the relaxed atmosphere. The lunchtime fixed-price menu is popular,
while the fashionable Parisians who
come here in the evenings can make a
choice between the low-calorie
menu or the more expensive gourmet
menu.

Au Quai d'Orsay *F*//
49 quai d'Orsay, 7e ☎ *45 51 58 58* ●
AE MC V ● *smart dress*
Just along the Quai from the foreign
ministry, this smart restaurant purrs
at lunch time with the confidential
chatter of diplomats, and at night is
graced by the *beau monde*, mainly
couples. They come for the
traditional *cuisine bourgeoise* and for
the wide variety of mushrooms, in
particular for the vast plateful of
wild mushrooms served as a starter.
Prices are reasonable, and there are
good value lunch and dinner
menus.

Le Régence *F*/////
Hôtel Plaza Athénée, 25 ave
Montaigne, 8e ☎ *47 23 78 33* ● *AE DC*
MC V ● *jacket and tie*
For those who want a glamorous
setting for their high-level business
entertaining, with maybe a film star
or two at the next table, then the
tasteful opulence of "le Plaza" could
be just right. The period furnishings
are matched by extreme comfort and
splendid service; at dinner there is
candlelight and a pianist; and on fine
days you can eat in the shade of red
parasols in the flower filled inner
courtyard. The cuisine is mainly
classical, and the wine list is excellent.

Le Relais Saint-Germain *F*
190 bd St-Germain, 7e ☎ *45 48 11 73*
● *MC V*
For a reasonably priced working
lunch on the Left Bank, Le Relais is
very good value and it is highly
popular with middle-rank civil
servants and publishers, for example.
There is no carte, just a set menu of
well-cooked classic dishes with plenty
of choice. The air-conditioned
basement is calmer than the crowded
entrance floor, on which there is a
covered terrace for watching the
world go by.

Robuchon (Jamin) *F*/////
32 rue de Longchamp, 16e
☎ *47 27 12 27* ● *closed Sat & Sun*
● *AE DC V* ● *jacket and tie preferred*
Behind an unassuming façade, down
a side-street near the Trocadéro, lies
arguably the best restaurant in Paris
today, thanks to the remarkable gifts
of its *patron*/chef Joël Robuchon. It
used to be called Jamin, but he has
now changed its name to his own –
but not out of vanity, for this
rigorous perfectionist is a shy man
who stays in his kitchen rather than
parading among his guests after
dinner. Reservations need to be made
a month in advance for lunch and two
to three months in advance for dinner
in one of his two small and very
comfortable dining rooms, where
some might find the theatrically

romantic decor a little fussy. But few would apply this word to a modern cuisine of great subtlety and invention.

Taillevent   _E_ ////
15 rue Lamennais, 8e ☎ *45 61 12 90 • closed Sat, Sun, Aug, 1 week Feb, nat hols • no credit cards • jacket and tie*
Just east of L'Etoile, Robuchon's friend Jean-Claude Vrinat also runs a luxurious establishment in the top gourmet bracket, reckoned by the senior politicians and industrialists who use it to be one of the city's four or five best. Tables need to be reserved weeks ahead, but once there you will not be patronized or intimidated. The decor is discreet and classical, the seating spacious and the atmosphere serious, as diners concentrate on business and their meal. The wine list is outstanding, and the cuisine is constantly evolving, including, for instance, hot oysters with leeks and truffles.

La Tour d'Argent   _E_ /////
15–17 quai de la Tournelle, 5e ☎ *43 54 23 31 • closed Mon • AE DC MC V • jacket and tie*
This is a penthouse where it is worth making a reservation well ahead to secure a table with a view across to the floodlit Notre-Dame and the Seine below. Security is tight and identities are carefully checked. Once inside, you are struck by the graceful dignity of this restaurant, where the waiters wear tails even at noon. The chandeliers, parquet floor and well-spaced yellow-clothed tables provide the setting for a cuisine under new chef Manuel Martinez of the highest quality that mixes modern and classical: duck in various guises is what the restaurant is famous for, but lamb and lobster are also first-rate, and the set menu at lunch is good value. The wine list is the best in Paris, and afterwards you can enjoy an armagnac or cognac in the lovely, atmospheric cellars. The service is courteously attentive.

Au Trou Gascon   _E_ ////
40 rue Taine, 12e ☎ *43 44 34 26 • closed Sat & Sun • AE DC MC V*
This delightful old bistro, owned by Alain Dutournier who has since set up the Carré des Feuillants (see above), is usefully located in an eastern area where a major new business quarter is fast growing up around Quai de Bercy but where there are few really good eating-places. The decor is late 19th century with mirrors and plenty of atmosphere. Under chef Bernard Broux the Gascon and Landais cooking is as excellent as ever, with some classic local dishes and some innovations. The set business lunch offers a good choice and the range of wines and armagnacs is spectacular.

Restaurant prices

The price symbol (_E_ to _E_ /////) given after the restaurant name is based on the cost at the time of going to press of a typical *à la carte* meal including half a bottle of wine, tax and service (see pages 6 and 7). Most restaurants offer at least one, and often several, fixed-price menus at considerably lower prices.

Brasseries
Brasseries are today more in vogue than ever with Parisians. Though generally too hectic and congested for high-level entertaining, they could often be the right choice for a more down-to-earth business meal. Prices are usually moderate and the cooking straightforward.

The fairly small *Le Balzar*, 49 rue des Ecoles, 5e ☎ 43 54 13 67, is a haunt of university professors and media people; *La Coupole*, 102 bd du Montparnasse, 14e ☎ 43 20 14 20, attracts into its famous high-ceilinged hall artists and ad-men, starlets and scribblers, tourists and grey-suited bourgeois, and the noise and fun go on well into the small hours;

Flo, 7 cour des Petites-Ecuries, 10e
☎ 47 70 13 59, noted for its Alsatian
food and draught beer, is trendy and
lively but has rather cramped seating;
Lipp, 151 bd St-Germain, 6e
☎ 45 48 53 91, remains the
celebrated meeting-place of the city's
political and intellectual elite; the
bustling *Le Muniche*, 27 rue de Buci,
6e ☎ 46 33 62 09, is popular with the
Left Bank media world (try for the
quieter alcoves) and open till 3am.

Non-French cuisines

Paris does not have many good
restaurants serving foreign cuisines,
but they are on the increase and you
may like to try one or two of the
following places.
American Joe Allen, 30 rue Pierre-
Lescot, 1er ☎ 42 36 70 13, is not a
place for business, but fun for any
homesick visitor seeking burgers and
apple pie in an authentic (well, fairly)
American atmosphere.
Chinese and Vietnamese These
proliferate, two of the best being
Chez Vong, 27 rue Colisée, 8e
☎ 43 59 77 12, which is fairly smart,
and *Tan Dinh*, 60 rue de Verneuil, 7e
☎ 45 44 04 84, with its pretty decor
and good French wines.
German The delightful *Au Vieux
Berlin*, 32 ave George-V, 8e
☎ 47 20 88 96, has style and
comfort, good German food, a pianist
in the evenings, and clients include
top French and German politicians.
Indian restaurants are still scarce, but
there is excellent tandoori cooking at
Raajmahal, 192 rue de la Convention,
15e ☎ 45 33 15 57.
Italian Best among the many good
ones are probably *Conti*, 72 rue
Lauriston, 16e ☎ 47 27 74 67, and
Sormani, 4 rue du Général-Lanzerac,
17e ☎ 43 80 13 91.
Japanese Kinugawa, 9 rue du Mont-
Thabor, 1er ☎ 42 60 65 07, is elegant
and friendly.
Russian Dominique, 19 rue Bréa, 6e
☎ 43 27 08 80, run by a White
Russian *émigré* family, serves bortsch,
blinis and other well-known dishes in
an "old Russian" decor.

OTHER RESTAURANTS

Paris has scores of atmospheric
bistros and romantic restaurants, too
down-to-earth or crowded for
business but good for relaxing with
friends. *Atelier Maître Albert*, 1 rue
Maître Albert, 5e ☎ 46 33 13 78,
offers low lighting, a good set dinner
and a young clientele. *Bistro de la
Gare*, 59 bd du Montparnasse, 6e
☎ 45 48 38 01, 30 rue St-Denis, le ☎
40 26 82 80, and at 73 ave des
Champs-Elysées, 8e ☎ 43 59 67 83,
are lively formula restaurants offering
a good set meal at a fair price with a
pretty decor. *Chartier*, 7 rue du
Faubourg-Montmartre, 9e
☎ 47 70 86 29, is an authentic
surviving late-19thC "soup kitchen"
with Art Nouveau decor and very low
prices. *Chez Joséphine*, 117 rue du
Cherche-Midi, 6e ☎ 45 48 52 40, is a
pleasantly atmospheric old bistro with
a good-value menu and a formidable
wine list. *Chez Toutoune*, 5 rue de
Pontoise, 5e ☎ 43 26 56 81, is lively,
friendly, very Parisian, with a copious
Provence-inspired set menu. *Le
Coupe-Chou*, 9 rue de Lanneau, 5e
☎ 46 33 68 69, is a romantic place in
a very old beamed building. *La
Marlotte*, 55 rue du Cherche-Midi, 6e
☎ 45 48 86 79, is animated, candlelit, much in vogue with yuppies and
has some well-known clients (Chirac
and Giscard among them) and
the food is good value. *Polidor*,
41 rue Monsieur-le-Prince, 6e
☎ 43 26 95 34, is a delightful warm
bistro with good bourgeois cooking
and upmarket clients. *Le Procope*, 13
rue de l'Ancienne-Comédie, 6e
☎ 43 26 99 20, is Paris's oldest café-
restaurant (1686): once the haunt of
Voltaire, Robespierre and Balzac, it is
under new management, which has
raised the quality of the food and the
prices. *Orestias*, 4 rue Grégoire-de-
Tours, 6e ☎ 43 54 62 01, is Greek-
run, down-to-earth, inexpensive and
excellent. *Le Trumilou*, 84
quai de l'Hôtel de Ville, 4e
☎ 42 77 63 98, provides good
country cooking in a warm friendly
atmosphere.

Bars and cafés

The French tend to work late in their offices, and generally prefer to do business over a leisurely meal rather than in bars. Nearly all the best cocktail bars for business talks are in the big hotels, frequented by foreigners, or attached to leading restaurants. Café-going on the other hand is an old Paris tradition, but it has waned in recent decades as the French have become more comfortably housed. The city's 10,000 cafés offer much the same range of alcoholic drinks as bars (apart from elaborate cocktails). Unlike bars, they usually have open terraces on the street, but they tend to be more cramped, noisy and casual than hotel bars, and therefore less suitable for a quiet business drink. Several of the bars and cafés mentioned on this page also feature in *Restaurants*.

Smart bars The luxury hotels have the best: the Bristol, Crillon (much used by journalists), George V, Inter-Continental, Lancaster, Plaza Athénée and the Ritz, whose very fashionable bar was "liberated" by Hemingway in 1944. The Concorde La Fayette has a stylish panoramic rooftop bar, as does the Hilton. The smooth and intimate bar of L'Hôtel International is popular with film and theatre people, and that of the Pont Royal with publishers and writers.

Among the best-known café-bars in restaurants are *Fouquet's*, on the Champs-Elysées, which is old-fashioned but still smart, *La Coupole*, always the focus of a trendy crowd, the *Closerie des Lilas*, still a haunt of literati, and *Chez Francis* at the Pont de l'Alma. The Foyer Bar of the *Café de la Paix*, 12 bd des Capucines, 9e, and the *Alexandre*, 53 ave George V, 8e, are frequented by a sophisticated and cosmopolitan crowd. And the famous *Harry's New York Bar*, 5 rue Daunou, 2e, still dispenses its 160 different types of whisky to wistful expatriates, as it did in the days when Scott Fitzgerald and Hemingway were coming here as regulars.

Wine bars These are bistros or taverns serving good wine by the glass, and also snacks and light dishes. *Le Henri-IV*, 13 pl du Pont-Neuf, 1er, is much used by actors, politicians and lawyers from the nearby courts; *Rubis*, 10 rue du Marché St-Honoré, 1er, is also popular. As the modern wine bar is less a Paris than a London phenomenon, it is not surprising that two of the best should be English-owned: Steve Spurrier's *Blue Fox*, Cité Berryer, 8e, and Mark Williamson's *Willi's*, 13 rue des Petits-Champs, 1er, are popular with the British and anglophile French.

Pubs Recent attempts to implant the British pub have been less successful. Several so-called pubs today serve English beers and pub food amid "typically English" decor. To English eyes these places may look phoney, yet some remain popular with Parisians – among them, *Le Pub St-Germain*, 17 rue de l'Ancienne Comédie, 6e, open all night, *Le Sir Winston Churchill*, 5 rue de Presbourg, 16e, and *Le Twickenham*, 70 rue des Saints-Pères, 6e, frequented by publishing people.

Cafés The most famous Paris cafés are side by side in St-Germain-des-Prés – the *Deux Magots* and *Le Flore*, 170 and 172 bd St-Germain, 6e, where Sartre and Camus used to meet. Today there are fewer writers and more tourists: but these are still lively places and could be suitable for a business chat in the mornings or mid-afternoons when they are least crowded. Much the same applies to the historic cafés on the bd de Montparnasse – *Le Select*, No. 99, *Le Dôme*, No. 108, and *La Coupole*, No. 102, which are still haunts of the art world. A similar role is played by the cafés of some brasseries, such as *Le Balzar* and notably *Lipp* (see *Brasseries*). The latest place for younger smart people is the slick and futuristic *Café Costes*, sq des Innocents, 1er, at Les Halles and *Café Beaubourg*, next to the Pompidou centre, 1er.

Entertainment

"Paris by night" (the term used even by the French) is mostly as glamorous as its reputation and certainly as varied. Full listings of events in the capital are published in two pocket-sized weeklies, *L'Officiel des Spectacles* and *Pariscope*. Your hotel should also have a copy of the free *Sélection Paris* booklet and you can dial ☎ 47 20 94 94 for a recorded message about current events in the city (☎ 47 20 88 98 in English and ☎ 47 20 57 58 in German).

Ticket agencies Obtaining tickets in advance is not an easy matter. Many theatres operate a system involving reservations and sales not more than one or two weeks in advance; they are reluctant to make telephone reservations and do not work with agencies. Your hotel may be able to obtain tickets for you and the following agencies are usually reliable: *Agence des Théâtres des Champs-Elysées* ☎ 43 59 24 60 and 43 59 80 39, *Night and Day* (in Méridien-Etoile Hotel) ☎ 47 59 92 82, *SOS Théâtre* ☎ 42 25 03 18 and 42 25 67 07.

Theatre Paris theatre is often a disappointment, with curiously old-fashioned and declamatory acting. The best-known subsidized theatre is the very beautiful *Comédie Française*, pl du Théâtre-Français, 1er ☎ 40 15 00 00, for which it is hard to obtain tickets; the *Odéon*, 1 pl Paul-Claudel, 6e ☎ 43 25 70 32, is subtitled "Théâtre de l'Europe" and often acts as a home for visiting foreign companies; the *Théâtre de la Ville*, 2 pl du Châtelet, 1er ☎ 42 74 22 77, is well known for its international theatre festival. The commercial theatres are mostly on the Right Bank, many near the Opéra, the experimental mostly on the Left Bank. The liveliest of the experimental theatres are Peter Brook's *Bouffes du Nord*, 37 bis bd de la Chapelle, 10e ☎ 42 39 34 50; the *Cartoucherie*, route de la Pyramide, in the Bois de Vincennes, 12e, ☎ 48 08 39 74, a converted ammunition factory; and the *Lucernaire Forum*, 53 rue Notre-Dame-des-Champs, 6e ☎ 45 44 57 34. Most of Paris's theatres close for at least a month during the summer.

The café-theatres – lively, uncomfortable and requiring a good knowledge of French and things French – are concentrated in the Beaubourg area: *Les Blancs Manteaux*, 15 rue des Blancs-Manteaux, 4e ☎ 48 87 15 84; *Café de la Gare*, 41 rue du Temple, 3e ☎ 42 78 52 51; *Petit Casino*, 17 rue Chapon, 3e ☎ 42 78 36 50; *Point Virgule*, 7 rue Ste-Croix-de-la-Bretonnerie, 4e ☎ 42 78 67 03. Others are on the Left Bank: *Café d'Edgar*, 58 bd Edgar-Quinet, 14e ☎ 43 20 85 11 and *Cave du Cloître Saint-Séverin*, 19 rue St-Jacques, 5e ☎ 43 25 37 63. *Au Bec Fin*, 6 rue Thérèse, 1er ☎ 42 96 29 35, usually offers a good dinner as well as a choice of several playlets.

Opera and dance The splendid *Opéra* ☎ 47 42 57 50 with its Chagall ceiling stages both opera and ballet but tickets are expensive and hard to obtain. The *Théâtre Musical de Paris*, better known as *Théâtre du Châtelet*, pl du Châtelet, 1er ☎ 42 33 00 00, has lavishly staged opera and dance at prices affordable by wider audiences, an aim that is also behind the newly opened *Opéra Bastille*. Dance is also staged at the Opéra, where the country's ballet company is based, but dance companies can be found in many venues all over Paris during the excellent winter season (mainly Nov and Dec): primarily the *Théâtre des Champs-Elysées*, 15 ave Montaigne, 8e ☎ 47 20 36 37; and huge places such as the *Palais des Congrès*, Porte Maillot, 17e ☎ 48 78 11 74 (information) and 48 78 75 00 (reservations); the *Palais des Sports*, Porte de Versailles ☎ 48 28 40 48; even the sports complex *Palais Omnisports de Paris Bercy*, 6 bd Bercy, 12e ☎ 43 46 12 21. During the Marais Festival (June) and the Festival de l'Ile de France (in the summer months) dance can be enjoyed in the courtyards of the mansions in Le Marais and historic buildings outside Paris.

Music The main venue for classical music is the *Salle Pleyel*, 252 rue du Faubourg St-Honoré, 8e ☎ 45 61 06 30 and 45 63 88 73. Concerts are also held at the *Maison de la Radio*, 116 ave du Président-Kennedy, 16e ☎ 42 30 15 16, and at the *Théâtre des Champs-Elysées*, 15 ave Montaigne, 8e ☎ 47 20 36 37. Much the pleasantest way of listening to classical music is to attend one of the frequent concerts held in beautiful churches such as the Gothic *Sainte-Chapelle* (reserve well in advance), *Saint-Germain L'Auxerrois*, *Saint-Germain-des-Prés*, *Saint-Julien-le-Pauvre*, *Saint Merri*, *Saint-Roch* and *Saint-Louis-en-L'Ile*. The cathedral of *Notre-Dame*, the church of the *Madeleine* and various historic buildings also stage occasional concerts. For contemporary music the best place is IRCAM, the experimental music centre inside the Pompidou centre ☎ 42 77 12 33. The main pop and rock venues are the huge *Palais des Congrès* ☎ 42 66 20 75, the *Palais des Sports* ☎ 48 28 40 90, the more recent *Palais Omnisports Bercy*, bd Bercy, ☎ 43 41 72 04 and the legendary *Olympia Music-Hall* ☎ 42 66 17 79.

Paris has dozens of jazz clubs, offering the whole range of styles. *New Morning*, 7–9 rue des Petites-Ecuries, 10e ☎ 45 23 51 41, has often been rated as the best in Europe. Other well-known clubs include *Caveau de la Huchette*, 5 rue de la Huchette, 5e ☎ 43 26 65 05; *Petit Journal*, 71 bd St-Michel, 5e ☎ 43 26 28 59; and *Slow Club*, 130 rue de Rivoli, 1er ☎ 42 33 84 30.

Cinema The latest films are a major topic of conversation in Paris and cinemas are frequently crowded throughout the week (reduced prices everywhere on Mon). The plush cinemas are on the Champs-Elysées and in the modern Forum des Halles, the art houses mostly on the Left Bank, in the Latin Quarter and Saint

Germain-des-Prés. In both these categories foreign films are shown in the original languages, generally with French subtitles (labelled *v.o.* for *version original* in the various listings); elsewhere in Paris films are dubbed (labelled *v.f.* for *version française*). The standard programme in the capital's 450-plus cinemas runs from 2pm to midnight (2am on Fri and Sat), with films showing at two-hour intervals. Paris has one *cinémathèque*, at the Palais de Chaillot, 16e ☎ 47 04 24 24, providing a non-stop feast of classics, both French and foreign. Usherettes expect a tip.

Nightclubs and casinos Paris has a number of very fashionable (and very expensive) private nightclubs whose doors tend to remain firmly closed to those not accompanied by habitués or famous faces. *Club Olivia Valère*, 40 rue du Colisée ☎ 42 25 11 68; *Elysée-Matignon*, 48 ave Gabriel, 8c ☎ 42 25 73 13; and the famous *Régine's*, 49 rue de Ponthieu ☎ 43 59 21 60, are all in the 8e arr near the Champs-Elysées. *Castel*, 15 rue Princesse, 6e ☎ 43 26 90 22, is the most exclusive.

The best dinner-and-show places are mostly very stylish, very expensive and more popular with foreigners than the French. They include the long-famous *Folies-Bergère*, 32 rue Richer, 9e ☎ 42 46 77 11; *Lido* 116 bis ave des Champs-Elysées, 8e ☎ 45 63 11 61; and *Moulin Rouge*, pl Blanche, 18e ☎ 46 06 00 19. Other well-known places are *Alcazar de Paris*, 62 rue Mazarine, 6e ☎ 43 29 02 20; *Cabaret 78*, 78 ave des Champs-Elysées, 8e ☎ 43 59 09 99; *Don Camillo*, 10 rue des Saints-Pères, 7e ☎ 42 60 82 84; *Eléphant Bleu*, 49 rue de Ponthieu, 8e ☎ 43 59 58 64; and the *Paradis Latin*, 28 rue Cardinal-Lemoine, 5e ☎ 43 25 28 28. *Crazy Horse Saloon*, a very upmarket strip club at 12 ave George-V, 8e ☎ 47 23 32 32, is popular for business entertainment.

The only casino in the Paris area open to visitors is at Enghien to the northwest of the city.

Shopping

Despite the mushrooming of hypermarkets in the suburbs, Paris still has a huge variety of small specialist shops, and for many visitors shopping is one of its main attractions. Window displays are stylish, the range of goods is excellent and shopping hours are long: roughly 9.30–7, Mon–Sat, though smaller shops may close for two hours at lunch time. Apart from the clusters of antique dealers and specialist bookshops on the Left Bank, Paris does not have as distinct shopping districts as some other cities.

Fashion is the main exception. The major old-established couturiers are in and around Avenue Montaigne, 8e (*Balmain, Dior, Courrèges, Givenchy, Laroche, Nina Ricci, Yves St Laurent, Ungaro*) or Rue du Faubourg St-Honoré, 8e (*Louis Férand, Lanvin, Torrenté*, with *Chanel* nearby in Rue Cambon, 1er). The more avant-garde designers prefer the Left Bank: *Sonia Rykiel*, 4 rue de Grenelle, 6e; *Chantal Thomass*, 5 rue du Vieux-Colombier, 6e. Many of the trendiest fashion boutiques are in Saint-Germain-des-Prés or in and around the Forum Les Halles.

Department stores Standard opening hours are 9.30–6.30, Mon–Sat. *Au Bon Marché*, 38 rue de Sèvres, 7e ☎ 45 49 21 22, is the only department store on the Left Bank and has a well-known antiques department. The huge *Galeries Lafayette*, 40 bd Haussmann, 9e ☎ 42 82 34 56, and its neighbour *Au Printemps*, 64 bd Haussmann ☎ 42 82 50 00, are full of chic boutiques and have useful facilities for visitors: shopping cards enabling purchases to be grouped together; 24hr pick-up facility; tax-recovery documentation; bureau de change; travel and theatre agency; restaurants; hairdressers. *La Samaritaine*, 19 rue de la Monnaie, 1er ☎ 40 41 20 20, less stylish but popular for its roof terrace with spectacular views over the Paris rooftops, is open till 8 on Wednesday.

Drugstores These stylish mini-shopping centres are open daily 9–1.30am, selling newspapers and magazines, gifts, books and records; all have restaurants, some have takeaway food service. *Drugstore Saint-Germain*, 149 bd St-Germain, 6e ☎ 42 22 80 00; *Drugstore Champs-Elysées*, 133 ave des Champs-Elysées, 8e ☎ 47 23 54 34; *Drugstore Matignon*, 1 ave Matignon, 8e ☎ 43 59 38 70.

Shopping centres and arcades There is a whole series of upmarket shopping malls or arcades leading off the north side of the Champs-Elysées, with fashion boutiques, restaurants and snackbars. *Forum des Halles*, 1er, is a smart shopping centre built in the late 1970s to replace the colourful food market; fashion boutiques and jewellery shops, restaurants, cafés, cinemas, sports facilities and Fnac store. *Palais des Congrès*, Porte Maillot, 17e, has art and antique shops, temporary craft stalls, bookshop, fashion boutiques, post office, restaurants and cafés. *Tour Maine-Montparnasse*, ave du Maine, 14e ☎ 45 38 32 32 is a large shopping centre adjoining the vast skyscraper, with dozens of shops (including a branch of the English owned store Habitat and Galeries Lafayette), restaurants and cafés as well as various leisure facilities.

Street markets Paris has many colourful open-air food markets. The best known are in Saint-Germain-des-Prés (Rue de Seine and Rue de Buci), the Latin Quarter (Rue Mouffetard), the Invalides area (Rue Cler), and Neuilly (Place du Marché, close to the Palais des Congrès).

There is a picturesque flower market on the Ile de la Cité near Notre-Dame; a market for stamps and postcards is held on Avenue Marigny and Avenue Gabriel, near the Champs-Elysées, on Thursdays, weekends and public holidays; and the famous flea-market (Marché aux Puces) at Porte de Clignancourt selling antiques, clothes and books is open from Saturday to Monday.

Sightseeing

Paris is full of monuments, old churches, elegant squares and picturesque streets, as well as scores of museums and galleries. Many of the major sights lie fairly close together near the stretch of the river between Notre-Dame and the Eiffel Tower. This central area is very compact and can be toured on foot. State museums are closed on Tuesday, many others on Monday: all are open on Sunday when many are free (on other days most charge modest admission fees). The tourist office ☎ 47 23 61 72 will give advice. For recorded details in English of the day's main events ☎ 47 20 88 98.

Arc de Triomphe Crowning the top of the Champs-Elysées, this impressive arch with its relief sculptures was built by Napoleon to commemorate French military victories. Below it, an eternal flame burns over the Tomb of the Unknown Soldier, honouring the dead of two world wars. Magnificent view from the platform at the top. *Pl Charles-de-Gaulle, 8e. Platform open 10–5.30.*

Assemblée Nationale (Palais Bourbon) The lower house of parliament meets in a semi-circular chamber in this 17thC mansion built by the Duchess of Bourbon. To attend a debate, and visit the fine library, apply in writing to 126 rue de l'Université, 75007.

Bibliothèque Nationale A fine 17thC mansion houses one of the world's greatest collections of maps, prints, manuscripts and books (9m volumes). The medals collection and splendid Mazarin Gallery are open to the public. *58 rue de Richelieu, 2e. Open 12–6.*

Conciergerie The keeper (concierge) of the king's household used to inhabit this section of the great 14thC palace built by Philip le Bel on the north side of the Ile de la Cité. Later it became notorious as a prison, especially during the Revolution, and one can visit the cells where Marie-Antoinette, Robespierre, Danton and others awaited the guillotine. *1 quai de l'Horloge, 1er. Open Wed–Mon, 10–5.*

Eiffel Tower Built in 1889 for the World Exhibition, long reviled but now placidly accepted as the city's best-known symbol, engineer Gustave Eiffel's tower of iron girders rises 315 metres/1,052ft above the city. The two lower platforms can be reached by lift or stairs, the top one by lift only: splendid panoramas. *Pont d'Iéna 7e. Open 10am–11pm.*

Gobelins tapestry factory Founded by Louis XIV, this state-owned enterprise still weaves tapestries for public buildings and for use as official gifts. *42 ave des Gobelins, 13e. Guided tours 2 and 3 Tue, Wed, Thu.*

Grand Palais This huge porticoed structure, built for the Universal Exhibition of 1900, now houses large-scale temporary art exhibitions and a science museum, the Palais de la Découverte. *Ave Winston-Churchill, 8e. Open Wed–Mon, 10–8 (Wed until 10).*

Hôtel de Ville Seat of the city government and office of its mayor, this great pompous pile was built in the 1870s as a pastiche of its Renaissance predecessor, burned down in 1871 by the Communards. The debates of the city council are open to the public; on Mondays there are guided tours of the reception rooms. *Pl de l'Hôtel de Ville, 4e. Reception open Mon–Sat, 9–6; tours Mon, 10.30.*

Les Invalides This massive complex of buildings was erected by Louis XIV in the 1670s to house his invalided soldiers. Today the main attraction is Napoleon's tomb. There are also museums of French military history and of the two world wars. *Open Apr–Sep, 10–6; Oct–Mar, 10–6.*

Jardin des Plantes Botanical garden dating from the 17th century and containing tropical plants, a natural history museum, including skeletons and fossils, and a small zoo. *Rue Geoffroy St-Hilaire, 5e. Open Wed–Mon, 10.30–5; Museum, 2–5.*

La Madeleine A handsome 18th–19thC church with Corinthian columns, a lovely marble interior and a famous organ. It is often used for concerts and smart weddings. *Pl de la Madeleine, 8e. Open 8.30–7.*

Maison de Balzac Of the various Paris homes of the great novelist, this one is now a museum, full of his possessions and steeped in his personality. *47 rue Raynouard, 16e. Open Tue–Sun, 10–5.30.*

Musée d'Art Moderne de la Ville de Paris Housed in the grandiose Palais de Tokyo. Braque, Dufy, Modigliani and Picasso are well represented. *11 ave du Président Wilson, 16e. Open daily exc Mon, 10–5.40; Wed 10–8.30.*

Musée Carnavalet A Renaissance building in the Marais, once the home of Madame de Sévigné, now a fascinating museum of Paris history, conveyed in models, paintings, maps and furniture. Many of the collections will be transferred to neighbouring *Hôtel Peletier St-Fargeau* while the Carnavalet is renovated.

Musée de Cluny One part of this museum is an archaeological site, the remains of the vast Gallo-Roman thermal baths of around AD200; the other part, the Hôtel de Cluny, built by rich abbots in the 15thC, houses a medieval collection including a set of marvellous 15thC tapestries. *6 pl Paul-Painlevé, 5e. Open Wed–Mon, 9.45–12.30, 2–5.15.*

Musée Grévin Waxworks of famous people ancient and modern; historical tableaux; distorting mirrors and other tricks. *10 bd Montmartre, 9e. Open daily, 10–7.*

Musée du Louvre France's leading museum, and one of the world's greatest, housed in a huge and majestic palace that was successively enlarged by various monarchs from François I to Napoleon III. The Greek, Roman and Egyptian antiquities include the *Venus de Milo* and *Winged Victory of Samothrace*; the Leonardo da Vinci collection, including *Mona Lisa*, is the world's finest; El Greco and Rembrandt are well represented. A controversial glass pyramid now provides a vast new entrance for the public. *Quai du Louvre, 1er. Open Wed–Mon, 10–6.30.*

Musée d'Orsay A huge and ornate late-19thC railway station, left derelict, has been transformed into a very beautiful museum of the arts, covering the period 1848–1914. All the Impressionists formerly in the Jeu de Paume have been transferred here. *1 rue de Bellechasse, 7e. Open Tue–Sun, 10–6; Thu, 10–9.45; Sun, 10–6.*

Musée Picasso (Hôtel Salé) A 17thC mansion in the Marais houses the artist's private collection of his own work, and of some other artists, which passed to the state in lieu of tax on his death. All his periods are represented. *5 rue de Thorigny, 3e. Open Thu–Mon, 9.15–5; Wed 9.15–10pm.*

Musée Rodin Much of the best work of the great sculptor, including *The Kiss* and *The Burghers of Calais*, is laid out in a fine 18thC mansion and its quiet garden. *77 rue de Varenne, 7e. Open Tue–Sun, 10–5.*

Musée Victor Hugo Memorabilia of the great novelist, with some of his own drawings and paintings. *6 pl des Vosges, 4e. Open Tue–Sun, 10–5.30.*

Notre-Dame Built in the 12th–14th centuries, sacked during the Revolution, then restored by Viollet-le-Duc, this architectural jewel lies at the heart of Vieux Paris. It has a richly sculptured façade and lovely rose windows; you can ascend its high twin towers. *Rue de l'Arcole, 4e. Open 8–9; towers open 10–5.*

Opéra Charles Garnier's ornate 1860s masterpiece has a marble stairway and an ornate auditorium, enhanced, or marred for some, by the addition of Chagall's painted ceiling. *Pl de l'Opéra, 9e. Open for visits 10–5; closed Sun and public holidays.*

Palais de Chaillot Built for the 1937 Exhibition, this huge colonnaded palace with its two curving wings today houses a state-run theatre and four interesting museums: the *Musée du Cinéma*, the *Musée de la Marine* (maritime subjects, including model ships), the *Musée des Monuments Français* (replicas of French monumental sculptures), and the *Musée de l'Homme* (pre-history and anthropology). *Pl du Trocadéro, 16e. Varied opening times, all closed Tue.*

Palais de l'Elysée Built in 1718, and since 1873 the French President's official residence and workplace. Not open to the public, but the courtyard can be glimpsed from the street. *Rue du Faubourg-St-Honoré, 8e.*

Palais de Justice The main Paris law courts occupy a huge building on the Ile de la Cité that was once a royal palace, then the seat of parliament till 1789. *4 bd du Palais, 1er. All courts and halls, except juvenile court, open to public weekdays, 9–7.*

Palais du Luxembourg The seat of the Senate (upper house of parliament) is a palace built for Marie de Medici in the 17th century, then much altered in the 19th. Guided tours include the council chamber, library (with paintings by Delacroix) and other rooms. *15 rue de Vaugirard, 6e. Not open the public.*

Palais Royal Cardinal Richelieu's 17thC palace, with its elegant colonnaded courtyard, was later the scene of orgies, political rallies, and prostitution. The palace itself is now offices, and Président Mitterrand has had the courtyard adorned with 260 black-and-white striped columns, an avant-garde piece of art that horrifies many Parisians. *Rue de Rivoli, 1er. Gardens open 7.30am–8.30pm.*

Panthéon The tombs of many illustrious Frenchmen, from Victor Hugo and Emile Zola to Resistance leader Jean Moulin, are housed in this rather fusty museum, at several times in its history a church, with its huge dome. Interesting paintings by Puvis de Chavannes. *Pl du Panthéon, 5e. Open 10–6.*

Père Lachaise cemetery Hundreds of famous people, from Molière and Chopin, Balzac and Rossini to Oscar Wilde and Edith Piaf, lie buried in the city's largest cemetery, laid out in 1804. *Bd de Ménilmontant, 20e. Open daily.*

Pompidou centre (Beaubourg) Sometimes described as "an arty oil refinery" because of its multi-coloured external piping, the giant cultural centre initiated by the late President Pompidou at first shocked Parisians. Now it pleases most of them, and attracts more visitors per day (25,000) than the Eiffel Tower and Louvre combined. As well as a library, industrial design centre and much else, it houses the splendid Musée National d'Art Moderne. Outside is a colourful parade of street entertainers. *Rue St-Martin, 4e. Open Wed–Mon, 12–10; Sat & Sun, 10–10.*

Sacré-Coeur This famous Paris landmark, gleaming white on the hill of Montmartre, was built in the late 19th century in response to a national vow after defeat in the war of 1870–71. Its neo-Byzantine style is not to all tastes: but the interior is elegant, with a superb mosaic above the altar. *Rue du Cardinal Dubois, 18e. Open 6am–10.45. Access to crypt 9–5.30; summer 9–6.30.*

Saint-Etienne-du-Mont A Latin Quarter church built between 1492 and 1632 in a strange variety of styles, with a notable roodscreen and fine stained-glass windows in the cloister. *Pl St-Geneviève, 5e.*

Saint-Eustache This large and lovely church built 1532–1637 at Les Halles is noted for its flying buttresses, lavish stained glass and superb organ. Often used for concerts. *Impasse St Eustache, 1er. Open 8–7pm.*

Saint-Sulpice A great 17th–18thC church in classical style, with masses of space and fine murals by Delacroix. Recitals are often given on its massive organ. *Pl St-Sulpice, 6e.*

Sainte-Chapelle Fine 13thC church tucked away in a courtyard of the Palais de Justice; possibly the loveliest church in Paris as well as one of the oldest. It consists of two chapels one above the other – the lower one a little gloomy, the upper one lit by marvellous stained-glass windows. *4 bd du Palais, 4e. Open 10–6.*

La Sorbonne The University of Paris was founded here by Robert de Sorbon in 1253 and the present imposing buildings date from the 17th century. They are now used for lectures and administration by several of the 13 university faculties scattered around the city. The great courtyard thronged with students, the baroque library and ornate lecture rooms are worth visiting. *Rue Sorbonne, 5e.*

UNESCO headquarters Imposing Y-shaped building dating from 1958 and containing works of art by Henry Moore, Picasso and others. Open to groups by prior arrangement. *9 pl de Fontenoy, 7e ☎ 45 68 10 00.*

La Villette: Cité des Sciences et de l'Industrie Just inside the Périphérique in the northeast of the city is an ambitious development which typifies the French love of grandeur. What is claimed to be the world's largest science museum of futuristic design, opened in 1986 in a huge building that was formerly the city's main abattoir. Displays are elaborate and ingenious, with the accent on French high-tech. The symbol of La Villette is the spherical Géode, next door, which houses a panoramic cinema using the Omnimax process. Nearby, on a 34ha/85-acre site, is a brand-new arts and leisure complex, with three concert halls and the new home of the Paris Conservatoire. *30 Ave Corentin-Cariou, 19e. Museum open Tue–Fri, 10–6; Wed, noon–9; Sat & Sun, noon–8.*

Guided tours

A guided tour by bus can probably provide the best quick introduction to Paris. Several companies run circular tours of the main sights or of certain specialized sights. These usually last about 2hr and include commentary in various languages. Operators include *American Express* ☎ 42 66 09 99, *Cityrama* ☎ 42 60 30 14, *Paris-Vision* ☎ 42 60 31 25, *SNCF* ☎ 43 87 61 89.

River trips The banks of the Seine are best seen from one of the cruise-boats that ply mainly the central stretch between the Eiffel Tower and Quai de Bercy. They also go after dark when the main buildings are floodlit. Apply to *Vedettes de Paris* ☎ 43 26 92 55. *(Easter–Nov), Bateaux–Parisiens Tour Eiffel* ☎ 47 05 50 00, or *Vedettes du Pont Neuf* ☎ 46 33 98 38. *Bateaux Mouches* ☎ 42 25 22 55 also run cruises that serve lunch or dinner.

Walking lecture tours on cultural and historical themes, with expert guides, are organized by *Arcus*, 3 rue Rousselet, 7e ☎ 45 67 68 01, and *Paris et son Histoire*, 82 rue Taitbont, 9e. ☎ 45 26 26 77.

Incentive tours Companies wanting to plan a group incentive visit for their staff could apply to *Incentive Congress Organization*, 22 rue Turbigo, 2e ☎ 42 96 81 11, or *Treasure Tours*, 15 rue de l'Arcade, 8e ☎ 42 65 05 69.

Parks and gardens
Central Paris has less greenery than many great cities, but there are quite big parks on its periphery. To the west, the Bois de Boulogne is rather heavily dissected by motor roads, but it contains several delightful and secluded smaller parks such as the Bagatelle and Pré Catelan as well as the Jardin d'Acclimatation, an amusement park. To the east, the Bois de Vincennes has a zoo, boating lakes, and on the north side a château with medieval keep and a chapel. Inside the city the best-known central parks are small and rather formal: the Jardin de Luxembourg with its baroque fountain and statues, and the Tuileries, elegant but a little dry and dusty. The charming little Parc Monceau in the 8e has been pleasantly landscaped and has some children's playgrounds. Those in search of more romantic green spaces should visit the Parc de Monsouris (14e) and the unusual Parc des Buttes Chaumont (19e) with its hilly woods and rocky island in a lake.

Spectator sports

Paris's major venue for spectator sports is the huge new complex called the *Palais Omnisports de Paris Bercy*, 8 bd de Bercy, 12e ☎ 43 46 12 21, which houses numerous sporting activities including boxing, cycling, motorcycle races and showjumping.

Cycling Paris–Roubaix race in the spring; Grand Prix Cycliste de la Ville de Paris, June; the Tour de France reaches its climax on the Champs-Elysées at the end of July.

Horse-racing The smart racecourses are *Auteuil* (steeplechasing) and *Longchamp* (flat racing), both in the Bois du Boulogne, 16e, and *Vincennes*, on the east of the city, is famous for its trotting races. The major race for aficionados is the *Prix de l'Arc de Triomphe*, which attracts the international set to Longchamp in early October.

Rugby and soccer The big Paris stadium is the *Parc des Princes*, Porte de Saint-Cloud, 16e ☎ 42 88 02 76. The top local soccer teams are *Paris Saint-Germain* and *Matra-Racing*.

Tennis The *Stade Roland-Garros*, ave Gordon-Bennett, 16e ☎ 47 43 48 00, hosts the French Open Championship in late May, early June.

Keeping fit

The French have recently taken to sport in a big way. Fitness centres, squash and tennis clubs are now fashionable, especially with young business executives of both sexes, and are often hard to get into. The places we list below will normally accept visitors, often for a high hourly or daily fee, but are usually crowded in the evenings and at weekends.

Fitness centres and health clubs The *Gymnase Club* requires payment for a minimum of ten visits to any one of its well-equipped clubs, which claim to offer 44 different activities ranging from aerobics to underwater gymnastics; most have pools, saunas, jacuzzi and UVA. Convenient addresses for business visitors are the *Gymnase Maillot*, 17 rue du Débarcadère, 17e ☎ 45 74 14 04;

the *Salle des Champs-Elysées*, 55 bis rue de Ponthieu, 8e ☎ 45 62 99 76 and the *Vitatop Fitness Club*, 118 rue de Vaugirard, 6e ☎ 45 44 38 01, which has pool, sauna, steam bath, solarium with pleasantly garden-like decor. The punningly named *Espace Vit'Halles*, 48 rue Rambuteau, 4e ☎ 42 77 21 71, which has plenty of space and facilities, offers anything from a day ticket to an annual subscription and is open seven days a week. (See also *Hotels*.)

Golf Weekday playing for a green fee is usually possible at clubs in nearby towns. The most private, and oldest, is Mortfontaine, near CDG airport. Play is by invitation only at *Racing Club de France*, La Boulie near Versailles ☎ 39 50 59 41, *Saint-Cloud*, 69 rue du 19 Janvier, Garches ☎ 47 01 01 85 and at *Saint-Nom-la-Bretèche*, Domaine de la Tuilerie ☎ 34 62 54 00. At *Saint-Germain-en-Laye*, route de Poissy ☎ 34 51 75 90 non members with a handicap of 24 or less can play Tuesday to Friday.

Riding There are three riding stables in the Bois de Boulogne: *Centre Hippique du Touring-club de France* ☎ 45 01 20 88; *Société d'Equitation de Paris* at the Porte de Neuilly ☎ 45 01 20 06; and *Société Equestre de l'Etrier*, route de Madrid-aux-Lacs ☎ 45 01 98 87; and one in the Bois de Vincennes: *Bayard UCPA Centre Equestre* ☎ 43 65 46 87.

Squash and tennis Clubs willing to accept visitors are mainly on the outskirts. *Club de Squash*, 45 bd des Bouvets, Nanterre ☎ 47 73 04 40, has 6 squash courts, plus fitness centre and sauna; and *Tennis Country Club*, 58 ave du Président-Wilson, Saint-Denis ☎ 48 09 22 69, has 20 indoor tennis courts and 5 squash courts.

Swimming Paris's public swimming pools are unpleasantly overcrowded. For pools in health clubs and hotels see above. *Piscine Robert Keller*, 14 rue de l'Ingénieur-Keller, 15e ☎ 45 77 12 12, is a private pool with a sauna.

Local resources
Business services
Paris has excellent facilities for conferences, seminars and meetings and an increasingly good range of services for individual business visitors. Your hotel may have good advice, since Paris hotel concierges are rightly famous for their ability to supply at speed (and for a consideration) any services guests require. *Assistance Démarches* ☎ 42 81 47 67 is a useful service offering help with administrative problems such as obtaining visas.

Companies offering short-term office accommodation include: *Acte*, 17 rue de la Baume, 8e ☎ 43 59 77 55; *Ibos*, 15 ave Victor-Hugo, 16e ☎ 45 02 18 00; *Locaburo*, 14 rue Anatole-France, La Défense ☎ 47 75 32 00; *Multiburo*, 34 bd Haussmann, 9e ☎ 47 70 47 70 ⊠ MBI 290266; *Orion Locations*, 39 rue de Surène, 8e ☎ 42 66 92 94; and *Le Satellite*, 8 rue Copernic, 16e ☎ 47 27 15 59. The *2A Service* at the airports (see *Arriving*) can also supply fully equipped and serviced offices for rent.

Photocopying and printing
Photocopiers are available in most post offices, at stations and airports, and in hundreds of copy shops, photography studios and stationers all over the city. *Rank Xerox* has copy shops at 80 bd de Sébastopol, 3e ☎ 48 87 03 31; 128 rue de Rennes, 6e ☎ 45 49 04 10; and 40 bd Malesherbes, 8e ☎ 42 66 10 53. *Organization Deb's*, 139 ave Charles-de-Gaulle, Neuilly ☎ 47 45 20 44 provides an efficient and comprehensive service midway between the Palais des Congrès and La Défense and has another branch at La Défense itself ☎ 47 78 40 65. *Secretarial* For all temporary staff, *Manpower* has offices all over Paris; for the nearest to your hotel consult the telephone directory or ☎ 47 66 03 03. *Intérim Nation* ☎ 43 45 50 00 is another company with many branches. Most large hotels can arrange for temporary

secretarial assistance. *Monique Deberghes*, 92 rue Saint-Lazare, 9e ☎ 42 81 07 63, specializes in supplying conference stenotypists and typing from tapes.
Translation and interpreting
Communications Internationales Rozbroj ☎ 47 64 10 00 ⊠ 640252 fax 47 66 36 86; *Eclair Courrier International* ☎ 42 25 86 10; *Express Traductions* ☎ 48 74 65 73; *Opéra Traductions* ☎ 47 42 06 43.

Communications
Local delivery Most Paris businesses have their own messenger or courier for collections and deliveries in and around the city and many also send their own staff to provincial cities. So any company you do business with will probably be able to provide this service. Large hotels can often supply a messenger for errands within Paris. The city's messenger services generally work on a subscription basis, or require you to buy a block of ten tickets. Also *Allo Frêt* ☎ 46 55 88 80; *Allo Postexpress* ☎ 40 23 65 45; *Delta Courses* ☎ 42 74 00 00; *TTL* ☎ 42 26 24 33; *Vit' Courses* ☎ 46 51 90 17.
Long-distance delivery Calberson-Calexpress ☎ 40 34 11 66; *DHL* ☎ 45 01 91 00; *Securicor France* (Europe only) ☎ 43 39 04 33.
Post offices Paris has one 24hr post office, 52 rue du Louvre, 1er ☎ 40 28 20 00; the office at 71 ave des Champs-Elysées is open Mon–Sat 8am–10pm. Outside Paris, the post office at *Orly Sud* airport is open 24hr, that at *CDG* airport Mon–Sat 6.30am–11pm, Sun and public holidays 8.30am–8.30pm. Normal post office opening hours in Paris are Mon–Fri 8–7, Sat 8–noon.
Telex and fax 24hr public telex information office is at 103 rue de Grenelle, 7e ☎ 45 50 34 34; to dictate a telex by telephone ☎ 42 47 12 12. The main fax office is in the Palais des Congrès, at Porte Maillot, 17e (on the lower ground floor); telex and fax are also available at the main post office in each *arrondissement*.

Conference/exhibition venues

Paris is one of the world's leading conference centres, and can offer a huge range of venues, from major convention hotels to prestige rooms in historic mansions and châteaux.

Palais des Congrès, 2 pl de la Porte-Maillot, 17e ☎ 46 40 22 22 and 40 68 22 22, is the largest conference centre, holding up to 4,100 people, with 19 meeting rooms, 2 exhibition halls of 1,250 sq metres, simultaneous translation equipment (for up to 6 languages) and a wide range of other facilities. It is conveniently situated in the same building as the Roissy/CDG air terminal. The *Parc des Expositions* at the Porte de Versailles, 15e ☎ 48 42 87 00, is Paris's major exhibition centre, with 8 exhibition halls covering a total of 220,000 sq metres, 20 meeting rooms seating up to 600 people, restaurant facilities for over 4,000, and 6,000 parking spaces. Of the many other conference halls and rooms available (a full list is available from the *Comité Parisien des Congrès*, see *Information sources*), the best-known central ones include, in *arrondissement* order, the *Salle de l'Espace*, 2 pl Maurice-Quentin, 1er ☎ 40 26 18 25; the *Maison de L'Europe de Paris*, 35 rue des Francs-Bourgeois, 4e ☎ 42 72 94 06; the *Centre de Conférence Panthéon*, 16 rue de l'Estrapade, 5e ☎ 43 25 11 85; *Maison de la Chimie*, 28 bis rue St-Dominique, 7e ☎ 47 05 10 73; *Centre Audiovisuel de l'Entreprise*, 21 rue Clément-Marot ☎ 47 20 65 32; *Centre Chaillot-Galliéra*, 28 ave George-V ☎ 47 20 71 50; *Maison des Centraux*, 8 rue Jean-Goujon ☎ 43 59 71 74; *Espace de Pierre Cardin*, 1 ave Gabriel ☎ 42 66 17 30 and *Pavillon Gabriel*, 5 ave Gabriel ☎ 42 68 18 18 – all in the 8e; and the new *Zénith* at La Villette, 19e ☎ 42 40 60 00. Outside Paris possibilities include historic châteaux such as *Vaux-le-Vicomte* ☎ 60 66 97 09 and *Breteuil* ☎ 30 52 05 11, the attractive *Moulin de Guérard* ☎ 64 04 77 55 and *Pavillon Henri IV* ☎ 34 51 62 62 at St Germain-en-Laye.

Emergencies

Bureaux de change Suprisingly few Paris banks have exchange counters and the few that do exist frequently close for lunch between 11.30 and 1.45, especially in July and Aug. The *Crédit Commercial de France* (CCF) has special exchange offices at 115 ave des Champs-Elysées, 8e ☎ 40 70 27 22 (Mon–Sat, 8.30–8), 2 carrefour de l'Odéon, 6e ☎ 43 25 38 66 (Mon–Sat, 9–7.30) and at Galeries Lafayette, 40 bd Haussmann, 9e ☎ 46 26 20 63 (Mon–Sat, 9.30–6). The *Union de Banques à Paris* (UBP) bureau de change operates Sat, Sun and public holidays 10.30–6. Bureaux de change at airports and stations are open till at least 8.30pm, and often till 11.30pm in summer.

Credit card loss or theft American Express ☎ 47 77 72 00; *Access/ Eurocard/MasterCard* ☎ 43 23 46 46; *Diners Club* ☎ 47 62 75 75; *Visa* ☎ 42 77 11 90.

Medical emergencies SOS *Médicins* ☎ 43 37 77 77 or 47 07 77 77; for cases of food or drug poisoning *Centre anti-poison* ☎ 40 37 04 04; for burns ☎ 47 72 91 91.

Hospitals British Hospital, 3 rue Barbès, Levallois-Perret ☎ 47 58 13 12; *Hôpital Américain de Paris* 63 bd Victor-Hugo, 92200 Neuilly-sur-Seine ☎ 47 47 53 00. *Hôpital Cochin* 27 rue du Faubourg St-Jacques, 14e ☎ 42 34 12 12. Automatic call boxes at main crossroads labelled *Police-secours* may also be used in emergencies.

Pharmacies Paris has one 24hr pharmacy: *La Pharmacie des Champs-Elysées* 84 ave des Champs-Elysées, 8e ☎ 45 62 02 41. The pharmacy counter in the *Drugstore Saint-Germain* (on the corner of Bd St-Germain and Rue de Rennes, 6e) is open daily to 2am. For pharmacists willing to make up prescriptions outside normal opening hours, contact the *Commissariat de police* of the *arrondissement*, where emergency prescriptions must also be stamped. *Police* ☎ 17. Préfecture de Police, 7 bd du Palais, 4e ☎ 42 60 33 22.

Government offices

Centre Français du Commerce Extérieur (CFCE), 10 ave d'Iéna, 16e ☎ 45 05 30 00: information about France's foreign trade. *Institut National de la Statistique et des Etudes Economiques* (INSEE), 18 bd Adolphe Pinard, 14e ☎ 45 40 01 12 or 45 40 12 12: Paris's "economic observatory;" *Ministère de l'Economie, des Finances et de la Privatization*, 93 rue de Rivoli, 1er ☎ 42 60 33 00 (*Commerce extérieur*, 41 quai Branly, 7e ☎ 45 50 71 11; *Commerce, Artisanat et Services*, 80 rue de Lille, 7e ☎ 45 56 24 24): information on all forms of income and other planning assistance to small businesses. *Ministère de l'Industrie, des P et T et du Tourisme*, 101 rue de Grenelle, 7e ☎ 45 56 36 36: information on postal, telex and fax services at 20 ave de Ségur, 7e ☎ 45 64 22 22. *Ministère de l'Interieur*, pl Beauvau, 8e ☎ 45 22 90 90: inquiries and information on immigration procedures, residence permits and matters of security.

Information sources

Business information *Chambre de Commerce et d'Industrie de Paris*, 27 ave de Friedland, 8e ☎ 42 89 70 00. *Chambre de Commerce Internationale*, 38 cours Albert 1er, 8e ☎ 45 62 34 56. *Assemblée Permanente des Chambres de Commerce et d'Industrie* (APCCI), 45 ave d'Iéna, 16e ☎ 47 23 01 11, provides information on local chamber of commerce activities throughout France. *Comité Parisien des Congrès*, Office de Tourisme, 127 ave des Champs-Elysées, 8e ☎ 47 20 12 55, offers a very full information service, free of charge, on all the technical aspects of organizing conferences, seminars, meetings, incentives in Paris; meeting rooms available; conference services include interpreting, accommodation, special reduction on rail and air travel within France; meetings can be set up with companies providing a wide range of services and the Committee will also put a whole conference project out to tender.

Local media The national press is based in Paris. The city is the home of the *International Herald Tribune*, but has no local daily. *Ville de Paris*, a monthly published by the Hôtel de Ville, gives information on local development projects and occasionally on local businesses but is geared to ratepayers rather than visitors. *Pariscope* and *L'Officiel des Spectacles* are the best source of information on local events. *Europe 1* news flashes often give information on traffic trouble spots and *Radio Tour-Eiffel*, a local radio station, is light-hearted but informative.

Tourist information The main *Office de Tourisme de Paris* is at 127 ave des Champs-Elysées, 8e ☎ 47 23 61 72 or 47 20 60 20 ⨶ 611984; for a recorded message giving details of current events in and around the capital ☎ 47 20 94 94 (English version ☎ 47 20 88 98, German version ☎ 47 20 57 58). Subsidiary tourist offices at Orly and Roissy/CDG airports, Gare d'Austerlitz, Gare de l'Est, Gare de Lyon, Gare du Nord and at the Eiffel Tower (May–Sep only). RATP (public transport) information ☎ 43 46 14 14.

Thank-yous

Credit card orders are not usually accepted by telephone in France but the concierge in your hotel may be able to arrange for payment to be added to your hotel bill.
Florists *Jardin de Vaugirard (Interflora)*, 239 rue de Vaugirard, 15e ☎ 43 06 11 91; *Pascal Martinet Fleurs Royal Vendome*, 231 rue St-Honoré, 1er ☎ 42 60 42 76.
Fruit It is chic these days to send baskets of exotic fruit instead of flowers: *Inter-fruits*, 89 ave de Wagram, 17e ☎ 47 63 10 55, does attractive arrangements.
Luxury foods *Fauchon*, 26 pl de la Madeleine, 8e ☎ 47 42 60 11.

LYON

City code ☎ included in numbers

Secretive, cautious, prosperous, self-confident – Lyon has always been, and remains, all of those things. But it has also recently become one of Europe's fastest growing and most innovative cities. About 14 years ago its ageing industrial base was steered through a radical overhaul by its long-serving mayor, Francisque Collomb. Today Lyon boasts no fewer than three dynamic *technopoles* (industrially-oriented research centres), at La Doua, Ecully and Gerland. Similarly, three major new industrial sites, at L'Isle d'Abeau, Plaine de l'Ain and Limonest, have been created close by. The new industrial climate has attracted a number of international firms to Lyon (among them Hewlett Packard, Schering-Plough and Lever). Another feather in the city's cap was the decision to move the headquarters of Interpol from Paris to Lyon. In addition, Lyon's celebrated silk industry, which started in the 15th century, continues to flourish alongside the growing man-made fibre industry.

Lyon is the capital of the thriving Rhône-Alpes region, and France's second most important city economically with a population of only 1.2m. Its banks, which first rose to prominence in the 16th century, remain thriving concerns. It has long been the base of big French corporations such as Rhône-Poulenc (chemicals) and Berliet (now Renault Véhicules Industriels). It also teems with smaller, high-growth French companies which have benefited from Lyon's booming unlisted securities market, which opened in 1983. However, the Bourse, founded in 1464, still has a long way to go before becoming an international financial market on the scale of Frankfurt Milan or Zürich.

Another tradition of Lyon is gastronomy. It is no myth that senior Lyonnais executives prefer to spend their money on lavish dining at top restaurants than on flashy status symbols. Lyon is a city, then, where the ice-breaking function of business entertainment can prove crucially important. While popular belief says it is hard to make an initial deal with Lyonnais business people, they are unswervingly loyal once you strike up a relationship and gain their trust.

Arriving

Lyon likes to call itself "the crossroads of France." The city is connected by the A6 autoroute to Paris (the Dijon–Lyon section can be congested in summer), Marseille, Grenoble, Saint-Etienne and Clermont-Ferrand. The autoroute linking Lyon with Geneva will be virtually completed by the end of 1989. There is a good range of direct scheduled air services to major European cities and all important French cities. But the quickest way from Paris to Lyon (centre to centre) is via the TGV (high-speed train).

Lyon-Satolas International airport
This is very much a business traveller's airport, as it offers connections to business cities and schedules departures and arrivals early and late in the day. Being 27kms/17 miles from the centre of Lyon, and under competition from the TGV, means that it is not much used to and from Paris. But there is considerable traffic with all other major French cities, as well as daily weekday direct flights from Amsterdam, Brussels, Copenhagen, Düsseldorf, Frankfurt, London, Milan, Munich, Turin, Vienna and

Zürich. The airport has two light, airy terminals containing cafés and bars, two brasseries and one high-class restaurant, La Grande Corbeille. Banking and currency exchange facilities are available in the central building Mon–Sat, 8.35–5; at other times up to 500Fr per passenger will be changed by the hostesses near Bloc 2 in the international terminal. There is a post office open weekdays, 8–8 and Sat, 8–noon.

The airport's *2A Service* (☎ 72 22 72 21 or 72 22 75 26) offers good business facilities including individual offices, meeting rooms with a capacity of up to 30, telephones, telex, secretarial services, slide projection and catering. Airport information and freight inquiries ☎ 72 72 72 21.

Nearby hotels *Sofitel Lyon Satolas* ☎ 72 22 71 61 ⊠ 380480 • AE DC MC V. Modern hotel in the airport's central building overlooking the runways and mountains beyond; all rooms soundproofed and air-conditioned. *Climat de France* ☎ 78 40 96 44 ⊠ 306725 • AE MC V. Modest modern hotel in the airport's freight section; free shuttle.

City link The long trip into town by taxi is expensive. Buses are a good alternative as they are frequent and nearly as quick as taxis.

Taxi The ride takes about 30mins. Taxis wait in front of each terminal. For reservations ☎ 78 71 90 90.

Car rental All the main car rental firms have desks at the airport. A car is necessary if you are making trips to the outskirts of Lyon.

Bus The bus fare is about one-fifth of the cost of a taxi. Buses leave every 20mins (every 30mins Sat pm and Sun) from Bloc 2 of the international terminal and Bloc 3 of the domestic terminal. You should get off either at Gare de la Part-Dieu (35mins), or at Gare Perrache (45mins), depending on your final destination. The bus driver can reserve a taxi (by radio), which will meet you at one of the stops in town and take you on.

Lyon-Bron airport
This private airport is 10kms/6 miles east of Lyon, next to the European exhibition centre. *2A Service* offers on-the-spot business facilities (fewer than at Satolas airport). All inquiries ☎ 78 26 81 09.

Railway stations
The TGV has revolutionized rail travel. The 425km/266-mile trip from Paris now takes a mere 2hrs. Over 20 TGVs a day run in each direction from about 6am to midnight. Lyon has two main stations: Gare de Perrache and Gare de la Part-Dieu. You must decide when buying your ticket which station is the more convenient for you (all seats on TGVs have to be reserved). For both stations: passenger inquiries ☎ 78 92 50 50; reservations ☎ 78 92 50 70.

La Part-Dieu This is the first stop for passengers from Paris. It has among other things an Avis desk and a currency exchange bureau. The station is in the middle of one of Lyon's two business quarters. To reach the other one, Cordeliers, take either the Métro (subway), changing at Charpennes, or a taxi. Leave by the station's Vivier-Merle exit for the taxis (turn left outside) and airport bus stop (straight ahead).

Perrache TGVs from Paris reach this station 10mins after leaving Gare de la Part-Dieu. There is a 3-stop subway connection with Cordeliers. Use the Terre-plein Central exit for taxis and for the airport bus (which is poorly signposted – look out for the vehicle itself rather than a bus stop).

Getting around
The centre of Lyon is quite large and often congested with traffic. Getting around usually requires a car, the subway, a taxi or a bus. Just crossing the river Rhône by one of the several bridges entails a walk of some 180 metres. But once you are in either of the two business quarters, La Part-Dieu or Cordeliers, the easiest way to get around is on foot.

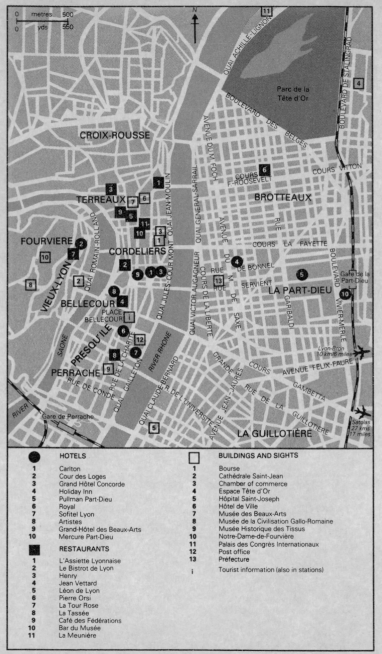

Taxis Although easily recognizable and plentiful, it is not immediately clear whether cabs are vacant. If one of the very small coloured lights under the word "taxi" is on, it means the taxi is occupied; if none of the lights is on, it is vacant. Taxis may be hailed or found at ranks (there are not many of these). They are relatively expensive. Radio cabs: *Taxi-Allô* ☎ 78 28 23 23, *Télé-Taxi* ☎ 78 28 13 14, *Taxi-Radio* ☎ 78 30 86 86.

Limousines *Compagnie Lyonnaise des Limousines* ☎ 78 85 64 10; *Avis* ☎ 72 33 99 14.

Driving Once you have got the hang of the traffic system (almost all streets are one-way), driving is easy except at rush hours and in the centre. Parking may prove difficult, but many hotels have their own parking facilities. All major car rental firms have offices in the city centre.

Walking This is safe in central Lyon and easy, as the Rhône and Saône rivers make orientation straightforward.

Subway Lyon's newish Métro network is clean, quiet and efficient. Tickets are best bought in sheets of six from vending machines, and should be stamped in the stamping machines on platforms before boarding the train. There are useful 2- and 3-day rover tickets valid for both the subway and buses.

Bus Certain bus lines are useful, particularly if you need to get to the suburbs. Subway and bus tickets are interchangeable and can be bought from the driver. They should be stamped in one of the machines on the bus. There are maps of bus lines at stops and in vehicles.

Area by area

The real centre of Lyon is located on what is known as Presqu'île (literally "peninsula"), a narrow tongue of land that runs between the Rhône and Saône rivers just before they join each other. Its districts, from north to south, are Terreaux, Cordeliers, Bellecour and Perrache. The older of Lyon's two business quarters lies on the east side of Presqu'île, in Cordeliers and adjoining parts of Terreaux and Bellecour. This is where the Lyon Bourse and the big finance and insurance companies are located.

The other main business quarter is in the new district of La Part-Dieu, on the east side of the Rhône. Here the emphasis is on engineering, computers and high-tech industries.

The largely 18thC quarter of Croix-Rousse, once the centre of Lyon's silk industry, lies to the north of Presqu'île. The oldest part of the city, Vieux-Lyon, huddles under the hill of Fourvière on the west bank of the Saône. The most desirable residential quarter in central Lyon is the northern part of Brotteaux, on the edge of the Parc de la Tête d'Or.

Districts Lyon is divided into nine *arrondissements*, and their numbers form the last digit of their zip codes. But the Lyonnais themselves prefer to use the old names of districts rather than the *arrondissement* number. To help you to find your bearings, here are the zip code equivalents of the districts mentioned above: Terreaux = 69001; Cordeliers = 69001 and 69002; Bellecour and Perrache = 69002; La Part-Dieu = 69003; Croix-Rousse = 69004; Vieux-Lyon = 69005; Brotteaux = 69006. Villeurbanne, although a different commune from Lyon itself (zip code 69100), is so close to the northeast of central Lyon that it is effectively an inner suburb.

The suburbs

The most sought-after residential areas on the outskirts of Lyon are to the northwest (Ecully, Dardilly). But many commute farther afield from the attractive hills (Monts du Lyonnais) southwest of the city.

Much heavy industry is based to the south of Lyon, particularly along the Rhône. There are three major new industrial sites within a 37km/23-mile radius of the city:

manufacturing firms (in particular Lever) are located at Plaine de l'Ain, while major computer and service companies are at L'Isle d'Abeau (Hewlett Packard) and Limonest.

Hotels

Lyon hotels are generally of a high standard, but there are relatively few of them. As though waking up to this fact, the city gained two new luxury hotels in 1987, the Cour des Loges and the Holiday Inn. All hotels given full entries have IDD telephones in every room. Most major hotels offer currency exchange. Parking is not a problem unless stated otherwise. Normally hotel accommodation is easy to find. If you experience problems, the tourist office ☎ 78 42 25 75 may be able to help you reserve a room (but not more than five days before your arrival).

Because of keen competition from the city's many restaurants, hotel catering is kept on its toes. All the main hotel restaurants referred to by name serve high-class cuisine in spacious and elegant surroundings.

Carlton $\boxed{F}$ /
4 rue Jussieu, 69002 ☎ *78 42 56 51* ⊠ *310787 fax 78 42 10 71 • Mapotel • AE DC MC V • 87 rooms, 1 bar, no restaurant*
The Carlton is one of Lyon's most pleasant older hotels, and is much appreciated by business travellers and visiting actors and musicians for its quiet, central location and discreet, friendly service. Its large rooms (including rotundas, a feature of turn-of-the-century French architecture) have traditional or modern furniture. Limited parking • 1 meeting room (capacity 10).

Cour des Loges $\boxed{F}$ ////
6 rue du Boeuf, 69005 ☎ *78 42 75 75* ⊠ *330831 • AE DC MC V • 53 rooms, 10 suites, 1 restaurant, 1 bar*
This new hotel in Vieux-Lyon within easy walking distance of Cordeliers, is an imaginatively converted series of Renaissance buildings. The less expensive rooms are on the small side, but this is made up for by the quality of their fittings and facilities (electronic safes, hairdryers, videos). Some larger rooms and suites have a private garden or fireplace. The bar-cum-restaurant, Tapas des Loges, managed by Philippe Chavent of La Tour Rose down the road (see

Restaurants), serves till 2am. 24hr room service, gift shop, newsstand, video library • pool, sauna, jacuzzi, gym • 4 meeting rooms (capacity up to 40).

Grand Hôtel Concorde $\boxed{F}$ //
11 rue Grôlée, 69002 ☎ *78 42 56 21* ⊠ *330244 fax 78 37 52 55 • AE DC MC V • 140 rooms, 3 suites, 1 restaurant, 1 bar*
A big, conveniently central hotel housed in a late-19thC building which is much used for seminars and conferences. The most congenial of its large, traditionally-furnished rooms (all of which have cable TV) overlook the Rhône. There is a particularly spacious and pleasant public area ideal for small informal meetings. 9 meeting rooms (capacity up to 200).

Holiday Inn $\boxed{F}$ ///
29 rue de Bonnel, 69003 ☎ *72 61 90 90* ⊠ *330703 fax 72 61 17 54 • AE DC MC V • 157 rooms, 1 suite, 1 restaurant, 1 bar*
Opened in mid-1987, this is without doubt the Lyon hotel that best caters for business travellers. There are computer facilities, as well as the usual range of business services. Rooms are well equipped

and there is a special executive floor. The building and decor are cautiously modern. Its Nouvelles Orléans restaurant bravely proposes genuine Louisiana cuisine. 24hr room service • sauna, jacuzzi, gym • 16 meeting rooms (capacity up to 400).

Pullman Part-Dieu *F*////
129 rue Servient, 69003 ☎ *78 62 94 12* [TX] *380088 fax 78 60 41 77* • *AE DC MC V* • *245 rooms, 7 suites, 2 restaurants, 1 bar*
Perched at the top of the huge Crédit Lyonnais skyscraper (locally nicknamed "the pencil") in the middle of the Part-Dieu quarter, this is Europe's tallest hotel. Its snug rooms are reached by galleries running around an atrium which is draped with tropical plants. They afford stunning views (ask for the Fourvière side when making your reservation), as does the restaurant, which is ideal for business entertaining at senior level. The bar, Le Panache, is also popular with business people. There are good business facilities and a special executive floor. Modular meeting room (capacity up to 250).

Royal *F*/
20 pl Bellecour, 69002 ☎ *78 37 57 31* [TX] *310785 fax 78 37 01 36* • *Mapotel* • *AE DC MC V* • *90 rooms, 1 restaurant, 1 bar*
The Royal, like its sister hotel, the Carlton, is one of the city's older hotels, with spacious rooms including some rotundas. On the whole its decor is pleasantly sober and the Royal enjoys a superb location overlooking one of Europe's largest squares, Place Bellecour. 1 meeting room (capacity 10).

Sofitel Lyon *F*////
20 quai Gailleton, 69002 ☎ *72 40 05 50* [TX] *330225 fax 72 40 05 50* • *AE DC MC V* • *195 rooms, 3 suites, 2 restaurants, 2 bars*
This large modern hotel is on the banks of the Rhône, not far from the Place Bellecour. Although rather

unprepossessing from the outside, it is most congenial within, with pleasant bedrooms, a delightful interior palm garden, luxury boutiques, an excellent rooftop restaurant, Les Trois Dômes, and a fashionable cocktail bar, Le Melhor. Simple food is served till 2am in the smart Sofi Shop restaurant on the ground floor: a good place for private conversations as tables are separated by smoked-glass partitions. Hairdresser • 17 meeting rooms (capacity up to 400).

OTHER HOTELS
Artistes *F*/ *8 rue Gaspard-André, 69002* ☎ *78 42 04 88* [TX] *375664 fax 78 42 93 76* • *AE DC MC V.*
Quiet, modestly priced hotel near Place Bellecour.
Grand-Hôtel des Beaux-Arts *F*/
75 rue du Président-Herriot, 69002 ☎ *78 38 09 50* [TX] *330442 fax 78 42 19 19* • *AE DC MC V.*
Recently modernized traditional hotel in the middle of Presqu'île. Also competitively priced.
Mercure Part-Dieu *F*//// *47 bd Vivier-Merle, 69003* ☎ *72 34 18 12* [TX] *306469 fax 78 53 40 69* • *AE DC MC V.* Large modern hotel in the middle of the Part-Dieu business quarter and a 3min walk from the Gare de la Part-Dieu. Prices are lower in Aug and at weekends.

Out of town
Those who prefer rural surroundings should consider the possibility of commuting to *Ostellerie du Vieux Pérouges* ☎ *74 61 00 88* in Pérouges (see *Sightseeing*), 39kms/24 miles northeast – a beautiful country hotel whose main St Georges et Manoir section is a perfectly preserved 15thC building.

Credit card abbreviations	
AE	American Express
DC	Diners Club
MC	Access/MasterCard
V	Visa

Restaurants

The Lyonnais regard their city as the gastronomic capital of the world. A slight exaggeration, perhaps, even if top-notch restaurants do lie extraordinarily thick on the ground. While members of the local business community, like all Lyonnais, love to linger over sophisticated *haute cuisine*, they also congregate in humbler establishments known as *bouchons*. Reservations are always advisable, even in these. All the major restaurants listed here have excellent wine lists and offer attractive set menus. (See also Cour des Loges, Pullman and Sofitel hotels.)

L'Assiette Lyonnaise *F*//
19 pl Tolozan ☎ *78 28 35 77* • *closed Sat L, Sun, Aug 1–14* • AE DC MC V
This recently redecorated, unpretentious restaurant full of potted plants and ventilated by a huge ceiling fan is ideal for the not-too-formal business lunch or late supper (last orders 11.30). There is a small terrace in summer, a rarity in Lyon. The food is traditional Lyonnais and very good value.

Le Bistrot de Lyon *F*///
64 rue Mercière ☎ *78 37 00 62* • V
This establishment in the lively Rue Mercière attracts a smarter clientele and serves more sophisticated cuisine than its bistro atmosphere and friendly prices would seem to indicate. Most unusually in a city that tends to pull down the shutters early, it serves until 1.30am.

Henry *F*//
27 rue de la Martinière ☎ *78 28 26 08* • *closed Sat L, Mon* • AE DC V
One of the very few Lyonnais restaurants suitable for important entertaining occasions which also takes orders until 11.30pm and is open on Sunday. In addition, its two private dining rooms with independent telephones make it possible to have lingering business lunches. Chef Pierre Balladone, a highly skilled but unflashy cook who is particularly at home with fish, offers good value top-flight cooking. The decor is sober and tasteful, the tables well spaced, and the service very friendly.

Jean Vettard *F*///
7 pl Bellecour ☎ *78 42 07 59* • *closed Sun, Jul 24–Aug 31* • AE DC V • *smart dress preferred*
A long established family-run restaurant on Place Bellecour whose superb *belle époque* decor and celebrated Lyonnais dishes – *quenelles de brochet Lyonnaise, poularde en vessie* – have remained unchanged down the generations. But Jean Vettard also offers several excellent and intelligently "modern" dishes of his own devising, including *turbot au fumet de menthe. The* place for really important business entertaining.

Léon de Lyon *F*////
1 rue Pleney ☎ *78 28 11 33* • *closed Mon L, Sun, Dec 20–Jan 6* • V
Jean-Paul Lacombe is a brilliant practitioner of generously served *nouvelle cuisine* that is inventive without being far-fetched. His wide-ranging menu, which explains each dish in detail, changes completely twice a year. The decor is typically Lyonnais, with stained-glass windows, wood panelling and low ceilings, and the service impeccable. The nonsmoking ground-floor dining room is the best place for quiet discussions.

Pierre Orsi *F*////
3 pl Kléber ☎ *78 89 57 68* • *closed Sun (also Sat, May–Sep)* • AE MC V • *no smoking till end of meal preferred*
Located between the two most chic shopping streets in Lyon, Cours Franklin-Roosevelt and Cours Vitton, this is the only really top-class

restaurant close to the Part-Dieu business quarter, and is much frequented by senior managers at lunch time. Pierre Orsi's classical cuisine is as refined and elegant as his salmon-pink decor.

La Tour Rose 🄵////
16 rue du Boeuf ☎ *78 37 25 90*
● *closed Sun* ● *AE DC MC V*
Owner-chef Philippe Chavent is an exponent of the highly imaginative – and occasionally over-the-top – *nouvelle cuisine* and a fan of rare Côtes-du-Rhône vintages. But dining at La Tour is more than a gastronomic event: Chavent is a discriminating collector of modern art, which graces his walls; the tablecloths are made of silk, no less; and the restaurant building itself is a fine example of Lyonnais Renaissance.

Restaurant price guide
For the meanings of the restaurant price symbols, see *Symbols and abbreviations* on pages 6 and 7.

Bouchons
These café-restaurants generally serve expertly cooked local dishes and Beaujolais of a quality rarely found outside the Lyon area, all for very reasonable prices. Business people traditionally organize informal meetings in their local *bouchon* over a bottle of wine and *mâchons* (a substantial snack taken at any time of day), or else sit down for an often lengthy set lunch, sometimes conducting business into the afternoon over the *bouchon*'s own telephone. Although such restaurants are casual, reservations are advisable; they are always closed on Sundays. The most celebrated *bouchon*, which has almost graduated to the status of a restaurant proper, is *La Tassée*, 20 rue de la Charité ☎ 78 37 02 35. The one where there is the greatest competition for a table is *Café des Fédérations*, 8 rue du Major-Martin

☎ 78 28 26 00. Two lesser known *bouchons* much frequented by bankers and insurance brokers are the convivial *Bar du Musée*, 2 rue des Forces ☎ 78 37 71 54 and, for those who like a Gargantuan atmosphere, *La Meunière*, 11 rue Neuve, ☎ 78 28 62 91.

Out of town
Some 12kms/7 miles out of Lyon, in Collonges-au-Mont-d'Or, there is a restaurant whose fame has travelled the world – as indeed has its eponymous owner, Paul Bocuse. The cuisine at *Restaurant Paul Bocuse* ☎ 78 22 01 40 is undoubtedly sublime, if you can bear the vulgarity of the decor. But the demure Lyonnais are not too keen on those who, like Bocuse, excel at self-publicity. So if you want to entertain an important local client out of town, head rather for Mionnay, 20kms/12 miles north of Lyon, which boasts one of the very finest restaurants in the whole of France, *Alain Chapel* ☎ 78 91 82 02. But take the precaution of reserving well in advance.

Bars
The two hotel bars most favoured by business people for a quiet drink are *Le Panache*, in the Pullman, and more particularly *Le Melhor*, in the Sofitel, which specializes in cocktails (see *Hotels*). Those in search of a really discreet atmosphere make for *Le Cintra*, 43 rue de la Bourse (opposite the Stock Exchange), a veritable cavern of leather seats, polished brass and varnished wood panelling. But many Lyonnais business people like to do their talking in *bouchons*.

Lyon also has two excellent wine bars which offer a wide range of vintages, from the humble to the most prestigious, by the glass: *Le Comptoir du Boeuf*, 3 pl Neuve-St-Jean and *Le Bouchon aux Vins*, 62 rue Mercière. The Rue Mercière has many other bars, which are more suitable for an evening off.

Entertainment

Lyon has quite a lively cultural scene. For essential listings buy the weekly *Lyon Poche*.

Theatre One of France's most celebrated theatres is Roger Planchon and Georges Lavaudant's *Théâtre National Populaire* (TNP), 8 pl Lazare-Goujon, Villeurbanne ☎ 78 84 70 74. Lyon is also regularly visited by touring companies from other cities.

Cinema The inventors of the cinema, Louis and Auguste Lumière, were from Lyon. Their house has been turned into *L'Institut Lumière*, 25 rue du Premier-Film ☎ 78 00 86 68. It holds photographic exhibitions and houses the Lyon Cinémathèque, which organizes regular showings of rare films. In commercial cinemas, many English-speaking films are shown with subtitles (*version originale*, or *v.o.*).

Music Lyon is a very musical city and attracts many big names in every department, from classical to jazz and rock. There are regular concerts by its own orchestra, the Orchestre National de Lyon (conductor: Emmanuel Krivine), usually at the *Auditorium Maurice-Ravel*, 149 rue Garibaldi ☎ 78 71 05 73. The important Festival International Berlioz alternates with the Biennale de la Danse (Sep). There are frequent organ recitals in churches.

Nightclubs Lyon was once famed as a city of early-to-beds. Things have changed, and there are now many nightspots. Among the more chic are *Le Piano*, 53 rue Mercière ☎ 78 92 89 16 and *Le Saint-Antoine*, 37 quai St-Antoine ☎ 78 37 01 35. The trendiest discos, which attract a younger, more dynamic crowd, are *L'Aquarius*, 47 quai Pierre-Scize ☎ 78 28 84 86, and especially *L'Actuel*, 30 bd Eugène-Deruelle ☎ 78 95 12 93 (Wed–Sat).

Casino There is a charming *belle époque* casino in the tiny spa of Charbonnières-les-Bains, ☎ 78 87 02 70, 8kms/5 miles west of Lyon on the N7.

Shopping

Fashion Not surprisingly in view of its tradition as a textile city, Lyon has a natural feel for clothes (especially silk). The best fashion shops are to be found in Cours Franklin-Roosevelt and its continuation Cours Vitton, not far from the Part-Dieu quarter, and in Rue du Président-Herriot, in Presqu'île. For good-value silk articles try *Maison des Canuts*, 10 rue d'Ivry, which is also a small museum.

Food Wander around the mouthwatering central food market, *Halles de Lyon*, 192 cours La Fayette, to see if anything takes your fancy. *Maurice Bernachon*, 42 cours Franklin-Roosevelt, is certainly the best known, and doubtless the best, maker of chocolates in Europe.

Department stores Au Printemps, 42 pl de la République, and two *Galeries Lafayette* stores, at 6 pl des Cordeliers and in the Centre Commercial de la Part-Dieu, a shopping centre which also houses a wide variety of other stores.

Antique markets The best is *Stalingrad*, 115 bd de Stalingrad, Villeurbanne. Top antique dealers operate in Rue Auguste Comte.

Sightseeing

The recently-renovated *Vieux-Lyon*, with its many 16th–17thC buildings, galleried courtyards, Florentine towers and interesting shops, is well worth exploring. Parts of it have been pedestrianized. Above Vieux-Lyon is perched the immense church of *Notre-Dame-de-Fourvière*, an important centre of pilgrimage and an unparalleled example of late-19thC extravagance (rare stones used in its construction, and a mixture of Byzantine, Assyrian, Gothic and Romanesque styles). At the south end of Vieux-Lyon is the stately Gothic *Cathédrale Saint-Jean*, which is remarkable for its three highly ornate doors and 13thC stained-glass windows.

To the north of Presqu'île the *Croix-Rousse* quarter, once the home of *canuts* (silk workers), should on no account be missed: it is honeycombed with *traboules*, covered passages, galleries or flights of steps connecting streets or houses to one another. These *traboules*, a word derived from the Latin *transambulare* (to walk through), enabled silk to be carried to and from workshops without being rained on – and *résistants* to escape their pursuers during the last war (a map of the *traboules* is available from the Office de Tourisme).

Lyon has only one central park, the pleasant and popular *Parc de la Tête d'Or*, just north of Brotteaux. It has a small zoo, a lake and a superb rose garden.
Musée des Beaux-Arts A large collection of sculpture and paintings, particularly strong in French 19thC and 20thC art. *20 pl des Terreaux. Open Wed–Mon, 10.45–6.*
Musée de la Civilisation Gallo-Romaine An intelligent display of relics from the time when Lyon was called Lugdunum. *17 rue Cléberg. Open Wed–Sun, 9.30–12, 2–6.*
Musée Historique des Tissus A fine collection of tapestries, fabrics and, above all, silks. *34 rue de la Charité. Open Tue–Sun, 10–12, 2–5.30.*

Guided tours
Office de Tourisme ☎ 78 42 25 75 offers a number of interesting walks. The 2hr tour of floodlit Vieux-Lyon includes access to private courtyards. *Taxi-Radio* ☎ 78 30 86 86 runs tours of Lyon by taxi with commentary, lasting up to 3hrs for the longest. There are river cruises Apr–Oct ☎ 78 42 96 81.

Out of town
Vienne, 30kms/19 miles south and easily reached by train or motorway, has superb Roman remains (temples, theatre, mosaics). Pérouges (see also *Hotels*), 39kms/24 miles northeast, with a good autoroute connection, is a perfectly preserved tiny medieval village, often used as a ready-made film set.

Spectator sports
Racing There are regular horse races at Hippodrome de Bron-Parilly ☎ 78 38 09 69.
Soccer Olympique Lyonnais (OL), a 2nd-division club, plays at the Stade Gerland, ave Jean-Jaurès. For information ☎ 78 58 64 22.

Keeping fit
Fitness centre The best and most comprehensively equipped centre open to visitors is *Le Mandala*, 9 rue Boissac ☎ 78 42 74 28.
Golf Two 18-hole golf courses are open to nonmembers (weekdays only): *Golf du Clou* ☎ 74 98 19 65, in Villars-les-Dombes, 30kms/ 19 miles northeast; and *Golf de Lyon-Verger* ☎ 78 02 84 20, 14kms/ 9 miles south.
Squash The *Squash Club de Lyon*, 20 rue Essling ☎ 78 95 13 25, has four courts and is open to nonmembers.
Tennis The only club that regularly accepts nonmembers (if you reserve 24hrs ahead) is LET ☎ 78 55 63 66. It is 8kms/5 miles northeast on exit slip-road 5 (for Beynost) off the A42 autoroute. There are outdoor and covered courts.

Local resources
Business services
The major hotels listed can either provide or organize most of the services you are likely to need.
Photocopying and printing Copy 200 ☎ 78 30 62 69, *J'Imprime* ☎ 78 95 10 92 and 78 24 45 04.
Secretarial Marcelle Genevier ☎ 78 86 04 09.
Translation Peter Brook ☎ 78 52 74 30.

Communications
Local delivery RAC ☎ 78 58 36 52, *Taxi-Colis* ☎ 72 04 68 00.
Long-distance delivery Taxi-Colis ☎ 72 04 68 00.
Post office Main office: Hôtel des Postes, pl Antonin-Poncet.
Telex and fax International Télex Assistance ☎ 78 83 46 87.

Conference/exhibition centres

Eurexpo ☎ 72 22 33 44 is Lyon's main exhibition centre. It is just off the A43 autoroute 13kms/8 miles east, next to Bron private airport and halfway to Satolas airport. Opened in 1984, it has 9 ha/23 acres of exhibition halls and, as befits Lyon, no fewer than six restaurants. Eurexpo can also accommodate conferences. During all exhibitions there is a bus shuttle service between Eurexpo and Gare de la Part-Dieu. For major events there is also a shuttle between Eurexpo and Satolas airport.

Central Lyon has two major conference centres: *Palais des Congrès Internationaux*, quai Achille-Lignon, 69006 ☎ 78 93 14 14, whose biggest auditorium has a capacity of 1,000; and the brand-new *Espace Tête d'Or*, 103 bd Stalingrad, 69100 Villeurbanne ☎ 78 94 69 00, which has a modular hall that can hold up to 3,000 people. For other conference inquiries, contact the *Bureau des Congrès* in the Office de Tourisme ☎ 78 42 25 75.

Emergencies

Bureaux de change Most major hotels will change currency, but give a rather poor rate. *Thomas Cook*, Gare de la Part-Dieu, daily, 8.30–6.30. *AOC*, 13 rue du Griffon, Mon–Sat, 9–6.

Hospitals 24hr emergency department: *Hôpital Saint-Joseph*, 9 rue du Professeur Grignard ☎ 78 69 81 82; *Hôpital Edouard-Herriot*, 5 pl d'Arsonval ☎ 78 53 81 11. These hospitals will give details of how to get emergency dental treatment during the day.

Pharmacies Pharmacie Blanchet, 5 pl des Cordeliers; open all the time. *Pharmacie Perret*, 30 rue Duquesne; open Mon–Sat, 8.30am–7pm.

Police Main station: *Hôtel de Police* 40 rue Marius-Berliet ☎ 78 00 40 40.

Government offices

Worth contacting are the city hall, *Hôtel de Ville*, pl des Terreaux

☎ 78 27 71 31, and the *Préfecture*, cours de la Liberté ☎ 78 62 20 26.

Information sources

Business information By far the most useful organization is ADERLY (Association pour le Développement Economique de la Région Lyonnaise), which is a department of the *Chambre de Commerce et de l'Industrie de Lyon*, 20 rue de la Bourse, 69002 ☎ 78 38 10 10. ADERLY will not only advise the visiting business traveller but give incoming firms practical help on the siting of their business, rental of premises, building permits, housing, schooling, and so on.

Local media The main daily newspaper is the *Progrès de Lyon*, which regularly carries local and national business news. There is also a monthly business magazine, *Entreprises Rhône-Alpes*.

Tourist information The *Office de Tourisme* has a single telephone number ☎ 78 42 25 75 and two bureaux, one of which opens longer hours in summer (Jun 15–Sep 15): pl Bellecour (in the middle of the square), Mon–Fri, 9–6 (9–7 in summer), Sat, 9–5 (9–6 in summer); Gare de Perrache, Mon–Sat, 9–12.30, 2–6. Information about local events and cultural listings will be found in the weekly *Lyon Poche*.

Thank-yous

Chocolates Maurice Bernachon, 42 cours Franklin-Roosevelt ☎ 78 24 37 98 (open Sun, closed Mon). Your Lyonnais client will appreciate a gift purchased from this world-famous maker of chocolates who has stubbornly turned down all offers to entice him away from his native city of Lyon.

Florists Interflora, 22 pl des Terreaux ☎ 78 28 85 39, will take telephone orders with credit card payment.

STRASBOURG

City code ☎ included in numbers

The pleasant and prosperous capital of Alsace is so attractive that many people think of it as a picture-postcard tourist spot; some even think of it as being in Germany. The local authorities are working hard to dispel Strasbourg's folksy image and to emphasize its importance as a major economic centre, an important port on the Rhine and the seat of such institutions as the Council of Europe, the European Court of Human Rights and the European Parliament.

Although not as industrialized as Mulhouse to the south, Strasbourg has a number of thriving industries, especially brewing (Kronenbourg, Heineken, Adelshoffen and Pêcheur), food (Suchard Tobler), cars (General Motors) and textiles. Some 500 new factories have been set up in Alsace since the early 1960s, many of them with foreign capital attracted by the Alsatian reputation for hard work.

The city is a major service centre, with particular importance in banking, finance and insurance; three large regional banks, the Sogénal, Crédit Industriel d'Alsace-Lorraine and the Banque Fédérative du Crédit Mutuel (BFCM) have their headquarters in Strasbourg. The presence of the European institutions has fostered the growth of a large diplomatic community: over thirty countries have consulates in the city. The city is also an academic centre; it has three universities and famous schools of medicine and theology.

Increasing emphasis is being put on high-tech research: a technopark is being set up in the southern suburbs at Illkirch. France's first World Trade Center was opened in Strasbourg in 1979, and the conference centre attracts more conferences than any other French city except Paris. Despite all this economic activity, despite the regular influx of Eurocrats, life seems to proceed at a pleasantly leisurely pace and this is not the least of Strasbourg's successes.

Arriving

Strasbourg's central position in Europe gives it good road links with Austria, the Benelux countries, Germany, Italy and Switzerland, as well as Paris. The journey from Paris takes 4–5hrs by car or train. The airport has some international flights but occasionally it may be more convenient to use Basle airport (145kms/90 miles away).

Strasbourg-Entzheim airport
There are domestic flights to Paris, Lille, Lyon, Marseille and Nice, and international flights to major European and some North African destinations (not all direct). Information *Strasbourg-Aviation*

☎ 88 68 91 99; helicopter services: *Europe Hélicoptères* ☎ 88 68 40 99.

Although small, this airport has a restaurant, bar, meeting room for up to 25 people, bureau de change, travel agency and duty-free shop. Airport information and reservations ☎ 88 78 40 99.

City link The airport is 12kms/ 7 miles southwest of the city on the D392; road journey takes about 20 min by car, 30mins by bus.

Taxis are normally available when scheduled flights arrive or may be ordered in advance ☎ 88 36 13 13.

Car rental All major rental companies have desks at the airport.

Bus There is an efficient service coinciding with scheduled flights.

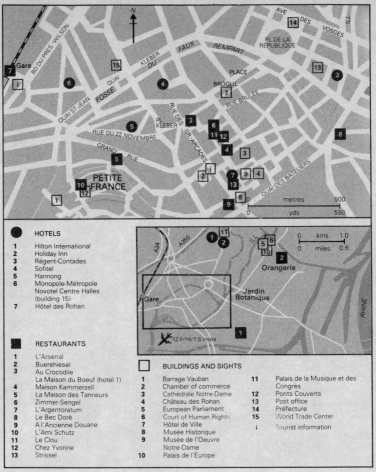

HOTELS

1 Hilton International
2 Holiday Inn
3 Régent-Contades
4 Sofitel
5 Hannong
6 Monopole-Métropole
  Novotel Centre Halles
  (building 15)
7 Hôtel des Rohan

RESTAURANTS

1 L'Arsenal
2 Buerehiesel
3 Au Crocodile
  La Maison du Boeuf (hotel 1)
4 Maison Kammerzell
5 La Maison des Tanneurs
6 Zimmer-Sengel
7 L'Argentoratum
8 Le Bec Doré
9 A l'Ancienne Douane
10 L'Ami Schutz
11 Le Clou
12 Chez Yvonne
13 Strissel

BUILDINGS AND SIGHTS

1 Barrage Vauban
2 Chamber of commerce
3 Cathédrale Notre-Dame
4 Château des Rohan
5 European Parliament
6 Court of Human Rights
7 Hôtel de Ville
8 Musée Historique
9 Musée de l'Œuvre
  Notre-Dame
10 Palais de l'Europe
11 Palais de la Musique et des
   Congrès
12 Ponts Couverts
13 Post office
14 Préfecture
15 World Trade Center
i Tourist information

Railway station

Strasbourg's large and busy station handles numerous international as well as domestic trains. It has an exchange counter, lockers and photocopying facilities. Taxis wait outside. Passenger inquiries and reservations ☎ 88 22 50 50 or ☎ 88 32 07 51.

Getting around

Walking is quick and pleasant in the city centre. There are several taxi ranks and an efficient bus service.

Taxis The main rank is in Place de la République. Other useful ones are in Place Kléber and outside the Novotel. For radio taxis ☎ 88 36 13 11 or 86 36 13 13.

Driving Traffic is not a major problem and parking is relatively easy. All the main car rental companies have offices.

Buses The Compagnie des Transports Strasbourgeois (CTS) has information kiosks outside the station and beside the town hall, or call *Allobus* ☎ 88 28 20 30.

Area by area

Strasbourg lies to the west of the Rhine, and the centre is encircled by the river Ill and its canals. At its heart is the lovely cathedral, and between here and the river are the city's major museums. The bustling commercial area runs from the cathedral west and north to Place Kléber and Place Broglie. The picturesque Petite France area is to the west.

Beyond the river to the west lies the station surrounded by hotels and small businesses, and to the north the leafy Place de la République, with monumental 19thC public buildings and the Palais du Rhin.

Avenue de la Paix leads north from the centre towards the modern conference centre and exhibition grounds. To the east of here are the European institutions and the lovely Orangerie park, whose surrounding streets form an exclusive residential area.

Another upmarket area is La Robertsau beyond the Orangerie, though some executives prefer the large western suburb of Oberhausbergen or the wine villages in the surrounding countryside. The northern suburb of Schiltigheim is industrial and several big breweries are based here.

Hotels

The business traveller is spoilt for choice in Strasbourg. During the European Parliament sessions, however (roughly one week per month), hotel accommodation becomes markedly scarce. Advance reservations are advisable at all times, as Strasbourg is a major tourist city as well as a business and Eurocrat centre. All hotels listed here have IDD telephones, 24hr room service, currency exchange and parking facilities. The first two are conveniently close to the conference centre.

Hilton International *F////*
ave Herrenschmidt ☎ *88 37 10 10*
[TX] *890363 fax 88 36 83 27* • *AE DC MC V* • *247 rooms, 5 suites, 2 restaurants, 1 bar*
The rooms are comfortable and air-conditioned; eight are reserved for nonsmokers. The hotel has a first-class restaurant, La Maison du Boeuf (see *Restaurants*); Le Jardin is more casual and serves lighter meals. The piano-bar, Le Bugatti, is convenient for meeting business colleagues travelling by car. Shops, courtesy coach to European Parliament • sauna, jacuzzi, relaxation room • 5 meeting rooms (capacity up to 450).

Holiday Inn *F////*
20 pl de Bordeaux ☎ *88 35 70 00*
[TX] *890515 fax 88 37 07 04* • *AE DC MC V* • *168 rooms, 2 suites, 2 restaurants, 2 bars*
The atmosphere here is comfortable and relaxed. All rooms are air-conditioned and fairly spacious, with

good working areas. Some, mainly on a special executive floor, have extra business facilities. The Louisiane restaurant is relaxed and cheerful; the bars are always busy. Shops • pool, sauna, jacuzzi, steambath, half-court tennis • modular meeting room (capacity up to 1,200).

Régent-Contades *F////*
8 ave de la Liberté ☎ *88 36 26 26*
[TX] *890641 fax 88 37 03 71* • *AE DC MC V* • *31 rooms, 1 suite, 1 bar; no restaurant*
This lovingly restored and very grand late 19thC mansion overlooking the Ill offers luxurious accommodation. The bedrooms are elegant and comfortable, the bathrooms well planned, and each has a hairdryer. The bar and small lounge are both pleasant. The beautiful panelled breakfast room doubles as a meeting room. A few dishes can be served in bedrooms 24hrs. Sauna, jacuzzi • 1 meeting room (capacity up to 20).

Sofitel _F_///
4 pl St-Pierre-le-Jeune ☎ _88 32 99 30_
TX _870894 fax 88 32 60 67_ • _AE DC
MC V_ • _158 rooms, 5 suites,
1 restaurant (closed Sun and first half
Aug), 1 bar_
The Sofitel, in the heart of
Strasbourg, is within walking distance
of most major sights and amenities.
The rooms are fairly small but have
the usual Sofitel comforts. The
restaurant and bar are frequently used
for business entertaining. Hairdresser
• 5 meeting rooms (capacity up to
120).

OTHER HOTELS
Hannong _F_// _15 rue du 22
Novembre_ ☎ _88 32 16 22_ TX _890551
fax 88 22 63 87_ • _AE DC MC V._
A small, central hotel within walking
distance of the station. It has a
popular wine bar. Two small meeting
rooms (capacity up to 60).
Monopole-Métropole _F_// _16 rue
Kuhn_ ☎ _88 32 11 94_ TX _890366
fax 88 32 82 55_ • _AE DC MC V._ The
best of the hotels near the station
with good old-fashioned service. No
restaurant. 1 meeting room (capacity
up to 30).
Novotel Centre Halles _F_//
Quai Kléber ☎ _88 22 10 99_

TX _880700 fax 88 22 20 92_ •
_AE DC MC V._ A somewhat impersonal
modern hotel in the World Trade
Center complex.
Hôtel des Rohan _F_/ _17 rue du
Maroquin_ ☎ _88 32 85 11_ TX _870047
fax 88 75 65 37_ • _MC V._ A delightful
little hotel near the cathedral. Few
business amenities but great charm.
No restaurant.

Out of town
Le Moulin ☎ 88 96 27 83,
13kms/8 miles northeast at La
Wantzenau, is in a lovely setting
on the banks of the Ill. There is a
delightful restaurant next door,
also called _Le Moulin._ A number
of Alsace's top restaurants are
within easy reach of Strasbourg by
car. At Marlenheim, 20kms/12
miles away, is _Hostellerie du Cerf_
☎ 88 87 73 73, closed Tue, Wed.
At Landersheim, 5kms/3 miles
farther away, is the Adidas
factory's famous staff canteen,
Auberge du Kochersberg
☎ 88 69 91 58, closed Sun D,
Tue, Wed; it is undoubtedly one
of the region's finest restaurants.
Visitors' lunches start at 1 on
weekdays.

Restaurants

The Strasbourgeois love their food and wine, so it is not surprising that
the city offers a wide choice of excellent restaurants. The two top
gourmet restaurants, Buerehiesel and Au Crocodile, have a mixed
clientele of Eurocrats, business people, wealthy tourists and locals. Few
restaurants are geared solely to business meals.

L'Arsenal _F_/
11 rue de l'Abreuvoir ☎ _88 35 03 69_
• _closed Sat, Sun D, 2 weeks
end Jan, L 4 weeks Jul/Aug_
• _AE DC MC V_
Small, attractive and impeccably run,
this restaurant is a favourite of
diplomats, 5mins by taxi from the
older part of town. Superb Alsatian
(but delicate) food at reasonable
prices, and an excellent wine list
punctiliously served.

Buerehiesel _F_////
4 parc de l'Orangerie ☎ _88 61 62 24_ •
_closed Tue (exc Tue L in summer),
Wed, 2 weeks Aug, Christmas, New
Year_ • _AE DC MC V_
An authentic 17thC Alsatian
farmhouse lovingly reconstructed in
the Orangerie park is the setting for
one of Strasbourg's finest restaurants.
The _nouvelle cuisine_ comes in
generous portions and the service is
pleasantly relaxed.

Au Crocodile *F* ////
10 rue de l'Outre ☎ *88 32 13 02 •*
closed Sun, Mon, 4 weeks Jul/Aug,
Christmas, New Year • AE DC MC
This elegant restaurant is more formal
than the Buerehiesel, but offers
equally accomplished cooking with
some interesting *nouvelle* versions of
filling regional dishes. Private dining
rooms available.

La Maison du Boeuf *F* ////
ave Herrenschmidt ☎ *88 37 10 10 •*
closed 2 weeks Aug • AE DC MC V
The Hilton's restaurant is one of the
best in town, offering excellent fish as
well as meat. In summer meals are
served on a pleasant terrace.

Maison Kammerzell *F* ////
16 pl de la Cathédrale ☎ *88 32 42 14*
• closed 3 weeks Jan/Feb • AE DC
MC V
Housed in a picturesque 15th–16thC
building with ornate woodcarvings,
this restaurant offers two types of
cuisine: Alsatian on the ground floor
and *nouvelle* upstairs.

La Maison des Tanneurs *F* /
42 rue du Bain-aux-Plantes
☎ *88 32 79 70 • closed Sun, Mon*
(open Sun L in May, Jun and Sep) •
AE DC MC V
This is a charming and very popular
restaurant in a 16thC tannery in
Petite France specializing in
Alsatian dishes. A good place for
business entertaining.

Zimmer-Sengel *F* //
8 rue du Temple-Neuf ☎ *88 32 35 01*
• closed Sat L, Sun and most of Aug •
AE DC MC V
An old-established restaurant near the
cathedral. It specializes in *nouvelle*
cuisine and the fixed-price "Allegro"
menu is good value.

Restaurant price guide
For the meanings of the restaurant
price symbols, see *Symbols and*
abbreviations on pages 6 and 7.

OTHER RESTAURANTS
The well-run station buffet
L'Argentoratum ☎ *88 32 68 28* is
often used for less formal business
entertaining (closed Wed); private
dining rooms are available. *Le Bec*
Doré, 8 quai des Pêcheurs
☎ *88 35 39 57*, overlooks
the river and is popular for both
business and more casual dining
(closed Mon, Tue). Also overlooking
the river is *A l'Ancienne Douane*,
6 rue Douane ☎ *88 32 42 19*, a large
and busy brasserie. The food, wine
and beer are all Alsatian at *L'Ami*
Schutz, 1 Ponts-Couverts
☎ *88 32 76 98*, where there is a
convivial atmosphere in the evening.

Winstubs
Somewhere between a German
Bierkeller and an English pub in
atmosphere, but very much an
Alsatian institution, the *Winstub* is a
congenial place to meet friends after
work over a jug of wine and a filling
local dish; most open from late
afternoon until the early hours.
Among the best is *Le Clou*, 3 rue
Chaudron ☎ *88 32 11 67*, but
traditionalists swear by *s'Burjerstuewel*
(also known, less tongue-twistingly,
as *Chez Yvonne*), 10 rue du Sanglier
☎ *88 32 84 15*. *Strissel*, 5 pl de la
Grande-Boucherie ☎ *88 32 14 73*, is
particularly atmospheric with its
rustic decor.

Bars
The bar in the World Trade Center is
useful for meeting business contacts,
though it closes at 6.30. The Sofitel's
bar is central, and the Hilton's
Bugatti piano-bar is handy for those
attending conferences. Local
businessmen are fond of the beer in
the bar of the Hôtel de France, 20
rue Jeu-des-Enfants. *Le Wyn Bar* in
the Hannong hotel is among the best
for food.

Entertainment
Strasbourg offers fine musical
entertainment, particularly during the
June music festival. There is little

nightlife other than discos, but Kehl, just across the German border, has a varied nightlife, much of it rather sleazy.

Theatre, dance, opera The *Théâtre Municipal*, pl Broglie ☎ 88 36 45 66, stages plays and has lively opera and operetta seasons by the Opéra du Rhin company. The *Théâtre National de Strasbourg*, 1 rue André Malraux ☎ 88 35 63 60, has a complicated season-ticket system that often makes it difficult for visitors to obtain tickets. The *Théâtre Alsacien de Strasbourg*, pl Broglie ☎ 88 75 48 00, specializes in plays in dialect. *Le Maillon*, pl André Malraux ☎ 88 26 16 17 or 88 26 12 66, is a lively arts complex offering theatre, jazz, modern dance and film.

Music The *Orchestre Philharmonique de Strasbourg* ☎ 88 22 15 60 performs in the municipal theatre or in the *Palais de la Musique et des Congrès*, ave Schutzenberger ☎ 88 35 03 00. Concerts are also held in the *Pavillon Joséphine* in the Orangerie park and, in summer, in the courtyard of the *Château des Rohan* (see *Sightseeing*).

Shopping

The narrow old streets near the cathedral – Rue du Dôme, Rue des Hallebardes, Rue des Orfèvres – are full of chic boutiques; Place de la Cathédrale itself is more touristy, with the accent on local wares. The Place Kléber area has the city's department stores – *Magmod*, *Printemps* and the *Fnac*. The *Centre Halles*, in the same complex as the World Trade Center, is a useful place for one-stop shopping.

The city is famous for its fruit brandies (*alcools blancs*) and its excellent *foie gras*.

Sightseeing

Strasbourg has many picturesque buildings, including one of the country's finest cathedrals, as well as several good museums. All museums open daily exc Tue, 10–12, 2–6; closed May 1st, Nov 1st, Christmas, New Year.

Cathédrale Notre-Dame Gothic cathedral in pinkish sandstone, with elaborate carvings, lofty spire and famous astronomical clock. *Son-et-lumière* (in French and German) is staged in the cathedral from about Easter to September.

Château des Rohan fine 18thC château (also known as Palais Rohan), now housing three museums: the *Musée Archéologique* (closed for renovation until 1990/91), the *Musée des Beaux-Arts* and the *Musée des Arts Décoratifs*. Also worth seeing in the château are the *Cabinet des Estampes* (open Thu pm only), with over 20,000 prints and drawings, and the *grands appartements*. *2 pl du Château* ☎ 88 32 48 95.

Musée Historique A local history collection. *3 pl de la Grande-Boucherie* ☎ 88 32 25 63.

Musée de l'Oeuvre Notre-Dame Alsatian art from the Middle Ages to the Renaissance. *3 pl du Château* ☎ 88 32 06 39.

Orangerie Attractive public gardens designed by Le Nôtre.

Palais de l'Europe The Council of Europe and the European Parliament can be seen from sightseeing boats, or visited by appointment. *Bd de la Dordogne* ☎ 88 37 40 01.

Petite France Picturesque area of half-timbered houses and quiet canals; attractive old streets are linked by three bridges, the *Ponts Couverts*; beyond them the *Barrage Vauban*, part of the old fortifications, affords a striking view of the old town. There is an enjoyable boat trip, starting with a tour of Petite France and then going right up to the Palais de l'Europe, which is worth fitting into even a busy schedule.

Out of town

The beautiful countryside around Strasbourg is well worth exploring. The imposing castle of Haut-Koenigsbourg, 60kms/37 miles southwest of the city, is an extraordinary folly built for Kaiser Wilhelm II in 1901 on the site of a medieval ruin; and all along the *Route de Vin de l'Alsace* (Wine Road), which starts at Marlenheim and meanders through 100kms/62 miles of vineyards, are picturesque villages such as Obernai, Ottrott, Ribeauvillé and Riquewihr, where the local wines can be tasted.

Spectator sports

Horse-racing The nearest racecourse, Hippodrome de Strasbourg-Hoerdt, is 16kms/10 miles north of the city ☎ 88 51 32 44; open Mar–Jun, Sep–Nov.
Soccer Extremely popular, even though the local team has not done well in recent years. The *Racing-Club de Strasbourg* stadium is at *Meinau* ☎ 88 34 12 18 and ☎ 88 34 08 47 at weekends; the *Association Sportive de Strasbourg* has another soccer stadium at *Tivoli-Wacken* ☎ 88 36 60 78.

Keeping fit

Fitness centres Two in the city centre are *L'Eau Vive*, 29 rue du Vieux-Marché-aux-Vins ☎ 88 22 36 55, which also offers aerobics and jazz classes; and *Energy Centre*, 2c rue Moll ☎ 88 22 12 44, which also has martial arts and aerobics. *Le Maintien*, in the suburbs at Neudorf ☎ 88 34 26 44, is open until 9 every evening. (See also *Hotels*.)
Golf The top local club is *Golf-Club de Strasbourg*, rte du Rhin, Illkirch ☎ 88 66 17 22.
Riding Centre Equestre, rue de l'Hippodrôme in the Parc du Rhin ☎ 88 61 67 35; *L'Etrier de Strasbourg*, 13kms/8 miles northeast at Le Wantzenau ☎ 88 96 60 57.
Squash and tennis There are courts near the exhibition grounds run by the *Association Sportive de Strasbourg* ☎ 88 35 29 23 (tennis), and ☎ 88 31 50 02 (squash); *Centre Halles* (2nd floor) ☎ 88 23 00 55 also has courts, sauna, bar and restaurant.
Swimming There is an olympic-size pool in the suburban *Centre Nautique de Schiltigheim* ☎ 88 33 24 40; an indoor municipal pool quite close to the city centre, bd de la Victoire ☎ 88 35 51 56 (open until 9.30 Tue;

closed Sun); outdoor pools in Wacken ☎ 88 31 49 10 and close to the Pont de l'Europe ☎ 88 61 92 30 (open until 11 Tue, Thu, Fri).

Local resources

Business services

France's first World Trade Center, the *Maison du Commerce International de Strasbourg* (MCIS), 4 quai Kléber ☎ 88 32 48 90 TX 890673 fax 88 75 51 23, was opened in 1979. It covers 5,000 sq metres on eight floors and offers a good range of business services; with shops, parking areas and hotels nearby.

Fully equipped office space can be rented from one day to three months, and meeting rooms are available. Services offered free to World Trade Center members, for a fee to others, include a well-stocked information library; legal, accounting and tax advice; telex and fax; photocopying. The centre has a restaurant and a bar, and companies in the same building can supply translating, interpreting and messenger services.

Photocopying and printing
Eclair Print 11 rue St Gothard ☎ 88 35 22 96; *SAID*, 43 fbg de Saverne ☎ 88 32 02 25; *Copies'stueb*, 1 pl du Foin ☎ 88 35 34 84.
Secretarial services
Allo Secrétariat, 9 pl Kléber ☎ 88 32 68 32; *Secrétariat no. 1*, 58 ave des Vosges ☎ 88 36 56 16.
Translating and interpreting
Interpretations Traductions Alsace ☎ 88 22 20 22 TX 890673 fax 88 75 64 29 is in the MCIS.

Communications

Long-distance delivery DHL (international) ☎ 05 11 95 31 (toll free); *Chronopost* ☎ 05 30 05 30 (toll free) or at main post office; *SERNAM* ☎ 88 28 00 12 (international), and ☎ 88 28 46 10 (national).
Post office Main office: 5 ave de la Marseillaise ☎ 88 23 44 00; others are at the station and Centre Halles.
Telex and fax At main post office; *International Telex Assistance* ☎ 88 22 20 22 TX 890673.

Conference/exhibition centres

The attractive *Palais de la Musique et des Congrès*, ave Schutzenberger ☎ 88 37 67 67 ⛶ 890666 is the third largest conference centre in France. Its current facilities include the 2,000-seat Salle Erasme auditorium, the 500-seat Salle Robert Schuman, and nine other rooms (capacity up to 350). Most rooms are air-conditioned and equipped with a wide range of facilities, including simultaneous interpreting equipment. The centre has bars, cafeteria, telex and telephone, a bank, travel agency, gift shop, infirmary and a photo lab. The 1,700 sq metre *Galerie de Marbre* (Marble Gallery) can be rented for exhibitions or banquets (capacity up to 1,000).

An extension scheduled to open in 1989 will include a 1,000-seat auditorium and 2,000 sq metres of exhibition space, plus a banqueting hall seating up to 1,400.

Close by is an exhibition centre, the *Parc des Expositions Strasbourg-Wacken* ☎ 88 36 63 55 ⛶ 870096.

Emergencies

Bureaux de change The exchange counter at the station is open 9–8 (sometimes later in summer); CMDP, 26 rue du Vieux-Marché-aux-Poissons ☎ 88 32 12 08, is open Sun to about 5.
Hospitals Emergencies ☎ 15; SAMU ☎ 88 33 33 33; *Hôpital Civil* ☎ 88 16 17 18; *Centre Hospitalier Régional*, ave Molière, Hautepierre ☎ 88 28 90 00.
Pharmacies The main police station has a list of pharmacies open outside usual business hours.
Police Main station: 11 rue de la Nuée-Bleue ☎ 88 32 99 08. Emergencies ☎ 17.

Government offices

Hôtel de Ville, 9 rue Brûlée ☎ 88 32 99 03; *Préfecture*, 5 pl de la République ☎ 88 32 99 00; *Douane* (regional customs office), 11 ave de la Liberté ☎ 88 35 48 40; *Comité Economique et Social d'Alsace*, 35 ave de la Paix ☎ 88 25 68 67.
EC offices Parlement Européen, ave de l'Europe ☎ 88 37 40 01; *Conseil de l'Europe*, ave de l'Europe ☎ 88 61 49 61.

Information sources

Business information The best source of information is the MCIS (see *Business services*), with its large information library. Local economic data can be supplied by *Chambre de Commerce du Bas-Rhin*, 10 pl Gutenberg ☎ 88 32 12 55; and INSEE's *Observatoire Economique de l'Alsace* ☎ 88 32 03 18.
Local media The main regional daily is *Les Dernières Nouvelles d'Alsace*. The chamber of commerce publishes *Le Point Economique* every two months, with articles on local business topics; and a monthly *Bulletin d'Opportunités Commerciales* which aims to match those seeking and offering business opportunities. *FR3 Alsace* is the regional station of the third television channel.
Tourist information Office de Tourisme de Strasbourg et sa Région, Palais des Congrès has three "welcome offices." Main office: Place de Gutenberg ☎ 88 32 67 07; others opposite the station ☎ 88 32 51 49 and at the Pont de l'Europe ☎ 88 61 39 23. Open winter Mon–Fri, 9–12.30, 1.45–6; summer 8–7 daily.

Thank-yous

Cakes Kohler-Rehm, pl Kléber ☎ 88 32 15 93, has an *"Intergâteaux"* dispatch service.
Confectionery Catalin, 4 pl de l'Homme-de-Fer ☎ 88 32 62 45; *Gross*, 24 pl des Halles ☎ 88 22 22 77; *Léonidas*, pl de la Cathédrale ☎ 88 32 19 81.
Florists Fuchs, 19 rue des Orfèvres ☎ 88 32 19 57.

GERMANY

A postwar "economic miracle" (*Wirtschaftswunder*) transformed West Germany from a bankrupt nation into the third largest economy in the world, a leading industrial and exporting country and a "motor" of world economic growth. The 1979 oil crisis and the global recession that followed made the economy falter; GDP growth was sluggish (averaging 2% a year) and unemployment rose. Yet the period 1980–88 saw low or negative inflation, a large current account surplus, an inexorable strengthening of the Deutschemark and substantial cuts in the budget deficit. These factors, combined with strong growth in capital investment and exports in 1989, have led to a renewed feeling of confidence in the West German economy as the country prepares itself for 1992 and the single European market.

Manufacturing remains the backbone of the West German economy, accounting for just over 40% to GDP and employing about 40% of the work force. The main areas of production are motor vehicles, machinery, electrical and electronic equipment, chemicals, food processing and metals. Most of these industries are dominated by a few large companies. Traditionally industrial activity has been concentrated in the iron and steel producing Ruhr. But recession and a consequent restructuring of many traditional industries have led to a shift in industrial activity southward, particularly to Hesse and Bavaria, the centre of the country's high technology and motor industries. Agriculture accounts for a small and declining 1.5% of GDP and employs just over 1% of the work force. But productivity is high and West Germany produces enough not only to satisfy domestic demand in some foodstuffs, but it is the fourth largest exporter of food and drink in the world – although also one of the largest importers. The service sector has grown at the expense of industry and agriculture and it now accounts for just over 50% of total output.

West Germany has relatively few natural resources and depends on imports for most of its basic raw materials and fuel resources, including over 90% of its oil needs. Since the 1973 energy crisis government policy has been aimed at reducing the nation's dependence on imported oil, which in 1986 accounted for 40% of energy consumption. It is strongly committed to nuclear energy, despite the controversy it arouses. In 1986 nuclear fuel provided 30% of total electricity output; its share is due to rise to 35% by the year 2000.

West Germany is the largest exporter in the world; exports of goods and services account for 30–35% of GDP. Manufactured goods dominate export trade, with finished goods accounting for 70% of earnings. The motor industry is West Germany's largest earner, with sales accounting for almost one-fifth of export earnings in 1987. Its other main exports are industrial machinery, chemicals and engineering products. Its main imports are food and drink, petroleum and natural gas, chemicals and other raw materials for industry. The percentage share of imported finished goods is increasing, due to rising consumer demand and the strength of the Deutschemark; in 1987 West Germany was the world's second largest importer after the United States (in US dollar terms) – a statistic which emphasizes its role as a "motor" of international economic growth.

Nearly half of West German trade is conducted with fellow EC members, France and the Netherlands being its major trading partners. Within the Community West Germany dominates trade with Eastern Europe; in 1987 it accounted for 44% of EC exports to the Soviet Union and 48% of those to East Germany.

Geography Germany is made up of 4 broad physical zones. The northern section is a plain cut by inland waterways; both the North Sea and Baltic coastline are indented with estuaries leading to the main ports. The central section contains wooded uplands and river valleys, including that of the northward flowing and extremely polluted Rhein. To the south there are the Alpine foothills rising to the Bavarian Alps, which form a natural frontier with Austria. The east and southwest are heavily forested and contain the coniferous Black Forest.

Climate The climate is temperate and variable. The northern areas have milder weather than the south but they have more rain. Winters are generally dull and wet, with average temperatures in January dropping to 1.5°C (35°F) in the northern lowland areas and much lower, about -6°C (18°F), in the Bavarian Alps. Summers are hot in the south and east, with average temperatures in July rising to 20°C (70°F), but slightly cooler and more changeable in the northern lowlands, with less sunshine. Spring and autumn are often overcast.

Population 61m.

Government The federal republic of Germany consists of 10 Länder (states) and West Berlin, all of which have legislative autonomy on matters that are not specifically assigned to the federal government (such as defence, foreign affairs and finance).

The legislature is split into 2 houses. The Bundestag, the lower house, has 518 members most of whom are elected by a mixed system of proportional representation and single-member constituencies for 4 years. It elects the head of the federal government and chief executive, namely the federal chancellor, on the recommendation of the federal president. The Bundesrat, the upper house, has 45 members appointed by the governments of the Länder. It plays a minor role in the legislative process.

The head of state is the federal president, who is elected for 5 years by an electoral college made up from the Bundesrat and regional legislatures.

Currency The unit of currency is the Deutschemark (DM), which is divided into 100 Pfennigs (Pfg).

West Germany is a founder member of the European Monetary System (EMS), formed in 1979. Periodic realignments within the exchange rate mechanism usually entail and effective revaluation of the Deutschemark against the participating countries.

Time Germany is on Central European Time, which is 1hr ahead of GMT. Summer time is in force from the end of Mar to the end of Sep; clocks are put forward, and Germany is then 2hrs ahead of GMT.

Dialling codes West Germany's IDD code is 49. Omit the initial 0 from the city code when dialling from abroad. To make an international call from west Germany, dial 00 before dialling the relevant country code.

Public holidays (* some Länder only) Jan 1, Jan 6*, Good Fri, Easter Mon, May 1, Ascension, Whit Mon, Corpus Christi*, Jun 17, Aug 15*, Nov 1*, Repentance Day, Dec 25, Dec 26.

BERLIN
City code ☎ 030

Geographically and politically, West Berlin is unique. Marooned in East German territory, it is separated by the Wall from East Berlin, the other half of the former Prussian and German capital. It became a political pawn during the Cold War tension of the 1950s, which eventually led to the building of the Wall in 1961, but since the Four Power Agreement of 1971 West Berlin has ceased to live in the eye of East-West confrontation.

Although West Berlin is strictly speaking a *Land* (state) of the Federal Republic, its deputies in Bonn have only limited voting rights. It has its own parliament, which elects a governing mayor (currently the young and ambitious Eberhard Diepgen). Bonn, in theory at least, has no direct say in the affairs of West Berlin, since supreme authority over the city is still held by the "protecting powers," France, Great Britain and the United States.

West Berlin's geographical position and curious status have had a direct bearing on its economic and social life. After World War II, almost all the major German companies that had had their headquarters in Berlin moved to the safety of other West German cities, and even after the easing of tension in 1971 they were reluctant to return. From 1970 to 1983, jobs in its manufacturing industry fell by 40%.

Yet West Berlin's output has risen steadily because of the heavy subsidies from Bonn to compensate for the disadvantages of its location and to keep it as a showcase for Western values. Just over half its budget is currently provided by West Germany; much of the money is used to provide generous incentives to lure companies to the city. Recently, long-standing Berlin-based employers such as Siemens, AEG, Schering and Daimler-Benz were joined by West Germany's most successful computer company, Nixdorf. A business drive aimed at attracting high-technology industries to Wedding has met with some success.

People are also encouraged to move to West Berlin. Not only does the city offer 30% lower personal taxes and other advantages, but its residents are not liable to military service. This has prompted many Greens and nonconformists to migrate to the city. They have set up a counter-culture in Kreuzberg and Neukölln, where they live in relative harmony with the large colony of Turkish workers. Berlin has a long tradition of immigration: at the end of the 17th century there was a massive influx of French Huguenots; they were later followed by Polish and Bohemian refugees.

West Berlin's diverse attractions have reversed population trends over the last five years, increasing the numbers by 50,000 to 1.9m. Over that same period, only about 30,000 new jobs were created and unemployment is higher here than in the country as a whole. Meanwhile, the rest of West Germany, put out by what it regards as the "feather-bedding" of West Berlin, waits expectantly for the next trick to be pulled out of the hat by the Berliners, famous in politics as in business for always having an eye to the main chance.

Arriving

Although most visitors from West Germany drive to Berlin, many business travellers prefer to fly there. There are scheduled flights to and from all major West German cities and about 20 world business capitals. Air passengers are not subject to East German controls. Regular but not very comfortable trains run between Berlin and Hamburg, Hanover, Frankfurt and Nuremberg. Passport control and the issue of transit visas are carried out on the train. Four *Autobahn* transit routes connect West Germany with Berlin: vehicles arriving from Hamburg (E15) enter Berlin at the Heiligensee checkpoint; those arriving from Hanover (E8), central West Germany (E63 and E6), and Nuremberg (E6) cross at the Drewitz/Dreilinden checkpoint. Drivers are advised to obey East German regulations (for example, no speeding, no hitchhikers). The speed limit, rigidly enforced, is 100km/63mph. Commercial traffic also goes by inland waterway.

Berlin-Tegel airport

Berlin-Tegel airport was originally intended to complement Berlin-Tempelhof airport, but in 1975 became the city's only civilian airport when Tempelhof was reserved almost exclusively for military use. Only six major airlines operate out of Berlin-Tegel (PanAm, TWA, British Airways, Euro Berlin, Air France and Dan Air; Lufthansa is not permitted to fly to West Berlin). There are daily services to 14 West German cities, including very frequent flights to and from Hamburg, Frankfurt and Munich. Cities served by direct international scheduled flights include Amsterdam, Brussels, Copenhagen, London, Oslo, New York, Paris, Stockholm and Zürich.

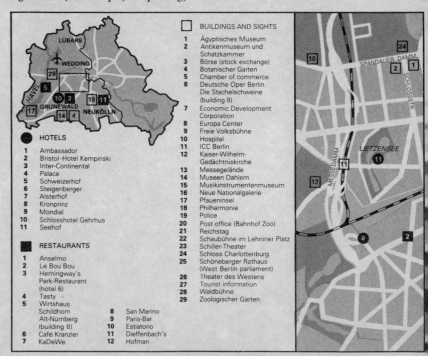

BUILDINGS AND SIGHTS
1   Ägyptisches Museum
2   Antikenmuseum and
    Schatzkammer
3   Börse (stock exchange)
4   Botanischer Garten
5   Chamber of commerce
6   Deutsche Oper Berlin
    Die Stachelschweine
    (building 8)
7   Economic Development
    Corporation
8   Europa Center
9   Freie Volksbühne
10 Hospital
11 ICC Berlin
12 Kaiser-Wilhelm-
    Gedächtniskirche
13 Messegelände
14 Museen Dahlem
15 Musikinstrumentenmuseum
16 Neue Nationalgalerie
17 Pfaueninsel
18 Philharmonie
19 Police
20 Post office (Bahnhof Zoo)
21 Reichstag
22 Schaubühne im Lehniner Platz
23 Schiller-Theater
24 Schloss Charlottenburg
25 Schöneberger Rathaus
    (West Berlin parliament)
26 Theater des Westens
27 Tourist information
28 Waldbühne
29 Zoologischer Garten

HOTELS
1   Ambassador
2   Bristol-Hotel Kempinski
3   Inter-Continental
4   Palace
5   Schweizerhof
6   Steigenberger
7   Alsterhof
8   Kronprinz
9   Mondial
10 Schlosshotel Gehrhus
11 Seehof

RESTAURANTS
1   Anselmo
2   Le Bou Bou
3   Hemingway's
    Park-Restaurant
    (hotel 6)
4   Tasty
5   Wirtshaus
    Schildhorn   8   San Marino
    Alt-Nürnberg   9   Paris-Bar
    (building 8)   10   Estiatorio
6   Café Kranzler   11   Dieffenbach's
7   KaDeWe   12   Hofman

The single terminal is compact and convenient. Its drive-in system means there is a very short distance between aircraft, passport control and the airport taxi rank and bus stop. Its facilities include currency exchange bureaux (which close just before the arrival of last flights), seven cafés and restaurants, a post office, conference rooms ☎ 41013232 and a branch of the tourist office, which runs a hotel reservation service. Airport information ☎ 41012307; freight inquiries ☎ 41011.

Nearby hotel *Novotel Berlin-Airport*, Kurt-Schumacher-Damm 202, 51 ☎ 4106-0 ⊤ₓ 181605 fax 4106 700 • AE DC MC V. Attractive modern hotel with good conference facilities, outdoor pool, sauna and solarium. Free airport shuttle service.

City link The airport is 7kms/4 miles north of the city centre, which can be reached by bus or, better, by taxi.

Taxi There are normally plenty of taxis immediately outside the main hall of the terminal. The journey into town takes about 15mins. Telephone reservations ☎ 6902, 261026, 216060 and 240202.

Limousine Limousine Service ☎ 3015040; Minex ☎ 8533091.

Car rental It is more convenient to rent a car at the airport, where Avis, Europcar, Hertz and interRent have desks, although they also have city offices.

Bus There is no airport bus. City bus No. 9 runs between the airport and the centre (Kurfürstendamm, Zoo and Budapester Strasse) but the journey is rather slow (25–35mins). Tickets (cheap) may be bought from the driver.

Railway station
Bahnhof Zoologischer Garten (almost always abbreviated to Bahnhof Zoo) is West Berlin's main

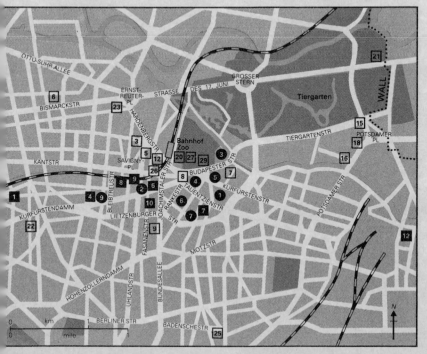

rail terminus, but still looks the suburban station it once was. Many trains continue into East Berlin and beyond, so do not be fooled by the station's appearance into thinking you have not yet arrived at your destination. Although the East German rail authorities who, paradoxically, run Bahnhof Zoo, have at last begun to renovate the terminus, it has few facilities apart from a currency exchange bureau (outside the station building) and a post office. There is a taxi rank in front of the station, and very good *U-Bahn* and *S-Bahn* train connections to all parts of the city. For those with not too much baggage, the station is within walking distance of several major hotels. Timetable inquiries ☏ 19419.

Getting around

The centre of Berlin, around the Europa Center and the eastern end of Kurfürstendamm, is where most of the major hotels are located. It is fairly compact and can be easily negotiated on foot. Outside this area you will need to take a taxi or use public transport.

Taxis Berlin has 350 taxi ranks, several big radio cab companies, little traffic congestion and taxi fares are about 15% lower than in the rest of West Germany. Radio taxis ☏ 6902, 261026, 216060, and 240202.

Limousines Limousine Service ☏ 3015040; *Minex* ☏ 8533091.

Driving Driving and parking do not present major problems although there are one-way streets. Car rental *Avis* ☏ 2611881, *Budget* ☏ 41012886, *interRent* ☏ 41013368, *Europcar* ☏ 2137097.

Walking Almost all streets are lined with trees, so walking is enjoyable except when smog periodically descends on the city. But take care to avoid the maroon cycle tracks.

Subway, bus The extensive and integrated network of fast and clean *U-Bahn* and *S-Bahn* trains and frequent buses is easy to use. You

must buy tickets, which are interchangeable, from one of the many vending machines before boarding a vehicle or from the bus driver. The simplest solution is to buy a 24hr rover ticket, valid for all forms of transport.

Area by area

West Berlin is curiously lopsided, with its centre huddled near its eastern boundary. Most of what is now West Berlin became part of Berlin only in 1920 and was still a suburb before World War II. Although now diminished as an economic force, it remains West Germany's largest industrial city and is dotted with factories and power stations. Surprisingly perhaps, one third of its large area is made up of parks, forests and lakes.

Europa Center area The modern Europa Center, an imposing business and entertainment centre, lies at the heart of Berlin's business, shopping and hotel quarter, which includes Budapester Strasse, the eastern end of Kurfürstendamm with its many cafés, and adjoining streets.

Wedding This once rather run-down industrial area of north Berlin was recently the site of a scheme to attract new high-tech businesses.

Siemensstadt An industrial district in the west, once the headquarters of the mighty Siemens and still the base of its Berlin subsidiary.

Dahlem This museum and university quarter in southwest Berlin, along with Zehlendorf, is the newly fashionable place to live.

Grunewald This western suburb, which borders on West Berlin's largest wood (of the same name), is where, prewar, the big businessmen used to live. Full of grand villas and large gardens, it is even now a much sought-after residential area.

Kreuzberg A still war-scarred district in the southeast, Kreuzberg is the centre of Berlin's thriving alternative culture, and the home of many of the city's 130,000-strong Turkish population.

Hotels

Almost all of the major hotels are clustered in the Europa Center area. There is no problem reserving rooms. All those listed here offer rooms with IDD telephones, TVs and minibars and can arrange for translation and secretarial help. Currency exchange, 24hr room service and hotel parking are commonly available.

Ambassador *DM* ////
Bayreuther Str 42–43, 30 ☎ *219020*
TX *184259 fax 21902380 or 21902199*
• *AE DC MC V* • *197 rooms, 3 suites,*
2 restaurants, 1 bar
Tucked away in a quiet side street, near the KaDeWe department store, the Ambassador is a pleasant, modern hotel with good-sized, light and bright rooms. The top-floor tropical pool, complete with exotic plants and poolside bar, is very congenial. One of its restaurants, the Conti-Fischstuben (closed Sat L and Sun), deserves its reputation as the best in the city for seafood. Hairdresser • pool, sauna, solarium, massage • 4 meeting rooms (capacity up to 200).

Bristol-Hotel Kempinski *DM* /////
Kurfürstendamm 27, 15 ☎ *884340*
TX *183553 fax 8836075* • *AE DC MC*
V • *325 rooms, 35 suites, 3 restaurants,*
1 bar
Berlin's most prestigious hotel is housed in an unexciting 1950s building and has a huge, stark entrance lobby a bit like a station concourse. But otherwise it leaves nothing to be desired. Service is good; the fairly large and traditionally furnished guest rooms (two for nonsmokers) were renovated in 1987, and equipped with hairdryers. There is a roomy piano bar with leather armchairs, as well as three excellent restaurants: the Kempinski Grill (French cuisine), the Kempinski Restaurant (local dishes; closed Mon), and the Kempinski Eck, a fashionable brasserie which spreads outside onto the Kurfürstendamm (and offers special business lunches).
Hairdresser, newsstand • pool, fitness centre, sauna, solarium, massage • 10 meeting rooms (capacity up to 600).

InterContinental *DM* ////
Budapester Str 2, 30 ☎ *26020*
TX *184380 fax 260280760* • *AE DC*
MC V • *600 rooms, 70 suites,*
3 restaurants, 3 bars
By Berlin Zoo, the city's largest luxury hotel is in typical InterContinental mould: the rooms are uniform, comfortable and unremarkable, and the service (24hr) is competent. While the international cuisine at its main restaurant, Zum Hugenotten, is appreciated by the top business people and politicians who eat there, its smallish tables are more suitable for informal discussions than for really important get-togethers. The large and airy Six Continents Lounge, by the entrance, is a favourite meeting place for local bankers. Shopping arcade • pool, sauna, massage, solarium • computer rental, 16 meeting rooms (capacity up to 2,000).

Palace *DM* ////
Europa Center, Budapester Str, 30
☎ *254970* TX *184825 fax 2626577* •
AE DC MC V • *256 rooms, 6 suites,*
2 restaurants, 1 bar
Ideally situated in the Europa Center, this up-and-coming hotel has black-and-cream rooms, variations on a pink and maroon theme in its public areas, and flowers and potted plants throughout. The main restaurant, La Réserve (D only), which offers excellent French cuisine and several set menus, has both an intimate atmosphere and well-spaced tables ideal for confidential discussions. Conference facilities are good and above all comfortable. At the end of the working day, the congenial Palace Bar attracts business people from outside. Hairdryers in rooms, telephones in some bathrooms, 24hr

room service • pool, fitness centre, sauna, massage, • 10 meeting rooms (capacity up to 800).

Schweizerhof *DM* ////
Budapester Str 21–31, 30 ☎ *26960* ⊠ *185501 fax 2696900 •* *InterContinental • AE DC MC V • 434 rooms, 26 suites, 3 restaurants, 3 bars*
Despite being one of the biggest major hotels in town, the Schweizerhof has a poky entrance lobby. Its rooms, which include special ones for women executives and nonsmokers, are not exactly large either, though their furniture (partly traditional, partly modern) and floral decor are attractive. Unless you find something romantic about the occasional roar of lions in the Zoo opposite, ask for a room at the back. The hotel's main restaurant, the Grill, which offers Swiss and Berlin cuisine and specializes in game, is a popular place for business lunches. Room service 6am–11pm. Hairdresser, shops • indoor pool, sauna, massage, jacuzzi •16 meeting rooms (capacity up to 700).

Steigenberger *DM* ////
Los-Angeles-Pl 1, 30 ☎ *21080* ⊠ *181444 fax 2108117 • AE DC MC V • 400 rooms, 29 suites, 2 restaurants, 4 bars*
Built in 1981, this new hotel is quiet and near the Europa Center. It competes with the Bristol-Hotel Kempinski for the custom of VIPs, and boasts a presidential suite with its own lift. The spacious rooms have a restful decor. Business people crowd the large Piano Bar in the evening, and the Park-Restaurant is one of Berlin's top eating places (see *Restaurants*). 24hr room service, shopping arcade • pool, sauna, solarium, massage • computer rental, 11 meeting rooms (capacity up to 600).

OTHER HOTELS
Of the other major hotels, two are located right in the city centre, one is very near the International Congress

Center (ICC) and Messegëlande, and the Kronprinz and the Schlosshotel Gehrhus have retained something of the atmosphere of prewar Berlin.

Alsterhof *DM* /// *Augsburger Str 5, 30* ☎ *219960* ⊠ *183484 fax 243949*
• AE DC MC V. A large modern hotel only 5min walk from Kurfürstendamm and the Europa Center. It has good conference facilities and an indoor pool, sauna, solarium and massage.

Kronprinz *DM* //
Kronprinzendamm 1, 31 ☎ *896030* ⊠ *181459 fax 8931215 • AE DC MC V.* The assets of this attractive hotel (built in 1894 but well-modernized) include excellent personalized service, massive breakfasts and a jolly beer-garden. It is within 15min walk of the ICC.

Mondial *DM* /// *Kurfürstendamm 47, 15* ☎ *884110* ⊠ *182839 fax 88411150 • AE DC MC V.* A moderate-sized, modern central hotel with an acceptable restaurant, and an indoor pool with solarium and massage.

Schlosshotel Gehrhus *DM* //
Brahmsstr 4–10, 33 ☎ *8262081 • AE DC MC V.* This secluded family hotel, set among spacious grounds in the Grunewald area, has kept much of the character, if not all the appurtenances, which it possessed when it used to be the Palais von Pannwitz.

Seehof *DM* //// *Lietzensee-Ufer 11, 19* ☎ *320020* ⊠ *182943 fax 32002251 • AE DC MC V.* The most convenient hotel for the ICC/ Messegeländé (5min walk), in a bucolic location overlooking a lake (Lake Lietzensee) with swans. Facilities include indoor pool, sauna and solarium.

Hotel and restaurant price guide

For the meanings of the hotel and restaurant price symbols, see pages 6 and 7.

Restaurants

Berlin restaurants are often more interested in mood and style, and staying open late, than in gastronomic perfection, so do not expect the culinary standards of, say, Munich. The most suitable places for top-flight business entertaining are hotel restaurants (see *Hotels*), especially the Steigenberger's Park-Restaurant. Except for special events, it is not normally necessary to make reservations.

Anselmo *DM* ////
Damaschkestr 17 ☎ *3233094 • closed Mon • no credit cards*
Anselmo Bufacchi's restaurant, just off the western end of Kurfürstendamm, has long been regarded as Berlin's classiest Italian restaurant. The clean, Milanese-style decor, the modern art on display and the smartly dressed clients make this a good place for not-too-formal business occasions. The cuisine is unfussy Italian at its best, and the wine list boasts, unusually, a large contingent of excellent Italian vintages.

Le Bou Bou *DM* ///
Kurfürstendamm 103 ☎ *8911036 •*
• AE MC
This high-ceilinged restaurant, round the corner from Anselmo, has a superbly austere *Jugendstil* (Art Nouveau) decor. It is a favourite lunching spot for executives from Siemens and Schering, while in the evening the candles come out and the atmosphere is more relaxed. The cuisine is a mixture of French, international and traditional German, the wine list solely French, and the service attentive.

Hemingway's *DM* ////
Hagenstr 18 ☎ *8254571 • closed Sat • AE DC MC*
This exclusive restaurant is tucked away in Grunewald. Its very individual and chic decor of white wicker armchairs, white trelliswork and a huge mirror on the ceiling is just right for a not-too-formal business celebration. The chef gives his *nouvelle cuisine* one or two interesting German touches (though the small portions are decidedly

unGerman). The wine list is excellent, and the bar congenial.

Park-Restaurant *DM* ////
Steigenberger hotel ☎ *2108855 • closed Mon • AE DC MC V*
Expect to rub shoulders with VIPs at the Park-Restaurant, the city's top restaurant for political and business entertainment. But it is as suitable for the brisk lunch as it is for protracted dining: every day a perfectly devised three-course, 60min business lunch is served. Make sure of reservations on Friday evenings for the 6-course champagne dinner (not expensive given that you can drink as much bubbly as you want). The excellent French cuisine is "modern" without being *nouvelle*, and the service impeccable.

Tasty *DM* //
Kurfürstendamm 53 ☎ *8839444 • closed Sun • no credit cards*
Don't be put off by the name or the café-like exterior; inside, you will find comfortable seats, beautifully designed chrome and marble tables, and a clientele to match: fashion designers and well-dressed business people. The French dishes on the short menu are refined and very skilfully executed, with the emphasis on seafood (especially lobster), and the wine list is short but well selected. Tasty has a high value-for-money ratio and is open from noon to midnight.

Wirtshaus Schildhorn *DM* ///
Strasse am Schildhorn 4A ☎ *3053111 • AE MC V*
Wirtshaus Schildhorn is one of Berlin's most countrified restaurants, on a peninsula jutting out into the

lake formed by the Havel river. From the outside, it looks a little like a day-trippers' café – low, half-timbered buildings, sprawling terraces, boats for rent, a jetty for river cruisers. This is deceptive, for within it is furnished with taste and offers imaginative "New German cuisine," which may explain why it is the haunt of the well-to-do and of prominent figures in the media and arts worlds. Open daily from 10am to midnight, it is ideal for off-duty relaxation.

OTHER RESTAURANTS
Berlin is packed with lively, casual places at which to eat, most of them open very late. Many of these establishments are clustered near the Europa Center. An invaluable standby for the quick business lunch is the very congenial *Alt-Nürnberg* ☎ 2614397, a basement restaurant in the Europa Center. The food is hearty and Bavarian, and the pine-panelled decor a most convincing replica of a tavern (private rooms available). Other good lunching places include the restaurant section of the historic *Café Kranzler*, Kurfürstendamm 18–19 ☎ 8826911, and the numerous luncheon bars in the department store *KaDeWe* (see *Shopping*).

One of the best of the many genuine Italian restaurants is *San Marino*, Savignypl 12 ☎ 3136086, which offers *pizze* and *calzoni* that are several cuts above average; in summer it is very pleasant to dine on the large and agreeable terrace which gives on to the quiet Savignyplatz. Not far from there is the fashionable and noisy *Paris-Bar* (not to be confused with Le Paris), Kantstr 152

☎ 3138052 (closed Sun), which has good modern art on its walls and attracts off-duty business people as well as musicians and intellectuals.

Many restaurants are closed for lunch but serve dinner until very late. Fashion-conscious yuppies like the clean white decor, temporary art exhibitions and straightforward fare at *Estiatorio*, Fasanenstr 70 ☎ 8818785. The classier western end of Kreuzberg is fast coming into fashion as a venue for relaxed dining out. Two reliable places are *Dieffenbach's*, Dieffenbachstr 11 ☎ 6945606, and *Hofmann*, Grossbeerenstr 18 ☎ 2156712, both of which offer short menus with a Mediterranean accent and are frequented by journalists, artists and other professional people.

Bars and cafés
Much informal business is done in the bars of Berlin hotels. In addition to the *Bristol* in the Bristol-Hotel Kempinski, the *Six Continents Lounge* in the InterContinental, the *Palace Bar* in the Palace, and the *Piano Bar* in the Steigenberger (see *Hotels*), there is the *Times-Bar* (open from 6) in the Savoy Hotel, Fasanenstr 9–10, one of the best cocktail bars in town, which is frequented by stockbrokers working nearby. Late diners can also sample excellent cocktails at the smart *Le Baronet*, Kurfürstendamm 190–192 (from 8). During the day, a stylish place for a rendezvous is the *Champagne Bar* on the sixth floor of the department store KaDeWe (see *Shopping*).

Berlin has many relaxed drinking places, such as the pub-like *Kneipen*. These are packed with people who sit drinking and talking through the night. In the Europa Center area it is usually quite safe to drop into any bar, even if you are a woman on your own. Worth trying are *Die Kleine Weltlaterne* (open from 8), Nestorstr 22; *Zur Kneipe* (open from 6), Rankestr 9, and *Tiago* (open during the day as well), Knesebeckstr 15.

Entertainment

Berlin's long tradition of *Kultur*, on which it rightly prides itself, has been kept alive on both sides of the Wall by generous subsidies. In some areas, political cabaret and established theatre, for example, East Berlin has the edge. But West Berlin still has a wealth of activities and several annual festivals (theatre, classical music, jazz and film). Details of all events will be found in *Tip* and *Zitty* which come out every fortnight. The agencies in the *Wertheim* or *KaDeWe* department stores (see *Shopping*) have ticket agencies or try *Wildbad-Kiosk*, Rankestr 1 ☏ 8814507.

Theatre The three established theatres are the *Schaubühne im Lehniner Platz*, Kurfürstendamm 153 ☏ 890023, the *Schiller-Theater*, Bismarckstr 110 ☏ 3195236 and, perhaps the best, the *Freie Volksbühne*, Schaperstr 24 ☏ 8813742. Many lively events are staged by West Berlin's alternative theatre groups, such as *Grips-Theater*, Altonaer Str 23 ☏ 3914004 and *Theater am Kreuzberg*, Möckernstr 66 ☏ 7851165. In order to see some political cabaret for yourself (if your German is *very* fluent) try *Die Stachelschweine*, Europa Center ☏ 2614795.

Opera, dance Under its director Götz Friedrich, the *Deutsche Oper Berlin*, Bismarckstr 35 ☏ 3410249, has become the leading venue for opera and dance. The *Theater des Westens*, Kantstr 12 ☏ 3121022, puts on some very high-class musicals. Alternative groups to see include *Tanzfabrik*, Möckernstr 68 ☏ 7865861, *Neuköllner Oper*, Karl-Marx-Str 131 ☏ 6376061, and *Die Etage*, Hasenheide 54 ☏ 6912095.

Cinema Berlin holds a March film festival and is one of the most rewarding West German cities for the dedicated filmgoer. It has some 80 cinemas, many of them art houses which show foreign films with German subtitles.

Music Musical life in Berlin is dominated by the towering figure of Herbert von Karajan, resident conductor of the world-famous Berlin Philharmonic Orchestra. They usually perform at the *Philharmonie*, Matthäikirchstr 1 ☏ 254880, a modern concert hall of unconventional design and superb acoustics. The city is also famed for its rock music and has several hundred active rock groups (for details see listings magazines). In summer, open-air performances of both classical and rock music take place at the *Waldbühne* in Ruhleben ☏ 8529056.

Nightclubs and casinos Berlin's legendary nightlife is still thriving: it boasts no less than 50 discos and a host of floor-shows (of variable quality). The more respectable discos include *Annabell's*, Fasanenstr 64 ☏ 8835220. But the really "in" place for business people who like to let their hair down after hours is *Dschungel*, Nürnberger Str 53 ☏ 246698.

There is a casino, the *Spielbank Berlin*, in the Europa Center (Budapester Strasse entrance).

Shopping

The Kurfürstendamm is commonly thought to be Berlin's top shopping street. But the really smart places to buy clothes, shoes, leather goods and so on are in adjoining streets such as Joachimstalerstrasse, Meinekestrasse, Fasanenstrasse, Uhlandstrasse and Bleibtreustrasse. The boutiques in the Europa Center are also worth exploring. Berlin has two department stores which deserve a visit, *Wertheim*, Kurfürstendamm 231, and *KaDeWe*, Tauentzienstr 21, the largest in Europe, whose staggering food department, which takes up the whole of the sixth floor, stocks some 25,000 different foods and has 22 tiny luncheon bars where you can sample the food.

Upmarket antique dealers will be found in the Eisenacher Strasse/ Motzstrasse area, in the antique market housed in the converted *U-Bahn* station at Nollendorfplatz

(closed Tue), and in Keithstrasse.
But you are more likely to find a
real bargain at the weekend flea
markets, *Trödelmarkt*, Strasse des 17
Juni, and *Krempelmarkt*, near
Potsdamer Pl.

Sightseeing

The most familiar sights of West
Berlin are not its most interesting, as
Berliners would agree. The *Kaiser-
Wilhelm-Gedächtniskirche* is a
shored-up ruin turned into a
memorial, which Berliners have
nicknamed "the lipstick and powder
compact," "the hollow tooth" and
worse. Near it stands the 90
metre/300ft-high *Europa Center*. The
broad and 3.5km/2.25 mile-long
Kurfürstendamm, or Ku'damm, is
lined with the free-standing showcases
of its many shops, groups of exotic
but docile punks posing for tourists,
and the occasional modern
monumental sculpture. The only
major building of prewar central
Berlin that is now in West Berlin is
Germany's former parliament
building, the *Reichstag*, stranded near
the wall not far from the
Brandenburg Gate and nicknamed the
"sleeping beauty." Between the
Reichstag and the Zoo lies the
Tiergarten, a vast park with many
trees, neat flowerbeds, and lakes.

West Berlin has much to offer the
art-lover, with over 50 public and
private galleries.
Ägyptisches Museum A superb
Egyptian collection which includes
the celebrated bust of Queen
Nefertiti. *Schlossstr 70. Open Sat–
Thu, 9–5.*
Antikenmuseum und Schatzkammer
A rich collection of Greek, Cretan
and Etruscan art and gold jewellery.
Schlossstr 1. Open Sat–Thu, 9–5.
Botanischer Garten One of the
largest botanical gardens in Europe,
with arboretum, mountain and steppe
vegetation and 16 glasshouses.
Königin-Luise-Str 6–8. Open daily 9–4.
Museen Dahlem A complex of eight
museums devoted to paintings,
etchings, sculpture, ethnography,

East Asian art, Islamic art, Indian art
and German folklore respectively.
*Arnimallee 23–27. Open Tue–Sun,
9–5.*
Musikinstrumentenmuseum
European and non-European musical
instruments from the 16thC to the
present. *Tiergartenstr 1. Open Tue–
Sat, 9–5; Sun, 10–5.*
Neue Nationalgalerie Designed by
Mies van der Rohe, this museum
houses a fine collection of 19thC and
especially 20thC paintings (mainly
German). *Potsdamer Str 50. Open
Tue–Sun, 9–5.*
Schloss Charlottenburg The former
summer residence of the Prussian
kings (early 18thC) contains the
famous rococo Golden Gallery and
interesting collections of arts and
crafts, porcelain and paintings.
Luisenpl. Open Tue–Sun, 9–5.
Zoologischer Garten The Berlin Zoo,
which has the largest number of
animal species of any zoo in the
world, has a notably successful
breeding record. *Hardenbergpl. Open
daily 9–7 or, in winter, until dusk.*

Suburbs

Although they live in an enclave,
West Berliners are certainly not cut
off from the countryside. Much of
outer Berlin consists of forests, lakes
and beaches, and even farmland.
Places to visit include the little old
village of *Alt-Lübars*, the *Havel* river,
the forest of *Grunewald* and the
traffic-free island of *Pfaueninsel*,
which has several 18thC and
early-19thC follies, peacocks, English-
style landscaped gardens and rare
trees. It can be reached by boat from
Wannsee *S-Bahn* station or from
Spandau.

Guided tours

Tours take anything from 30mins to
4hrs. Operators include BBS
☎ 2134077, BVB ☎ 8822063, *Severin
& Kühn* ☎ 8831015, and *Berolina*
☎ 8833131.

Boat excursions along the network
of canals, rivers and lakes are
organized by *Riedel* ☎ 6913782

East Berlin

When Berlin was divided up among the Four Powers after the last war, the heart of the city (Berlin-Mitte), where the Brandenburg Gate, Unter den Linden, and most major buildings and museums were located, became part of the eastern sector. You can go on a sightseeing trip organized by West Berlin limousine or coach operators (see *Getting around* and *Sightseeing*). These tours, lasting about 4hrs, reduce the checkpoint formalities and avoid the usual obligation to buy East German currency, but rush through the museums. If you decide to go as a pedestrian, the best crossing point is Friedrichstrasse (the terminus of *S-Bahn 3*); vehicles cross at Checkpoint Charlie. Avoid Saturday or Sunday mornings, when there can be a long wait. To cross, you need a passport, DM5 for a visa and a minimum of DM25 which is changed into East German currency and has to be spent in East Berlin. You may take Western currency with you, but you have to declare it. Your hotel will provide you with further tips and details of regulations governing your trip to East Berlin.

Sightseeing

In the 1970s, and more particularly during the years leading up to East Berlin's 750th anniversary, in 1987, the East German authorities at last began to rebuild and refurbish the many ruined public buildings and housing. After strolling up the impressively broad *Unter den Linden*, the main artery of the prewar capital, and taking a look at that hackneyed symbol of the divided city, the *Brandenburg Gate*, you should try to visit the best of East Berlin's superb museums.
Bode-Museum A rich collection ranging from Egyptian and Byzantine antiquities to coins and 14th–18thC sculpture and paintings. *Monbijou-Brücke. Open daily exc Mon, 9–6 (Thu, 9–8; Fri, 10–6).*
Pergamonmuseum One of the greatest museums of Mesopotamian, Greek and Roman antiquities in the world. It also houses impressive Islamic and Far Eastern collections. *Museumsinsel (entrance in Am Kupfergraben). Whole museum open Wed–Sun, 9–6 (Fri, 10–6); Western Asian and Architecture rooms also open Mon, 1–6 and Tue, 9–6.*
Potsdam The historic town of Potsdam, which lies in East Germany just west of West Berlin, should on no account be missed if you have a little time. It contains one of Germany's architectural gems, the rococo *Schloss Sanssouci*, built by Frederick the Great in 1747.

(including an eye-opening summer tour starting in run-down Neukölln by the Wall and traversing the city to the Havel lake), *Winkler* ☎ 3917010 and *Stern und Kreisschiffahrt* ☎ 8038750.

Keeping fit

There are fitness centres for residents in several hotels (see *Hotels*).
Fitness centres Engelbert Dörbandt, Kurfürstendamm 182–183 ☎ 8826301; *Work Out Sports*, Lützowstr 105–106 ☎ 2627017.
Squash Squash-Tennis Nord (7 courts), Wittenauer Str 82–86 ☎ 4024031; *Squash Point Siemensstadt* (8 courts), Jugendweg 5 ☎ 3823030.
Swimming Olympia-Schwimmstadion, Olympischer Pl ☎ 3040676 (open air) and *Blub*, Buschkrugallee 64 ☎ 6066060.
Tennis Preussenpark (11 courts), Kamenzer Damm ☎ 7751051.

Local resources

Business services

The major hotels listed can provide or organize most of the services you

are likely to need. Otherwise try
Bürotel Büroservice ☎ 8827031 or BDS
☎ 8029079.
Photocopying and printing Unikopie
KG ☎ 3142785.
Secretarial A.-M. Hoffmann
☎ 6025140.
Translation Übersetzen Berlitz
☎ 3239047.

Communications
Local and long-distance delivery
DHL ☎ 8315026.
Post office Bahnhof Zoo open 24hrs
(except for parcels). Tegel airport
open daily, 6.30am–9pm.
Telex and fax Fernmeldeamt 1,
Winterfeldtstr 21 ☎ 2181 open 24hrs.
Fax also at all large post offices.

Conference/exhibition centres
The ICC *Berlin*, the city's international
congress centre, built in 1979 to a
futuristic design, is not only the
world's biggest centre of its kind, but
its high-tech facilities are some of the
best in the world. They include
modular auditoria (maximum capacity
5,000), 20 halls (capacity up to 900),
80 smaller rooms, a newsstand, post
office, bank, bars, restaurants and
huge parking facilities. Adjoining the
ICC building, and under the same
management, is the *Messegelände*
(exhibition centre), whose 15 main
halls and 12 pavilions offer about
63,000 sq metres/650,000 sq ft of
display space. The congress and
exhibition centre is very conveniently
located next to the Funkturm (radio
tower) in western Berlin, at the point
where the *Autobahnen* coming
through the Drewitz/Dreilinden and
Heiligensee checkpoints join up with
West Berlin's A10 ring road.
Inquiries AMK *Berlin*, Messedamm 22,
B19 ☎ 30381.

Emergencies
Bureaux de change Late opening:
Post office, Tegel airport, 6.30–9;
Berliner Bank, Tegel airport, 8–10;
Wechselstube, Bahnhof Zoo (entrance
outside the station building), Mon–
Sat, 8–9; Sun, 10–6.

Hospitals 24hr emergency
department *Klinikum Westend,*
Spandauer Damm 130 ☎ 30351.
Medical emergency service ☎ 310031.
Dental emergency treatment ☎ 1141.
Pharmacies To find out the names
and addresses of pharmacies which
open late and at weekends ☎ 1141.
Police Main station *Polizeipräsidium,*
Tempelhofer Damm 1 ☎ 6991.

Government offices
The *Wirtschaftsförderung Berlin* (Berlin
Economic Development Corporation),
Budapester Str 1, 30 ☎ 26361,
advises on incentives available to
incoming firms, and puts out an
informative booklet called *Setting up
in Berlin (West).*

Information sources
Business information The *Industrie-
und Handelskammer zu Berlin*
(chamber of commerce),
Hardenbergstr 16–18, 12 ☎ 31801, is
a good source of information on local
business activity, and publishes a
useful brochure called *Business
Contacts in Berlin.*
Local media Berliner Morgenpost
covers financial and economic news.
But the business community's
required reading, as elsewhere in
West Germany, are *Frankfurter
Allgemeine Zeitung (FAZ)* and
Handelsblatt.
*Tourist information Verkehrsamt
Berlin* (Berlin tourist office) has
three branches: Tegel airport, open
7.30–10.30 ☎ 4101-3145; Europa
Center (Budapester Strasse
entrance), open 7.30–10.30
☎ 2626031; Bahnhof Zoo, open 8–11
☎ 3139063. The monthly *Berlin
Programm* lists entertainments, air
and train timetables, details of
museums and so on (see also
Entertainment).

Thank-yous
Wertheim and *KaDeWe* (see *Shopping*)
have the biggest choice of gifts. For
that extra-special gift, try *Present
Goldberg*, Kurfürstendamm 12, or
Kamphüs, Ansbacher Str 21.

DÜSSELDORF

City codes zip 4000 ☎ 0211

In 1946 when the British forces occupying northwest Germany amalgamated two states to create North Rhine Westphalia, Düsseldorf became its capital, to the delight of its citizens.

Düsseldorfer like to be a step ahead, in business as in day-to-day living. Appearances matter and it is no coincidence that they are among the most fashion conscious in West Germany; the Königsallee is the country's smartest boulevard for buying and showing off fine clothes. Though lacking the reassurance of a long cultural history like Cologne's, they are proud that their city was the symbol of West Germany's postwar miracle and keen to exploit its convenient location. Though the population is only 580,000, the city is responsible for around 10% of West Germany's foreign trade, enabling its citizens to earn over 20% more than the national average.

The industrial revolution gave Düsseldorf its reputation as the *Schreibtisch* of the Ruhr, the administrative headquarters of Germany's traditionally most productive industrial area; two-thirds of its 350,000-strong workforce are white-collar workers. The city's prosperity has been closely linked with the Ruhr; in the buoyant years of steel and coal output it boomed. Today the unemployment rate is higher than the national average though lower than that of the Ruhr itself.

Chemicals, machinery, steel tubing and vehicle production are the city's major industries, and Daimler-Benz, Henkel, Krupp, Salzgitter and Thyssen all have important centres there. Diversification has helped to cushion the recession in steel. Mannesmann, for instance, is now stronger in electronics than in heavy engineering. In banking and insurance, Düsseldorf trails behind Frankfurt and Cologne, though its service sector – advertising and consultancy firms – is significant. Trade fairs, mostly in capital goods, are also big earners.

More than 3,000 foreign companies have an administrative base in the city, twice as many as in Frankfurt, its nearest rival. Most are American, the next most numerous being Dutch and Japanese companies. A DM180m Japan-Center has been built and sales by some 300 Japanese enterprises, encompassing electronics, engineering and commerce, are valued at DM7bn. The city is now Japan's main European base, and about 6,000 Japanese live there. Significantly, Düsseldorf has been actively pursuing links with the Chinese, hoping to become Europe's base for China as well.

Arriving

Düsseldorf is the gateway to north Germany, with its international airport 8kms/5 miles south of the city centre. *Autobahnen* from Holland, Belgium and France join the busy German network near the city. Express trains run hourly to other major cities.

Düsseldorf-Lohausen airport
The airport, which handles nearly 10m passengers a year, half of whom are on charter flights, is Germany's third largest for freight. There are over 840 scheduled flights each week, connecting with 76 cities across four continents. The newly built terminal has two wings for scheduled flights

and one for charter. Distances between check-in and boarding are short. There is a bureau de change, open daily, 6.15am–10pm, and a bank, open Mon–Fri, 6am–10pm. Other facilities include post office, florist and hairdresser, conference and banquet rooms, and VIP lounge. Airport information ☎ 421223; freight inquiries ☎ 421551.

City link Train is the quickest means of transport into town but many business travellers take a taxi.

Taxi Cabs wait outside the terminal building. There are fixed fares to the city centre (DM16) and for the 5min ride to the NOWEA exhibition grounds (DM10).

Limousine Autohansa and Artus Buchholz have desks in the arrivals hall.

Car rental Autohansa, Avis, Europcar, interRent, Hertz and Budget have desks. Only rent a car if you plan to go out of town.

S-Bahn Trains run every 20mins to the Hauptbahnhof, journey time 13mins, and then on to Solingen-Ohligs (36mins).

Bus During fairs the No. 896 departs at 20min intervals for the NOWEA exhibition grounds 3kms/2 miles away.

Railway station

Düsseldorf Hauptbahnhof is on the east side of the city centre, a 15min walk from the main shops and business areas. Intercity services run to some 60 major European cities; these include 13 daily to Amsterdam (2hrs 40mins), 16 to Brussels (3hrs 20mins), 14 to Milan (11hrs 30mins) and 9 to Paris (5hrs 50mins). Lufthansa operates express services for its passengers to Frankfurt airport (2hrs 35mins) four times daily. Local commuter *S-Bahn* trains run to 19 stations within the city and throughout the Ruhr area.

The smart, modern station has a large central concourse lined with an impressive array of shops and cafés, a post office, bureau de change, pharmacy, florist and photocopying

service; *interRent* car rental has a desk in the centre of the concourse. Buses and trams leave from the front of the main entrance. Timetable inquiries 6am–8.30pm ☎ 58228.

Getting around

Walking within the main business and shopping area centred on Königsallee is practical, but elsewhere take a taxi or use public transport which serves the main areas and hotels efficiently.

Taxis White Mercedes taxis can be picked up at the station, airport or NOWEA exhibition grounds and there are numerous ranks in the city centre. Reservations ☎ 33333.

Limousines The main car rental firms offer limousine service. Other companies are *Auto Posern* ☎ 423666 and *Artus Buchholz* ☎ 325040.

Driving Four *Autobahnen* run into the city across the Rhein from the east. There are also two from the north and one from the south. Heavy traffic frequently causes long delays on the bridges at rush hours, 7–8.30 and 4.30–6. Parking can be difficult in the centre, although the city has 48 parking areas, several beside the Rhein, in addition to meters and hotel garages. Car rental firms include *Autohansa* ☎ 325040, *Avis* ☎ 132055, *Budget* ☎ 360401, *Hertz* ☎ 357025, *interRent* ☎ 767261; and sports cars from *Erdmann* ☎ 375827.

Walking While it is easy and safe to find one's way round on foot, distances between different areas of the city can be considerable. The Altstadt is pedestrianized.

Bus, tram and train VRR (Verkehrsverbund Rhein-Ruhr) bus, tram and *S-Bahn* train services are quite fast and frequent between the city centre, suburbs, and the NOWEA exhibition grounds. They link up with Deutsche Bundesbahn train services throughout the Rhein-Ruhr region. Train tickets on the different services are interchangeable. Single bus or tram tickets can be bought when you board, or from ticket offices.

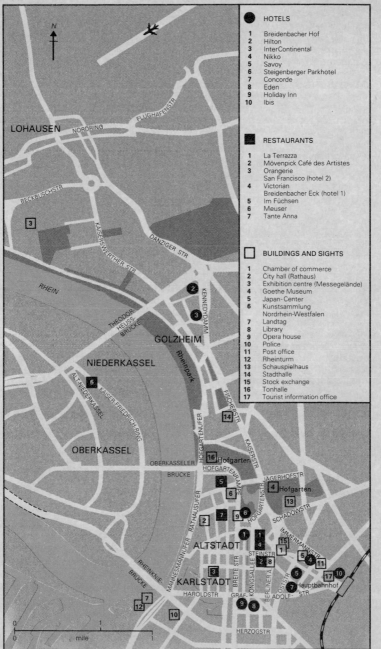

HOTELS

1 Breidenbacher Hof
2 Hilton
3 InterContinental
4 Nikko
5 Savoy
6 Steigenberger Parkhotel
7 Concorde
8 Eden
9 Holiday Inn
10 Ibis

RESTAURANTS

1 La Terrazza
2 Mövenpick Café des Artistes
3 Orangerie
  San Francisco (hotel 2)
4 Victorian
  Breidenbacher Eck (hotel 1)
5 Im Füchsen
6 Meuser
7 Tante Anna

BUILDINGS AND SIGHTS

1 Chamber of commerce
2 City hall (Rathaus)
3 Exhibition centre (Messegelände)
4 Goethe Museum
5 Japan-Center
6 Kunstsammlung
  Nordrhein-Westfalen
7 Landtag
8 Library
9 Opera house
10 Police
11 Post office
12 Rheinturm
13 Schauspielhaus
14 Stadthalle
15 Stock exchange
16 Tonhalle
17 Tourist information office

VRR 24hr passes are good value. Route maps are available from the tourist office opposite the Hauptbahnhof.

Area by area

The city centre is a 3km/2-mile area lying between the Rhein, on the west, and the main railway station. In the middle, Königsallee, the city's most famous boulevard, runs south from the extensive Hofgarten park to Graf-Adolf-Platz. The 200-year-old "Kö," as it is called, is lined with chestnut and plane trees, and smart shops and street cafés. The other main streets run parallel on either side. Postwar rebuilding followed the previous grid pattern of broad straight streets. Some old buildings were restored to their heavy Germanic style but many more were replaced by undistinguished modern buildings in the 1950s. The Thyssen headquarters, a slender mass of glass and concrete overlooking the Hofgarten park, was Germany's first skyscraper. Across the canalized river Düssel, on the western side, are the headquarters of many large companies. The city centre's business quarter is sandwiched behind them in Breite Strasse and Kasernenstrasse. Many banks cluster around Blumenstrasse, behind the Kö, to the east. Japanese businesses are concentrated on Immermannstrasse where the Japan-Center is situated.

The Altstadt, the oldest part of the city, between Heinrich-Heine-Allee and the Rhein, is a quaint pedestrianized area of narrow streets, baroque churches and old houses. It is particularly lively at night, as it is crammed with beer halls, restaurants and jazz cellars.

The suburbs

Almost a third of Düsseldorf's workforce commutes, some travelling as far as 65kms/40 miles. Close to the trade fair grounds overlooking the Rhein, Lohausen and Kaiserswerth have remained sought-after residential areas despite the airport's proximity; and Angermund is an exclusive residential area just outside the city, 8kms/5 miles north of the airport.

Japanese business people have moved in force into Oberkassel in a loop of the Rhein's west bank, while neighbouring Niederkassel has become a fashionable area for dining out.

In Golzheim, until recently farmland between the city and the airport, high-rise office blocks house insurance, computer and fashion companies.

Heavy industry is concentrated to the east of the main station in Flingern-Süd, Lierenfeld and Gerresheim. There are also large pockets of heavy industry in Derendorf and Rath, to the south and southeast of the airport, as well as on the city's southern borders at Holthausen and Benrath and on the west bank in Heerdt (ceramics).

Hotels

The city is keen to promote itself as a key business centre and has several very well-equipped hotels. Pride of place goes to the Breidenbacher Hof. The big modern hotels run by international chains are farther out, in the more recently developed business districts. The large number of foreign visitors, including many Japanese, helps to keep standards of service and prices high, especially during major trade fairs when it is essential to make reservations well in advance. The tourist office ☎ 350505 has a computer reservations service. Bedrooms usually have an IDD telephone, a minibar and multichannel TV. Most hotels offer secretarial and other office facilities. The main recommendations have 24hr room service and parking space.

Breidenbacher Hof *DM* /////
Heinrich-Heine-Allee 36, D1 ☎ *303-0*
TX *8582630 fax 1303830* AE DC MC V
• *135 rooms, 30 suites,*
3 restaurants, 2 bars
Düsseldorf's oldest and most elegant
hotel, right in the city centre, in the
banking district. The large, thickly
carpeted lobby and bar-lounge are
furnished with antiques and oil
paintings, and uniformed staff are on
hand to attend to the needs of guests,
most of whom are business people.
Rooms are individually decorated in
lavish style, with gold-leaf fittings as
well as practical details like good
lighting and spacious worktops.
Airport limousine service • 6 meeting
rooms (capacity up to 80).

Hilton *DM* /////
Georg-Glock-Str 20, D30 ☎ *4377-0*
TX *8584376 fax 4377650* • AE DC
MC V • *376 rooms, 18 suites,*
2 restaurants, 2 bars
This is the city's largest hotel, built
in 1970 and now surrounded by high-
rise office blocks. Its lobby buzzes
with business executives and showbusiness personalities, and middle-
eastern royalty make frequent use of
the top-floor suites, one of which has
a grand piano. All bedrooms are air-
conditioned and have recently been
renovated. One floor is reserved for
nonsmokers. The San Francisco (see
Restaurants) is one of Düsseldorf's
leading restaurants. Shops • pool,
sauna, solarium, massage • in-house
secretaries and translators, extra
telephone lines available, 24hr
courier, Reuters service, 14 meeting
rooms including the 1,500-seat
Rheinlandsaal.

InterContinental *DM* /////
Karl-Arnold-Pl 5, D30 ☎ *45530*
TX *8584601 fax 4553110* • AE DC MC
V • *290 rooms, 19 suites, 2 restaurants,*
1 bar
Like the neighbouring Hilton, the
InterContinental is modern and
international in style, catering mainly
to business people visiting or working
in the immediate area. The Les

Continents restaurant, with side
rooms available for small groups, is
eminently suitable for working meals,
with three- or four-course executive
menus at lunch time. The smart, long
lobby area, divided into sections, is a
useful meeting point. Hairdresser,
gift shop, newsstand, Lufthansa
check-in • pool, fitness centre, sauna,
solarium, jacuzzi, massage, 11
meeting rooms (capacity up to 400).

Nikko *DM* /////
Immermannstr 41, D1 ☎ *8340*
TX *8582080 fax 161216* • AE
DC MC V • *285 rooms, 16 suites,*
2 restaurants, 1 bar
This modern luxury hotel is in the
district where many Japanese
companies have established their
offices. Standards of service are high
and there is a comprehensive range of
business facilities including news and
share-price monitors in the large
lobby area. There is an executive
floor and 10 rooms are reserved for
nonsmokers. The Benkay restaurant
has Japanese rooms where diners sit
on the floor, as well as Western
seating and set menus. Hairdresser,
gift shop, fashion boutique,
newsstand • pool, exercise
equipment, 2 saunas, solarium,
jacuzzi, Japanese massage • 7 meeting
rooms (capacity up to 700) with
simultaneous translation facilities.

Savoy *DM* /////
Oststr 128, D1 ☎ *360336* TX *8584215*
fax 360336 • AE DC MC V
• *Günnewig* • *130 rooms, 1 suite,*
1 restaurant, 1 bar
The centrally situated Savoy appeals
to those who demand high standards
of accommodation but prefer a
smaller, more individual hotel. Its
guest rooms have considerable charm
and the comfortable bar area is very
suitable for informal business
meetings. Another useful rendezvous
is the hotel's Konditorei-café, next
door. Newsstand • pool, fitness
centre, sauna, massage, solarium
• 4 meeting rooms (capacity up to
150).

Steigenberger Parkhotel *DM* ////
Corneliuspl 1, D1 ☎ *8651* ⊠ *8582331*
fax 131679 • *AE DC MC V* • *160
rooms, 12 suites, 1 restaurant, 1 bar*
The Parkhotel overlooks the wooded
Hofgarten and is one of the city's
finest old buildings. It offers an
efficient, willing service that business
visitors clearly appreciate. Bedrooms
and extensive lounge areas were
restored to their turn-of-the-century
glory after World War II damage and
are furnished in period. Rooms have
cable TV; some also have safes and
trouser presses, and a few have
saunas. Suites have large drawing
rooms, which are ideal for private
conferences, and a second telephone
in the bathrooms. Staff will arrange
for the services of secretaries and
interpreters or the despatch of
packages. Nonsmoking rooms,
newsstand • 10 meeting rooms
(capacity up to 250).

OTHER HOTELS
Concorde *DM* // *Graf-Adolf-Str
60, D1* ☎ *369825* ⊠ *8588008*
• *Rema* • *AE DC MC V.* Small hotel
with well-equipped rooms.
Eden *DM* // *Adersstr 29–31, D1*
☎ *3891-0* ⊠ *8582530 fax 3897777*
• *Best Western* • *AE DC MC V.*
Situated close to the Kö, with newly
renovated rooms and conference
facilities.
Holiday Inn *DM* //// *Graf-
Adolf-Pl 10, D1* ☎ *38730* ⊠ *8586359
fax 3873390* • *AE DC MC V.* At the
end of the Kö, with the usual
Holiday Inn facilities, including a
pool, exercise equipment and good
conference services.
Ibis *DM* // *Konrad-Adenauer-Pl
14, D1* ☎ *16720* ⊠ *8588913
fax 1672101* • *AE DC MC V.* No-frills
accommodation in part of the main
station building; rooms overlook a
quiet courtyard.

Restaurants

It is fashionable to dine on *nouvelle cuisine* in up-to-the-minute surroundings, but many local business people prefer heartier indigenous dishes such as *Schweinshaxe*, knuckle of pork, *Sauerbraten*, a beef dish with
a piquant sauce, or cabbage with *Mettwurst* – a local sausage – served in
unpretentious beer hall restaurants. Few of the Altstadt's restaurants are
suitable for business entertaining. The main hotel dining rooms are a safe
choice and those on Königsallee are usually reliable and more lively. Reservations are strongly advised, especially during trade fairs.

La Terrazza *DM* ///
Königsallee 30 ☎ *327540* • *closed Sun*
• *AE DC MC V* • *jacket and tie*
Well-spaced tables, with trailing
plants, white wicker chairs on a
black-and-white tiled floor and
picture windows which overlook the
Kö all help to make La Terrazza a
favourite with business people. Italian
food with an emphasis on regional
and fish dishes.

Hotel and restaurant prices
For the meanings of the price
symbols, see pages 6 and 7.

**Mövenpick Café des
Artistes** *DM* ////
Kö-Galerie, Steinstr 13 ☎ *320314*
• *AE DC MC V*
The glittering modern Kö-Galerie,
which contains several restaurants, is
spread over two hexagonal floors
decked with palms and linked by a
striking perspex elevator. In a quiet
corner on the lower floor is the Café
des Artistes, which is popular with
both local business people and
shoppers. Good-value French menus
with an Italian influence change every
day depending on what is available at
market, and the wine list is
impressive.

Orangerie *DM* ////
Bilker Str 30 ☎ *131828* • *closed Sun except during fairs* • *DC* • *jacket and tie*
Serving classic *haute cuisine* in commensurately rich surroundings, the Orangerie is the place to be seen, particularly during fashion fairs. It attracts jet-setters and successful business people out for a celebratory evening. The recommended six-course menu changes every day. Less expensive menus and *à la carte* dishes are available in the Bistro section.

San Francisco *DM* ////
Hilton hotel ☎ *4377741* • *AE DC MC V* • *jacket and tie*
This restaurant is much used for business entertaining by executives from the nearby offices of international corporations such as IBM. The cuisine is American; prime rib, imported direct from the United States and carved on the trolley, is a popular choice. Four-course lunches including wine are particularly good value for money.

Victorian *DM* ////
Königstr 3A ☎ *320222* • *closed Sun and hols* • *AE DC MC V* • *formal dress*
Günter Scherrer, one of West Germany's leading chefs, created the Victorian in 1984 to meet the needs of business people: quality cuisine at the right price, an impressive wine list, efficient service and quiet surroundings. The upstairs Salon, discreet in sober Victorian style, offers a menu featuring German and French dishes, with the emphasis on *nouvelle cuisine*. A private room is available and at lunch there is a fixed-price three-course menu. Downstairs

there is a less formal Lounge restaurant. If entertaining important clients, be sure to specify the Salon when making your reservation.

OTHER RESTAURANTS
The ambience and view from the café restaurants along the Kö make them very suitable for informal business lunches. The *Breidenbacher Eck*, Heinrich-Heine-Allee 36 ☎ 8601, is as popular with executives working in the neighbourhood as with opera-goers in the evening. Its alcove seating is informal but private. *Im Füchsen*, Ratinger Str 28 ☎ 84062 is a typical brewery beer hall with rows of long, unvarnished wooden tables and tiled walls. *Meuser*, Alt-Niederkassel 75 ☎ 51572, is an old country inn on the fashionable west bank specializing in *Speckpfannkuchen* (bacon pancakes). *Tante Anna*, Andreasstr 2 ☎ 131163, housed in a 16thC building, is the city's oldest wine-cellar; straightforward Continental food and beer as well as wine are available until midnight.

Bars and cafés
The local beer is *Altbier*, a strong, dark-brown brew with a malty flavour, which is often served straight from the barrel. It is drunk in large beer halls, with stone floors and rows of bare ashwood tables. They are frequented by both managers and workers, equally attracted by a love of good beer.
    In the Altstadt, nicknamed the "world's longest bar counter," more than 200 brewery bars, restaurants, cafés and discos are concentrated in an area of about one square kilometre with not a strip club in sight. In summer large numbers of tourists join the regulars.
    The cocktail bars along the Kö are much more sophisticated than those in the Altstadt. Bankers mingle with journalists at *NT*, short for *Nachtrichten Treff*, beside newspaper offices at Königsallee 77; electronic news displays flash overhead and newspapers are provided.

Credit card abbreviations

AE	American Express
DC	Diners Club
MC	Access/MasterCard
V	Visa

Carnival

Hundreds of fancy-dress balls and other lively events take place in the weeks preceding Lent. During the last six days of the carnival season, colourful parades of decorated floats take over the streets. The main one, the Rosenmontag (Rose Monday) procession, is over 3kms/2 miles long. Spectators watch from large stands that are erected along the route and also spend a lot of time on the streets, dancing and singing in fancy dress. Sweets and other small gifts are showered from the floats. Very little serious business is done during these few days.

Entertainment

Düsseldorf's main cultural reputation is for painting and sculpture but its opera and music also attract audiences from outside the city. The Altstadt provides informal entertainment and the nightclubs around Königsallee a more sophisticated variety.

Listings appear in the monthly *Düsseldorfer Hefte*, available from newsstands, *TOP Tips* and *Düsseldorf-Führer*, available free at hotels, and in the daily newspapers. Information ☎ 11516. Opera and concert performances tend to get sold out well in advance, but the tourist office ☎ 350505 has a special allocation.

Theatre, dance, opera The *Deutsche Oper am Rhein*, Heinrich-Heine-Allee 16 ☎ 370981, has a combined Düsseldorf/Duisburg repertory company performing a wide-ranging programme (Sep–Jun), including ballet. The *Düsseldorfer Schauspielhaus*, Gustaf-Gründgens-Pl 1 ☎ 363011, has large and small theatres staging classic and modern plays. *Kom(m)ödchen*, in the Kunsthalle, Hunsrückenstr ☎ 325428, is famous for its political cabaret but a good knowledge of German is essential.

Music There are 20 concerts a month (Sep–mid-Jun), in the acoustically excellent *Tonhalle*, Ehrenhof 1 ☎ 8996123, beside the Rhein. The Düsseldorfer Symphoniker performs regularly, and leading international orchestras on occasion. Classical concerts also take place in the *Robert-Schumann-Saal*, Ehrenhof 4a ☎ 8993829, and rock concerts in the *Philips-Halle*, Siegburger Str 15 ☎ 8993679, which seats up to 6,000.

Nightclubs The smartest nightclubs are in the Königsallee area and include *Chequers Club* at No. 28 ☎ 327521 with a cabaret, and *Sams West* at No. 27 ☎ 328171.

Shopping

Düsseldorf's claim to be the smartest, most fashionable city in West Germany is reflected in its shops. The east side of Königsallee is lined with exclusive fashion shops and jewellers, antique and bookshops. Several chic new shopping arcades lead off on either side, such as the Kö-Galerie and Trinkhaus Galerie.

Along Schadowstrasse are the largest department stores and as many as 20 shoe shops. There is also a compact new shopping precinct, Carsch-Haus, under the Heinrich-Heine-Allee.

Sightseeing

In addition to glamorous Königsallee (see above), the other main area which should be explored on foot is the Altstadt. The city has a long tradition as a major art centre. Many leading artists and sculptors have taught at its art academy. Special exhibitions are staged regularly in the *Städtische Kunsthalle*, Grabbepl 4 ☎ 8991 and also in the many smaller galleries, particularly around Bilker Strasse in the Altstadt.

Goethe Museum Devoted to Goethe and his time, featuring the writer's original manuscripts. *Schloss Jägerhof, Jacobistr 2. Open Tue–Sun, 11–5; Sat, 1–5.*

Hofgarten At the end of the Kö, a huge park with ornamental gardens

and fountains. Most of the city's art galleries are around it.
Kunstsammlung Nordrhein-Westfalen State art collection, with a fine selection of modern paintings, notably works by Paul Klee but also by Pablo Picasso, Georges Braque and Marc Chagall. *Grabbepl. Open Tue–Sun, 10–6.*
Rheinturm Just by the Rhein and the parliament buildings, this new telecommunications tower has a 234-metre/768-ft high viewing platform, revolving restaurant and the world's largest decimal clock. *Stromstr 20. Open daily, 10am–midnight.*
Schloss Benrath This 200-year-old castle has recently been magnificently restored. It is 12mins by tram No. 701 from Jan-Wellem-Pl. *Benrather Schlossallee 104. Open Tue–Sun, 10–5.*

Guided tours
Bus tours depart daily at 2.30 mid-Apr–mid-Oct (otherwise Sat only) from Friedrich-Ebert-Str, opposite the Hauptbahnhof. The 2hrs 30mins tour includes a visit to the Rheinturm and a boat trip. Reservations at the tourist office ☎ 350505.

Out of town
The hilly countryside of *Bergisches Land* about 29kms/18 miles to the southeast is dotted with half-timbered houses, country inns, picturesque churches and castles. Near Solingen, *Schloss Burg* ☎ (0212) 42098 is a medieval castle with fine views over the Wupper valley and a collection of antique furniture and weapons.
Neandertal, the valley where prehistoric human remains were found, lies 18kms/11 miles east of the city; museum ☎ (02104) 31149.

Spectator sports
Horse-racing The *Grafenberg* racecourse, 5kms/3 miles out, has weekly meetings May–Oct ☎ 353666.
Ice hockey Federal League matches every week at the *Eisstadion Düsseldorf*, Brehmstr 27 ☎ 627101.
Soccer and football The home soccer team, Fortuna, plays at the

Rheinstadion, Europapl 4 ☎ 8995216. There is a strong following here for the Panthers American football team.
Tennis Exhibition matches at the *Rochus Club*, Rolander Weg 15 ☎ 623676.

Keeping fit
Details of sports facilities are available from *Sportamt* ☎ 8995204. A useful leaflet is *Tips für Freizeit-Sportler* from the tourist office.
Fitness centres The newest and most luxurious centre is the *Kö-thermen*, inside the Kö-Galerie, Königsallee 80 ☎ 139950, which even has a jogging track. Others include the *Olymp-Fitness-Center*, Tempelforterstr 47 ☎ 354664, and the *Business-Communication-Club*, Graf-Adolf-Str 92 ☎ 353229, which has exercise equipment, sauna and squash courts.
Golf West Germany's only public course (two 9-hole rounds) is *Golfplatz Lausward*, Auf der Lausward ☎ 396617; season Mar–Nov.
Ice skating *Eisstadion Düsseldorf*, Brehmstr 27 ☎ 627101.
Swimming *Wellenbad Stadtmitte* indoor pool is at Grünstr 15 ☎ 8216413. The Nikko and Savoy hotel pools are open to nonresidents.
Tennis Reservations for public courts at the *Freizeitpark*, Ulenbergstr 11 ☎ 152520 and (summer only) the *Rheinstadion* ☎ 8995216.

Local resources
Business services
Photocopying Available at department stores and the Hauptbahnhof.
Printing *Druckerei Vialon*, Ronsdorfer Str 11 ☎ 7336139.
Secretarial *Arbeitsamt Düsseldorf*, Fritz-Roeber Str 2 ☎ 8226513.
Translation *Messmer*, Hüttenstr 6 ☎ 379839. Also *Arbeitsamt Düsseldorf* ☎ 8226513.

Communications
Local delivery Taxis will deliver.
Long-distance delivery *City Cars Courier* ☎ 334471; *DHL* ☎ 49080 or

474081; *Postkurierdienst* at the main post office ☎ 19619 and *IC Kurierdienst* at the Hauptbahnhof ☎ 3680524. Also *Federal Express*, Wanheimer Str 61 ☎ 424632. *Post offices* Main post office: Immermannstr 51 ☎ 1630. *Telex and fax* At main post office.

Conference/exhibition centres
Thirty major trade fairs attracting nearly 22,000 exhibitors, over half from abroad, take place each year in Düsseldorf. They include four international fashion fairs (IGEDO), and those for footwear and catering. The boat show and DRUPA (printing and paper) are the largest of their kind in the world.

The Düsseldorf trade fair organization, *NOWEA*, Stockumer Kirchstr ☎ 45601 or 4560555 (press and information) has 15 interconnected halls with a total of 155,300 sq metres of exhibition space, plus another 58,000 sq metres/626,400 sq ft outdoors. The connected exhibition congress centre (*MKC*), between the city and the airport, includes conference rooms with capacity for up to 1,200. All have simultaneous translation facilities (6 languages) and video transmission.

The numerous other conference venues include the *Stadthalle*, Fischerstr 20 ☎ 8993806, *Philips-Halle*, Siegburger Str 15 ☎ 8993679 and the *Palais Wittgenstein*, Bilker Str 7–9 ☎ 89995781. The *Hilton* has the biggest hotel conference complex.

Emergencies
Bureaux de change At the airport, open daily, 6.30am–10pm, and at the Hauptbahnhof, 7.30am–8pm.
Hospitals Emergencies ☎ 3888989. 24hr emergency *Städtische Krankenanstatten*, Gräulinger Str 120 ☎ 28001.
Pharmacies At the Hauptbahnhof, open Mon–Fri, 8am–9pm; Sat, 8–2. The address of the nearest duty pharmacy is posted up at other times.
Police Main station: Jürgenspl 5 ☎ 8701.

Government offices
Landesregierung des Landes Nordrhein-Westfalen (state government), Haroldstr 2 ☎ 83701. The *Bezirksregierung* (district government offices) are at Cecilienallee 2 ☎ 49771.

Information sources
Business information Industrie-und Handelskammer zu Düsseldorf (Chamber of commerce), Ernst-Schneider-Pl ☎ 35571. Stock exchange: *Rheinisch-Westfälische Börse*, Ernst-Schneider-Pl 1 ☎ 8621. Central library: *Bücherei Stadtmitte*, Bertha-von-Suttner-Pl ☎ 8994399. Useful business listings appear in the sales guide available free from the *Werbeamt*, Mühlenstr 29 ☎ 8993864. The editorial offices of *Handelsblatt*, the leading business daily, are at Kasernenstr 67.
Local media The serious-minded, daily *Rheinische Post* carries extensive national and local business coverage.
Tourist information Verkehrsverein der Stadt Düsseldorf, Konrad-Adenauer-Pl ☎ 350505, opposite the Hauptbahnhof (open Mon–Fri, 8–6; Sat, 8–1). Accommodation and information office at the Hauptbahnhof (open Mon–Sat, 10–10; Sun, 4–10).

Thank-yous
Confectionery Walter Cordes, Im Kö-Karree, Königsallee 58 ☎ 80246.
Florists Numerous shops in every district. There is one at the Hauptbahnhof, open 8am–10pm; and *Blumen Muschkau* is at the airport as well as at Berliner Allee 48 ☎ 371702.
Gifts Hella B, Hohe Str 46 ☎ 132626; and from several shops in the Garsch-Hans basement, Heinrich-Heine-Allee.

FRANKFURT

City code ☎ 069

Frankfurt am Main is not the largest city in Germany, but it is the centre of German business and, in particular, the undisputed centre of banking. Albert Speer once called Frankfurt a small provincial city town but, with a population of just over 600,000, its achievement in becoming the show-case of the West German economic miracle is impressive. The establishment here of the Deutsche Bundesbank (central bank) after World War II attracted the financial community. Today, 370 banks (many of them foreign), employing a total of 42,000 people, have headquarters or offices in Frankfurt, thus earning it the obvious nickname of "Bankfurt." The city's booming stock exchange (*Börse*) is the most important in West Germany, though its turnover is far short of that of New York, Tokyo or London.

Frankfurt benefited from the partition of Germany, becoming the geo-graphical centre of the Federal Republic. Its already considerable role as a crossroads of European trade was thereby enhanced, which helps to explain its other economic successes: its Messe, one of Europe's leading trade fair centres; and its airport, which handles more freight than any other in Europe and employs over 40,000 people. It is also the home of a number of well-known companies, of which by far the largest is the big chemicals group Hoechst. Other international companies headquartered here include Metallgesellschaft, AEG (now a part of Daimler-Benz), Degussa and Philipp Holzmann. The reputation of Frankfurters for being hardworking, dour and hard-nosed is not entirely unjustified; local business people, for instance, do not like their day to be interrupted by too protracted a lunch.

For years, Frankfurt has suffered from a poor image. According to one opinion poll, 57% of its inhabitants would prefer to live somewhere else. It has been voted "Europe's most boring city" by readers of a business magazine. Yet the city council has lavished money on theatre and music and built a string of new museums along the Main river. More than 10% of the city's budget, which is partly funded by a local corporation tax, goes on culture. But Frankfurt's image is rapidly changing. A recent (1986) European Community study concluded that it is one of the most successful cities in the whole Community. The city is on the verge of a new building boom. Companies and financial organizations want to be in the centre, so the trend is to build upwards. The tallest building in Europe, the Messeturm, designed by the German/American Helmut Jahn, has already been started. When it is finished, at 250 metres tall, it will dwarf the buildings of today. By the mid-1990s there will be ten sky-scrapers of a size equal to that of "Jahn Turm." Frankfurt will then really live up to its nickname "Mainhatten."

Arriving

Frankfurt is almost exactly in the middle of West Germany. It has first-class road and rail links with the rest of Germany and with neighbouring countries. Most visitors from abroad come in via Flughafen Frankfurt Main, the second largest airport in Europe after London's Heathrow.

Frankfurt Main airport
There are regular direct flights to Frankfurt Main airport from over 200 cities worldwide. Twenty million people use the airport annually and the rapid increase in numbers which has recently caused delays has led to an accleration of the plans for a new runway and terminal. It is difficult to find porters and trolleys and there is a long walk to the baggage claim area. But the facilities of this huge three-level terminal include 36 cafés and restaurants, over 100 shops, 5 banks, 2 post offices, 2 pharmacies, a clinic (☎ 6906767 ext. 3000), a dentist's surgery (☎ ext. 3228), a nursery, 3 cinemas, one of which shows English-language films, a police station, a non-denominational chapel and a discotheque (see *Entertainment*.) The airport's Europe City Club (ECC) provides a special lounge for first-class passengers of airlines which do not have their own VIP lounge ☎ 69070314. Also available are conference rooms with catering, telephones, telex and fax ☎ 69070066/7. In 1988 the 47,000-sq metre Frankfurt Airport Centre, a business, exhibition and communications complex was opened. The special "meeting point" (arrival level section B) is a useful place for a rendezvous or from which to be collected. Airport information ☎ 6903051. Freight inquiries ☎ 6906969.
Nearby hotels Sheraton, Hugo-Eckener-Ring 15, Am Flughafen ☎ 69770 ⊤⊠ 4189294 fax 69772209 • AE DC MC V. Connected by a covered passageway with the terminal, this Sheraton is one of Europe's biggest hotels.
Steigenberger Airporthotel, Unterschweinstiege 16, F75 ☎ 69851 ⊤⊠ 413112 fax 69851 • AE DC MC V. Large hotel 5min drive from the airport near the greenery of the Frankfurter Stadtwald. Sauna and indoor pool. *Novotel Frankfurt Rhein-*

Main, Am Weiher 20, Kelsterbach 6092 ☎ (06107) 75050 ⊤⊠ 4170101 fax 8060 • AE DC MC V. Quiet, 10min drive from the airport, with sauna, indoor pool, solarium and good conference facilities.

A free minibus shuttle runs to the Steigenberger Airporthotel and the Novotel from the back end of the taxi rank to the left of the arrival level exits.
City link The airport is only 9kms/ 5.5 miles southwest of Frankfurt. *S-Bahn* trains from the station underneath the terminal to the Hauptbahnhof main station are frequent and speedy (journey time 11min), if you have little baggage, although they are crowded in rush hours. If you are heavily laden, a taxi will be more convenient although it will take longer (journey time 20–35min). Renting a car can be useful if you have out-of-town places to visit. But the excellent network of fast *S-Bahn* trains should suffice for most destinations around Frankfurt.
Taxi There are usually plenty of taxis at the various exits of the arrival level; the downtown ride costs DM30–40. For reservations call ☎ 230001.
Limousine Avis ☎ 6902777.
Car rental All major car rental firms have desks on the arrival level of Section A.
S-Bahn The journey by the two *S-Bahn* lines into central Frankfurt costs about a tenth of the taxi fare. The S15 runs about every 15min to the Hauptbahnhof, while the slightly less frequent S14 serves both the Hauptbahnhof and Hauptwache, the centre of the city.

Railway station
Frankfurt's Hauptbahnhof, which is very large and very busy, has hourly mainline train connections over 18 hours of the day with all major German cities. It forms the hub of 22 *U-Bahn* (subway) and *S-Bahn* lines, reaching the whole city, the suburbs and most of the neighbouring towns. The Hauptbahnhof is quite central,

BOCKEN-HEIM

GRUNEBURGWEG

WESTEND

BOCKENHEIMER LANDSTR.

SENCKENBERGANLAGE

KETTENHOFWEG

REUTERWEG

HOCHSTR

OPERN-PL

HAUPT-WACHE

ZEIL

HAMBURGER ALLEE

FRIEDRICH-EBERT-ANLAGE

SAVIGNYSTR

TAUNUSANLAGE

LANDSTR

MAINZER

TAUNUSSTR

ROSSMARKT

BERLINER STR

KAISER-

THEATER-PL

STR

AM HAUPTBAHNHOF

Hauptbahnhof

BASELER STR

WILHELM-LEUSCHNER-STR

SCHAUMAINKAI

UNTERMAINKAI

UNTERMAIN BRÜCKE

MAIN

ALTE BRÜCKE

ALT-SACHSENHAUSEN

SCHWEIZER STR

SACHSEN-HAUSEN

TEXTORSTR

10 km/6 miles

3 km/2 miles

9.5 km/5.75 miles

500 metres

0 metres 500
0 yds 550

	HOTELS				
1	Frankfurter Hof	4	Humperdinck	4	Goethehaus
2	Hessischer Hof		Restaurant Français (hotel 1)	5	Historisches Museum
3	Intercontinental	5	Mövenpick	6	Hospital
4	National	6	Maredo	7	Jahrhunderthalle Hoechst
5	Parkhotel	7	Dippegucker	8	Kommunales Kino
6	Savigny	8	Zum Gemalten Haus	9	Liebieghaus
7	Arabella-Hotel	9	Wagner	10	Messe Frankfurt
8	Frankfurt Plaza	10	Germania	11	Museum für Kunsthandwerk
9	Holiday Inn	11	Kanonesteppel	12	Naturmuseum Senckenberg
10	Mozart	12	Florian	13	Office of Economic Development
		13	La Posada		Opernkeller (building 1)
	RESTAURANTS	14	Tse-Yang	14	Palmengarten
		15	Kikkoman	15	Police
1	Bistrot 77			16	Post office (24 hr)
2	Da Bruno		BUILDINGS AND SIGHTS	17	Post office (main office)
	Frankfurter Stubb			18	Römerberg
	(hotel 1)	1	Alte Oper	19	Städelsches Kunstinstitut
3	Gallo Nero	2	Börse (stock exchange)	20	Städtische Bühnen
			Chamber of commerce (building 2)	21	University
		3	City Hall (Rathaus)		

but is a good 20min walk, or more, from many of the leading hotels, the Messegelände (exhibition centre) and the banking quarter. A streetcar (*Strassenbahn*), which can be picked up outside the station, passes the Messe. On the three levels of the Hauptbahnhof are a wide range of shops, many cafés and brasseries, several banks, a post office and the tourist office, which will help you find a hotel room. The rank in the forecourt usually has plenty of taxis.

There are, however, no porters and the exit is a long walk from arrival platforms. There is an interRent office in the station ☎ 291028. Timetable inquiries ☎ 19419.

Getting around
Distances between business districts in Frankfurt are too far to be covered on foot although, if you have appointments in the banking quarter and are staying at one of the central hotels, walking may be the best way

of getting around. When visiting the suburbs, take either a taxi or an *S-Bahn* train to the station nearest your destination, then a taxi from there.

Taxis Taxis are available only from outside the Hauptbahnhof, outside the major hotels or by phoning for one, which may take 10min to arrive. They become very scarce at key hours during major trade fairs and a wait of anything up to half an hour outside the Messegelände in the evening is not unusual. Radio taxi ☎ 230001, 250001, 230033 or 545011.

Limousines Limousine-Travel-Service ☎ 230492/5.

Driving There are no particular problems here except for many one-way streets and the traffic-free streets in the centre. The map in the tourist office's useful *Information and Tips for the Visitor* indicates parking facilities. All the major car rental firms have offices in central Frankfurt. *Avis* ☎ 230101, *Budget* ☎ 290066, *Europcar* ☎ 234002, *interRent* ☎ 291028 and *Hertz* ☎ 233151.

Walking is generally safe, although single women should avoid the red-light district at night around the Kaiserstrasse.

Public transport Frankfurt has an integrated and interchangeable, although confusing, public transport system of *U-* and *S-Bahn* subway trains, trams and buses. When finding taxis is a problem (see above), public transport (especially trams) can take you near your destination fairly quickly.

Buy a ticket from a vending machine at the stop before boarding. Fares vary depending on the time of day, so the simplest solution may be to buy a 24hr rover ticket valid for all forms of transport. Some maps provided by the tourist office are out of date because of extensions to the *U-Bahn* network and the phasing out of some bus and tram routes.

Area by area
The heart of Frankfurt is a compact area centred on the pedestrian square, Hauptwache. Only about 1.6kms/1 mile across, it is bordered on three sides by a string of gardens where the city walls once stood and on its south by the river Main. It was almost totally rebuilt after World War II. Some corporations are based there, but the chief business and banking quarter, along Kaiserstrasse, is a little farther to the west, towards the Hauptbahnhof. Northwest of the main station is the vast Messegelände (exhibition centre).

Westend, which is north of the city centre, is a much sought-after residential area as well as the home of many publishers, advertising agencies and computer systems companies. Up-and-coming residential areas include Bockenheim, northwest of the centre which is conveniently connected with the banking quarter by the new *U-Bahn* lines 6 and 7, and the quiet district of Bornheim northeast of the centre.

Sachsenhausen, on the south side of the river, is partly residential and partly the entertainment quarter for Frankfurters as well as for tourists.

The suburbs About half of the 400,000 people who work in Frankfurt commute daily from its extensive and often pleasant suburbs. Niederrad, on the immediate outskirts of the city south of the river, combines a new business district with an unspoilt old quarter. Similarly, Höchst, a little farther out to the west, is both the seat of the eponymous chemical giant (spelt Hoechst) and an old town with several historic buildings. To the northwest, the little town of Königstein and the fashionable spa of Bad Homburg in the Taunus hills are where many senior executives live.

Hotel and restaurant price guide
For the meanings of the hotel and restaurant price symbols, see pages 6 and 7.

Hotels

The major hotels are scattered in or near the centre, the banking quarter and the Messegelände. Between major fairs half of the city's rooms are unoccupied (and special terms can often be arranged). But during the Motor Show or Book Fair it can be impossible to find accommodation in Frankfurt itself, and prices rise steeply. Rooms then have to be sought as far afield as Bad Homburg (17km/11 miles), Darmstadt (35km/22 miles), Mainz or Wiesbaden (40km/25 miles), but road and rail connections from these towns to Frankfurt are very good.

All the main hotels listed here have IDD telephones; currency exchange is standard and parking facilities are generally available, but a charge may be made.

Frankfurter Hof *DM* /////
Am Kaiser pl, F1 ☎ *21502* ⊠ *411806 fax 215900 • Steigenberger • AE DC MC V • 360 rooms, 38 suites, 4 restaurants, 2 bars*
This is the doyen of Frankfurt's hotels (opened 1876) and undoubtedly offers the best and most comprehensive services of them all. Located not too far from the banking quarter, it provides a full range of in-house business facilities. The rooms, which are spacious and well soundproofed, are tastefully decorated in different colours. The Aperitif Bar and especially the duck-blue Lipizzaner Bar (from 5pm), which has nightly live music, are favourite spots for informal business discussions. Of the four restaurants, two, the Restaurant Français and the Frankfurter Stubb (see *Restaurants*), attract customers from outside the hotel, while the Hofgarten is a popular venue for business lunches. 24hr room service, hairdresser, newsstand • 16 meeting rooms (capacity up to 500).

Hessischer Hof *DM* /////
Friedrich-Ebert-Anlage 40, F1 ☎ *75400* ⊠ *411776 fax 7540924 • AE DC MC V • 153 rooms, 7 suites, 1 restaurant, 2 bars*
A rather stern late-40s exterior, opposite the Messegelände, conceals a hotel that ranks near the Frankfurter Hof. Customers appreciate the staff's friendly and personal service, and the fact that their room preferences are

noted down for next time. The decor of its spacious rooms is old-fashioned in the best sense. Public areas are almost museum-like in their decor, with several fine old masters, attractive prints and a collection of Sèvres porcelain as well as other antiques. The lobby bar is a favourite meeting place (from 3pm), while the other bar, Jimmy's, is one of the city's most elegant nightspots. The restaurant's well-spaced tables make for discreet business entertaining although it is too dark in the evenings for detailed negotiations. Newsstand • 11 meeting rooms (capacity up to 300).

Intercontinental *DM* /////
Wilhelm-Leuschner-Str 43, F1 ☎ *26050* ⊠ *413639 fax 252467 • AE DC MC V • 800 rooms, 64 suites, 3 restaurants, 1 bar*
Close to the banking quarter, this recently renovated hotel has two wings. Business travellers are usually accommodated in the older building overlooking the river. In return for its high prices, the hotel offers comfortable rooms and the most modern conference rooms in Frankfurt. The other side of the coin is its rather anonymous atmosphere. The Prolog/Epilog bar behind the lobby is a good place to meet. 24hr room service, hairdresser, florist, gift shop, newsstand • pool, sauna, solarium, fitness centre, massage • 9 meeting rooms (capacity up to 800).

National *DM* ////
Baseler Str 50, F1 ☎ *234841*
TX *412570 fax 234460* • *Best Western*
• AE DC MC V • *71 rooms,*
1 restaurant, 1 bar
Like the Hessischer Hof, the
National is housed in a rather
unprepossessing postwar building.
But its rooms and public areas have
antique furniture and carpets. Its
leisurely, discreet atmosphere,
friendly staff and very reasonable
prices obviously appeal to its regular
customers. The hotel is opposite the
main railway station and not very far
from the headquarters of the big
banks. The best rooms face the
back, but those overlooking the
busy station forecourt have
soundproofing. 24hr room service,
newsstand • 4 meeting rooms.

Parkhotel *DM* /////
Wiesenhüttenpl 28–38, F1 ☎ *26970*
TX *412808 fax 26978849* • *Mövenpick*
• AE DC MC V • *263 rooms, 17 suites,*
3 restaurants, 1 bar
The Parkhotel, which is as usefully
located as its neighbour, the National,
is the choice for many guests visiting
the Messe. It has two sections: the
main body of the hotel (built 1970),
for which a major renovation was
completed in 1989, and the more
exclusive Tower (built 1905 and
recently refurbished). The hotel is
notable more for its service, attention
to regular customers and comfort
than for its grandeur. There are 25
rooms for nonsmokers, and a
particularly helpful concierge. The
hotel's main restaurant, La Truffe
(closed Sat and Sun), which is highly
suitable for business entertaining, is
rather sombre but serves fine French
cuisine and remarkable wines. The
Casablanca piano bar, although

crowded, is a popular rendezvous.
Newsstand, gift shop • sauna,
solarium, exercise equipment • 13
meeting rooms (capacity up to 230).

Savigny *DM* /////
Savignystr 14–16 F1 ☎ *75330*
TX *412061 fax 7533175* • *Pullman* •
AE DC MC V • *120 rooms, 2 suites,*
1 restaurant, 1 bar
This modern hotel is tucked away in
a quiet street halfway between the
Messe and the banking quarter. Since
being taken over by Pullman in 1986,
it has been refurbished in good taste
throughout. There is a large public
area with a relaxed light grey decor,
and many of the rooms have
balconies. The restaurant is good for
business meals of a very private
nature, as sections of it can be
partitioned off. Newsstand, gift shop
• 4 meeting rooms (capacity to 80).

OTHER HOTELS
Arabella-Hotel *DM* //// *Lyoner*
Str 44–48, 71-Niederrad ☎ *66330*
TX *416760 fax 6633666* • AE DC MC
V. This modern hotel is in the new
business district of Niederrad. Its
facilities include a large swimming
pool and a jogging track.
Frankfurt Plaza *DM* /////
Hamburger Allee 2–4, F1 ☎ *79550*
TX *412573 fax 79552432* • *Canadian*
Pacific • AE DC MC V. At the top of a
skyscraper (except for reception) and
opposite the Messe, it offers the usual
facilities of a luxury hotel but has
little character.
**Holiday Inn Conference
Center** *DM* ///// *Mailänder Str 1,*
F70 ☎ *68020* TX *411805 fax 6802333*
• AE DC MC V. A 26-floor tower with
fine views, on the edge of
Sachsenhausen with extensive
conference facilities.
Mozart *DM* //// *Parkstr 17, F1*
☎ *550831* • *closed Christmas–*
NewYear • AE DC MC V. A modest,
modern and friendly hotel, in a leafy
street on the edge of the Westend
area. For those who prefer discretion
and quiet rather than business
facilities. No restaurant.

Credit card abbreviations	
AE	American Express
DC	Diners Club
MC	Access/MasterCard
V	Visa

Out of town

There are two luxury hotels near Frankfurt that appeal to those in search of relaxation in a stylish setting rather than a convenient location. *Gravenbruch Kempinski*, Frankfurt 6078/Neu-Isenburg 2 ☎ (06102) 5050 is a large hotel, set in spacious grounds, 11kms/7 miles south of the city and within easy reach of the airport by *Autobahn* (free shuttle service). It has a health farm, indoor and outdoor pools, a tennis court and excellent food at its Gourmet-Restaurant. The *Schloss-Hotel*, Kronberg im Taunus 6242 ☎ (06173) 70101 is an imposing 19thC castle-hotel, surrounded by a park with an 18-hole golf course. The rooms are large and furnished with antiques. Dining in its majestic restaurant is a memorable event. Kronberg is reached in about 20min by *S-Bahn* 4 from Frankfurt. The

Sonnenhof, Falkensteiner Str 9 ☎ (06174) 29080, although not quite in the same class, is a pleasant hotel in a very quiet location 23kms/14 miles away in Königstein. It has a pool and sports facilities.

In case you are unable to find suitable accommodation in Frankfurt, here are some suggestions in nearby towns: the *Maritim-Kurhaus-Hotel* in Bad Homburg ☎ (06172) 28051, a comfortable hotel with sauna and pool a stone's throw from the Kurpark, where guests can take the waters, and visit the casino; the *Mainzer Hof* in Mainz; and the *Nassauer Hof* ☎ (06131) 233771 in Wiesbaden, containing the best restaurant in Wiesbaden, Die Ente Vom Lehel ☎ (06121) 133666; and the *Maritim* in Darmstadt ☎ (06151) 80041, a hotel with sauna and pool, right next to the station.

Restaurants

Hotel restaurants in Frankfurt offer remarkably high standards and value for money. In addition to the Restaurant Français and Frankfurter Stubb described below, the main restaurants of the Hessischer Hof, the Parkhotel and the Savigny (see *Hotels*) are eminently suitable for business entertaining. When important fairs and exhibitions are held here, service in all restaurants may be very slow, restaurants crowded and reservations are essential.

Bistrot 77 `DM` ////
Ziegelhüttenweg 1 ☎ *614040* • *closed Sat L, Sun and 3 weeks Jun–Jul* • *AE DC MC*
In Sachsenhausen, but well away from the brash touristy quarter, Bistrot 77 is one of the best French restaurants in town. The cuisine of its Alsatian chef, Dominique Mosbach, is sensibly *nouvelle*. The top advertising executives and showbiz celebrities who dine at this restaurant like its cool, white-tiled modern decor and pleasant terrace.

Da Bruno `DM` ///
Elbestr 15 ☎ *233416* • *closed Sun (open Sun D during major fairs) and Jul 15–Aug 15* • *AE DC MC*
This restaurant has long been a

favourite with bankers (many of whom work round the corner), no doubt because of its almost club-like atmosphere. Some of the tables are set in private booths. The food is straightforward, top-quality Italian, the ambience perhaps more suitable for a business lunch than an evening out.

Frankfurter Stubb `DM` //
Frankfurter Hof Hotel ☎ *21502* • *closed Sun (open Sun D during major fairs), 3 weeks Jul and Dec 24–Jan 3* • *AE DC MC V*
This rustic cellar restaurant, with its alcoves and waitresses in traditional German costume, is very different in style from the hotel in which it is housed. It is the haunt of local

business people who like genuine German cuisine of the highest quality. In addition to Frankfurt's own herb sauce, the delicious *Grüne Sosse*, you can also sample dishes made from forgotten recipes dug up from old cookbooks.

Gallo Nero   *DM* //
Kaiserhofstr 7 ☎ *284840 • closed Sun (exc during major fairs) •* AE DC MC V
Young executives like the terrace (weather permitting) of this Italian restaurant near the Alte Oper, and the small alcove tables inside are ideal for private meetings and negotiation. Both the very good and imaginative food and the service are typically Italian.

Humperdinck   *DM* /////
Grüneburgweg 95 ☎ *722122 • closed Sat L, Sun and 3 weeks Jun–Jul •* AE DC MC V
Some find Humperdinck's a bit pretentious, but there is no denying its very high standards and its suitability for the most important occasions. Good taste prevails throughout, from the mainly French cuisine to the restful decor and occasional live classical music. There are several interesting set menus, including a special business lunch. The restaurant, which is on the edge of the Westend business quarter, is in the house where there once lived the composer Engelbert Humperdinck, who wrote *Hansel and Gretel*.

Restaurant Français   *DM* /////
Frankfurter Hof Hotel ☎ *21502 • closed Sun (except during major fairs) and Jul •* AE DC MC V *• jacket and tie*
A sumptuous golden and green decor, oil paintings, very well-spaced tables, silver tableware and legions of well-trained waiters help to make the Restaurant Français *the* place for a really important business celebration. To top everything, the French cuisine is among the best in Frankfurt, and the wine list is staggering.

OTHER RESTAURANTS
Many Frankfurt business people prefer not to linger over lunch, so they frequent quite simple restaurants. Two favourites, partly because of their convenient locations, are the *Mövenpick*, Opernpl 2 ☎ 20680, which is a cluster of different types of restaurant (including a nonsmoking one), and the *Maredo*, Taunusanlage 12 ☎ 7240795, a steakhouse on the first floor of the handsome two-towered Deutsche Bank building (from which it draws many of its customers: reservations advisable at lunchtime). A useful standby opposite the station is *Dippegucker*, Am Hauptbahnhof 4 ☎ 234947, which is more congenial than it seems from the outside and offers good, honest German fare. All these restaurants serve food continuously from noon to midnight.

For more relaxed eating out, locals often choose one of the taverns in Sachsenhausen to enjoy *Rippchen* (salted pork chops) and *Handkäs mit Musik* (cheese with onions), washed down with *Apfelwein* (*Ebbelwoi or Ebbelwei* in local dialect), a dry, almost still cider with a deceptively strong punch. They avoid Alt-Sachsenhausen (the northeast end), which is full of tourists and off-duty US soldiers, preferring instead the establishments on and off Schweitzer Strasse. These include: *Zum Gemalten Haus* ☎ 614559 and its neighbour *Wagner* (the most fashionable of all) ☎ 612565, at 67 and 71 Schweitzer Strasse respectively, and, round the corner, *Germania* ☎ 613336 and *Kanonesteppel* ☎ 611891, at 16 and 20 Textorstrasse.

For foreign food, there are two Italian restaurants worth a visit. In Westend, and frequented by the banking and advertising sets at both lunch and dinner, is *Florian*, Kettenhofweg 59 ☎ 722891. And *La Posata*, Schlossstr 126 ☎ 777274, is an atmospheric Italian restaurant only a few minutes' walk from the Messe. The best of those offering

Chinese food is *Tse-Yang*, Kaiserstr 67 ☎ 232541 and one of the newest Japanese restaurants *Kikkoman*, Friedberger Anlage 1 ☎ 4990021, which serves Washoku and Teppan, is also the most reliable.

Out of town
It is well worth going out of Frankfurt to the restaurant of the *Sonnenhof* in Königstein or to sample the superb food in three other hotels, the *Gravenbruch* at Neu-Isenburg, the *Nassauer Hof* in Wiesbaden, and the *Schloss-Hotel* in Kronberg (see *Hotels*). But for the special occasion, locals will suggest you go 13kms/8 miles south of Frankfurt to *Gutsschänke Neuhof* in Dreieich-Götzenhain ☎ (06102) 3214, a 500-year-old half-timbered manor house, with log fires, lawns and weeping willows.

Bars
The bars of the major hotels are convenient and congenial places to meet, particularly the *Lipizzaner* in the Frankfurter Hof, the *Prolog/Epilog* in the Intercontinental and the *lobby bar* of the Hessischer Hof.

Besides the cider taverns (see *Restaurants*), two pleasant meeting places in the traffic-free centre which have terraces in summer are *Volkswirt*, Kleine Hochstr 9 (from 4pm), which provides 32 excellent wines (mainly German) by the glass and is usually jammed with yuppies, and *Das Cafehaus*, Grosse Eschenheimer Str 13, which, unusually for Frankfurt, is open 6am–3am.

Entertainment
Frankfurt has a lively and varied cultural life. Most listings except film programmes will be found in the tourist office's monthly *Monatsprogramm*. Otherwise consult the local editions of *Frankfurter Allgemeine Zeitung* or the *Frankfurter Rundschau*.
Theatre, dance, opera Theatre, particularly of an experimental and

avant-garde nature, has long flourished in Frankfurt, and there is plenty for the playgoer who understands German. Of the three municipal companies (reservations ☎ 236061) based in the *Städtische Bühnen*, Theaterpl 1, the opera enjoys the highest international reputation.
Cinema Frankfurt has plenty of good cinemas, and, unusually for West Germany, shows some foreign films in their original versions. The *Kommunales Kino* is a cinema in the *Filmmuseum*, Schaumainkai 41 ☎ 2128830.
Music The *Alte Oper*, Opernpl, for many years a bomb-scarred ruin, was converted in 1981 into a multipurpose, modular hall with superb acoustics for all kinds of concerts (classical, jazz, rock), as well as conferences. Concert reservations ☎ 1340400. Many other musical events are held in the *Jahrhunderthalle Hoechst*, Pfaffenwiese, Höchst ☎ 3601244.

Frankfurt is one of Europe's main jazz centres. A number of clubs regularly feature top performers. There are frequent jazz concerts in the *Opernkeller* (the bistro beneath the Alte Oper ☎ 13400), the courtyard of the *Historisches Museum*, Saalgasse 19 ☎ 2125599, and the *Palmengarten*, Palmengartenstr ☎ 2123382.
Nightclubs and casinos It is best to avoid the second-rate and sometimes risky nightlife in the notorious red-light area in and around Kaiserstrasse, which is due to be cleaned up (or moved to the other side of town) in the near future. Frankfurt's classiest nightspot is *Jimmy's* in the Hessischer Hof (see *Hotels*). But for a little more life – and noise, in its disco section – try the jet-setters' favourite, the *Dorian Gray* ☎ 6902212 in Terminal C of Frankfurt airport.

There are two famous casinos not too far away, in Wiesbaden ☎ (06121) 526954 (private pick-up service available), and in Bad Homburg ☎ (06172) 20041; there is a frequent bus shuttle service from the southside of the Hauptbahnhof stopping on the way opposite the Messe.

Shopping

There are many large department stores as well as clothing and shoe shops in the pedestrianized Zeil, the shopping street with the highest turnover in West Germany. Fashion boutiques are in Schillerstrasse and especially Goethestrasse, though the really smart place to go is Bad Homburg. Frankfurt is renowned for its furs, and the best shops cluster around Düsseldorfer Strasse opposite the main railway station.

Sightseeing

Frankfurt's modern and largely traffic-free centre is pleasant enough, although the Römerberg, with its faithfully reconstructed 15thC houses, looks a little like a film set. Sachsenhausen has retained much of its prewar atmosphere, though its older part, Alt-Sachsenhausen, has become rather brash as a result of the tourist trade. But the lack of sights is amply made up for by the seven museums along the Schaumainkai, on the south bank of the river.

Goethehaus Goethe's birthplace (rebuilt after World War II), furnished in period, with memorabilia in the small adjoining museum, the Goethemuseum. *Grosser Hirschgraben 23. Open Apr–Sep, Mon–Sat, 9–5.50, Sun, 10–1; Oct–Mar, Mon–Sat, 9–4, Sun, 10–1.*

Liebieghaus A remarkable sculpture museum with exhibits from antiquity to the present day. *Schaumainkai 71. Open Tue–Sun, 10–5 (Wed, 10–8).*

Museum für Kunsthandwerk Arts and crafts exhibited in a beautifully designed new museum. *Schaumainkai 17. Open Tue–Sun, 10–5 (Wed, 10–8).*

Naturmuseum Senckenberg A natural history museum with an extraordinary paleontological collection. *Senckenberganlage 25. Open Mon, Tue, Thu, Fri, 9–5; Wed, 9–8; Sat, Sun, 9–6.*

Städelsches Kunstinstitut One of the world's major collections of paintings from the Middle Ages to the 20thC. *Schaumainkai 63. Open Tue–Sun, 10–5 (Wed, 10–8).*

Zoologischer Garten Founded in 1858, Frankfurt Zoo has some 700 species of animal and is widely regarded as one of the finest in the world. In the Exotarium conditions suitable for many species have been recreated. *Alfred-Brehm-Pl. Open summer 8–7, spring and autumn, 8–6, winter 8–5. Exotarium open 8am–10pm.*

Guided tours

The Ebbelwei-Express (with cider and pretzels), a converted old tram which can be boarded anywhere on its circular route, is a good way of seeing the main sights. Inquiries: *Stadtwerke Frankfurt/Main* ☎ 13682425. The *Tourist office* ☎ 2128849/51 or 2128708/9 organizes 2–3hr tours, starting from the Hauptbahnhof, the airport and the Römerberg.

Out of town

The spa of *Bad Homburg*, 17kms/ 11 miles north, with its chic boutiques, casino and park, is definitely worth a visit. Less well-known is the smaller spa *Bad Nauheim*, 36kms/23 miles north, whose 1910 buildings form a perfect example of *Jugendstil* (German Art Nouveau). The celebrated part of the *Rhein valley* from Wiesbaden to the Lorelei rock can be explored by car or on a day trip by river cruiser. Boats leave from the footbridge on Mainkai. Operator: *Köln-Düsseldorfer* ☎ 282420.

Spectator sports

Horse-racing From March to November at the *Niederrad racetrack*, Schwarzwaldstr 125 ☎ 6787018.

Soccer Eintracht Frankfurt plays at *Waldstadion*, Mörfelder Landstr 362 ☎ 678040. The tourist office's two branches also sell advance tickets.

Keeping fit

For general information on sports facilities, contact *Sport- und Badeamt* ☎ 2123565. Most of the major hotels are equipped with sports facilities.

Fitness centres United Sporting Club, Mainzer Landstr 150A ☎ 735050; *Sportstudio P&W*, Schwalbacherstr 54 ☎ 7380045.

Golf Players of a reasonable standard with their club card can play at *Frankfurter Golf-Club*, Golfstr 41 ☎ 6662318 and *Hanau Wilhelmsbad*, Wilhelmsbader Allee 32, 6450 Hanau 1 ☎ (06181) 82071. There are several courses in Bad Homburg.

Squash Squash Zentrum Ost (9 courts), Ostparkstr 25 ☎ 434756.

Swimming Many hotels have pools. The heated 50-metre-long *Garten Hallenbad Rebstock*, August-Euler-Str 7 ☎ 6311012, also has saunas and a solarium.

Tennis Waldstadion (20 outdoor courts), Mörfelder Landstr 362 ☎ 678040, or *Tenniszentrum Klüh* (2 indoor and 16 outdoor courts), Im Uhrig 29 ☎ 525118.

Local resources

Business services

The major hotels can provide or organize most of the services you will need. *Messe-Servis* ☎ 75750, caters particularly for trade fair visitors.

Photocopying and printing Photocopying facilities in the main hotels. Printing: ABC *Druck* ☎ (06196) 600521.

Secretarial Das Textstudio ☎ 288833.

Translation KERN ☎ 740821.

Communications

Local delivery Non-stop Kurier ☎ 610671.

Long-distance delivery Skypak ☎ (06107) 61066.

Post office At the Hauptbahnhof and airport Departure Hall B. Both are open 24hrs.

Telex and fax Main post office: Zeil 108 ☎ 2110; open Mon–Fri, 8–6, Sat, 8–noon. Airport reception

hall (telex only): open Mon–Sat, 8–9, Sun, 8–5.30.

Emergencies

Bureaux de change Late opening: *Deutsche Verkehrs-Kredit-Bank*, Hauptbahnhof, daily 6.30–10. Some airport banks are open daily 7–9.30.

Hospitals 24hr emergency department: *Uniklinik*, Theodor-Stern-Kai 7 ☎ 63011. Emergency doctor ☎ 79502200. Emergency dental treatment ☎ 6607271.

Pharmacies To find out pharmacies open late ☎ 11500.

Police Main station: Friedrich-Ebert-Anlage 9–11 ☎ 25551.

Government offices

Wirtschaftsförderung Frankfurt GmbH (City of Frankfurt am Main's Office of Economic Development), Grüneburgweg 102 ☎ 153080, puts out an informative booklet called *Frankfurt – Preferred by Decision-Makers*. It also provides information and gives advice to incoming firms on setting up business.

Information sources

Business information The *Industrie-und Handelskammer Frankfurt am Main* (chamber of commerce), Börsenpl 6 ☎ 21970, publishes *Metropole Frankfurt am Main* which gives a broad picture of local business activity and *Frankfurt – Das Wirtschaftszentrum* provides details of hundreds of leading companies based in Frankfurt.

Local media The *Frankfurter Allgemeine Zeitung (FAZ)* is the bible of the West German business establishment. The other locally based paper is the *Frankfurter Rundschau*.

Tourist information Verkehrsverein (tourist office) is at the Hauptbahnhof ☎ 2128849/51, open Mon–Sat, 8–9 (8–10 Apr–Oct), Sun, 9.30–8 and at Römerberg 27 ☎ 2128708/9, open Mon–Fri, 9–7, Sat & Sun, 9.30–6. Its *Information and Tips for the Visitor* is a useful booklet.

Thank-yous
Confectionery Plöger, Grosse
Bockenheimer Str 30 ☎ 20941.
Florists Blumen Beuchert, Rathenaupl

☎ 282663.
Wine merchants Frankhof (in the
Frankfurter Hof, see *Hotels*)
☎ 21502.

Messe Frankfurt

Messe Frankfurt is one of West
Germany's top three trade fair and
exhibition centres. Its fairs attract
about 1m visitors annually, rising to
2m in the years when big biennial
events are held. In addition to the
Book Fair, Fur Fair, Music Fair,
various textiles fairs and the
biennial IAA (International Motor
Show), there are many smaller,
more specialized events. Since 1980
there has been a policy of steady
investment: the *Festhalle* (built
1907) has been refurbished for use
as a conference and concert hall; the
Messe's exhibition halls are now
linked by the Via Mobile, a covered
system of travelators and escalators
almost 1km in length: and work on
Europe's highest office skyscraper, a
250-metre tower, should be
completed in time for the Messe's
750th anniversary in 1990.
Getting there At Ludwig-Erhard-
Anlage 1, F1 ☎ 75750 ⓉⓍ 411558,
the Messe is a 5–10min taxi ride
from the centre of town, the main
station, the Westend and banking
quarters. It can also be reached by
trams 16 and 19 from the main
station.

Clear signposts from the
Autobahn network direct cars to the
Messe's Rebstock parking facilities
for over 20,000 vehicles. From
there a bus shuttles to and from the
fairground. There are 3,000 parking
spaces (mostly booked by
exhibitors) in or in front of the
Messe itself.
Exhibition space The Messe's
ten exhibition halls are divided
into three self-contained sections,
so that several small fairs can be
held simultaneously. In all, there
areabout 260,000 sq metres/

2.8m sq ft of display space.
Facilities The hub of the Messe is
the recently built Tarhaus, where
the facilities include a post office, a
travel agency, a baby-minding
service, a medical centre, several
banks, and 27 bars and restaurants.
Temporary office accommodation is
available in the central Torhaus.

Conferences are an expanding
part of Messe Frankfurt's business.
There is a wide range of conference
facilities, with 42 rooms and halls,
including the Festhalle, which holds
8,000.

There are two large hotels
opposite the Messe, the Hessischer
Hof and the Frankfurt Plaza (see
Hotels). Accommodation during
major fairs is a problem, so contact
the *Messe Frankfurt Accommodation
Bureau*, Ludwig-Erhard-Anlage 1,
F1☎ 75756222 ⓉⓍ 411558 in good
time. The bureau puts out a very
useful booklet called *Hotelania
Frankfurt–Hotelania Rhein-Main*,
which lists over 500 hotels in
Frankfurt and the surrounding
Rhein-Main area.

Additional conference facilities
Two other important venues in and
around Frankfurt are: the *Alte Oper
Frankfurt*, Opernpl, F1 ☎ 13400
ⓉⓍ 412890, which has rooms for up
to 700 and a main hall with a
capacity of 2,400; and the
Jahrhunderthalle Höechst,
Pfaffenwiese 6230, F80
☎ 3601211, which has rooms for up
to 200 and a main hall with a
capacity of 2,000.

HAMBURG ·

Hamburg is both a city and one of the ten *Länder* which go to make up the Federal Republic. With 1.6m people, it is second only to West Berlin in size, and as a port its pre-eminence remains unchallenged. It is also one of the greatest concentrations of commerce in the country, and its industrial base is substantial.

Hamburg has been an important port for 800 years, although it is 104km/65 miles from the open sea on the river Elbe. A leading member of the Hanseatic League in the 14th century, in the 19th century it expanded to become Europe's gateway to the United States and Latin America. It remains important for transhipment and is one of the world's largest free ports. Blohm u. Voss is still the major shipbuilder and repairer, but the focus of engineering has shifted: Airbus Industrie's German participant, MBB, has its main plant here and Lufthansa's technical centre is at Fuhlsbüttel airport. Electronics is well established; Philips makes instruments, while Valvo, its component subsidiary, turns out silicon chips. Several international oil companies have their German headquarters in Hamburg, including BP, Conoco, Esso, Mobil, Shell and Texaco. The biggest firm is BAT, not only manufacturing cigarettes but diversifying into food processing. Another large employer in Hamburg is Unilever and its subsidiaries, making toiletries and cosmetics.

Forty per cent of Germany's magazines and newspapers are published in Hamburg, including *Stern*, *Der Spiegel* and *Bild-Zeitung*, and two leading record labels, Deutsches Grammophon and Polygram, have manufacturing plants locally.

Industrial activity is supported by excellent research facilities. There are three universities – Hamburg, Hamburg-Harburg technical university and that of the federal armed forces – in addition to DESY, Germany's nuclear physics centre. Bio-technology and lasers, oceanography, timber and soil sciences and process technology are just some of the wide range of disciplines that are researched by Hamburg institutions.

Unemployment is above the national average at 12%. Industrial growth has not matched decline because of containerization at the docks and the loss of shipbuilding contracts. Yet trade and industry have an international outlook: 200 US and 100 Japanese companies have their German headquarters here. Indeed, Hamburg sees itself as Germany's window on the world.

Arriving

Hamburg is the communications centre of northern Germany and is well served by road, rail, air and sea. Euroroutes E3 and E4 (*Autobahnen* A1 and A7) from the south meet at Hamburg and continue into Scandinavia. Euroroute E15 (*Autobahn* A24) brings traffic from Berlin and eastern Europe. Just south of the city is Maschen, site of one of the largest railway marshalling yards in Europe.

Hamburg-Fuhlsbüttel airport
A DM350m upgrade of the present

airport is in progress and this may cause some disturbance. The terminal facilities are relatively limited for the airport of a city of Hamburg's size.

The main terminal is reserved for international services and an adjoining one is for domestic flights. There are only two air jetties so passengers are usually bussed between terminal and aircraft. Clearing the airport takes 20–30mins on average. The Deutsche Bank bureau de change is open daily, 6.30–10.30pm. Shops and stalls include a post office, hairdresser and florist. The duty-free shop is small but well stocked. Passenger inquiries ☏ 5082557 or 5082558, freight ☏ 5082639 or 5082699.

Nearby hotel Airlines Hotel, Zeppelinstr 12, H63 ☏ 505043 • AE MC V. About 800 metres from the airport.

City link The airport is 8km/5 miles north of the city centre and a taxi is the quickest way to get into town.

Taxi There are ranks outside each section of the terminal with cabs usually waiting. However, the ranks officially close at 11pm. The fare to the centre is around DM25 and the journey takes about 20–30mins, depending on traffic.

Limousine Avis Chauffeur-Drive ☏ 6700309.

Car rental Auto-Hansa, Avis, Europcar, Budget, Hertz and interRent all have desks near international arrivals. Renting a car makes sense if your appointments are in the outer suburbs.

Bus There are bus stops outside each section of the terminal. The Airport-City-Bus leaves every 20mins for the Hauptbahnhof (journey 35mins), stopping at Hamburg Messe (trade fairs) and Atlantic-Hotel among other places en route. The fare is DM8.

Credit card abbreviations	
AE	American Express
DC	Diners Club
MC	Access/MasterCard
V	Visa

Train and subway The Airport Express (no. 110 bus) runs every 10min to Ohlsdorf station, with *S-Bahn* and *U-Bahn* connections to the centre. A through ticket costs DM3.10 and the total journey time is 30–35min. The last bus to connect leaves the airport at 11.14pm.

Railway stations
Hamburg has two main stations. Direct hourly services run to the main Ruhr cities and to Cologne (4hrs), Frankfurt (4hrs 30mins), Mannheim (5hrs 20mins) and Munich (7hrs 20mins). There are also important connections with Berlin and East Germany and with Scandinavia. Inquiries ☏ 19419 for both stations.
Hauptbahnhof The station is on the eastern side of the inner city zone. Originally the main station, the Hauptbahnhof is now primarily used for suburban lines, although intercity trains stop at platforms 11–14. Facilities include two bureaux de change, a hotel reservations desk, an interRent counter and several shops and stalls. There are taxi ranks on both sides of the building and two *U-Bahn* stations.
Altona This extensive, modern station is the main terminus, well to the west of the inner city. Facilities include information office, bureau de change, florist, tobacconist, refreshment stall, cafeteria, newsstands, shoe repairer and department store. It is also a motor rail loading point.
Dammtor The station for the Congress Centrum, with both *S-Bahn* and mainline connections. Many intercity trains stop here.

The Landungsbrücken
The passenger landing-stages in the St Pauli district are used for local river services and for the car ferry to and from England. Within the ticket hall are an information office, bureau de change, refreshment stalls and restaurants. Landungsbrücken station has both *S-Bahn* and *U-Bahn* services. Inquiries ☏ 313977.

Getting around

Hamburg's well-organized public transport system provides an easy and convenient method of getting around.

Taxis The cabs are all beige, usually Mercedes, and must be picked up at a rank or ordered by telephone. At peak times, try the ranks at the Hauptbahnhof; otherwise call *Autoruf* ☎ 441011, *Hansa* ☎ 211211, *Radio Taxi* ☎ 6562011 or *Taxiruf* ☎ 611061.

Limousines *Richter* ☎ 666670, *Telecar* ☎ 249141.

Driving Traffic is rarely very congested but finding the way is not always easy. Three concentric ring roads are signposted to avoid the city centre, but at most times of the day it will prove quicker to select a direct route. The main car rental companies have offices in the city including *Avis* ☎ 341651, *Europcar* 244455, *Hertz* ☎ 230045, *interRent* ☎ 362221 and *Budget* ☎ 5082305.

Walking The inner city is best covered on foot. It is generally quite safe, with the exception, particularly at night, of the St Pauli and St Georg districts.

Public transport *U-Bahn* and *S-Bahn* both come under the Hamburger Verkehrsverbund (HVV). There are three fare zones; ticket machines display the fares to most points and give change. Tickets, which can also be bought from bus drivers, are valid for transfers between bus, train and subway.

Plans of the train and subway network are displayed at all stations. There are three *U-Bahn* and six *S-Bahn* lines, with trains every 10mins to all parts of the city. In the late evening you may be troubled by drunks; certain station passageways are especially hazardous. Inquiries ☎ 322911.

Area by area

The residential and business centres of Hamburg are concentrated to the north of the river Elbe, and the port occupies the southern bank where the river divides into two. This district is called Harburg. The inner suburbs around the Alster lake are the most prestigious.

Innenstadt The city centre, and chief business and shopping centre, lies between the river Elbe and the old city wall. It is split in two by the river Alster, with the Altstadt on the east and Neustadt on the west. The Binnenalster and the "Fleete" network of canals lend a Venetian flavour to the district. Little remains of the old city, save in areas such as Peterstrasse, with its brick and half-timbered houses.

The restored stock exchange on Adolphsplatz is the focus of the financial sector, and insurance and other commercial companies cluster around the Hauptbahnhof.

The most striking feature of the shopping district is the attractive network of *Passagen*, covered arcades where people can stroll, protected from traffic and the weather; the Alster arcades, lit by old-fashioned lanterns, date from the last century, while others, such as the Hanse-Viertel complex with its glass barrel roof and cupolas, are much more recent.

St Pauli and St Georg These two areas, respectively to the west and east of the city centre, exemplify the libertine atmosphere often unjustly attributed to the city as a whole. The main streets, the Reeperbahn and Steindamm, otherwise known as *Sündige Meile* (mile of sin), blaze with neon at night, offering all forms of lively entertainment from sex shows and nightclubs to the famous Hansa variety theatre.

Pöseldorf is a trendy part of the high-class residential area, Harvestehude, on the west of the Alster lake. Stylish boutiques, art galleries, discos and restaurants now occupy former sheds and stables centred on the Pöseldorf market.

Eppendorf, around the head of the lake, has attracted many quality shops and restaurants although it is not as affluent as Pöseldorf.

Uhlenhorst, on the eastern side of the

lake, traditionally the "wrong" side, is nevertheless a select middle-class residential area and the base for the activities of many sailing and rowing clubs.

Altona The DESY nuclear research centre is here but it is mainly residential and, along the Elbchaussee, are some of the most expensive mansions with grounds in the city.

The outer suburbs

Blankenese The former fishing village of Blankenese is built on a steep and wooded hillside, 14kms/9 miles west of the centre. It has been taken over by affluent commuters who have built splendid villas and gentrified the fishermen's cottages, but the old centre retains an attractive, rustic atmosphere.

City-Nord This area of high-rise office blocks about 5kms/3 miles north of the city centre dates from the mid-1960s. More than 20 distinctive complexes house multinational companies such as BP, IBM, Hoechst, Esso, Shell and Texaco, altogether giving employment to some 2,000 people.

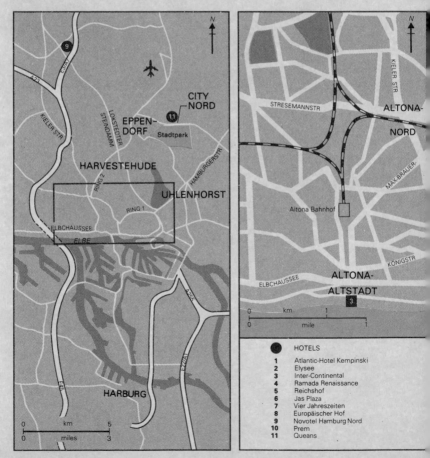

	HOTELS
1	Atlantic-Hotel Kempinski
2	Elysee
3	Inter-Continental
4	Ramada Renaissance
5	Reichshof
6	Jas Plaza
7	Vier Jahreszeiten
8	Europäischer Hof
9	Novotel Hamburg Nord
10	Prem
11	Queans

Hotels

In a city where international tourism is not highly developed, most hotel clients are business people. Recently there has been expansion at the top end of the scale and one hotel, the Vier Jahreszeiten, is ranked among the best in the world.

All of the main hotels listed have TVs and IDD telephones in the guest rooms and provide currency exchange and parking.

Atlantic-Hotel
Kempinski [DM] ////
An der Alster 72, H1 ☎ *28880*
TX *2163297 fax 247129* ● *AE DC*
MC V ● *265 rooms, 13 suites,*
2 restaurants, 2 bars
Built at the beginning of the century

by the Alster lake, the Atlantic was originally intended to attract the North Atlantic luxury liner business and resembles "a glittering ocean liner at anchor." Its spacious lobby and public rooms are in a grand style, and its clients include political figures

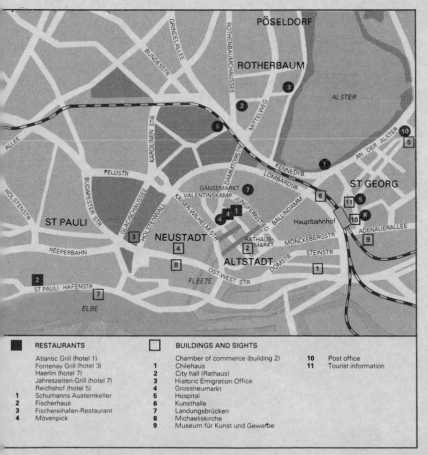

RESTAURANTS

Atlantic Grill (hotel 1)
Fontenay Grill (hotel 3)
Haerlin (hotel 7)
Jahreszeiten-Grill (hotel 7)
Reichshof (hotel 5)
1 Schumanns Austernkeller
2 Fischerhaus
3 Fischereihafen-Restaurant
4 Mövenpick

BUILDINGS AND SIGHTS

Chamber of commerce (building 2)
1 Chilehaus
2 City hall (Rathaus)
3 Historic Emigration Office
4 Grossneumarkt
5 Hospital
6 Kunsthalle
7 Landungsbrücken
8 Michaeliskirche
9 Museum für Kunst und Gewerbe

10 Post office
11 Tourist information

and leading business people. The corner bar, called Atlantic Mühle, and both restaurants overlook the Alster (see *Restaurants*). There is a new atrium bar. The suites are all overlooking the lakeside and all of the elegantly furnished guest rooms have well-equipped bathrooms and video. 24hr room service, florist, gift shop, boutique, hairdresser, newsstand • pool, health club, massage, solarium; tennis and squash at a nearby club • 15 meeting rooms (capacity up to 300).

Elysee   *DM* ////
Rothenbaumchaussee 10, H13
☎ *414120* ⊤Ⓧ *212455 fax 41412733*
• *AE DC MC V* • *300 rooms, 6 suites,*
2 restaurants, 2 bars
This modern hotel has achieved wide popularity since its opening in 1985. Half the guests are here for business purposes and the remainder are in Hamburg as tourists. They appreciate its light and streamlined decor as well as the brasserie and *Stube* which provide informal meals. 24hr room service • pool, sauna, jacuzzi, massage • 6 meeting rooms (capacity up to 750).

InterContinental   *DM* /////
Fontenay 10, H36 ☎ *414150*
⊤Ⓧ *211099 fax 41415186* • *AE DC*
MC V • *284 rooms, 6 suites,*
3 restaurants, 1 bar
The efficient 12-floor Inter-Continental stands in a quiet street at the edge of fashionable Pöseldorf. Its spacious entrance hall is flanked by a small shopping arcade. There is a large ballroom and conference facilities are available on the tenth floor. The comfortable bedrooms, decorated in pastel shades, have cable TV. On the top floor are the well-regarded Fontenay Grill (see *Restaurants*) and the Hamburg casino. 24hr room service, Lufthansa check-in, gift shop, shoe shop, men's outfitters, newsstand, hotel transport • pool, health club, massage, solarium • business centre, 9 meeting rooms (capacity up to 450).

Ramada Renaissance   *DM* /////
Grosse Bleichen, H36 ☎ *349180*
⊤Ⓧ *2162983 fax 34918431* • *AE DC*
MC V • *204 rooms, 7 suites,*
1 restaurant, 1 bar
The Renaissance is modern, but constructed in traditional Hamburg brick, blending into the adjacent Hanse-Viertel shopping arcade. The public rooms are furnished in sombre style; in contrast, the bedrooms are pleasantly light and spacious. One whole floor is given over to the Renaissance Club which has its own check-in service and lounge. 24hr room service, newsstand • sauna, massage, solarium • 5 meeting rooms (capacity up to 200).

Reichshof   *DM* ///
Kirchenallee 34–36, H1 ☎ *248330*
⊤Ⓧ *2163396 fax 24833588* • *AE DC*
MC V • *294 rooms, 6 suites,*
1 restaurant, 1 bar
The Reichshof, run by the third generation of the founding family, is right opposite the Hauptbahnhof. It has a fine Edwardian-style exterior and a spacious marble reception and lounge area. Rooms come in three grades: business rooms are the best appointed, with larger TV, desk and additional seating; economy rooms have TV, radio, shower and minibar. The most spacious bedrooms are at the front. Useful restaurant for casual meals (see *Restaurants*). Gift shop, newsstand • 12 meeting rooms (capacity up to 150).

SAS Plaza   *DM* /////
Marseiller Str 2, H36 ☎ *35020*
⊤Ⓧ *214400 fax 35023333* • *SAS* • *AE*
DC MC V • *549 rooms, 21 suites,*
2 restaurants, 2 bars
The 32-floor Plaza is the biggest hotel in Hamburg. Well served by public transport, it is only a few metres from Dammtor station. It is in a complex which includes the Congress Centrum Hamburg and draws many of its clients from there. Two floors are reserved for nonsmokers, and all guest rooms are comfortable and

newly furnished in modern style. Extras include video. 24hr room service, hairdresser, gift shop, newsstand • pool health club, jacuzzi, sauna, solarium, • Business centre, 9 meeting rooms (capacity up to 700).

Vier Jahreszeiten *DM* /////
Neuer Jungfernstieg 9–14, H36
☎ *34940* ⊤ *211629 fax 3494602*
• *AE DC MC V* • *170 rooms,*
4 restaurants, 2 bars
This top-class hotel, with its white façade, looks out over the inner Alster lake. Founded in 1897 by Friedrich Haerlin, it is now run by the third generation of the Haerlin family. The six-floor building is on a triangular site with an inner courtyard; outer rooms are mainly doubles and inner ones singles. The Vier Jahreszeiten is furnished throughout in 19thC style, with chandeliers, ormolu clocks, dark paintings and tapestried chairs. The impressive function rooms include the appropriately named Gobelin-Saal, which is lined with fine tapestries. The Haerlin and Jahreszeiten-Grill

are both notable (see *Restaurants*). 24hr room service, newsstand, hairdresser • 5 meeting rooms (capacity up to 120).

OTHER HOTELS
Europäischer Hof *DM* //
Kirchenallee 45, H1 ☎ *248171*
⊤ *2162493 fax 24824799* • *Golden Tulip* • *DC MC V*. Opposite the Hauptbahnhof. Comfortable, if a little unimaginative.
Novotel Hamburg Nord *DM* ///
Oldesloer Str 166, H61 ☎ *5502073*
⊤ *212923 fax 5592020* • *MC V*.
Modern, low-rise hotel on the north side of the city, next to *Autobahn* exit Schnelsen-Nord.
Prem *DM* //// *An der Alster 8–10,*
H1 ☎ *241726* ⊤ *2163115*
fax 2803851 • *AE DC V*. Much smaller than the nearby Atlantic. Popular with business people although lacking business facilities.
Queens *DM* /// *Mexikoring 1, H60*
☎ *6305051* ⊤ *2174155 fax 6322472*
• *AE DC MC V*. Well-equipped modern hotel, adjacent to the City-Nord office complex.

Restaurants

Hamburg is famous for its seafood, although no fish now come from the river Elbe because of pollution. Some fish restaurants beyond the city limits are well-known but, generally, the best restaurants are in the main hotels. Reservations are advisable.

Atlantic Grill *DM* ////
Atlantic Hotel ☎ *28880* • *AE DC MC V*
• *jacket and tie*
The Atlantic hotel's main restaurant, with views across the Alster lake, has a relaxed atmosphere which appeals to both business and private patrons. The menus are seasonal, with an emphasis on fish dishes.

Fontenay Grill *DM* ////
Inter-Contintental Hotel ☎ *443430 or 414150* • *closed Sat L* • *AE DC MC V*
• *jacket and tie*
This relatively small restaurant is much used for high-level business entertaining. Classic French food and some superb Bordeaux wines.

Haerlin *DM* /////
Vier Jahreszeiten Hotel ☎ *34940* •
closed Sun • *AE DC MC V* • *jacket and tie*
The elegant Haerlin restaurant offers a wide choice of international *haute cuisine*. Well-spaced tables, gilt mirrors and bronze-coloured carpets are set off by white walls. It is eminently suitable for top-level business entertaining and a fixed-price lunch menu is available.

Jahreszeiten-Grill *DM* //
Vier Jahreszeiten Hotel ☎ *34940* • *AE DC MC V*
The linen napkins and fine china clearly indicate that this is not the

average *Stube*, though the rustic furniture and oak fittings are in style. The menu is similar to that of the Haerlin, but the atmosphere is more relaxed and less ostentatious. Prices are also lower.

Reichshof *DM* ///
Reichshof Hotel ☎ *248330* • *AE DC MC V*
The Reichshof is not suitable for high-level entertaining, but it is well used by business people generally. One of its virtues is a gallery which is divided into a series of private rooms; another is that the full menu is available continuously between noon and midnight. The food is international.

Schümanns Austernkeller *DM* //
Jungfernstieg 34 ☎ *346265 or 345328*
• *closed Sun and hols* • *no credit cards*
• *reservations essential*
More than a century old, Schümanns is known for its unusual layout. It consists entirely of booths and private rooms seating up to 30, with names such as "Dutch Room" or "Hunter's Room" and with antique furnishings to match. The menu is German and the wines are mainly white.

OTHER RESTAURANTS
There are dozens of good eating places all over Hamburg. *Fischerhaus*, St Pauli-Fischermarkt 14 ☎ 314053, heads the list of fish restaurants. Farther along the river at Grosse Elbstrasse 143, the *Fischereihafen-Restaurant* ☎ 381816, with a fine view of the port, is just as popular. In the centre of town, in the basement of the Hanse-Viertel, is the Mövenpick which features four different theme restaurants: *Mövenpick, Café des Artistes, Backstube* and *Weinkeller* ☎ 351635.

Hotel and restaurant price guide
For the meanings of the hotel and restaurant price symbols, see *Symbols and abbreviations* on pages 6 and 7.

Bars
Bars range from elegant cocktail establishments to down-to-earth *Kneipen*. The cocktail bars in the main hotels – notably *Hansa Kogge* (Inter-Continental), *Simbari* (Vier Jahreszeiten), *Noblesse* (Ramada), *Piano Bar* (Reichshof) and the *Atlantic-Bar* (Atlantic) – are all suitable for drinks in the early evening. For the beer connoisseur, the *Börsen Treff*, Alten Wall 36, opposite the stock exchange, serves ten beers from the wood, and is quiet enough for informal business discussions. There are half a dozen casual bars on and near the Grossneumarkt, and the Eppendorf area is worth exploring for good *Kneipen*.

Entertainment
Hamburg offers classical music and drama performed to the highest standards (as well as less exalted entertainment in the Reeperbahn area). Many events are detailed in the monthly *Hamburger Vorschau*, which can be obtained from the tourist information offices at Bieberhaus am Hauptbahnhof (Kirchenallee exit), at the airport (Ankunftshalle D) and at the St-Pauli-Landungsbrücken 3. Tickets can be reserved from theatres and the following ticket agencies: *Collien*, Eppendorfer Baum 25 ☎ 483390, *Gerdes*, Rothenbaumchaussee 77 ☎ 453326, *Schumacher*, Colonnaden 37 ☎ 343044.
Theatre, dance, opera Out of some 40, the three main theatres are *Deutsches Schauspielhaus u. Malersaal*, Kirchenallee ☎ 248713, opposite the Hauptbahnhof, and *Thalia-Theater*, Raboisen 67 ☎ 322666, both with a repertoire of serious drama, but to enjoy performances a good understanding of German is needed; and the *Hamburger Kammerspiele*, Hartungstr 9 ☎ 445162, which puts on lighter plays. The *Hamburgische Staatsoper* ☎ 351555, one of the world's leading opera houses, is located at Grosse Theaterstrasse. It

also stages performances by the Hamburg Ballet company. Variety shows with international acts are presented at the *Hansa-Theater*, Steindamm 17 ☎ 241414. The *Operettenhaus* ☎ 27075270, in the Reeperbahn, stages popular musicals.

Cinema Two downtown cinemas offering feature films are *Broadway* in Gerhofstrasse ☎ 343175, and *Metropolis* in Dammtorstrasse ☎ 342353, both near the Gänsemarkt. The *Amerika-Haus*, Tesdorpfstr 1 ☎ 4106292, shows American films in the original version. *The British Council Film Club* has shows (2–5) at Rothenbaumchaussee 34 ☎ 446057. There are many *Sex Kinos* in St Pauli and St Georg.

Music Concerts are regularly given by Hamburg's three resident orchestras – the Symphoniker, the Philharmonisches and the Sinfonie – at the *Musikhalle*, Karl-Muck-Pl ☎ 346920. Jazz is played mostly in *Kneipen* and small clubs. There are regular jazz, rock and pop concerts at *Fabrik*, Barnerstrasse ☎ 391563.

Nightclubs and casinos The main districts for nightlife are St Pauli and St Georg. It is important to take care here: leave valuables in the hotel safe, do not go alone, carry money in small denominations, order your own drinks and pay for them on receipt. Less risky are the other nightlife areas: Pöseldorf, Eppendorf and Grossneumarkt, which is only an 8min walk from the Rathausmarkt and has plenty of cheerful bars and bistros in which to absorb the local atmosphere.

The only licensed casino in Hamburg is in the InterContinental Hotel (other places are only fruit machine halls). It is open 3pm–3am and a passport is required. Roulette, baccarat and blackjack are played. Stylish discos include the one in the Vier Jahreszeiten Hotel and *Blue Satellite*, on the 26th floor of the Hamburg Plaza Hotel.

Shopping

The main shopping area is in the city centre. The big department and clothing stores such as *C & A, Hennes u. Mauritz, Horten, Jäger & Mirow, Karstadt* and *Peek u. Cloppenburg* are along the Mönckebergstrasse, the wide street that runs from the Hauptbahnhof to Rathausmarkt. Across the Alster from the Rathaus is Neustadt, where you will find smaller, individual shops as well as *Alsterhaus*, an upmarket department store. *Schüler* is a men's tailor trading from an old-fashioned shop in the Alsterarkaden. The network of *Passagen* makes this area popular for window shopping.

Sightseeing

Leaflets and maps are available from tourist offices see *Information sources*). A free booklet, *Where to go in Hamburg*, is published monthly.

Historic Emigration Office This part of the Museum für Hamburgische Geschichte (Hamburg history museum) contains the names of all who emigrated to the USA via the port of Hamburg between 1850 and 1914. For a fee, any ancestors can be traced and details supplied of their journeys. *Holstenwall 24. Open Tue–Sat, 10–1, 2–5.*

Kunsthalle One of the most important collections in Germany, covering European art comprehensively to the 20th century. Of major interest are the world-famous 14thC altar paintings and the works from the German Romantic movement. *Glockengiesserwall. Open Tue–Sun, 10–5.*

Michaeliskirche This landmark, near the port, is considered to be the finest late-baroque church in north Germany. *Krayenkamp 4C. Open daily, 9–5.30 (summer); Mon–Sat, 10–4, Sun, 11.30–4 (winter).*

Museum für Kunst und Gewerbe The art and industry museum has a large collection of medieval, oriental and Islamic art. Also rooms furnished in *Jugendstil* (Art Nouveau). *Steintorpl. Open Tue–Sun, 10–5.*

Port The port (*Hafen*) covers 100 sq km/39 sq miles and has berths for 500 ocean-going ships along 39km/24 miles of quayside. Guided tours (see below) depart from near the Landungsbrücken.

Rathaus The late-19thC city hall is a splendid example of the Nordic Renaissance style. It contains the seat of the Hamburg Senate and the city administrative offices. It has 647 rooms, including a series of noteworthy ceremonial halls. *Rathausmarkt. Open Mon–Fri, 10–3; Sat–Sun, 10–1; tours in English hourly.*

Other notable buildings The curiously-shaped ten-floor office block in Burchardplatz, known as the *Chilehaus*, was built in the 1920s. The *St Pauli Elbtunnel*, constructed in about 1910, was featured in the film *The Odessa File*; this twin tunnel runs from near the Landungsbrücken into the free port area. Descent and ascent at each end is in cages for both people and vehicles (open non-stop).

Guided tours
Boat trips *Alster Touristik* ☎ 341141 or 341145 operates sightseeing boats from Jungfernstieg on the Alster lake and canals from April to October. *HADAG Line* ☎ 37680024 and other operators run tours (1hr) around the port; *English Cruise* ☎ 564523. Point of departure for all trips is St-Pauli-Landungsbrücken.
Bus tours *Jasper* ☎ 22710610, and others, operate 2hr or 2hr 30min bus tours of the city.

Spectator sports
Horse-racing The German Derby and other racing and showjumping events are held at the *Klein Flottbeck* racecourse, Derby Pl, Baron-Voght-Str 59 ☎ 828182, and trotting races at the *Trabrennbahn Am Volkspark*, Luruper Chaussee 30 ☎ 894004.
Soccer Hamburg's most famous team, HSV, plays at the *Volksparkstadion*, Sylvesteralle ☎ 837001.
Tennis The *Club der Alster* courts in Rothenbaum ☎ 445078 are used for the German open championships.

Keeping fit
Detailed advice on sports facilities may be obtained from *Hamburger Sportbund* ☎ 41211.
Fitness centres About 60 clubs in Hamburg offer fitness training, bodybuilding, sauna, solarium and even martial arts, all open to visitors. The Atlantic, Plaza, Inter-Continental, Elysee and Ramada hotels, in that order of preference, have fitness centres open to nonresidents.
Golf The most attractive course is the *Hamburger Golf-Club Falkenstein*, In de Bargen 59 ☎ 812177. The *Golf-Club auf der Wendelohe*, Oldesloer Str 251 ☎ 5505014, is open to nonmembers.
Squash Recommended clubs in the suburbs are *Squash-Hof*, Cuxhavener Str 66 ☎ 7962079, *Squashland*, Barsbütteler Str 33 ☎ 6530017, and *Squash Rackets Center*, Hans Henny Jahnweg 63 ☎ 2205519.
Swimming The best equipped public pool is the *Alster Schwimmhalle*, Ifflandstr 21 ☎ 223012. Also recommended are the *Bismarckbad*, Ottenser Hauptstr 2 ☎ 397601, and *Holthusenbad*, Goernerstr 21 ☎ 474754.

Local resources
Business services
Most of the larger hotels provide or will arrange photocopying and other business services. *Rent-an-Office*, Schauenberger Str 15 ☎ 3281080, can provide furnished or unfurnished offices for rental periods from a few hours to several weeks, supported by secretarial, telex and fax services.
Photocopying and printing *Fix Fotokopien* at Mönckebergstr 11 ☎ 324709 is the most central. *G.F. Scharlau* has a shop at Hühnerposten 14 ☎ 231313 and three other branches. *Copyshop*, Grindelallee 132 ☎ 443679, also has a fast printing service.
Secretarial *Hamburg City Büro Service* at Spalding 1 ☎ 231175; *Multi-Büro-Service* at Billstr 30 ☎ 784449; both open Mon–Fri.

Translation Büro R.K. Lochner, An der Alster 26 ☎ 244654.

Communications
Local delivery Courier Express ☎ 6770011, *Der Kurier* ☎ 291919. *Long-distance delivery* DHL ☎ 55410, XP ☎ 501212, *Federal Express* ☎ 5082941, TNT ☎ 7320626 and *World Courier* ☎ 505055 have offices at the airport.
Post office Main office at Hühnerpostern 12 ☎ 2395224. The office in Hauptbahnhof is open 24hr.
Telex and fax City Büro Service ☎ 231175, Mon–Fri.

Conference/exhibition centres
The *Congress Centrum Hamburg* (CCH) at Dammtor ☎ 35690 comprises 17 air-conditioned halls of different sizes. On the other side of the Botanical Gardens is the *Messegelände*, Jungiusstr 13 ☎ 35691, exhibition grounds with 13 halls. The biggest fair held there is the annual German international boat show.

Emergencies
Bureaux de change Deutsche Verkehrs-Kredit-Bank upstairs in the Hauptbahnhof is open daily, 7.30–10; it provides emergency cash on all credit cards.
Hospitals Nearest to the centre is *Allgemeines Krankenhaus St Georg*, Lohmühlenstr 5 ☎ 248801. Emergency doctor ☎ 228022. Emergency dental service ☎ 11500.
Pharmacies Police stations or the emergency doctor can advise on pharmacies that open late. Foreign drugs are stocked by *Internationale Apotheke*, Ballindamm 39 ☎ 335333 and *Roth's Alte Englische Apotheke*, Jungfernstieg 48 ☎ 343906. Both are near Jungfernstieg station.
Police Headquarters at Beim Strohause 6 ☎ 2838520.

Government offices
Hamburg Tourist Board at Burchardstr 14, H1 ☎ 30051-0 is the first source of general guidance on business matters in Hamburg. *Behörde für*

Wirtschaft, Hans-Ulrich Witt, Alter Steinweg 4, H11 ☎ 34912427 is the local department of trade and industry. The *Behörde für Wissenschaft u. Forschung*, Hamburger Str 37, H76 ☎ 291881 deals with science and research. Neither of these bodies handles promotions or liaison, which are the responsibility of the chamber of commerce.

Information sources
Business information The *Handelskammer Hamburg* (chamber of commerce) is in the stock exchange (part of the Rathaus) at Adolphspl 1, H11 ☎ 361380.
Local media Hamburger Abendblatt has the best local business coverage. The national daily, *Die Welt*, has a local section on Hamburg. The regional radio and TV organization, NDR, broadcasts from Hamburg.
Tourist information The main tourist information office is in Bieberhaus, opposite the Hauptbahnhof ☎ 30051-245. The counter in the Hauptbahnhof itself operates a hotel reservations service ☎ 30051-230. Other tourist offices are at the airport ☎ 30051-240, at Hanse-Viertel ☎ 30051-220 and St-Pauli-Landungsbrücken 3 ☎ 30051-200.

Thank-yous
Chocolates Paulsen, Poststr, sells fine chocolates.
Florists Blume Eppendorf, Eppendorfer Baum 20 ☎ 474793, is a high-class florist with three other branches. *Blumen Gaworski*, Lübecker Str 85 ☎ 252918, is well-established.
Gifts Möhring, Neuer Wall 25–31 ☎ 376040, has a wide selection of gifts; credit cards are taken.
Wine merchants Cordx Stehr, Mohlenhofstr 3 ☎ 337961, and C.C.F. *Fischer*, Hahntrapp 2 ☎ 366924.

MUNICH (München)

City code ☎ 089

If you ask Germans where, if they had to move, they would most like to live and work, Munich comes top of the list. The city is a cultural and economic magnet. The beautifully restored architecture, the choice of theatre, music, art galleries, restaurants and shops, and the nearby Alps all give Munich a head start. The dynamic Franz Josef Strauss, Bavaria's minister-president for 15 years until his death in 1988, lobbied tirelessly to bring in leading-edge industries, and helped to create a city that is go-ahead as well as attractive.

Munich's success dates back over a century to when the Wittelsbach kings promoted education and science; the technical university was founded in 1868 and later a great scientific library and museum, and the German patent office. Mechanical and electrical engineering, alongside brewing and insurance, became Munich's chief industries. Siemens, BMW and MAN had plants here before World War II, and Siemens moved its headquarters from Berlin to Munich in 1945, bringing suppliers in its wake. Later BMW concentrated its operations on Munich. Today, major companies in the city include aerospace specialists Deutsche Airbus and MBB, and Motorola and Texas Instruments in the field of electronics, as well as much of Germany's software industry. At the research complex at Garching 4,000 scientists and technicians work with some of the world's most powerful experimental hardware. In manufacturing output, Munich is now the top city in Germany, and the insurance giants, Allianz and Münchener Rückversicherung (or Munich Re), with their vast investment funds have helped make the city a major financial centre. Additionally, Munich leads in Germany's softer industries, notably fashion, advertising, printing and publishing, and the country's biggest film studios, Bavaria-Film, are also located here.

Tourism is a big revenue earner, particularly since the 1972 Olympics, and Munich is an important venue for congresses and trade fairs. The city has invested heavily in infrastructure to serve its population of nearly 1.5m. The problem now is an acute shortage of office and industrial space. A new business park is being developed in north Munich, and fully equipped small-business 'nurseries' are being created in a run-down pocket of the city, but the long-term solution lies with the closure in 1991 of the existing airport to which the exhibition centre and several of the breweries will move, releasing valuable inner-city sites. This is typical of Munich's ambitious and far-sighted approach. Yet underneath the glitter, the old Munich is still very much alive, with its Fasching (carnival), Oktoberfest and seasonal markets.

Arriving

Munich is Germany's second busiest airport in scheduled passenger volume, after Frankfurt. There are direct international flights from 70 cities world-wide, and domestic links with 15 cities are excellent, with about 20 flights a day from Frankfurt. The main Intercity railways from Hamburg, the Rhein-Ruhr area and Frankfurt terminate here, and five *Autobahnen* converge.

Munich airport (Riem)

The 1939-built airport, which is 8km/5 miles east of the city, is too small. It will be closed in 1991 and replaced by a new, larger one at Erding, 30kms/20 miles northeast of Munich. Departing and arriving passengers use separate buildings. On arrival, immigration and customs clearance takes 10–40mins. In the arrivals hall there are information desks for Lufthansa and general flight information, and a city tourist office (*Fremdenverkehrsamt*) which provides a hotel reservations service. The bureau de change is open daily, 7.30–10. A snack bar is open daily, 7–12. The departure building has more extensive and better facilities including a large restaurant and two smaller adjoining ones. In addition, there are four snack bars open daily, 4.30am–9pm. Several airlines have lounges and there is a choice of shops, with a modest duty-free section. Airport information ☎ 92110. Freight inquiries ☎ 92118528.

City link For the short ride into the centre a taxi is best.

Taxi The journey takes 15–25mins and the fare is DM20–25. There are always cabs outside the terminal.

Car rental It is not worth renting a car unless you have appointments in the industrial suburbs. Hertz, Avis, Europcar and several German firms have desks at the airport.

Bus and train. A shuttle bus service between the airport and the Hauptbahnhof, which takes about 25mins, leaves every 15mins or so, 6–9.30 (airport), 5–9 (Hauptbahnhof). The fare is DM5.

Railway stations

München Hauptbahnhof This is a terminus for many Intercity routes from northern and central Germany, and trains to and from Italy and Austria stop here. There are almost hourly services to many central and southern German cities. The station has a restaurant, shops, a DB (Deutsche Bundesbahn) travel centre, city tourist office, Bavarian state travel agency and bureau de change with a Eurocard cash dispenser. Taxis are plentiful and there are ranks and bus and streetcar stops in front of the main exit. An underground concourse of shops leads to the *U-Bahn* and *S-Bahn* station. Timetable inquiries ☎ 592991.

Bahnhof München-Pasing A busy junction in the western suburbs where Intercity trains from Stuttgart and the Rhein stop. It is also served by four *S-Bahn* lines.

Getting around

The city is large and distances between centres of activity are considerable. In the Altstadt (part of which is pedestrianized) and within the government and banking districts it is practical to walk between appointments. If venturing farther afield take a taxi (expensive) or get to know the excellent public transport system; a map and timetable can be obtained from the city tourist office at the Hauptbahnhof or most bookshops. All public transport has an interchangeable automated ticket system. A 24hr unlimited ticket covers a 10kms/6-mile radius; cost DM6.50.

Taxis can be picked up at one of 150 ranks (identified on easily available street maps) or called ☎ 21611 (24hr). Note that some drivers are *Gastarbeiter* (foreign workers) or students, with a hazy knowledge of the city.

Driving Traffic flows freely at most times, except on Friday afternoons. The fast outer city ring road links all five *Autobahnen*. Driving in the Altstadt is not recommended. There are parking facilities, many multilevel, particularly west of the Altstadt, off Sonnenstrasse. Car rental: *Avis* ☎ 12600020, *Budget* ☎ 223333, *interRent* ☎ 557145.

Walking The city centre, formerly a haunt of prostitutes, is now safe at all hours, but along Goethestrasse and on the western edge of the city, sex clubs and hookers are much in evidence.

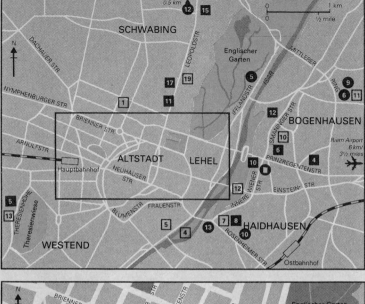

HOTELS		3	Chesa Rüegg	2	Asamkirche
		4	Da Pippo	3	Chamber of commerce
1	Bayerischer Hof	5	Le Gourmet	4	Deutsches Museum
2	Continental	6	Käfer-Schänke	5	Europäisches Patentamt
3	Königshof		Königshof (hotel 4)	6	Frauenkirche
4	Palace	7	La Piazzetta	7	Gasteig
5	Park Hilton	8	Preysing-Keller	8	Haus der Kunst
6	Sheraton	9	Sabitzer	9	Hofbräuhaus
7	Vier Jahreszeiten	10	Tai Tung	10	Hospital
8	An der Oper		Restaurant (hotel 7)	11	Hypo-Bank building
9	Arabella	11	Bistro Terrine	12	Landtag
10	City Hilton	12	Bogenhauser Hof	13	Messegelände
11	Eden-Wolff	13	Kay's Bistro	14	Michaelskirche
12	Holiday Inn	14	Die Kulisse	15	Nationaltheater
13	Penta	15	Pizzeria Italy	16	Neues Rathaus
		16	Extrablatt	17	Police headquarters
	RESTAURANTS			18	Residenz
			BUILDINGS AND SIGHTS	19	Siegestor
1	Aubergine			20	Theatinerkirche
2	Boettner	1	Alte and Neue Pinakothek	21	Tourist information

Subway and rapid transit The *U-Bahn* (white 'U' on blue sign) and the *S-Bahn* (green 'S' on white) use the same stations in the centre, with *S-Bahn* routes running east-west between the Hauptbahnhof and Ostbahnhof (by a large industrial zone to the east). The *U-Bahn* routes run mainly north-south, with interchanges onto the *S-Bahn* at the Hauptbahnhof Karlsplatz, Marienplatz and Ostbahnhof. An important new route links the centre with residential Bogenhausen and the office and hotel complex at Arabellapark, to the northeast.

The *S-Bahn* lines run out to commuter towns and industrial areas, roughly within a 35km/22-mile radius. *U-Bahn* inquiries ☎ 238030; *S-Bahn* inquiries ☎ 557575.

Streetcars and buses Strassenbahnen (streetcars) are slow and generally to be avoided.

Area by area

The city owes its present shape to the post-1945 policy of re-creating its historic form. There are no skyscrapers and office and hotel development has had to find space where it can, often in outer districts. Most of the city lies west of the small river Isar but, with improved public transport, business, hotels and entertainments are spreading to east-bank Bogenhausen and Haidhausen.

City centre The Altstadt (old town), with its narrow winding streets and buildings dating from the Middle Ages to the Renaissance, is still defined by three ancient gates and a ring road following the old walls. In the centre is a pedestrianized area around Marienplatz, where beautiful old churches and public buildings blend with shops, restaurants and *Bierkeller*. The main shopping street, Kaufingerstrasse, and its continuation, Neuhauser Strasse, run west to the Karlstor and Karlsplatz (or Stachus), the hub of city traffic. Running north from Marienplatz, another traffic-free shopping street, Theatinerstrasse, leads into the main

north-south axis, Ludwigstrasse, flanked by formal public buildings as far as the Siegestor which looks like a triumphal arch.

To the east of Marienplatz a maze of narrow streets, now being restored to create studios and boutiques, surrounds the famous Hofbräuhaus beer hall. Just north of this is Maximilianstrasse, Munich's most exclusive shopping street, which runs east from the Residenz palace and opera house, past the very grand Vier Jahreszeiten hotel, to the Bavarian parliament building across the Isar.

Business districts Business is scattered throughout the city, although traditionally the banking, insurance and professional district is the area west of Ludwigstrasse. The headquarters of Siemens is also here, in Wittelsbacher Platz, and the striking dark-blue steel and glass complex of the Landesbausparkasse (LBS) is on Oskar-von-Miller-Ring. Other prestigious addresses are Barer Strasse, Brienner Strasse and Jägerstrasse. Some of the best restaurants and nightclubs, as well as the Continental hotel, are on or near Maximiliansplatz; to its south, Promenadeplatz, with the elegant Bayerischer Hof hotel, has some of the oldest private banks.

Another business and administrative area is the Lehel, the former Jewish quarter between the Altstadt and the river, where the fairly narrow streets are lined with ornate late-19thC houses. Several state government offices are here, including the Staatsministerium für Wirtschaft und Verkehr (Ministry of Economics).

Across the river, on the far side of Bogenhausen, an important new development is under construction at Arabellapark. Already completed are the Sheraton and Arabella hotels, a conference centre, the startlingly modern high-tech headquarters of the Hypo-Bank (now the tallest building in Munich) and many other office blocks.

Schwabing This is Munich's Latin quarter. North of the Siegestor, Ludwigstrasse becomes tree-lined Leopoldstrasse with pavement cafés; the university, Academy of Arts, boutiques and small theatres are all here, as well as an increasing number of businesses and many restaurants. In the quiet side streets are sought-after 19thC apartment houses, once occupied by artists and writers such as Thomas Mann.

Theresienwiese and Westend On the west side of the city is the Theresienwiese, site of the annual Oktoberfest. Next to it is the Messegelände (exhibition centre), and the surrounding district is home for many foreign workers. The city council is rejuvenating the area with small enterprise zones and townscaping.

The suburbs

The most exclusive inner suburb is Bogenhausen, across the Isar. Haidhausen, just south of it, is being gentrified and is the site of an impressive new cultural complex, the Gasteig. Nymphenburg, near the royal palace, is another desirable residential area a couple of miles to the west.

Many executives live farther out, particularly in Grünwald to the south, or along the *S-Bahn* line to Starnberg or in the suburbs beyond the airport.

Industrial areas Industry is spread right around the perimeter and along the main railway lines. Siemens' main plant is at Obersendling in the south, but it also has works at Neuperlach in the southeast and at Freimann in the north, and it is building a big new plant at Poing in the northeast. Also at Freimann is the Euro-Industriepark. At Karlsfeld in the northwest are MAN and MTU; Junkers and Krauss-Maffei are at Allach in the west, and BMW is near the Olympiapark in the north of the city. New industries are being established in the northern corridor of the two *Autobahnen* to Landshut and Ingolstadt, both important industrial centres.

Hotels

The 1972 Olympics gave a great boost to Munich's hotel building; there then followed a lull, but new hotels are opening again, particularly in the northeast around Bogenhausen. In the city centre a handful of long-established German-owned hotels with both charm and cachet dominate the scene.

All rooms in the hotels listed have bath or shower, an IDD telephone and TV. Most hotels offer exchange facilities for major currencies. Parking is not a problem.

Bayerischer Hof/Palais Montgelas *DM* ////
Promenadepl 2–6, M2 ☎ *21200*
Ⓧ *523409 fax 2120906* • *AE DC MC V* • *440 rooms, 45 suites, 3 restaurants, 4 bars*
This busy hotel is one of the hubs of Munich's social and commercial life. At the edge of the Altstadt, the main hotel has a postwar façade, but the adjoining neo-classical Palais Montgelas was acquired in 1969 and lavishly restored to provide palatial reception rooms. The public areas are furnished with antiques and tapestries, and the bedrooms have recently been luxuriously renovated, those facing south over the square are best. The Grill restaurant is very popular as a business lunch venue, and the Palais-Keller serves Bavarian food. There is also a nightclub and a theatre (the Kleine Komödie). Hairdresser, beauty salon, gift shop, jeweller, newsstand, fashion boutiques, fur shop, travel agents

• rooftop pool, solarium, sauna, jacuzzi, massage • 17 meeting rooms (capacity up to 1,280), 11 other banqueting rooms.

Continental *DM* ////
Max-Joseph-Str 5, M2 ☎ *551570*
☒ 522603 fax 55157500 • Royal Classic • AE DC MC V • 135 rooms, 12 suites, 3 restaurants, 1 bar
The 'Conti,' convenient for the business district has been substantially renovated. The accent is on understated luxury and attentive service, and regular guests include big names in fashion, finance and industry. The rather utilitarian architecture is well disguised with antiques, paintings, tapestries and oriental rugs and the larger guest rooms are elegant, often with wood panelling or fabric-covered walls. All have video with a choice of English or German films, and 80% look onto a grassy courtyard. The Kaminrestaurant has a big open fire and there is a garden restaurant for summer dining, as well as the rustic Tiroler Stuben. Hairdresser, florist, newsstand • 4 meeting rooms (capacity up to 200).

Königshof *DM* ////
Karlspl 25, M2 ☎ *551360* ☒ *523616 fax 55136113 • AE DC MC V • 97 rooms, 9 suites, 1 restaurant, 1 bar*
The Königishof, on Munich's busiest square, close to the Altstadt and Hauptbahnhof, more than compensates for its undistinguished exterior with *trompe-l'oeil* panelling, leather seating and much gilt. This decor extends to the guest rooms (which vary widely in price according to size and comfort) but not to the bar or to the restaurant, which is one of the best in Munich. Rooms have air conditioning and soundproofing. 4 meeting rooms (capacity up to 100).

Palace *DM* ////
Trogerstr 21 (corner Prinzregentenstr), M80 ☎ *4705091* ☒ *528256 fax 4705090 • AE DC MC V • 67 rooms, 6 suites, 1 restaurant, 1 bar*

Opened in September 1986, this is one of Munich's newer luxury hotels, in Bogenhausen, a 7min drive from the airport and 8min from the city centre. It has grandeur on an intimate scale, with marble floors, classical statuary and spotless white decor, and has already established a reputation. International musicians are among the regular guests. Most of the rooms overlook a central courtyard and are decorated in pastel colours. Some suites have a private sauna. 24hr room service • terrace with solarium and jacuzzi, exercise equipment, massage • 6 meeting rooms (capacity up to 100).

Park Hilton *DM* ////
Am Tucherpark 7, M22 ☎ *38450 ☒ 5215740 fax 38451845 • AE DC MC V • 480 rooms, 21 suites, 3 restaurants, 1 bar*
Built in 1972 and refurbished in 1987, this is probably now the best Hilton in Europe. Just a 10min drive from the centre, it has superb views, proximity to the lovely Englischer Garten and access to all of the suburbs using the ring road. The lobby with its tapestries, mirrors and gilding is undeniably flamboyant, but the pastel decor of the guest rooms is more restful, and the suites range in style from Laura Ashley to Royal Bavarian. All of the rooms have scenic views either to the Alps or over river and parkland. 24hr room service, hair and beauty salons, boutiques, newsstand, gift shop, medical centre, shuttle-bus to the city • pool, sauna, solarium, massage, gym, free loan of golf clubs, other sports available locally • Courier, 9 meeting rooms (capacity up to 1,000).

Credit card abbreviations	
AE	American Express
DC	Diners Club
MC	Access/MasterCard
V	Visa

Sheraton *DM* /////
Arabellastr 6, M81 ☎ *92640*
TX *522391 fax 916877* • *AE DC MC V*
• *650 rooms, 3 restaurants, 2 bars*
This 22-floor tower is in the rather
bleak Arabellapark complex, about a
10min drive or subway ride from the
airport and the city. The rooms are
pleasant and functional, and it has
extensive conference facilities.
Nightclub, hairdresser, shops, Avis
desk • pool, sauna, exercise room •
10 meeting rooms.

Vier Jahreszeiten *DM* /////
Maximilianstr 17, M22 ☎ *230390,*
TX *523859 fax 23039693* • *Kempinski*
• *AE DC MC V* • *345 rooms,*
20 suites, 3 restaurants, 1 bar
The Vier Jahreszeiten is the grandest
hotel in Munich and there has been
some necessary refurbishment of its
time-honoured decor. On the city's
most exclusive shopping street,
conveniently close to the opera house
and national theatre, its original
mid-19thC frontage has been carefully
preserved and its softly lit, panelled
lounge is a society haunt. The best
bedrooms overlook the Residenz. The
service is civilized and welcoming.
The famous restaurant is not for
everyday eating (see *Restaurants*), but
the cheaper Bistro-Eck is popular for
business lunches. The ornate private
rooms are better for receptions than
conferences. Hairdresser, gift shop,
newsstand, Lufthansa check-in desk •
pool, sauna, massage, exercise
equipment • 10 meeting rooms.

OTHER HOTELS
An der Oper *DM* // *Falkenturmstr*
10, M2 ☎ *2900270* TX *522588* • *AE*
DC MC. A small hotel with
comfortable, modern rooms and a
good restaurant.
Arabella *DM* ///// *Arabellastr 5,*
M81 ☎ *92321* TX *529987*
fax 92324449 • *AE DC MC V.* A 300-
room tower near to the Sheraton,
adjoining the congress centre. Pool
and exercise centre.
City Hilton *DM* ///// *Rosenheimerstr*
15, M 80 ☎ *48040* TX *529437*
fax 48044804 • *AE DC MC V.* New
Hilton in Haidhansen, 10mins walk
from the centre.
Eden-Wolff *DM* //// *Arnulfstr*
4–8, M2 ☎ *551150* TX *523564*
fax 55115555 • *AE DC MC V.* Big,
comfortable hotel beside the
Hauptbahnhof. Rooms vary widely in
price; the best are away from the
street and station. Well-equipped
meeting rooms.
Holiday Inn *DM* //// *Leopoldstr*
194, M40 ☎ *381790* TX *5215439*
fax 3617119 • *AE DC MC V.* North of
Schwabing, near the ring road and
Nuremberg *Autobahn.* Pool and usual
Holiday Inn facilities. There is a
cheaper Holiday Inn in Sendling,
near the Siemens plant.
Penta *DM* ///// *Hochstr 3, M80*
☎ *4485555* TX *529046 fax 4488277* •
AE DC MC V. Big, modern tower in
Haidhausen, handy for the airport
and close to the centre. Pool, sauna
and well-equipped meeting rooms.

Restaurants
There is a wide choice of foreign cuisine – French, Italian, Balkan and
Chinese – in the city centre, Schwabing and Bogenhausen and all levels of
formality are catered for. Bavarians are fond of meat and fish; local dishes
include *Leberkäse,* a liver pâté often served in hot slices, and fish grilled
on a skewer, *Steckerlfisch.* Reservations up to two days in advance for the
main restaurants described are strongly advised.

Aubergine *DM* /////
Maximilianspl 5 (entrance in Max-
Joseph-Str) ☎ *598171* • *closed Sun,*
Mon, 3 weeks in Aug, hols • *MC* •
jacket and tie

Master chef Eckart Witzigmann, ex-
Paul Bocuse and Washington's Jockey
Club, owns and sometimes cooks in
this restaurant, which is famous
throughout Germany. This is

the place to celebrate a major coup or give a big thank-you, but you must reserve 2–3 weeks ahead. The costly decor of deep purple carpet, chandeliers, mirrors, white and metallic walls is a blend of classic and high-tech modern. The dozen tables are well spaced, and there is a small upstairs bar (with a selection of 80 whiskies). The *nouvelle cuisine* fixed-price menu is slightly cheaper for lunch than dinner. The wine list is superb and the service impeccable.

Boettner   *DM* ////
Theatinerstr 8 ☎ 221210 • closed Sat D, Sun, hols • AE DC MC V • jacket and tie
This central restaurant, club-like and intimate, and furnished with antiques, has been a lunch-time watering-hole for top business people and politicians since 1901. It still retains the atmosphere of those days, and the founder's grandson, Roland Hartung-Boettner, is in genial attendance. Although busiest at lunch, the ten tables are often full during the evening interval of the nearby opera house. The rich menu offers old-fashioned German and French *haute cuisine*. The bar doubles as a wine shop and delicatessen, where you can buy oysters and caviar to eat there or take away.

Chesa Rüegg   *DM* //
Wurzerstr 18 ☎ 297114 • closed Sat, Sun, hols • AE DC MC V • jacket and tie
The Chesa Rüegg has become a popular lunch and dinner haunt of the business and media fraternity, with its rustic Alpine decor, reasonable prices and convenient location just off Maximilianstrasse. But its 30 tables are closely spaced and it can be noisy. Mainly Swiss menu.

Price guide
For the meanings of the price symbols, see pages 6 and 7.

Da Pippo   *DM* //
Mühlbaurstr 36 ☎ 4704848 • closed Sat L, Sun, Aug 1–21, Dec 23–Jan 2 • DC MC
This spacious, informally elegant restaurant in a leafy Bogenhausen street is for social rather than business entertaining. In the evening, mirrors and candlelight give it a romantic atmosphere. Sophisticated Italian cooking and good Sicilian wines.

Le Gourmet   *DM* /////
Ligsalzstr 46 ☎ 503597 • D only; closed Sun and 2 weeks in Jan • AE DC MC V
The only good restaurant close to the Messegelände (exhibition centre), Le Gourmet's ten tables are in two small ornately furnished rooms. The top-class cooking is both *nouvelle* and Bavarian. The cellar has over 300 French classified *crus*.

Käfer-Schänke   *DM* ////
Prinzregentenstr 73 ☎ 41681 • closed Sun, hols • AE DC MC
A large, old-established, family-owned restaurant, the Käfer-Schänke is a Munich institution and is usually crowded and noisy. It is better for a lively evening than a working lunch, though it has private rooms. Famous faces are seen here. The food is good value though prices are fairly high.

Königshof   *DM* ////
Königshof hotel, Karlspl 25 ☎ 551360 • AE DC MC V • jacket and tie
Probably the best hotel restaurant in town, the restfully decorated and spacious dining room of the Königshof has a soundproofed picture window overlooking the Stachus. The cuisine is *nouvelle*, with dishes like coquille St Jacques and calf's liver with shallots in red wine sauce. A wide selection of excellent wines.

La Piazzetta   *DM* //
Oskar-von-Miller-Ring 3 ☎ 282990 • closed Sat L • AE DC MC V
A fashionable restaurant in the business district (in the LBS

building). Comprising three adjoining rooms and a separate brasserie, many of its tables are in alcoves, ideal for a discreet business rendezvous. The Florentine menu allows a wide choice of antipasti and fish dishes and the extensive Italian wine list includes reasonably priced bottles. A new attraction is the piano bar, open until 6 in the morning.

Preysing-Keller [DM] ////
Innere Wiener Str 6 (Haidhausen)
☎ *481015 • D only; closed Sun and Dec 22–Jan 6 • no credit cards*
This spacious restaurant, deep in a 300-year-old vault, with bar and comfortable lounge, is a splendid refuge on a winter's night. Near the parliament house and Gasteig arts centre, it is only a short ride from the city. The food is international and ambitious and the wines excellent.

Sabitzer [DM] /////
Reitmorstr 21 ☎ 298584 • closed Sat L, Sun • AE DC MC
This is one of Munich's most respected establishments. Outside it sports gleaming stucco and awnings, while inside there are sparkling chandeliers and flowers on every table. The cuisine is *nouvelle* Bavarian with dishes such as soufflé of pike with basil sauce and haunch of rabbit with tarragon. The wine list is appropriately grand. A good choice for a business meal, with less expensive set lunches.

Tai Tung [DM] //
Prinzregentenstr 60 ☎ 471100 • closed Sun • AE DC MC
The oldest and best Chinese restaurant in southern Germany, Tai Tung is in an inviting scarlet and black lacquer basement beneath the Stuck Villa, a *Jugendstil* (Art Nouveau) museum and gallery.

Vier Jahreszeiten restaurant [DM] /////
Vier Jahreszeiten hotel ☎ 23039599 • closed L, Sun Aug • AE DC MC V • jacket and tie
This elegant rococo restaurant – until recently known as Walterspeil – has long been patronized by members of the government and aristocracy. As a business venue, it still has considerable cachet, but it is now only open in the evenings. The Bavarian cuisine has had mixed reports.

OTHER RESTAURANTS
Bistro Terrine, Amalienstr 89 (entrance Amalien-Passage) ☎ 281780 is newish but much praised. In Bogenhausen, the *Bogenhauser Hof*, Ismaningerstr 85 ☎ 985586, is an old hunting lodge where Bavarian food is served in traditional surroundings. *Kay's Bistro*, Utzschneiderstr 1 ☎ 2603584, has a showbiz clientele, live music and good food. *Die Kulisse*, Maximilianstr 26 ☎ 294728, is a busy after-theatre restaurant in the style of a Viennese coffee-house. The popular *Pizzeria Italy*, Leopoldstr 108 ☎ 346403, offers Italian cooking at reasonable prices.

Bars and cafés
The Münchner has a habit of sitting down to eat, drink and talk at any time of the day, and there are numerous rendezvous in the business district. The bars of the top hotels are a good rendezvous. *Harry's New York Bar* in Falkenturmstrasse is old-established and more Munich than Manhattan. Probably the most "in" place is *Schumann's*, Maximilianstr 36, which is open to the small hours. The trendy *Extrablatt*, in Schwabing, Leopoldstr 7 ☎ 333333, is furnished with original pieces from long gone *belle époque* hotels. For a drink at any time of day the *Augustiner-Gaststätte*, Neuhauser Str 16, has spacious rooms and a leafy beer-garden behind a small 16thC façade.

Credit card abbreviations	
AE	American Express
DC	Diners Club
MC	Access/MasterCard
V	Visa

Entertainment

Munich has the richest variety of opera, theatre and music of any city in Germany, particularly during the festival months of June and July. The best source of information is the official monthly programme, *München: offizielles Monatsprogramm.* Tickets for theatre, concerts and sports events (but not for the Staatsoper, Staatstheater and Kammerspiele) can be bought from agencies including ABR-*Theaterkasse*, Neuhauser Str 9 ☎ 1204421, and *Max Hieber*, Liebfrauenstr 1 (by the cathedral) ☎ 226571.

Opera, musicals, dance Richard Wagner and Richard Strauss still feature strongly in the repertoire of the Staatsoper at the *Nationaltheater*, Max-Joseph-Pl (box office Maximilianstr 11 ☎ 221316), and occasional productions are staged in the beautiful *Cuvilliéstheater*, Residenzstr 1 ☎ 221316. The *Staatstheater am Gärtnerplatz*, Gärtnerpl 3 ☎ 2016767, offers a wider range of opera, ballet and musicals, and the *Deutsches Theater*, Schwanthalerstr 13 ☎ 593427, has a programme of operetta, musicals and international solo stars.

Theatre Traditional productions of the classics are staged by the Staatsschauspiel company at the *Residenztheater*, Residenzstr 1, and *Marstalltheater*, Max-Joseph-Pl ☎ 221316 (for both), and more adventurous stagings of classic and contemporary plays are performed by the Kammerspiele at the *Schauspielhaus*, Maximilianstr 26 ☎ 237210. For satirical comedy, there is the famous *Münchner Lach-und Schiessgesellschaft*, Ursulastr 9 ☎ 391997. More in vogue is the *Münchner Rationaltheater*, Hesselohestr 18 ☎ 334050.

Cinema Most of the popular cinemas are to the west of the city or in Schwabing. Foreign-language films are shown at *Atlantik-Filmpalast Fremdsprachenkino*, Schwanthalerstr 2–6 ☎ 555670.

Music The recently opened *Gasteig* centre, Rosenheimer Str 5 ☎ 41810, stages international concerts and recitals. The Bavarian Radio Symphony Orchestra under Rafael Kubelik gives concerts (Thu, Fri) in the *Herkulessaal* of the Residenz, and chamber music is performed in the *Max-Joseph-Saal*, Residenzstr 1 ☎ 224641. There are summer concerts in the *Schloss Nymphenburg* ☎ 220868.[1]

Nightclubs Munich's nightspots are numerous but mainly aimed at the young. Perennially 'in' despite or because of its spartan interior is *P1* (pronounced *peh eins*), Prinzregentenstr 1 ☎ 294252 (open 9.30–4, closed Mon), once the tea rooms of the Haus der Kunst. In summer, drink on the terrace overlooking the Englischer Garten.

Shopping

Munich is Germany's headquarters for the fashion industry, art and antiques. The most exclusive shops are in Maximilianstrasse and adjoining streets.

Department stores For less expensive shops, try Kaufinger and Neuhauser Strasser; *Karstadt*, *Kaufhof* and *Woolworth* are here. *Hertie* is in Schützenstrasse.

Gifts Dallmayr, Dienerstrasse, is a fresh food shop and delicatessen that once supplied royalty.

Fashion In Maximilianstrasse *Gucci*, *St Laurent* and *Jil Sander* are represented; *Guy Laroche* is in Falckenbergstrasse, along with top names in shoes, jewellery and men's clothes. Traditional dirndls are stocked at *Beck am Rathauseck*, Marienplatz.

Sports equipment The superb *Sport-Scheck*, Sendlinger Str 85, also leases equipment.

Antiques The antiques trade clusters around the Viktualienmarkt; art dealers are in Ottostrasse (Kunstblock), north of Maximiliansplatz. The top art auctioneers, *Neumeister*, is in Barerstrasse.

Schwabing is known for

antiquarian books and prints (Amalienstrasse), and it has dozens of boutiques and galleries.

Sightseeing

The galleries, museums, churches and palaces are among the finest in Europe. For recorded information in English ☎ 239162 (galleries and museums) ☎ 239172 (other sights).

Altstadt landmarks Within a short walk of Marienplatz are the earliest royal residence, the *Alter Hof*, a quiet medieval courtyard open at all times; the *Altes Rathaus*, the old town hall, from Gothic to baroque in style; the red-brick Gothic cathedral and centrepiece of the city, *Frauenkirche*; the 16thC *Hofbräuhaus*, Platzl 9, with its oom-pah band; and the *Michaelskirche* in Neuhauser Strasse, the greatest Renaissance church north of the Alps. On the Marienplatz is the ornate neo-Gothic *Neues Rathaus*, whose famous Glockenspiel draws a big crowd every day at 11am (also 12am and 5pm in summer).

Alte Pinakothek Built in 1827 to house the royal collection, this is now one of the world's foremost art galleries, with virtually all major 14th–18thC painters represented. *Barer Str 27. Open Tue–Sun, 9–4.30; also Tue and Thu, 7pm–9pm.*

Asamkirche The narrow 18thC façade of this church conceals a riot of pink, white and gold stucco. *Sendlingerstr. Open daily.*

Deutsches Museum Built in 1903 on an island in the river, and dedicated to science and technology, it ranks with the Smithsonian. *Isarinsel. Open 9–5.*

Englischer Garten This informal park, so named because an Englishman advised on its layout in 1785, is a haven for cyclists, joggers, sunbathers (often nude) and lovers; drinkers gather at the *Chinesischer Turm* pagoda. *Entrance in Prinzregentenstr. Open 24hr.*

Haus der Kunst In one of the few surviving public buildings of the Nazi era, where the notorious 'Decadent Art' show was held, there is now an

excellent 20thC collection from Pablo Picasso and Marc Chagall to Pop and Minimal art. *Prinzregentenstr 1. Open Tue–Sun, 9–4.30; also Thu, 7pm–9pm.*

Neue Pinakothek A striking modern building, completed in 1980, housing late-18th and 19thC works, including some by the German Romantics, English landscape painters and French Impressionists. *Theresienstr. Open Tue–Sun, 9–4.30.*

Nymphenburg palace The Bavarian Versailles. Built as a royal summer residence between 1664 and 1715, its ornate public rooms look onto an ornamental park. *In M19, 6km/4 miles west of centre. Open May–Sep, Tue–Sun, 9–12.30, 1.30–5; Oct–Apr, 10–12.30, 1.30–4.*

Olympiazentrum Impressive sports complex open to the public (see *Spectator sports*), built for the 1972 Olympics. The huge tent-like roof, made up of 8,000 acrylic plates, is 75,000 sq metres in area. *On U-Bahn 3.5kms/2 miles north of centre. Guided tours on request.*

Residenz Max-Joseph-Pl 3. A collection of imposing 16th–19thC buildings where the Wittelsbach kings lived. The *Cuvilliéstheater* (Residenzstr 1, entrance in Brunnenhof) is a sumptuous red and gold rococo auditorium with four tiers of balconies (*open Mon–Sat, 2–5; Sun, 10–5*). North of the Residenz, the *Hofgarten*, Hofgartenstr, is a formal 17thC garden enclosed by colonnades on two sides (*open 24hr*). The magnificent courtyards and state apartments of the palace now form the *Residenzmuseum*, housing the crown jewels and other treasures (*Max-Joseph-Pl, open Tue–Sat, 10–4.30; Sun, 10–1; guided tours*).

Schwabing Just north of the pagoda in the Englischer Garten, Thiemestrasse takes you into the side streets of Schwabing. If you have a spare hour, walk up to Wedekindplatz, then through to Münchener Freiheit and back down Leopoldstrasse.

Siemens-Museum Has several thousand exhibits connected with the

development of electronics. *Prannerstr 10. Open Mon–Fri, 9–4; Sat–Sun, 10–2.*
Theatinerkirche An elegant ochre-washed baroque basilica with twin spires. *Theatinerstr. Open May–Sep, 10–1, 3–5.*

Guided tours
Panorama Tours City & Country ☎ 591504 runs daily 2hr 30min bus tours of main city sights from Bahnhofplatz.

Out of town
Dachau, 17kms/10.5 miles northwest of city, is the site of the notorious concentration camp. The one remaining building is a museum ☎ (08131) 1741.
Starnbergersee 30kms/19 miles southwest of Munich. The most easily reached of Munich's lakes, set in wooded hills with a view of the Alps. A steamer leaves on regular trips ☎ Starnberg Staatliche Schiffahrt (08151) 12023.

Munich's festivals
Oktoberfest is an annual beer-drinking festival at the end of September, which has developed from celebrations held in 1810 to mark a royal wedding and now attracts some 6m visitors. It lasts just over two weeks. *Fasching,* Munich's carnival season, runs from January 6 until Shrove Tuesday, four to six weeks later, and includes some 2,000 costume balls. Outdoor events take place around the Viktualienmarkt.

Spectator sports
Athletics, cycling, soccer Soccer is predominant and Bayern-München is one of the strongest teams in Europe. Their home ground is the *Olympiastadion,* also used for major athletic and cycling events. Tickets ☎ 30613577.
Horse-racing Meetings are held on Wed and Sat at *Daglfing* (trotting) and *Riem* (flat racing) ☎ 9300010.

Skiing International competitions in downhill, slalom amd jumping are held at *Oberstdorf,* 160km/100 miles southwest of Munich. *Ideal-Tours* organizes excursions ☎ 268011.

Keeping fit
Fitness centres Club Vitaprop, Berg-am-Laimstr 91 ☎ 433061.
Fitnessstudio Arabellapark, Arabellastr 15 ☎ 911891. *Body Up,* Dachauer Str 50 ☎ 596293.
Golf A most attractive course is at *Feldafing* on the Starnbergersee ☎ (08157) 1305.
Jogging The Englischer Garten offers ample scope.
Skiing Sport-Scheck ☎ 21660 organizes day and weekend excursions.
Squash Bavaria Squash Center, Bavariastr 16 ☎ 774181, has 14 courts.
Swimming The open-air pool at *Prinzregentenbad,* Prinzregentenstr 80 ☎ 474808, is fashionable and has a restaurant. Visitors can use the pool at the *Olympiazentrum* ☎ 30613390.
Tennis Sport-Scheck ☎ 21660 runs courts, now as popular as the private clubs, especially the ones at *Herzogpark* in Bogenhausen.

Local resources
Business services
Companies offering fully furnished, equipped and staffed offices for short-term use include *Günther Bureau Service System,* Leopoldstr 28 ☎ 333200.
Photocopying and printing Hansa-Print, Thalkirchner Str 72 ☎ 530195; *Top Kopie,* Gabelsberger Str 73 ☎ 5234598; *Copyland,* Amalienstr 46 ☎ 288275.
Secretarial Petra Fischer, Einsteinstr 111 ☎ 4707071 (Mon–Fri, 8.30–5.30); *Lydia Morawietz Büro-Service,* Zeppelinstr 73 ☎ 4488496 (Mon–Fri, 8.30–5.30). *Allround* ☎ 8595055 for English and foreign languages (Mon–Fri, 10–8).
Translation The *Industrie- und Handelskammer* ☎ 51160 can

recommend interpreters and translators.

Communications

Local delivery City Car ☎ 555444; *CentroCar* ☎ 770077.
Long-distance delivery DHL ☎ 909050; TNT ☎ 3106006.
Post office Main post office: Residenzstr 2 ☎ 2177302; 24hr service at Bahnhofpl 1 ☎ 5598406.
Telex and fax Günther Bureau Service ☎ 333200 handles telex, fax and data processing; also *International Business Services* ☎ 4313005 ⊠ 5213379.

Conference/exhibition centre

The *Messegelände* beside the Theresienwiese, on the west side of the city, comprises 19 halls with a total of 105,000 sq metres, and a further 200,000 sq metres of open-air space. It hosts some 20 fairs and 60 conferences each year. Contact *Münchner Messe- und Ausstellungs GmbH*, Theresienhöhe 13, M72 ☎ 51070. The *Arabella Konferenz-Zentrum*, in Arabellapark, M81, has 11 rooms on two floors, seating up to 560. For audiences of up to 2,400, the *Kongresssaal* of the *Deutsches Museum* ☎ 2179241 is often used. For all conference information contact *Fremdenverkehrsamt*, Rindermarkt 5 ☎ 2391216.

Emergencies

Bureau de change Hauptbahnhof (railway station), open daily, 6–11.30.
Hospitals Emergency admissions at *Krankenhaus Rechts der Isar*, Ismanninger Str ☎ 41401. Heart emergencies ☎ 41402239. Ambulance ☎ 222660. Doctors on emergency ☎ 558661, and dentists ☎ 7233093.
Pharmacies For pharmacies open after hours and on Sun ☎ 594475.
Police Ettstr 2 ☎ 2147211.

Government offices

The economic department of the City Council, *Wirtschaftsamt der Landeshauptstadt München*, Blumenstr 17, M2 ☎ 2334872, deals with companies wanting to set up here. At state level, contact the *Staatsministerium für Wirtschaft und Verkehr*, Prinzregentenstr 28, M22 ☎ 216201.

Information sources

Business information The *Industrie- und Handelskammer*, Max-Joseph-Str 2, M2 ☎ 51160, runs a computer database of products and suppliers in Oberbayern and Munich, and advises on all regulations. *Europäisches Patentamt*, Erhardstr 27, M5 ☎ 23990, is the central patent office for the EC, and the *Deutsches Patentamt*, Zweibrückenstr 12, M2 ☎ 21951 for the Federal Republic. *Bayerische Staatsbibliothek*, Ludwigstr 16, is the central reference library.
Local media The *Süddeutsche Zeitung* is one of Germany's leading papers. Its politics are liberal, left of centre and its business coverage is excellent. The *Münchner Merkur* has a more regional appeal and is loyal to the CSU government. *Bayerischer Rundfunk* is the local station for both radio and TV.
Tourist information Amtliches Bayerisches Reisebüro for tours outside Munich, at the Hauptbahnhof ☎ 12040. *Fremdenverkehrsamt München* for the city, at the Hauptbahnhof, south exit ☎ 2391256.

Thank-yous

Confectionery Café Kreutzkramm, Maffeistr 4.
Florists Blumen-Schmidt, in the precinct under Karlspl ☎ 597739.
Wine merchants La Maison du Vin, Hohenzollernstr 34 ☎ 341400.

STUTTGART

City code ☎ 0711

Stuttgart is a comparative latecomer to the league of big German cities, having neither a long mercantile tradition, nor, until just a century ago, any industrial importance. It began to emerge around 1750 when it became the permanent seat of the dukes and, in 1806, the kings of Württemberg. Several palaces were built, a bureaucracy was established, and an excellent educational system was set up. The poet Schiller and Hegel the philosopher were both pupils here. In the early 19th century Stuttgart was still chiefly a market for local farmers and wine-growers; publishing was the only organized industry of national importance. The advent of the railway ended the city's relative isolation, and its advanced schools produced two of Germany's great industrial pioneers, Gottfried Daimler and Robert Bosch. Their companies, founded in the 1880s, still dominate Stuttgart's industry. Today, about 80% of the city's output is in engineering – automobile, electrical and mechanical – represented by Daimler-Benz, Porsche, Bosch, SEL and Bauknecht. Other industries include optics, instrumentation, furniture, textiles, chemicals and food processing. The German headquarters of IBM is here, and Nixdorf has a plant. Yet Stuttgart is still an important centre for agriculture and for publishing, with more than 170 firms including the Holtzbrinck-Gruppe, Klett and the Deutsche Verlagsanstalt.

The old kingdom of Württemberg has become the federal *Land* of Baden-Württemberg (population 9.3m) and Stuttgart remains the region's political and administrative capital. Although the city itself has only 550,000 inhabitants, its immediate hinterland, the economically buoyant mid-Neckar region, has a population of 2.3m. It is being said that West Germany's future economic growth will be based on a Stuttgart–Munich corridor, well away from the Rhein-Ruhr area. Stuttgart is already a cultural rival to Munich, with two universities, theatre, opera and a world-class ballet company. Under the enlightened Oberbürgermeister Manfred Rommel, son of the World War II general, an elegant, efficient city has risen from the ruins of 1945. Yet it is still undeniably provincial, and its people, the Swabians, who have a strong sense of identity, are akin to the Swiss in their Protestant tradition, capacity for hard work and technical aptitude. Despite a wariness of outsiders, they have made Stuttgart a significant international business centre; of all German cities it is second only to Munich in the value of its exports, and hosts many major trade fairs and exhibitions.

Arriving

There are scheduled air services from about 25 cities outside Germany, mainly via Frankfurt or other major German airports. Direct connections exist with Brussels, Copenhagen, London, Madrid, Milan, Nice, Paris, Turin, Vienna and Zürich.

Domestic air links with major cities are comprehensive, with 6 flights a day from Hamburg (1hr 10mins), 7 from Düsseldorf (1hr), 5 from Frankfurt (45mins), though only 2 from Munich (55mins). Rail links are also good: 24 services a day from Munich (2hrs 12mins), 22 from Mainz (2hrs 8min), and 23 from Mannheim (1hr 27mins). Stuttgart is well placed in the *Autobahn* network at the junction of the E11 Karlsruhe–Munich and E70 Würzburg–Switzerland but traffic congestion is a problem, especially in summer.

Stuttgart airport
The airport is small and inadequate. Plans for a new terminal and longer runway are in hand, and a rapid-transit rail link to the city is being constructed, for completion in the early 1990s. Checking-in can be slow at peak times (7–9 and 3.30–6), but flight arrival procedures rarely take more than 30mins. Facilities include a modest restaurant, the Top Air, a buffet, coffee shops and a bureau de change, open Mon–Sat, 7.30am–10pm; Sun, 8.30am–10pm. Flight information ☎ 7901388.
Nearby hotel Mövenpick, Flughafen, 23 ☎ 79070 ⓉⓍ 7245677 fax 793585
● AE DC MC V. Less than 200 metres from the terminal, with a free bus connection, the Mövenpick was renovated in 1986 and the rooms are all well equipped.
City link The airport is at Echterdingen, 13kms/8 miles south of the city. Until the *S-Bahn* link is ready in 1990, the choice is airport bus or, probably more convenient, taxi (about 25mins to the city centre, 35mins in rush hours).
Taxi Cabs line up outside the terminal; there is rarely a shortage.
Car rental Avis, Hertz and interRent offices are in huts facing the terminal exit, but driving is not recommended unless you have an appointment outside the city centre.
Bus Services, operated by Stuttgarter Strassenbahnen (SSB), run every 20–30mins, 4.55am–00.15am; fare DM6. The pick-up point is outside the exit. Drop-off points are the city air terminal in Lautenschlagerstrasse and the main railway station.

Railway station
The *Hauptbahnhof* is the hub of the city, close to the two best hotels and

main shopping and business areas. More than 1,000 trains a day serve the 16 platforms, including the relatively new rapid-transit (*S-Bahn*) links to the industrial suburbs. The entrance to this system is down an escalator, where you also find the *U-Bahn*. At ground level in front of the station there are stops for many city buses including those to the airport and exhibition centre. There are always taxis in three ranks in front and beside the country bus terminus. In the concourse is a bureau de change, open Mon–Sat, 8–8.30, Sun, 9–8; and an information desk with English-speaking staff, open daily 6am–10pm ☎ 19419.

A large underground shopping precinct is immediately outside the station in the Arnulf-Klett-Platz, where there is a helpful city tourist office (*Verkehrsamt*) ☎ 2228240.

Getting around
The centre of Stuttgart is fairly compact, and short-term visitors should rely on walking or taxis. The city and inner suburbs are served by the rapid and cheap streetcar (*Strassenbahn*) system, part of which runs underground. Driving in the city is difficult, and for journeys to industrial suburbs such as Zuffenhausen, Feuerbach, Untertürkheim and Vaihingen, the *S-Bahn* is quicker (but note that it does not go to Sindelfingen).
Taxis It is best to pick up a cab at one of the many ranks at places in the centre, including the railway station, the Planie and the Rotebühlplatz. Otherwise call *Taxi-Auto-Zentrale* ☎ 566061.
Limousines Rolf Brunold ☎ 771992.
Driving As much of the centre is traffic-free and other streets are congested, driving in Stuttgart is not easy. The main traffic arteries are Konrad-Adenauer-Strasse and Theodor-Heuss-Strasse, linked by Schlossstrasse which crosses the centre in an underpass with complex multilevel junctions at either end. Street parking is very limited, but

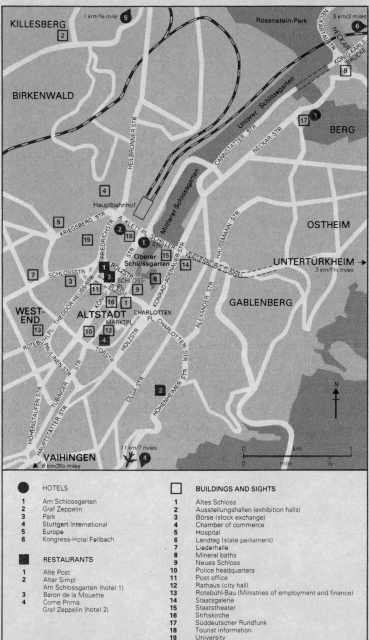

KILLESBERG
2

BIRKENWALD

KILESSBERG

Rosenstein-Park

NECKARTALSTR

5 km/3 miles
6

KÖNIG-KARLS-BRÜCKE

8

1 km/⅝ mile
5

HEILBRONNER STR

Unterer Schlossgarten

CANNSTATTER STR

NECKAR-STR

BERG

17   3

Mittlerer Schlossgarten

Hauptbahnhof
4

OSTHEIM

KRIEGSBERG STR
5

19

A.-KLETT-PL.
2

FRIEDRICHSTR

SCHILLER STR

18   1

STR

Oberer Schlossgarten
15

14

HAUSSMANN-STR

WAGENBURG TUNNEL

UNTERTÜRKHEIM →
3 km/1¾ miles

SCHLOSSSTR
3

7

SCHLOSS-PL.
1   3   6

BOLZSTR

KÖNIG-STR

PLANIE

9

11

16   1

WEST-END

ROTEBÜHL PL.

THEODOR-HEUSS-STR

PAULINEN STR

13

ALTSTADT

MARKTPL.

10   12   4

KONRAD-ADENAUER-STR

CHARLOTTEN PL.

CHARLOTTEN STR

HOLZSTR

TORSTR

HOHENSTAUFEN STR

HAUPTSTÄTTER STR

TÜBINGER STR

OLGA-STR

HOHENHEIMER STR

ALEXANDER STR

GABLENBERG

2

VAIHINGEN
6 km/3¾ miles

11 km/7 miles
4

N

0   km   1
0   mile   ½

●	HOTELS		□	BUILDINGS AND SIGHTS
1	Am Schlossgarten		1	Altes Schloss
2	Graf Zeppelin		2	Ausstellungshallen (exhibition halls)
3	Park		3	Börse (stock exchange)
4	Stuttgart International		4	Chamber of commerce
5	Europe		5	Hospital
6	Kongress-Hotel Fellbach		6	Landtag (state parliament)
			7	Liederhalle
■	RESTAURANTS		8	Mineral baths
			9	Neues Schloss
1	Alte Post		10	Police headquarters
2	Alter Simpl		11	Post office
	Am Schlossgarten (hotel 1)		12	Rathaus (city hall)
3	Baron de la Mouette		13	Rotebühl-Bau (Ministries of employment and finance)
4	Come Prima		14	Staatsgalerie
	Graf Zeppelin (hotel 2)		15	Staatstheater
			16	Stiftskirche
			17	Süddeutscher Rundfunk
			18	Tourist information
			19	University

there are over 30 multilevel or underground garages whose addresses are on a list obtainable from the tourist office. The main car rental firms all have city centre offices, including *Hertz* ☎ 643044.

Walking A large part of the city centre is accessible only on foot. The main axis, Königstrasse, is traffic-free as are Schlossplatz and many adjoining streets and squares. Walking at night presents no problems, but you might want to avoid the sex-bars around Leonhardsplatz.

Streetcars Streetcars and stops (marked either by 'U' or 'H' signs) are being modernized. A map is available from the vvs (Stuttgart transport) office in the Arnulf-Klett-Passage. Tickets for all methods of public transport are sold only from orange vending machines at streetcar and *S-Bahn* stations and bus stops.

Buses There is a frequent service from the railway station to the exhibition centre at Killesberg.

Trains The *S-Bahn*, identified by green 'S' signs, can be picked up for the industrial suburbs at the railway station or Rotebühlplatz; and taxis are available at main suburban stations.

Area by area

Stuttgart lies in a narrow valley. Its compact centre divides neatly into four zones. East of Königstrasse, Schlossplatz and Oberer Schlossgarten provide a setting for the Staatstheater, Landtag (state parliament), Neues Schloss and other impressive public buildings. South of this are the most exclusive shopping streets such as Calwer Strasse, Marktplatz and Hirschstrasse, on both sides of the Königstrasse. To the east, beyond the main traffic route of Holzstrasse, is the "low-life" area, with remnants of the old Stuttgart still visible. To the west of the pedestrianized shopping district is the main business area, between Schlossstrasse and Theodor-Heuss-Strasse, where 1970s glass and steel mingle with 19thC neo-classical

buildings. The stock exchange and state ministries of finance, economics, and employment are here, together with banks, insurance companies and professional offices.

The suburbs

The steep valley sides have winding streets of expensive and sober suburban houses only a few minutes from the city. Gablenberg and Degerloch on the east side, and Birkenwald and Killesberg on the west side, are desirable places to live. In Killesberg, the Weissenhof-Siedlung is a famous estate of houses designed in 1927 by Le Corbusier, Walter Gropius, Mies van der Rohe and other leading architects. On the surrounding plateau, woods or agricultural land provide an attractive backdrop for commuter villages such as Botnang and Sillenbuch.

Just north of the city, not far from the working class suburbs and gasworks and stockyards of Ostheim and Gaisburg, is the Berg district, an elegant enclave around the Villa Berg palace and gardens. Across the river is ancient Bad Cannstatt, whose warren of narrow old streets is popular with the young.

The industrial areas

The older industrial areas are along the Neckar. At Untertürkheim, upriver, is the main Daimler-Benz plant, and at Obertürkheim an inland harbour built in 1958 gives Stuttgart access to the Rhein and North Sea. Down the valley are Feuerbach (Bosch) and Zuffenhausen (Porsche). On the high ground to the south, Vaihingen has an important new industrial zone and the IBM headquarters. Linked to the city by the *S-Bahn* are the industrial outer boroughs – or mid-Neckar region – including Fellbach, Esslingen and Waiblingen to the east, Böblingen to the southwest, Leonberg to the west and Kornwestheim and Ludwigsburg to the north.

Hotels

No great hotels in Stuttgart survived the war, and well-known international chains have appeared only in recent years, with an Inter-Continental which opened in late 1988 and a Holiday Inn which was due to open in late 1989. Otherwise, there are German-owned hotels, most of which were built in the 1950s and 1960s.

All the hotels listed are well maintained and comfortable. They have room service to 11pm or later, with TV/radio in every room and a choice of *en suite* bath or shower.

Am Schlossgarten *DM* ////
Schillerstr 23, 1 ☎ *20260* ⊤ₓ *722936 fax 2026888 • LEGA • AE DC MC V • 125 rooms, 4 suites, 2 restaurants, 1 bar*
Close to the railway station and Königstrasse, with views over the park and the Staatstheater, this discreet, courteously run hotel is the first choice for visiting politicians, celebrities and senior executives. The wood-panelled public rooms and lobby are in an elegant, modern and sober style. The lounge and bar are useful for informal discussions, while the main restaurant (see *Restaurants*) has an excellent reputation. Bedrooms are light and attractively decorated, though not very spacious; the most pleasant overlook the park. 6 meeting rooms (capacity up to 120).

Graf Zeppelin *DM* /////
Arnulf-Klett-Pl 7, 1 ☎ *299881* ⊤ₓ *722418 fax 292141 • Steigenberger • AE DC MC V • 260 rooms, 20 suites, 3 restaurants, 2 bars*
Almost next door to the Am Schlossgarten, the Graf Zeppelin is less prestigious but larger and caters more directly for business people. Behind its bleak modern exterior an effort has been made to re-create the grand style, with mirrored surfaces, high-quality reproduction furniture and a wealth of textures and colours. Bedrooms are comfortable and well equipped, with cable TV, soundproofing and individual air conditioning. Two of the four restaurants in the hotel specialize in local cuisine, and there is a nightclub with live entertainment. Currency exchange • pool, sauna, massage • 11 meeting rooms (capacity up to 500).

Park *DM* ////
Villastr 21, 1 ☎ *280161* ⊤ₓ *723405 fax 284353 • AE DC MC V • 80 rooms, 3 suites, 2 restaurants, 1 bar*
This hotel in Berg, 2.5kms/1.5 miles from the centre and midway to Daimler-Benz, attracts a clientele which includes business and media people; Süddeutscher Rundfunk (South German Radio and TV) is next door. It is also used regularly by the local CDU party. It is owned and run by a husband-and-wife team, with an accent on personal service. The public areas are predominantly white, with oriental rugs and simple, modern furnishings, while the bedrooms are light and welcoming; ask for one overlooking the park. One of the two restaurants is Swabian-style, and the snug bar in the basement is agreeable for informal conversation. Newsstand • 4 meeting rooms (capacity up to 120).

Stuttgart International *DM* ////
Plieninger Str 100, Möhringen, 80 ☎ *720211* ⊤ₓ *7255763 fax 7202210 • AE DC MC V • LEGA • 167 rooms, 33 suites, 3 restaurants, 1 bar*
This 1960s high-rise hotel has the most comprehensive facilities of any in the Stuttgart area, but is 8kms/5 miles south of the city. The airport and the *Autobahn* are only 5mins by road, and it is handy for the Vaihingen industrial area and IBM. The hotel's excellent conference facilities are much used. There is, in

summer, an open-air beer-garden. Hairdresser, newsstand, currency exchange • pool, fitness centre, sauna, solarium, massage, bowling •13 meeting rooms (capacity up to 1,000).

OTHER HOTELS

Europe _DM_ /// _Siemensstr 26, Feuerbach, 30_ ☎ _815091_ TX _723650 fax 854082 • Europe Hotels International • AE DC MC V. The nearest hotel to the Killesberg exhibition complex and to Bosch but not within easy walking distance of either. A modern tower with a mix of decors. Much used for conferences._

Kongress-Hotel Fellbach _DM_ ///
Tainerstr 7–9, 7012 Fellbach ☎ _5859 0_ TX _7254900 fax 5859304 • AE DC MC V. About a 10min drive east of Stuttgart, this spacious, low-rise hotel built in 1984 caters specifically for visitors to the new Schwabenlandhalle exhibition and conference centre._

Hotel and restaurant price guide
For the meanings of the hotel and restaurant price symbols, see pages 6 and 7.

Restaurants

There are few restaurants in Stuttgart that will suit a major occasion and for more routine business meals some Italian ones are reliable. The native Swabian cuisine is among the best in Germany, being lighter and more varied than elsewhere, with less _Wurst_ and pickled products and, as in Switzerland, more emphasis on eggs and cheese. People working in the suburbs tend to eat at country inns.

Alte Post _DM_ //
Friedrichstr 43 ☎ _293079 • closed Sun, Mon L, Sat L • DC MC V • jacket and tie • reservations essential_
This panelled restaurant in the heart of the city is the most exclusive in town, with a mainly dark-suited and earnest clientele. Although it is generally full, it is never noisy and is an eminently suitable venue for important business meals. The menu is international _haute cuisine_, with dishes like lobster in vin jaune, and medaillions of venison in cranberry sauce.

Alter Simpl _DM_ ////
Hohenheimer Str 64 ☎ _240821 • D only; closed Sun • no credit cards_
The intimate Alter Simpl, with its beams and paraffin lamps, is just a 5min taxi ride from the city centre. Its thick 19thC walls muffle the noise of the traffic on the busy road outside. The cooking is _nouvelle_ German, based on skilful use of fresh seasonal ingredients. Suitable

for either business occasions or relaxation, the restaurant stays open till 1am.

Am Schlossgarten _DM_ ////
Am Schlossgarten hotel ☎ _2026830 • AE DC MC V • jacket and tie_
This restaurant is an absolutely dependable choice for an important lunch or dinner, and you can use the hotel's elegant bar and lounge for discussions before and after your meal. The large, panelled restaurant overlooks the gardens. The tables are widely spaced and the service polished. The menu includes international and local dishes, and the wine list is well chosen.

Credit card abbreviations

_AE_	American Express
_DC_	Diners Club
_MC_	Access/MasterCard
_V_	Visa

Baron de la Mouette *DM* ///
Kleiner Schlosspl 11 ☎ *220034* • *AE
DC MC V*
In the pedestrianized centre of
Stuttgart the Swiss Mövenpick group
runs a complex of five restaurants, of
which the Baron de la Mouette is the
most stylish. Many local business
people eat here, attracted by the
good-value, light international
cuisine, with its emphasis on fresh
ingredients. The restaurant is a useful
choice for a working meal, especially
if time is limited.

Come Prima *DM* ///
Steinstr 3 ☎ *243422* • *closed Mon* •
AE DC MC V
Media and theatre people in
particular frequent Maurizio Olivieri's
light, uncluttered Italian restaurant in
a quiet location not far from the
Rathaus. The short, well-chosen
menu includes home-made pasta and
interesting fish dishes; in summer
there are tables outside.

Graf Zeppelin *DM* //
Graf Zeppelin hotel ☎ *299881* • *closed
Sat, Sun, mid-Jul–early Aug,* • *AE DC
MC V* • *jacket and tie*
The Graf Zeppelin hotel's spacious,
elegant and international restaurant is
used almost exclusively by business
people. Its seasonally changed menu
ranges from classic to *nouvelle*,
with dishes such as quails with
marinated chanterelles, medaillons
of lobster with basil and noodles
and, for the more diet-conscious,
poached veal fillet in vegetable
stock. The excellent wine list
includes some agreeable local bottles,
and the service is discreet and
attentive.

Out of town
Country restaurants and inns are very
popular, especially when time is not
pressing. Visitors, however, may feel
uneasy entertaining a client on his or
her home ground, but two places can
be recommended for a gastronomic
treat.
The *Ulrichshöhe*, in Nürtingen-

Hardt ☎ (07022) 52336, is about a
30min drive southeast of Stuttgart. It
has a terrace with a splendid view and
a menu which has earned a *Michelin*
rosette, including *loup de mer* in olive
sauce and rack of lamb with
rosemary.
The *Traube* (closed at weekends)
is an 18thC inn in the semi-rural
suburb of Plieningen ☎ 454833.
It serves such dishes as quail
consommé with truffles, ragout of
crayfish with chanterelles and passion
fruit sorbet as well as typical Swabian
dishes.

Weinstuben
Weinstuben are a special feature of the
Stuttgart scene. Open only in the
evenings, they are cheerful, noisy
places, often in attractive old
buildings with rough wooden
furniture, where local wines are
served from the barrel. The food is
exclusively Swabian and includes such
dishes as *Maultaschen* (like large
ravioli) or *Spätzle* (buttered noodles).
Zur Kiste, Kanalstr 2 ☎ 244002, is
the best known, but it is small and
usually crowded. In the same area,
near Charlottenplatz, is the
Schellenturm, Weberstr 72 ☎ 234888,
a 16thC tower with rough stone walls
and beamed ceilings.
Just 3.5kms/2 miles out of town, at
Bad Cannstatt, is another cluster of
Weinstuben including the *Klösterle*,
Marktstr 71 ☎ 568962, a former
monastery which claims to be the
oldest occupied building in the
Stuttgart area.

Bars and cafés
For a quiet discussion, there are
really only the bars in the *Am
Schlossgarten* and *Graf Zeppelin* hotels.
Fashionable wine bars include *Emilie*,
Mozartstr 49 ☎ 6491900, which is
popular with artists, journalists and
students; and *Fresko*, Konrad-
Adenauer-Str 28 ☎ 233613, in the
avant-garde new wing of the
Staatsgalerie, which is candlelit at
night and has a grand piano for
customers to play.

Entertainment

For German-speakers and music-lovers, Stuttgart offers top-class theatre, opera, dance and concerts. Tickets (except for the Staatstheater) and a free listings booklet, *Monatsspiegel*, with some English text, from the tourist office in Arnulf-Klett-Passage ☎ 2228243. Like all big German cities, Stuttgart also has a large number of sex-bars with live or filmed entertainment.

Theatre, dance, opera The *Staatstheater*, Oberer Schlossgarten 6 ☎ 2032444, is used for opera, with orchestras and singers of international standing, and for productions by the Stuttgart Ballet, founded by Britain's John Cranko, and now, under Marcia Haydée, one of the world's best. The *Kleines Haus* and the *Kammertheater* (in the new Staatsgalerie) offer outstanding German and international drama of all periods. The home of satire and cabaret is the *Renitenz-Theater*, Königstr 17 ☎ 297075.

Classical music Stuttgart has its world-famous chamber orchestra, its Melos Ensemble, and is the base for Helmut Rilling's Bach choral festival. *Liederhalle*, Berliner Pl 1 ☎ 2589710.

Cinema Most of the big cinemas are on or close to Königstrasse.

Nightclubs Stuttgart's nightlife lacks variety and sophistication. Apart from the *Scotch Club* in the Graf Zeppelin hotel, the only chic nightspot is the exclusive *Perkins Park*, Stresemannstr 39, Killesberg ☎ 252062. Two notable exceptions to the rather sleazy establishments around Leonhardsplatz are *The Four Roses*, Leonhardspl 24 ☎ 242837 and the *Moulin Rouge*, Kronprinzstr 15 ☎ 294705.

Shopping

All the best shops are concentrated around Königstrasse, near the south end of which is the attractive Calwer Passage, a restored period arcade of small boutiques. Porcelain, glass, furs, leather goods and jewellery are very good quality, though expensive. *Hertie*, on the corner of Schulstrasse and Königstrasse, and *Breuninger* in Marktplatz, are the most notable department stores. *Kamal und Silbermann*, Hindenburgbau, sells simple modern jewellery, while *Maas*, Schillerplatz, has antique jewellery and silver. *Schatzinsel*, Untere Königstrasse, is a leading oriental antique dealer; and among dozens of private art galleries, *Valentien* in Königsbau is one of the best-known. *Spielwaren-Kurtz*, Marktplatz, offers a wide selection of toys. For designer clothes, try *Modus*, Klett-Passage, and *Uli's*, Stiftstrasse.

Sightseeing

The 217-metre-high Fernsehturm (television tower) in the hilltop suburb of Degerloch provides an impressive view of the whole city. Its important historical buildings, such as the Altes Schloss and the Neues Schloss, a late-18thC royal palace, have been restored since World War II and are within walking distance of each other.

Motor museums The *Daimler-Benz Museum*, Mercedesstr 136, Untertürkheim (open Tue–Sun, 9–5); and the *Porsche Museum*, Porsche-Str 42, Zuffenhausen (open Mon–Fri, 9–12, 1.30–4).

Staatsgalerie Important collections of medieval German, Dutch and Italian painting and, in the new wing designed by James Stirling, of 20thC art, with German artists well represented. *Konrad-Adenauer-Str 30–32. Open 10–5; Tue and Thu, 10–8.*

Stiftskirche Late-Gothic premier Protestant church of Württemberg. In a side chapel is the tomb of Count Ulrich (d.1265) and his wife, founders of the Württemberg dynasty. *Schillerpl. Open daily, 8–5.30 (Thu, 12–5.30). Church music performed Fri 7pm.*

Württembergisches Landesmuseum in the Altes Schloss, a handsome Renaissance castle with a central galleried courtyard. Mainly archeological and regional exhibits. *Schlosspl/Karlspl. Open Tue–Sun, 10–5 (Wed, 10–7). Guides available.*

Out of town

Burg Hohenzollern ☎ (07471) 2428, 60kms/37 miles south near Hechingen, is a vast castle (completed 1867) with a panoramic view, and custodian of imperial treasures such as the Prussian crown of 1889. *Esslingen*, 14kms/9 miles southeast, has a picturesque marketplace, a 15th–16thC former town hall and two interesting Gothic churches. At *Ludwigsburg*, 16kms/10 miles to the north, there is a magnificent baroque palace and gardens ☎ (07141) 1411. Northeast of the city, *Maulbronn Zisterzienser-kloster* ☎ (07043) 7454, founded in 1147, is the best-preserved monastery in West Germany. And the old university town of *Tübingen*, 40kms/25 miles south of Stuttgart, has medieval buildings, many half-timbered.

Spectator sports

Details of sports fixtures from the *Sportamt*, Eberhardstrasse 33 ☎ 2162141.
Athletics International events are held at two venues. *Neckarstadion*, Mercedesstr ☎ 2164661, seats 70,000; tickets from the tourist centre ☎ 2228243 or *Kartenhäusle*, Kleiner Schlosspl. A new covered stadium next door, the *Hanns-Martin-Schleyer-Halle*, box office ☎ 561565, is also used for tennis, gymnastics, show-jumping and indoor soccer.
Soccer VFB Stuttgart plays at *Neckarstadion*.

Keeping fit

The clubs listed below do not require membership.
Fitness centres Sportstudio City Fitness Pfarrstr 1 (off Leonhardsplatz) ☎ 243327.
Golf The *Stuttgarter Golf Club* is 40kms/25 miles away at Mönsheim ☎ (07044) 5852.
Jogging Stuttgart's forest jogging tracks (*Waldsportpfade*) are marked with posts. Nearest to the city, one starts and ends at Geroksruhe, in Gablenberg, at the terminus of the No. 15 streetcar.

Mineral baths Stuttgart has a greater volume of natural spring water than anywhere else in western Europe. *Mineralbad Leuze*, An der König-Karls-Brücke ☎ 283224, is open daily, 6–8; the warm, invigorating, carbonated water feeds 6 swimming and plunge pools; saunas, solarium and restaurant.
Swimming In addition to the pool at the *Stuttgart International* hotel, which is open to non-residents (see *Hotels*), there are indoor public pools in the suburbs, but none in the city. In Killesberg, the *Höhenfreibad* is an outdoor pool, near the exhibition centre.
Tennis, squash The *Rems-Murr-Center* ☎ 582868 has 6 tennis and 6 squash courts. Nearer the city are the public courts of *Tennisanlage Cannstatter Wasen* ☎ 2164181.

Local resources

Business services

Of the various conference centres, only the Messe- und Kongresszentrum at Killesberg (see below) offers the fullest range of business services including word processing, modems, audiovisual equipment, teleconferencing, secretaries, translators and interpreters.
Photocopying and printing Copy-Shop ☎ 225391, near the railway station.
Secretarial Mon–Fri, *Büro-Service Burth* ☎ 769067; *ib personal* ☎ 220059.
Translators and interpreters Kern GmbH Language Services ☎ 235066, Mon–Fri.

Communications

Local delivery Tele-car ☎ 561104.
Long-distance delivery Express Parcels Systems ☎ 8567666.
Post office Hauptpostamt, Kleiner Schlosspl/Fürstenstr ☎ 20671, open Mon–Fri, 8–6; Sat, 8.30–12.30; also at the railway station, open Mon–Sat 7–11; Sun, 8–10.
Telex and fax At the station post office above.

Conference/exhibition centres
Stuttgart now hosts important trade
events. A booklet from the Kongress-
und Tagungsbüro Stuttgart, Villa
Scheuffelen, Stafflenbergstr 37
☎ 233988, gives full details of
9 major venues and lists over 40
other conference sites, including
hotels.

The main venue is the *Messe
Stuttgart*, Am Kochenhof 16 ☎ 25891
Ⓣ 722584, which is 4kms/2.5 miles
north of the centre, in Killesberg. It
has 36,500 sq metres/395,000 sq ft of
exhibition space. Annual fairs include
GARN (yarn and fibre), CAT (computer-
aided technology), and INTERGASTRA
(hotels and catering). The conference
centre has 7 rooms seating 50–990
and a hall for 8,000.

Hanns-Martin-Schleyer Halle,
Mercedesstr 69 ☎ 552067/69 is a
covered arena 3kms/2 miles from the
city centre, which can seat
3,000–10,000, with 4 smaller rooms
for 50–200. Right in Stuttgart, the
Liederhalle at Berliner Pl 1
☎ 2589710 has 2,000 sq metres/2,160
sq ft of exhibition space, 3 rooms for
150–2,000, audiovisual equipment
and a restaurant. *Medienzentrum Alte
Stuttgarter Reithalle*, Forststr 2
☎ 22144043, also centrally located,
offers 4 rooms for 30–800, full
audiovisual equipment, 2 sound
studios and film and video editing
facilities. *Schwabenlandhalle* in
Fellbach, Tainer Str 7 ☎ 580055 is
10kms/6 miles east of the city. Its
superbly designed, asymmetrical halls
can seat up to 1,400.

Emergencies
*Bureaux de change Deutsche
Verkehrs-Kredit-Bank* at the airport
and railway station, open late and at
weekends.
Hospitals In the city centre:
Katharinenhospital ☎ 20341. Serious
emergencies ☎ 280211. Dental
treatment ☎ 7800266.
Pharmacies Every pharmacy
(*Apotheke*) displays a notice with the
address of the nearest all-night
pharmacy.

Police Headquarters: Schmale
Str 11 ☎ 89902101.

Government offices
Staatsministerium Baden-Württemberg,
Richard-Wagner-Str 15 ☎ 21531
deals with very big projects only. The
*Ministerium für Wirtschaft und
Technologie, Baden-Württemberg*,
Kienestr 18 ☎ 1230 handles import,
export, cooperation between foreign
and local companies, and foreign
companies setting up subsidiaries
locally. Those setting up in the city
should consult the *Bürgermeisteramt
der Stadt Stuttgart (Wirtschafts-referat)*,
Marktpl 1 ☎ 2163570.

Information sources
Business information The regional
chamber of commerce is the *Industrie-
und Handelskammer Mittlerer Neckar*,
Jägerstr 30 ☎ 20051. A
documentation centre and patent
library, showing the best of local
products, is provided by the
Landesgewerbeamt Baden-Württemberg,
Kienestr 18 ☎ 1230. Public libraries
include the *Württembergisches
Landesbibliothek*, Konrad-Adenauer-
Str 8 ☎ 2125424 and the
Universitätsbibliothek, Holzgartenstr
16 ☎ 1212222.
Local media The *Stuttgarter
Nachrichten* has excellent economic,
political and arts coverage.
Süddeutscher Rundfunk (South
German radio and TV) is based in
Stuttgart.
Tourist information The
Verkehrsamt *i-Punkt* (information
point) ☎ 2228240 is in the Arnulf-
Klett-Platz, the precinct in front of
the railway station. At the east exit of
the precinct is the city transport
information office, VVS ☎ 66061.

Thank-yous
Florists Blumen-Gugeler in the railway
station and also in the Arnulf-Klett-
Passage ☎ 295690; *Blumen-Fischer* in
the Königsbau arcade, Schlosspl
☎ 295833. Both will deliver.
Wine merchants Benz-Wein, Urbanstr
1 ☎ 240947.

GREECE

After 25 years of strong growth, the Greek economy was hit badly by the world recession of the early 1980s. A two-year stabilization plan (1985–87) helped the economy to stage a modest recovery; growth is expected to remain above 2.5% a year into the 1990s. Even so, the current account deficit on the balance of payments is still large, the level of foreign debt is high and the rate of inflation over 10%.

Traditionally agriculture has played a major role in the economy, and it is still an important sector, even though its overall importance in the economy has declined since the 1960s. Today it employs about 25% of the work force and accounts for about 15% of GDP and over 20% of export earnings.

Industry (including mining and construction) and services expanded rapidly in the 1960s and 1970s, with government incentives encouraging investment; by 1979 they accounted for around 30% and 50% of GDP respectively. A decade later, however, manufacturing's share had fallen to 15% and productivity was about half the EC average. The "crisis" of the early 1980s was caused primarily by a heavy debt burden and price controls. Many small firms became unprofitable and went under; 44 loss-making industries were taken over by the government in 1983. Since then the government has said that it will transfer some of them back to the private sector. The main areas of production (in terms of value added) are food products, beverages and tobacco, textiles, clothing and footwear, chemicals and metal products. The fastest growing sectors are mining and quarrying, oil refining, and the manufacture of clothing and some agricultural products.

Manufactures (mainly textiles, clothing and footwear) account for about 50% of all exports, food and food products for about 25%. Greece's main imports are consumer goods, food products, capital machinery and petroleum. About two-thirds of foreign trade is conducted with other EC countries. Greece's large trade deficit is partly offset by earnings from services, notably from tourism and shipping, and EC transfers.

Geography A country of mountainous peninsulas and rugged islands. The only lowland areas are the river valleys, small basins in the mountains and coastal plains.
Climate Summers are hot and dry; average temperatures in Athens reach 28°C (82°F) in July. Winters are mild in the south but cooler in the north and inland areas.
Population 9.9m.
Government Greece is a republic. The parliament, the Vouli, has 300 members elected every 4 years. The president is elected by parliament for a term of 5 years; he appoints the majority leader in parliament as prime minister.
Currency Drachma (Dr).
Time 2hrs ahead of GMT; end Mar-end Sep, 3hrs ahead of GMT.
Dialling codes Greece's IDD code is 30. Omit the initial 0 from the city code when dialling from abroad. To make an international call from Greece, dial 00 before dialling the relevant country code.
Public holidays Jan 1, Jan 6, Mon before Shrove Tue, Mar 25, Greek Orthodox Good Fri–Easter Mon, May 1, 7th Mon after Easter Mon, Aug 15, Oct 28, Dec 25, Dec 26.

ATHENS

City code ☏ 01

The cradle of Western civilization and birthplace of democracy (and the capital of modern Greece since 1834) is today a noisy, polluted and not very beautiful city. One-third of Greece's population is packed into Greater Athens – just over 3m people.

Much of Greece's industry is concentrated around Athens: oil refineries, steelworks, mines, papermills and breweries. The shipyards at Eleusis are the biggest in the Mediterranean and employ around 5,000 people. The largest and most profitable companies include Aluminium de Grèce, Heracles General Cement, Greek Powder & Cartridge, Titan Cement and Hellenic Shipyards. Textiles, chemicals and pharmaceut-icals, electrical equipment and food are other important manufacturing industries. Many major companies, like Papastratos (tobacco) and Hel-lenic Steel, have factories elsewhere but headquarters here. Banking, insurance and the press are also based in the capital. Shipping is at nearby Piraeus and the great names – Goulandris, Livanos, Niarchos, Onassis – are still the best examples of private enterprise in this predomi-nantly state-run economy.

Tourism is a big earner, though many tourists spend only a day or two in the capital itself. Enclosed on three sides by mountains, Athens is set in a bowl which traps smog caused by industrial pollution and fumes from around 1m motor vehicles. The average temperature is around 30°C from June to September and the summer heat and humidity has become increasingly uncomfortable over the years.

Greek hospitality is legendary, and much business entertaining is done in the evening. On the whole, Greeks have an easy-going, Mediterranean attitude to life, but methods of doing business differ between the gener-ations. Older people are more chauvinistic and attach importance to ritual; the younger technocrats who have studied abroad tend to be more Western in their manners and less oblique.

Arriving

Most business visitors fly into Athens, but there are frequent passenger services by sea to Piraeus from France and Italy. Car ferries from eastern Italy provide easier access than the road through Yugoslavia (the border is 640kms/400 miles from Athens).

Hellenikon airport

This airport is divided into two terminals several kilometres apart and linked by an Olympic Airways shuttle service (hourly, 8–8). The East terminal handles foreign international flights and has better facilities than the West terminal, which handles all Olympic airways flights (including domestic services). The freight terminal is between the two: inquiries
☏ 989 2631 (international)
☏ 989 2604 (domestic).

West terminal Arriving here is tiresome: the building is run-down, there are few baggage trolleys (though they can be found in the arrivals hall), and long lines for clearing customs. The departures area of the terminal is not much better, though some improvements are in progress. The only restaurant is outside (opposite the arrivals exit). Facilities include banks and bureaux de change (open daily, 7am–10.30pm or 11) a business-class lounge, information desk and limited duty-free shop. Passenger inquiries ☏ 981 1201/2/3/4;

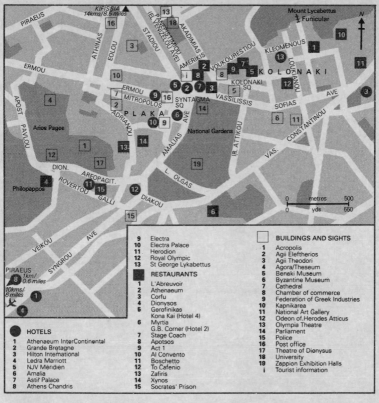

PIRAEUS
14kms/8.6 miles KIFISSIA
Mount Lycabettus
Funicular
N

9	Electra	
10	Electra Palace	
11	Herodion	
12	Royal Olympic	
13	St George Lykabettus	

RESTAURANTS

1	L'Abreuvoir
2	Athenaeum
3	Corfu
4	Dionysos
5	Gerofinikas
	Kona Kai (Hotel 4)
6	Myrtia
	G.B. Corner (Hotel 2)
7	Stage Coach
8	Apotsos
9	Act 1
10	Al Convento
11	Boschetto
12	To Cafenio
13	Zafiris
14	Xynos
15	Socrates' Prison

BUILDINGS AND SIGHTS

1	Acropolis
2	Agii Eleftherios
3	Agii Theodori
4	Agora/Theseum
5	Benaki Museum
6	Byzantine Museum
7	Cathedral
8	Chamber of commerce
9	Federation of Greek Industries
10	Kapnikarea
11	National Art Gallery
12	Odeon of.Herodes Atticus
13	Olympia Theatre
14	Parliament
15	Police
16	Post office
17	Theatre of Dionysus
18	University
19	Zappion Exhibition Halls
i	Tourist information

HOTELS

1	Athenaeum InterContinental
2	Grande Bretagne
3	Hilton International
4	Ledra Marriott
5	NJV Meridien
6	Amalia
7	Astir Palace
8	Athens Chandris

Olympic Airways reservations ☎ 961 6161; (domestic) ☎ 929 2444.

East terminal Facilities for all foreign airline passengers are better here than at the West terminal: restaurant (open 24hrs), Greek national tourist board (EOT) office ☎ 961 2722 (open irregularly Mon–Sat), information desk and hotel reservations service, souvenir and duty-free shops. The departures hall has a post office and desk for long-distance telephone calls. There are usually plenty of taxis waiting outside. Passenger inquiries ☎ 900 9466.

Nearby hotels There are many hotels very near Glyfada (and consequently they are noisy). The *Emmantina*, 33 Possidonos ☎ 898 0683 ⓉⓍ 210615,

and the *Regina Maris*, 11 Diadohou Pavlou ☎ 894 0468 ⓉⓍ 219420 ● AE DC MC V, are modern and air-conditioned, with pools.

City link The airport is on the coast 10kms/6 miles south of the city centre. A taxi or limousine is the most comfortable and convenient way into town. Buses offer a bone-shaking, but cheap and frequent, service to the centre (useful if there are long lines for taxis and your hotel is near Syntagma Square).

Taxi A cab costs Dr600–700 but drivers sometimes overcharge. At the West terminal (especially 5–8pm) be prepared to wait for a taxi and for drivers to be choosy about their destinations.

Limousine ☎ 323 3957.
Car rental Major firms have offices here but driving in central Athens is not recommended.
Bus Bus services run to 4 Amalias Ave, just off Syntagma Square, every 20mins (hourly after midnight) and (No. 19) to Piraeus (Karaiskaki Sq). Olympic Airways' buses leave from the West terminal for their offices at 96 Syngrou Ave every 30mins: journey time 20–30mins, more in rush hours; fare Dr100.

Railway and bus stations
The railway and long-distance bus systems are run by Greek State Railways (OSE); the stations are adjacent and a short taxi ride from the centre. Buses are generally more comfortable than trains (travel first class). Inquiries ☎ 522 2491 (train) ☎ 524 0519 (bus).
Larissa station Services from Europe and northern Greece. Fast trains and buses to Salonika take about 7hrs 30mins ☎ 821 3882.
Peloponnese station Trains to the Peloponnese.

Getting around
Taxis and limousines are widely used, and public transport is generally disdained by affluent Athenians. Foreigners find the bus and trolleybus system difficult unless they can read the Greek alphabet; the subway is simpler but of limited use. A map with street names in Greek and English is helpful, though most street signs in the centre are written in both alphabets. Confusion arises where streets have two names; Athenians use the older ones, for example Panepistimiou, not El Venizelou Ave, and Patission, not 28 Oktovriou, but maps give both.
    All vehicles, including taxis, may drive in central Athens only on alternate days, indicated by their licence-plates, so not all cabs from Piraeus will be able to go into town.
Taxis are cheap and, unless you are going to Piraeus or the suburbs, the minimum fare (Dr200) may apply.

They can be scarce at rush hours. All drivers understand, and usually speak, some English. Ranks are few but cabs stop if hailed. Sharing is common; would-be passengers shout their destinations at passing taxis. Tipping with small change is usual.
    It may be worth reserving a cab for several hours to cover all appointments, and you may be able to negotiate a rate. Radio taxis: *Taxi* ☎ 411 5200, *Ikaros* ☎ 321 4058, *Proodos* ☎ 643 7198. There is a minimum call-out fare and it is difficult to reserve taxis when shifts change (2–4pm).
Limousines Rank in Voukourestiou ☎ 323 3957 or 322 7142.
Driving Restricted entry to the centre, traffic congestion and major parking problems discourage most visitors from driving in Athens. International firms *Avis* ☎ 322 4951 and *Hertz* ☎ 994 2850 are more reliable than the numerous local car rental agencies on Syngrou Avenue.
Walking is advisable in the centre for short distances, especially during rush hours. Unaccompanied women should avoid the Omonia Square area at night.
Bus There is a comprehensive and frequent bus and trolleybus service. Buses (5am–midnight or 0.30) are old-fashioned but reasonably comfortable, except during peak hours. The exact fare of Dr30 must be put into a box beside the driver. A useful line is No. 40 to and from Piraeus (dark green bus).
Subway There is a swift "subway" (mostly above ground) from Kifissia (12kms/7.5 miles north), through the centre, to Piraeus; fare Dr30.

Area by area
Syntagma (Constitution) Square, dominated by the Parliament building, is the central hub of Athens geographically and politically. It is also the main business quarter; streets leading off it include Panepistimiou, lined with banks, Vassilissis Sofias Avenue, running east, where grand villas are now embassies, and Ermou,

to the west, a busy commercial and shopping street. To the northeast is the smart, airy residential district of Kolonaki, on the slopes of Mount Lycabettus. To the southwest is the Plaka, or Old Town, now much restored, and beyond and above it the Acropolis.

An increasingly important focus of international business is the seemingly endless Syngrou Avenue which leads to Piraeus. There are three large modern hotels here and several multinational company headquarters.

The most densely populated and polluted area is between Patission and the stations. There are still small factories making a wide range of goods between here and Piraeus.
Piraeus The modern port of Piraeus is just 10mins' drive from Syngrou or a subway ride from Omonia Square. Life revolves around the bustling quays and the shipping offices of Akti Miaouli. There is a residential area on the hill and a picturesque port at Mikrolimano (see *Restaurants*).

The suburbs Although many Athenians choose to live out of the centre, the journey into town, even from nearby suburbs like Filothei or Psihiko, can take up to an hour.

The most attractive residential districts to the north are Halandri, Maroussi, Kifissia (a summer resort some 14kms/8.5 miles from the centre) and Ekali. This is an up-and-coming area for clean industry and new businesses, and residents can commute to Piraeus without going into Athens.

The splendid Apollo coast, from Faliro to Sounion, is now much built-up. Glyfada (15kms/9 miles), close to the airport and the US Hellenikon base, has many American residents. More appealing is Vouliagmeni (25kms/15.5 miles), where the finest villas have views of the lovely bay.

Industry, major shipyards and oil refineries are concentrated northeast towards Salonika and west towards Corinth.

Hotels

Athens has one traditional and several modern luxury hotels (plus one at Vouliagmeni). Except for the Hilton, all the hotels which have main entries are on Syntagma Square (near most central businesses) or on Syngrou Avenue (convenient for Piraeus). Facilities include currency exchange, newsstands, laundry and 24hr room service; most secretarial needs can be met. All hotels listed are air-conditioned, with IDD telephones in bedrooms, and those with pools are not confined to the luxury category.

Corporate rates are usually negotiable, and many hotels offer discounts in winter. For reservations contact the Hellenic Chamber of Hotels, 2 Karagiorgi Servias ☎ 323 7193 (after arrival) or 24 Stadiou ☎ 323 6962 (before departure).

Athenaeum InterContinental *⬚////*
89–93 Syngrou Ave, GR-117 45
☎ *902 3666* ⊠ *221554 fax 921 7653*
● *AE DC MC V* ● *510 rooms, 50 suites,*
5 restaurants, 2 bars
The InterContinental prides itself on its conference facilities, the largest and most efficiently organized in the city; each bedroom has a separate working area suitable for small

meetings (5 business suites have fax machines). Modern Greek art decorates the vast public areas. There are several theme restaurants: the rooftop Premier (with 21 kinds of shish-kebab and fabulous views of the Acropolis), the Rotisserie (French), the Kublai Khan (Mongolian) and the popular Pergola coffeeshop overlooking the pool. Nonsmoking rooms, shops, shuttle service to the centre • pool, fitness centre, sauna • business centre with secretarial, word processing and translation facilities, 12 meeting rooms (capacity to 2,000).

Grande Bretagne $\boxed{D}$////
Syntagma Sq, GR-105 63 ☎ *323 0251* ☒ *215346 or 219615 (reservations only) fax 322 8034 • AE DC MC V • 380 rooms, 25 suites, 2 restaurants, 2 bars*
The grand old lady of Athens, built in 1872, is the most prestigious venue for grand gatherings, banquets and balls. Presidents, Heads of State and VIPs always stay here, but lesser mortals are not disdained. Bedrooms are cream-coloured, spacious and traditional, with marble bathrooms. Many have balconies; those at the top have the biggest and best ones, with Acropolis views; front rooms are sound-proofed. The bar is rather dark; better to meet at the Winter Garden, the formal dining room or the ever-popular G.B. Corner (see *Restaurants*). No parking facilities. Hairdresser, shops • 4 meeting rooms (capacity up to 450).

Hilton International $\boxed{D}$////
46 Vassilissis Sofias Ave, GR-106 76 ☎ *722 0201* ☒ *215808 fax 721 3110 • AE DC MC V • 453 rooms, 19 suites, 3 restaurants, 3 bars*
A landmark of Athens, the city's first modern international hotel recently celebrated its 25th anniversary with some rejuvenation to the decorations. It has an executive floor and is the most convenient major hotel for those with business in Maroussi or Kifissia. The airy Byzantium restaurant/ coffeeshop, with a salad buffet, is popular for an informal business lunch, as is the pool restaurant (open Apr–Oct). Ta Nissia is a more formal Greek restaurant (D only). The vast lobby-lounge is another good meeting place. Bedrooms are spacious, calm and virtually identical except for the views: even numbers face the Acropolis. Hairdresser, shops • pool, sauna, massage • business centre, 8 meeting rooms (capacity up to 1,550).

Ledra Marriott $\boxed{D}$////
115 Syngrou Ave, GR-117 45 ☎ *934 7711* ☒ *221833 fax 935 8603 • AE DC MC V • 242 rooms, 15 suites, 4 restaurants, 4 bars*
Opened in 1983, the Ledra Marriott has established a reputation for quality and smooth service, attracting the shipping and banking communities and executives of multinational companies. It is well-equipped for conferences, and the Kona Kai (see *Restaurants*) is one of the city's most sophisticated dining spots. The Ledra Grill, specializing in seafood and US beef, is ideal for dinner and private lunches. The Zephyros is more of a coffeeshop, and the seasonal Panorama, by the rooftop pool, has a view that lives up to its name. Quality furnishings and neutral colour-schemes are used in the bedrooms. The nonsmoking rooms are all on the first floor. Limited parking facilities. Hourly shuttle bus to city centre, hairdresser, gift shop • pool, jacuzzi • secretarial, word processing and translation services, 7 meeting rooms (capacity up to 300).

NJV Meridien $\boxed{D}$////
Syntagma Sq, GR-105 64 ☎ *325 5301* ☒ *210568 fax 323 5856 • AE DC MC V • 166 rooms, 16 suites, 2 restaurants, 1 bar*
This is the best modern, luxury-class hotel in the centre, and it attracts business visitors, mostly from other countries in Europe. It has lovely big bedrooms, whose light decor with classical features and splashes of bright colour, is inspired by the colours of Greece. The best rooms overlook the square, have uninterrupted views of the Acropolis, and are well sound-proofed. The Brasserie des Arts serves French and international cuisine and is a good choice for a drawn-out business meal; service is reputedly slow. Valet parking. Shops • business centre with secretarial, word processing and translation facilities, 1 meeting room (capacity up to 100).

OTHER HOTELS

Amalia _D/_ _10 Amalias Ave,_
_GR-105 57_ ☎ _323 7301_ ⊤ᴸ _215161_
fax 323 8792 • _AE DC MC V._ A
pleasant, well-run hotel overlooking
the Ethnikos Kipos (National
Gardens); convenient for the Zappion
Exhibition Halls.

Astir Palace _D/////_ _Panepistimiou_
& Vassilissis Sofias, GR-106 71
☎ _364 3112_ ⊤ᴸ _222380 fax 364 2825_
• _AE DC MC V._ A gleaming reflecting
glass block overlooking Syntagma
Square; lots of space, moderate
service. Convention facilities.

Athens Chandris _D//_ _385 Syngrou_
Ave, GR-175 64 ☎ _941 4824_
⊤ᴸ _218112 fax 942 5082_ • _AE DC MC_
_V._ Owned by the famous shipping
company, this is the nearest top-class
hotel to Piraeus. Facilities include a
swimming pool and restaurant on the
rooftop.

Electra _D/_ _5 Ermou, GR-105 63_
☎ _322 3223_ ⊤ᴸ _216896 fax 322 0310_
• _AE DC MC V._ A central hotel used
by business people and tour groups;
the bar is a useful meeting place but
bedrooms are dull and poorly lit.

Electra Palace _D/_ _18 Nikodimiou,_
_GR-105 57_ ☎ _324 1401_ ⊤ᴸ _216896_
fax 324 1875 • _AE DC MC V._ Near the
Plaka area not far from the Acropolis,
with a pool. Under the same
management as the Electra.

Herodion _D/_ _4 Rovertou Galli,_
_GR-117 42_ ☎ _923 6832_ ⊤ᴸ _219423_
fax 923 5851 • _AE DC MC V._ A
comfortable, efficiently-run hotel near
the Acropolis.

Royal Olympic _D/_ _28–32_
Diakou, GR-117 43 ☎ _922 6411_
⊤ᴸ _215753 fax 923 3317_ • _AE DC MC_
_V._ A modern hotel with traditional
interior, popular with the British.
Noisy location; request a room
overlooking the quieter courtyard and
pool.

St George Lykabettus _D/_ _2_
Kleomenous, GR-106 75 ☎ _729 0711_
⊤ᴸ _214253 fax 729 0439_ • _AE DC MC_
_V._ A pleasant Kolonaki district hotel
on the slopes of Mount Lycabettus, a
short taxi ride from the centre.
Romantic views from bedrooms and
the rooftop restaurant and pool.

Out of town

Astir Palace _D////_ _Vouliagmeni_
Beach, GR-166 ☎ _896 0211_ ⊤ᴸ
215013 fax 896 2582 • _AE DC MC V._
A modern resort hotel in a superb
setting, with its own beaches, leisure,
sports and conference facilities (see
Keeping fit). Popular at weekends with
smart Athenians and well-equipped
for the commuting business visitor.

Pentelikon _D//_ _66 Deligiani,_
Kefalari, Kifissia ☎ _801 2837_
⊤ᴸ _224699 fax 801 0314_ • _AE DC MC_
_V._ A quiet, old-style hotel, with pool
and a superb, expensive restaurant, in
a pleasant suburb, convenient for
some businesses.

For the meanings of the hotel
and restaurant price symbols,
see pages 6 and 7.

Restaurants

The restaurants of the top hotels are suitable for expense-account entertaining and their coffeeshops for less formal meals: the Pergola at the
InterContinental, Byzantium at the Hilton and the category-defying G.B.
Corner. The Mikrolimano seafood restaurants are 15mins by taxi from
central Athens.

A typical Greek meal begins with _mezedakia_ or _mezé_ (hors d'oeuvres)
ordered for the whole table, followed by a main course which is often
grilled lamb or fish. Desserts, like _baklava_ (honey-nut pastry), are very
sweet. The local drinks are ouzo, an aniseed-flavoured aperitif, and
retsina, a resinated wine.

Business lunches with foreign guests normally start between 1.30 and 2.30 and dinner from 8.30 or 9.30, but locals may eat after 10. Many restaurants only serve dinner. Reservations are essential in hotels, advisable 24hrs in advance elsewhere.

L'Abreuvoir *D*////

51 Xenokratous ☎ *722 9061* • *AE DC MC V* • *reservations essential*
Once a humble bistro, this smart French restaurant in fashionable Kolonaki is favoured both for business and social entertaining, especially in the evenings. The decor is cool and sophisticated, and there is a delightful canopied terrace. Cooking is classic French. Should you fail to get a table, or feel like a change, try *Je Reviens*, next door at No.49 ☎ 721 0535.

Athenaeum *D*////

8 Amerikis ☎ *363 1125* • *closed Sun, Jul, Aug* • *AE DC MC* • *tie preferred*
An old-fashioned establishment, proclaimed only by a discreet brass plaque, the Athenaeum is a good choice for formal business entertaining. The elegant, classical dining room has a fine fireplace and well-spaced tables. There is excellent Greek and European food, a reasonably priced buffet and a separate cocktail bar.

Corfu *D*

6 Kriezotou ☎ *361 3011* • *AE DC V*
Open daily from midday to midnight, the Corfu is most popular for weekday lunches, especially with politicians, lawyers and the local business community. Greek and Corfiot cooking; efficient service.

Dionysos *D*/

43 Rovertou Galli ☎ *923 3182* • *AE DC MC V* • *reservations advisable*
Despite the undistinguished food, Dionysos attracts Athenians as well as tourists with its superb picture-window view of the Acropolis; government ministers often bring their foreign counterparts here. The decor is semi-formal, the clientele predominantly male. There is another

Dionysos on Lycabettus (☎ 722 6374); also under the same ownership are the popular downstairs café and famous Zonar's in Panepistimiou (see *Bars and cafés*).

Gerofinikas *D*////

10 Pindarou ☎ *362 2719* • *AE DC MC V* • *reservations essential*
A classic Athenian restaurant, where many foreign visitors are entertained. The twin pivots of the rather dark, wood-panelled restaurant are the trunk of a palm tree (from which it takes its name) and the refrigerated counter (from which you can choose your food). Typical, and very good, are the stuffed vine leaves, oriental rice and sticky Greek puddings, and there is always fresh fish. A good choice for large parties.

Kona Kai *D*/////

Ledra Marriott Hotel ☎ *934 7711* • *closed L, Sun* • *AE DC MC V* • *reservations essential*
Enormous rattan armchairs, tropical plants and little streams contribute to the exotic atmosphere of this subterranean restaurant, serving Polynesian food. The Bali lounge and bar serves cocktails, and there is a Japanese *teppanyaki* corner serving sushi.

Myrtia *D*////

35 Markou Moussourou ☎ *701 2276* • *closed L, Sun, Aug* • *AE DC MC V* • *reservations essential*
The original Myrtia, Athens' most famous taverna (now with a branch in

---

Credit card abbreviations

AE	American Express
DC	Diners Club
MC	Access/MasterCard
V	Visa

Monte Carlo), is in the village-like residential area of Pangrati. Here, locals rub shoulders with top politicians, filmstars and executives of multinationals and their guests. There are often tourist groups in the garden in summer.

OTHER RESTAURANTS
Half-bar, half-restaurant, and with the atmosphere of an English pub crossed with a mid-West saloon, *G.B. Corner*, in the Grande Bretagne Hotel ☎ 323 0251, is a regular meeting place for Athenians and foreigners alike, especially for lunch; food is European and overpriced. Those set on hamburgers or steaks repair to the similar *Stage Coach* at 14 Voukourestiou ☎ 363 5145 (the smarter part is upstairs). *Apotsos*, 10 Panepistimiou ☎ 367 7046, is a smoky, bohemian turn-of-the-century *ouzerie* (local inn) popular with artists and journalists (and some lawyers and politicians) for its off-beat atmosphere and basic Greek dishes (L only; no credit cards). *Act 1*, 18 Akadimias ☎ 360 2492, is a favourite of after-theatre socialites, with a cocktail bar, piano and singing (D only).

In Kolonaki *Al Convento*, 4–6 Anapiron Polemou ☎ 723 9163, serves quite good Italian food (always crowded; arrive early). There are two recent additions to the scene: the informal and chic *Boschetto* ☎ 721 0893, in the little park opposite the Hilton, serving Italian *cucina nuova*, and *To Cafenio*, 26 Loukianou ☎ 722 9056, where elaborate hors d'oeuvre are served in smart yet spartan surroundings (no credit cards).

Two safe choices in the touristy Plaka (reservations essential) are *Zafiris*, 4 Thespidos ☎ 322 5460, an excellent game restaurant, with a colourful atmosphere and establishment clientele (open D, Oct–May only), and *Xynos*, 4 Agelou Geronta ☎ 322 1065, with a garden (D only). In the Makrigiani district, south of the Acropolis, *Socrates' Prison*, 20 Mitseon ☎ 922 3434, is also an authentic taverna.

Out of town
At Piraeus, the expensive seafood restaurants of Mikrolimano harbour are popular with the shipping fraternity at lunch time. *Zefiros* ☎ 417 5152, is considered by many to be the best; Athenians flock here in the evenings. There are two very exclusive clubs in Piraeus, the Marine and the City, to which those in shipping may be invited.

In the northern suburbs try the *Blue Pine* in Kifissia ☎ 807 7745, which has a garden for summer dining. *Psaropoulos* in Glyfada ☎ 894 5677 is a popular seafront fish restaurant for lunch.

Bars and cafés
The international business community congregates in the bars or coffeeshops of hotels: in the Hilton's lobby-lounge or *Byzantium*, at the Chandris, in the Ledra Marriott's *Crystal Lounge* or *Hellenic Bar* and the InterContinental lobby. Some Greeks frequent *ouzeries* like Apotsos (see *Restaurants*) or *Athinaikon* in Euripidou.

Zonar's 1930s-era café on Panepistimiou is always full and has an adjoining restaurant offering over 100 Greek dishes. *Ellinikon* on Kolonaki Square is popular for a light lunch.

Entertainment
The Athens Festival runs from June to September, with ancient drama, opera, music and ballet performed in the *Odeon of Herodes Atticus*. The ticket office is at 4 Stadiou (in the arcade) and tickets are sold up to 10 days in advance. It is not possible to reserve seats by telephone, but for advice on availability ☎ 322 1459. A summer festival of ancient drama is held at Epidaurus (a 2hr drive). Sound and Light, presented in English, French and German from April to October, is a less exalting experience. The *Athens News* gives daily listings.
Theatre The *National Theatre*, 20 Agiou Constantinou ☎ 522 3243, stages classical and modern plays.

Athenians enjoy *epitheorissi* (comedy and political satire).

Music and opera A concert hall is being built next to the US embassy. Meanwhile there are regular concerts given at the *Pallas Theatre*, 1 Voukourestiou ☎ 322 8275. The National Opera Company performs at the *Olympia Theatre*, 59 Akadimias ☎ 361 2461, and in summer at the Athens festival.

Dance Folk dancing by the Dora Stratou company at the *Philopappus Theatre* ☎ 324 4395 or 921 4650, May–Sep.

Cinema Foreign films have original soundtracks with subtitles. There are many open-air cinemas.

Nightclubs and casino For typical Greek entertainment dine at a taverna or visit a lively seafront *bouzoukia*. The smartest discotheque is the *Nine Muses* at the Astir Palace Hotel in Vouliagmeni (see *Hotels*), open summer only. The winter version is the *Nine Plus Nine*, 14 Agras ☎ 722 2325, although more popular for dining than dancing. The *Parnes Casino* is in the Mount Parnes Hotel ☎ 246 9111 at the highest point around the city, 40kms/22 miles to the north.

Shopping

The best shopping is around Syntagma Square and in the Kolonaki district. Most shops open Mon & Wed, 9–5; Tue, Thu, Fri, 10–7; Sat, 8.30–3.30. Mid-Jun–Sep they are open until 1.30pm and re-open Tue, Thu & Fri evenings. Tourist shops sell arts and crafts (worry beads, fluffy woollen rugs or *flokati* and embroidered articles) and may stay open until midnight. Furs (in Mitreopoulos or from *Sistovaris* in Ermou), jewellery (*Lalaounis*, 6 Panepistimiou) and real sponges (on sale at stalls) make the best gifts, and shoes are good value (Ermou and Kolonaki). The Benaki Museum (see *Sightseeing*) sells copies of original artifacts. There is a flea-market in Monastiraki (best on Sundays but crowded).

Sightseeing

If you see nothing else, visit the Acropolis, preferably early in the morning. Wander the back streets of the Plaka or take the funicular (or footpath) up Mount Lycabettus. It is probably more rewarding to take a day trip to the classical sites of Attica or Argolis, or to the islands (see *Out of town*), than to visit any but the major museums. Check opening hours with the tourist office.

Acropolis Monumental complex (being restored) including the *Erectheion*, with famous caryatids, the majestic Doric *Parthenon*, where classical Greek architecture reaches the summit of perfection, and the Ionic *Temple of Athene Nike*. The *Museum* displays sculptures from the site. There are fine views of the ancient *Theatre of Dionysus* and the *Odeon of Herodes Atticus* below. *Open Mon, 11–5; Tue–Fri, 8–5; Sat & Sun, 8.30–3.*

Agora The focal point of civic life in ancient times, with extensive ruins and a good *Museum*. The 5thC BC *Theseum* (Temple of Hephaestus) is the best preserved Doric temple in Greece. Best seen from the *Areopagus*, below the Acropolis, where St Paul preached in AD 51. *Open Tue–Sun, 8.30–3. Entrance on Adrianou.*

Archeological Museum Outstanding classical sculpture, plus gold jewellery and masks from Mycenae, Attic vases and other finds from all over the ancient Greek world. *44 Patission. Open Mon, 11–5; Tue–Fri, 8–5; Sat & Sun, 8.30–3.*

Benaki Museum Byzantine icons, jewellery and ancient artifacts in a neo-classical mansion. *1 Koumpari (entrance on Vassilissis Sofias Ave). Open Mon, Wed–Sun, 8.30–2.*

Byzantine churches The most remarkable include the tiny *Agii Eleftherios* on Mitropolos Square (next to the *Cathedral* or *Metropoli*), *Kapnikarea* on nearby Ermou and *Agii Theodori*, a few streets north.

Byzantine Museum Icons and treasures from early-Christian to post-Byzantine times. *22 Vassilissis Sofias*

Ave. Open Tue–Sun, 8.30–3.
National Art Gallery Greek and
other European paintings especially
by El Greco. *50 Vassilissis
Constantinou Ave. Open Tue–Sat, 9–3;
Sun, 10–2.*
Other sites The *Roman Agora*, with
the octagonal *Tower of the Winds* and
Hadrian's Library; the *Monument of
Lysicrates* (Diogenes' Lamp); the
Temple of Olympian Zeus and
Hadrian's Arch, which marks the
entrance to the ancient city.

Guided tours
Chat Tours, 4 Stadiou ☎ 322 3137,
and *Key Tours*, 2 Ermou ☎ 323 2520,
both run daily morning tours lasting
about 4hrs (and also evening
"nightlife" tours).

Out of town
Chat Tours, *Key Tours* and travel
agents run half-day trips to the
Temple of Poseidon at Sounion (43
miles/69kms) – taxis charge about
Dr6,000 for the round trip. *Delphi*
and *Corinth*, *Mycenae* and *Epidaurus*
are available as one-day bus tours.

Other ancient sites near Athens
include *Eleusis* (22kms/13.5 miles but
now an industrial area), *Marathon*
(38kms/23.5 miles), *Brauron*
(38kms/23.5 miles), *Amphiareion*
(45kms/28 miles) and *Rhamnous*
(49kms/30 miles). There are
remarkable Byzantine churches and
old monasteries at *Kessariani*
(6kms/3.5 miles) and *Daphni*
(11kms/7 miles).

Key Tours organizes one-day cruises
of the islands of the Bay of Athens,
Aegina, *Poros* and *Hydra*, but there
are regular hydrofoil and ferry
services from Piraeus (Flying
Dolphins ☎ 452 7107).

Spectator sports
Soccer at the Olympic stadium in
Maroussi ☎ 683 4000; *basketball* at
the Peace and Friendship Stadium in
Neo Faliro ☎ 481 9513.

Keeping fit
The *Ekali Club* has a pool, tennis

court and a restaurant ☎ 813 2685.
The *Astir Palace Hotel* at Vouliagmeni
(see *Hotels*) offers tennis courts, three
pools, watersports and a health centre
with sauna. The Greeks are not much
interested in strenuous exercise.
Fitness centres Nonresidents can use
the pool, sauna and fitness equipment
at the *Athenaeum InterContinental
Hotel*.
Golf *Glyfada Golf Club* ☎ 894 6820
and 894 6875.
Riding *Athens Riding Club*, Gerakas,
Agia Paraskevi ☎ 661 1088, is nearest
to the centre of town. *Hellenic Riding
Club* ☎ 681 2506.
Sailing *Hellenic Sailing Federation*
☎ 323 6813 or 413 7351. *Hellenic
Open Sea Sailing Club* ☎ 412 3357.
Yacht hire through *Yacht Brokers &
Consultants Association* ☎ 981 6582.
Skiing North of Athens ☎ 321 2429
(3hrs).
Swimming Vouliagmeni has the most
appealing, and cleanest, beaches. The
Hilton pool is open to nonresidents.
Tennis *Athens Tennis Club*, 2
Vassilissis Olgas ☎ 923 2872 or, in
the suburbs, the ACS *Tennis Club*
☎ 639 2000 at Halandri, the AOK
Tennis Club ☎ 801 3100 at Kifissia or
the *Attica Tennis Club* ☎ 681 2557 at
Filothei. Information from *EFOA
Tennis Federation* ☎ 821 0478.
Waterskiing Contact the *Waterskiing
Federation* ☎ 523 1875 or 522 9729.
Windsurfing *Greek Windsurfing
Association* ☎ 323 2877. Skinias at
Marathon is a good beach.

Local resources
Business services
Executive Services Ltd offers
secretarial, translating and
interpreting services, conference
planning and PR ☎ 778 3698.
Photocopying and printing At hotels
and neighbourhood copy shops. *Rank
Xerox Copy Service*, 23–25 Leka
☎ 324 9930, is central.
Secretarial *International Business
Service* ☎ 724 5541.
Translation *Commissioners
International: Gordon A. Ball Ltd*
☎ 672 4284 or *Dominique Thomson*,

c/o Hotel Grande Bretagne
☎ 323 0251.

Communications
Local delivery ACS ☎ 522 4072 or
523 7202; *DMB* ☎ 922 3618 or
324 9941.
Long-distance delivery DHL
☎ 982 9691; *World Courier Hellas*
☎ 362 6885.
Post offices Main offices: 100 Eolou
and Syntagma Sq, open Mon–Fri,
7.30–8; Sat & Sun, 9–1.30. *ELTA*
(express mail service) ☎ 524 2502.
Telex and fax Telex at main post
offices. Also *Photo Express*,
4 Athinion, Glyfada ☎ 894 1391.

Conference/exhibition centres
The Athenaeum InterContinental and
Hilton Hotels have excellent facilities
(including catering). Also used are the
huge *Peace and Friendship Stadium* at
Neo Faliro ☎ 481 9512 and the
Zappion Exhibition Halls, Amalias
Ave ☎ 323 1660 or 322 4610, the
main venues for trade fairs.

Emergencies
Bureaux de change Normal bank
hours are Mon–Thu, 8–2; Fri,
8–1.30. The National Bank of Greece
in Syntagma Square is open Mon–Fri,
8am–9pm; Sat & Sun, 8–8.
Hospitals Ambulance/First Aid
☎ 166. *KAT Hospital for Accidents*, 2
Nikis, Kifissia ☎ 801 4411; *Hygeia
Hospital*, Kifissias Ave ☎ 682 7940
(private) or 723 3782 (24hr medical
assistance for visitors with insurance
cover). Dental emergencies
☎ 643 0001 (open 10pm–6am).
Pharmacies For a list of those which
are open late, check the *Athens News*
or ☎ 107.
Police ☎ 100 or (English-speaking)
171; 7 Syngrou Ave ☎ 921 4392.
Emergency multilingual advice
☎ 171.

Government offices
Ministry of Commerce, Kanningos Sq
☎ 361 6251; *Ministry of Industry,
Energy and Technology*, Odos
Zalokosta 10 ☎ 363 0911.

Information sources
Business information Chamber of
commerce and industry, 7 Akadimias,
GR-106 75 ☎ 362 4280; *Federation of
Greek Industries* (*SEB*), 5 Xenofontos
☎ 323 7325 (government/business
relations); *ICAP*, 64 Vassilissis Sofias
Ave, GR-115 28 ☎ 721 5792 (financial
directory of Greek companies; market
research and other services); *Piraeus
Chamber of commerce and industry*,
Loudovikou 1 ☎ 417 7241; *Piraeus
Port Authority* ☎ 451 1411.
Local media National dailies include
Kathimerini (right-wing morning), *Ta
Nea* (Socialist, afternoon) and
Naftemboriki (financial, especially
shipping). *Ekonomikos Tachidromos* is
an economic weekly.

Athens News (daily) and *Greece's
Weekly* are in English, as is the
weekly summary of financial news in
Express (available by subscription).
The Athenian is a monthly general and
cultural magazine.
Tourist information Greek National
Tourist Organization *EOT*, 2 Karageorgi
Servias (inside National Bank)
☎ 322 3111, and at 1 Ermou ☎ 325
2267. Information available in several
languages: ☎ 171 (headquarters at
Syngrou Ave ☎ 923 9224). *Aliens
Bureau* ☎ 646 8103 (for visas and
information on residence). *The Week
in Athens* and *This Week in Athens*
both give some general tourist
information.

Thank-yous
Confectionery/cakes Floca, 1 Veikou
☎ 922 9633; *Fresh*, 1 Sekeri
☎ 364 2948; *La Chocolatiere*, 32
Skoufa ☎ 722 0200 and at the Hilton
Hotel.
Florists Ponirakis, 45 Patriarchou
Ioachim ☎ 722 0662 or 721 8182 or
Skarentzos in Voukourestiou.

IRELAND

After a decade of recession, rising unemployment and mounting budget and balance of payments deficits, the Irish economy has begun to pick up; GDP is growing strongly, inflation is falling, the balance of payments has moved into surplus and the large budget deficit has been reduced. But some of the government's austerity measures have proved very unpopular and unemployment remains high (nearly 19% in 1988), despite growth in manufacturing output and investment.

Traditionally agriculture has been the most important sector of the economy. Today it is less important, although it still accounts for over 10% of GDP and employs 13% of the work force. Livestock farming is the main activity; production accounts for over 80% of agricultural output. Over 50% of total output is exported.

Industrial growth, largely financed by foreign capital, has been lead by modern manufacturing industries (such as electronics, pharmaceuticals and machinery), producing goods for export. Traditional industries (such as textiles, clothing, footwear and leather), mostly Irish-owned and producing goods for the domestic market, have been hit by foreign competition and are declining in importance. Meanwhile, tourism, which is now Ireland's third largest foreign exchange earner, other service industries and construction have expanded.

Ireland is heavily dependent on external trade; exports of goods and services account for about 60% of GDP. Manufactured goods (mainly machinery and transport equipment but now including chemicals and electrical office equipment) account for over 60% of total exports, while food and food products account for about 25%. Imports consist mainly of machinery and transport equipment, manufactures and components, chemicals, petroleum and its products. Over two-thirds of external trade is conducted with other members of the EC, of which UK remains the dominant trading partner.

Geography The centre of Ireland is a fertile plain, dotted with lakes and low hills and drained by slow, winding rivers. Most of the high ground is located around the coast. The east coast is more sheltered than the west.
Climate A mild, equable climate greatly influenced by the Gulf stream. Rain throughout the year.
Population 3.6m.
Government Ireland has been a republic since 1949. The parliament consists of the Senate (the upper house), with 60 members, and the Dail (the lower house), with 166 members elected by proportional representation every 5 years. The prime minister (Taoiseach) is the leader of the majority party in the Dail. The president is elected by direct vote every 7 years.
Currency Punt, or Irish pound (I£).
Time GMT; end Mar–end Sep, 1hr ahead of GMT.
Dialling codes Ireland's IDD code is 353. Omit the initial 0 from the city code when dialling from abroad. To make an international call from Ireland, dial 16 (03 for UK) before dialling the relevant country code.
Public holidays Jan 1, Mar 17, Good Fri–Easter Mon, 1st Mon in Jun, 1st Mon in Aug, last Mon in Oct, Dec 25, Dec 26.

DUBLIN

Dublin, with a population of 1.25m, is Ireland's administrative and financial centre. Banks and insurance companies, unions and industry federations all have their headquarters in the city. Industry itself tends to be small-scale and located on the outskirts of Dublin.

After a decade of economic distress, the result of overborrowing and fiscal laxity, the Irish economy seems to be on the mend. But there is still a shortage of jobs and many graduates and skilled young workers emigrate to countries where employment opportunities are greater. Helping to stem this flow is the Industrial Development Authority, an energetic body which has succeeded in attracting substantial foreign investment through incentives such as tax breaks and grants.

While welcoming overseas investors, the Dublin business community believes that long-term wealth and job creation depend on the growth of indigenous companies. It is hoped that Dublin can become an important European financial centre, and the city is not short of entrepreneurial and business ability. Michael Smurfitt (of Jefferson Smurfitt) turned a small corrugated paper company into a multinational, whose activities range from banking to distribution; and Tony O'Reilly (of US giant Heinz but with substantial interests in Ireland) has proved even more skilful in business than he was on the rugby pitch when playing for his country.

One of the pleasures of doing business in Dublin is the loquacious charm of the people, which should not be mistaken for a lack of commercial shrewdness. If you can, allow half a day for sightseeing in the Georgian city and a few days for exploring farther afield. Even Kerry in the southwest is only a few hours' drive away.

Arriving

Dublin is easily reached by air. There are frequent flights from many airports in Britain, and also frequent scheduled flights from Amsterdam, Brussels, Copenhagen, Düsseldorf, Frankfurt, Madrid, Milan, Moscow, Paris, Rome, Zurich and several US cities, including New York, Boston, Atlanta, Chicago and Los Angeles.

There are car ferry services from Holyhead in Wales and Liverpool in northeast England.

Dublin airport

Clearance formalities rarely take long at Dublin's efficient airport, where the facilities include a well-stocked shopping arcade and duty-free shop, bar, restaurant, telephones and an information desk, which offers an accommodation reservation service. The post office is open daily, 9–12.30 and 1.30–5, banks open 6.45am–9.00pm (9.30 Fri). Airport inquiries ☎ 370191.

Nearby hotels Dublin International ☎ 379211 Ⓣ 32849 *fax* 425874 AE DC MC V. A sound-proofed 200-bed hotel run by Trusthouse Forte, opposite the terminal.

City link The airport is located 6 miles/10kms north of the centre. Taxis provide the swiftest link.

Taxi There are usually plenty of cabs in front of the terminal. The journey into town via the N1 road takes 15–20mins, slightly longer during rush hours, 8–9.30 and 4.30–6.

Car rental Major firms have desks in the arrivals hall.

Bus An express service runs every 30mins, 8am–9.30pm, taking 25mins to reach the Central Bus Station in Amiens Street. The ordinary city bus can take twice as long.

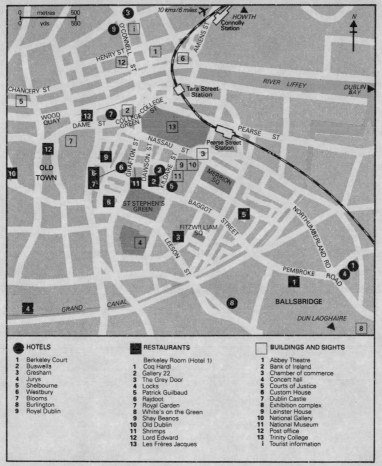

HOTELS

1 Berkeley Court
2 Buswells
3 Gresham
4 Jurys
5 Shelbourne
6 Westbury
7 Blooms
8 Burlington
9 Royal Dublin

RESTAURANTS

Berkeley Room (Hotel 1)
1 Coq Hardi
2 Gallery 22
3 The Grey Door
4 Locks
5 Patrick Guilbaud
6 Rajdoot
7 Royal Garden
8 White's on the Green
9 Shay Beanos
10 Old Dublin
11 Shrimps
12 Lord Edward
13 Les Frères Jacques

BUILDINGS AND SIGHTS

1 Abbey Theatre
2 Bank of Ireland
3 Chamber of commerce
4 Concert hall
5 Courts of Justice
6 Custom House
7 Dublin Castle
8 Exhibition complex
9 Leinster House
10 National Gallery
11 National Museum
12 Post office
13 Trinity College
i Tourist information

Getting around

The city centre is compact and easily covered on foot. To get to Ballsbridge and places farther out, it is best to take a cab or use public transport.
Taxis All taxis carry a prominent yellow roof sign, lit up at night. Officially they are not allowed to stop when hailed. Taxis wait in major streets and squares. You can telephone the nearest rank (see Taxi Cab Ranks in the Yellow Pages) or call National Radio Cabs ☎ 772222 or 776528.
Limousines Dial-a-Merc ☎ 373333;

Liam Ormsby Chauffeur Drive ☎ 401257.
Driving Traffic drives on the left and there is a 30mph/48kph speed limit within the city. The main routes into and through the city are congested on weekdays. Parking is difficult and theft is a problem. Central parking is available in Marlborough Street (parallel to O'Connell Street), Drury Street and Setanta Place.
Car rental Avis ☎ 776971; *Budget* ☎ 370919; *Murray's Europcar* ☎ 681777; *Hertz* ☎ 767476.
Walking In most parts of the centre –

on the south side of the Liffey, at least – walking is easy and pleasurable. Along the quays traffic is an irritant.

Bus and train The bus system is cheap and reasonably easy to understand, but services are too irregular to be convenient.

By contrast, the Dublin Area Rapid Transit system (DART) provides a frequent and efficient train service between the northern town of Howth and the southern town of Bray, via the city centre and Dun Laoghaire. Key central stations are at Connolly (Amiens Street), Tara Street and Pearse Street.

Area by area

Dublin is divided roughly in two by the River Liffey. The main street of the unfashionable north side is O'Connell Street. Halfway along this wide avenue is the imposing classical-style General Post Office; at the northern end is the monument to Charles Stewart Parnell, founder of the Home Rule movement. To the west is Henry Street, with its busy daily market, and the Courts of Justice in Chancery Street. To the east is the renowned Abbey Theatre and the Custom House, dwarfed by the ugly Liberty Hall, built in the 1960s as headquarters of the powerful Transport and General Workers' Union.

On the fashionable south side of the Liffey many of the city's most important buildings are crowded into a few blocks. The stately Bank of Ireland, built in the 18th century as the Irish Parliament, faces the entrance of Trinity College, also known as the University of Dublin. From here, Grafton Street, traditionally the city's smartest shopping area, stretches south to St Stephen's Green.

East, off Grafton Street, is the new and luxurious shopping mall, Royal Hibernian Way, on the site of the much lamented Royal Hibernian Hotel. One block farther east is Leinster House, built as a private mansion in 1745, and now the seat of the Dáil, Ireland's Parliament. It is surrounded by ministerial buildings, and the National Museum is located in the same complex.

To the east again are Fitzwilliam and Merrion Squares, Georgian Dublin at its finest. Most of the houses are now offices for companies and professionals.

Farther south, the Grand Canal marks the limit of the Georgian city and the beginning of the Victorian residential suburb of Ballsbridge. Here too, many of the spacious detached houses are now offices. The US Embassy is in Ballsbridge, along with most of the city's best modern hotels.

West of St Stephen's Green is Old Dublin, where the Vikings founded the city around AD841. Much of the area was bulldozed and redeveloped in the 1960s and 1970s – now an admitted mistake. Substantial remains of the early settlement were discovered when Irish Life were preparing to build their new headquarters on Wood Quay in the early 1980s.

Industrial suburbs New industrial developments are concentrated north of the city, along the airport road. There are plans to rejuvenate the redundant port area due east of the city for smaller manufacturing enterprises.

Residential suburbs Many of the city's professional and business classes now live out along Dublin Bay, in Blackrock, Monkstown, Dun Laoghaire and Dalkey or even farther south.

Hotels

The Shelbourne, on St Stephen's Green, is by tradition Dublin's classiest hotel, while the Berkeley Court is the best of the cluster of well-equipped modern hotels with large parking areas in Ballsbridge. Hotels are busiest in summer but are also packed in winter when there is a weekend rugby international at Lansdowne Road. The Tourist Board offices at the airport and in O'Connell Street provide a hotel reservations service.

Berkeley Court *P*////
Lansdowne Rd, 4 ☎ *601711* ⊤ₓ *30554 fax 617238* • *AE DC MC V* • *200 rooms, 10 suites, 2 restaurants, 1 bar*
Monarchs and prime ministers have stayed at the Berkeley Court, built in the mid-1970s in the Ballsbridge suburbs. The opulent decor of oil paintings, antique furniture and deep pile carpets recreates an atmosphere of *fin-de-siècle* elegance. Service is polished and the spacious rooms are luxuriously furnished. The quiet lounge and Lobby Terrace are both excellent for informal business meetings, and the Berkeley Room restaurant, specializing in fish, is often used by high-ranking politicians and business people for entertaining. Parking, hairdresser, shopping arcade • pool, sauna • 3 meeting rooms (capacity up to 250).

Buswells *P*
Molesworth St, 2 ☎ *764013* ⊤ₓ *90622 fax 762090* • *AE DC MC V* • *70 rooms, 1 restaurant, 2 bars*
Buswells is a small hotel owned and run by the Duff family. It was converted from a group of houses in a fine 18thC terrace and, despite its small rooms, is popular with politicians and business travellers because of its personal service and its central location opposite the Dáil. 2 meeting rooms (capacity up to 150).

Gresham *P*//
23 Upper O'Connell St, 1 ☎ *741114* ⊤ₓ *32473 fax 787175* • *AE DC MC V* • *183 rooms, 6 suites, 1 restaurant, 2 bars*
This old and atmospheric hotel, with its fine Art Deco lobby, was fashionable in the 1960s when President Eisenhower and Elizabeth Taylor were regular guests. Its fortunes flagged but have revived again under the management of the Ryan Group. Strong points are the central location, hospitable staff, comfortable rooms and a quiet, relaxed atmosphere which many prefer to the bustle of Dublin's bigger hotels. Parking, newsstand • 1 meeting room (capacity up to 250).

Jurys *P*///
Ballsbridge, 4 ☎ *605000* ⊤ₓ *93723 fax 605540* • *AE DC MC V* • *380 rooms, 8 suites, 3 restaurants, 2 bars*
Jurys is a big modern hotel in Ballsbridge, often used by visitors attending trade fairs at the nearby Royal Dublin Society exhibition halls. The hotel also has its own extensive conference facilities that are used by local firms for sales seminars, exhibitions and fashion shows. It has a busy atmosphere and friendly staff, and aims to keep guests happy with a nightly cabaret and a swimming pool complex under a glass-roofed pavilion. Parking, shops • 9 meeting rooms (capacity up to 850).

Shelbourne *P*////
St Stephen's Green, 2 ☎ *766471* ⊤ₓ *93653 fax 616006* • *THF* • *AE DC MC V* • *168 rooms, 17 suites, 1 restaurant, 1 bar*
The Shelbourne (pronounced Shelburn) was built in 1824 and overlooks Dublin's spacious and leafy St Stephen's Green, close to the Dáil and the key ministries. The lobby with its marble-lined walls, chandeliers and portraits of the Irish aristocracy sets the tone of this grand hotel. However, it is necessary to reserve a suite if you want to be sure of elegant accommodation. Politicians meet in the Horseshoe Bar; the club-like Aisling restaurant is a popular place for business entertaining, and the rooms in which the Irish Constitution was drafted are now used for private functions. Parking • 5 meeting rooms (capacity up to 550).

Westbury P////
Grafton St, 2 ☎ *791122* ⊠ *91091
fax 797078* • *AE DC MC V* • *150
rooms, 6 suites, 2 restaurants, 1 bar*
Located just off Dublin's most
fashionable shopping street, the
Westbury is a modern hotel furnished
with reproduction antiques. The
extensive upper Terrace lounge,
carpeted with deep pink, hand-made
rugs, is a popular meeting for the
business community, and the
Sandbank Seafood Bar quickly fills in
the early evening with local
executives. Parking, shops.

OTHER HOTELS
Bloom's P///   *Anglesea St, 2*
☎ *715622* ⊠ *31688 fax 715997* •
AE DC MC V. Small and popular with
tourists, but very central.

Burlington P//   *Upper Leeson St, 4*
☎ *605222* ⊠ *93815 fax 605064* •
AE DC MC V. This modern hotel in
suburban Ballsbridge is Dublin's
biggest. Very popular for its dinner
and cabaret (in summer) and
Annabelle's disco.
Royal Dublin P//   *40 Upper
O'Connell St, 1* ☎ *733666* ⊠ *32568
fax 733120* • *AE DC MC V*. Small
hotel on the less popular north side of
the Liffey, but modestly priced and
comfortable. Parking.

Hotel and restaurant price guide
For the meanings of the hotel and
restaurant price symbols, see
Symbols and abbreviations on pages
6 and 7.

Restaurants

The Irish have a well-deserved reputation for being great talkers and a lot
of business is done over lunch or dinner. Many of Dublin's restaurants
specialize in seafood and most of the best ones are small.

Berkeley Room P//
Berkeley Court Hotel ☎ *601711* •
AE DC MC V
This superior hotel restaurant, which
specializes in seafood followed by
Irish mist *soufflé*, is a favourite with
the high fliers of Dublin society.

Coq Hardi P////
35 Pembroke Rd ☎ *689070* • *closed
Sat L, Sun, 2 weeks Aug* • *AE DC MC V*
An elegant restaurant in a converted
Georgian house, decorated with
antiques and oil paintings. Manager
John Howard's interest in horse-
racing – and the possibility of picking
up a useful tip for the races – is one
reason why many leading business
guests return regularly. Other good
reasons are the excellent seafood and
fine wines.

Gallery 22 P//
22 St Stephen's Green ☎ *686169* •
closed Mon D, Sun • *AE DC MC V*
Intimate cellar restaurant whose
central location makes it a popular

choice for a quick and informal
lunch. You choose from a menu of
excellent home-made soups, smoked
salmon and game.

Grey Door P////
23 Upper Pembroke St ☎ *763286* •
closed Sat L, Sun • *AE DC MC V*
Dublin professionals with offices in
the nearby Georgian houses of
Fitzwilliam and Merrion Squares are
regular diners in the high-ceilinged
Grey Door. The cuisine is described
as Russian/Scandinavian: dishes are
served with rich sauces containing
soured cream and caviar.

Locks P//
1 Windsor Ter ☎ *538352* • *closed Sat
L, Sun* • *AE DC MC V*
This former pub, serving excellent
fish, attracts businessmen as well as
rock musicians. The location, by the
side of the Grand Canal in the rather
seedy Portobello suburbs, is off-beat,
but parking is easy and a private
room is available.

Patrick Giulbaud P////
46 James Pl ☎ *601799* • *closed Sat L,
Sun* • *AE DC MC V*
This is a chic restaurant in an
unpromising location, a scruffy mews
close to the Bank of Ireland's
headquarters, from which it draws
much custom. The dining room
resembles a conservatory, with
baskets of lush tropical greenery
cascading from the high glass ceiling.
The menu is traditional Irish à la
Giulbaud.

Rajdoot P////
26–28 Clarendon St ☎ *794274* • *closed
Sun L* • *AE DC MC V*
Considered to be one of Europe's top
Indian restaurants, Rajdoot has the
sophisticated ambience that attracts
even the most choosy, and its spicy
North Indian cuisine is of the highest
quality.

Royal Garden P/
Westbury Centre, Clarendon St
☎ *791397* • *AE DC MC V*
Near to the Rajdoot, at the rear of
the Westbury Hotel, the Royal
Garden serves authentic Cantonese
cuisine using local fish and prawns.

White's on the Green P////
119 St Stephen's Green ☎ *751975* •
closed Sat L, Sun • *AE DC MC V*
White's splendid Georgian interior,
with views over St Stephen's Green,
has been host to guests as diverse as
President Mitterrand and Peter
Ustinov. Chef Michael Clifford has
made his name by applying
sophisticated twists to traditional Irish
dishes such as stew and roast lamb
and complementing them with a fine
wine list.

OTHER RESTAURANTS
In town, other restaurants to try
include *Shay Beanos*, 37 Lower
Stephen St ☎ 776384, smart but
small – which means that you cannot
expect privacy; and the nearby *Old
Dublin*, 90 Francis St ☎ 542028, in a
cobbled back street surrounded by
antique shops, whose menu includes

some imaginative vegetarian dishes
and the Russian-influenced Fillet à la
Novgorod. *Shrimp's Wine Bar*, 1
Anne's Lane ☎ 713143, just off
Grafton Street, offers excellent fish
dishes at reasonable prices. *Lord
Edward*, 23 Christchurch Pl
☎ 542420, is also noted for its
seafood. *Les Frères Jacques*, 74 Dame
St ☎ 794555, is popular with
theatregoers and serves classic French
cuisine.
  There are also several
recommendable restaurants within a
short drive of the centre. *The Park*,
26 Main St, Blackrock ☎ 886177,
specializes in local salmon and game
dishes. *Le Relais des Mouettes*, Marine
Parade, Sandy Cove, Dun Laoghaire
☎ 809873, serves high-quality French
cuisine and imports cheese from
France. *King Sitric*, East Pier,
Harbour Rd, Howth ☎ 325235,
enjoys sweeping views and serves
excellent fish.

Bars and cafés
You must not leave Dublin without
visiting one of its traditional pubs.
They are open 10.30am–11.30pm.
Doheny and Nesbitt's, 5 Lower Baggot
St, is the atmospheric haunt of
politicians, journalists and barristers.
McDaid's, 3 Harry St, is a literary
pub, once favoured by Brendan
Behan and the Dublin bohemians.
Davy Byrne's, 21 Duke St, was
mentioned in James Joyce's *Ulysses*.
Under new management it has been
modernized and is now the haunt of
young professionals, many of whom
come for breakfast meetings over
smoked salmon and scrambled eggs.
More like the pubs that Joyce knew is
Mulligan's, 8 Poolbeg St, 200 years
old and another journalistic
rendezvous. On the north side of the
Liffey, the *Tilted Wig*, 1 Chancery Pl,
near the Four Courts, is popular with
lawyers. *Mitchell's Wine Bar*, 21
Kildare St, lists interesting wines and
serves inexpensive bar meals.
Opposite the Dáil, and close to
ministerial offices, it attracts
politicians and civil servants.

The best hotel bars for business entertaining are the *Horseshoe Bar* at the Shelbourne and the *Terrace Bar* at the Westbury.

The café has traditionally played an important part in Dublin's social life. Perennial favourites for tea, coffee and talk are the branches of *Bewley's* in Grafton Street, Westmoreland Street and South Great George's Street.

Entertainment

Dublin has a rich cultural tradition, with many "Irish" offerings. Listings are given in the fortnightly magazine *In Dublin*.

Theatre, dance and opera The *Abbey*, Lower Abbey St ☎ 787222, was founded in 1898 by W.B. Yeats and others as the national playhouse. The modern theatre, rebuilt in 1966 after a fire, specializes in works by Irish playwrights such as Synge, Shaw, O'Casey and Wilde. The downstairs sister theatre, the *Peacock*, puts on new plays and experimental drama. Orson Welles made his first stage appearance at the *Gate*, Parnell Sq ☎ 744045, a small repertory theatre with a high reputation. The *Gaiety*, South King St ☎ 771717, is a colourful Victorian building, used by visiting and local opera, ballet and drama companies.

Classical music Major performances are given at the *National Concert Hall*, Earlsfort Ter ☎ 711888 (information) and 711533 (credit card reservations).

Traditional music O'Donghue's, 15 Merrion Row ☎ 762807, is regarded as Dublin's best spot for traditional Irish music. Other pubs with regular traditional music nights are *An Béal Bocht*, 58 Charlemont St ☎ 755614, and *Kitty O'Shea's*, 23 Upper Grand Canal St ☎ 609965.

Nightclubs, most of which are upmarket discos, are concentrated along Leeson Street, where *Bojangles* ☎ 789428, *Parkers* ☎ 765620, *Samantha's* ☎ 765252, *Strings* ☎ 613664 and *Suesey Street* ☎ 686674 are all found.

Shopping

Most shops open Mon–Sat, 9–5.30, with late-night opening to 8 on Thu. Increasingly book and gift shops are now opening on Sunday afternoons. For the visitor, the area to concentrate on is around Grafton Street. The best department stores are *Brown Thomas* and *Switzer's*, both on Grafton Street itself. The best shopping complexes are the Powerscourt Townhouse Centre, off Clarendon Street, and Royal Hibernian Way, off Dawson Street.

Art and antiques James Adam, 26 St Stephen's Green, is the city's main auction house, but there are scores of antique shops along Ormond Quay. Saturday's *Irish Times* covers forthcoming auctions.

Books Waterstone's, 7 Dawson St, has a vast stock and is open every day. *Fred Hanna Ltd*, 27–29 Nassau St, the town's university bookshop, has a fine academic and general stock. For those wishing to browse, there are numerous second-hand bookshops in the city, many of them near Trinity College.

Crafts The *Kilkenny Shop*, 2 Nassau St, is the national design authority's showcase for the best of Ireland's jewellery, porcelain, glass, textiles and home furnishings.

Crystal Switzer's department store, 92 Grafton St, stocks a comprehensive range of Irish crystal.

Irish linen Paul Costelloe's *haute couture* suits and blouses are stocked by *Brown Thomas*, 15 Grafton St. Dublin high society also patronizes *Ib Jorgensen*, 53 Dawson St.

Men's tailoring Joseph Monaghan, 98 St Stephen's Green, and *Louis Copeland*, 30 Lower Pembroke St, are fine old-fashioned tailors. *Alias Tom*, 2 Duke Lane, is the best place to try for ready-to-wear linen shirts and classic suits.

Woollens Traditional sweaters in striking and colourful patterns from *Irish Cottage Industries*, 44 Dawson St, *The Sweater Shop*, 9 Wicklow St, or *Blarney Woollen Mills*, 21–23 Nassau St.

Sightseeing

Chester-Beatty Library and Gallery of Oriental Art contains a world-famous collection of Oriental prints and manuscripts. *20 Shrewsbury Rd. Open Tue–Fri, 10–5; Sat, 2–5.*

Dublin Castle Originally built in 1204, the Castle served as the home of the English viceroys who ruled Ireland until 1922. The State Apartments are lavishly decorated with frescoes, portraits, Venetian chandeliers and Chippendale furniture. *Dame St. Open Mon–Fri, 10–12.15, 2–5; Sun, 2–5.*

National Botanic Gardens Founded in 1795 and famous for its large and gracious 19thC greenhouses, protecting giant Amazonian water lilies, and a fine collection of roses. *Botanic Rd, Glasnevin. Open (summer) Mon–Sat, 9–6; Sun, 11–6; (winter) Mon–Sat, 10–4.30.*

National Gallery Few Old Masters but of interest for Irish portraits and paintings. *Merrion Sq. Open Mon–Sat, 10–6 (9 Thu); Sun, 2–5.*

National Museum The main room of the museum is devoted to Irish antiquities, including finds from the recently excavated Viking harbour, along Wood Quay. The Treasury contains masterpieces of early Celtic art and jewellery, including the 13thC Tara Brooch. *Kildare St. Open Tue–Sat, 10–5; Sun, 2–5.*

Phoenix Park, to the west of the centre, is one of the largest city parks in Europe. Laid out in the 18th century, it offers fine views and is a popular place for relaxation.

Trinity College Library The Long Room, built 1712–32, is lined with galleried bookcases and is used to display the richly illuminated Book of Kells, written around AD800. *College St. Open Mon–Fri, 9.30–4.30; Sat, 9.30–12.30.*

Churches Dublin has hundreds of churches and two cathedrals, *St Patrick's* and *Christ Church*. At *St Michael's*, in Church St, you can visit the vaults containing 17thC mummified remains.

Guided tours Guided walks of historic and literary Dublin led by knowledgeable residents ☎ 556970. *Tour Guides Ireland* ☎ 794291. *City Tours* by bus ☎ 302222. The *Guinness Brewery* offers tours Mon–Fri, 10–3 ☎ 536700.

Out of town

The coast of Dublin Bay is a pleasure to explore, from the castle at Howth to the James Joyce Museum, housed in a Martello tower at Sandycove.

Farther afield, places within an hour's drive that are particularly worth visiting include, to the north, the 14thC *Malahide Castle*, where the majority of paintings of the National Portrait Collection are on display; to the west, *Jigginstown House*, a ruined 17thC mansion, and *Castletown House*, the finest Palladian building in Ireland. The best scenery lies to the south in County Wicklow; here *Powerscourt* has magnificent formal terraced gardens, and at *Glendalough* a slender round tower marks the site of a 7thC cathedral.

Spectator sports

Horse-racing At *Phoenix Park* ☎ 381411, north of the city, and *Leopardstown* ☎ 893607, south. The big events are held elsewhere; the 2,000 Guineas (May) and St Leger (Oct) at the *Curragh*, in County Kildare, and the Irish Grand National (Easter Monday) at *Fairyhouse*, County Meath.

Rugby Internationals are played at *62 Lansdowne Rd* ☎ 684601.

Gaelic football and hurling Important matches are played at *Croke Park* ☎ 363222.

Keeping fit

Fitness centres *City Gym*, Eden Quay ☎ 788100.

Golf Numerous courses, many in areas of natural beauty, are accessible from Dublin, but weekends are always very busy. *Royal Dublin Golf Club*, Bull Island, Dollymount ☎ 337153, is 3.5 miles/5.5kms from the city centre. *Dun Laoghaire Golf Club*, Eglinton Pk, Tivoli Rd

☎ 803916, is 7 miles/11kms south.
Full details of all courses, facilities
and fees are published by the *Irish
Tourist Board* ☎ 747733.
Squash Squash Ireland Ltd, Phoenix
Park ☎ 385850.
Swimming The most central pools
are in Sean McDermott St ☎ 720752
and Townsend St ☎ 770503. Clean
sandy beaches are within easy reach
of the city at Sandymount, Merrion,
Dollymount and Howth.
Tennis Herbert Park, Ballsbridge
☎ 684364.

Local resources
Business services
Companies offering serviced offices
for rent include *Hogan House*,
15 Hogan Pl ☎ 613022, and
Northumberland House,
44 Northumberland Rd ☎ 688244.
Photocopying and printing
Prontaprint has offices throughout the
city, including 38 Upper Baggot St
☎ 609500 and 164 Capel St
☎ 734352.
Secretarial Co Sec, IDA Enterprise
Centre, Pearse St ☎ 775487.
Translation Askus, 19 Duke St
☎ 779954.

Communications
Local delivery City Courier Ltd
☎ 787440; *Hurricane* ☎ 531577;
Pageboy ☎ 901885.
Long-distance delivery DHL
☎ 424622; *Federal Express*
☎ 482299.
Post office The *General Post Office*,
O'Connell St ☎ 728888, is open
Mon–Sat, 8–8; Sun, 10.30–6.
Telex and fax If your hotel cannot
help, faxes can be sent from all
branches of *Prontaprint* (see above).

Conference/exhibition centres
Major trade fairs are held at the
*Royal Dublin Society Exhibition
Complex*, Ballsbridge ☎ 680645. Of
the hotels, *Jurys* is well-equipped for
sizable conferences. Prestige functions
often take place at the converted
17thC *Royal Hospital Kilmainham*,
west of the city ☎ 718666.

Emergencies
Bureaux de change Banks are open
Mon–Fri, 10–12.30; 1.30–3 (5 on
Thu). The bureau de change at the
General Post Office, O'Connell St, is
open Mon–Sat, 8–8; Sun, 10.30–6.30.
The *Bank of Ireland's* airport branch
is open daily, 6.45am–9.30pm.
Hospitals Emergencies ☎ 999. The
Jervis St hospital ☎ 723355 has a
casualty department.
Pharmacies The *O'Connell
Pharmacy*, 55 Lower O'Connell St
☎ 730427, is open daily until 10pm.

Government offices
Foreign Affairs Department, 80 St
Stephen's Green ☎ 780822.
Department of Industry and Commerce,
Kildare St ☎ 614444. *Customs and
Excise*, Great George St South
☎ 792777.

Information sources
*Business information Dublin Chamber
of Commerce*, 7 Clare St ☎ 614111.
The *Industrial Development Authority
(IDA)*, Wilton Park House, Wilton Pl
☎ 686633, is responsible for
attracting overseas investment
through development grants and
subsidies. It also runs small business
enterprise centres and four major
industrial developments on the
outskirts of the city.
Local media The daily *Irish Times*
has good coverage of business and
economic news. Many Dubliners read
the *Sunday Tribune* for its political
analysis and arts coverage.
*Tourist information Dublin and East
Tourism*, 14 Upper O'Connell St
☎ 747733. Open Mon–Fri, 9–6; Sat,
9–1.

Thank-yous
Chocolates Leonidas, 16 Royal
Hibernian Way, off Dawson St
☎ 795915.
Flowers Florianna, 25 Dawson St
☎ 776693, or *Aeroflora* at the airport
☎ 379900 ext 4747.
Wine Mitchell's, 21 Kildare St
☎ 760766.

ITALY

Despite few natural resources and a heavy dependence on imported raw materials, the Italian economy has grown rapidly since World War II. An economic miracle was achieved during the 1950s and 1960s, when output doubled. The oil shocks of the 1970s affected Italy more seriously than many of its West European neighbours and the economy faltered, hit by inflation and balance of payments problems. The 1980s, however, have seen a return to prosperity: to the extent that, by 1987, the Italians were claiming to have overtaken the UK to become the world's fifth-largest industrial power.

This success has been built on unpromising foundations. Mineral resources are extremely limited; 80% of energy requirements is imported – twice the West European average; agricultural production has long failed to meet demand. A strong export performance is vital to pay for the country's import needs; manufactured goods make up 90% of exports. Italy is Europe's largest exporter of clothing and shoes and a major force in the world market for industrial machinery, office machinery, motor vehicles and chemicals. Its large construction firms are active around the world.

The state has a substantial role in the economy, through energy giant ENI and the industrial corporation IRI, which has holdings in over 140 companies employing over half a million people. IRI has a stake in three major banks, the national airline Alitalia and the autostrade as well as steel, engineering, aerospace, telecommunications and shipbuilding companies. Large private companies are relatively few in number, although those that do exist – such as Fiat (automobiles), Olivetti (office machinery and computers), Pirelli (tyres) and Zanussi (domestic appliances) – are often major international forces in their sector. Small firms are at least as important as an engine of growth as their larger counterparts, dominating vital sectors such as the clothing industry and maintaining employment in difficult times when larger companies cut back. The flourishing black economy, too, is a significant creator of wealth; estimates put its contribution at anything from 10% to 50% of GDP.

But the benefits of Italy's postwar economic miracle remain unevenly distributed. The income gap between the rich industrialized north and the poor underdeveloped south – the Mezzogiorno – remains vast. The average income in Calabria, the poorest region, is only 45% of that in Lombardy; unemployment is twice as high in the south as it is in the north and centre. Substantial sums have been invested in efforts to create new industries in the south, but the industries chosen, such as steel and chemicals, were set up just as their world markets went into decline. The north/south divide has begun to widen again in recent years, with demand for migrant labour in the north falling as industries modernize and automate.

The buoyant Italian economy of the late 1980s has yet to make much impact on unemployment levels in the south. The new-found prosperity enjoyed by much of the country has also made it difficult for Italy's weak and short-lived governments to take what might amount to unpopular measures to tackle the economy's underlying problems: notably the huge budget deficit, which is running at the equivalent of more than 10% of GDP and is far higher, in relative terms, than those of its European competitors or of the United States. However, high levels of domestic savings and a low foreign debt burden make even this problem less pressing than it might otherwise be and the outlook for the Italian economy remains healthy, barring sharp increases in energy and raw material prices.

Geography Italy is for the most part upland. The peaks and glaciers of the Alps form the northern border with France, Switzerland, Austria and Yugoslavia. The limestone Apennines run the entire length of the Italian peninsula. The most important lowland area is the valley of the Po, in the east. It is the main agricultural region and contains the major industrial centres of Milan and Turin; about one-third of the population lives there.

Climate The north has a temperate climate; the south and centre have a Mediterranean climate, with long dry summers and mild winters. The average temperatures are around 25°C (77°F) in summer and 8°C (46°F) in winter. There are local variations according to altitude.

Population 57.1m.

Government Italy has been a republic since 1946. It consists of 20 administrative regions, all of which have considerable autonomy on matters of health, education and the police.

The head of state is the president of the republic, who is elected for a term of 7 years by an electoral college consisting of members of parliament and delegates from each of the country's regions.

Legislative power is held by a bicameral parliament, comprising a chamber of deputies with 630 members and a regional senate with 315 members. Both of these chambers are elected by proportional representation, and they have equal powers. Executive power lies in the hands of the council of ministers, whose leader is known as president of the council.

No political party has held an absolute majority in parliament since 1953. As a result there has been a string of coalition governments, each formed by between three and five political parties. But these coalitions have not led to political stability. Between 1945 and 1988 there were about 50 different governments; some of these held office for a few years, but many lasted for only a matter of weeks.

Currency The unit of currency is the Italian lira (L).

Italy is a member of the European Monetary System (EMS). The lira is allowed to fluctuate more widely from the central rate than other currencies participating in the exchange rate mechanism − by 6% compared with 2.25%, although central bank policy is to keep lira movements within a narrower band.

Time Italy is on Central European Time, which is 1hr ahead of GMT. Summer time is in force from the end of Mar to the end of Sep; clocks are put forward, and Italy is then 2hrs ahead of GMT.

Dialling codes Italy's IDD code is 39. Omit the initial 0 from the city code when dialling from abroad. To make an international call from Italy, dial 00 before dialling the relevant country code.

Public holidays Jan 1, Jan 6, Easter Mon, Apr 25, May 1, May 12, Aug 15, Nov 1, Nov 6, Dec 8, Dec 25, Dec 26.

ROME (Roma)

Rome was a provincial town of some 200,000 inhabitants before becoming the capital of Italy just over a century ago. Today it covers more than 1,500 sq km/580 sq miles and is the largest Italian city in population (3m, plus some 1.3m visitors a year) and in area. Rome struggles to preserve the mystique (and fabric) of the ancient centre of civilization and of the Eternal City, focal point of the Roman Catholic faith, alongside its role of modern European capital.

Although the main international financial market is in Milan and industry is concentrated in the North, Rome remains the decision-making base. It is the seat of government, the embassies, the Banca d'Italia, the state-controlled holding companies, ENI (hydrocarbons), EFIM and IRI (Institute for the Reconstruction of Industry), with the head offices of its subsidiaries Alitalia, RAI (television and radio) and Finsider (steel). National corporations have administrative headquarters here and most Northern companies have an agent or office in Rome. Many international companies are based at Mussolini's planned suburb, EUR (Esposizione Universale di Roma), or at nearby Castello della Magliana: these include Colgate, Digital, Esso, General Motors, Hewlett Packard, Mobil, Procter & Gamble and Squibb.

Rome is Italy's third largest industrial conurbation in terms of employees in industry. Pomezia, about 40 minutes' drive to the south, is the main industrial complex; factories, notably pharmaceutical (Johnson & Johnson) and electronic, were set up here with aid from the Cassa per Il Mezzogiorno. High technology is concentrated along the Via Tiburtina, towards Tivoli, and includes the state-owned Selenia and Contraves, a subsidiary of Oerlikon.

Roman laziness and lethargy are legendary. But while it is true that the average Roman has something of a Southern mentality – liking siestas, street life and feast days – there is more of a get-up-and-go spirit in the city today. Public Rome and private business are sharply divided. While bureaucracy remains slow moving and corrupt, lots of thriving small businesses have sprung up since the early 1980s. These new Romans work normal business hours, and like everyone else, civil servants included, criticize state inertia and inefficiency.

In business, string-pulling is necessary, and personal clout counts for everything: foreigners usually need to operate through agents, especially as English is less widely spoken than in Milan. Romans are more easy-going (and less punctual) than the Milanese, but getting things done can be stressful. Meetings with bureaucrats and politicians (only available midweek) should be before lunch.

The 1970s and early 1980s were depressing. Terrorism was rife, governments came and went more frequently than ever, and the famous film industry based at Cinecittà declined. Now the Brigate Rosse ringleaders are behind bars, Cinecittà is back in business (just), monuments are being restored (slowly) and problems are being recognized if not resolved. The Rome capital project includes the transfer of all government ministries to Centocelle, due east of the centre, and the development of the Tiber into a navigable waterway. Funds are awaited. Vast improvements to the airports are planned for the early 1990s but it has been estimated that by the year 2005 air traffic will have doubled.

Arriving

The main airport, Leonardo da Vinci airport at Fiumicino, is often strike-bound. Ciampino, which handles domestic and international charter flights, is closer to the centre but has poor transport links. Rome is connected to the North (via Florence and Milan), to the South and east of Italy by autostrada but the national rail network provides faster and more convenient access to other centres (4hrs from Milan).

Leonardo da Vinci airport (Fiumicino)

Europe's fourth busiest airport handles up to 50,000 passengers a day, nearly half on domestic flights. It is being greatly enlarged and a rail link with central Rome is under construction.

Facilities at the international terminal are not very convenient for arriving passengers. Airside, near passport control, are a bank (very high commission charges, open 7.30–11pm) and tourist information and hotel desks (not always staffed); baggage collection is near the exit. In the main arrivals hall facilities are basic: one bar, telephones, a bureau de change (24hr; more convenient than the bank). The bus ticket counter is beyond the exit (there is an automatic machine near baggage reclaim, sometimes out of order). The departures hall has a pharmacy, post office and telephone room. The departures lounge has two new duty-free shopping centres (one for designer fashion), the only airport restaurant (closes 10.30pm), a 24hr bar, a telex and telegram service (8–noon) and a VIP lounge.

Flight information inquiries ☎ 60123640; passenger information and airline offices ☎ 6010; Alitalia international flights ☎ 60103358,

national flights ☎ 60103204; recorded information on Alitalia flights 5456; baggage information 60124252. All numbers are often busy.

Nearby hotels Satellite Palace, Vle delle Antille 49, 00121, Roma Lido ☎ 5693941 ⊤Ⅹ 611469 • Fezia Hotels • *AE DC MC V*. Large modern hotel with pool, convention facilities and airport shuttle (takes 20mins).
Sheraton (see *Hotels*).

City link Fiumicino is 36km/22 miles southwest of Rome. Until the railway is completed, a taxi is the best way to get into the city, but beware the "pirate" versions.

Taxi The ride into central Rome takes about 45mins and costs around L65,000. Official ranks are outside the terminals. Reservations from the airport ☎ 60124310.

Limousine There is a limousine desk in the arrivals hall.

Car rental Not recommended for central Rome, but convenient for business at EUR or at Pomezia (30km/18 miles south). Major companies have offices in the arrivals hall.

Bus The ACOTRAL airport bus runs every 10mins 7–12.45, then on the hour; tickets (L5,000) from counters in both arrivals halls (or from automatic machines in the international arrivals hall). Allow 1hr for the journey. The terminal is in Via Giolitti, beside the main Stazione Termini.

Ciampino airport

Ciampino handles international charters and some domestic and private flights. Strikes here are very uncommon. Passenger inquiries ☎ 724241.

City link Ciampino is 16km/10 miles southeast of Rome. It is simplest to take a taxi to the centre as there are no airport shuttle buses and public transport is slow and inconvenient.

However, you may have to wait for a cab.

Taxi The journey to the city centre takes about 40mins and costs L25-30,000.

Car rental Avis, Budget, Hertz and Maggiore have desks.

Bus and train The ride by ACOTRAL bus to Anagnina takes 20mins; from there take the subway to the centre.

Urbe airport

Small airport for private and military planes, north of the city. It is 30mins by taxi from the centre ☎ 8120524 or 8120571.

Railway stations

Stazione Termini A huge monument of 20thC architecture, and the hub of the country's rail network. There are good, fast trains from Milan every hour during the day taking 5hrs 10 mins, and the Pendolino leaves at 7am and 7pm and takes 4hrs. Reserve sleepers on services to major cities through travel agents. The tourist information office is accessible only from the platforms and facilities are poorly indicated. There is access to both subway lines and outside in the Piazza dei Cinquecento is a bus terminal for city and suburban services. Buses from both airports arrive alongside the station in Via Giolitti. This is a seedy area; beware pickpockets and pirate cabs. There are often long lines waiting for taxis.

Inquiries ☎ 4775 but usually busy; reservations ☎ 110 but it is more reliable to use a travel agent; sleeper information ☎ 4741750.

Getting around

Rome's traffic is notoriously noisy and congested; it is a relief to walk in the traffic-restricted parts of the historic centre. Taxis are most useful for business appointments since the subway system is too limited and, at rush hours, buses are too crowded.

Taxis Taxis usually wait at ranks on main piazzas but they can be hard to find when shifts change (1–3.30pm and 8.30–9pm). A small tip (10%) is normal practice. To order in advance consult the Yellow Pages for the local rank or call *Radio Taxi* ☎ 3570, *Radio Taxi Roma* ☎ 3875, *Radio Taxi La Capitale* ☎ 4994 or *Radio Taxi Cosmos* ☎ 8433.

Limousines Sapres ☎ 4745389, *Avis* ☎ 31512143 or 6441969, *Bevilacqua* ☎ 462896.

Driving Traffic jams are endemic and the centre is closed to nonresidents. There is 24hr parking at Villa Borghese and Piazza San Bernardo (others are open 7–9) costing about L2,000 per hour, L10,000 per day.

Walking is the best (often the only) way to get around the fairly compact but confusing historic centre; elsewhere the noise, the hills and, in summer, the heat can be wearing. It is usually safe to walk in the centre at night but it is sensible to avoid ill-lit or empty streets. The station area and backstreets of Trastevere can be sinister: dropouts and *drogati* congregate here. Bag-snatching is now less prevalent (the current sport is to snatch casually-flung fur coats) but shoulder bags are at risk, even in daylight. Avoid wearing valuable jewellery.

Bus The bus system is useful for the longer-term visitor and those who know the city well. Tickets are bought from main bus terminals, tobacconists, newsstands and bars and half-day tickets are available. Most buses run till midnight.

Subway There are two lines: A is useful for short hops from the Prati area or Piazza di Spagna to the business area (Barberini, Repubblica, Termini), B for EUR. Tickets are available from machines at some stations or the usual outlets like bars. Services stop before midnight.

Area by area

Ancient Rome was defined by the river Tiber (Tevere) and the city walls, of which there are extensive remains. The focus of life has shifted gradually north from the medieval, Renaissance and baroque heart of the city towards the northeast,

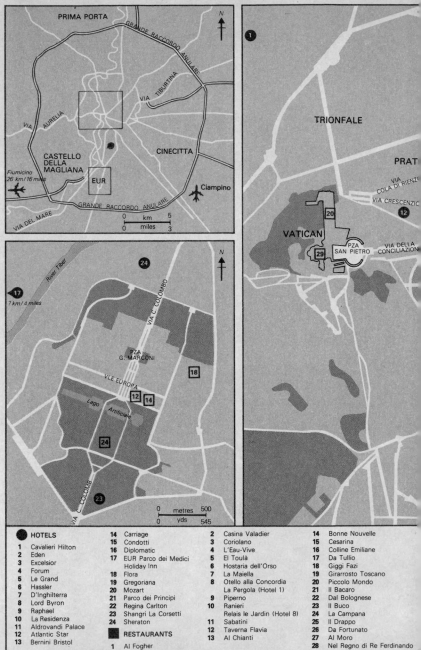

ITALY

PRIMA PORTA

GRANDE RACCORDO ANULARE

VIA TIBURTINA

VIA AURELIA

CASTELLO DELLA MAGLIANA

CINECITTA

Fiumicino 26 km / 16 miles

EUR

GRANDE RACCORDO ANULARE

Ciampino

VIA DEL MARE

0 — km — 5
0 — miles — 3

River Tiber

7 km / 4 miles

VIA C. COLOMBO

PZA G. MARCONI

VLE EUROPA

Lago Artificiale

VIA C. COLOMB

0 — metres — 500
0 — yds — 545

TRIONFALE

PRAT

VIA COLA DI RIENZO

VIA CRESCENZIO

VATICAN

PZA SAN PIETRO

VIA DELLA CONCILIAZION

HOTELS	14	Carriage	2	Casina Valadier	14	Bonne Nouvelle

HOTELS

1 Cavalieri Hilton
2 Eden
3 Excelsior
4 Forum
5 Le Grand
6 Hassler
7 D'Inghilterra
8 Lord Byron
9 Raphael
10 La Residenza
11 Aldrovandi Palace
12 Atlantic Star
13 Bernini Bristol

14 Carriage
15 Condotti
16 Diplomatic
17 EUR Parco dei Medici Holiday Inn
18 Flora
19 Gregoriana
20 Mozart
21 Parco dei Principi
22 Regina Carlton
23 Shangri La Corsetti
24 Sheraton

■ **RESTAURANTS**

1 Al Fogher

2 Casina Valadier
3 Coriolano
4 L'Eau-Vive
5 El Toulà
6 Hostaria dell'Orso
7 La Maiella
8 Otello alla Concordia
La Pergola (Hotel 1)
9 Piperno
10 Ranieri
Relais le Jardin (Hotel 8)
11 Sabatini
12 Taverna Flavia
13 Al Chianti

14 Bonne Nouvelle
15 Cesarina
16 Colline Emiliane
17 Da Tullio
18 Giggi Fazi
19 Girarrosto Toscano
20 Piccolo Mondo
21 Il Bacaro
22 Dal Bolognese
23 Il Buco
24 La Campana
25 Il Drappo
26 Da Fortunato
27 Al Moro
28 Nel Regno di Re Ferdinando

208

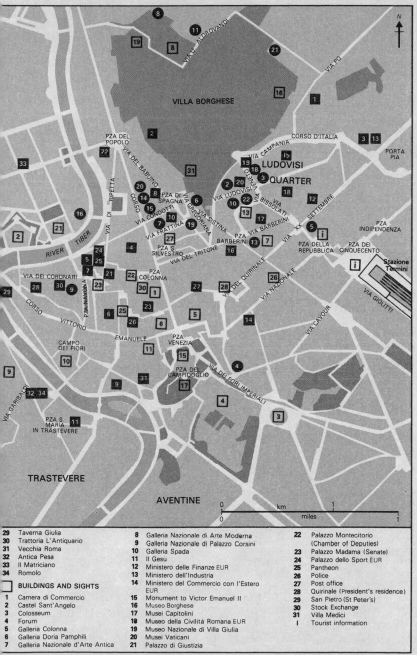

redeveloped in the 19th century.

Much of business, commercial and diplomatic Rome lies north of the walls, where smart residential areas extend beyond the Tiber. Planned suburbs and industrial areas have been developed to the south and southwest, notably at EUR, with several state companies and ministeries. The city (including EUR) is enclosed by the Grande Raccordo Anulare (GRA), or ring road.

Ludovisi, Borghese and the station
The curving, café-lined Via Veneto, scene of the *dolce vita* of the 1960s, is no longer very glamorous. But the *Ludovisi quarter* (either side of the Via Veneto) has the largest number of traditional hotels in Rome. Most major international airlines are in Via Bissolati, Via Barberini or Via Veneto and the Ministero dell'Industria and IRI are on Via Veneto.

The Ludovisi quarter extends to Via XX Settembre, site of important government ministries (notably Agriculture, Defence and the Treasury), and Via del Quirinale, with the presidential palace. Beyond is a busy commercial district around the Via Nazionale, with the Banca d'Italia, Via Cavour and the run-down area around the station. To the east, Via Tiburtina leads towards the Tiburtina Valley and Rome's burgeoning high-tech industry.

North of the ancient walls and the main traffic artery, Corso d'Italia, is a lively commercial district around Via Po (banks and trades union offices) and Via Salaria. East is *Nomentana*, mainly residential but with hospitals and the university nearby.

North of the large heart-shaped park of Villa Borghese (which has several museums) is *Parioli*, long the smartest address in Rome. In this area, which is becoming popular for offices, many of the detached villas are embassies. Farther north is the Olympic village, where some 8,000 government employees are now housed.

The historic centre The Corso, which the ancient Romans used for

horseracing, is still the capital's main high street, lined with shops, bars, the head offices of banks and the scene of the evening *passeggiata*. It runs from Piazza del Popolo (designed as a triumphal entrance to the city) to Piazza Venezia (with the hideously prominent monument to Victor Emanuel II known as the "Typewriter"). Half is closed to traffic; most of the streets off it are also traffic-restricted. On the Corso, Piazza Colonna and the adjacent Piazza Montecitorio are the centre of political life: Palazzo Chigi is the prime minister's headquarters and Palazzo Montecitorio houses the Chamber of Deputies. A few minutes' walk away, in Palazzo Madama, is the Senate.

West of the Corso, Renaissance and baroque Rome nestle in a kink of the Tiber. Here are narrow lanes full of artisans' workshops, piazzas, stately palaces (notably Palazzo Farnese, now the French Embassy) and famous churches. Café tables overlook the lively baroque Piazza Navona and the ancient Pantheon. The Borsa is incorporated in the ruins of an ancient temple behind the Piazza del Parlamento. The remains of the so-called Jewish ghetto are also in this corner of old Rome. The area west of the Corso is a popular place to live, especially among well-to-do single people and expatriates.

East of the Corso life revolves around the colourful Spanish Steps and the fashionable shopping streets around Via Condotti and Via Frattina. Newspaper offices are by Piazza San Silvestro and the Corso.

Most of the remains of ancient Rome, including the Colosseum and the Forum (but not the Pantheon), lie to the south around the Aventine, Palatine and Esquiline hills. *Aventino* is a peaceful residential district.

Trastevere and Prati *Trastevere* has a bohemian reputation but is now fashionable. Although artists and intellectuals live here, the Trasteverini, who claim to be the original Romans, are largely a working-class community. North of the Vatican is *Prati*, a professional residential area, with apartments and rather dilapidated 19thC villas, and a popular shopping street, Via Cola di Rienzo. There is a subway connection to the centre.

Many lawyers are based here, close to the grandiose Palazzo di Giustizia (Italy's supreme court) and to the Tribunale and Prefettura (lower courts). The head office of RAI 2 (television) is in Via Mazzini. Farther north are the residential areas of *Trionfale* and airy *Monte Mario*, with apartment blocks overlooking the city.
The Vatican On the west side of the Tiber, the Vatican covers about 44ha/ 100 acres, most of it inaccessible to the public. A ceremonial approach, the Via della Conciliazione, was cut through the original medieval quarter in 1929 to commemorate the establishment of a separate city state. This leads to the magnificent Piazza San Pietro, designed by Bernini.

The suburbs
To the north are the smart residential districts of *Fleming* and *Vigna Clara* around the Via Cassia and Via della Camilluccia. Here detached villas with gardens and condominiums with pools are popular with foreign residents. The Ministry of Foreign Affairs is nearby. *Olgiata* is a security-guarded suburb with villas and a famous golf club.

To the south, EUR, planned by Mussolini as a modern civic showcase for Fascism, was completed in the 1950s. This is an orderly, spacious but soulless business and residential district with ministries (notably Finance, Foreign Trade, and Post and Telecommunications) and headquarters of major companies. It is about 20mins by subway from the city centre and about 20mins drive from Fiumicino airport.

Castello della Magliana, with other company headquarters and hotels, is some 6km/4miles to the west of EUR.

Hotels

Rome's proudest old hotels are in or around the Via Veneto and the wide 19thC thoroughfares of the business district, especially Via Cavour. Many are relics of a grander age; period interiors have become shabby and double-glazing fails to keep out the noise of traffic. Still in the top league however are the Grand, Excelsior, Eden and, nearby, the Hassler. For more modern luxury, and quiet bedrooms, the two best hotels are a short taxi ride from the centre: the small, elegant Lord Byron, or the vast, airy Hilton. Hotels in the Borghese and Nomentana areas are not as grand as some of their names suggest (like Aldrovandi Palace and Parco dei Principi). A new Holiday Inn, in the shell of an old hotel on Piazza Minerva, is due to open in 1989.

Around the traffic-restricted Piazza di Spagna there are several attractive places to stay. Rooms in these smaller hotels should be reserved well ahead in the peak tourist season (Easter to September). At EUR and Castello della Magliana most needs are catered for by a Holiday Inn and Sheraton and several smaller hotels.

Luxury and most other better hotels are air-conditioned and offer 24hr room service, concierge, currency exchange and a daily laundry service. Parking is usually with a local garage. Standard features in bedrooms are IDD telephones, radio and TV (often with foreign news channels and/or video) and minibars. Major hotels will do photocopying and send telexes and fax messages for clients, but, except for the Hilton and the Sheraton which have convention centres, will use agencies for full secretarial services. Most luxury hotels charge 19% IVA (VAT) and a small city tax on top of rates, and breakfast is usually extra.

Cavalieri Hilton 🖿 /////
Via Cadlolo 101, 00136 ☎ *31511*
🆇 *625337 fax 3151* • *AE DC MC V* •
355 rooms, 19 suites, 2 restaurants,
2 bars
The Hilton scores high among business people for its facilities and efficient service. It is in Monte Mario but there is a frequent air-conditioned shuttle bus service to the centre (15mins), and regular visitors appreciate the space and the quiet, especially in summer when there is often a cool *ponentino* (westerly) breeze. The beautifully landscaped pool, surrounded by palm trees, attracts incentive tours, and convention delegates can get their hair cut or buy newspapers and presents without having to go into the centre at all. Recent renovations to the decor have cost US$12m. Old Masters and antiques add class to the huge lobby, and bedrooms have been stylishly updated. They are spacious and restful, well-equipped without being too functional. The La Pergola restaurant has superb views (see *Restaurants*). Hairdresser, newsstand, travel agent, car rental offices, boutiques, shuttle bus to centre and airport • pool, sauna, tennis, jogging track, massage, Turkish bath • convention centre with secretarial and translation services, 5 meeting rooms (capacity up to 350, 2,000 in convention centre).

Eden 🖿 ////
Via Ludovisi 49, 00187 ☎ *4743551*
🆇 *610567 fax 4742401* • *THF* • *AE DC MC V* • *93 rooms, 17 suites,*
2 restaurants, 2 bars
The Eden (pronounced "Edden"), near the Villa Borghese and now run by Britain's Trusthouse Forte group, has been one of Rome's top hotels for a century, attracting diplomats and top business people. Ministers, and even the president, often lunch in the delightful roof terrace restaurant.

Public rooms and the majority of bedrooms are large and old-fashioned with some "modern" additions already showing their age; newer bedrooms (about 40%) are more sophisticated (marble bathrooms, push-button telephones). The suites are the height of luxury; some have enormous baths with hydro-massage. Hairdresser • 3 meeting rooms (capacity up to 120).

Excelsior 🖿 ////
Via Veneto 125, 00187 ☎ *4708*
🆇 *610232 fax 4756205* • *CIGA* •
AE DC MC V • *325 rooms, 45 suites,*
1 restaurant, 1 bar
Opened with ceremony in 1906, the Excelsior is the most famous hotel on the Via Veneto. It featured in Fellini's *La Dolce Vita*, and was long the haunt of film stars and exiled heads of state. Now it is an efficient hotel with more *movimento* (action) than the even grander Grand. Public rooms retain the original opulent neo-classical decoration; the balcony of the small Sala d'Oro dining room offers some privacy for business lunches and the winter garden is used for fashion shows. The best bedrooms have been refurbished in the standard CIGA Empire style; rooms overlooking the US Embassy and Via Boncompagni are the quietest; singles tend to be small. Most bedrooms are classified de luxe or super de luxe; opt for standard and you will be upgraded subject to availability. The Caffè Doney outside on Via Veneto is now owned by CIGA. Hairdresser • sauna, Turkish bath • 11 meeting rooms (capacity up to 1,500).

Forum 🖿 ////
Via Tor de' Conti 25, 00184 ☎ *6792446*
🆇 *622549 fax 6799337* • *AE DC MC V*
• *74 rooms, 6 suites, 1 restaurant, 1 bar*
A converted villa incorporating an old church tower, the Forum is one of Rome's most unusual hotels, with good views of the main trading place

of the ancient Romans. Its mainly business clientele includes employees of Fiat, General Motors, IBM and the World Bank; corporate rates are offered and the location is relatively convenient for EUR. Politicians and other VIPs appreciate the security here (police are in evidence outside) and the service is deferential and personal. Bedrooms are comfortable and elegant with antique desks and Murano chandeliers. The roof restaurant (genuine local cooking) is chic, with parquet floors, cane-backed chairs and cool dove-grey tones; there is a separate room (no view) for private meals. Shuttle bus to airport • 3 meeting rooms (capacity up to 100).

Le Grand *⊡||||||*
Via V.E. Orlando 3, 00185 ☎ *4709* ⊠ *610210 fax 4747307* • *CIGA* •
AE DC MC V • *133 rooms, 35 suites, 2 restaurants, 1 bar*
Still the most prestigious hotel in Rome, the Grand is in a narrow, noisy street off Via XX Settembre. It is not a chic area at night but the sort of people who stay here – royalty and heads of state, politicians, diplomats and top-ranking business people – are usually cocooned in limousines as soon as they step outside. Inside, all is reassuringly civilized from the vast, formal salon (rather dowdy for some tastes) to the intimate panelled restaurant and the more informal, summery Pavillion, where buffet lunches are served. Bedrooms are mostly old-fashioned, dark and rather noisy, bathrooms are big but not luxurious. Unless you can afford a suite, you stay here for the service (impeccable) and the status, not the standard or style of the bedrooms. Hairdresser • sauna, massage • 13 meeting rooms (capacity up to 650).

Hassler *⊡||||||*
Pza Trinità dei Monti 6, 00187 ☎ *6782651* ⊠ *610208 fax 6799278* •
AE • *87 rooms, 12 suites, 4 restaurants, 1 bar*
The legendary Hassler occupies a prime site at the top of the Spanish

Steps, a peaceful refuge from the city. The faithful customers (45% from the USA) know that little changes at this comforting hotel where the staff take a pride in personal service. Furnishings may be unfashionable and worn, the food may be notoriously dull and expensive, but the place has character and the views from the rooftop restaurant and suites are beyond price. Romans will be impressed if you stay here. Favourite rooms are often reserved several months in advance (singles are all on the back; request single occupancy in a double on the front for a better room). Only the suites are luxurious and some are very pretty with sparkling bathrooms; the presidential suite and roof terrace can be rented for meetings. Room service, 7–11, hairdresser • 3 meeting rooms (capacity up to 50).

D'Inghilterra *⊡|||||*
Via Bocca di Leone 14, 00187 ☎ *672161,* ⊠ *614552 fax 672161* •
AE DC MC V • *95 rooms, 8 suites, 1 restaurant, 1 bar*
This exclusive, rather aristocratic hotel does not encourage an ordinary expense-account clientele. It has a long tradition of hospitality to intellectuals, artists, politicians and men of letters, as well as royalty and popes. But for those who appreciate the atmosphere of a country residence, full of antiques, paintings and fresh flowers, with courteous service, this is a most civilized base in a convenient and smart district. The tiny, club-like Morland bar and the small, enchanting Roman Garden restaurant, with separate meeting room, are suitable for business encounters. Limited parking facilities. 2 meeting rooms (capacity up to 20).

Lord Byron *⊡||||||*
Via G. de Notaris 5, 00197 ☎ *3609541* ⊠ *611217 fax 3609541* • *Ottaviani* •
AE DC MC V • *44 rooms, 6 suites, 1 restaurant, 1 bar*
For luxury in a friendly atmosphere, the Lord Byron has no equal in Rome. A rather ordinary villa in quiet

Parioli has been converted into an immaculate little hotel without losing the charm of a private residence. There are gracious flower-filled public rooms (a delicious buffet breakfast is served in the bar) and spacious, fresh-looking bedrooms with splendid marble bathrooms. Service is superlative. The elegant Relais le Jardin restaurant (see *Restaurants*) is the best place to take important Roman clients. 1 meeting room (capacity up to 40).

Raphael *L////*
Largo Febo 2, 00180 ☎ *650881* TX *622396 fax 6878993* • *AE DC MC V* • *85 rooms, 1 restaurant, 1 bar*
A good mid-price choice, the Raphael is the best hotel in the Piazza Navona area. Regular guests include lawyers, senators, people in media and entertainment and foreign business guests as well as tourists. Ex-Prime Minister Bettino Craxi lives in the penthouse apartment, so the entrance is guarded by armed police. Restructuring will be complete by the end of 1989. Public rooms are individual, with a cluttered assortment of antiques and oil paintings.

La Residenza *L/*
Via Emilia 22-24, 00187 ☎ *460789* TX *410423 fax 972565* • *no credit cards* • *21 rooms, 6 suites, 1 bar*
A small hotel close to the US Embassy patronized by a cosmopolitan clientele. The decor combines casual modern with antique. The atmosphere is that of an elegant but unstuffy private house; hence the name. Bedrooms are well-equipped and some have small balconies. Splendid buffet breakfasts make a good start to the working day.

OTHER HOTELS
Aldrovandi Palace *L////* *Via Ulisse Aldrovandi 15, 00197* ☎ *8841091* TX *616141 fax 879435* • *AE DC MC V*. Old-fashioned, rather drab Parioli hotel with new convention centre, used mainly by

Italian companies. The pool and Relais Piscine restaurant attract outsiders.
Atlante Star *L////* *Via Vitelleschi 34, 00193* ☎ *6564196* TX *622355* • *AE DC*. Smart, well-equipped hotel near the Vatican, with roof-garden restaurant, conference and business facilities.
Bernini Bristol *L////* *Pza Barberini 23, 00187* ☎ *463051* TX *610554 fax 4750266* • *AE DC MC V*. Sound business-oriented hotel in a noisy location. Standard bedrooms, quite elegant public rooms and well-equipped meeting rooms; used by major Italian companies.
Carriage *L///* *Via delle Carrozze 36, 00187* ☎ *6794106* TX *626246 fax 6799106* • *AE DC MC V*. Appealing small hotel with smartly refurbished rooms in fashionable area near the busy Spanish Steps; comfortable and quiet.
Condotti *L/* *Via Mario de' Fiori 37, 00187* ☎ *6794661* TX *611217* • *Ottaviani* • *AE DC MC V*. Simple but personal, welcoming and quiet, with an elegant entrance hall.
Diplomatic *L///* *Via Vittorio Colonna 28, 00193* ☎ *6542084* TX *6561734* • *AE DC MC V*. Well-run small hotel near the Vatican.
EUR Parco dei Medici Holiday Inn *L///* *Via Castello della Magliana 65, 00148* ☎ *5475* TX *613302* • *AE DC MC V*. Well-equipped modern block close to Esso at Castello della Magliana.
Flora *L////* *Via Veneto 191, 00187* ☎ *497821* TX *622256* • *AE DC V*. A traditional hotel with a good reputation.
Gregoriana *L/* *Via Gregoriana 18, 00187* ☎ *6794269* • *no credit cards*. Sophisticated small hotel in high-fashion street with spacious bedrooms. No restaurant.
Mozart *L/* *Via dei Greci 23b, 00182* ☎ *6787422* • *no credit cards*. Elegant and popular small hotel; rooms on the Corso can be noisy.
Parco dei Principi *L///* *Via Mercadente 15, 00198* ☎ *8841071* • *AE DC V*. Dated 1960s block near the

Villa Borghese, with pool.
Regina Carlton ⬚*L*|||| *Via V.*
Veneto 72, 00187 ☎ *476851*
🆇 *610517 fax 8445104* • *AE DC MC V.*
A comfortable, classic Via Veneto
hotel.
Shangri La Corsetti ⬚*L*|| *Vle*
Algeria 141, 00144 ☎ *5916441*
🆇 *614664* • *AE DC MC V.* At EUR and
well-positioned for Squibb, Procter &
Gamble and Colgate. Pool.
Sheraton ⬚*L*|||| *Vle del Pattinaggio,*
00144 ☎ *5453* 🆇 *626073* • *AE DC MC*
V. Ugly situation off the main road to
Fiumicino airport, but convenient for
Castello della Magliana and EUR. Pool.
Alitalia check-in. Conference halls.

Clubs

The most aristocratic and exclusive
men's clubs in Rome are the *Circolo
della Caccia* and the *Circolo degli
Scacchi* but nonmembers enter by
invitation only. It is smart to belong
to a rowing or golf club, and business
discussions are often held over a
round of golf. Those who want their
own working base in Rome should
consider membership of the American
Express *Consul Club*, Pza di Spagna 35
tel 6786795, with business services,
formal and informal meeting rooms and
a small roof terrace.

Restaurants

Rome does not offer as great a range of restaurants in type and cuisine as
some other European capitals or even Milan. The roof-top restaurants of
the major hotels – the Eden, Forum, Hassler and Hilton – are prestigious
places for business entertaining. The garden theme restaurants at the
D'Inghilterra and Lord Byron hotels are also pleasant.

It is acceptable to take local business guests to good trattorias for less
expensive meals, and for appealing surroundings the best restaurants are
behind the Pantheon and Piazza Navona. In summer many restaurants
offer al fresco dining; but the outside tables attract tourists. Similarly,
some widely advertised trattorias in Trastevere are to be avoided. Most
restaurants are closed on Sundays. For a quick business lunch in the Via
Veneto try the Café de Paris or Harry's Bar. At EUR most people go to the
Shangri La or Sheraton.

Roman cooking is robust rather than refined. Typical dishes include
pasta with bacon (*spaghetti alla carbonara* or *all'amatriciana*), oxtail (*coda
alla vaccinara*) and *saltimbocca alla romana*. Deep fried artichokes (*carciofi
alla giudea*) are often served as a first course. A popular new summer
starter is cold pasta with tomato and basil. Some of the best restaurants
specialize in regional cuisines, from Abruzzo to the Veneto. For fish, and
especially shellfish, stick to restaurants with a good reputation.

Lunch (around 1.30pm) is the main business meal, dinner (8.30 or
9pm, often later in summer) being mainly for friends and family. Same
day reservations will often suffice, but for a choice of table reserve further
ahead.

Al Fogher ⬚*L*|
Via Tevere 13b ☎ *857032* • *closed Sun*
• *AE DC* • *jacket and tie* • *reservations*
essential
In the business district, convenient for
the major hotels, the small (but not
cramped) Al Fogher has a pleasantly
countrified atmosphere: antique
furniture and cooking from the
Veneto region, with Friulian wines.

Signora Gaspardis d'Eva, the extrovert, blonde proprietress, welcomes her business custom mainly at lunch time and will organize fixed menus for groups.

Casina Valadier $\boxed{L}////$
Al Pincio, Villa Borghese ☎ *6792083* •
closed L, Mon, Aug • *AE DC MC V* •
jacket (and tie preferred) for D
High prices and indifferent food do not deter smart Romans from this delightful restaurant in a Napoleonic villa on the airy Pincian hill. Those staying in the best hotels eat here in the company of ministers and Banca d'Italia chiefs; and the chic lunch-time crowd on the terrace is likely to include artists, journalists, politicians and aristocrats. Favoured customers get the inner tables which have the most shade; in cold weather, or for greater privacy, they can retreat to the elegant Empire-style *sala romana*. The evening ambience is serious and formal; romantic on the candlelit upper terrace, or cloistered in the private salons.

Coriolano $\boxed{L}////$
Via Ancona 14 ☎ *8449501* • *closed Sun, Aug* • *AE DC MC* • *reservations essential*
Convenient for the Via Po and for Via XX Settembre, this civilized small restaurant, seating just 40, is appreciated by bankers, industrialists and politicians for its calm atmosphere and good food. Produce fresh from the market includes *funghi porcini* (from October to January) and fish; pasta is home-made. Gleaming silver plates, large sparkling glasses and fresh flowers indicate attention to detail.

L'Eau-Vive $\boxed{L}/$
Via Monterone 85a ☎ *6541095* • *closed Sun, Aug* • *AE MC V* • *jacket and tie preferred* • *no smoking*
In an old *palazzo* close to the Pantheon, this is a French restaurant run by missionaries, popular for business lunches; converts include local politicians. Dishes number many

French classics – try the *tournedos* with champagne and mushrooms or the *crêpes Grand Marnier* – accompanied by specially imported wines including exclusive *grands crus classés*. Waitresses are multilingual (Spanish-speaking from South America, French-speaking from Africa, English-speaking from the Philippines), and an Ave Maria is sung at about 10.30pm. Despite the original decorated ceilings, the atmosphere upstairs is canteen-like; opt instead for a ground-floor table or reserve in advance the small private room (up to 8 people). Classical music.

El Toulà $\boxed{L}////$
Via della Lupa 29b ☎ *6873498* •
closed Sun, Aug • *AE DC MC V* • *jacket and tie*
A classic business venue offering international and Venetian cuisine and an impressive wine list. The surroundings are luxurious, the service faultless.

Hostaria dell'Orso $\boxed{L}////$
Via dei Soldati 25 ☎ *6864250* • *closed L, Sun, mid Jul–end Aug* • *AE DC V* • *reservations essential*
An opulent establishment guaranteed to impress – unless your guest is a gourmet. In this 15thC *palazzo*, a one-time simple tavern now offers palatial decor, a piano bar and nightclub (upstairs). Popular with tycoons and trendies, stargazers and American tourists, but open only in the evenings.

La Maiella $\boxed{L}/$
Pza Sant'Apollinare 45 ☎ *6864174* •
closed Sun, 2 weeks Aug • *AE DC V* • *reservations essential*
A well-known and respected restaurant near Piazza Navona, with tables outside in fine weather. Politicians and other public figures are often seen here on weekdays and the place is usually packed in the evenings as well as at lunch time. Cooking is from Abruzzo, with truffles and seafood in season.

Otello alla Concordia *⌐L⌐/*
Via della Croce 81 ☎ *6791178* • *closed*
Sun • *DC*
This well-known Roman trattoria does
a brisk trade; arrive early to sit in the
pleasant covered courtyard (for which
reservations are not taken).
Journalists, artists, tourists and people
from the nearby centres of the fashion
and the antiques trades find Otello
convenient for a quick, cheap lunch;
sit inside (in the older, more
characteristic part) if you prefer not to
feel hurried or overheard. Food is
usually quite good, seldom
outstanding; wines are simple – from
Tuscany or the Castelli Romani.

La Pergola *⌐L⌐////*
Cavalieri Hilton ☎ *31511* • *closed Sun*
• *AE DC MC V* • *reservations essential*
Although the Hilton's roof terrace
restaurant has been closed for security
reasons, La Pergola still offers
splendid penthouse views over Rome.
The reputation for superb cooking
and fine wines attracts Roman diners
as well as hotel guests. Piano bar.

Piperno *⌐L⌐//*
Monte Cenci 9 ☎ *6540629* • *closed*
Sun D, Mon, Aug • *AE DC* •
D reservations essential
The best of the restaurants in the
so-called Jewish ghetto area. Both
food and service here are reliable and
there is plenty of space, with tables
outside on the tiny piazza in summer.
Popular with locals as well as tourists.

Ranieri *⌐L⌐//*
Via Mario de' Fiori 26 ☎ *6791592* •
closed Sun • *AE DC MC V* • *jacket*
and tie
This conservative establishment is
named after Queen Victoria's cook
(who started it in 1843). The interior
is little changed: several small rooms
with brocaded silk walls, gilded
mirrors and crystal chandeliers.
Cooking has recently been rejuvenated
by the arrival of a new chef. Regulars
include politicians, financiers and
diplomats, elderly aristocrats and
tourists. Private rooms are available.

Relais le Jardin *⌐L⌐////*
Lord Byron Hotel ☎ *3609541* • *closed*
Sun • *AE DC MC V* • *ties preferred* •
reservations essential
Considered by some the best
restaurant in Rome, Le Jardin attracts
a clientele which includes the
president, ministers and top business
people. Its airily elegant atmosphere is
just right for lingering business
lunches or romantic dinners, and the
adjacent bar is a delightful place for
an *aperitivo* or coffee. Expect
imaginative, Italianized *nouvelle cuisine*
and outstanding service.

Sabatini *⌐L⌐////*
Pza Santa Maria in Trastevere 18
☎ *5818307* • *closed Tue* • *AE DC MC V*
• *D reservations essential*
The best restaurant in Trastevere, a
good choice for business entertaining,
but also touristy. Roman cooking.

Taverna Flavia *⌐L⌐//*
Via Flavia 9 ☎ *4745214* • *closed Sun*
• *AE DC V* • *reservations essential*
A favourite with IRI bosses, politicians
from the nearby ministries, journalists
and guests of the Grand Hotel, this
simple but expensive taverna has
stayed fashionable since the 1950s
when it was patronized by the film
stars whose signed photographs still
hang on the walls. *Insalata Veruschka*,
a salad with truffles, is the pride of
this high-class establishment, and the
wine list is outstanding.

OTHER RESTAURANTS
The following restaurants, listed by
area, all offer reliable cooking.

Ludovisi/Borghese
Al Chianti, Via Ancona 17 ☎ 861083.
Tuscan cooking in Porta Pia district.
Bonne Nouvelle, Via del Boschetto
73-74 ☎ 486781. Fish restaurant.
Cesarina, Via Piemonte 109
☎ 460073. Bolognese cooking, near
Via XX Settembre.
Colline Emiliane, Via degli Avignonesi
22 ☎ 4817538. Quiet trattoria off
noisy Via del Tritone; cooking from
Emilia-Romagna.

Da Tullio, Via S. Nicola da Tolentino
26 ☎ 4745560. Tuscan cooking, near
Piazza Barberini.
Giggi Fazi, Via Lucullo 22 ☎ 464045.
Near the US Embassy, Roman food.
Girarrosto Toscano, Via Campania 29
☎ 493759. Touristy, Tuscan
restaurant convenient for the Ludovisi
quarter.
Piccolo Mondo, Via Aurora 39d
☎ 485680. Well-known Ludovisi
quarter restaurant; hotly-contested
outside tables, elegant interior,
Roman cooking.

Central Rome

Il Bacaro, Via degli Spagnoli 27
☎ 6864110. Fine wines and good
food; popular with journalists;
evenings only except Sun.
Dal Bolognese, Pza del Popolo 1
☎ 3611426. Bolognese cooking;
convenient for RAI, the art galleries of
Via del Babuino and the cocktail set
from Rosati's (see *Bars and cafés*).
Il Buco, Via Sant'Ignazio 7–8
☎ 6793298. Excellent Tuscan
trattoria near the Borsa, with outside
tables.
La Campana, Vicolo della Campana 18
☎ 6867820. Sound, old, no-frills
Roman trattoria between the Tiber
and the Parliament.
Il Drappo, Vicolo del Malpasso 9
☎ 6877365. The best Sardinian
restaurant in Rome.
Da Fortunato, Via del Pantheon 55
☎ 6792788. Classic Roman trattoria
frequented by politicians and business
people.
Al Moro, Vicolo delle Bollette 13
☎ 6783495. Crowded restaurant near
Trevi fountain; sound Italian cooking.
Nel Regno di Re Ferdinando, Via dei
Banchi Nuovi ☎ 6541167. A rustic
but sophisticated Neapolitan taverna;
evenings only.
Taverna Giulia, Vicolo dell'Oro 23
☎ 6869768. Elegant, good service and
Genoese food; till 2am.
Trattoria dell'Antiquario, Pza San
Simeone 27 ☎ 6879694. Good service
and quite good traditional food;
pleasant tables outside on the Via dei
Coronari; evenings only.

Vecchia Roma, Pza Campitelli 18
☎ 6864604. Pretty restaurant in an
airy Renaissance palace, with al fresco
dining on a lovely square near the
Jewish ghetto area; closed Wed.

Across the Tiber

Antica Pesa, Via Garibaldi 18
☎ 5809236. Trastevere trattoria,
typical Roman dishes.
Il Matriciano, Via dei Gracchi 55
☎ 317810. Very Roman atmosphere;
popular with lawyers and film
industry people. Near the Vatican.
Romolo, Via di Porta Settimiana 8
☎ 5818284. Trastevere restaurant
with delightful interior garden
bounded by the Aurelian wall.

Out of town

There are good seafood restaurants at
Fiumicino (30km/18 miles), near the
airport. Romans flock here at
weekends. *Bastianelli al Molo*
☎ 6440118, in Via di Torre
Clementina, is generally considered
the best. Restaurants at Frascati
(22km/13.5 miles) are also popular for
an excursion.

Bars and cafés

Most Roman bars cater for a quick
drink standing at the counter; for a
business discussion it is better to meet
at a hotel, preferably the *Grand*.
Alternatively, sample the garden bar
of the *Eden* or the drawing-room
atmosphere of the *Lord Byron* or the
D'Inghilterra. *Casina Valadier* (see
Restaurants) is a smart place to be
seen. Romans prefer *spumantino* or
white wine to spirits before dinner.
     There are some café-bars suitable
for a business encounter. The old-
fashioned *Rosati* on Piazza del Popolo
is a classy rendezvous. *Antico Caffè
Greco*, Via Condotti 86, a famous
haunt of 19thC *literati*, and the quaint
Babington's Tea Rooms, at the foot of
the Spanish Steps, close before dinner
but are fine for an afternoon chat or
an early aperitif. On the Via Veneto
Harry's Bar, the *Café de Paris* or
Doney's are good places for a drink or
light meal.

In your leisure time you might try a chocolate *tartufo* at *Tre Scalini* on Piazza Navona or visit one of the ice-cream shops near the Pantheon.

Entertainment

The monthly newsletter and events list *Carnet* is distributed free by the tourist office. *A Guest in Rome* is also available free in hotels.

Ticket agencies *Orbis*, Pza del Esquilino ☏ 4744776 or 4751403.

Opera The season lasts from November to May at the *Teatro dell'Opera di Roma*, Pza Beniamino Gigli 8 ☏ 463641 (but standards are variable). In July and August there is an open-air season in the ruins of the Baths (*Terme*) of Caracalla; for good seats reserve ahead through Teatro dell'Opera or Carriani Tours ☏ 460510 or 4742501.

Theatre The season runs from October to May but in summer there are some outdoor performances. Italian classics (Pirandello and Goldoni) are regularly featured as well as Shakespeare in translation.

Music The Accademia Nazionale di Santa Cecilia plays at *Auditorio Pio*, Via della Conciliazione 4 ☏ 6541044, box office open Thu, 5–8, Fri, 9–1. In June, evening concerts are held in the beautiful setting of the Campidoglio, although the acoustics are poor. Advance tickets from Via della Conciliazione 4, Mon–Fri, 9–2.

The RAI orchestra performs from October to June at *Auditorio del Foro Italico*, Pza Lauro de Bosis 1 ☏ 6541044. The *Teatro Ghione*, Via delle Fornaci ☏ 6372294, is a venue for concerts and operettas.

Concerts are often held in the city's countless churches and at the Villa Medici (French Academy), Vle Trinità dei Monti 1 ☏ 67611; these are usually advertised on posters.

Pop and rock concerts are held in EUR at the *Pala EUR* or at the *Palaein*, Pzle dello Sport ☏ 5925205.

Cinema *Pasquino*, Vicolo del Piede 19 ☏ 5803662, shows frequently changing programmes of English-language films.

Nightclubs There are several stylish nightclubs and discotheques in Parioli and around Via Veneto. Most nightspots are closed in July and August.

Smart discotheques with dining include classic, touristy *Jackie' O*, Via Boncampagni 11 ☏ 461401, and *Open Gate*, Via San Nicola da Tolentino ☏ 4750464, frequented by politicians and grand Romans. *Gilda*, Via Mario de' Fiori 97 ☏ 6784838, and *Histeria*, Via R. Giovanelli ☏ 864587, are also recommended for dancing.

At *Arciliuto*, Pza Montevecchio 5 ☏ 6879419, the owner/entertainer sings poems to music, slipping from Neapolitan to English and appealing to a cosmopolitan clientele. Also in the Piazza Navona area is *Hemingway*, Pza delle Coppelle 10 ☏ 6544135, a bar popular with young Romans, actors and famous faces.

At Fregene (38km/23.5 miles) *Il Miraggio* ☏ 6462655 is a fashionable disco/nightclub, open in summer only.

Shopping

Milan may be Italy's capital of fashion but Rome still leads for *alta moda* (*haute couture*); among designers based here are Renato Balestra, Roberto Capucci, Rocco Barocco, Gianfranco Ferrè and Lancetti. The best shopping areas are compact and traffic-free. Near the Spanish Steps, and around Via Condotti, Via Borgognona and Via Frattina are the most exclusive fashion boutiques (including those selling jewellery, shoes and other accessories). *Alta moda* workshops are concentrated in nearby Via Gregoriana and Via Sistina. Via del Babuino is the best address in the city for art dealers and for Persian carpets, and parallel Via Margutta has several artists' studios and galleries. Antiques can also be found in Via Giulia and Via dei Coronari (west of the Corso there are many craftsmen making picture frames and restoring furniture).

Linens and lingerie, leather gloves and shoes are worth looking out for,

as are prints and picture frames.
Classic made-to-measure shirts are
also good quality.

Customers from outside the EC can
reclaim IVA on objects costing over
L525,000 at shops displaying the
"Tax Free System" sign. Take the
invoice to the customs office at
Fiumicino airport and obtain a cash
refund at the Santo Spirito bank there
(or apply by post).
Books *Lion Bookshop*, Via del
Babuino 181 ☎ 3605837. *Feltrinelli*,
Via Vittorio Emanuele Orlando 84–86
☎ 484430, opposite the Grand Hotel,
has an excellent English selection.
Fashion *Laura Biagiotti*, *Fendi*, *Ferrè*,
Pancaldi and *Versace* (for men) are in
Via Borgognona; *Battistoni* (made-to-
measure), *Beltrami* (shoes and
leathergoods), *Cucci* and *Gucci* in Via
Condotti. The Milanese designer
Giorgio Armani has shops in Via del
Babuino, and top Parisian names like
Balenciaga, *Courrèges* and *Yves St
Laurent* are in Via Bocca di Leone.
The most famous Roman designer is
Valentino; his atelier is on Via
Gregoriana 24 (women's boutique, Via
Bocca di Leone 15; men's, Via
Condotti at the corner of Via Mario
de' Fiori).
Gloves *Merola*, Via del Corso 143.
Jewellery *Buccellati* and *Bulgari* are
the best-known Italian jewellers in Via
Condotti; also there are *Cartier*,
Capuano, *Carlo Eleuteri* and *Massoni*.
Furst is in Via Veneto, *Petochi* on
Piazza di Spagna.
Lingerie and linens *Emilia Bellini*,
Pza di Spagna 77, *Cesari*, Via
Barberini 3, for the former; and
Brighenti, Via Frattina 3, for the
latter.
Street markets Lively street markets
include the Sunday flea market at
Porta Portese and the food market on
Campo de' Fiori, daily except
Sundays. On Piazza Fontanella
Borghese there are stalls selling old
prints and books (daily except Sun).

Sightseeing

Rome's history provides an exhausting
sightseeing challenge. There are

extensive remains and monuments.
There are early Christian catacombs
and churches (some of the most
ancient being *fuori le mura*, outside the
walls), and scores of important High
Renaissance and baroque churches by
architects such as Bramante, Bernini
and Borromini. There are numerous
palaces, some with extensive art
collections, and the many lovely
piazzas and exuberant fountains are
particularly characteristic of the city.
St Peter's and the Vatican are rich in
art treasures and there are many
museums and galleries. If you have
only a limited amount of time for
sightseeing you will want to take in St
Peter's and the Sistine Chapel, and
then perhaps some of the other sights,
according to your choice.
Castel Sant' Angelo Built as a
mausoleum for the Emperor Hadrian
(135–39), later a medieval fortress and
now an art and military museum.
*Lungotevere Castello. Open Tue–Sat,
9–2; Sun, 9–1.*
Colosseum Built 72–96 by the
Flavian emperors, this is the most
important monument and symbol of
ancient Rome, originally used for
gladiatorial combats and "circuses."
Nearby is the *Arch of Constantine*,
built in 315 to celebrate his victory
over Maxentius at Ponte Milvio. *Open
daily, 9–3.30; summer 9–7.*
Forum The Roman Forum, focus of
public life in the ancient capital,
comprises the remains of temples,
triumphal arches, public buildings
and private villas overlooked by the
Palatine hill. *Via dei Fori Imperiali.
Open Tue–Sat, 9–3; summer, 9–6;
Sun, 9–1.*
Galleria Colonna Rich Renaissance
art collection of the Colonna princes.
*Via della Pilotta 17. Open daily, 9–1;
closed Aug.*
Galleria Doria Pamphili Superb
private collection of 15th–17thC
Italian and other European works of
art. *Pza del Collegio Romano 1a. Open
Tue, Fri–Sun, 10–1.*
Galleria Nazionale d'Arte Antica
The National Gallery, housed in
Palazzo Barberini. Mainly 13th–16th

centuries. *Via IV Fontane 13. Open Tue–Sat, 9–2; Sun, 9–1.*

Galleria Nazionale d'Arte Moderna 19th and 20thC Italian art, beside the Villa Borghese gardens. *Vle delle Belle Arti 131. Open Tue–Sat, 9–2; Wed, Fri, 3–6; Sun, 9–1.*

Roman churches

Among the many churches worth visiting, the following is a selection of the most outstanding.

Early Christian and Byzantine *Santa Maria in Trastevere, Santa Prassede* and *San Clemente* for Byzantine-influenced mosaics; the best are at *Santa Costanza*, Via Nomentana, about 2.5km/1.5 miles from the centre. *Santa Maria Maggiore* has early Christian mosaics.

Renaissance Bramante's *tempietto* at San Pietro in Montorio; a perfect Renaissance building.

High Renaissance/baroque *Il Gesù*, the main Jesuit church in Rome, and a prototype of the baroque style, famous for its façade and exuberant ceiling painting; exquisite *Santa Maria della Pace*; the façade by Carlo Maderno of *Santa Susanna*; Borromini's *Sant'Ivo alla Sapienza* and *San Carlo alle Quattro Fontane*, both masterpieces of virtuoso design; *Sant'Andrea al Quirinale* by Bernini; *Sant'Andrea della Valle* and *Sant'Ignazio*, both with unbelievably opulent ceilings.

Among those with great works of art are *Santa Maria sopra Minerva* (Michelangelo's *Redeemer*; frescoes by Filippino Lippi); *San Pietro in Vincolo* for Michelangelo's *Moses*; *San Luigi dei Francesi* (famous early works of Caravaggio); *Santa Maria del Popolo* (frescoes by Pinturicchio, masterpieces of Caravaggio); *Santa Maria della Vittoria* (Bernini's *Ecstasy of Saint Teresa*); and the 16thC ceilings in *San Giovanni in Laterano*.

Galleria Nazionale di Palazzo Corsini Corsini collection of 16th and 17thC art now belonging to the state, but displayed in the family *palazzo*. *Via della Lungara 10. Open Tue–Sat, 9–7; Mon, 9–2; Sun 9–1.*

Galleria Spada A small but fine collection of baroque paintings in the same *palazzo* as the Council of State. *Pza Capo di Ferro 3. Open Tue–Sat, 9–2; Sun, 9–1.*

Museo Borghese In the palace of the Villa Borghese gardens. Only the sculpture rooms are open. *Pza Scipione Borghese 5. Open Tue–Sat, 9–7; Sun–Mon, 9–1.30.*

Musei Capitolini Large collection of antique sculpture in Palazzo Nuovo; more sculpture and paintings in the *Museo del Palazzo dei Conservatori* opposite. *Pza del Campidoglio 1. Open Tue–Fri, 9–2; Sat, Sun, 9–1; Tue, Thu, 5–8; Sat, 8.30pm–11pm.*

Museo della Civiltà Romana The history of Rome and its influence; worth seeing if you are at EUR. *Pza G. Agnelli 10. Open Tue, Wed, Fri, Sat, 9–1; Thu, 9–1.30, 4–7; Sun, 9–1.*

Museo Nazionale di Villa Giulia Important pre-Roman, notably Etruscan, remains in a 16thC papal villa. *Pzle di Villa Giulia 9. Open Mon–Sat, 9–2; Sun, 9–1.*

Musei Vaticani Extensive papal collections, many museums, and Michelangelo's ceiling in the Sistine Chapel, recently and controversially cleaned. Raphael's *Stanze* and the Borgia apartments can be visited on the way. Treasures of the picture gallery (*Pinacoteca*) include works by Giotto, Florentine masters, Raphael (*Transfiguration*) and Caravaggio. The *Pio-Clementino museum* contains important classical sculpture including the *Apollo Belvedere*, the *Belvedere Torso* and the *Laocoon*. Other museums show ancient art (*Museum of Ancient Egypt, Etruscan Museum*) and religious subjects. *Vle Vaticano. Open Mon–Sat, 8.45–1; last Sun in month 9–1; Easter, summer, Mon–Fri, 8.45–4.*

Pantheon Marvellously preserved 2ndC BC temple, consecrated as a Christian church in 606 and

containing the tomb of Raphael. The dome, whose diameter is equal to its height, is an extraordinary engineering feat. *Pza della Rotonda. Open Mon–Sat, 9–1, 2–5; Sun, 9–1.*
San Pietro (St Peter's) This magnificent focus of the Catholic faith, built over the tomb of St Peter, is the largest church in the world, with a dome by Michelangelo and colonnades by Bernini. Inside see Michelangelo's *Pietà* and Bernini's ornate *baldacchino*. Fine views from the roof. *Open daily, 7–6.*

Guided tours
American Express, Pza di Spagna 38 ☎ 67641; *Carrani Tours*, Via V.E. Orlando 95 ☎ 460510; *CIT*, Pza della Repubblica 68 ☎ 47941; *Pioneer Line*, Via Filippo Turati 43 ☎ 734234. Half- and full-day coach tours include entry to selected sights. For a surface-scratching view of the city *ATAC* operates an unguided 2hr tour on bus route 110 from Piazza dei Cinquecento ☎ 46954444.

For authorized guides contact the tourist office or *Sindicato Nazionale CISL Guide Turistiche*, Rampa Mignanelli 12 ☎ 6789842. For incentive tours contact *Eurotravel* ☎ 5926025 (EUR office) or ☎ 858592 (Parioli office).

Out of town
Typical tours include Tivoli (Roman Villa Adriana, gardens of the Villa d'Este), and the Castelli Romani (towns of the Alban Hills, known for their wines). There are also day trips by coach to Assisi, Florence and Naples.

Spectator sports
Major sporting events are held at several grounds equipped for indoor and outdoor sports from swimming to athletics and skating to soccer: the *Foro Italico*, at the foot of Monte Mario, the *Palazzetto dello Sport* and stadium at Flaminio and the *Palazzo dello Sport* and *Tre Fontane* at EUR.

Soccer Local teams are Roma and Lazio. They play at *Stadio Olimpico* ☎ 36851 or 3966733 or at Flaminio. Tickets available at the stadium.
Racing *Ippodromo delle Cappanelle*, Via Appia Nuova 1255 ☎ 7993143 or 794359; *Ippodromo di Tor di Valle*, Via del Mare ☎ 5924205 (trotting); some evening races.

Keeping fit
The sporting facilities at Foro Italico, at EUR and at Acqua Acetosa, Via dei Campi Sportivi 48 ☎ 36851, are open to all. There are several exclusive golf, rowing and tennis clubs where visitors might be invited: the snobbiest is the *Circolo Aniene*, which does not allow women.
Fitness centres *American Workout Studio*, Via Massimo d'Azeglio 3 ☎ 6799751. *American Health Club*, Largo Somalia 60 ☎ 8394488, has reciprocal membership arrangements and is associated with *Roman Sport Center*, Via del Galoppatoio 33 ☎ 3601667. *Navona Health Center*, Via dei Banchi Nuovi 39 ☎ 6530104.
Golf To play at *Circolo del Golf di Roma*, Via Appia Nuova 716a (Acquasanta) ☎ 783407, *Country Club Castelgandolfo*, Via Santo Spirito 13 ☎ 93112301 or *Golf Club Olgiata*, Largo dell'Olgiata 15 ☎ 3789141, you need membership of any other golf club in the world.
Riding *Villa Borghese*, Via del Galoppatoio 25 ☎ 360679, requires membership.
Swimming The pools at the Cavalieri Hilton and Aldrovandi Palace (see *Hotels*) can be used by visitors. There is an outdoor pool at EUR, *Piscina delle Rose*, Vle America ☎ 5926717. The best beaches are at Circeo, a 2hr drive south of Rome, and 2hrs north at Ansedonia.
Tennis *Tennis Club Parioli*, Largo de Morpurgo Umberto 2 ☎ 836408, is the most exclusive tennis club (also with pool and gym; by invitation only). *Circolo Canotieri e Tennis Lazio*, Lungotevere Flaminio 25 ☎ 3606853, offers 15-day season tickets, at the invitation of a member. *Società*

Ginnastico di Roma, Via Muro Torto 5 ☎ 465566, was opened in 1890 and is used by MPs, US diplomats, actors and journalists. *Circolo della Stampa*, Via Brunelleschi 13 ☎ 3960790, owned by a team of journalists, requires only a fee of L12,000. Anyone with government contacts might be invited to play at the *Circolo di Montecitorio* or the Foreign Ministry's sports centre at Acqua Acetosa. *Circolo Tennis EUR*, Vle dell'Artigianato 35 ☎ 5924693, is a prestigious club (members and guests only).

Local resources

Business services

Consul Club, Pza di Spagna 35 ☎ 6786795; *Executive Service*, Via Savoia 78 ☎ 853241, rents offices, equipment and staff; *Pinciana Office*, Via di Porta Pinciana 4 ☎ 4814143 ⊤ⓧ 621489 (instant offices).
Photocopying Photocopying is available at hotels; otherwise use office suppliers or business services.
Secretarial Rome at your service, Via Orlando 75 ☎ 484583.
Translation World Translation Centre, Via XX Settembre 1 ☎ 4812723; *EGA Congressi*, Vle Tiziano 19 ☎ 3960341; *Centro Pilota*, Via Palestro 68 ☎ 4453317; *Congressi* (*STOC*), Via Laurentina 203 ☎ 5401758.

Communications

Local delivery Pony Express ☎ 3309; *Roman Express* ☎ 3398048. *Piana* ☎ 7316451 delivers nationally.
Long-distance delivery DHL ☎ 72421; *Emery International Cargo System* ☎ 6454247; *Domenichelli* ☎ 43671 to Milan; *TNT Traco* ☎ 6888980.
Post offices Central office: Pza San Silvestro (24hr telex and telegram service ☎ 6795530), open Mon–Fri, 8.30–9; Sat, 8.30–noon, with facilities for international telephone calls. Area post offices open Mon–Fri, 8.15–2 (Sat to noon); principal sub post offices (including that at Fiumicino airport) open till 6pm for parcels and 8pm for telegrams and registered

letters. The Vatican post office is sometimes better for outgoing mail.
Telex and fax The telex office in the international departures lounge at Fiumicino is open daily, 8.25–1.50, 2–5 ☎ 601623 or 601631. Fax at the central post office.

Conference/exhibition centres

Rome offers a wide range of venues from convention hotels and specially built convention centres to historic buildings. The *Grand* provides splendid rooms with efficient organization. The *Sheraton Roma*, Vle del Pattinaggio, 00144 ☎ 5453 ⊤ⓧ 614223, hosts international conferences throughout the year. *International Congress Office*, Via Rubicone 27, 00198 ☎ 8441185 ⊤ⓧ 812277, organizes exhibitions.
In the centre is the *Congressi Residenza di Ripetta*, Via di Ripetta 231 ☎ 672141 (capacity up to 300); *Castel Sant'Angelo* and *Palazzo Barberini* (capacity up to 200); *Palazzo Brancaccio* can take conferences of at least 120 participants; and *Villa Miani* at Monte Mario is popular for gala dinners and receptions.
At EUR, the *Auditorium della Tecnica* (capcity up to 1,000), the *Fiera di Roma*, *Pala EUR* (capacity up to 14,000) and the *Palazzo dei Congressi* (capacity up to 1,500) cater for enormous international conferences.

Emergencies

Bureaus de change Open outside normal office hours and Sat: *Banca Nazionale del Lavoro*, Pza Venezia 6 (also open Sun), *Credito Italiano*, Pza di Spagna 19. Bureaus de change at Termini station and *American Express*, Pza di Spagna 38, are open all day weekdays and Sat am and 24hrs at Fiumicino airport.
Hospitals Ambulance (Red Cross) ☎ 5100. 24hr medical service ☎ 4756741. For private medical treatment *Salvator Mundi International Hospital*, Vle delle Mure Gianicolensi 67 ☎ 586041 (telephone in advance). *Policlinico Umberto I*, Vle del

Policlinico 155 ☎ 49971, *San Camillo*, Circonv. Gianicolense 87 ☎ 58701, *San Giovanni*, Via Amba Aradam 9 ☎ 7705, and *Sant'Eugenio*, Pzle dell'Umanesimo (EUR) ☎ 5904, have emergency facilities.
Pharmacies For details of pharmacies open see daily newspapers or ☎ 1921. *Internazionale*, Pza Barberini 49 ☎ 462996, *Imbesi*, Vle Europa 76 ☎ 5925509 (EUR), are open all night. For English or American pharmaceutical products try *Evans*, 63 Pza di Spagna ☎ 6790626, or the pharmacy at the Vatican.
Police *Questura*: Via San Vitale 15 ☎ 4686.

Government offices
Ministero degli Affari Esteri, Pzle della Farnesina 1 ☎ 36911 (Foreign Affairs); *Ministero delle Finanze*, Vle America (EUR) ☎ 5997 (Finance); *Ministero dell'Industria, del Commercio e dell'Artigianato*, Via Vittorio Veneto 33, 00100 ☎ 4705 (Industry, Commerce and Crafts); *Ministero del Commercio con l'Estero*, Vle America (EUR), 00144 ☎ 5993 (Foreign Trade); *Ministero del Tesoro*, Via XX Settembre 97 ☎ 47611 (Treasury).

Information sources
Business information *Camera di Commercio*, Via de'Burrò 147, 00186 ☎ 6783280; *Camera di Commercio Internazionale*, Via XX Settembre 5 ☎ 462575; CED (*Centro Elettronico de Documentazione*), Via D. Chiesa ☎ 3308 (legal data bank); *Confindustria*, Vle dell'Astronomia 30, 00144 ☎ 59031 (General Confederation of Italian Industry which helps members through representation to government and other groups); *Consiglio Nazionale delle Ricerche* (National Research Council), Pzle Aldo Moro 7, 00185 ☎ 49931; *European Communities Information Office*, Via Poli 29, 00187 ☎ 6789722; *Istituto Nazionale per il Commercio Estero*, Via Liszt 21, 00144 ☎ 59921 (promotes export of Italian goods); *Istituto per la Cooperazione Economica Internazionale e i Problemi*

dello Sviluppo, Via Cola di Rienzo 11 ☎ 383169 (promotes international economic cooperation and development). The Rome Yellow Pages (*Pagine Gialle*), in English, can be bought from international bookshops.
Local media *Il Messaggero* and *Il Tempo* are the main Italian dailies published in Rome; *L'Espresso* is the main news weekly magazine. *La Repubblica* has Rome and Milan editions. Other national and international newspapers are widely available, the latter by 2pm on the day of publication.

Tele MonteCarlo broadcasts CBS evening news the next morning (7.15 and 7.45) and 24hr Cable Network News is available at major hotels. On radio the Voice of America, the BBC and Vatican News are in English.
Tourist information Via Parigi 11 ☎ 461851, and branches at Termini station, in the baggage claim area at Fiumicino airport and at autostrada exits. *Vatican City information office*, Pza San Pietro ☎ 6984866.

Public transport information, bus maps, passes from ATAC, Pza dei Cinquecento ☎ 4695.

Thank-yous
Books *Rizzoli*, Largo Chigi 15 ☎ 6796641; *Mondadori*, Via Veneto 140 ☎ 462631.
Confectionery *Moriondo & Gariglio*, Via della Pilotta 2 ☎ 6786662.
Florists *Valle Fiori*, Via V.E. Orlando 90a ☎ 460209; *Teleflor International*, Via Scirè 14 ☎ 8313447.

BOLOGNA
City code ☎ 051

Bologna, site of one of the oldest universities in Europe and capital of Emilia-Romagna, has developed from a thriving agricultural market town into the fifth most important industrial complex in Italy with a population of nearly 500,000. Its position has always been important and it commands a network of trade routes from the Northern plain, from Ravenna and from the South.

The prosperity of the city and its environs is based on Bologna's role as a focus for the distribution of goods in central Italy, on trade in the rich produce of the Po valley, notably in grain and fruit, and on industry including food processing, especially pasta and chocolates, furniture making, electronics, the manufacture of automobile components, electrical equipment, steel and chemicals; the electro-mechanical sector employs 50% of the work force. Technical expertise and flexibility have been key elements in companies that have responded swiftly to competition; GD, for example, which started as a manufacturer of motorcycles, has become a world leader in making machinery for the packaging of confectionery, soaps and cigarettes. Most industrial concerns are medium to small and many, including some of the larger ones, are family enterprises. Only five companies employ more than 500 people, headed by Marposs, producing precision instruments, most of which are exported.

Economic growth in the last 20 years has been stimulated by the construction of the increasingly important Fiera exhibition and fair ground; it hosts about 30 fairs a year, 16 of which are of international importance including the fashion, shoe, and children's book fairs. In 1987 its visitors numbered 700,000 of whom 60,000 were foreigners.

The left has been politically dominant in Bologna since World War II, despite the city's bourgeois values, and cooperatives, which have sprouted throughout the region, have collaborated successfully with private enterprise. The city's economy is flourishing, yet life seems to proceed at a pleasantly leisured pace. The Bolognese like to work hard, and are patient and courteous. It is not for nothing that the city is known as *Bologna la Grassa* ("the Fat"). It has an abundance of good restaurants and long and leisurely meals are a business tradition.

Arriving
Bologna is not well served by regular international flights but is a vital road and rail junction, linking major Northern Italian cities with the centre and South.

Guglielmo Marconi airport
By 1990, when Italy hosts the soccer World Cup, Bologna's small airport will have grown considerably. Prior to its enlargement facilities were limited to a café, a snack bar, banking and exchange facilities, a self-service restaurant (in a separate building), and a VIP lounge. Flights connect daily with Paris, Frankfurt and London and six days a week with Munich as well as Milan, Rome, Naples, Alghero and Palermo. Summer charter flights bound for the Adriatic cause congestion. Inquiries ☎ 311578 or 312259.
City link The city centre is 8km/5 miles to the southeast.
Taxi It is best to take a cab and you

rarely have to wait long for one; the
journey to the centre takes only
15–20mins, fare L15,000.
Car rental Europcar, Hertz and Avis
have desks at the airport.

Railway station
Bologna's busy and often crowded
station, north of the city centre,
handles numerous domestic and
international trains. Florence is just
70mins away and a project is under
way to speed up links to Milan and
Rome (currently 2hrs 30mins away).
The journey time to Venice is 2hrs.
Facilities include a cafeteria, 24hr
currency exchange, information and
SIAT tourist offices. The station is
about a 15min walk from the centre.
There is a regular bus service to all
parts of the city, including the Fiera
site. Getting a taxi is usually easy.
Inquiries ☎ 246490.

Getting around
The centre is quite compact and the
most sensible way to get round the
city is on foot, with 35kms/21 miles
of arcade for shelter from rain and
excessive heat. Taxis are the easiest
alternative but there is also a fast,
cheap bus network.
Taxis Radio Taxis ☎ 372727 or
534141 provide a reliable service;
otherwise there are ranks in Piazza Re
Enzo, Piazza Galvani and Via Rizzoli.
You can hail them in the street, but
they are hard to find during the big
fairs.
Limousines Baratta ☎ 522763, *CAB*
☎ 553415.
Driving A car is a positive drawback
unless you are visiting sites outside
the city. The centre (which is a maze
of one-way streets) is closed to traffic
during the weekends and parking in
central streets is not permitted.
Walking Orientation is easy and
walking safe except in deserted areas
at night. Watch out for bag-snatchers.
Bus The bus network is useful for
places outside walking distance,
especially the Fiera, but the system
can be confusing in the evenings
when lines shorten or change routes

and at weekends when the centre is
closed to most buses.

Area by area
The main streets of Bologna radiate
from Piazza Maggiore towards the
city gates and the *viali*, the circle of
avenues which follows the ancient
walls. Despite the intrusion of
postwar architecture in the northeast,
the core remains remarkably medieval
in character: red-brick *palazzi* and
mansions and arcades flank many
streets.

The indisputable heart of the city
has always been the Piazza Maggiore
and the adjoining Piazza del Nettuno.
This magnificent square, bordered by
grand *palazzi* and the huge church of
San Petronio, was (and to a certain
extent still is) the place where
Bolognese gathered for speeches,
ceremonies, meetings and protests.
But the long-standing symbol of the
city is the Piazza di Porta Ravegnana
and its two acutely·leaning medieval
towers (*Due torri*). The university
area, with its graffiti-streaked walls
and socialist posters, lies northeast
along the Via Zamboni.

Business development has largely
been outside the *viali* ring road. The
Fiera site north of the old city is an
avant-garde complex of exhibition
pavilions, a business centre and
soaring towers with offices, agencies,
banks and shops. Close by is the
Palazzo dei Congressi conference
centre. Farther north, Castel
Maggiore is another important
commercial quarter, whose
Centergross is a large wholesale depot
for a wide range of goods.
The suburbs The most desirable
residential quarters are the quiet
wooded hills (the Colli district) to the
south of the city, where top business
executives own luxury villas. The
industrial suburbs to the north and
east, between the city centre and the
tangenziale (outer ring road), are less
prestigious. In the southwest,
Casalecchio di Reno, another
industrial and commercial centre, is
now almost a part of Bologna.

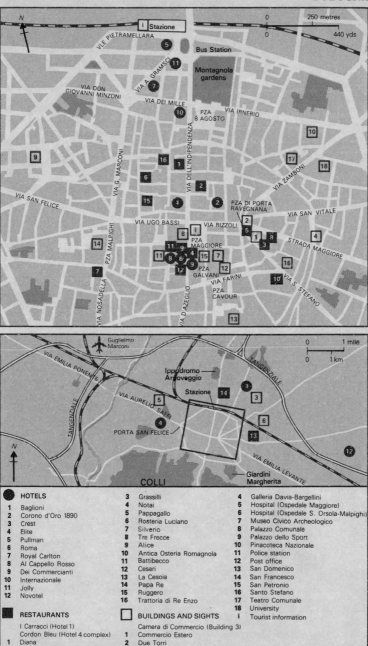

i Stazione

0 | 250 metres
0 | 440 yds

VLE PIETRAMELLARA

Bus Station

Montagnola gardens

VIA DON GIOVANNI MINZONI

VIA A. GRAMSCI

VIA DEL MILLE

PZA 8 AGOSTO

VIA IRNERIO

VIA G. MARCONI

VIA DELL'INDIPENDENZA

VIA ZAMBONI

VIA SAN FELICE

PZA DI PORTA RAVEGNANA

VIA SAN VITALE

VIA UGO BASSI

VIA RIZZOLI

PZA MAGGIORE

STRADA MAGGIORE

PZA MALPIGHI

PZA GALVANI

VIA FARINI

VIA S. STEFANO

VIA NOSADELLA

VIA D'AZEGLIO

PZA CAVOUR

Guglielmo Marconi

VIA EMILIA PONENTE

Ippodromo Arcoveggio

TANGENZIALE

Stazione

VIA AURELIO SAFFI

PORTA SAN FELICE

TANGENZIALE

VIA EMILIA LEVANTE

COLLI

Giardini Margherita

0 | 1 mile
0 | 1 km

●	**HOTELS**		3	Grassilli		4	Galleria Davia-Bargellini
1	Baglioni		4	Notai		5	Hospital (Ospedale Maggiore)
2	Corono d'Oro 1890		5	Pappagallo		6	Hospital (Ospedale S. Orsola-Malpighi)
3	Crest		6	Rosteria Luciano		7	Museo Civico Archeologico
4	Elite		7	Silverio		8	Palazzo Comunale
5	Pullman		8	Tre Frecce		9	Palazzo dello Sport
6	Roma		9	Alice		10	Pinacoteca Nazionale
7	Royal Carlton		10	Antica Osteria Romagnola		11	Police station
8	Al Cappello Rosso		11	Battibecco		12	Post office
9	Dei Commercianti		12	Cesari		13	San Domenico
10	Internazionale		13	La Cesoia		14	San Francesco
11	Jolly		14	Papa Re		15	San Petronio
12	Novotel		15	Ruggero		16	Santo Stefano
			16	Trattoria di Re Enzo		17	Teatro Comunale
						18	University
■	**RESTAURANTS**		□	**BUILDINGS AND SIGHTS**		i	Tourist information
	I Carracci (Hotel 1)			Camera di Commercio (Building 3)			
	Cordon Bleu (Hotel 4 complex)		1	Commercio Estero			
1	Diana		2	Due Torri			
2	Franco Rossi		3	Fiera			

Hotels

Some new hotels have been built on the outskirts of Bologna, but the demand for accommodation still exceeds the supply. During trade fairs and conventions every room is taken and prices rise by 15–20%.

All hotels listed have IDD telephones in every room, currency exchange and parking arrangements.

Baglioni *L*////
Via dell'Indipendenza 8, 40121
☎ *225445* [TX] *510242 fax 234840 •*
Palace • AE DC MC V • 117 rooms,
8 suites, 1 restaurant (separate
management), 1 bar
Bologna's grandest hotel, which reopened only in 1987 after a closure of ten years, is in the city centre. Today it is a regular rendezvous for the most affluent Bolognese, many of whom come to dine in the very expensive I Carracci (see *Restaurants*). The public rooms have been restored to their former splendour with frescoed walls, moulded ceilings and grand chandeliers. Bedrooms combine classical charm and modern luxury although some are small. The palatial suites are furnished with antiques and include marble bathrooms with jacuzzis. Parking arrangements are cumbersome. 24hr room service, hairdresser • 5 meeting rooms (capacity up to 75).

Corona d'Oro 1890 *L*//
Via Oberdan 12, 40124 ☎ *236458*
[TX] *224657 fax 262679 • AE DC MC V*
• 34 rooms, 1 suite, 1 bar
A pleasing small hotel, the Corona d'Oro dates back to the 14th century and is said to have housed Italy's first printing works. The Renaissance portico and 16thC coffered ceilings have been preserved, and the former winter garden transformed into an elegant Art Nouveau entrance hall. On a cobbled, traffic-free street close to the famous leaning towers, the hotel is popular with academics, actors and artists and well suited to business visitors who are happy with a central base offering personal attention but limited working facilities. 1 meeting room (capacity up to 45).

Crest *L*///
Pza della Costituzione 1, 40128
☎ *372172* [TX] *510676 fax 357662*
• AE DC MC V • 164 rooms, 1 suite,
1 restaurant, 1 bar
The Crest is adjacent to the exhibition and trade centres and is a good option for a working lunch and for those attending the Fiera. It has an unprepossessing exterior but is welcoming and well-equipped, one of the few hotels in the city with a garden and a pool. Executive rooms are larger and better-equipped than standard rooms, others are kept for nonsmokers and some are decorated and furnished in attractive floral fabrics. It can be difficult to get a taxi into the city centre. 24hr room service • pool • 7 meeting rooms (capacity up to 350).

Elite *L*///
Via Aurelio Saffi 36, 40131 ☎ *437417*
[TX] *510067 • AE DC MC V • 60 rooms,*
20 suites, 1 restaurant (separate
management), 1 bar
Modern, comfortable and well-appointed, the Elite is just outside the *viali* to the west, only a 10min taxi ride from the city centre and not far from the airport. It attracts a mainly business clientele. The suites are large (some have self-catering facilities) and the restaurant, the Cordon Bleu (see *Restaurants*), is superb. There is also a nightclub. Closed late Jul–late Aug. 3 meeting rooms (capacity up to 150).

Pullman *L*/
Vle Pietramellara 59, 40121 ☎ *248248*
[TX] *214822 fax 249421 • Pullman •*
AE DC MC V • 240 rooms, 1 restaurant,
1 bar
A large and sober 19thC building facing the station, the Pullman is

surprisingly modern and light inside with stylish public rooms and a comfortable bar for meeting business contacts; it was completely rebuilt in the early 1980s. The bedrooms have adequate working space, and are furnished with well-planned, pretty, modern fabrics, reproduction antiques and attractive lighting. The quietest rooms are at the back, overlooking a garden (not part of the hotel). 3 meeting rooms (capacity up to 90).

Roma *L*
Via d'Azeglio 9, 40123 ☎ *274400* ⊤ₓ *583270* • *AE DC MC V* • *87 rooms, 3 suites, 1 restaurant, 1 bar*
Low prices and a civilized atmosphere have made the Roma one of the most sought-after hotels in Bologna, attracting actors, discerning tourists and business travellers who appreciate charm, character and personal service. Another bonus is the quiet position on a smart traffic-free shopping street, just a few steps from the Piazza Maggiore. Public rooms are furnished with antiques and chintz, guest rooms with light floral patterns. Advance reservations essential. 1 meeting room (capacity up to 30).

Royal Carlton *L*///
Via Montebello 8, 40121 ☎ *249361* ⊤ₓ *510356 fax 249724* • *Gamma* • *AE DC MC V* • *250 rooms, 20 suites, 1 restaurant, 1 bar*
The Royal Carlton is a large, luxury hotel standing in its own garden not far from the station. Inside, the

emphasis is on space, modern comforts and cool efficiency. The lobby is furnished in brown and beige with mock-leather seating, the large bedrooms are stylish and the suites are luxurious. The bar is the best business rendezvous in Bologna. 24hr room service, hairdresser, secure underground parking • conference centre with 10 meeting rooms (capacity up to 1,000).

OTHER HOTELS
Al Cappello Rosso *L*/// *Via de' Fusari 9, 40123* ☎ *261891* ⊤ₓ *583304* • *AE DC MC V*. Central, quiet old *palazzo* with ultra-modern rooms.
Dei Commercianti *L*/ *Via de'Pignattari 11, 40124* ☎ *233052* ⊤ₓ *224657 fax 224733* • *AE DC MC V*. Small, recently refurbished hotel with limited facilities on quiet, central street.
Internazionale *L*/// *Via dell'Indipendenza 60, 40121* ☎ *254454* ⊤ₓ *511038* • *Gamma* • *AE DC MC V*. Central with comfortable modern bedrooms, but somewhat gloomy lobby. Rooms at the back are quieter.
Jolly *L*/ *Pza XX Settembre 2, 40121* ☎ *248921* ⊤ₓ *510076 fax 249764* • *AE DC MC V*. Big, ugly hotel near the station. Dull public areas in 1950s style; functional modern bedrooms.
Novotel *L*/// *Via Villanova 31, 40055* ☎ *781414* ⊤ₓ *213412* • *AE DC MC V*. Huge modern complex 8kms/5 miles east of the centre with Olympic-size pool, 4 tennis courts, conference and meeting rooms.

Restaurants
The Bolognese love their food and their city is justifiably regarded as a mecca of traditional Italian gastronomy. Reservations are essential during trade fairs.

I Carracci *L*///
Baglioni Hotel ☎ *270815* • *closed Sun, 4 weeks Jul–Aug* • *AE DC MC V* • *reservations essential* • *jacket preferred*
A 16thC room with a beautifully frescoed ceiling is the setting for this

sophisticated restaurant which serves rich regional dishes. It occupies part of the Baglioni Hotel and, though under separate management, is a favourite among the upper strata of the business community, particularly for lunch.

Cordon Bleu *L*////
Via Aurelio Saffi 38 ☎ *437417* ●
closed Mon L, Sun, 4 weeks Jul–Aug
● *AE DC MC V* ● *jacket preferred*
This long-established restaurant
continues to produce what many
consider the best food in town. A
particularly popular lunchtime
rendezvous for the business
community, it lies just outside the
Porta San Felice, in the same
complex as the Elite Hotel but under
separate management. Pierantonio
Zarotti has a bold approach when it
comes to introducing new dishes to
the Bolognese scene: some are
modern adaptions of the classics,
others are imported from central and
Southern Italy, and a few are entirely
his own invention. The choice of fish
is excellent and there is a very well
stocked cellar.

Diana *L*//
Via dell'Indipendenza 24 ☎ *231302* ●
closed Mon, Jan 1–12, most of Aug ●
AE DC V
Diana opened at the beginning of the
century and still serves authentic
Bolognese cooking at reasonable
prices. In one of the main shopping
streets of the centre, it is a cheerful
restaurant with big mirrors and bright
chandeliers. A good choice for truffle-
lovers and for informal meals, but
usually too busy for discreet
conversation.

Franco Rossi *L*///
Via Goito 3 ☎ *279959* ● *closed Sun,
May–Aug; Tue, Sep–Apr; July* ● *AE
DC V* ● *jacket and tie*
One of the most appealing restaurants
in the city, for both ambience and
cuisine, this smart, family-run
establishment offers carefully
prepared, imaginative dishes suitable
for both business or social occasions.
Tables are prettily laid, always with
fresh flowers and homemade bread;
the menu changes frequently and for
those in a hurry at lunch time there is
the option of a *piatto del giorno*. A
private room for 10 is available for
business meetings.

Grassilli *L*//
Via dal Luzzo 3 ☎ *222961* ● *closed
Wed, mid-Jul–mid-Aug* ● *AE DC V*
A charming setting and a club-like
atmosphere – photographs on the
walls of artists and intellectuals give
the place a slightly arty character –
combine to make this tiny restaurant
very popular among professionals. It
is tucked away in a small street in a
very old part of the city. Traditional
Italian cuisine features strongly on the
menu, as well as international dishes
such as fillet steaks prepared in
different ways.

Notai *L*//
Via de'Pignattari 1 ☎ *228694* ● *closed
Sun (except during fairs)* ● *AE DC MC V*
Some of the Bolognese argue that the
Notai is not what it was, that
standards in food and service have
dropped and prices are too steep.
However it is still high on the list
among foreign visitors, thanks
perhaps to its position opposite San
Petronio, the Art Nouveau decor and
well spaced tables. Food is regional
and there is a 6-course *menu
degustazione*. A piano provides
background music.

Pappagallo *L*//
Pza della Mercanzia 3c ☎ *232807* ●
closed Sun D, Mon, Aug ● *AE DC V*
Opinions are divided about this well-
known establishment, one-time
symbol of Bolognese gastronomy. It is
appreciated for its sophistication, its
attentive service and its setting in an
old *palazzo* near the two leaning
towers, but the Art Nouveau decor is
a touch garish and the quality of the
food these days is variable and seldom
matches that of Gianluigi Morini's
other restaurant, the San Domenico
at Imola. The cooking is a blend of
nouvelle and traditional Bolognese
cuisines, and the wines classic Italian.
Set menus are available at lunch time.

Rosteria Luciano *L*//
Via Nazario Sauro 19 ☎ *231249* ●
closed Tue D, Wed, Aug ● *AE DC MC V*
A small restaurant with excellent

regional dishes, the Luciano is central and nearly always packed. Even so it provides an ideal background for discussions of a general nature over lunch. The exterior may not be very impressive but inside the restaurant is smart and modern. It also offers a good wine list.

Silverio *L*∥
Via Nosadella 37a ☎ *330604 • closed Mon, Aug • AE V*
Silverio's is the place nowadays in Bologna to see and be seen. In company with the fashionable, the beautiful and the intellectual, you can be sure that even the most elaborate dishes will retain the virtues of their natural ingredients. The conversation tends to dwell more on the creativity of the cuisine than on business, or even the exhibitions of modern art that grace the walls.

Tre Frecce *L*∥
Strada Maggiore 19 ☎ *231200 • closed Sun D, Mon, Aug • AE DC V*
The wooden-columned portico and ancient arches of an old town mansion form the entrance to this small, attractive restaurant which is popular with business people for both lunch and dinner. In one of the oldest parts of the city, it consists of a main dining area decorated with old paintings, and a gallery above reached by a wooden staircase. The food is Bolognese but light, with an imaginative use of vegetables. The *tortelloni* with ricotta and walnut sauce is an established favourite.

OTHER RESTAURANTS
There are many less expensive and more informal restaurants. *Alice*, Via d'Azeglio 65b ☎ 583359, is small, serves superb food, and is always lively with a cosmopolitan crowd of diners from soccer to movie stars. *Antica Osteria Romagnola*, Via Rialto 13 ☎ 263699, specializes in Neapolitan food (reservations are recommended) and *Battibecco*, Via Battibecco 4 ☎ 275845, is animated

and known for its fish. *Cesari*, Via de' Carbonesi 8 ☎ 237710, is highly regarded for its authentic Bolognese fare. *La Cesoia*, Via Massarenti 90 ☎ 342854, is excellent value and popular. For a reliable haven from the Fiera at lunch time try *Papa Re*, Pza dell'Unità 6 ☎ 366980. *Ruggero*, Via degli Usberti 6 ☎ 236056, a perennial favourite with locals, serves excellent fresh fish cooked on embers on Thursday and Friday. *Trattoria di Re Enzo*, Via Riva di Reno 79 ☎ 234803, is small but has well-spaced tables.

Out of town
At Casteldebole, 7km/4.5 miles west of central Bologna, the *Antica Trattoria del Cacciatore* ☎ 564203 serves traditional Bolognese cuisine at high prices in an attractive rustic setting and decor. At Imola, 32km/20 miles southeast of Bologna, the *San Domenico* ☎ (0542) 29000, in a 16thC Dominican convent, is the regional temple of gastronomy; its cuisine ranks among the best in Europe. Space is limited; reservations are essential.

Bars and cafés
The more exclusive hotel bars, particularly the *Royal Carlton* and the cocktail bar of the *Baglioni*, are best for serious discussions. For an informal chat over coffee or Fortnum & Mason tea and cakes, go to *Zanarini* in Piazza Galvani. The most sophisticated bar for a drink and pasta is *Zelig*, Via Porta Nuova 9, which serves good wine and beer. However the authentic Bolognese meeting places are the *osterie*, long-estabished venues for social encounters or cultural activities. Many offer full meals and/or provide entertainment such as cabaret, jazz or films. Most are open until after midnight.

Entertainment
Bologna has a long cultural tradition and is proud of its music.
Theatre Small theatres perform

comedies and high-quality avant-garde drama from (Oct–May) but there is no permanent civic theatre.
Music The most important venue is the *Teatro Comunale*, Largo Respighi, with an elaborate 18thC auditorium. Symphony concerts and opera take place Sep–Jun; reservations ☎ 529999. Concerts are also organized in other city theatres, in churches and at the *Conservatorio Giambattista Martini*, Pza Rossini 2 ☎ 221483. Jazz can be heard in many *osterie*, notably at *Dell'Orsa*, Via Mentana 1 ☎ 270744.
Cinema The *Adriano*, Via San Felice 52 ☎ 555127, shows original language films every Monday, Oct–May.
Nightclubs Among the more fashionable clubs are the *Black Shadow Club*, Vicolo Broglio 1 ☎ 229704, with disco, orchestra and cabaret, and *La Fontanina*, a short drive out of town at Via Roncrio 10 ☎ 581070, with dinner and show.

Shopping
The Galleria Cavour (access by Via Foscherai or Via Farini) boasts some of the biggest names in Italian design, but there are boutiques throughout the historic centre, many in beautifully restored old buildings. The Bolognese shoe designer Bruno Magli has shops at Piazza Mercanzia 1 and Via Ugo Bassi 5. The city's food shops are a treat. The biggest market for fresh produce is the *Mercato delle Erbe*, Via Ugo Bassi 25. Also worth exploring is the area of Via Pescherie Vecchie (off Piazza Maggiore) and Via Drapperie.

Sightseeing
The charm of Bologna can only be appreciated by walking unhurriedly through the old city and in the university district.
Galleria Davia-Bargellini Intriguing collection of 15th–19thC paintings and applied arts displayed in a splendid *palazzo*. *Strada Maggiore 44. Open Tue–Sat, 9–2; Sun, 9–12.30.*
Museo Civico Archeologico Ancient Egyptian, Etruscan, Greek and Roman finds. *Via dell'Archiginnasio 2. Open Tue–Sat, 9–2; Sun, 9–12.30.*
Palazzo Comunale, Collezioni Comunali d'Arte Bolognese paintings (the *trecento* to late baroque) in impressive ex-papal *palazzo*. *Pza Maggiore. Open Mon, Wed–Sat, 9–2; Sun, 9–12.30.*
Pinacoteca Nazionale Mainly Bolognese art from Gothic to baroque. Important works by Vitale da Bologna, Giotto and Raphael. Rooms devoted to works by the Carracci family, Guercino and Guido Reni. *Via Belle Arti 56. Open Tue–Sat, 9–2; Sun and hols, 9–1.*
San Domenico Huge 13thC Dominican basilica, reconstructed in the 18th century. Contains Nicola Pisano's vividly carved marble tomb (Arca di San Domenico). *Pza San Domenico.*
San Francesco Imposing 13thC Franciscan church with flying buttresses and chapels radiating from the main altar. *Pza San Francesco.*
San Petronio Massive basilica, whose unfinished Gothic brick façade dominates the main piazza. Finely carved reliefs on the central portal by 15thC Sienese Jacopo della Quercia, and other 15thC works of art inside. *Pza Maggiore.*
Santo Stefano Picturesque group of 8th–13thC sanctuaries, cloisters and crypts, on a square of old houses and *palazzi*. Tiny museum and a shop selling honey and liqueurs made by the monks. *Via Santo Stefano 24.*
University museums There are 24 university museums, containing rare scientific teaching materials from the 16th century on. Guided tours only; ☎ 512151. Most fascinating is the *Museo Ostetrico Givan Antonio Galli* (obstetrics museum) containing life-size terracotta, wax and glass babies used to train midwives (Via Zamboni 33; open Mon–Fri, 9–4; Sat; 9–1). The *Museo di Anatomia Umana Normale* (museum of human anatomy) has wax models of the human muscular system (many life size), as used by 18thC students (Via Irnerio 48; open Mon–Fri, 9–1).

Spectator sports

Basketball The most popular sport in the city. Bologna's two professional teams (Virtus and Fortitudo) play in championship leagues. Matches take place at the *Palazzo dello Sport*, Pza Azzarita 8 ☎ 557283; tickets are not easy to obtain.
Horseracing Popular trotting races take place at the *Ippodromo Arcoveggio* Sep–May. Information ☎ 371505.

Keeping fit

Fitness centres The *Crest* and the *Novotel* have sports facilities, but most good private clubs require membership of at least one month. *Villa Ghigi Club*, Via Mezzacosta 1 ☎ 331701, accepts nonmembers.
Golf The *Golf Club Bologna*, Monte San Pietro, Via Sabattini 69 ☎ 969100, is the most exclusive and requires membership of another club.
Squash Muncipal *Squash Center*, Via Amendola 8 ☎ 553528.
Tennis Call *Federazione Tennis*, Via Martelli 31 ☎ 530348.

Local resources

Business services
Executive Service, Via A. Saffi 15 ☎ 522578, provides in-house staff, equipment and offices.
Photocopying and printing Emiliana Macchine Ufficio ☎ 522370 or 522366; *Gestetner* ☎ 392872 or 399731.
Secretarial and translation Palazzo dei Congressi 5c ☎ 6435111.

Communications
Local delivery Radio Taxis ☎ 372727 or 534141, *Pony Express* ☎ 222888, *Mini Tras* ☎ 323032.
Long-distance delivery Express ☎ 373878 and *Nircoop* ☎ 503107 deliver to major Italian cities, *DHL* ☎ 578927 internationally.
Post office Posta Centrale, Pza Minghetti 1 ☎ 223598 (open Mon–Fri, 8.15–6.30 for letters; Sat, 8.15–2), at the station and the Fiera.
Telex and fax Errepi, Via S. Donato 66/13 ☎ 514001 or 501616.

Conference/exhibition centres
The large modern exhibition and trade fair site, the *Fiera* (Pza Costituzione 6, 40128 ☎ 282111), hosts about 20 fairs (including international exhibitions of children's books, footwear and leather, agricultural machinery, technology and equipment for the building trade) and provides 85,000 sq metres of covered exhibition area. The Centro Servizi provides banks, computer terminals, meeting rooms and press room. The nearby Palazzo dei Congressi has an auditorium seating 1,400 and many smaller rooms. The *Palazzo Albergati*, Via Masini 46, Zola Predosa ☎ 750247, has capacity for up to 2,000.

Emergencies
Bureaux de change facilities at the railway station (24hrs).
Hospitals 24hr emergency at *Ospedale Maggiore*, Largo Nigrisoli 2 ☎ 382984, and *Ospedale S. Orsola-Malpighi*, Via Massarenti 9 ☎ 6363111.
Pharmacies Sunday and overnight rota details from pharmacies, newspapers or ☎ 192.
Police Pza Galileo Galilei ☎ 337111.

Information sources
Business information The *Camera di Commercio*, Palazzo degli Affari, Pza della Costituzione ☎ 515131, in the Fiera complex.
Local media The *Bologna Economica* is a monthly business paper, published by the chamber of commerce.
Tourist information, Pza Maggiore 6 ☎ 239660, at the railway station ☎ 246541, both open Mon–Sat, 9–7, Sun, 9–1, and at the Fiera (during fairs).

Thank-yous
Chocolates Confetteria Majani, Via Carbonesi 5 ☎ 234302.
Florist Romano, Logge del Pavaglione 4 ☎ 221820, or Via Rizzoli 9 ☎ 222523.

MILAN (Milano)

Milan is essentially a central European city, just 48kms/30 miles south of the Alps and a strategic trading post for centuries. Successive domination by the Spanish, Austrians and French has helped to shape a cosmopolitan city which commercially and financially is the capital of Italy. With a population of 1.7m (3.1m including suburbs), Milan is second to Rome in size but accounts for much more of Italy's national income; the average Milanese is over twice as rich as the average Southerner.

Milan's economy is now based on the service sector which employs more than half the work force. It is the centre of banking and the Milan Borsa is the main stock market in Italy. The Americans, British and Swiss are the chief foreign investors, with the Japanese showing increasing interest.

Tertiary industries like advertising, marketing, PR and broadcasting, particularly private television companies, flourish. Silvio Berlusconi, the media magnate, is one of several dynamic business figures. Carlo De Benedetti, of Olivetti fame, directs his wide-ranging business empire from here and Raul Gardini heads several of the heavier industries. There are five universities, three of which are private, including Luigi Bocconi, a business and economics university.

Local industries include machine tools, car components, furniture and paper, textiles and garments, gold and silver jewellery, leather goods and foodstuffs. Firms employing under 100 people are still the backbone of Milan's commercial success. The annual April Fiera is the largest general trade fair in Europe with well over 1m visitors. Specialist trade fairs, especially fashion, are of increasing importance.

Among the major industries are chemicals and petrochemicals (Montedison, now controlled by Gardini), bio-engineering and textiles (SNIA), electro-engineering (Magneti Marelli at Sesto San Giovanni, employing over 8,000 people), steel (Falck, employing 10,000), rubber and cables (Pirelli, Italy's fourth largest private-sector company, employing over 30,000 here, with a tyre factory at Bollate) and agro-industrial products (notably Ferruzzi, also run by Gardini). Pharmaceuticals include Carlo Erba at Limito, Enichem at San Donato, Milanese and Formenti at Vimodrone plus Beecham, Glaxo and ICI. IBM employs over 12,000.

For ready-to-wear (*pronta moda*) fashion, many cognoscenti say that Milan has overtaken Paris; the biggest name is Giorgio Armani. Milan leads Europe in furniture design (Artemide's research headquarters are at Pregnara) and manufacture with factories in the Brianza area. Publishing is important (Fabbri, Feltrinelli, Garzanti, Mondadori – at Segrate – Olympia Press, Rizzoli, Rusconi, *La Repubblica*, Sperling & Kupfer and others), and the Italian art market is also based here.

A relatively small proportion of inhabitants are true *milanesi* (the descendants of at least three generations). After the war there was a concerted emigration from the poor Mezzogiorno and Southerners still comprise much of the work force (and many of those out of work) at the bottom of the social pile. Next come the industrious *piccoli borghesi*, then the English-speaking, go-getting workaholics and yuppies. Old aristocrats, entrepreneurial industrialists and *nuovi ricchi* head the hierarchy.

The Milanese work feverishly hard, enjoy making deals, pride themselves on their efficiency and are frustrated that the lazier Romans make the decisions. They joke that the Mediterranean, if not Africa, begins at Rome and complain that they are the Romans' new slaves. It is important, at all costs, to cut a *bella figura*: fur coats are more than a protection against the cold winters; high-profile security is a status symbol. Smart *milanesi* have villas on the Lakes or yachts at Portofino, and in August the elite are at St Tropez or on the Costa Smeralda.

Research and technology are to be boosted with the creation of Montecity (for Montedison's chemical works) and Centro-direzionale. Pirelli's old plant at Bicocca will become Tecno-city, Europe's largest science park for high-tech firms, by the early 1990s. And by 2000 airport facilities will be improved and Malpensa connected to Milan by train.

Arriving

Milan has two international airports, neither very large nor well-equipped for the volume of business-oriented traffic which comprises nearly 90%, some 10m passengers a year. Malpensa is 1hr by road from central Milan (but well-placed for Varese or Como); Linate is more convenient. There is no regular link between the two airports, although Alitalia can arrange transfers for groups if its connecting flights are involved. General flight information (both airports but often busy) ☎ 74852200; recorded information on operations and check-in times ☎ 7491141.

Autostrada and rail connections with Europe and the rest of Italy are excellent; Milan is 1hr by road from the Swiss border (60kms/37 miles) and 4hrs by high-speed train from Rome (570kms/354 miles).

Linate airport

Linate handles European and domestic flights, plus Middle Eastern destinations, with regular flights from capitals and other major cities. Facilities are often very crowded. They include a restaurant, pharmacy, bars, limited shops (but an excellent food emporium for last-minute gifts), car rental and a tourist office. There is a Visa automatic cash dispenser in the baggage collection area; expect a wait (though not necessarily poor rates of exchange) at the banks, which are open 8–9. The Fiera welcome desk on the left of the exit provides information and advice on major trade fairs.

Linate is often plagued by strikes and understaffing may cause delays at passport control or baggage collection. Allow 1hr or more for check-in on departure as passengers are often "bumped." Those with hand baggage only may collect boarding passes in the boarding area and so avoid the check-in procedures. Inquiries ☎ 7485313 or 3129; (tickets) ☎ 74852250, (international departures) ☎ 7381312, (freight) ☎ 7384393.

City link The airport is just 10kms/6 miles east of the centre; a taxi to Piazza Duomo or a bus to the Stazione Centrale take about 20mins in average traffic. Bus tickets are sold inside the airport (left of the exit).

Taxi There are usually plenty of taxis outside the terminal. The fare to central Milan is at least L20,000 and to the Fiera allow 40mins and L25,000. There is an extra charge of L15,000 to the Padiglione Sud exhibition pavilion (30kms/18 miles). A "private taxi" service charges double for journeys into central Milan.

Car rental A car is no use in central

Milan but Hertz (open 7.30–11.30
☎ 868001) and other car rental firms
are represented here.
Bus The blue SEAV bus service to the
central station (and Porta Garibaldi)
runs every 15–20mins and costs
L2,000. The orange ATM (public
transport) bus No. 73 goes to the
central Piazza San Babila. There is a
free bus service to Padiglione Sud
during major fairs.
Helicopter ATA ☎ 7381051.

Malpensa airport
Flights from major US cities, notably
New York (several daily), some other
international and long-haul
destinations and charter flights from
Europe arrive here. Facilities include
a post office, restaurant, bar, car
rental desks and bureau de change.
Inquiries ☎ 868028, (air freight)
☎ 868096, (passengers)
☎ 74852200.
Nearby hotels Jet Hotel, Via Tiro a
Segno 22, Gallarate, 21013 Varese
☎ (0331) 785534 (with pool), takes
major credit cards. *Astoria*, Vle Duca
d'Aosta 14, Busto Arsizio, 21052
Varese ☎ (0331) 636422, has a
restaurant and meeting room (AE
only).
City link The airport is 46kms/29
miles northwest of Milan, so a taxi is
expensive; the bus service, which
connects with flights, is much cheaper
and scarcely less convenient.
Taxi Allow 1hr for the journey to
central Milan, and at least L80,000.
Car rental It can be cheaper to rent a
car for a day than take a taxi to
central Milan if you are sure you can
park and deliver it. Europcar
☎ 868017, Hertz ☎ 868001,
InterRent ☎ 868124, Maggiore
☎ 868036, Tirreno ☎ 868023.
Bus The bus to Stazione Centrale (via
Porta Garibaldi station) takes 45mins
and costs L5,000. For outward
journeys report to Stazione Centrale
2hrs 30mins before the flight
departure.
Helicopter or jet Executive Jet
☎ 7380951, Ciga Aviation ☎ 733316,
Gitanair ☎ 717468 or 7426954.

Railway stations
Stazione Centrale Milan's grandiose
main station in Piazzale Duca d'Aosta
provides national and international
services. Despite the name it is not in
the city centre, although conveniently
close to some major hotels. It
provides a tourist office, bars,
restaurants, newsstands,
photocopying facilities, computerized
multilingual information booths and
information desks for different
foreign languages. The shops, bank
and tourist office are closed at lunch
time. Travel agencies, on the
concourse or just outside, advertise
cut-price European fares and will
make wagon-lits and hotel
reservations.
The nonstop Milan–Rome express
(Il Pendolino) runs at 6.55am and
7pm and takes 4hrs. It has first-class
carriages, restaurant cars and
multilingual stewardesses. A faster
version, the ETR 500, due for
inauguration in 1990, will have
telephones, telex and fax.
There are buses to both airports
(tickets from Agenzia Doria, Piazza
Luigi di Savoia, to the east of the
building). Take a taxi to the city
centre; there is usually a steady flow
of cabs. Until the completion of line
3, the subway journey involves
changing lines. Rail inquiries
☎ 67500.
Porta Garibaldi Some international
arrivals from the north (especially
motorail from, for example, Paris);
also from Turin, Pavia, Rome and
Florence.
Stazione Nord Commuter trains from
Brianza, Como and Varese.

Getting around
In the centre of Milan restricted
traffic makes walking easy but taxis
are plentiful. The public transport
system is comprehensive, well
integrated and cheap.
Despite or perhaps because of the
layout of Milan, with its concentric
ring roads and streets radiating from
the Duomo, the city is confusing to
drive in. One-way systems, tramlines

and the restricted central zone (closed to nonresidents 7.30–1, 7.30–6 in summer) are additional complications. *Piste ciclabili* (cycle lanes) have been added to some roads.

Public transport runs from 6.15am to just after midnight (some buses until 1am). Day tickets for unlimited travel on both the ATM (bus and tram) and MM (subway) can be bought at the ATM offices in the subway stations at Piazza Duomo (open Mon–Sat, 8–8) and the Stazione Centrale. ATM information ☎ 89010797.

Taxis There are always plenty of taxis in the centre and at ranks in the main piazzas. They can sometimes be hailed on the street. They are metered but fares are usually rounded up, so tipping is not obligatory. Drivers rarely speak English and may look up quite straightforward destinations. Radio taxis: *Arco* ☎ 6767, *Autoradiotaxi Velasca* ☎ 8585, *Esperia* ☎ 8388.

Limousines Pacifico Deluxe cars ☎ 864664, *Mose' Bellina* ☎ 3080180, *VIP Limousine* ☎ 6592158 (including cars with telephones).

Driving Not only is driving restricted and complicated but break-ins are common. Hotels should issue permits to enter the central zone. Car rental from *Hertz* ☎ 6598151, *Eurodrive* ☎ 6704582, *Avis* ☎ 6981. Guarded car-parking is indicated by a white P on a blue background in the city centre, near the station and in the Fiera districts.

Walking Milan's streets are relatively safe and pleasant, although you may be bothered by hawkers, especially near the station. Women alone at night, especially in the Castello and Parco Sempione areas, may be propositioned.

Bus and tram The surface transport system is efficient and the same stops are used by bus and tram. Useful lines include the *circonvallazione* tram line (Nos 29 or 30) which runs around the *viali* (until 1am). A bus tours the vast Fiera area during exhibitions.

Tickets are bought from bars, tobacconists or newsstands displaying the ATM sign and from coin-operated machines at some bus-stops. They are valid for 75mins from the moment they are time-stamped.

Subway The Metropolitana Milanese (MM) system is simple to use, with swift, frequent and clean trains. There are two lines, 1 (red) and 2 (green), and a third (yellow) is due to open in the first half of 1990.

Tickets are valid for the bus and tram. They can can be used for more than one trip within 70mins, but only for one metro journey, which must be the first. They can be bought from machines at stations and from bars.

Area by area

Milan is laid out like a target, with the Piazza Duomo as the bull's-eye. Within the inner circle or Cerchia dei Navigli (following the original medieval walls) are the banking and business areas, the smartest shopping streets, the main historical sights and the most expensive residential districts.

A second *circonvallazione*, the *viali* or *bastioni*, encloses other fashionable residential and business areas.

The areas between the *viali* and the *circonvallazione esterna* (ring road), are becoming more acceptable as districts to live in. The gates of the original walls have given their names to the surrounding areas.

Beyond the ring road are working-class suburbs, factories and modern office and residential complexes such as Milanofiori to the southwest, Segrate, Milano San Felice and Milano 2 to the east, near Linate airport. These areas are now incorporated in Greater Milan.

Piazza Duomo/the centre The Duomo is still the heart of the city. From it the vaulted Galleria Vittorio Emanuele II, a popular meeting-place with cafés and shops, leads to La Scala. To the west is the banking and business area around Piazza Affari (site of the Stock Exchange), Via Mercanti and Piazza Cordusio. To the

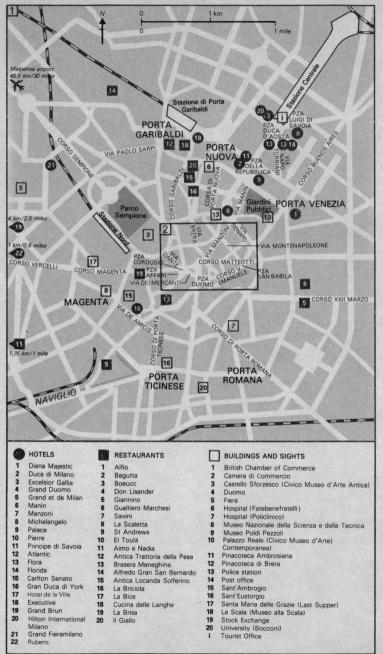

HOTELS

1. Diana Majestic
2. Duca di Milano
3. Excelsior Gallia
4. Grand Duomo
5. Grand et de Milan
6. Manin
7. Manzoni
8. Michelangelo
9. Palace
10. Pierre
11. Principe di Savoia
12. Atlantic
13. Flora
14. Florida
15. Carlton Senato
16. Gran Duca di York
17. Hotel de la Ville
18. Executive
19. Grand Brun
20. Hilton International Milano
21. Grand Fieramilano
22. Rubens

RESTAURANTS

1. Alfio
2. Bagutta
3. Boeucc
4. Don Lisander
5. Giannino
6. Gualtiero Marchesi
7. Savini
8. La Scaletta
9. St Andrews
10. El Toulà
11. Aimo e Nadia
12. Antica Trattoria della Pesa
13. Brasera Meneghina
14. Alfredo Gran San Bernardo
15. Antica Locanda Solferino
16. La Briciola
17. La Bice
18. Cucina delle Langhe
19. La Brisa
20. Il Giallo

BUILDINGS AND SIGHTS

1. British Chamber of Commerce
2. Camera di Commercio
3. Castello Sforzesco (Civico Museo d'Arte Antica)
4. Duomo
5. Fiera
6. Hospital (Fatebenefratelli)
7. Hospital (Policlinico)
8. Museo Nazionale della Scienza e della Tecnica
9. Museo Poldi Pezzoli
10. Palazzo Reale (Civico Museo d'Arte Contemporanea)
11. Pinacoteca Ambrosiana
12. Pinacoteca di Brera
13. Police station
14. Post office
15. Sant'Ambrogio
16. Sant'Eustorgio
17. Santa Maria delle Grazie (Last Supper)
18. La Scala (Museo alla Scala)
19. Stock Exchange
20. University (Bocconi)
i. Tourist Office

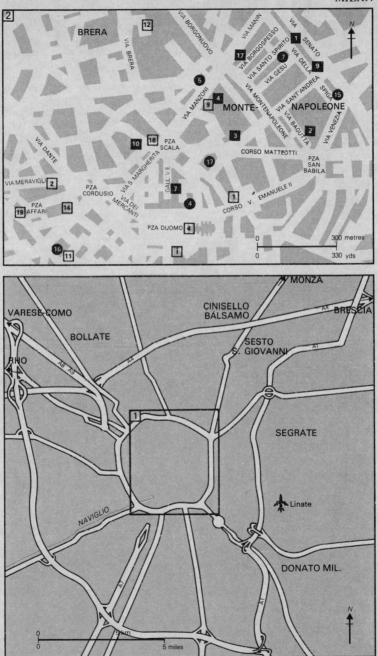

east a traffic-free shopping street, Corso Vittorio Emanuele, leads to the modern Piazza San Babila, with insurance and other offices.

Brera A small area north of the Duomo and around the Brera gallery. Derelict and the home of penniless artists and drug addicts in the 1970s, it is now gentrified and trendy, Milan's answer to Greenwich Village. *Corriere della Sera* and other newspaper offices are based here.

Montenapoleone Fashionable central Milan around Via Montenapoleone, with exclusive shops and aristocratic palace façades hiding courtyards and gardens.

Magenta Wide avenues and turn-of-the century apartment blocks give this area west of the Duomo a rather Parisian feel. It has long been a fashionable residential district, traditionally the home of Lombard nobility.

Porta Romana Shops, offices and housing; a fairly well-to-do district south of the Duomo, soon to have MM (line 3) access.

Porta Garibaldi This commercial district by the station is developing fast, thanks to rocketing prices. Via Paolo Sarpi is Milan's Chinatown.

Stazione Centrale The central station area (Porta Nuova and Porta Venezia) is also commercial, and the base for the wholesale rag trade. Corso Buenos Aires is the main traffic artery and shopping street with a large population of Moroccan immigrants. The elegant Pirelli building became a symbol of modern architecture after it was completed in 1960.

Fiera A residential and business area around the Fiera exhibition halls.

Porta Ticinese Run-down until five years ago, this is the area for the unconventional, artists and even young brokers and yuppies. There are some expensive bars and nightclubs and good restaurants. Along the *Naviglio* (canal) are dilapidated shuttered *palazzi* with balconies.

The suburbs
Commuting is relatively new, although the wealthy Milanese have traditionally kept villas near the Lakes. Monza and Brianza have become virtual suburbs of Milan. Como and Varese, less than 1hr by train from Milan, are becoming dormitory towns.

Hotels

Milan has nearly 400 hotels, and most of the guests are here on business. Hotels are generally well-equipped and comfortable, with meeting rooms for conferences, and employees normally speak excellent English. In-house business services are rare but staff will arrange photocopying, telex and fax for you.

The most prestigious hotels are those in the CIGA chain (but none is really central) and some grand old hotels (the elegant Marino alla Scala is being extensively renovated). Prices tend to be very high but there are comfortable, efficient and moderately priced hotels near the Stazione Centrale.

For major international fairs (especially the April trade fair and September furniture fair), reserve accommodation up to a year ahead; for minor fairs a month should suffice. Those who have not made reservations may have to stay outside Milan in Bergamo, Como or Varese, all within about 55kms/35 miles. Rooms can be reserved at the tourist office in the Stazione Centrale, at Linate airport and through Hotel Reservation Milan ☎ 706095. As a rule, breakfast is not included in room prices. Many hotels are closed for two weeks in August.

Diana Majestic *L*//
Vle Piave 42, 20129 ☎ *202122*
TX *333047* • *CIGA* • *AE DC MC V* •
94 rooms, 1 bar
A comfortable old-fashioned hotel
being upgraded to CIGA standards but
retaining some of its Art Deco
features. Used by models, designers
and others in the fashion trade. 24hr
room service.

Duca di Milano *L*/////
Pza della Repubblica 13, 20124
☎ *6284* TX *325026 fax 6555966* •
CIGA • *AE DC MC V* • *10 rooms, 50*
suites, 1 restaurant, 1 bar
Quieter and calmer than its grander
neighbour the Principe, the Duca is
ideal for those needing a working
base and popular with merchant
bankers. Each of the comfortable
suites has a separate desk and seating
area suitable for small meetings; the
single rooms are unusually spacious.
Civilized public rooms include a
dining area. Stock exchange prices are
transmitted for the benefit of guests.

Excelsior Gallia *L*////
Pza Duca d'Aosta 9, 20124 ☎ *6277*
TX *311160 fax 6277* • *THF* • *AE DC*
MC V • *266 rooms, 14 suites,*
1 restaurant, 1 bar
This traditional grand old hotel,
whose heyday was in the 1930s, has
recently been taken over by Trust
House Forte. Although the grandeur
is faded in places the Excelsior is still
a prestigious business hotel, with
good facilities. It is a few minutes'
walk from the bus terminal for the
airports and from the station. Sauna,
massage, solarium • 7 meeting rooms
(capacity up to 400).

Grand Duomo *L*///
Via San Raffaele 1, 20121 ☎ *8833* TX
312086 fax 872752 • *MC V* • *160*
rooms, 18 suites, 1 restaurant, 1 bar
The central location of this well-
known hotel overlooking the Piazza
del Duomo attracts many foreign
business people and tourists, and the
spacious lobby is a good meeting
place. Rooms (with some inadequate

small exceptions) are well-equipped
for the working visitor and some have
splendid views. The split-level suites
are ideal for small meetings.

Grand et de Milan *L*/////
Via A. Manzoni 29, 20121 ☎ *801231*
TX *334505 fax 872526* • *AE DC MC V*
• *79 rooms, 10 suites, 1 restaurant, 1 bar*
The Grand is an aristocratic hotel; old
tradition (since 1865) and old money
mingle with the new fashion brigade.
The *belle époque* interior is being
completely restructured. Verdi was
among the illustrious guests and
composed some of his masterpieces in
the ornate studio (in which he also
died): the hotel is a traditional
favourite with La Scala stars. The
tiny restaurant is primarily for the
convenience of guests. No hotel
parking.

Manin *L*////
Via Manin 7, 20121 ☎ *6596511*
TX *320385 fax 655216* • *AE DC MC V*
• *105 rooms, 5 suites, 1 restaurant, 1 bar*
Well-respected as a sound family-run
hotel, giving good value and personal
service and with a pleasant location
opposite the public gardens. There is
an open bar area suitable for quiet
meetings and a formal restaurant.
Bedrooms are spacious and plain
(quietest at the back, but with
terraces on the front). A covered
verandah leads to a private garden
and the conference rooms. 3 meeting
rooms (capacity up to 230).

Manzoni *L*/
Via Santo Spirito 20, 20121 ☎ *705697*
• *no credit cards* • *52 rooms, 1 bar*
A superior small hotel with a good
address. The Manzoni offers few
facilities and services but has
comfortable bedrooms at a sensible
price. Old photographs of Milan add
a certain charm. Garage.

Michelangelo *L*/////
Via Scarlatti 33, 20124 ☎ *6755*
TX *340330 fax 6694232* • *AE DC MC*
V • *250 rooms, 10 suites, 1 restaurant,*
1 bar

A tall modern hotel with its own high-tech convention centre. In the basement is the Ghirlandaio restaurant, with a menu created by Gualtiero Marchesi (see *Restaurants*). Bedrooms (nearly half of which are singles) are functional and well equipped; they are being gradually refurbished from the top floor, which has fine views, downwards. Bus service to both airports • 8 meeting rooms (capacity up to 750).

Palace $\boxed{L}////$
Pza della Repubblica 20, 20124
☎ *6336* TX *311026 fax 654485 •*
CIGA • AE DC MC V • 184 rooms,
7 suites, 1 restaurant, 1 bar
The best-known business hotel in Milan (many visiting stockbrokers stay here) is a stark modern block opposite the Principe. The public areas are modern, but dated. By contrast bedrooms (and the Casanova restaurant) are luxurious, in neo-classical style. The roof garden is used for receptions.

Pierre $\boxed{L}////$
Via de Amicis 32, 20123 ☎ *8056221*
fax 8052157 • AE DC MC V • 47
bedrooms, 6 suites, 1 restaurant, 1 bar
A sophisticated, chic new hotel which has yet to establish its market. The Pierre is not geared to executive-level meetings but aims to combine ultra-luxurious accommodation with friendly personal service. For those who enjoy remote-control gadgetry and monogrammed towelling robes. No hotel parking. 1 meeting room (capacity up to 30).

Principe di Savoia $\boxed{L}/////$
Pza della Repubblica 17, 20124
☎ *6230* TX *310052 fax 6595838 •*
CIGA • AE DC MC V • 269 rooms,
18 suites, 1 restaurant, 2 bars
If the Palace is for business, then the Principe, a good 20min walk from the centre, is for VIPs. The presidential suite is just that. The 85 or so super de-luxe rooms have Empire-style furniture and pastel ragged walls and 100 modern de-luxe rooms have teak

walls and fittings. The rest (merely "superior," although some are very small) are being refurbished. A busy hotel with variable service.

OTHER HOTELS
Near the station there are some efficient small hotels:
Atlantic $\boxed{L}///$ *Via Napo Torriani*
24, 20124 ☎ *6691941* TX *321451*
fax 6706533 • AE MC V.
Flora $\boxed{L}$ *Via Napo Torriani 23,*
20124 ☎ *650242* TX *312547 • AE DC V.*
Florida $\boxed{L}$ *Via Lepetit 33, 20124*
☎ *6705921* TX *314102 • Best Western*
• AE DC MC V.
In the centre but reasonably priced:
Carlton Senato $\boxed{L}///$ *Via Senato 5,*
20121 ☎ *798583* TX *331306*
fax 5456043 • AE MC V. Quiet back bedrooms overlook Via delle Spiga.
Gran Duca di York $\boxed{L}/$ *Via*
Moneta 1A, 20100 ☎ *874863 • AE.*
Modest, old-fashioned hotel near the Borsa.
Hotel de Ville $\boxed{L}///$ *Via Hoepli*
☎ *867651* TX *312642 fax 866609 •*
AE DC MC V. Central and convenient if a bit dated.
Well-equipped for the business visitor, but not central are:
Executive $\boxed{L}////$ *Vle Sturzo 45,*
20154 ☎ *6294* TX *310191 fax 653240*
• Interhotel • AE DC MC V. Opposite Porta Garibaldi station. Adjacent convention centre with facilities for up to 1,200.
Grand Brun $\boxed{L}////$ *Via Caldera 21,*
20153 ☎ *45271* TX *315370*
fax 4526055 • Gamma hotels • AE DC
MC V. Luxury modern hotel near San Siro.
Hilton International Milano $\boxed{L}/////$
Via Galvani 12, 20124 ☎ *6983*
TX *330433 fax 6071904 • AE DC MC*
V. Standard Hilton, with plans under way for an executive business centre.
Near the Fiera are two functional hotels:
Grand Fieramilano $\boxed{L}////$ *Vle*
Boezio 20, 20145 ☎ *3105* TX *331426*
fax 314119 • Interhotel • AE DC MC V.
Rubens $\boxed{L}///$ *Via Rubens 21, 20148*
☎ *405051* TX *333503 fax 48193114 •*
AE DC MC V.

Clubs

There are several exclusive men's clubs to which visitors might be invited, and which have affiliations with a few similar clubs abroad. The *Società del Giardino*, Via San Paolo 10, is the oldest with the finest decor (see the fencing room) and a garden. It has some women members. *L'Unione*, Via Borgonuovo, is the most aristocratic and old-fashioned. *Il Clubino*, Via Omonima 3, has a separate dining room where women may be entertained.

Restaurants

There are typically old-fashioned Milanese restaurants (where the reputation is more legendary than the food) and friendly trattorias serving traditional Lombard cooking, although *nouvelle cuisine (la cucina nuova)* has several brilliant disciples, in particular Gualtiero Marchesi. Perhaps surprisingly, Milan has the best fish restaurants in the country (but fish is very expensive). Hotel restaurants are not generally highly regarded, and it would not be considered good form to entertain Italian guests at a foreign restaurant. Most of the best restaurants are closed in August.

Reservations are not necessary for lunch. Most Milanese now prefer a quick snack at a bar to the traditional midday meal. However, at the classic business lunch venues it is sensible, and sometimes essential, to make a reservation in the morning. Friday and Saturday nights are busiest and, in the evenings, it is quite usual for businessmen to entertain without their wives. Because of the fashion clientele, suits are not usually *de rigueur* but jackets should be worn in smarter restaurants.

Traditional Milanese dishes are saffron risotto, *cotoletta alla milanese* (*Wiener Schnitzel*) and *vitello tonnato* (veal in cold tuna sauce) plus various stews (including *osso buco, cazzoeula*). Lighter food is generally appreciated now, especially at lunch time, but it is worth remembering that some Italians remain suspicious of *nouvelle cuisine*.

Alfio *L*////
Via Senato 31 ☏ *700633* • *closed Sun L, Sat* • AE DC MC V
One of the top restaurants in Milan, attracting US and Japanese bankers, Italian industrialists and brokers and journalists from nearby Piazza Cavour. Alfio serves excellent pasta and the best seafood in town; choose swordfish, salmon or a *misto*. The splendid buffet and light setting are most attractive in summer.

Bagutta *L*//
Via Bagutta 14 ☏ *702767* • *closed Sun, Aug* • AE DC MC V • *reservations essential*
A large, casual and cluttered Tuscan trattoria, with walls decorated with caricatures and a garden at the back. Literati, art collectors and dealers, media and PR people, stars from the opera and ballet, and some publishers and journalists, are attracted by the atmosphere rather than particularly special food. Ask for a table at the rear if you want to talk business.

Boeucc *L*//
Pza Belgioioso 2 ☏ *780224 or 782880* • *closed Sun L, Sat, Aug* • AE • *reservations a day in advance*
Used by grand old businessmen, by politicians (Craxi, Goria), journalists, the Mayor of Milan, La Scala stars and Raul Gardini whose office is next door. Boeucc is elegant and understated with well-spaced tables, ideal for confidential business discussions (request a quiet table). The seafood is good and the verandah and garden are a bonus.

Don Lisander *L*////
Via Manzoni 12A ☎ *790130* • *closed*
Sat D, Sun • *AE DC MC V* •
reservations essential
Known as a business restaurant,
elegant remodelled Don Lisander is
popular with top bankers and Fiat
executives from Turin. Tables are
close together but al fresco dining in
a delightful garden courtyard is a
major attraction in summer. Cooking
is traditional but leans towards *la
nuova cucina*; fixed-price menus
offered are a *piatto unico*, suitable for
a quick lunch, and a 7-course *menu
degustazione*.

Giannino *L*/////
Via Amatore Sciesa 8 ☎ *5452948* •
closed Sun • *AE DC MC V*
A favourite with foreign bankers,
business guests and tourists rather
than locals. The layout is spacious,
with a winter garden and several large
private rooms. Representative dishes
from all the Italian regions come out
of the open-plan kitchen. Suitable for
an extended lunch or dinner,
especially for groups of 6–10 people.

Gualtiero Marchesi *L*//////
Via Bonvesin de la Riva 9 ☎ *741246*
• *closed Mon L, Sun, Aug* • *AE DC
MC V* • *jacket and tie*
Ultra-expensive, ultra-serious temple
of modern Italian cooking, the only
restaurant in the country to boast
three Michelin rosettes. From the
individual modern sculptures on each
table to the saffron risotto with gold
leaf, everything is calculated to
challenge conventional tastes. The
atto unico is a theatrical single fixed-
price dish suitable for a business
lunch. Marchesi is more popular with
Americans than with the Ambrosiani,
but the ambience is suitable for
business entertaining.

Savini *L*/////
Galleria Vittorio Emanuele II
☎ *8058364* • *closed Sun, mid Aug* •
AE DC MC V • *jacket and tie* • *D
reservations advisable Sep–Nov*
Legendary Savini's offers bland

cuisine in velvet, mirror and gilt
surroundings little changed since the
19th century. This is definitely the
safest place to invite local business
contacts if you want to impress, but
may be too stuffy and uninspiring for
some tastes. The glassed-in area
under the awning is more public, and
slightly less formal than the exclusive
interior. Upstairs there are several
elegant private dining rooms. The
formidable wine list includes 100
French wines.

La Scaletta *L*///
Pzle Stazione Genova 3 ☎ *8350290* •
closed Sun, Mon • *no credit cards* • *D
reservations essential*
Pina Bellini's delicious, highly
inventive cooking is considered by
some to be the best in Milan. The
elegant but informal surroundings,
with just nine tables, and the off-
centre location make La Scaletta more
suitable for a leisurely dinner than a
business lunch. For some privacy
request the table by the bar. There is
a selection of excellent, often *recherché*
wines.

St Andrews *L*/////
Via Sant'Andrea 23 ☎ *793132* • *closed
Sun* • *AE DC MC V* • *jacket and tie* •
reservations essential
The sombre modern decor of this
international-style restaurant makes it
ideal for business lunches. Food is
excellent, with the emphasis on
luxuries (caviar, oysters, Scotch
smoked salmon); menus come in five
languages and wines vary from local
to French *grands crus*. The location,
on the corner of Via Spiga, attracts
the fashion fraternity as well as
business people. The dark *enoteca* in
the cellars is an excellent place for
confidential meetings or parties of
25–30 people.

El Toulà *L*////
Pza Paolo Ferrari 6 ☎ *870302* •
closed Sun • *AE DC MC V* • *D
reservations essential.*
Second only to Savini in prestige,
sophisticated El Toulà has a

conventional, club-like atmosphere conducive to top-level business discussions (Agnelli and De Benedetti lunch here). Proximity to La Scala also attracts evening opera-goers for whom there is an after-theatre supplement. Inoffensive continental cuisine – the *filet mignon* could be in London or New Jersey – but an excellent wine cellar.

OTHER RESTAURANTS

Superb creative cooking in elegant surroundings 15mins by taxi from the centre is provided by *Aimo e Nadia*, Via Montecuccoli 6 ☎ 416886: an excellent place for an evening excursion when enjoyment is more important than business. *Antica Trattoria della Pesa*, Vle Pasubio 10 ☎ 6555741, is an old favourite, serving typical, rather heavy Lombard cooking. *Brasera Meneghina*, Via Circo 10 ☎ 808108, is similar, with a pleasant garden. *Alfredo Gran San Bernardo*, Via G.A. Borghese 14 ☎ 3319000, offers the best in classic Lombard cooking, a little way from the city centre. In the Brera area, *Antica Locanda Solferino*, Via Castelfidardo 2 ☎ 6599886, is a chic bistro. Nearby, *La Briciola*, Via Solferino 25 ☎ 6551012, is popular with media people.

Fashion-crowd favourites include *La Bice*, Via Borgospesso 12 ☎ 702572/795528, now with a twin in New York, and *Cucina delle Lange*, Corso Como 6 ☎ 6595180, with conservatory dining. In the evening trendies eat late at chic but pretentious *La Brisa*, Via Brisa 15 ☎ 872001, which has a garden (popular at weekends), or at *Il Giallo*, Via Milazzo 6 ☎ 6571581, in the Brera area.

Out of town

For a gastronomic excursion make the short journey (20kms/12.5 miles) southwest to *Antica Osteria del Ponte* ☎ (02) 9420034 at Cassinetta di Lugagnano, which is regarded by Italian and foreign gourmets as the best restaurant in Italy.

Bars and cafés

Hotel bars are convenient for business meetings and are generally quiet in the afternoon. The atmospheric and elegant old cafés (*Sant' Ambroeus, Cova, Del Bon, Taveggia*) are good places to meet over an *aperitivo* and there are also several cafés in the Galleria, for example *Biffi*. *Baretto*, Via Sant' Andrea 3, is popular with merchant bankers; in the same street the bar of *St Andrews* restaurant is a good place to meet for discussions (open outside mealtimes).

Entertainment

If you are lucky enough to get tickets for an evening of opera at *La Scala*, from personal contacts, you have a scoop. Ticket agencies do not exist.

For listings see the free fortnightly *Night and Day Milano* or the monthly *Spettacolo a Milano* or *What's On in Milan*.

Opera The season runs from 7 Dec (St Ambrose Day) to the end of May. For tickets you can try writing 60 days in advance to the box office: Botteghino, La Scala, Via dei Filodrammatici 2. If international stars have cancelled at short notice try the box office (open daily 10–12.30, 3.30–5.30, performance days 5.30– 9.30 ☎ 807041) for returns.

Theatre The main theatres are *Teatro Manzoni*, Via Manzoni 42 ☎ 790543, *Teatro Nazionale*, Pza Piemonte 12 ☎ 4396700 (classic Italian drama and visiting international companies), *Piccolo Teatro*, Via Rovello 2 ☎ 8690631, under the brilliant manager/director Giorgio Strehler, and *Teatro Lirico*, Via Larga 14 ☎ 866418, the largest in Lombardy. *Music* There are concerts at the *Angelicum*, Pza Sant' Angelo 2 ☎ 6592748, the *Conservatorio Giuseppe Verdi*, Via Conservatorio 12 ☎ 701755, and the *Piccolo Scala*, Via Filodrammatici. The concert season at La Scala is June and Sep–Dec. The main venue for rock concerts is the *Palatrussardi* close to the Fiera district ☎ 3340055.

Cinema Films in the original

language are shown at *Angelicum*, Pza Sant' Angelo 2 ☎ 6551712 (Wed–Sun). *Cinema Anteo*, Via Milazzo 9 ☎ 6597732, is among the art cinemas (*cinema d'essai*).

Nightclubs One of the most exclusive members-only nightclubs is *Agora*, Via San Marco 33A. Discotheques include *Nepentha*, Pza Diaz 1 ☎ 804837, and *Plastic*, Vle Umbria 20, the current hits among the gilded (and sometimes tarnished) youth of Milan. Otherwise nightlife revolves mainly around the bars (open until about 2am) of the Brera and Naviglio areas. Friendly jazz bars (*locali*) and piano bars include *Biblo's*, Via Madonnina 17 ☎ 8051860 (with a basement discotheque).

Shopping

Shops in Milan are now among the finest in Europe, and are comparable with the best in New York. The most sophisticated and elitist shopping streets are the Via Montenapoleone and surrounding streets (between Via Manzoni, Corso Matteotti and Via della Spiga). Fashion boutiques predominate but there are also furriers, jewellers, shops selling fine leather goods and antique dealers.

The arcaded, traffic-free Corso Vittorio Emanuele is another major shopping street.

Shops open Mon–Sat, 9 or 9.30–12.30 or 1 and 3.30–7 or 7.30.

Antiques Antique shops are in the Montenapoleone, Brera and Naviglio areas. The Brera market is held every third Sat in the month from 10am between Via Fiori Chiari and Via Madonnina.

Art galleries Milan is the leading city in Italy for contemporary art, with hundreds of commercial galleries. *Studio Marconi*, Via Tadino 15, is well-established. More avant-garde are *Studio Carlo Grossetti*, Via dei Piatti 9, *Cannaviello*, Via Cusani 10, and *Toselli*, Via del Carmine 9.

Philippe Daverio, Via Montenapoleone, shows good Italian 20thC art.

Bookshops There are bookshops all over town, but conveniently in the Galleria Vittorio Emanuele (*Garzanti*, *Rizzoli*), Via Manzoni (*Feltrinelli*) and Corso Vittorio Emanuele (*Mondadori*). *The American Bookstore* is opposite the Castello Sforzesco and *The English Bookshop* is at Via Mascheroni 12.

Fashion Among the famous names in Italian fashion (for women) in the Via Montenapoleone area are *Giorgio Armani* (Via Sant'Andrea), *Laura Biagiotti* (Via Borgospesso), *Gianfranco Ferrè*, *Krizia* and *Gianni Versace* (Via della Spiga), *Mila Schön* and *Missoni* (Via Montenapoleone) and *Valentino* (Via Santo Spirito).

Food Gourmets will enjoy the stores in Via San Marco, Via Spadari (*Peck*, with a restaurant in Via Victor Hugo and Via Speronari). The irresistible *Salumaio di Montenapoleone*, Via Montenapoleone 12, also has mouth-watering window displays.

Furniture The best modern furniture showrooms are between the Brera and Piazza San Babila, notably in Via Borgogna, Via Durini and Via Manzoni.

Jewellery The most famous names are in Via Montenapoleone: *Buccellati*, *Calderoni*, *Faraone* and others. On Via Manzoni *Gioelli di Burma* makes copies of classic jewellery.

Leather goods Another area of fine craftsmanship and design; the big names are *Nazareno Gabrielli*, *Gucci*, *Trussardi* and *Valextra* in the Via Montenapoleone and Corso Vittorio Emanuele area. Some of the best shoe shops (*Beltrami*, *Ferragamo*, *Fratelli Rossetti*, *Tanino Crisci*) are on the Via Montenapoleone.

Menswear Famous names in Italian menswear are *Armani*, Via Sant'Andrea 9, and *Ermenegildo Zegna*, Via Verri 3. Italians buy English-style clothing from *Bardelli*, Corso Magenta 13; and *Brigatti*, with shops in Corso Venezia and Galleria Vittorio Emanuele, is famous for classic sportswear. Tailors include *Tindaro de Luca*, Via Durini 23 ☎ 794394. *Truzzi*, Corso Matteotti 1, is the smartest shirt-maker. *Cravatti*

Nazionali, Via San Pietro all' Orto, has a vast range of ties and *Lorenz*, Via Napoleone 12, sells masculine accessories made from horn, leather and other natural materials.

Pasticcerie The best confectionery and pastry shops are *Galli*, Corso Porta Romana 2 (for *marrons glacés*), *Marchesi*, Via Santa Maria alla Porta 13, and *Taveggia*, Via V. di Modrone 2. *Cova*, Via Montenapoleone 8, and *Sant'Ambroeus*, Corso Matteotti 7, have prettily-packaged chocolates.

Wine At the atmospheric old *Taverna Moriggi*, Via Morigi 8 ☎ 807752, you can buy and taste fine wines with salami and cheese. *N'Ombra de Vin*, Via San Marco 2 ☎ 6552746, is another good wine merchant.

Sightseeing

Although not primarily a tourist city, Milan has important museums and art collections and some fine churches. Top priority for those with little time is Leonardo da Vinci's *Last Supper*, in the refectory of the church of Santa Maria delle Grazie (about 15mins by taxi from the Piazza del Duomo).

Castello Sforzesco The castle of the Sforza dynasty houses the *Civico Museo d'Arte Antica*. Lombard painting and sculpture, furniture and tapestries, musical instruments, ivories, glass and ceramics, mainly from the Renaissance and later, and Michelangelo's last work, the Rondanini Pietà. *Pza Castello. Open Tue–Sun, 9.30–12.15, 2.30–5.30.*

Duomo Vast, ornate Gothic cathedral begun in 1386 (the façade was completed only in 1809). Splendid views from the roof (elevator). *Pza Duomo.*

Museo Poldi Pezzoli Charming city collection, with paintings (by Bellini, Botticelli, Guardi, Pollaiuolo), glass, ceramics, Persian rugs, clocks, bronzes and other treasures. *Via Manzoni 12. Open Tue–Sat, 9.30–12.30, 2.30–5.30 or 6 (Thu 9–11pm); Sun, 9.30–12.30.*

Pinacoteca Ambrosiana Old Master collection of Cardinal Federico Borromeo, with rooms devoted to

Leonardo da Vinci and his followers and to Venetian and Dutch art. Fine paintings by Titian and Caravaggio. *Pza Pio XI 2. Open Sun–Fri, 9.30–5.*

Pinacoteca di Brera One of the world's greatest art collections with many Italian masterpieces. *Via Brera 28. Open Tue–Thu, 9–5.30; Fri, Sat, 9–1.30; Sun, 9–12.30.*

Santa Maria delle Grazie Renaissance church with a dome by Bramante and the refectory where in 1495 Leonardo painted the *Last Supper*. *Pza Santa Maria delle Grazie. Refectory open Tue–Sat, 9–1.30, 2–6.30; Sun, 9–3.*

Other museums include the *Museo alla Scala*, Pza della Scala, with opera memorabilia, the *Museo Nazionale della Scienza e della Tecnica*, Via San Vittore 21, with models by Leonardo da Vinci, and the *Civico Museo di Arte Contemporanea*, an expanding collection of modern art in the Palazzo Reale.

Romanesque churches include the 9thC *Sant'Ambrogio*, a superb example of the style, and *Sant'Eustorgio*, with the fine Renaissance Portinari chapel.

Guided tours

Basic guided tours of the city by bus leave from Piazza Duomo.

The stock exchange can be visited on weekday mornings: arrangements by the *Comitato Direttivo Agenti di Cambio di Milano*, Pza degli Affari 6 ☎ 85344632.

Out of town

A number of interesting smaller cities are within easy reach, *Bergamo* being the most appealing and nearest. About 30kms/18.5 miles south is the famous *Certosa di Pavia*, an ornate Renaissance monastery.

Lake Como is the nearest of the major Italian Lakes, although traffic is bad at weekends and *Lake Maggiore* (with resort accommodation at Stresa) may be more easily accessible. *Lago d'Orta* is one of the most charming lakes and less visited than its larger neighbours. Day trips to the

Lombard Lakes (bus and boat) depart daily Apr–Oct from Piazza Castello or the Stazione Centrale. *Bellagio*, on a promotory between Lake Como and Lake Lecco, is a pleasant weekend resort with spectacular scenery and good walking country.

Spectator sports

Soccer is the most popular spectator sport, followed by "basket," of which the Italians are European champions.
Horse-racing Racing and trotting at *Ippodromo di San Siro* ☎ 4084350.
Motor racing The Grand Prix circuit at Monza is 15kms/10 miles from the centre of Milan ☎ (039) 22366.
Soccer Milan and Inter play on Sundays on the western outskirts at the *Stadio San Siro*, Via Piccolomini 5 ☎ 4077279 or 4031235.

Keeping fit

The Milanese are becoming fanatical about keeping fit. The best municipal sports centre (with gyms, tennis courts, pools, skating rinks and more) is the *SAINI*, Via Corelli 136.
Fitness centres American Contourella at Via Montenapoleone 10 ☎ 705290 and Pza della Repubblica 1A ☎ 6552728 (aerobics, body-building, yoga, swimming). *Club Francesco Conti*, Via Cerva 4 ☎ 700141 and branches, accepts monthly membership.
Golf Country Club Barlassina, Birago di Camnago ☎ (0362) 560621, and *Golf Club Milano*, Parco di Monza ☎ (039) 303081, are the nearest full golf courses (green fees required).
Country Club Carimate ☎ (031) 790226 (membership of another club required) is on the Como road.
Jogging The *Giardini Pubblici*, an English-style park, and the *Parco Sempione* are the most central parks.
Riding Contact *Associazione Nazionale Turismo Equestre*, Via Piranesi 44B ☎ 7384615 for information.
Squash Club Milano, Via Piranesi 9 ☎ 7382437 (entry fee required); *Giambellino Squash Club*, Via Giambellino 5 ☎ 4225979.

Local resources

Business services

Executive Service, Via Vincenzo Monti 8 ☎ 5456331, provides fully-equipped offices with multilingual secretaries, photocopiers, telex, fax and meeting rooms. *International Business Centre*, Corso Europa 12 ☎ 656093, has offices for rent.
Photocopying and printing There are copy shops all over Milan.
Secretarial MGR, Pza S. Ambrogio 16 ☎ 809621, and *CTI*, Via Palestrina 31 ☎ 719244, offer typing in several languages. *MGR* also organizes conferences.
Translation Language Consulting, Via Lanzone 6 ☎ 8057846; *Cooperativa Traduttori Interpreti*, Via Don Gnocchi 19 ☎ 4044826; *Associazione Italiana Traduttori ed Interpreti* ☎ 48193195.

Communications

Local delivery Mototaxi ☎ 5434, *Pony Express* ☎ 5493.
Long-distance delivery Airborne Express ☎ 5064946, *DHL International* ☎ 5080, *ITK* ☎ 3072.
Post office Main office: Via Cordusio 4 ☎ 875452, open 8.15–7.40 and to midnight for some services.
Telex and fax Telex service at the 24hr telegraph office of the main post office.

Conference/exhibition centres

The vast *Centro Congressi Milanofiori*, 20090, Milanofiori ☎ 824791, has 9 meeting rooms for up to 2,500 people. The *Fiera di Milano*, Largo Domodossola 1, 20145 ☎ 49971, has meeting rooms for up to 500 people and is the venue for the April industrial and consumer goods fair, and for specialized international exhibitions including several for fashion.
Camera di Commercio Industria Artigianato e Agricoltura di Milano, Via Meravigli 9B ☎ 85151, and the *Centro Meravigli*, Via G. Negri 8 ☎ 8693520 (capacity up to 200 people) are central. Also central are *Palazzo Acerbi*, Corso Porto Romana 3, and *Palazzo delle Stelline*, Corso

Magenta 61 ☎ 4818503, providing historic venues (capacity up to 120 and 250 respectively). *Castello di Macconago*, on the outskirts of the city at Via Macconago 38 ☎ 5694819, can accommodate up to 80 participants and is also available for receptions.

Emergencies
Bureaux de change At Linate and Malpensa airports and major stations. Open normal office hours are *Cambio Milano*, Pza Affari ☎ 8053927, *Cambival*, Via Cantù 3 ☎ 864101, *Urgnani*, Via Cordusio 2 ☎ 807490.
Hospitals Ambulance ☎ 7733, Red Cross ☎ 3883, dental assistance (9am–noon) *Odontomil*, Pza Loreto ☎ 2829808. *Fatebenefratelli*, Corsa Porta Nuova 23 ☎ 63631, has a 24hr first aid service. *Policlinico*, Via Francesco Sforza 35 ☎ 5511655.
Pharmacies Ambreck, Via Stradivari 1 ☎ 209401, *Bracco*, Via Boccaccio 26 ☎ 4695281, *Ferrarini*, Pza V Giornate 6 ☎ 5451471, and *Formaggia*, Corso Buenos Aires 4 ☎ 203320, are open 24hrs. The *Italo-English Chemist's Shop*, Corso Europa 18 ☎ 701828, is open during shop hours. The pharmacy in the departures hall at the Stazione Centrale is open 8.30–12.30, 3.30–7.30 with an emergency night service bell.
Police Questura: Via Fatebenefratelli 11 ☎ 62261; city police emergencies 77271 (Uigili Urbani).

Information sources
Business information Camera di Commercio, Via Meravigli 9B, 20123 ☎ 875109; *Assistenza e documentazione operatori esteri*, Via Ansperto 5 ☎ 85155248 or 85155212 (help and information for foreign entrepreneurs). *The British Chamber of Commerce for Italy*, Via Agnello 8, 20121 ☎ 877798, offers research and business facilities to members, who are not necessarily British.
Local media Milan publishes the *Corriere della Sera* (Via Solferino), a national heavyweight, and *La Repubblica* has editorial offices in Milan. *Il Sole-24 Ore* is a prestigious business daily read by entrepreneurs and professionals, *Milano Finanza* a weekly international digest of finance, economy and politics. *Panorama*, published by Mondadori, is a Milanese *Time* or *Newsweek*. The major publishing group Rusconi publishes a magazine called *GenteMoney*. There are three major private TV networks; Canale 5, Italia 1 and Retequattro.
Tourist information The main office is at Via Marconi 1 ☎ 809662 (open 9.45–12.30, 1.30–6), with branches in the Stazione Centrale and at Linate airport.

Thank-yous
Chocolates Cova, Via Montenapoleone 8.
Florists Radaelli, Via Manzoni 16 ☎ 702876.

TURIN (Torino)   *City code* ☎ 011

Turin is Fiat. Not only is Fiat the biggest vehicle manufacturer in Europe, but the Agnelli empire, now diversified into sectors such as banking, steel mills, newspapers and leisure, employs directly or indirectly nearly half of Turin's work force. Fiat makes 80% of Italian cars (including Alfa Romeo, Lancia and Ferrari) and accounts for much of the production of commercial, agricultural and earth-moving vehicles, employing some 300,000 people overall. Also in Turin are manufacturers of car parts (ATI, MEC, Siette) and car designers (Bertone, Giugiaro, Pininfarina). The international motor show takes place in even years, drawing over 500,000 visitors.

Turin, with its population of just over 1m, has overtaken Milan as the main centre of Italian industry, and not just of cars and engineering. There are many clothing and textile companies here too. Gruppo Finanziario Tessile (GFT), with Marco Rivetti at the helm, has 14 factories employing some 7,500 workers and makes garments for designers like Armani, Ungaro and Valentino. Confectionery (notably Ferrero), coffee (Lavazza) and printing and publishing are also major employers, and the famous vermouth firms, Martini, Carpano and Cinzano, have their main offices in central Turin. Insurance is another important sector (SAI, Toro and Reale Mutua among others).

Turin-based companies have taken to sponsoring exhibitions and have poured much-publicized funds into local restoration projects, thus drawing international attention to the city and proclaiming their faith in its future. Recent projects have included the reorganization of the Egyptian Museum (Istituto Bancario San Paolo), the restoration of Juvarra's baroque, palatial hunting-lodge, a few kilometres out of the city, Stupinigi (Fiat and the Cassa di Risparmio) and of the Accademia delle Scienze (Italgas).

The old Fiat factory at Lingotto is being transformed into a high-tech exhibition, conference and research centre with heliport and restaurant. The whole project is expected to be completed around 1994, jointly financed by public and private money with Fiat providing half the funds, estimated at L400bn. Other major projects include the new stadium for the World Cup in 1990.

But, compared with Milan, Turin is still a provincial town, with a provincial mentality. The influx of some 50,000 workers from the South in the 1960s profoundly affected its social fabric. The dwindling aristocracy retreated behind the shutters of gloomy *palazzi*, the rich industrialists barricaded themselves in their villas in the hills, with guard dogs and closed circuit television. Still only 100,000 people live in the noble but rather run-down centre of Turin, one-time capital of the princes of Savoy and of a united Italy.

Arriving

There is direct road access to Turin from the north (St Bernard Pass, Mont Blanc tunnel) but there is still no autostrada from the French border. The city is bounded to the north, west and south by the *tangenziale* ring road and forms the westernmost apex of the triangle of autostrada routes linking the main cities of Northern Italy. Rail connections are also good. There are flights from some European cities but many business visitors have to fly to Milan.

Caselle airport
Scheduled direct flights link Turin daily with Frankfurt, London and Paris, several times a week with Munich, Düsseldorf, Stuttgart and Zürich and with Rome, Naples, Palermo and Pisa. Facilities are fairly basic but a staffed business centre, the first of its kind in the country, is planned and general improvements are under way to cope with the growing traffic. The bank on the main concourse is open Mon–Fri, 6.25–4.50, 5.25–11.15. Inquiries ☎ 5778431, recorded flight information ☎ 5778361/2/3/4 and ☎ 57781 (12–6am). Reservations ☎ 5778372.
Nearby hotels Atlantic, Via Lanzo 163, Borgaro Torinese 10071 ☎ 4701947 Ⓣ 22140 fax 4701783 • AE DC MC V. Modern hotel on the main road to Turin with SADEM bus stop nearby; restaurant, meeting rooms, pool, sauna and gym. *Jet Hotel*, Via della Zecca 9, Caselle Torinese 10072 ☎ 9963733 Ⓣ 215896 fax 9961544 • AE DC MC V. Popular hotel with meeting rooms, garden and good restaurant, the Antica Zecca (see *Restaurants*).
City link The airport is 16kms/10 miles northwest of Turin. It's best to take a taxi into the centre. Buses operate directly between the Alitalia terminal at Via Lagrange 35 ☎ 55911 and Milan's Malpensa airport to connect with Alitalia flights (journey time 2hrs, cost L10,000).
Taxi There are usually plenty of cabs on the rank in front of the airport; allow 25–35mins for the journey and about L30,000.
Car rental The major car rental firms have desks at the airport, but a car is

a drawback in the city.
Bus SADEM runs a regular service (every 20–30mins) of air-conditioned buses to the terminal (outside the centre) in Corso Inghilterra, also stopping on request at Porta Susa station (journey time, 30–45mins).
Helicopter Interavia ☎ 4703938 or 578630 is based at Caselle; 2-seaters cost from L600,000 an hour.

Railway stations
Stazione Porta Nuova is very central, opposite the end of Via Roma, and serves national and continental destinations. In the reservations hall there are separate windows for sleepers, for international services and for credit card payment (AE V). The best facilities are on the modern main concourse. The taxi rank on the left of the exit is a better bet than the one on the other side. Hotel reservations can be made at the information desk (open 9–3) ☎ 531327. Rail inquiries ☎ 517551.

Getting around
Visitors staying for only a day or two will find walking (in the centre) and taxis (for farther afield) the easiest answer.
Taxis wait at ranks (in main squares and streets, marked with blue-and-white signs) and can be ordered by telephone: *Central Taxi* ☎ 5744 (AE, free wake-up call), *Radio Taxi* ☎ 5730, *Pronto Taxi* ☎ 5737. For advance reservations, *Radio Taxi Avvenire* ☎ 5748. Surcharges are levied for baggage and at weekends, and journeys to the hills round Turin are double rate for single trips.
Limousines Autoservizi Mentana ☎ 446027 or 6691229.
Driving Not recommended; parking is difficult and buses and taxis have priority lanes.
Walking is convenient (and the many arcades offer shelter from sun and rain) but the main through streets are extremely noisy and you can encounter drunks, tramps and hawkers in some areas.

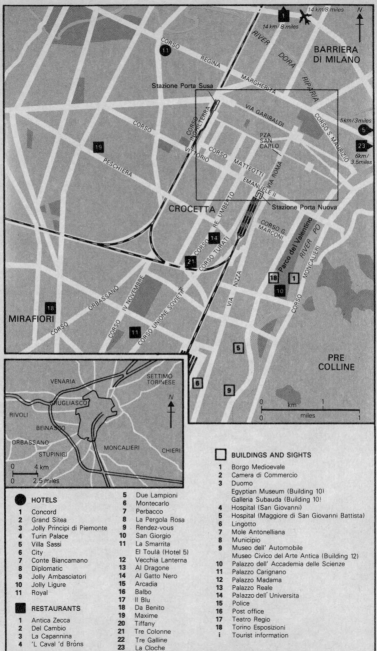

BARRIERA DI MILANO

14 km/8 miles

RIVER DORA RIPARIA

CORSO REGINA MARGHERITA

Stazione Porta Susa

VIA GARIBALDI

CORSO INGHILTERRA

5km/3miles

CORSO

VITTORIO

CORSO MATTEOTTI

PZA SAN CARLO

6km/3.5miles

PESCHIERA

VIA ROMA

EMANUELE II

CROCETTA

CORSO RE UMBERTO

Stazione Porta Nuova

CORSO G. MARCONI

Parco del Valentino

RIVER PO

CORSO TURATI

CORSO MONCALIERI

CORSO MONCALIERI

VIA NIZZA

MIRAFIORI

CORSO ORBASSANO

CORSO IV NOVEMBRE

CORSO UNIONE SOVIETICA

PRE COLLINE

0 km 1
0 miles 1

VENARIA

SETTIMO TORINESE

GRUGLIASCO

RIVOLI

BEINASCO

ORBASSANO

STUPINIGI

MONCALIERI

CHIERI

0 4 km
0 2.5 miles

	HOTELS
1	Concord
2	Grand Sitea
3	Jolly Principi di Piemonte
4	Turin Palace
5	Villa Sassi
6	City
7	Conte Biancamano
8	Diplomatic
9	Jolly Ambasciatori
10	Jolly Ligure
11	Royal

	RESTAURANTS
1	Antica Zecca
2	Del Cambio
3	La Capannina
4	'L Caval 'd Brons
5	Due Lampioni
6	Montecarlo
7	Perbacco
8	La Pergola Rosa
9	Rendez-vous
10	San Giorgio
11	La Smarrita
	El Toulà (Hotel 5)
12	Vecchia Lanterna
13	Al Dragone
14	Al Gatto Nero
15	Arcadia
16	Balbo
17	Il Blu
18	Da Benito
19	Maxime
20	Tiffany
21	Tre Colonne
22	Tre Galline
23	La Cloche

BUILDINGS AND SIGHTS

1	Borgo Medioevale
2	Camera di Commercio
3	Duomo
	Egyptian Museum (Building 10)
	Galleria Subauda (Building 10)
4	Hospital (San Giovanni)
5	Hospital (Maggiore di San Giovanni Battista)
6	Lingotto
7	Mole Antonelliana
8	Municipio
9	Museo dell' Automobile
	Museo Civico del Arte Antica (Building 12)
10	Palazzo dell' Accademia delle Scienze
11	Palazzo Carignano
12	Palazzo Madama
13	Palazzo Reale
14	Palazzo dell' Universita
15	Police
16	Post office
17	Teatro Regio
18	Torino Esposizioni
i	Tourist information

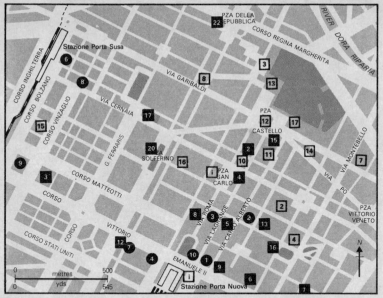

Bus and tram Routes are constantly changed in an effort to improve the system so get an up-to-date map from the tourist office or the ATM headquarters at Corso Turati 19B ☎ 500900. Tickets are sold by tobacconists displaying the blue-and-white ATM sign and at the kiosk in the underground passage in front of Porta Nuova station.

Sleek modern trams (*metropolitana leggera*) are replacing the old-fashioned ones now that plans for a subway have been shelved.

There are bus services to the main provincial towns, mostly from the terminals in Corso Inghilterra and Corso Marconi.

Area by area
The centre of Turin, laid out in a grid, lies west of the river Po and south of the river Dora Riparia, its main axis being the Via Roma, leading from the station to the Piazza Castello. The banking and business area is to the west of the Via Roma, around Piazza Solferino. West of the station is Crocetta, the most prestigious residential area in the

centre, where rich Torinese live in detached villas with gardens.

The outskirts of Turin have distinct characteristics. North of the Corso Regina Margherita is the Barriera di Milano, home to immigrants from the South of Italy, as is Le Vallette, to the northwest, site of the World Cup soccer stadium. To the south are densely-populated areas close to the Fiat factory at Mirafiori, and the former Fiat factory at Lingotto, now an important exhibition centre, used for the international motor show. Further development will include a research centre for advanced industry, incorporating the scientific departments of Turin university, a conference centre, apartments and shops.

A contrast to the dreary suburbs is the area east of the Po where the remains of Turin's aristocracy and the newer rich have their villas. The Pre Colline, immediately east of the centre, is a residential extension of it, a district of restored old buildings inhabited by artists and successful single people.

The suburbs

The conurbations of Beinasco (metallurgy), Collegno and Grugliasco to the west; Moncalieri and Nichelino to the south; Settimo Torinese (with GFT's largest single ready-made clothing factory in Europe) and Venaria to the north are all now incorporated in Turin. They are close to the ring road, and have a population of around 300,000. The aeronautics (Alitalia) zone is around Corso Francia, towards Collegno to the west.

Hotels

There is a wide gap between Turin's best hotels – the Turin Palace and the Principi di Piemonte in the centre vie for top spot – and the rest. In general, officially classified 4-star hotels are fairly well equipped for the business traveller, with modernized bedrooms and several meeting rooms, but 3-star hotels are of a poor standard.

All the hotels listed have IDD telephones, a concierge, but rarely 24hr room service, and at least one meeting room. Those with a full entry also have air conditioning, several conference rooms and parking facilities. None have shops, sports or keep-fit equipment or on-site business facilities – and changing money may not be easy.

It is not difficult to find a room except during major fairs, but it is essential to reserve accommodation well in advance for the bi-annual international car show.

Concord *L‖*
Via Lagrange 47, 10123 ☎ *5576756*
☒ *221323 fax 5576305 • Atahotels •*
AE DC MC V • 140 rooms, 4 suites,
1 restaurant, 1 bar
A rather impersonal but quite comfortable and central hotel used by business travellers which prides itself on its well-equipped convention centre. Bedrooms, of which about half are singles, are spacious with high ceilings and modern comforts. All are sound-proofed but it is still advisable to request one on the courtyard. The lobby (writing desk, newspapers) is a good meeting place and the Lagrange restaurant, although rather claustrophobic, is suitable for business lunches. Popular with visiting soccer teams. 6 meeting rooms (capacity up to 230).

Grand Sitea *L‖*
Via Carlo Alberto 35, 10123
☎ *5570171* ☒ *220229 fax 548090 •*
AE DC MC V • 117 rooms, 3 suites,
1 restaurant, 1 bar
A well-established hotel in the grand style, in a rather dour 19thC building. It has been modernized but retains some period features and a sedate atmosphere. Recent renovation has included the restaurant, in imperial style. The Sitea is close to the Teatro Regio and attracts visiting actors and musicians. Courtyard garden. 5 meeting rooms (capacity up to 100).

Jolly Principi di Piemonte *L‖‖*
Via P. Gobetti 15, 10123 ☎ *532153*
☒ *221120 • AE DC MC V • 99 rooms,*
8 suites, 1 restaurant, 1 bar
A marble-faced detached block set back from the central Via Roma, this is the flagship of the Jolly chain. Although it does not enjoy official luxury status, like the Palace, its public rooms and meeting rooms have more old-fashioned elegance and charm. The recently refurbished bedrooms are very comfortable and well equipped with desks and hairdryers and telephones in the bathrooms. The few single rooms, although spacious, have small bathtubs. Suites include marble bathrooms and small sitting-rooms. 4 meeting rooms (capacity up to 250).

Turin Palace *L̲‖‖*
Via Sacchi 8, 10128 ☎ *515511*
ⓉⓍ *221411 fax 5612187* • *Italhotels* •
AE DC MC V • *121 rooms, 2 suites,*
1 restaurant, 1 bar
Turin's only 5-star hotel is, although
opposite the station, considered the
smartest place to stay. The guestbook
lists VIPs from rock stars to royalty.
The lacquered, oriental-style bar is a
calm venue for business meetings.
The restaurant, serving regional and
international cuisines, has a separate
banqueting room and offers a sensibly
priced 3-course set meal and *à la
carte*. 5 meeting rooms (capacity up to
200).

Villa Sassi *L̲‖‖*
Strada Traforo del Pino 47, 10132
☎ *890556* ⓉⓍ *225437 fax 890095* •
Relais et Châteaux • *AE DC MC V* •
16 rooms, 1 suite, 1 restaurant,
1 bar
Only a short taxi ride from the
centre, Villa Sassi is a noble 18thC
villa, secluded in its own tranquil
parkland. It retains the atmosphere of
a country house, with antique
furniture and Old Master paintings.
A comfortable place to stay, and a
prestigious venue for dining, club
reunions, and fashion shows or
conferences. 4 meeting rooms
(capacity up to 500).

OTHER HOTELS
City *L̲‖* *Via Filippo Juvarra 25,*
10122 ☎ *216228* ⓉⓍ *216228* • *AE DC*
MC V. Small, neat, modern hotel near
Porta Susa station.
Conte Biancamano *L̲‖* *Corso*
Vittorio Emanuele 73, 10128
☎ *513281 fax 513281* • *AE DC MC V*.
Appealing little family-run hotel with
elegant sitting-room. No restaurant.
Diplomatic *L̲‖* *Via Cernaia 42,*
10122 ☎ *5612444* ⓉⓍ *225445*
fax 540472 • *AE DC MC V*. A new
hotel near the business area and main
bus terminal, with comfortable well-
decorated and equipped bedrooms
(mostly singles with shower only) and
4 meeting rooms. No restaurant.
Jolly Ambasciatori *L̲‖* *Corso*
Vittorio Emanuele 104, 10121 ☎ *5752*
ⓉⓍ *221296 fax 544978* • *AE DC MC V*.
Near the bus terminal.
Jolly Ligure *L̲‖‖* *Piazza Carlo*
Felice 85, 10123 ☎ *55641* ⓉⓍ *220617*
fax 535438 • *AE DC MC V*. Second
choice in the Jolly trinity. Central,
comfortable and functional, with a
spacious lobby lounge.
Royal *L̲‖* *Corso Regina Margherita*
249, 10144 ☎ *748444* ⓉⓍ *220259*
fax 748393 • *AE DC MC V*. Well-
equipped but charmless hotel on the
way out to the western *tangenziale*
and the aeronautics area. Conference
room for up to 600.

Restaurants
Turin executives avoid long business lunches and most restaurants are
closed by 3pm. Favoured places are brisk Tuscan trattorias, but there are
many more formal places suitable for confidential discussions or for
evening entertaining. Restaurants and old Torinese trattorias are concentrated near the markets, east of Via Roma and around Porta Palazzo. It is
advisable to make reservations in advance for dinner and the same day for
lunch.

Summer dining in the hills east of the Po is popular, and there are
some excellent restaurants around Alba, 59kms/36.5 miles south of
Turin; Italian guests will appreciate a gastronomic excursion there during the autumn truffle season.

Piedmontese cooking is regaining favour but now chefs try for quality
rather than quantity. Traditional dishes tend to be rich, and include
agnolotti (ravioli filled with truffles) and *brasato al Barolo* (beef braised in
Barolo wine).

Antica Zecca *L*///
Via della Zecca 9, Caselle Torinese
☎ 9961403 • *closed Mon, Aug* • AE
MC DC V
Near the airport at Caselle, this is a
sophisticated restaurant, in a
converted old mint, often crowded
with business people, especially at
lunch. Cooking, which is superb,
features unusual Piedmontese dishes
and excellent local wines.

Del Cambio *L*////
Pza Carignano 2 ☎ 546690 • *closed
Sun, Aug* • AE DC V • *jacket and tie*
A famous restaurant with original late
18thC mirror and gilt interior. Under
the present ownership, Del Cambio's
flagging gastronomic reputation has
been revived: dishes (like *brasato al
Barolo*) are traditional but interpreted
with flair, and the wine list has been
improved. Service is formal without
being starchy. Foreign visitors come
here out of curiosity, especially in the
evenings.

La Capannina *L*///
Via Donati 1 ☎ 545405 • *closed Sun,
Aug* • *no credit cards*
The Gallina brothers run a rustic-
style trattoria famous for its
Piedmontese food from the Langhe
region, south of Alba (where there is
another branch). A good place for an
informal evening.

'L Caval 'd Brôns *L*/////
Pza S. Carlo 157 ☎ 553491 • *closed
Sun, Aug* • AE V • *jacket and tie* •
reservations essential
Turin's most exclusive restaurant, on
the *piano nobile* above the café of the
same name, was restored in 1988 after
ten years of neglect. The atmosphere
is discreet and club-like; there is no
name or menu outside, just a
doorbell. Bankers snap up the tables
(there are only 8) at lunch time.

Due Lampioni *L*///
Via Carlo Alberto 45 ☎ 546721 •
closed Sun, Aug • V • *jacket and tie* •
reservations essential
Carlo Bagatin's long-established

restaurant has well-spaced tables, is
ideal for groups of four people, and
serves regional and international
cooking in comfortable though not
grand surroundings.

Montecarlo *L*///
Via San Francesco da Paola 37
☎ 830815 • *closed Sat L, Sun, Aug* •
AE DC MC V • *reservations essential*
A vaulted restaurant with a serious
atmosphere and modern cooking,
much frequented for mid-price
business lunches and dinners. Good
wine list.

Perbacco *L*/
Via Mazzini 31 ☎ 882110 • *closed
Mon L, Sun, Aug* • AE DC V
An attractive and fashionable new
restaurant in an old mansion, but
with a no-frills interior and fairly
cramped tables. The menu is
inventive, with surprising culinary
combinations. Popular with
journalists.

La Pergola Rosa *L*/
Via XX Settembre 18 ☎ 546534 •
closed Sun, Aug • V
A simple Tuscan trattoria with 1940s
decor and snob appeal. Fiat directors
lunch here.

Rendez-vous *L*///
Corso Vittorio Emanuele 38 ☎ 8396961
• *closed Sat L, Sun, Aug* • AE DC MC
V • *jacket and tie* • *reservations
essential*
A large restaurant, popular with
business people and ladies out for
lunch. Tables are well spaced, but it
can be noisy; there is a separate
private room (10–14 people).

San Giorgio *L*///
Borgo Medioevale al Valentino
☎ 6692131 • *closed Wed L, Tue, Aug*
• AE MC V
An elegant restaurant in the mock
medieval castle on the Po. Candlelit
dining (till 2am), with an orchestra
and formal service, attracts the
tourists. There are special salons for
banquets and receptions.

La Smarrita *L*////
Corso Unione Sovietica 244 ☎ *328488*
• *closed Mon* • *AE DC MC V* •
reservations essential
Close to Fiat and sometimes used by
Gianni Agnelli, La Smarrita is a
small, smart place for *nouvelle* Tuscan
food. The waiters are dressed like
monks. Good wines.

El Toulà *L*////
Villa Sassi Hotel ☎ *890556* • *closed
Sun, Aug* • *AE DC MC V*
A calm, countrified setting close to
the centre for formal business
gatherings or a romantic summer
evening. Reserve well in advance for
a table on the terrace. Area reserved
for nonsmokers.

Vecchia Lanterna *L*////
Corso Re Umberto 21 ☎ *537047* •
closed Sat L, Sun, 10–20 Aug • *AE DC
MC V* • *jacket required* • *D reservations
essential*
Armando Zanetti is one of Italy's
best-known chefs and attracts those
with a palate for the 7-course *menu
degustazione* (changed every 15 days).
Senior business executives and
ministers lunch here (the round tables
are good for small groups), and in the
evening the clientele is often younger.
Brocaded walls and Venetian lace
tablecloths create a traditional
atmosphere but the cooking is
modern and seasonal. Downstairs,
opposite the kitchens, is the Sala
Inglese, which is used for private
banquets.

OTHER RESTAURANTS
Al Dragone, Via Pomba 14 ☎ 547019,
is a brick-vaulted, taverna-type
trattoria. *Al Gatto Nero*, Corso Turati
14 ☎ 590414, is a well-known
seafood restaurant with a Tuscan
chef. The *Arcadia*, Galleria Subalpina
16 ☎ 532029, is pretty and smart and
full of executives at lunch time.
Balbo, Via Andrea Doria 11
☎ 511743, serves international and
local cuisine. *Il Blu*, Corso Siccardi
15B ☎ 545550, specializes in salads,
is chic and speedy. For the best fish

try the informal *Da Benito*, Corso
Siracusa 142 ☎ 3090353, close to the
Fiat factory, and *Maxime*, Via
Verzuolo 40 ☎ 4475677, whose
Egyptian owner adds exotic spices.
The elegant *Tiffany*, Pza Solferino 16
☎ 540538, is near the business and
banking area; *Tre Colonne*, Corso
Rosselli 1 ☎ 587029, with summer
service in the garden, is another safe
choice. *Tre Galline*, Via Bellezia 37
☎ 546833, is a typical old Torinese
trattoria. *La Cloche*, Strada al Traforo
del Pino 106 ☎ 894213, serves good
Piedmontese cooking on a rustic
covered verandah some 6kms/3.5
miles east of Turin.

Restaurants in the hills
Bastian Contrario, Strada Moncalvo
102, Moncalvieri ☎ 6968388,
panoramic views, vast array of
antipasti. *Il Ciacolon*, Vle xxv Aprile
11 ☎ 6610911, Venetian cooking and
antipasti, good fixed-price menus.
Pigna d'Oro, Via Roma 130, Pino
Torinese ☎ 841019, lovely terrace,
exclusive atmosphere, average food.
Tromlin, Via alla Parrocchia 7,
Cavoretto ☎ 697804, intimate,
family-run, with typical Piedmontese
food; open weekends and evenings.
Villa Montforts, Strada de' Luogo 29,
Castiglione Torinese ☎ 9606214,
18thC villa with classic cooking and
fine French wines (about 15kms/9
miles from Turin).

Bars and cafés
Turin's delightful 19thC coffee houses
are civilized places for semi-formal
business discussions where you can
drink the vermouth, take a light
lunch or snack and try the local
confections. *San Carlo* and *Caffè
Torino* in Piazza San Carlo and *Baratti*
and *Mulassano* in Piazza Castello have
splendid original interiors, with
chandeliers, mirrored or wood-
panelled walls, and a profusion of
gilt, velvet and stucco. The brasserie
in *Caffè Platti*, Corso Vittorio
Emanuele 72, has just the right
atmosphere for longer lunch-time
meetings.

Entertainment

Turin is rather quiet at night; the Torinese like to meet in cafés and piano bars.

In July and August there are open-air performances (*punti verdi*) in the parks and there is a music festival in September.

Theatre, opera, dance Teatro Regio, Pza Castello 215 ☎ 548000, puts on opera, concerts, ballets and plays Nov–mid Jun.

The other main theatres are the *Teatro Alfieri*, Pza Solferino 4 ☎ 535440, and the *Teatro Carignano*, Pza Carignano 6, which stages plays that require a good knowledge of Italian (tickets ☎ 544562).

Music Concerts are given at the recently facelifted *Conservatorio Giuseppe Verdi*, Via Mazzini 11 ☎ 878458, and in the RAI auditorium, Via Rossini 15 ☎ 8800.

Discotheques Bogart, Via Sacchi 34 ☎ 547530, with a piano bar, is one of the more reliable discotheques.

Shopping

Arcaded Via Roma and the traffic-free Via Garibaldi are the smart shopping streets, exhibiting the designs of the famous names in Italian fashion. Parallel to Via Roma is Via Lagrange, with mouth-watering food shops including *Defilippis* (for pasta), *Baita del Formagg* (for cheese) and *Castagno*, a superb delicatessen. At *Casa del Barolo*, Via Andrea Doria 7 ☎ 532038, you can taste and buy a large range of Italian wines. All over Turin are *pasticcerie*, displaying the confectionery, especially *gianduie* (chocolates), for which the city is famous. *Peyrano*, Corso Vittorio Emanuele II 76 ☎ 538765, sells probably the best chocolates in Turin; just up the road is *Platti*, a close rival. Shopping hours are 9–12.30 and 3–7.30. Food shops shut on Wed pm.

Street markets Porta Palazzo is a general market, the *Fiera del Gran Balon* an antique market held the second Sunday in the month. Both near the Piazza della Repubblica.

Sightseeing

Turin is a city of museums, monuments, churches and palaces.

Duomo The *Cappella della Santa Sindone*, containing the rarely displayed Holy Shroud, dated in 1988 to medieval times, is inside the cathedral. *Pza San Giovanni. Chapel open Tue–Fri, 8.30–12, 3–7; Sat–Sun, 9.45–10.30, 11.30–12.*

Mole Antonelliana Turin's odd pagoda (city emblem) affords fine views of the Alps on a clear day. *Via Montebello 20. Elevator Tue–Sun, 9–7.*

Museo dell'Automobile A fine collection of historic cars. *Corso Unità d'Italia 40. Open Tue–Sun, 9.30–12.30, 3–7.*

Palazzo dell'Accademia delle Scienze Palace by Guarini containing, in the *Galleria Sabauda*, an important picture collection with Italian and Flemish masterpieces, and the outstanding *Egyptian Museum. Via Accademia delle Scienze 6. Open Tue–Sat, 9–2, 3–7; Sun, 9–2.*

Palazzo Carignano Also by Guarini, the birthplace of Victor Emanuel II and seat of the first parliament of a united Italy. *Pza Carignano. Open Mon–Sat, 9–7; Sun, 9–1.*

Palazzo Madama Juvarra's majestic baroque façade hides a fortified medieval palace containing the Gothic and Renaissance collection of the *Museo Civica d'Arte Antica. Pza Castello. Open Tue–Sat, 9–7; Sun, 10–1, 2–7.*

Palazzo Reale Royal palace of the princes of Savoy, with opulent decoration and furniture. *Pza Castello. Open Tue–Sun, 9–2.*

Parco Valentino Broad park on the banks of the Po with a French-style *château* and the *Borgo Medioevale*, a 19thC reconstruction of a feudal village and castle. *Open Tue–Sat, 9–4; Sun, 10–4.*

Guided tours

Tours, some including lunch and a boat trip on the Po, leave in summer and during exhibitions from the station and some major hotels. Details at the tourist office and travel agents.

A private half-day tour of the robotic-assembly Fiat factory at Mirafiori can be made Mon–Sat. Chambers of commerce will organize group visits ☎ 33331.

Out of town
Basilica di Superga Juvarra's imposing basilica contains the tombs of the Savoy dynasty and the kings of Sardinia; 10kms/6 miles to the east. *Open Sat–Thu, 10–12.30, 3–5* ☎ 890083.
Castello di Rivoli Museum of contemporary art in handsome baroque interiors; 14kms/8.5 miles west. *Open Tue–Sun, 10–7* ☎ 9581547.
Sagra di San Michele Impressive fortified monastery at the entrance to the Susa valley, 25kms/15.5 miles to the east.
Stupinigi Hunting lodge conceived on a grand scale by Juvarra, also known as a *palazzo*, now gloriously restored, 9kms/5.5 miles southwest of Turin ☎ 3581220.

Spectator sports
Soccer by Juventus, Turin's most successful team is sponsored by Agnelli and supported by most middle management. Torino is the people's team. Matches are played at the Studio Comunale ☎ 352600.
Basketball, played at the Palazzo dello Sport ☎ 337416, and *rowing* (on the Po) are also popular spectator sports. *Horseracing and polo* take place at the *Ippodromo*, Vinovo, near Stupinigi, mostly at weekends ☎ 9651356.

Keeping fit
Fitness centres The Gym and Squash Club, Corso Trapani 57 ☎ 380835, and *Sport City*, Corso Dante 17A ☎ 3190884. *The American Club*, with 4 branches (including Corso Trapani 46 ☎ 337109), offers monthly membership and pools and tennis.
Golf Visitors who are members of other clubs may play at *I Roveri*, La Mandria ☎ 9235667, 18kms/11 miles to the north. There are other courses at Stupinigi and Vinovo.

Skiing Sestrière and Sauze d'Oulx are within 2hrs drive of Turin.

Local resources
Business services
Multilingual secretaries, telex and fax, word processing and other office facilities are offered by *AV*, Corso Siccardi 15 ☎ 533740 ☒ 225557 fax 515563, and *Executive Service*, Via Magenta 44A ☎ 531740, both with branches in other major cities. A local set-up is *CFT*, Via Ceva 47 ☎ 4731113. *International Office Service*, Via Egeo 18 ☎ 55811, is equipped for meetings and conferences.
Photocopying and printing Most hotels will photocopy for guests and there are numerous copy shops near the university and in business areas. *Elektra*, Pza Solferino 3 ☎ 531961, is central and open Mon–Fri, 8.30–7, Sat, 8.30–12.30. *TarServi* is near the aeronautics zone, Corso Marche 12 ☎ 715346.
Secretarial Copisteria Agostino, Via S. Agostino 4 ☎ 535657, offers word processing, translating (and offset printing) and will collect and deliver.
Translation ATID, Via Vittorio Amedeo II ☎ 519571, for notarized translations. *Inlingua*, Corso Vittorio 68 ☎ 532912 ☒ 225272 fax 5576297.

Communications
Local delivery Defendini, Via San Francesco d'Assisi 23d ☎ 55401; *Pony Express*, Via San Francesco di Paola 15-17 ☎ 8123618.
Long-distance delivery There are firms specializing in transporting anything from cars to computers to pianos; see the Yellow Pages. *DHL*, Via Saluzzo 42 ☎ 6502275, for letters and packets.
Post office Main office: Via Alfieri 10 and Via Arsenale 13, open Mon–Sat, 8–8 ☎ 547097.
Telex and fax At the main post office.

Conference/exhibition centres
The main exhibition hall, *Torino Esposizioni*, Corso Massimo d'Azeglio

15, 10126 ☎ 6569 (during exhibitions 6504970) ⊠ 221492 fax 6509801, has 9 meeting rooms and conference facilities for up to 3,000. Among the most important international shows held here are those on new technology, leisure and sport, food and trade equipment. Other central conference venues include the *Centro Incontri della Cassa di Risparmio di Torino*, Corso Stati Uniti 23 ☎ 57661, with a capacity of up to 300; the *Centro Congressi SEAT*, Via Bertola 34 ☎ 541096, which has 4 meeting rooms with a capacity of up to 300; and the *Sala Congressi dell'Istituto Bancario di San Paolo*, Via Santa Teresa ☎ 5551, with a meeting room accommodating up to 290 people; they have more conference facilities (capacity up to 200) at Via Lugaro 15 ☎ 5551. The *Museo dell'Automobile*, Corso Unità d'Italia 40 ☎ 677666, has 2 rooms (capacity up to 340). The international motor show is held every two years at *Centro Espositivo Lingotto*, Corso G. Ferraris 61, 10128 ☎ 5761.

Outside the centre there are attractive convention facilities at *Villa Gualino*, Vle Settimio Severo 65 ☎ 6502565, with panoramic views, and a meeting room for 80 people at *Castello di Rivoli*, Pzle Castello ☎ 9587256 (see *Sightseeing*), and at *Villa Sassi* (see *Hotels*). Receptions can be held at *Stupinigi* (see *Sightseeing*).

The *Centro Congressi Internazionale* Corso Tassoni 32 ☎ 761870, will organize conferences.

Emergencies
Bureaux de change Porta Nuova station information office, open 7–9, 12–2 and 3–9.30.
Hospitals Ospedale San Giovanni, Via Cavour 31 ☎ 57541; *Ospedale Maggiore di S. Giovanni Battista*, Corso Bramante 88/90 ☎ 6566, is the main university hospital; in emergency ☎ 5747, emergency surgery ☎ 633722.
Pharmacies Open at night and on holidays: *Boniscontro*, Corso Vittorio

Emanuele 66 ☎ 541271, *Maffei*, Pza Massaua 1 ☎ 793308, and *Pescarmona*, Via Nizza 65 ☎ 6699259. Some others stay open until 10.30.
Police Questura: Corso Vinzaglio 10 ☎ 55881.

Information sources
Business information Camera di Commercio, Via San Francesco di Paola 24 ☎ 57161. *Centro Estero Camere Commercio Piemontesi*, Via Ventimiglia 165 ☎ 6960096 ⊠ 214159 fax 6965456 (chamber of commerce for Piedmont region). *Centro Internazionale di Perfezionamento Professionale e Tecnico*, Corso Unità d' Italia 125 ☎ 633863. *Federazione delle Associazioni Industriali del Piemonte*, Corso Stati Uniti 38 ☎ 549246 (federation of industrial associations of Piedmont). *Biblioteche Civiche e Raccolte Storiche*, Via della Cittadella 5 ☎ 7653900 (public library).
Local media The influential Turin-based *La Stampa* is read all over Italy. The supplement *Torino Sette* details the week's cultural events. RAI television headquarters are also in Turin.
A Guest in Torino is distributed free in hotels and has information and advertising.
Tourist information Tourist offices are at at Via Roma 226 ☎ 535181 and Porta Nuova station ☎ 517551 or 531327.

Thank-yous
Chocolates Peyrano (see *Shopping*).
Florists T. Cichetti, Via Cernaia 34-36 ☎ 540054, *Fiorir di Fiori*, Corso Vittorio Emanuele 78 ☎ 544775; *Gabri*, Corso Palermo 25 ☎ 237993 or 284544.

THE NETHERLANDS

Large reserves of natural gas (which provide more than 50% of domestic energy requirements) helped the Netherlands weather the recession of the early 1980s better than most other European countries; GDP growth is above the OECD average, inflation is firmly under control and the balance of payments current account is in healthy surplus. Yet the budget deficit threatens to undermine long-term growth – public spending as a share of GDP is the highest in the EC, and unemployment remains high.

Whether the Dutch economy can produce the rates of growth needed to reduce unemployment will depend on the competitiveness of its manufacturing industries. Many of these industries have undergone extensive restructuring and in the late 1980s output, investment and profitability were all rising. The major industrial sectors are food, drink and tobacco, chemicals, machinery, eletrical and electronic products, and transport equipment. In many of these sectors the Netherlands has produced major multinational companies, including such world leaders as Philips, Unilever and Shell.

Agriculture (including market gardening and dairy farming) still plays an important role in the economy. The Netherlands is the world's second largest exporter of farm produce and the world's largest exporter of flowers and bulbs.

Historically the Netherlands is a trading nation, largely because of its lack of raw materials and small domestic market; today exports and imports of goods and services are still equivalent to about 60% of GDP. Most manufacturing and agricultural output is exported. Trade deficits in the 1970s have been replaced by healthy surpluses in the 1980s as world trade has picked up. Over two-thirds of foreign trade is with EC countries. West Germany and Belgium/Luxembourg are the Netherlands main trading partners.

Geography The Netherlands is almost totally flat and is criss-crossed by a network of inland waterways. Much of the land, especially in the west, is below sea level, protected by dykes and dunes. Some 7,700 sq kms (3,000 sq miles) of land have been reclaimed from the sea.
Climate The weather is generally temperate, with relatively cool summers and mild winters, although termperatures can drop to -17°C (10°F).
Population 14.5m.
Government The Netherlands is a parliamentary monarchy. The legislature, the Staten-Generaal, has 2 chambers: the Eerste Kamer (the upper chamber) with 75 members

elected by provincial councils for 6 years; and the Tweede Kamer (the lower chamber) with 150 members who are directly elected by proportional representation for 4 years.
Currency Guilder (G) or florin.
Time 1hr ahead of GMT; end Mar–end Sep, 2hrs ahead of GMT.
Dialling codes The Netherland's IDD code is 31. You should omit the initial 0 from the city code when dialling from abroad. To make an international call from the Netherlands, dial 09 before dialling the relevant country code.
Public holidays Jan 1, Good Fri–Easter Mon, Apr 30, May 5, Ascension, Whit Mon, Dec 25.

AMSTERDAM

City code ☎ 020

Amsterdam is a historic city and the unofficial capital of an area, known as *De Randstad*, that includes Haarlem, The Hague (the official capital), Rotterdam and the Europort, Utrecht and Hilversum. At least 50% of the nation's GNP is generated here, and the only major centres of industry outside are Eindhoven and the mining district of Limburg.

This whole region is not much larger than London, and travelling between centres of industry, offices and rural homes results in road and rail congestion. Many big employers, including Heineken and the Post Office, have relocated, and if the rapid growth of industry along the arterial routes continues the suburbs of these cities will soon merge.

The development of Schiphol airport's freight handling capacity has been crucial. It is now a major distribution point for European imports and exports, and an increasing number of overseas companies choose the Netherlands as a base for their pan-European activities. The ability to fly perishable produce inexpensively all over Europe has greatly benefited domestic agriculture. The airport has attracted high-tech industry in the southeast and to the west of the city, but development land is becoming expensive and future growth will probably concentrate on the redundant western harbour and the docks north of the North Sea Canal, which are significant as a transit port for coal, wood and cars.

The city of Amsterdam is an important banking and financial centre. Dutch banking was traditionally a closed world, dominated by the domestic ABN and Amro banks and the pension funds, but it was opened up by the liberalization measures of 1986. They led to the creation of a giant Postbank (a merger of the old government savings bank and the post office savings bank), which combined in 1989 with the NMB Bank, and the entry or expansion of operations by foreign banks. Liberalization was also introduced into the stock exchange system – the Amsterdam Stock Exchange, one of the oldest and largest in Europe, and the newer European Options Exchange, which deals in gold, silver, stock and currency.

Arriving

Although Amsterdam is an easy drive from Belgium, northern France and West Germany, most visitors fly to Schiphol. There are flights from all the European business capitals (several daily) and direct from many cities world wide. Train services run to Amsterdam from the major cities in Belgium and from Cologne, Munich, Hanover and Paris.

Amsterdam Schiphol airport
Over the last decade the Dutch airport authority and the state airline, KLM, have succeeded in turning Schiphol into one of the world's best and busiest airports. The modern, airy and spacious terminal has extensive shopping facilities, executive lounges with fax, telex and secretarial services operated by the major airlines, a post office, cafés and restaurants. The banks open daily, 7am–11pm, and hotel reservations can be made at the information desk. Domestic flights are operated by NLM City Hopper ☎ 17 09 31. Airport inquiries ☎ 601 09 66; for freight contact airlines.
Nearby hotels Barbizon Schiphol, Kruisweg 495, 2132 NA Hoofddorp

☎ (02503) 64422 ⊠ 74546 fax
(02503) 37966 • Golden Tulip •
AE DC MC V. This comfortable modern
hotel next to the airport is popular
with buyers attending the world's
largest daily flower and plant auction
at nearby Aalsmeer. Restaurants are
open very long hours to cater for
early and late arrivals, and the rooms
are large. Conference centre for up to
500, airport shuttle, fitness centre and
sauna. *Hilton International Schiphol*,
Herbergierstr, Schiphol Centrum,
1118 ZK ☎ 603 45 67 ⊠ 15186
fax 48 09 17 • AE DC MC V. Within the
airport complex and convenient for
the high-tech industrial estates of
southwest Amsterdam. Conference
facilities (with a/v equipment),
business centre (word processing,
translation and couriers), airport
shuttle, indoor pool and sauna.
City link The airport is 12kms/7.5
miles southwest of the city centre
with an excellent and rapid round-
the-clock train link.
Taxis There are always plenty of
taxis. The journey takes about
20mins, and the fare is about G30.
Car rental All the major firms have
offices in the arrivals area.
Train The station is below arrivals.
Trains to main Dutch cities leave
frequently from 5.25am to 0.15 and
hourly (to Centraal Station only,
journey time 20mins) through the
small hours; fare G4.40. The trains
are clean, punctual and comfortable.
Services connect with Amsterdam
Centraal, Amsterdam Zuid (South) in
the southern suburbs (for the Hilton)
and Amsterdam RAI for the
Congresgebouw conference centre and
the Okura Hotel. Train inquiries
☎ 601 05 41.

Railway station
Amsterdam Centraal, modernized in
1983, is used by commuters as well as
visitors and is very busy during the
8–9 and 5–6 rush hours. It is well
signposted and efficient, with a bank
(open 24hrs), post office (open
Mon–Fri, 8.30–9; Sat, 9–noon),
shops and a first-class restaurant.

Netherlands Railways (NV,
Nederlandse Spoorwegen) runs a
comfortable, swift and efficient
service to all the country's principal
towns. Opposite the station is the
head office of the Amsterdam tourist
board (VVV), which operates a hotel
reservations service. Many hotels are
only 5mins away by cab. The station
is well served by bus, tram and
metro. Railway inquiries ☎ 23 83 83.

Getting around
Because of parking restrictions and
the risk of damage and theft a car is a
disadvantage in central Amsterdam; it
is best to walk. For longer journeys
take a taxi. If you need to travel in
the suburbs a car would be useful.
Taxis will not stop if hailed in the
street, but wait at hotels, in main
streets and squares and near tourist
sights. Drivers usually speak English
and know their way around. A small
tip is expected. To order a cab
☎ 77 77 77.
Driving If you come into the city,
park at *Europarking*, in the northwest,
a short walk from the centre, at
Marnixstr 250 ☎ 23 66 94, which is
well-guarded. The highway
(*autosnelweg*) system linking
Amsterdam to the suburbs is well
developed but traffic congestion is
serious during the rush hours. *Avis*
☎ 83 60 61, *Budget* ☎ 12 60 66,
Europcar ☎ 83 21 23, *Hertz*
☎ 12 24 41, *InterRent* ☎ 73 04 77.
Walking The centre of Amsterdam is
compact and relatively free from
traffic; cyclists are the main problem.
Bus, subway and tram Amsterdam
has an integrated bus, tram and
metro system that may be useful for
excursions to the suburbs. Tickets
bought from bus and tram drivers
cost more than the multistrip tickets
(*strippenkaart*) purchased at
newsstands and tobacconists, post
offices and metro stations. These
must be punched at the start of a
journey. A *dagkaart* is valid for
unlimited travel for up to 3 days.
Most routes begin or end at Centraal
Station.

Area by area

The heart of Amsterdam is bordered by horse-shoe shaped waterways, the Grachtengordel, or canal girdle. At the north is the inlet known simply as the Ij (pronounced eye). On its north bank is the commercial port, linked to the sea by means of the 20km/12.5 mile North Sea Canal, which is still important and the principal European entry point for Japanese-made motor vehicles.

On the south bank Centraal Station forms the focal point of downtown Amsterdam. The broad Damrak runs from the station past the Art Deco stock exchange building to Dam square, dominated by the 17thC Koninklijk Paleis (Royal Palace), which also served as the City Hall until the new and controversial Stadhuis and Muziektheater on Waterlooplein was completed in the early 1980s.

The area east of Damrak is known as Oude Zijde (Old Side). It is the most ancient port of the city but rather shabby; the 13thC Oude Kerk (Old Church) is now in the heart of one of several red-light districts.

Nieuwe Zijde (New Side) is an area of late-19thC buildings and filled-in canals west of Damrak, but it backs onto the northwestern section of the canal ring, lined by warehouses, many of which have been converted into desirable apartments. Farther west again is the Jordaan district, criss-crossed by narrow lanes, once the working-class neighbourhood of Amsterdam, then in the 1960s and 1970s a centre of radicalism, artists and hippydom and now fast becoming fashionably residential.

Going farther south along the canal rings, the canal-side houses become grander. Many serve as offices for lawyers, architects and consultants. The stretch of Herengracht from Leidsestraat to Vijzelstraat, where the headquarters of the ABN Bank are located, is known as the "Golden Bend" because of the large number of insurance company offices in the palatial 18thC houses.

Farther around to the east at Utrechtsestraat there are the head offices of the Amro Bank at one end, in Rembrandtsplein, and De Nederlandsche Bank NV at the other, in Frederiksplein. Many major business premises lie in between.

The outermost canal, bordered by Mauritskade, Stadhouderskade and Nassaukade, marks a sharp division between the historic city and the 19thC suburbs. An important district is the museum quarter, which surrounds the three major art museums, and includes Vondelpark and the Concertgebouw concert hall. This is one of the city's most desirable residential districts, an area of gracious Art Deco apartments, cafés and restaurants of character and elegant shopping streets.

Equally prestigious is the adjoining district of Amsterdam Zuid (South), whose 1920s detached houses, in large gardens, are only for the very wealthy. They are being converted to offices, stimulated by the development of a business district around the World Trade Center (WTC) and RAI Congresgebouw (conference centre) on the city's southern limits.

Suburbs

The success of Schiphol airport has brought rapid growth to the southeastern suburbs, now the focus for high-technology manufacturing and businesses involved in freight and distribution. Lesser concentrations of industry are distributed all the way along the A4 highway and the railway lines that link Amsterdam to Schiphol and south to Rotterdam and The Hague.

The shortage of quality housing in Amsterdam itself means that many people commute, causing major traffic problems that even the completion of the new outer ring road has not relieved. Those who can afford it live in the wooded countryside as far east as Bussum and Hilversum, or west in Haarlem or Heemstede. The northern suburbs of Amsterdam are traditionally working-class.

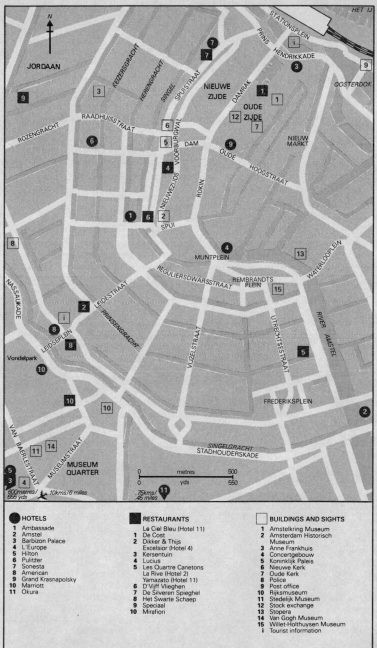

HET IJ

STATIONSPLEIN

JORDAAN

KEIZERSGRACHT

HERENGRACHT

SINGEL

SPUISTRAAT

NIEUWE ZIJDE

DAMRAK

PRINS HENDRIKKADE

OOSTERDOK

ROZENGRACHT

RAADHUISSTRAAT

NIEUWEZIJDS VOORBURGWAL

DAM

ROKIN

OUDE ZIJDE

OUDE HOOGSTRAAT

NIEUW MARKT

SPUI

MUNTPLEIN

REGULIERSDWARSSTRAAT

REMBRANDTS PLEIN

WATERLOOPLEIN

NASSAUKADE

LEIDESTRAAT

PRINSENGRACHT

LEIDSEPLEIN

Vondelpark

VIJZELSTRAAT

UTRECHTSESTRAAT

RIVER AMSTEL

FREDERIKSPLEIN

VAN BAERLESTRAAT

MUSEUMSTRAAT

MUSEUM QUARTER

SINGELGRACHT
STADHOUDERSKADE

| | metres | 500 |
| 0 | yds | 550 |

600metres/
655 yds

10kms/6 miles

.75kms/
.45 miles

HOTELS
1 Ambassade
2 Amstel
3 Barbizon Palace
4 L'Europe
5 Hilton
6 Pulitzer
7 Sonesta
8 American
9 Grand Krasnapolsky
10 Marriott
11 Okura

RESTAURANTS
Le Ciel Bleu (Hotel 11)
1 De Cost
2 Dikker & Thijs
   Excelsior (Hotel 4)
3 Kersentuin
4 Lucius
5 Les Quartre Canetons
   La Rive (Hotel 2)
   Yamazato (Hotel 11)
6 D'Vijff Vlieghen
7 De Silveren Spieghel
8 Het Swarte Schaep
9 Speciaal
10 Mirafiori

BUILDINGS AND SIGHTS
1 Amstelkring Museum
2 Amsterdam Historisch
   Museum
3 Anne Frankhuis
4 Concertgebouw
5 Koninklijk Paleis
6 Nieuwe Kerk
7 Oude Kerk
8 Police
9 Post office
10 Rijksmuseum
11 Stedelijk Museum
12 Stock exchange
13 Stopera
14 Van Gogh Museum
15 Willet-Holthuysen Museum
i Tourist information

Hotels

In Amsterdam the choice of a hotel depends on the area in which you want to stay. In the central historic area crossed by canals, which has the more distinctive restaurants, bars and shops, the best hotels are the prestigious L'Europe, the modern Pulitzer or the well-equipped Sonesta. For better access to the RAI Congresgebouw, the World Trade Center and the city's offices and factories, many of which are in the southern suburbs, it may be more convenient to choose the modern out-of-town Hilton or the Okura.

The standard of the main hotels is uniformly high. All provide currency exchange and 24hr room service, and rooms have IDD telephones, TVs with a choice of cable channels and in-house movies and minibars. Parking is not generally available. In summer it is advisable to reserve rooms several weeks ahead. There are scores of clean, comfortable and inexpensive hotels in the museum quarter and near Centraal Station, but the latter is a dubious night-time area, and because of drugs-related crime many small hotels lock their doors at night. Reservations can be made at the airport information desk, or at the tourist office opposite the station.

Ambassade *G//*
Herengracht 341, 1016 AZ ☎ *26 23 33*
Ⓣ *10158 fax 24 53 21* • *AE DC MC V*
• *42 rooms, 5 suites*
This small and charming hotel occupies a row of 17thC houses along the Herengracht (gentleman's canal) close to the financial district. Sensitive conversion has ensured that it retains much of its original character, including staircases of ladder-like steepness (like so many of the older hotels) but also spacious, beamed rooms with tall multipaned windows. The public rooms are furnished with antiques, the atmosphere is relaxed and the staff are friendly. Many of the guests are regulars, and reservations should be made well in advance. No restaurant. Gift shop • 2 meeting rooms (capacity up to 15).

Amstel *G////*
Prof. Tulpplein 1, 1018 GX
☎ *22 60 60* Ⓣ *11004 fax 22 58 08* •
InterContinental • *AE DC MC V* •
92 rooms, 19 suites, 2 restaurants,
1 bar
Opened in 1867, the Amstel is the *grande dame* of Amsterdam hotels, a palace set in riverside gardens on the edge of the Old Town and used by the Dutch royal family for state receptions. The same building houses the Amsterdamse Club, whose members include all the city's most important financiers and industrialists. The entrance hall has a sweeping staircase, under a vaulted ceiling, which leads up to a balustraded balcony, and the best of the bedrooms are equally splendid, with velvet drapes framing the views of canals, trees and red brick, panelled walls and reproduction furniture, including a large desk. Service is friendly and faultless. Parking, newsstand, gift shops • 7 meeting rooms (capacity up to 200).

Barbizon Palace *G////*
Prins Hendrikkade 5972, 1012 AD
☎ *556 45 64* Ⓣ *10187 fax 24 33 53*
• *Golden Tulip* • *AE DC MC V* •
265 rooms, 3 suites, 2 restaurants,
3 bars
Opened in May 1988, the Barbizon Palace is opposite Centraal Station; visitors from out of town find it convenient for informal meetings. The exterior incorporates the façades of 19 old buildings, and the interior is a striking neo-classical creation of

imitation marble pillars and white walls, used to hang Dutch masters on loan from city museums. Innovations include a private guest-only lounge and the Henry Hudson Club, which has a library, open fireplace and butler service. Old beams and materials salvaged from demolished houses have been used to give character to the bedrooms, and the distinctively decorated restaurants frequently play host to guest chefs offering cuisines as different as Chinese and classical Burgundian. Valet parking, nonsmoking rooms, apartments, shops, hairdresser • fitness centre, sauna, massage • secretarial, word processing and translation services, 13 meeting rooms (capacity up to 200).

L'Europe G////
Nieuwe Doelenstr 2–8, 1012 CP
☎ *23 48 36* ⊤ⅹ *12081 fax 24 29 62* •
AE DC MC V • *102 rooms, 12 suites,*
2 restaurants, 1 bar
The Hotel de l'Europe was built in the grand style in the 19th century on the site of a medieval bastion and at the junction of several canals so that it is surrounded almost entirely by water. This setting can be viewed from the spacious rooms, many of which have balconies, and from the opulent, Empire-style dining rooms. Exclusive and prestigious, the hotel offers much of the same elegance and ambience as the Amstel, but in a more central location, and it has a new wing containing the city's only hotel swimming pool. Parking, gift shop • pool, sauna, fitness centre • secretarial and word processing facilities, 6 meeting rooms (capacity up to 200).

Hilton G////
Apollolaan 138–140, 1077 BG
☎ *78 07 80* ⊤ⅹ *11025 fax 662 66 88* •
AE DC MC V • *258 rooms, 16 suites,*
2 restaurants, 1 bar
The best of the out-of-town hotels, the Hilton is a large, modern, high-rise building in the southern suburbs, close to the RAI Congresgebouw and

World Trade Center. It is primarily for business travellers. To compensate for its suburban location the hotel incorporates a lively discotheque and a casino. Next door, in the Garden Hotel, is the Kersentuin (see *Restaurants*), which serves some of the best food in the city. Parking, shopping arcade • business centre with courier and secretarial services, offices and 10 meeting rooms (capacity up to 600).

Pulitzer G////
Prinsengracht 315–331, 1016 GZ
☎ *22 83 33* ⊤ⅹ *16508 fax 27 67 53*
• *Golden Tulip* • *AE DC MC V* •
234 rooms, 7 suites, 2 restaurants,
1 bar
Over 20 merchants' houses and warehouses, most dating from the 17th century, the Golden Age of Dutch architecture, have been combined to create this distinctive hotel in which every room is different; some face Prinsengracht or Keizersracht, two of the city's most peaceful canals; others the quiet and rambling courtyards and gardens in between. Once owned by newspaper proprietor Joseph Pulitzer, the hotel is an active sponsor of the arts, hosting exhibitions of painting and sculpture in its own art gallery, as well as concerts in the gardens and a music festival in August, when barges are used to create a floating stage in front of the hotel. All this makes it popular with tourists as well as business travellers. Parking, nonsmoking rooms, apartments, gift shop • secretarial and word processing services, 7 meeting rooms (capacity up to 150).

Sonesta G////
Kattengat 1, 1012 SZ ☎ *21 22 23*
⊤ⅹ *17149 fax 27 52 45* • *AE DC MC V*
• *425 rooms, 10 suites, 1 restaurant,*
1 bar
The port and railway station are nearby, but the Sonesta faces a quiet back street and gives the impression of being much smaller than it is, thanks to sensitive modern design;

public areas are divided into smaller spaces, suitable for meetings, and enlivened by a large collection of paintings and sculptures. Some of the rooms, also decorated with modern art, have garden terraces and views across gabled rooftops. The 17thC Koepelzaal, or round church, opposite, with its magnificent baroque organ and to which the hotel is linked by a passage, has been converted into a conference centre capable of seating 500 and equipped with the latest a/v technology; it is also used for concerts every Sunday. The Sonesta has the best fitness centre in the city (open to nonresidents), with a gym, sauna, trainers and training classes. Rooftop parking, nonsmoking rooms, hairdresser, shops, disco • secretarial and word processing services, 10 meeting rooms (capacity up to 500).

OTHER HOTELS
American G/// *Leidsekade 97, 1017 PN* ☎ *24 53 22* ⊠ *12545 fax 25 32 36* • *AE DC MC V.* A splendid Art Deco hotel. Much of its character has been spoiled by modernization, but the Café Americain retains its Tiffany lamps and glowing stained glass, and the Nightwatch bar is a popular late-night rendezvous. Limited parking.

Grand Krasnapolsky G/// *Dam 9, 1012 JS* ☎ *554 91 11* ⊠ *12262 fax 22 86 07* • *Golden Tulip* • *AE DC MC V.* A quiet, stately, old-world hotel well protected from the bustle of the city's main square. Behind is a series of gardens, and a glass-roofed 19thC Winter Garden is being converted for conferences.
Marriott G/// *Stadhouderskade 19–21, 1054 ES* ☎ *83 51 51* ⊠ *15087 fax 83 38 34* • *AE DC MC V.* Busy, mainly tourist hotel, very close to the city's nightlife. Spacious, well-furnished rooms; efficient service. Parking.
Okura G/// *Ferdinand Bolstr 333, 1072 LH* ☎ *78 71 11* ⊠ *16182 fax 71 23 44* • *AE DC MC V.* A suburban tower-block with swift access to highways and high-tech industrial development, good parking and popular conference facilities. Excellent Japanese restaurants and the highly regarded Ciel Bleu (see *Restaurants*).

Hotel and restaurant price guide
For the meanings of the hotel and restaurant price symbols, see pages 6 and 7.

Restaurants

In recent years the standard of cooking in Amsterdam's restaurants has risen. Lunch generally is not an elaborate meal, and most business entertaining is done in the evening. The most suitable places for high-level entertaining are the Kersentuin or La Rive; everywhere advance reservations are essential.

Le Ciel Bleu G/
Okura Hotel ☎ *78 71 11* • *D only* • *AE DC MC V* • *jacket and tie*
The view from the Okura Hotel's top-floor restaurant over old and new Amsterdam is superb especially in the evening. Polished service and attractive *nouvelle cuisine* appeal to executives from the southern suburbs. Excellent seven-course *menu prestige*, and special *flambé* dishes. Private rooms available.

De Cost G///
Oude Brugsteeg 16 ☎ *24 70 50* • *closed Sat L, Sun* • *AE DC MC V*
The name of this 17thC harbour-side restaurant comes from the proverb starting "De Cost..." (Nothing ventured...), which is written in letters several feet high around the eaves. It is an appropriate motto, for the stock exchange is next door. Excellent French-influenced Dutch cuisine, such as wild duck, salmon

and pheasant with *sauerkraut*, bacon and sausage. Private room available.

Dikker & Thijs G/
Prinsengracht 444 ☎ *26 77 21* • *closed Sat L, Sun* • AE DC MC V
Founded by and named after a grocer and a chef who trained under Escoffier, this restaurant and the delicatessen on the entrance floor have been part of the Amsterdam restaurant scene since 1915, and both are patronized by leading members of the establishment. The cooking is in the classical French tradition. The menu is brief, the wine list expansive.

Excelsior G//
Hôtel de L'Europe ☎ *23 48 36* • *closed Sat L* • AE DC MC V • *jacket and tie*
Recently refurbished, the elegant mirrored and chandeliered Excelsior offers panoramic views from its large windows over the River Amstel. Regulars include members of the business community, and the service is friendly and discreet. The cuisine is French, with an emphasis on seafood and game.

Kersentuin G/
Garden Hotel, Dijsselhofplantsoen 7 ☎ *664 21 21* • *closed Sat L, Sun* • AE DC MC V
Chef Jon Sistermans has made the Kersentuin one of the most prestigious eating places in Holland. It is in the Oudzuid district, surrounded by gardens and beamed buildings now converted into offices for lawyers, architects and consultants. The decor has hints of Japan, but the cooking is French; even the ingredients, the langoustines, pintade, duck, lamb and kid are imported, and the wine list is probably the best in Amsterdam.

Lucius G
Spuistr 247 ☎ *24 18 31* • AE DC MC V
Deliberately frugal, this is nevertheless Amsterdam's best fish restaurant and attracts even senior business executives. The wooden beams and blue and white tiles are redolent of old Amsterdam, and the menu is written on blackboards. Service is attentive and the seafood excellent.

Les Quatre Canetons G/
Prinsengracht 1111 ☎ *24 63 07* • *closed Sat L, Sun* • AE DC MC V
Bankers and consulate staff are among the regulars of this restaurant run by chef/owner Wynand Vogel, who has received many plaudits since it opened in a converted warehouse in 1968. The name is a pun: Vogel specializes in duck but in Dutch "four ducks" sounds like "four ones," the address of the premises.

La Rive G/
Amstel Hotel ☎ *22 60 60* • *closed Sat L, Sun* • AE DC MC V • *jacket and tie*
When privacy and ambience are paramount La Rive is a sound choice. Leading members of the Amsterdam business community make it their exclusive retreat. Alcove tables and walls lined with wood-panelling and books contribute to its air of distinction. In summer the restaurant opens out onto the hotel's riverside garden terrace. At lunch time the seasonal menu changes daily and in the evening concentrates on hearty classical French dishes.

Yamazato G
Okura Hotel ☎ *78 71 11* • AE DC MC V
As elsewhere in the West, Japanese food is in vogue in Amsterdam. The chefs at Yamazato perform with flair, and the ingredients are said to be flown in daily from Japan. The reasonably priced business lunch is popular, and if this restaurant is full the hotel's Teppan Yaki Steakhouse is an acceptable alternative.

OTHER RESTAURANTS
Three of Amsterdam's best known restaurants are tourist haunts, but they are perfectly acceptable for informal dining. *D'Vijff Vlieghen* (Five Flies), Spuistr 294 ☎ 24 83 69

(D only), which is owned by the Grand Hotel Krasnapolsky, occupies several gabled 17thC houses with numerous small wood-panelled rooms. Similar in style is *De Silveren Spieghel*, Kattengat 4 ☎ 24 65 89, a traditional restaurant with small rooms off a labyrinth of blue-tiled passageways, serving fish and game with *nouvelle* influences. *Het Swarte Schaep* (The Black Sheep), Korte Leidsedwarsstr 24 ☎ 22 30 21, alone among the fast-food takeaways maintains high culinary standards on Amsterdam's busiest square. Reasonably priced Dutch food is served in heavily beamed rooms; excellent for late-night dining.

Speciaal, Nieuwe Leliestr 142 ☎ 24 97 06 (D only), is one of the best of the many Indonesian restaurants for the range and authenticity of its *rijsttafel* (a large variety of spicy side dishes served with rice). It is a welcoming family-run restaurant, unsophisticated and inexpensive, and one of the few that still grills its *saté* over charcoal.

Mirafiori, at Hobbemastr 2 ☎ 662 30 13, is an old-established Italian restaurant close to the banking district and popular for informal business lunches.

Out of town
For important out-of-town entertaining, Amsterdammers head for one of two restaurants. Closer to the centre, in the southern suburb of Amstelveen, is *Molen de Dikkert*, Amsterdamseweg 104A ☎ 41 13 78, in a 17thC mill where the cuisine combines the classic French and Dutch traditions. North of Utrecht, and some 35kms/22 miles south of Amsterdam, at Bosch en Duin, is *De Hoefslag*, Vossenlaan 28 ☎ (030) 28 43 95, run by the Fagel brothers, Martin and Gerard. Their light and refined style of cooking has made this, in the opinion of many, the Netherlands' top restaurant.

Bars
The best and most elegant international-style bars are *Le Bar* at the Hôtel de l'Europe and the *Amstel Bar*, a delightful terrace, with piano music, overlooking the river at the Amstel Hotel.

For authentic Amsterdam life you should visit one of the city's numerous, cheerful and often crowded "brown cafés," so called because, by tradition, wood predominates: bare floorboards, panelled walls and old tables and chairs. Here Amsterdammers meet friends, play chess, read newspapers or eat snacks over coffee, or beer and *jenever*, Dutch gin served neat either *oude* (old and mellow) or *jonge* (young) or flavoured with lemon, berries or spices. One of the most interesting is *De Frie Fleschjes* (The Three Flasks) in Gravenstraat 16, an ancient establishment where many a local company has casks of old brandy or gin marked for its private use. Others to try are *Eijlders*, Korte Leidsedwarsstr 47, once a well-known haunt for artists and still used for exhibitions of contemporary painting, and *Hooghoudt Proeflokaal*, Reguliersgracht 11, a cask-lined cellar popular with bankers. For a quiet and comfortable atmosphere, try a so-called "sitting room" bar in the museum quarter of the city.

Entertainment
Amsterdammers have a reputation for a radicalism that is displayed in their support for the contemporary arts. Stockhausen and Schoenberg are more frequently performed than Mozart, and a very full arts calendar is dominated by the modern and experimental. *Amsterdam This Week* details events. *Amsterdams Uitburo* (*AUB*) ticket agency, Leidseplein 26 ☎ 21 12 11.

Music The *Concertgebouw*, Van Baerlestr 98 ☎ 71 83 45, was recently restored, and the resident orchestra is well known for its classical repertoire. Tickets are much in demand, and the audience tends to dress formally.

Theatre, dance and opera The new *Stopera*, Amstel 3 ☎ 25 54 55, caused headline news in the late 1970s when violent demonstrations took place against housing shortages and the destruction of the former Jewish ghetto on whose site the complex was built. Now it houses the Muziektheater, the National Ballet and Netherlands Opera.

The atmospheric 19thC *Theater Carré*, Amstel 115 ☎ 22 52 52, close to the Amstel Hotel, is the main venue for drama, usually in Dutch, but touring ballet and theatre companies also perform here.

Cinema Films are shown in the original languages, with subtitles. Several cinemas have superb Art Deco interiors, such as *Tuschinski*, Reguliersbreestr 26 ☎ 26 26 33, which shows all the latest releases. Mainstream films are also shown at the *Cineac*, Reguliersbreestr 31 ☎ 24 36 39, and the *City*, Klein Gartmanplantsoen 13 ☎ 23 47 79. The *Kriterion*, Roetersstr 170 ☎ 23 17 08, shows art movies.

Nightclubs and casinos In the main red-light area, east of the Damrak, there are sex clubs, films and shops catering to a variety of tastes. Discos, nightclubs and live shows are near Leidseplein and Rembrandtsplein.

The Hilton Hotel has the monopoly on upmarket nightlife, with its *Juliana's* discotheque ☎ 73 73 13 and *Casino Amsterdam* ☎ 664 99 11. Jazz is popular, and in BIM *Huis*, Oudeschans 7377 ☎ 23 33 73, you can hear modern styles. Survivors of fast-moving trends include the suave and elite *Club la Mer*, Korte Leidsedwarsstr 73 ☎ 24 29 10, and the more avant-garde *Mazzo*, Rozengracht 114 ☎ 26 75 00.

Shopping

Shopping hours are Mon, 1–6; Tue–Fri, 9–6 (Thu to 8.30); Sat, 9–5. If you simply want to browse, wander along any of the streets running out of the city centre that link the four main canals. Here are small shops selling everything from antiques to ethnic art, posters and postcards to original paintings and sculpture.

The principal shopping streets are Kalverstraat (traffic-free, and rather touristy) and Nieuwendijk, parallel to Rokin and Damrak, and Heiligeweg and Leidsestraat. The most upmarket district lies just north of the museum quarter: Van Baerlestraat and P. C. Hooftstraat are centres for couturiers, chic boutiques, art galleries and interior design stores.

Antiques are mainly concentrated in Spiegelgracht and Nieuwe Spiegelstraat near the Rijksmuseum, where good buys include clocks, scientific instruments, tiles and Arts Nouveau and Deco lamps and ornaments.

Books *Athenaeum Boekhandel*, Spui 14–16, has an Art Nouveau interior and a large stock of foreign-language books.

Cheese *Wout Arhoek*, Damstraat 23, has the biggest range.

Delftware *Flocke & Meltzer*, P. C. Hooftstr 65–67, or Kalverstr 76, sells Delftware and Dutch porcelain.

Department stores *De Bijenkorf*, Damrak 90A, is a trend-setting department store; those with more conservative tastes go to the elegant *Maison de Bonneterie*, Kalverstr 183 and Beethovenstr 32, or *Metz*, Keizersgracht 455, renowned as a champion of modern design.

Diamonds The diamond trade was introduced to Amsterdam in the 16th century. Many outlets demonstrate diamond cutting and polishing and sell loose diamonds and finished jewellery, including the *Amsterdam Diamond Center*, Rokin 15, and the upper-crust *Coster*, Paulus Potterstr 24. *Hans Appenzeller*, a leading jeweller, is at Grimburgwal 15.

Markets Of the city's markets the best are for flowers along the Singel, west of Muntplein, the flea-market on Waterlooplein and the book market opposite the University.

Sightseeing

Amsterdam is a delight for its varied, brick architecture, traditional wooden bridges over slow-flowing canals, trees and small specialized shops. The most

stately houses are along Herengracht.
Amstelkring Museum A 17thC house
of the Golden Age of Dutch
architecture, just like an Old Master
painting; contains a secret attic
church dating from 1581. *Oudezijds
Voorburgwal 40. Open Mon–Sat, 10–5;
Sun, 1–5.*
Amsterdam Historisch Museum The
origins and development of the city
from a fishing village and marsh to
empire and prosperous port.
Kalverstr 92. Open daily, 11–5.
Anne Frankhuis preserves the room
in which the 14-year-old Jewish girl
hid and kept her diary for 25 months
before she and her family were sent
to Bergen-Belsen concentration camp,
where she died. *Prinsengracht 263.
Open Mon–Sat, 9–5; Sun, 10–5.*
Rijksmuseum The huge national
museum embraces painting,
sculpture, glass, textiles, porcelain
and furniture from the 15th to late
19th centuries. Highlights include
Rembrandt's *The Night Watch*, works
by Vermeer, Frans Hals and Jacob
van Ruysdael. *Stadhouderskade 42.
Open Tue–Sat, 10–5; Sun 1–5.*
Stedelijk Museum Modern art,
including works by the De Stijl (The
Style), founded 1917, and the postwar
COBRA group. *Paulus Polterstr 13.
Open daily, 11–5.*
Tropenmuseum Anthropological
museum enlivened by reconstructed
streets (with authentic sounds and
smells) from different regions of the
developing world. *Linnaeusstr 2. Open
Mon–Fri, 10–5; Sat & Sun 12–5.*
Van Gogh Museum One of the city's
top attractions; expect to wait at the
entrance during the summer. A small
selection of the vast collection is
displayed chronologically, with
biographical notes. *Paulus Polterstr 7.
Open Tue–Sat, 10–5; Sun, 1–5.*
Willet-Holthuysen Museum Two
gracious 18thC residences, with
contemporary furnishings, family
portraits and formal garden.
*Herengracht 605. Open Tue–Sat, 10–5;
Sun, 1–5.*
Guided tours *Holland International*
☎ 22 77 88, bookable through hotels,

run tours of Amsterdam by
motorlaunch or day-long coach trips
taking in Delft, Edam, The Hague or
the dyke enclosing the Ijsselmeer.

Spectator sports
Soccer Ajax is one of the top
European clubs. Tickets for games at
the *Ajaxstadion*, Middenweg 401, in
the east suburbs, are available at
hotels, agents (try Cruyff, Leidsestr
75 ☎ 22 88 82) or at the gate.

Keeping fit
Fitness centres *Splash*, at the Sonesta
Hotel ☎ 27 10 44 and at
Looiersgracht 26–30 ☎ 24 84 04, is
open to nonmembers.
Golf For information on courses open
to nonmembers contact *The Dutch
Golf Federation*, Soestdijkerstraatweg
172, Hilversum ☎ (35) 83 05 65.
Swimming *Zuiderbad*, Hobbemastr
26 ☎ 79 22 17, or the recently
renovated *De Mirandabad*, De
Mirandalaan, near the Amstel and not
far from RAI, with a nice old café.
Tennis *De Tennispool* ☎ 91 16 07 for
information.

Local resources
Business services
All the hotels listed have or can
arrange business support services.
Euro Business Center, Keizersgracht
62 ☎ 26 57 49, provides copying,
word processing, a telephone
message service and meeting rooms
or offices.
Photocopying and printing Post
offices and many small shops have
photocopying machines. For bigger
jobs try *Printerette*, Spuistr 128
☎ 662 70 66, or *Multicopy*,
Weesperstr 65 ☎ 24 62 08.
Secretarial *Manpower* ☎ 662 56 26
and *Randstad Uitzendbureau*
☎ 662 80 11 are at the World Trade
Center.
Translation Specialists in particular
languages and technical, legal or
commercial translation are in the
Yellow Pages under *Vertaalbureaux*.
Vertaal Buro Regeer is a leading allround firm ☎ 664 03 59.

Communications
Local delivery Holland Koeriers
☎ 92 40 45; *Abacus* ☎ 48 42 36.
Long-distance delivery DHL
☎ (06) 05 52 (toll free); *Federal
Express* ☎ 43 73 87; XP *Express
Parcels System* ☎ 91 23 46.
Post office Main post office:
Nieuwezijds Voorburgwal 182
☎ 555 89 11, open Mon–Fri, 8.30–6;
Sat, 9–12, and Oosterdokskade, by
the station, open until 9pm.
Telex and fax at the *Telehouse*,
Raadhuisstr 46–50 ☎ 74 36 54, open
24hrs.

Conference/exhibition centres
All the principal trade fairs and
conferences are held at the *Amsterdam
RAI Congresgebouw*, Europaplein
☎ 549 12 12, in the southern suburbs
and served by its own railway station,
9kms/5 miles from Amsterdam
Centraal Station. Other venues
include the nearby *World Trade
Center*, Strawinskylaan 1 ☎ 575 91 11,
as well as the *Hilton, Amstel* and
Sonesta Hotels. Many of the country's
most important trade fairs are held at
Utrecht, 35kms/22 miles south of
Amsterdam, at the *Koninklijke
Nederlandse Jaarbeurs* (Royal
Netherlands Industries Fair),
Jaarbeursplein, 3521 AL, Utrecht
☎ (30) 95 59 11.

Emergencies
Bureaux de change Banks normally
open Mon–Fri, 9–4. The *GWK Bank*
at Centraal Station is open 24hrs and
gives good rates.
Hospitals Emergencies (24hrs) for
doctors and dentists ☎ 664 21 11.
The main hospital is in the southeast,
Academisch Medisch Centrum,
Meibergdreef 9 ☎ 56 69 111. The
dental practice, AOC, at WG-Plein is
open daily, 6am–2am.
Pharmacies are open late and at
weekends on a rota. Details are
available from any pharmacy
or ☎ 94 87 09.
Police (*Politie*) Emergency ☎ 22 22
22. Headquarters: Elandsgracht 117
☎ 559 91 11. There is a lost property

office at Waterlooplein 11
☎ 559 80 05.

Government offices
Local government information can be
obtained from the City Hall,
Stadhuis, Oudezijds Voorburgwall
☎ 552 91 11.

Information sources
*Business information Kamer van
Koophandel* (Chamber of commerce)
is at Kon. Wilhelminaplein 13
☎ 17 28 82. Useful places to start are
the *Amsterdam Trade Information
Center*, Strawinskylaan 5 ☎ 57 53
140, the information office at the
Amsterdam City Hall, the Stadhuis, at
Oudezijds Voorburgwall 197 ☎ 552
91 11, and the *Holland Industrial
Expo*, World Trade Center,
Strawinskylaan 1–5 ☎ 54 53 368.
Local media Dutch-language papers
with local and national business
coverage are *Het Financieele Dagblad*,
NRC *Handelsblad* and *De Telegraaf*. A
leading daily paper is *de Volkskrant*.
Foreign newspapers are on sale the
day of publication in hotels and on
newsstands, and most hotels receive
British programmes and satellite news
from the USA.   ·
Tourist information The main VVV
(tourist office), opposite Centraal
Station, Stationspl 10 ☎ 26 64 44, is
open Mon–Fri, 9–6; Sat, 9–7; Sun,
10–1, 2–5; telephone service Mon–
Sat, 9–5. The VVV at Leidsestr 106 is
smaller and open shorter hours.

Thank-yous
Chocolates Berkhoff, Leidsestr 46
☎ 24 02 33, for homemade patisserie
and confectionery, or *Holtkamp*,
Vijzelgracht 15 ☎ 24 87 57.
Florists Flowershop Ivy, Leidseplein
33 ☎ 23 65 61; *De Roos* ☎ 16 86 85;
both accept credit cards.
Food and wine Dikker & Thijs,
Prinsengracht 444 ☎ 26 77 21, will
make up up attractive wine and food
hampers. *Hart's Wijnhandel*,
Vijzelgracht 27 ☎ 23 83 50, stocks a
good range of French wines and
Dutch liqueurs.

THE HAGUE (Den Haag)
City code ☎ 0703

The Hague is the administrative capital of the Netherlands, the seat of government and of the Permanent Court of Arbitration and the International Court of Justice. Populated by ministers, civil servants, lawyers and diplomats, it is peaceful, unhurried and civilized. It includes leafy, desirable suburbs and unspoiled coastal resorts. Several leading companies are based nearby, including Nutricia, Holland's biggest dairy company, and Heineken now at Zoeterwoude, 8kms/5 miles northeast.

Delft, 15mins by road, is charming and a base for vegetable oil and margarine processing, porcelain production and optical technology.

Arriving

Overseas visitors usually reach The Hague via Amsterdam's Schiphol airport, a journey by train, taxi or car which takes under an hour. The excellent highway and rail systems connect with other cities of the Netherlands, northern France, Belgium and West Germany.

Amsterdam Schiphol airport (see *Amsterdam*)
City link The Hague is 48kms/30 miles southeast of Schiphol. The rail link is fast and inexpensive. Airport information ☎ (20) 601 09 66.
Taxi The rank in front of the terminal always has plenty of cabs. Hague-based drivers offer a fixed-price fare of around G100.
Car rental All major rental firms have desks in the arrivals hall.
Train Trains run from below the terminal at 15min intervals from 6.30am to midnight and hourly during the night (fare G9.40, journey time 45mins). There are two stations: the Hague CS (Centraal) and The Hague HS (Hollands Spoor) in the southern suburbs, from which there are frequent services to The Hague CS.

Railway stations
The Hague CS is near the town centre, a big modern station with a KLM check-in, bank, post office (open Mon–Fri, 8.30–5.30; Sat, 9–noon). The Babylon shopping centre, and a tourist information and hotel reservations office, are alongside.
The Hague HS is served by trains from Amsterdam, Rotterdam and

Utrecht, Belgium and France to the south and West Germany to the east. Train inquiries (both stations) ☎ (06) 899 11 21 (toll free).

Getting around

Streets get congested, particularly at rush hours, and walking is a practical way to get around. Journeys outside the city require a taxi or car.
Taxis wait at squares and principal streets; they do not stop if hailed. A tip of small change is expected. For journeys at night or to the suburbs ☎ 90 77 22.
Driving The town centre has extensive all-day traffic-free zones and one-way systems. *Avis* ☎ 95 06 98, *Budget* ☎ 82 06 09, *Europcar* ☎ 85 17 08, *Hertz* ☎ 46 95 15.
Bus and tram Most trams and buses pass or depart from one of the two main railway stations; maps and tickets at most tobacconists, newsstands and post offices.

Area by area

The Hague has a downtown area of little more than 1km/0.6 miles across. At the centre is the Hof Vijver, a small lake, dismissed by some as a "village pond," and by it the Binnenhof (including Parliament and ministerial offices). To the west is the traffic-free shopping district and to the east the Haagse Bos, an extensive parkland stretching to the city limits within which is the Huis Ten Bosch or Koninklijk Paleis (Royal Palace). Beyond lies desirable, residential Wassenaar.
 The southern edge of the centre is

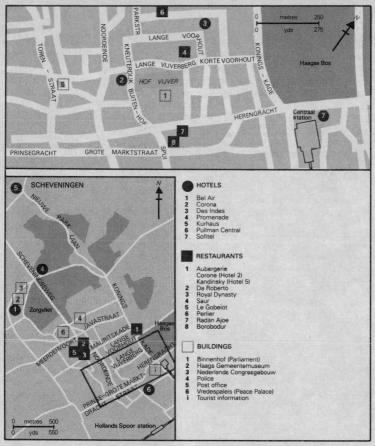

Prinsegracht/Grote Marktstraat.
Beyond this avenue is the poorest
part of the city and the red-light
district; it is being improved, and the
area between Spui and Centraal
Station now has new hotels, an arts
complex, offices and the Babylon
shopping centre. Farther south much
new industrial development and
construction is in progress along the
A12 highway to Utrecht.

The northern section of the city,
with its parks and tree-lined avenues,
is most appealing. The elegant 18thC
and 19thC houses of Lange
Vijverberg and Lange Voorhout are
occupied by publishers, lawyers, PR
and advertising consultants, as well as
by embassies. Beyond Mauritskade lie
19thC residential suburbs, the
Vredespaleis (Peace Palace), home of
the International Court of Justice and
the Congresgebouw conference
centre.

From here the 2km/1.3 mile-long
Scheveningseweg leads to the beach at
Scheveningen, a fishing village until
the 19th century when the stylish
Kurhaus Hotel and pier made it
fashionable; its elegance is now
diminished by modern housing and
theme parks. The small resort of
Kijkduin, 2kms/1.3 miles farther
west, is much more exclusive.

Hotels

The Hague has two hotels with character, Des Indes and the Corona, both quite small and in demand. Otherwise there are several efficient, modern hotels out of the centre. Prices are much lower in small establishments. All hotels listed offer parking, currency exchange, 24hr room service, and rooms have IDD telephones, TV and minibars.

Bel Air *G*//
Johan de Wittlaan 30, 2517 JR
☎ *50 20 21* TX *31444 fax 51 26 82 •*
AE DC MC V • 342 rooms, 8 suites,
2 restaurants, 2 bars
Beside the Nederlands Congresgebouw, this is a popular choice for anyone attending exhibitions and trade fairs. Rooms are pleasant and comfortable, with views over the Zorgvliet park. Shops, hairdresser • pool • 7 meeting rooms (capacity up to 200).

Corona *G*//
Buitenhof 39–42, 2513 AH ☎ *63 79 30*
TX *31418 fax 61 57 85 • AE DC MC V*
• 26 rooms, 2 restaurants, 1 bar
The small Corona looks onto a quiet and historic square. Its large rooms are tranquil, in pastel shades, and have reproduction antique furniture. The service is personal and friendly. Guests of the ministries, embassies and offices nearby find it welcoming. The hotel's restaurant is a favourite for business entertaining (see *Restaurants*). 3 meeting rooms with a/v equipment (capacity up to 100).

Des Indes *G*///
Lange Voorhout 54–56, 2514 EG
☎ *63 29 32* TX *31196 fax 45 17 21 •*
AE DC MC V • 75 rooms, 5 suites, 1 restaurant, 1 bar
Little has changed since this former palace, built in the 1850s, was converted into a hotel. The rooms are vast and furnished with reproduction antiques, and the marbled bathrooms are splendid. The Imperial Suite (expensive), includes an office with fax machine and photocopier and a meeting room with a/v equipment. The centrepiece of the hotel is the lounge, where diplomats and their visitors take tea amid the marbled

splendour. 7 meeting rooms (capacity up to 150).

Promenade *G*//
Van Stolkweg 1, 2585 JL ☎ *52 51 61*
TX *31162 fax 54 10 46 • Best Western*
• AE DC MC V • 97 rooms, 4 suites, 3 restaurants, 2 bars
Midway between the city centre (5mins by taxi) and the Strandweg at Scheveningen, the modern Promenade is surrounded by parks and woodland. The bar and bistro restaurant spill outside in summer. Popular with business travellers because of efficient service and choice of good restaurants, including the excellent La Cigogne. Shops, hairdresser • 5 meeting rooms (capacity up to 225).

OTHER HOTELS
Kurhaus *G*/// *Gevers*
Deynootplein 30, 2586 CK,
Scheveningen ☎ *52 00 52* TX *33295*
fax 50 09 11 • AE DC MC V. A splendid seafront hotel at Scheveningen where you can eat some of the city's best cooking in the Kandinsky (see *Restaurants*). For business guests who don't mind families and tourists.
Pullman Central *G*// *Spui 180,*
2511 BW ☎ *61 49 21* TX *32000*
fax 63 93 98 • AE DC MC V. In the new, large office and arts centre complex, with expanses of glass and concrete, but equipped with business suites, a fitness centre and several good restaurants, including the smart Japanese Shirasagi.
Sofitel *G*// *Koningin Julianaplein*
35, 2595 AA ☎ *81 49 01* TX *34001*
fax 82 59 27 • AE DC MC V. Another new hotel next to Centraal Station. Special business rooms and facilities for meetings.

Restaurants

French cooking and seafood predominate. For important entertaining the Corona or Kandinsky are best; for charm go to the Sauer. Most of the restaurants listed are small; reservations are advisable.

Aubergerie *G/*
Nieuwe Schoolstr 19 ☎ *64 80 70* •
D only, closed Tue • *AE DC MC V*
An attractively decorated restaurant next to the Theatre Pepyn. Theatregoers and business people come here for huge plates of *fruits de mer*, oysters and steaks of wild hare.

Corona *G/*
Corona Hotel ☎ *63 79 30* • *AE DC MC V*
Chef Robert Kranenborg is responsible for the Corona's reputation, which extends well beyond the capital. Elegant and sophisticated and with polished service, it attracts diplomats and the business community. French cooking and superb seafood.

Kandinsky *G/////*
Kurhaus Hotel ☎ *54 64 36* • *AE DC MC V*
The Kandinsky is one of The Hague's top restaurants for smart social, diplomatic and business occasions for its sea views and tranquil setting. Kandinsky's paintings decorate the walls; they complement the *nouvelle cuisine*, which is largely fish-based.

Da Roberto *G/*
Noordeinde 196 ☎ *46 49 77* • *closed Sat, Sun, Tue* • *AE DC MC V*
Roberto de Luca is an advocate of Italian *cucina nuova* and his very brief menu of highly original dishes based on homemade pasta has won a loyal local following.

Royal Dynasty *G*
Noordeinde 123 ☎ *65 25 98* • *closed Mon* • *AE DC MC V*
Parasols, potted palms and Chinese ceramics give this smart restaurant an oriental ambience, and it combines the culinary traditions of Thailand, Indonesia and Canton.

Saur *G/*
Lange Voorhout 51 ☎ *46 33 44* •
AE DC MC V
Saur is famous beyond the Netherlands and is patronized by staff from the nearby ministries and embassies. The emphasis is on seafood: six kinds of oysters, lobster served five different ways and a wide range of fish are served with flair in the club-like atmosphere. The oyster bar, with its huge circular copper-topped bar, is a popular alternative to the restaurant upstairs.

OTHER RESTAURANTS
Noordeinde is the culinary main street of The Hague. *Le Gobelot*, at No. 143 ☎ 46 58 38, draws on the cuisines of both East and West. *Perlier*, Nieuwe Schoolstr 13D ☎ 65 08 87, is a smart bistro and serves a short but inventive fish menu. Of The Hague's numerous Indonesian restaurants the *Radàn Ajoe*, Lange Poten 31 ☎ 64 45 92, is the smartest; the generous helpings and *rijsttafel* (rice with numerous spicy morsels) are inexpensive. Others prefer the small *Borobodur*, Bagijnestr 2325 ☎ 65 96 91.

Out of town
The *Auberge de Kieviet*, Stoeplaan 27 ☎ (01751) 19232, is 3kms/2 miles east of the city centre at Wassenaar. Rural surroundings add to polished service and creative French cuisine.

Bars and cafés

Mata Hari came to eavesdrop at the Hotel des Indes; and diplomats and business executives still meet and talk at *Le Bar*, the hotel's wood-panelled cocktail bar. Atmospheric cafés include *Le Duc*, 137 Noordeinde, decorated with antiques and mellow woodwork, *De Prins Taverne*, Noordeinde 65, which serves food, and *De Posthoorn Bodega*, Lange Voorhout 39A, the after-work retreat of the younger diplomatic set.

Entertainment

Den Haag Day by Day is available from the tourist office and hotels. There are outdoor concerts and festival events throughout June, the big North Sea Jazz Festival in July, with participants from around the world performing at the *Nederlands Congresgebouw*, Churchillplein 10, and huge firework displays nightly (Aug) on the front at Scheveningen. Tickets from *vvv* ☎ 54 62 00.

Music and opera The main concert hall is the *Dr Anton Philipszaal*, Houtmarket 17 ☎ 60 98 10, where the resident and Concertgebouw (from Amsterdam) orchestras perform regularly. *St Jacobskerk* is used for big choral works and the *Kloosterkerk* has a Bach choir and orchestra.

Theatre and dance Performances at the *Koninklijke Schouwburg* (Royal Theatre), Korte Voorhout 3 ☎ 46 94 50, are in Dutch, but London and Broadway hits are staged in English at the *Circustheater*, Gevers Deynootpl 50 ☎ 55 88 00. Modern dance and classical ballet are given at the *Danstheater aan't Spui*, Schedeldoekshaven 60 ☎ 60 49 30.

Cinema Recent releases with original soundtracks are shown at central cinemas; art films and classics at *Haags Filmhuis*, Denneweg 56 ☎ 45 99 00.

Nightclubs and casinos Nightlife is concentrated around the late-night bars and music cafés, like *Jazz Café Le Musicien*, Van Bylandtstr 191 ☎ 46 36 31 (live bands Wed & Fri, 10.30–1), and *La Velletta*, Nieuwe Schoolstr 13A ☎ 64 45 43. *Golden Gate Night Bar*, Bleijenburg 6 ☎ 63 97 27, has a disco and dance floor. The casino at the *Kurhaus Hotel*, Scheveningen ☎ 51 26 21, is open 2pm–2am.

Shopping

Shopping hours are Mon, 1–6; Tue–Fri, 9–6 (Thu to 9); Sat, 9–5. The main shopping street is Grote Marktstraat. The department store *De Bijenkorf* is worth visiting for its fine 19thC architecture and interiors. Behind it are many little streets and covered passages where small shops sell everything from designer underwear to fishing tackle. The chic *Bonneterie en Pander* department store is on Gravenstraat. Noordeinde is lively and lined with couturiers, antiquarian booksellers, art galleries, antique shops and restaurants.

Sightseeing

Binnenhof Medieval castle by the Hof Vijver enclosing the *Ridderzaal* (Knights' Hall) begun in the 13th century and the seat of the Dutch Parliament since the 16th century. The main chamber is now only for state occasions; much government business is conducted in the surrounding assembly rooms. *Tours hourly Mon–Sat, 10–4; Sun, 10–4 in summer.* In an adjacent building is the *Mauritshuis*, Royal Picture Gallery, a handsome 17thC brick building, containing an important collection of Dutch masters. *Plein 29. Open Tue–Sat, 10–5; Sun, 11–5.*

Haags Gemeentemuseum Contains salvaged and reconstructed rooms from 18thC and 19thC houses and modern paintings, including works by Monet and Mondriaan, and the seascapes and landscapes of the Impressionist Hague School. *Stadhouderslaan 41. Open Tue–Fri, 10–5; Sat & Sun, 12–5.*

Vredespaleis (Peace Palace) Completed 1907, with funds from the steel magnate, Andrew Carnegie, as the International Court of Arbitration and now also the International Court of Justice. *Carnegieplein 2. Open Mon–Fri, 10–12, 2–4.*

Guided tours Afternoon tourist office bus tours (3hrs), Mar–Sep ☎ 54 62 00. *Rondvaartbedrijf*, Spui 279A ☎ 46 24 73, organizes group bus and boat tours of The Hague and nearby cities.

Spectator sports

Horse-racing Mid-March–mid-November (Wed & Sun) at *Duindigt Renbaan*, Waalsdorperlaan 29, Wassenaar ☎ 24 44 27.
Soccer FC Den Haag plays at *Zuiderpark*, Mr P Droogleever.

Keeping fit

Fitness centre Splash, Pullman Hotel ☎ 61 49 21.
Golf Contact the *Dutch Golf Federation*, Soestdijkerstraatweg 172, Hilversum ☎ (035) 83 05 65.
Swimming Wavepool Scheveningen, Strandweg 13 ☎ 54 21 00, and *De Regentes*, Weimarstr 63 ☎ 63 27 40.
Tennis and squash Haags Tenniscentrum, Jaap Edenweg 2 ☎ 21 22 10; *Westvliet Racketcenter*, Westvlietweg 55 ☎ 86 44 40.

Local resources

Business services

International Business Center, Prinsengracht 63–65 ☎ 80 83 33, and *The Hague Business Center*, Parkweg 2 ☎ 52 09 54.
Photocopying and printing The Printer, Dr Kuyperstr 17 ☎ 64 41 22. *Multi Copy*, Parkstr 67 ☎ 64 75 60.
Secretarial Karola Grunenbaum Services, Jan van Nassaustr 84 ☎ 24 92 32, or *Wissenraet*, Van Stolkweg 34 ☎ 50 59 95.
Translation Vertaal Buro Regeer, Laan Van Meerdervoort 96B ☎ 46 42 00.

Communications

Local delivery Koeriers 2000, Deimanstr 306 ☎ 99 41 88.
Long-distance delivery DHL ☎ (06) 05 52; *Federal Express* ☎ (06) 022 23 33 (both toll-free).
Post office Main office: Kerkplein; open Mon–Fri, 8.30–7; Sat, 9–noon.
Fax and telex At the main post office and all hotels listed here.

Conference/exhibition centre

The main venue for trade fairs and conferences is the large *Nederlands Congresgebouw*, Churchillplein 10, Postbus 82000, 2508 EA ☎ 54 88 00 ⊠ 31700 fax 520407.

Emergencies

Bureaux de change Banks open Mon–Fri, 9–4; at Centraal Station, Mon–Sat, 8–9; Sun, 10–6.
Hospitals Emergency doctor ☎ 45 53 00 or 46 96 69 at night. Dental emergencies: *Dental Practice*, Anna Paulownastr 103 ☎ 65 46 46, open daily, 7am–midnight.
Pharmacies display details of those open out of normal hours or ☎ 45 10 00.
Police Emergency ☎ 22 22 22, otherwise ☎ 10 49 11. The police at Burg Patijnlaan 35 ☎ 10 80 15, handle lost and found articles.

Government offices

Ministerie van Economische Zaken (Economics Ministry), Bezuidenhoutseweg 30 ☎ 79 63 25, has a trade information department; *Export Bureau* ☎ 79 60 39.

Information sources

Business information Kamer van Koophandel (Chamber of commerce), A. Gogelweg 16 ☎ 79 57 95. Other trade-promotion organizations are based at *Holland Trade House*, Bezuidenhoutseweg 181, including *British Chamber* ☎ 47 88 81, *American Chamber* ☎ 47 82 34 and *French Chamber* ☎ 82 05 51. The *German Chamber* is at Nassauplein 30 ☎ 61 42 51.
Local media The daily *Haagsche Courant* covers business and international affairs. Hotel TVs receive British programmes and American satellite news.
Tourist information VVV at Koningin Julianaplein 30, by Centraal Station ☎ 54 62 00; open Mon–Sat, 9–8; Sun, 10–5.

Thank-yous

Chocolates Leonidas, Passage 74 ☎ 64 96 08, or *Godiva*, Plaats 24 ☎ 60 56 56.
Florists A'Corus Bloemen, Molenstr 7 ☎ 46 40 20, or *Jac. Heemskerk*, Bankastr 70 ☎ 55 85 44.
Food and wine Saur, Lange Voorhaut 47–53 ☎ 46 92 22.

ROTTERDAM
City code ☎ 010

The world's busiest port, Rotterdam handles some 250m tonnes/275m US tons of goods annually. West Germany, linked via the Rhine (Rijn), is an important source of, and destination for, these goods. Oil, its storage and refining and petrochemical research, is the other principal industry, and almost all the world's petroleum companies, led by Shell, have refining facilities in the Europort. Other significant employers are Unilever, Procter & Gamble, the insurance company Nationale Nederlanden, Credit Lyonnais and multinationals RDM and Akzo.

Rotterdam is a working city, busy by day and quiet at night; nobody lives in the centre if they can afford not to, and there is a drugs problem.

Arriving
Most overseas visitors fly to Amsterdam's Schiphol airport and take the train here. There are trains hourly from Antwerp, Brussels, Ghent and Bruges in Belgium, every two hours from Cologne and six a day from Paris. The city is linked by fast highways to Belgium, northeastern France and West Germany.

Rotterdam Zestienhoven airport
The small airport is 6kms/4 miles northwest of the city. It handles mainly freight but there are useful scheduled flights from Amsterdam, London's Heathrow and Paris. Standard facilities for a small airport. Information ☎ 415 7633. For freight inquiries contact carriers.

Amsterdam Schiphol airport (see *Amsterdam*)
City link Schiphol is 56kms/35 miles north of Rotterdam. The best way of reaching the city is by train from the airport station. Schiphol airport inquiries ☎ (20) 601 09 66.
Taxi Rotterdam-based taxis charge around G120 for the 1hr journey, cheaper than the metered fare.
Car rental All the major firms have desks in the arrivals hall.
Train InterCity trains depart every 15mins (hourly 1am–5am) for Rotterdam from the station below the arrivals (cost G18, time 55mins).

Railway station
Centraal Station is in the heart of the city, and many hotels are within walking distance. Trains leave every 15mins for Amsterdam (1hr), The Hague (15mins) and the suburbs. The modern concourse has a bank, cafés, shops and tourist information and hotel accommodation desks. Buses leave from in front of the main entrance. Rail inquiries ☎ 899 1121.

Getting around
It is convenient to walk around the centre; much of the shopping district is traffic-free.
Taxis The principal ranks are at Centraal Station, the square by the Stadhuis (City Hall), Stadhuisstraat, and outside hotels. Central reservation service ☎ 436 1222. Drivers expect to keep small change.
Driving A car is useful if you need to visit the port, which extends for miles to the southwest. Metered parking spaces are difficult to find in the centre, but not elsewhere. Roads are congested only at rush hours. Car rental firms include *Avis* ☎ 433 2233, *Budget* ☎ 411 3022, *Europcar* ☎ 411 4860, *Hertz* ☎ 465 1144 and *InterRent* ☎ 466 8811.
Walking Avoid unlit or deserted areas at night because of drug dealers.
Train Useful for journeys to the Hook of Holland and to the suburbs across the River Maas.
Bus, tram and subway Tickets for use on all public transport can be bought from tobacconists and newsstands. Most buses and trams start from outside Centraal Station. The subway reaches areas such as Oudehaven and Delfshaven.

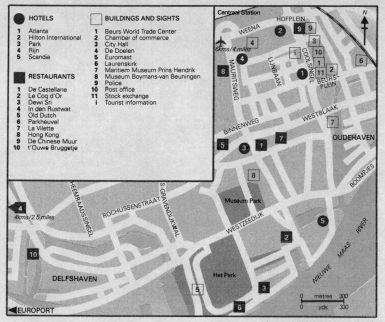

HOTELS

1 Atlanta
2 Hilton International
3 Park
4 Rijn
5 Scandia

RESTAURANTS

1 De Castellane
2 Le Coq d'Or
3 Dewi Sri
4 In den Rustwat
5 Old Dutch
6 Parkheuvel
7 La Vilette
8 Hong Kong
9 De Chinese Muur
10 t'Ouwe Bruggetje

BUILDINGS AND SIGHTS

1 Beurs World Trade Center
2 Chamber of commerce
3 City Hall
4 De Doelen
5 Euromast
6 Laurenskirk
7 Maritiem Museum Prins Hendrik
8 Museum Boymans-van Beuningen
9 Police
10 Post office
11 Stock exchange
i Tourist information

Area by area

Present-day Rotterdam was largely rebuilt after the heavy bombardments of 1940. The centre is a square: Weena, to the north, is lined with office tower-blocks; on Coolsingel, in the east, the Stadhuis (City Hall) stands next to the stock exchange and World Trade Center, housing Rotterdam's spot market for oil; Westblaak is to the south; and Mauritsweg on the west. The principal shops and the De Doelen arts complex lie within this area.

Immediately to the east is the rapidly developing old port, Oudehaven. Warehouses along the Boompjes and Haringvliet are being transformed into fashionable homes, and old bomb sites into futuristic

buildings. New shops, restaurants and cafés have recently opened but the port remains a working harbour. Farther east are the attractive suburbs of Kralingen and Hillegersberg.

Far less salubrious are the northern and western suburbs, reputed to be dangerous because of drug dealers.

The old port area of Delfshaven to the southwest was one of the few areas to escape bombing, and the recent extension of the metro line here is expected to stimulate the regeneration of this picturesque but run-down district. The massive, modern Europort starts here and stretches for some 16kms/10 miles along the Nieuwe Maas River to its North Sea estuary at the Hook of Holland.

Hotels

Nearly all Rotterdam's hotels are modern. Those listed are central and not far from the port and business districts. Currency exchange, 24hr room service and parking are standard unless specifically stated, and rooms have IDD telephones, multichannel TV and minibars.

Atlanta *G|*
Aert van Nesstr 4, 3012 CA
☎ *411 0420* ⊤ᵡ *21595 fax 413 5320*
● *AE DC MC V* ● *165 rooms, 2 suites,*
1 restaurant, 1 bar
Opposite the Beurs World Trade
Center and surrounded by the
characterless buildings of new
Rotterdam, the Atlanta's touches of
1930s Art Deco are a welcome
change. Rooms are modestly priced,
and a spacious business suite costs
little more than a standard room at
other central hotels. The bedrooms
have recently been modernized. Many
of the staff have been here for years,
and the service is courteous. 5
meeting rooms (capacity up to 400).

Hilton International *G|||*
Weena 10, 3012 CM ☎ *414 4044*
⊤ᵡ *22666 fax 411 8884* ● *AE DC MC V*
● *224 rooms, 24 suites, 1 restaurant, 1*
bar
Rotterdam's leading business hotel is
near the station. The well-equipped
conference rooms and the restaurant
are much in demand by local
companies for seminars and for
entertaining; and the disco and casino
enliven the small hours for
Rotterdam's young and not-so-young.
More space and bigger desks are
provided in the rooms on the top two
executive floors. Shops, hairdresser ●
courier, secretarial services, 6 meeting
rooms with a/v and translation
equipment (capacity up to 280).

Park *G|||*
Westersingel 70, 3015 LB ☎ *436 3611*
⊤ᵡ *22020 fax 436 3611* ● *AE DC MC V* ●
157 rooms, 2 suites, 2 restaurants, 2 bars
This is the most distinctive large

hotel in the city, and it appeals to
business travellers and affluent
tourists alike. Some rooms have
balconies overlooking the hotel's own
gardens. The older part of the hotel
retains many Art Deco flourishes in
the chandeliers, doorframes and
ceilings, and linking passages are used
as an art gallery. The only hotel in
Rotterdam to have a fitness centre,
sauna, solarium and massage. Room
service 7am–11pm, nonsmoking
rooms, shops ● 4 meeting rooms with
a/v equipment (capacity up to 80).

Rijn *G|*
Schouwburgplein 1, 3012 CK
☎ *433 3800* ⊤ᵡ *21640 fax 414 5482* ●
AE DC MC V ● *96 rooms, 4 suites,*
1 restaurant, 1 bar
This concrete and glass tower-block
has a welcoming interior and
refurbished bedrooms. The De
Doelen concert and conference centre
is opposite, and the hotel's Rhapsodie
restaurant is popular with
theatregoers. No parking. Hairdresser
● 9 meeting rooms with a/v facilities
(capacity up to 250).

OTHER HOTEL
Scandia *G|* *Willemsplein 1, 3016*
DN ☎ *413 4790* ⊤ᵡ *21662*
fax 412 7890 ● *AE DC MC V*. In the
port area, an inexpensive hotel
popular in the shipping business.
Friendly staff. Good value large
suites.

Hotel and restaurant price guide
For the meanings of the hotel and
restaurant price symbols, see
pages 6 and 7.

Restaurants

Rotterdam is packed with small, mainly ethnic (Indonesian, Chinese and
Indian) places to eat but only a handful are suitable for business entertaining. The ones listed stand out, but those in the main hotels are also
satisfactory. The usual business meal is lunch.

De Castellane *G|*
Eendrachtsweg 22 ☎ *414 1159* ● *AE*
DC MC V ● *reservations essential*

This smart restaurant in a converted
canal-side residence has a bar famous
for its original cocktails. The light

airy dining rooms, widely spaced tables and polished service are valued for business entertaining. The award-winning chefs specialize in serving imaginative seafood dishes.

Le Coq d'Or *G*/

Van Vollenhovenstr 25 ☎ *436 0242 • closed Sat L, Sun • AE DC MC V • smart dress preferred*

Le Coq d'Or is the only Dutch restaurant to have been awarded a Michelin star every year since the Netherlands guide was first published over 30 years ago, and such is its reputation that it no longer displays a menu outside. In a grand house in the old port area, it has a beamed interior decorated with old paintings. There is a garden for summer dining. The menu changes regularly, and vegetarian dishes are prepared with as much flair as the 7-course *menu gastronomique*.

Dewi Sri *G*

Westerkade 2022 ☎ *436 0263 • closed Sat & Sun L • AE DC MC V*

One of the two Indonesian restaurants in Holland to have carved out a loyal business clientele. The interior is more like a colonial club with polished wood, leather, palms and ceiling fans, than an Indonesian longhouse. The menu lists four different *rijsttafels* (many different exotic morsels eaten with rice), all magnificent and colourful. Large parties are regarded as a welcome challenge by the staff.

In den Rustwat *G*/

Honingerdijk 96 ☎ *413 4110 • closed Sat & Sun • AE DC MC • D reservations advisable*

This 16thC farmhouse restaurant in the leafy Park Honingen, about 5kms/3 miles east of the centre, is almost rustic. It has an immaculate garden that is a considerable attraction in summer. The menu, based on seasonal ingredients and chosen with care, features oysters, fresh fish and wild game in season. A pianist plays in the evening.

Old Dutch *G*/

Rochussenstr 20 ☎ *436 0242 • closed Sat & Sun • AE DC MC V*

A comfortable old restaurant with heavy beams and rustic charm incongruously surrounded by modern housing. The brasserie fills up for the lunch-time buffet, but the main restaurant is used for more formal occasions. Traditional Dutch food, such as rabbit and bean casseroles, is an alternative to light and imaginative fish and vegetarian dishes. Parking outside.

Parkheuvel *G*//

Heuvellaan 21 ☎ *436 0530 • closed Sat L, Sun • AE DC MC V*

The Parkheuvel is Rotterdam's premier restaurant for business entertaining. Here the captains of companies sit and watch their cargoes go in and out of the port, cocooned in this club-like, Bauhaus-style building on the edge of Het Park. The menu lists an ample choice of creatively presented fish, game and vegetarian dishes. In summer you can dine on the terrace.

La Vilette *G*//

Westblaak 160 ☎ *414 8692 • closed Sat L, Sun • AE DC MC V*

Surrounded by banks and insurance company offices, this is one of Rotterdam's leading restaurants for business entertaining. Chef Udo Vonno is responsible for the outstanding *nouvelle cuisine* served in the quiet, ultramodern dining room. Extensive wine list, fine vintage ports and friendly service.

OTHER RESTAURANTS

Numerous Chinese restaurants line a short stretch of Westersingel. One of the best serving authentic Cantonese food is *Hong Kong*, Westersingel 15 ☎ 436 6463. *De Chinese Muur*, Kruiskade 1 ☎ 412 5622, serves Indonesian food. Overlooking the canals and bridges of the old port area, *'t Ouwe Bruggetje*, Voorhaven 6 ☎ 477 3499, has character and serves familiar Dutch dishes and fish.

Bars

Hotel bars are best for a business rendezvous, especially the *Lobby Bar* at the Hilton. The *Park's Cocktail Bar* is quieter and more atmospheric. *Ramblas*, Delftsestr 15, near the Shell building, has charm and serves meals. There are modern bars in the old port along Oudehavenkade and Haringvliet, many with waterfront cafés.

Entertainment

Listings appear in *Rotterdam This Month*, available in most hotels. Regular events include the Film Festival (Jan & Feb) and the very popular Heineken Jazz Festival (Sep).

Music and opera at *De Doelen*, Schouwburgplein 50 ☎ 413 2490, home of the Rotterdam Philarmonic Orchestra and the venue for concerts by visiting artists.

Theatre and dance The main theatre is the *Rotterdamse Schouwburg*, Schouwburgpl 25 ☎ 411 8110, but nearly all performances are in Dutch. The main Dutch dance companies also perform here. The *Luxor Theatre*, Kruiskade 10 ☎ 413 8326, stages West End and Broadway hits.

Cinemas Films are shown with their original soundtracks. Those on Coolsingel show recent releases; *'t Verlster*, Gouvernestr 129 ☎ 436 4998, shows classics and art movies.

Nightclubs Conventional night life revolves around jazz clubs and cafés; some, like the *Harbour Jazzclub*, Delfsestr 15 ☎ 411 4958, and *Jazzcafé Dizzy*, s-Gravendijkwal 127 ☎ 477 3014, engage leading bands on Fridays and Saturdays and local groups on other nights.

Le Bateau is a smart disco at the Hilton Hotel patronized by people of all ages. The *Bluetiek-In*, Karel Doormanstr 12 ☎ 433 2067, is trendy and has video and laser shows.

Of the many nightclubs which feature striptease, one of the more respectable is *Mayfair*, Mathenesserlaan 471 ☎ 425 4155.

Casino At the Hilton Hotel ☎ 414 7799, open 2pm–2am.

Shopping

Most stores are national or international chains and open Mon, 1–5.30; Tue–Thu, 9–5.30; Fri, 9–9; Sat, 9–5. The main shopping areas are in Beursplein (department stores), the partly covered mall, Winkelpromenade, Lijnbaan and Binnenwegplein (small shops, fashion boutiques). There is a general market at *Mariniersweg*, in the old port (Tue & Sat, 9–5), east of the centre, with antiques and craft stalls.

Sightseeing

Even for those who are not in shipping, *Rotterdam Harbour* has appeal. Spido operates 1hr 45min tours through the docks and container ports from Willemsplein; luxury motor cruisers for 10 to 300 people can be rented ☎ 413 5400.

The picturesque waterways of *Delfshaven* are filled with old fishing boats and houseboats. The *Pilgrim Fathers' Church* stands where the pilgrims embarked for the New World on board the *Speedwell* in 1620, and later set sail aboard the *Mayflower* from Plymouth. The *Euromast*, Parkhaven 20, 176metres/ 560ft high, offers a crow's-nest view from its two restaurants (☎ 436 4811).

In Oudehaven is some spectacular modern architecture: see the glass pyramid of the *Gemeentebibliotheek* (public library) and the post-modernist cube-houses of Piet Blom, on Overblaak 70, one of which is furnished and open to the public.

Maritiem Museum Prins Hendrik shows the history of the port and shipping, and the 1868 Dutch Royal Navy vessel *Buffel*. Leuvehaven 1. *Open Tue–Sat, 10–5; Sun, 11–5.*

Museum Boymans-van Beuningen The very fine art collection includes Pieter Breuhgel's *Tower of Babel*, works by Bosch, Rubens and Rembrandt as well as by Monet, Picasso, Dali, Klee and Kandinsky. *Mathenesserlaan 18–20. Open Tue–Sat, 10–5; Sun, 11–5.*

Guided tours Orientation tours (early Apr–end Sep) are run by the *Tourist office*, Coolsingel 67 ☎ 413 6000. Inexpensive circuits of the city, port and nearby bulbfields for parties of 3 or 5 by plane are run from Rotterdam airport ☎ 415 7855.

Spectator sports

First division *Feyenoord FC* plays soccer twice a week in season at Olympiaweg 50 ☎ 419 5711. Major events (indoor soccer, tennis, squash, gymnastics) are held at *Ahoy'*, Zuiderparkweg 2030 ☎ 410 4204.

Keeping fit

Fitness centres Splash, Park Hotel ☎ 436 3611. *American Fitness Studio*, Oostzeedijk 230 ☎ 452 8794. *Golf Kralingseweg* 200 ☎ 452 7646. *Swimming Oostervant*, Oostervantstr 25 ☎ 477 2003, has an indoor pool, tennis courts and bowling alley. *Tennis Tennisstadion Rotterdam*, Ommoordsestr 341 ☎ 421 7262.

Local resources

Business services

Actual Business Services, Business Center Rotterdam, Stationsplein 45 ☎ 413 8116, rents offices and equipment.
Printing and photocopying Copy Shop, Pijnackerplein 19 ☎ 465 6261; *Multi Copy*, Westblaak 26 ☎ 414 1446.
Secretarial Uiterwijk and Partners, Vierhavensstr 17 ☎ 477 1370.
Translation Vertaal Buro Regeer, Schoonordstr 33B ☎ 467 1611.

Communications

Local delivery Active Koerier ☎ 467 0407.
Long-distance delivery TNT Skypak ☎ 411 7727. *DHL* ☎ (06) 0552 and *Federal Express* ☎ (06) 0222 333 (both toll free).
Post offices Central office: Coolsingel 42, next to the City Hall ☎ 454 2221, open Mon–Thu, 8.30–7; Fri, 8.30–8.30. The office at Delftplein 31 ☎ 454 2219 is open Mon–Fri, 8.30–9; Sat 8.30–noon.
Telex and fax At most hotels and post offices.

Conference/exhibition centres

Trade fairs and exhibitions are held at the *Ahoy' Exhibition Center* in the southern suburbs at Zuiderparkweg 20–30 ☎ 410 4204, which has 6 exhibition halls with 20,000 sq metres/216,000 sq ft of space. *De Doelen*, Schouwburgplein 50, is also used for conventions ☎ 414 2911. Smaller meetings and seminars are held at the *Beurs World Trade Center*, Beursplein 37 ☎ 405 4444.

Emergencies

Bureaux de change Banks open Mon–Fri, 9–4 (and Fri, 6.30pm–8pm). The bank at Centraal Station is open Mon–Sat, 7.30–10; Sun, 9–10.
Hospitals Emergency medical advice ☎ 420 1100; dental problems ☎ 455 2155. The most central hospital is the *Van Dam Ziekenhuis*, Westersingel 115 ☎ 436 4644.
Pharmacies Late and weekend opening is on a rotating basis. Details from pharmacies or ☎ 420 1100.
Police Emergency ☎ 414 1414. Station: Haagseveer 23 ☎ 424 2911.

Government offices

Information on business in Rotterdam from the *Municipal Library*, Hoogstr 110 ☎ 433 8911.

Information sources

Business information Kamer van Koophandel (Chamber of commerce), Beursplein 37 ☎ 405 7777.
Local media The local Dutch-language daily papers are the *Rotterdams Nieuwsblad* and *Rotterdams Stadsblad*.
Tourist information The main office is opposite the City Hall, Coolsingel 67, open Mon–Thu, 9–6; Fri, 9–9; Sat, 9–5; Sun, 10–4 (summer only) ☎ 413 6000. The office at Centraal Station is open Mon–Sat, 9–10; Sun, 10–10 ☎ 413 6006.

Thank-yous

Chocolates Leonidas, Stadhuisplein 28 ☎ 413 2727.
Florists Centrafleur Bloemsierkunst, Stationsplein 45 ☎ 411 0995.

NORWAY

The Norwegian economy is heavily dependent on oil and natural gas, which together account for about 10% of GDP and 40% of export earnings. Oil revenues have funded high public spending aimed at promoting full employment and maintaining social and welfare services. Rising energy exports and high public investment have contributed to GDP growth rates averaging about 4% a year since 1983 (well above the West European average) and per capita income levels that are among the highest in Europe. However, high inflation and skill shortages have been two consequences of the policy of keeping unemployment low.

The collapse of oil prices in 1986 and an increase in service payments (due to heavy foreign borrowing and investment in the 1970s to finance oil and gas development) have contributed to a balance of payments current account deficit, equivalent to about 4% of GDP. The government has responded by adopting measures to try to curb consumer spending and reduce the trade deficit, and to encourage traditional export industries and so make the economy less vulnerable to fluctuations in oil prices.

Manufacturing and mining's share of GDP has fallen to about 15%, partly reflecting a rise in the relative share of the oil and gas sector. But engineering, the largest manufacturing industry, has suffered from the high value of the krone; and shipbuilding is in decline, although oil platform production has increased. Industries that exploit the country's natural resources, such as wood processing, chemicals and metallurgy have fared better, partly due to use of cheap hydroelectric power. Norway's small agricultural sector is in decline as is its fishing industry, although fishing is still important as an employer and an export earner.

Oil, gas and related products will remain Norway's major exports in the early 1990s, and longer if higher oil prices make the development of northern reserves viable. Other export items are machinery, ships and oil platforms, non-ferrous metals, chemicals, fish and fish products, and pulp and paper. Norway's main imports are machinery and transport equipment, chemicals, food, drink and tobacco, ships and oil platforms, and clothing. Its main trading partners are fellow EFTA member Sweden, then West Germany and the UK.

Geography Norway is a mountainous country with an intricate coastline and a densely forested interior.
Climate The west experiences a marine climate with cool but mild summers and freezing winters. Inland is warmer in summer and even colder in winter.
Population 4.2m
Government Norway is a constitutional monarchy. The parliament, the Storting, has a 157 members elected every 4 years.

Currency Norwegian krone (NKr).
Time 1hr ahead of GMT; end Mar–end Sep, 2hrs ahead of GMT.
Dialling codes Norway's IDD code is 47. Omit the initial 0 from the city code when dialling from abroad. To make an international call from Norway, dial 095 before dialling the relevant country code.
Public holidays Jan 1, Maundy Thu, Good Fri, Easter Mon, May 1, May 17, Ascension, Whit Mon, Dec 25, Dec 26.

OSLO

Oslo, with a population of barely half a million, is a small, quiet city; while it covers an area of 450 sq kms/175 sq miles, only 12% of the land is built upon. Few capitals are so rich in natural beauty; it is ringed by mountains and forest, on the edge of Oslo Fjord, and unspoiled beaches, islands and country are less than 20mins drive away.

North Sea oil and gas have injected considerable prosperity into the capital. Norway's reserves will last well beyond the year 2000 but Oslo is concerned at its dependence on these two commodities; the mid-1980s' fall in oil prices had a serious effect on the country's balance of payments. The other industries – chemicals, computers, timber processing, ship-building and agricultural machinery – are all vulnerable to competition, especially from a more commercially aggressive Soviet Union.

Arriving

Many European cities and New York are linked by air with Oslo, which has two airports: most visitors arrive at Fornebu, but flights direct from the USA and Canada land at Gardermoen. Passenger car ferries (DFDS) sail overnight between Oslo and Copenhagen, and there are infrequent ferries from Britain.

Oslo-Fornebu airport
This is a modern airport with all the usual services: well-stocked gift and food shops, banks, a post office, restaurant, left baggage and a desk for information and accommodation reservations, all of which open Mon–Sat, 8–10; Sun, 11–10.

There are inexpensive services between Oslo and the principal towns of Norway: Braathen Safe ☎ 597000; SAS ☎ 427900 (business class); ☎ 427550 (economy); and Widerøe ☎ 427760.

There is an SAS lounge for its business-class passengers, with fax, telex and typing facilities for small jobs, and the Caravelle Conference Centre ☎ 596150. Airport inquiries ☎ 596716; for freight inquiries contact carriers.
Nearby hotel SAS *Park Royal*, Oslo N-1324, Lysaker ☎ 120220 ⊠ 78745 fax 120011. Just 2mins from the airport and 10mins from the city centre, it has a conference centre and good sports facilities.
City link Fornebu is 9km/5 miles

southwest of Oslo. Buses are frequent and nearly as quick as taxis.
Taxi The ride to town takes 15mins and costs around Nkr100.
Car rental The main firms have desks at the airport, but you do not need a car in central Oslo.
Bus Buses leave for the central station every 10–15mins until 11pm, stopping at the Scandinavia Hotel and the National Theatre, from which most other hotels are only a short walk.

Oslo-Gardermoen airport
Gardermoen is 50kms/31 miles to the north. Services include a bank, telephone and postal facilities, and duty-free and other stores all generally open daily, 7am–10pm, or to coincide with flights. The taxi ride takes 45–60mins (fare Nkr500). Alternatively, SAS operates a shared limousine service and an airport bus (fare Nkr50) that calls at the Scandinavia Hotel and the central railway station. Avis has a car rental office here. Airport inquiries ☎ (06) 978130.

Railway stations
Sentralbanestasjonen is very modern. Services include banks, a post office, restaurants and many small shops (open late and Sun). There is one train each way daily between Oslo and Stockholm and Oslo and Copenhagen (a 9hr 30 min journey). Express trains go south to

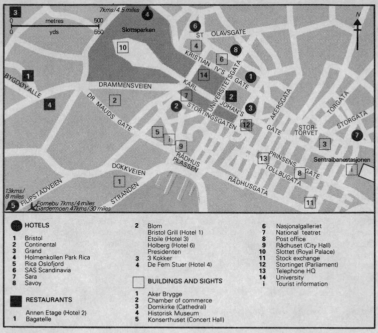

HOTELS

1. Bristol
2. Continental
3. Grand
4. Holmenkollen Park Rica
5. Rica Oslofjord
6. SAS Scandinavia
7. Sara
8. Savoy

RESTAURANTS

1. Annen Etage (Hotel 2)
   Bagatelle

2. Blom
   Bristol Grill (Hotel 1)
   Etoile (Hotel 3)
   Holberg (Hotel 6)
   Presidenten
3. 3 Kokker
4. De Fem Stuer (Hotel 4)

BUILDINGS AND SIGHTS

1. Aker Brygge
2. Chamber of commerce
3. Domkirke (Cathedral)
4. Historisk Museum
5. Konserthuset (Concert Hall)
6. Nasjonalgalleriet
7. National teatret
8. Post office
9. Rådhuset (City Hall)
10. Slottet (Royal Palace)
11. Stock exchange
12. Stortinget (Parliament)
13. Telephone HQ
14. University
i. Tourist information

Kristiansand, west to Bergen and Stavanger and north as far as Bodø. Inquiries ☎ 416221.

Getting around

The centre of Oslo is so compact that most destinations can be reached in minutes on foot.

Taxis Plentiful during the day and in the evening, but hard to find later at night. Cabs will stop if hailed or can be reserved an hour or more in advance ☎ 388080 or ordered at once from *Oslo Taxisentral* ☎ 388090. They are expensive and useful for journeys to the port area or suburbs or when the weather is really bad. Drivers do not always expect tips.

Limousines Bislet Limousine ☎ 350133.

Driving Parking in the centre is restricted, and spaces at meters are hard to find. There is multistorey parking beside the Scandinavia Hotel. *Avis* ☎ 849060; *Hertz* ☎ 200121; *InterRent* ☎ 557438.

Walking is safe and pleasant, especially in summer. In winter, appropriate footwear is needed for icy surfaces or melting snow.

Bus, tram and subway Tram routes cross the city centre, and a subway system operates to the eastern and western suburbs, with buses serving the hillier north. Tickets purchased from the driver, or in subway stations, are valid for 1hr on any form of public transport. An Oslo Card (*Oslokortet*) allows unlimited travel and other concessions for up to 3 days.

Ferries run frequently (twice every hour, Jun–Aug) around the Oslo Fjord; information ☎ 334386.

Area by area

Oslo is built around the northern bend of the Oslo Fjord, encircled by low wooded hills to the east and west and higher mountains to the north. The suburbs stretch for more than 40kms/25 miles around the shore.

The principal street, Karl Johans gate, is less than 1.5kms/1 mile long and most public buildings lie along or just off it. At the western end on a slight rise and surrounded by parkland is the Slottet (Royal Palace), the residence of the King of Norway from November to May. The Nationalteateret, centre of the city's cultural life, and the University administration in a handsome neo-classical building, lie outside the Palace gates.

Farther east is the yellow-brick Stortinget, Norway's Parliament. Beyond, Karl Johans gate is traffic free. From here onwards are the city's principal shops and department stores, the Domkirke (Cathedral) and the Sentralbanestasjonen. Nearby is the Børsen (stock exchange).

Traffic is routed around the centre and along the shores of the Fjord where it weaves a course through the docks, past the Rådhuset, or City Hall, and out to the suburbs. This road, Dokkveien, is the focus of business development. Offices are scattered through the near suburbs, often occupying typical Norwegian timber buildings converted from homes. Industry is along the road to Fornebu airport, to the northwest of the city and up the valley of the River Akerselva in the northeast. The most desirable properties are those by the Fjord to the southwest and in the mountains to the northwest.

Hotels

Oslo has several hotels with character, but the Bristol is the grandest, closely followed by the Continental. It is always best to make advance reservations, especially in the spring and autumn when the major fur sales and trade fairs are held. The SAS information desk at Fornebu airport will reserve accommodation. All hotels listed have IDD telephones, 24hr room service, currency exchange, parking and TV and minibars in all rooms.

Bristol *K*/////
Kristian IV's gate 7, N-0164 Oslo 1
☏ *415840* TX *71668 fax 428651* •
AE DC MC V • *141 rooms, 4 suites,*
2 restaurants, 2 bars
This grand 19thC hotel is full of surprises. Stepping in from one of Oslo's principal shopping streets, the visitor enters a Moorish-style lobby with great pillars and peacock-feather frescoes, an atmospheric setting for many an informal business breakfast, coffee or afternoon tea. By contrast, the rooms are decorated with contemporary Scandinavian fabrics and reproduction antique furniture. The guests are here mainly for business or are wealthy tourists. The staff are young, helpful and friendly. The Bristol Grill is one of the city's premier dining rooms (see *Restaurants*) but in the pleasant Spanish El Toro the food is also good and prices reasonable. Gift shop, hairdresser • banquet hall (capacity up to 250), 10 meeting rooms (capacity up to 25).

Continental *K*/////
Stortingsgaten 24–26, N-0161 Oslo 1
☏ *419060* TX *71012 fax 429689* •
AE DC MC V • *157 rooms, 12 suites,*
3 restaurants, 1 bar
This is a classic hotel of great style and elegance, established in 1909 and now run by Ellen Brochmann, granddaughter of the original founders. The Continental occupies a central place in Oslo life; it is used to accommodate guests of state, for meetings and business entertaining at the grand Annen Etage (see *Restaurants*), or for relaxing and watching the town go by in the splendid Viennese-style Theatercaféen. Rooms are large and comfortable. Standards of service are high, especially for regular guests. Shops, hairdresser • ballroom, 5 meeting rooms (capacity up to 40).

Grand K////
Karl Johans gate 31, N-0159 Oslo 1
☎ *429390* TX *71683 fax 421225* •
AE DC MC V • *267 rooms, 35 suites,*
5 restaurants, 3 bars
Opposite the Stortinget on Oslo's
central thoroughfare. The Grand is an
old palace-style hotel with modern
facilities, such as a large rooftop pool
in a modern extension; up here also is
the Etoile, one of the best restaurants
in Oslo (see *Restaurants*). Art Deco in
the public areas gives way to
contemporary-style decor in the
spacious bedrooms, including the
recently converted Tower Suite in the
clock tower, with its magnificent
views and a vast sunken bath. More
traditional is the Nobel Suite,
reserved for the winner of the Nobel
Peace Prize, presented in early
December. Official receptions for
visiting heads of state are often held
in the rococo banqueting hall. Shops
• pool, fitness room, sauna, solarium
• 11 conference rooms with a/v
facilities (capacity up to 300).

Holmenkollen Park Rica K////
Kongeveien 26, N-0390 Oslo 3
☎ *146090* TX *72094 fax 146192* •
AE DC MC V • *183 rooms, 8 suites,*
2 restaurants, 1 bar
The hotel is 8kms/5 miles north of
the city, 350 metres/1,150ft up in the
mountains with superb views and the
international ski-jump arena next
door. New wings have recently been
built but the attraction for conference
delegates who like sport is the
ornamented old timber mansion.
Nonsmoking rooms, transport to city
and airport, nightclub, hairdresser •
pool, sauna, fitness room • conference
centre with a/v and simultaneous
translation equipment, 33 meeting
rooms (capacity up to 160).

Rica Oslofjord K////
Sandviksveien 184, Sandvika N-1301
☎ *545700* TX *74345 fax 542733* •
AE DC MC V • *228 rooms, 15 suites,*
2 restaurants, 2 bars
Some 7kms/4 miles west of the
airport and 15kms/9 miles west of the
city, this hotel is beside the
convention centre, with mountains
behind and near several islands with
clean beaches linked to the mainland
by causeways. The rooms are around
a large marble-lined atrium.
Nonsmoking rooms, nightclub,
hairdresser • sauna, fitness room •
secretarial and word processing
facilities, 10 meeting rooms.

SAS Scandinavia K////
Holbergs gate 30, N-0166 Oslo 1
☎ *113000* TX *79090 fax 113017* •
AE DC MC V • *500 rooms, 19 suites,*
3 restaurants, 3 bars
This modern deluxe hotel is Norway's
largest and, at 21 floors, one of the
tallest buildings in Oslo. Views from
the Royal Club executive rooms and
the Summit 21 Bar embrace the
whole capital, the Oslo Fjord and the
mountains beyond. Like all SAS
hotels, the Scandinavia targets
business travellers, and has an
excellent restaurant, the Holberg (see
Restaurants). Shops, hairdresser •
pool, fitness room, sauna, solarium •
secretarial services, offices and
computers for rent, 10 meeting rooms
with a/v and simultaneous translation
equipment (capacity up to 1,000).

OTHER HOTELS
Sara K//// *Biskop Gunnerus' gate 3,*
N-0106 Oslo 1 ☎ *429410* TX *71342*
fax 424622 • *AE DC MC V*. A large
modern hotel close to the railway
station and the new Oslo Spectrum
(sports, concerts, conferences), due to
open May 1991. Comfortable rooms.
Savoy K// *Universitetsgata 11,*
N-0164, Oslo 1 ☎ *202655* TX *76418*
fax 112480 • *AE DC MC V*. One of the
smaller and less expensive central
hotels, with a restaurant and bar and
tastefully furnished rooms.

Credit card abbreviations	
AE	American Express
DC	Diners Club
MC	Access/MasterCard
V	Visa

Restaurants

When it comes to business entertaining in Oslo the hotel dining rooms nearly always win; most other restaurants cater to tourists. The Annen Etage is best for special occasions. Lunch is usually a short meal, and several of the listed restaurants open only for dinner, which begins at 6pm. Norwegian dishes tend to consist of lamb, sausages and meat patties.

Annen Etage K/////
Continental Hotel ☎ *419060* • *AE DC MC V*
With its turn-of-the-century *belle époque* decor and atmosphere of leisurely indulgence, Annen Etage provides the best venue for top-level entertaining in Oslo. Politicians and senior business executives discuss the issues of the day at well-spaced tables over dishes that combine the best of Norwegian ingredients – crayfish, stag, capercallie (large grouse) – prepared in French style.

Bagatelle K/////
Bygdøy allé 3–5 ☎ *446397* • *closed Sun, 3 weeks Jul–Aug* • *AE DC MC V*
Abstract paintings decorate the walls of Oslo's top gastronomic restaurant, and the furnishings are the very latest in design. The chefs excel at fish, and the daily *menu dégustation* is always imaginative. Excellent if highly priced wine list.

Blom K////
Karl Johans gate 41B ☎ *427300* • *closed Sun* • *AE DC MC V*
Blom is an institution, and its old-fashioned atmosphere has survived a recent move into a modern building. The ancient woodwork, oil paintings and armorial bearings that hang from the walls (symbolizing Norwegian cultural figures) lend it the atmosphere of a provincial Norwegian inn. A favourite haunt of today's artists and writers. The *smørbrød* open sandwich, buffet lunch is popular with the local business community.

Bristol Grill K/
Bristol Hotel ☎ *415840* • *AE DC MC V*
The Grill serves a sumptuous lunch-time buffet as well as charcoal-grilled

meat and fish. The quiet club-like atmosphere and unobtrusive service make it a good choice for business entertaining.

Etoile K//
Grand Hotel ☎ *429390* • *AE DC MC V*
The ultramodern Etoile is on the top floor of the Grand Hotel's recent extension, under a glass roof that gives diners the illusion of being outside. The style finds favour with Oslo's younger executives. The cooking is more than competent.

Holberg K/////
SAS Scandinavia Hotel ☎ *113000* • *closed L, Sun* • *AE DC MC V*
Chef Lars Erik Underthun has helped to transform a lack lustre restaurant into one of Norway's finest. The walls are decorated with scenes from the works of Holberg (a 19thC playwright), and the menu features typically Norwegian dishes, salmon, game and lamb from the mountain pastures. Inspired cheeseboard and wide choice of high-priced wines.

Presidenten K//
President Harbitz' gate 4 ☎ *558770* • *closed L, Sun* • *AE DC MC V*
Owner Simon Yuern and chef Inage Masaru of this restaurant in Oslo's western suburbs describe their cooking style as a combination of French and Oriental. There is a very limited *á la carte*, and the two daily set menus feature an eclectic range of dishes from pheasant mousse to oriental seafood. The two spacious dining rooms are decorated with contemporary Chinese watercolours and Scandinavian textiles. Exclusive and fashionable, yet good value, including the choice of fine wines.

3 Kokker [K]////
Drammensveien 30 ☎ *442650 • closed
L, Sun • AE DC MC V*
Founded in 1969 by Norwegian TV
personality Hror Dege, the 3 Kokker
is run by a team of three chefs, hence
its name. Some claim the restaurant is
past its prime, but there are others
who still regard it as the best in Oslo.
The uninviting exterior, a modern
office block, gives no hint of the
civilized interior. Spacious seating,
stylish service and an inventive six-
course *grand menu* make it very
suitable for discreet business
entertaining.

OTHER RESTAURANTS
The *Grand Café* and the
Theatercaféen, at the Grand and
Continental Hotels respectively, are
like Middle European coffee houses,
opening early and closing late and
serving everything from a sandwich
and beer, coffee and cakes to a full
meal with wine. Both are Oslo
institutions, with elegant turn-of-the-
century decor, polite service and
yards of window from which to
observe the street life outside. The
Grand is favoured by the younger set,
and the Theatercaféen is just right for
an informal business lunch.

The Holmenkollen Park Hotel's
main restaurant, *De Fem Stuer*
☎ 146090, is a retreat in summer and
a charming winter haven; fish and
game dishes.

Bars and cafés
Hotel bars are the best places for
informal meetings (Norway has a
powerful temperance movement). By
far the most civilized, and a popular
business rendezvous, is the club-like
Library Bar at the Bristol Hotel. A
close second is the *Continental Bar*,
decorated with prints and paintings.
Fru Blom, Karl Johans gate 39
(closed Sun), is a smart, upmarket
wine bar with outdoor tables that also
serves inexpensive meals. Nearby, the
Victoria, Karl Johans gate 35, is for
the young and chic. *The Scotsman*,
Karl Johans gate 17, serves meals.

Entertainment
Events are listed in the free *What's on
in Oslo*. Theatre tickets from theatres
or *Teatersentralen*, Youngstorget 5
☎ 418560.
Theatre All plays are performed in
Norwegian. Those by Henrik Ibsen
are frequently at the *Nationalteateret*,
Stortingsgaten 15 ☎ 412710.
Dance and opera Excellent
performances are staged at the *Den
Norske Opera*, Stortingsgaten 23
☎ 429475 (Oct–mid-Jun).
Music The Oslo Philharmonic and
visiting orchestras perform at the
Konserthuset, Munkedamsveien 14
☎ 416065 (information) ☎ 209333
(box office).
Cinema Films are in original
languages with subtitles. Central box
office, *Kinosentralen*, Stortingsgaten 16
☎ 418390.
Nightclubs The *Restaurant Humla*,
Universitetsgata 26 ☎ 424420, has
the best cabaret. At the Scandinavia
and Grand Hotels the restaurant
dance bands play late at the *Galaxy*
and the *Bonanza* respectively.
Sardines, Munkedamsveien 15
☎ 830075, is Oslo's liveliest disco.

Shopping
Stores are generally open Mon–Fri,
9–5 (Thu until 7); Sat, 9–2. Those in
the central station stay open late and
all weekend.

Most of Oslo's best shops are
concentrated in the two parallel
streets of Kristian IV's gate and Karl
Johans gate. Where these two avenues
meet, in Stortorvet, by the Cathedral,
is *Glasmagasin*, which sells the best of
Norway's, and Scandinavia's glass,
ceramics and furnishing fabrics.
Porsgrund porcelain and Hadeland
glass are distinctively Norwegian.
Also on display are Norwegian
pewter, from "antiqued" items to the
contemporary works of designers like
Gunnar Havstad.

Smaller shops selling locally made
products include furriers *Brødrene
Thorkildsen*, Øvre Slottsgate 18;
jeweller *David-Andersen*, Karl Johans
gate 20 and Steners gate 1, who

specializes in peacock-blue enamel wear; and the *Husfliden*, Møllergata 4, stocks handicrafts including Norwegian sweaters and embroidered folk costumes. At *Aker Brygge*, on the Stranden, are small shops in the 200-year-old shipbuilding halls. Entertainers and cafés make it an entertaining experience. When buying goods ask about tax concessions.

Sightseeing

In the summer expect to encounter tourists. Museums vary their opening hours according to the daylight; check at the tourist office.

Akershus Festning Restored 14thC fort containing state apartments and a museum devoted to the World War II resistance movement. *Festningspl. Open May–mid-Sep, Mon–Sat, 10–4; Sun, 12.30–4.*

Domkirke The cathedral was built 1694–99 but restored several times. Striking modern stained glass and ceiling frescoes. *Stortorvet.*

Frogner/Vigeland Huge park scattered with 650 granite and bronze sculptures by Gustav Vigeland (1869–1943), illustrating man's lifecycle and range of emotions.

Historisk Museum Oslo University's collection of archeological finds, notably some fine Viking jewellery and artifacts. *Fredriks gate. Open Tue–Sun, 12–3.*

Kon-Tiki Museet Contains the balsawood raft on which Thor Heyerdahl sailed from Peru to Polynesia in 1947 and his papyrus *Ra II* used to cross from Morocco to Barbados in 1970. In a separate building is the *Fram*, which sailed to both poles between 1893 and 1912. *Bygdøynes. Open daily, winter, 10.30–4; summer, 10–6.*

Munch Museet Paintings, drawings, prints and sculptures which Edvard Munch (1863–1944) bequeathed to the city. *Tøyengata 53. Open Tue–Sat, 10–8; Sun, 12–8.*

Nasjonalgalleriet Packed with paintings and sculpture, including works by Munch. *Universitetsgata 13. Open Mon–Fri, 10–4 (Tue, Thu, also 6–8); Sat, 10–3; Sun, 12–3.*

Norsk Folkemuseum Historic Norwegian buildings in a large park, including some 150 wooden farmhouses and a 13thC stave-church. *Museumsveien 10, Bygdøy. Open daily, winter, 11–4; summer, 10–6 (Sun, 11–6).*

Stortinget (Parliament) Built in neo-Romanesque style; rich interiors. *Open in summer recess.*

Vikingskiphuset At Bygdøy (15mins by road or 20mins by ferry from the City Hall) the Viking ship museum contains three Viking ships and funerary objects, 9th and 10thC, well displayed. *Hukvaveny. Open daily, winter, 11–3; summer, 10–6.*

Guided tours HMK *Tours* ☎ 208302. *Fjord Cruises* ☎ 419996 runs trips in Oslo Fjord; *Norway Yacht Charter* ☎ 414323 for cruise boats.

Spectator sports

Horse-racing The *Øvrevoll*, Vollsveien 132 ☎ 240190, is at Eiksmarka in the northwest. Trotting at *Bjerke Travbane*, Trondheimsveien ☎ 646050.

Skiing International skiing events are held at the *Holmenkollen Ski Arena* ☎ 141690 in the hills 8kms/5 miles north, within reach by tram.

Keeping fit

Daily membership at clubs is usually available.

Fitness centres Fitness Network, Olaf Helseths vei 2 ☎ 297016, and *The Workout*, Thereses gate 31 ☎ 604771.

Golf Oslo Golfklubb ☎ 240567 at Bogstad, 10kms/6 miles north of central Oslo, open May–Oct; members of recognized clubs welcome.

Squash Sagene Squash-senter, Sagveien 2 ☎ 355511, or *Sentrum Squash*, Thor Olsens gate 5 ☎ 207060.

Swimming Bislet Bad, Pilestredet 60 ☎ 464176, has a large indoor pool. Beaches on Langøyene island can be reached by ferry opposite City Hall.

Tennis Oslo Tennis Klubb, Hyllveien 5 ☎ 556981, and *Njårdhallen*, Sørkedalsveien 106 ☎ 141592.

Local resources

Business services

The SAS *Scandinavia Hotel* has a well-equipped business centre.
Photocopying and printing Weberg's Printshop, Pilestredet 1 ☎ 428643.
Secretarial Manpower, Dr Maudsgate 10 ☎ 115100.
Translation Forenede Translatører, Kongens gate 15 ☎ 425640 handles business and technical work.

Communications

Local delivery Securitas Express ☎ 679010; *Budbiler Tiny* ☎ 180680.
Long-distance delivery DHL ☎ 463470.
Post office Main office: Dronningens gate 15, open Mon–Fri, 8–10; Sat, 9–3.
Telex and fax At Kongens gate 21, open daily, 8–9.

Conference/exhibition centres

The *Oslo Convention Bureau*, Rådhusgata 23 ☎ 422982, provides free information on facilities and major events. Most of these take place at the *Info-Rama Convention Centre*, Sandviksveien 184, Sandivika ☎ 546090 ⊤⨯ 72690, next to the Rica Oslofjord Hotel. The centre has 5,000 sq metres/54,000 sq ft of space and meeting rooms for up to 2,500.

The principal trade fairs take place at *Norges Varemesse* (or *Sjølystsenteret*), Drammensveien 154 ☎ 438080 ⊤⨯ 78748: 5 exhibition halls (17,000 sq metres/183,600 sq ft) and a conference hall for up to 300. Fur trade exhibitions are held at the *Skinnsentret Kongress*, Økern Torgvei 13 ☎ 644150.

The *Caravelle Conference Centre*, Fornebu, Oslo Lufthavn, N-1330 ☎ 596150, has meeting rooms with a/v equipment for up to 100.

Emergencies

Bureaux de change Normal bank hours are Mon–Fri, 8.15–3.30 (Sep–May); 8.15–3 (Jun–Aug). The bank at the central railway station is open Mon–Fri, 8–8.30; Sat, 8–2 (Oct–May); daily, 7–11 (Jun–Sep). The bank at *Fornebu airport* is open Mon–Fri, 6.30–9; Sat, 7.30–7; Sun, 7–10am; and at *Gardermoen airport* Mon–Fri, 6–9; Sat, 6–8; Sun, 6–6.30.
Hospital 24hr emergency: *Oslo Kommunale Legevakt*, Storgatan 40 ☎ 201090. Dental treatment, *Oslo Kommunale Tannlegevakt*, Tøyen Senter, Kolstadgata 18 ☎ 674846; open Mon–Fri, 8pm–11pm; Sat & Sun, 11am–2pm, 8pm–11pm.
Pharmacy Jernbanetorgets Apotek, Jernbanetorget 4 ☎ 412482, 24hrs.
Police Headquarters: *Oslo Politikammer* and *Politistasjon*, Grønlandsleiret 44 ☎ 669966 (24hrs); foreign visitors' daytime line ☎ 669050. Emergency ☎ 002.

Government offices

The *Ministry of Industry*, POB 8014, Dep.,N-0030, Oslo 1 ☎ 349090; *Ministry of Trade and Shipping*, POB 8113 Dep. N-0032, Oslo 1 ☎ 314050.

Information sources

Business information Oslo Handelskammer (Chamber of commerce), Drammensveien 30 ☎ 557400. *Norges Industriforbund*, Middelthunsgate 27 ☎ 603290, gives information on investing in Norway.
Local media The main daily newspaper is *Aftenposten*.
Tourist information The main tourist office at *City Hall*, Rådhuset ☎ 334386, is open Mon–Fri, 8.30–4; Sat, 8.30–2.30 (Jan–May and Sep–Dec); Mon–Sat, 8.30–7; Sun, 9–5 (Jun–Aug). The information desk at the central station is open daily, 8–11.

Thank-yous

Chocolates Freia hand-made confectionery at *Freia på Karl Johan*, Karl Johans gate 31 ☎ 427466.
Florists Hoegh, Stortingsgata 26 ☎ 421736, and *Scandinavia Blomster* ☎ 112366 (Scandinavia Hotel).
Wines and spirits are sold only from state-run shops (*Vinmonopolet*) open Mon–Fri, 10–4; Sat, 9–1. The most central are at Fridtjof Nansens plass and Universitetsgata 7.

PORTUGAL

After severe balance of payments problems and spiralling debt in the mid-1980s the Portuguese economy is making a recovery: growth rates are above the EC average, unemployment is falling and inflation is high but under control. Severe difficulties remain, however.

Agriculture has steadily diminished in importance and currently contributes less than 10% to GDP, although it still accounts for 25% of export earnings and employs over 20% of the work force. The size of the average farm is small, methods of production are outdated, soil quality is generally poor and rainfall variable, and so productivity is very low by West European standards.

After initial rapid growth in the 1960s and early 1970s, domestic-owned manufacturing industries have performed poorly and need restructuring, especially the steel, chemicals and oil refining industries. Much of the impetus for modernization comes from abroad. Foreign investment in industry (and services) has increased significantly since Portugal joined the EC in 1986. Several multinationals are now based there, attracted by low labour costs. As agriculture and domestic-owned industry have declined in importance, service industries have recorded strong growth and now contribute about 50% to GDP and employ over 40% of the work force. The highest growth has been in tourism and banking. Portugal also has a flourishing black economy.

A vast majority of Portugal's foreign trade is with EC countries. Its exports are still dominated by low technology products, of which the main ones are textiles, clothing and footwear, machinery and transport equipment, wood, cork, paper and pulp, and food products. The main imports are machinery and transport equipment, food products, chemicals, mineral fuels and oil. Portugal regularly runs a deficit on its visible trade account, which is largely offset by tourism earnings, EC transfers and remittances from migrant workers.

Geography Portugal is divided into two by the River Tagus. The north consists of mountains and plateaux. The south has rolling lowlands. Much of the Portugal is covered by forest. The coast is dotted with capes and sandbars.

Climate Winters are cool and wet, summers are warm and dry. The south is prone to drought; the north has the highest rainfall.

Population 10.3m.

Government Portugal is a republic. The president is directly elected for a term of 5 years. The single chamber legislature, the assembly of the republic, has 250 members elected for 4 years. The prime minister is the leader of the majority party in the assembly.

Currency Escudo (Esc).

Time GMT; early Apr–end Sep, 1hr ahead of GMT.

Dialling codes Portugal's IDD code is 351. Omit the initial 0 from the city code when dialling from abroad. To make an international call from Lisbon dial 00 (for European countries) or 097 (for countries outside Europe) before dialling the relevant country code.

Public holidays Jan 1, Shrove Tue, Good Fri, Apr 25, May 1, Corpus Christi, Jun 10, Jun 13 (Lisbon), Jun 24 (Oporto), Aug 15, Oct 5, Nov 1, Dec 1, Dec 8, Dec 25.

LISBON (Lisboa)

City code ☎ 01

Portugal's capital had its heyday in the late 15th and 16th centuries, when its prosperity was based on the expanding Empire and trade in gold and diamonds, spices and slaves. This was the era of the great discoverers (Cabral, Magellan, Bartholomew Diaz and Vasco da Gama) and of King Manuel I, who gave his name to an architectural style unique to Lisbon. Invasion and earthquakes eventually undermined the confidence of the city and the prosperity of the country, but Lisbon retains some of the air of a grand capital: the centre was rebuilt in stately style after the great earthquake of 1755 reduced it to rubble. Now its fine 18thC buildings are looking somewhat dilapidated. In 1974 Lisbon was the scene of the bloodless Carnation Revolution (the graffiti can still be seen), and it received many *retornados* from the last colonies a year later. At the most recent census the population was still under 1m, but commuters from beyond the city limits swell it daily to around 1.5m. Its international importance has declined, but membership of the EC has encouraged foreign investment, and many multinationals have affiliated companies or joint ventures here. It is Portugal's main import centre.

Industries around Lisbon include steel (Siderurgia Nacional, 20kms/12 miles away), engineering, cement (Cimpor, Secil), chemicals (Quimigal) and vehicle assembly. Petrogal, the top company for sales, has a refinery at Cabo Ruivo. The port, at the estuary of the Tagus, is still the site of Portugal's main shipyards (Setenave, Lisnave, Soponata).

Portugal has the lowest standard of living in western Europe and it shows, even in the capital. There are scant funds for the improvement of public transport and roads or the restoration of the centre, but membership of the EC has began to pay economic dividends. For the visitor, the beauty of the setting, on seven hills overlooking the Tagus, the sunny climate and the relaxed, friendly nature of the people make Lisbon a pleasant place to do business.

Arriving

Lisbon is served by TWA, Air Canada, the main European airlines, some African ones and Varig (Brazilian airlines). Air Portugal (TAP) flies direct from New York and Boston, Montreal and Toronto, Rio de Janeiro and São Paolo as well as European and some African cities. Domestic flights from Porto (Oporto), which is 315kms/195 miles north, are numerous and take about 45mins.

There are overnight trains from Paris (15hrs 30mins) and Madrid (11hrs 15mins). There is also a good service from Porto (much quicker than driving: the Auto-Estrada do Norte is incomplete and the journey takes about 5hrs 30mins). The road from Madrid is better and the drive can take under 8hrs. Lisbon is connected by highway with Setúbal, to the south, and there are some short stretches of highway to the west of the city.

Portela airport

The airport is small and arriving passengers can often be at their hotel or in the centre of town within 50mins of landing. Facilities are few but adequate and include a tourist office ☎ 88 59 74, VIP lounge and duty-free shops. Domestic routes operated by LAR include daily flights from Porto and Bragança. Passenger inquiries ☎ 80 45 00 or 88 91 81; freight inquiries ☎ 88 11 01.

City link The airport is 8kms/5 miles north of the centre. The drive takes about 20mins; 45mins in rush hours.
Taxi Cabs wait outside arrivals. Heavy baggage is subject to a 50% surcharge – but the journey will not cost more than Esc500.
Car rental Several firms have offices near the exit.
Bus The green line (*linha verde*) express bus runs to the centre and Santa Apolónia station, and there are also buses to Cais do Sodré station via central Lisbon.

Railway stations
There are express trains from most major Portuguese towns. Santa Apolónia is the main station for international trains and trains from Porto. Many commuters use Cais do Sodré (the train journey is more convenient and pleasant than the drive from Cascais or Estoril). Information ☎ 87 70 92.
Santa Apolónia station Trains from Porto (3hrs 40mins) and the north, plus twice-daily services from Madrid and Paris, with sleepers. There is a tourist office ☎ 86 78 48 and car rental offices. You often have to wait for a taxi; a bus to the centre of town may be quicker. Inquiries ☎ 87 60 25 or 86 41 81.
Cais do Sodré station Regular commuter trains run along the coast from Cascais, Estoril and Belém. Inquiries ☎ 37 01 81.
Rossio station Trains from Sintra (every 20mins) and the west. Inquiries ☎ 36 50 22.
Sul e Sueste station Trains from the south and southwest: InterCity trains from Faro (Algarve) take 4hrs 20mins. Ferry connection for trains to the south and southwest from Barreiro across the Tagus. Inquiries ☎ 36 76 31.

Getting around
Lisbon's distinctive taxis (black with pale green roofs) are cheap, convenient, but are sometimes scarce. Buses and the subway are easy to use; the bus network is more extensive.

The Tagus is crossed by Europe's longest suspension bridge (with tolls) or by ferry.
Taxis Cabs will usually stop if hailed in the street, except on the main avenues where traffic is fast-flowing. They also wait in the street, and cabs can be called: *Radio Taxis* ☎ 82 50 61–5 or *AutoCoop* ☎ 73 27 56. Tip 10% or round up the fare.
Limousines Fredauto ☎ 52 68 70; *Samar* ☎ 76 61 48.
Driving Traffic and parking can be tiresome and Lisboans often become aggressive behind the wheel. People arriving by car may find it easier to park it (at their hotel or the Praça dos Restauradores) and use taxis for getting around town. For those with business outside the centre, many hotels have car rental representatives. Local car rental firms are cheap: *Euroauto* ☎ 54 27 11; *Monomotor* ☎ 66 85 07; *Rupauto* ☎ 77 80 86 (branches in Spain); *Turim* ☎ 54 41 64; *Viata* ☎ 73 31 48. International firms include *Avis* ☎ 36 26 76 (or at several hotels); *Europcar* ☎ 52 45 58.
Walking The main avenues can seem interminable on foot. Save your energies for exploring the narrow, steep alleys of the Bairro Alto and the Alfama districts. The Bairro Alto can be reached by the Santa Justa elevator or by funicular from Praça dos Restauradores.
Bus and tram Bus (and tram) stops are marked *Paragem*, and have clear diagrams of routes. Tickets are bought when you board, or you can buy a 4- or 7-day tourist card (also valid on the subway) from the stand under the Santa Justa elevator or in Largo do Rato or outside Cais do Sodré station.
Subway The subway is cheaper than either bus or tram. The line runs in a 12km/7 mile loop from the Zoo at Sete Rios, via Rotonda (Praça da Pombal) and Rossio to the newer parts of the city in the north, with an extra branch from Rotonda to the University. The service is quite fast and frequent, but crowded at rush hours; beware of pickpockets.

Ferry There are ferries across the Tagus from Praça do Comércio and Cais do Sodré to Cacilhas and Barreiro, and from Belém.
Train Commuter trains run along the coast every 20mins from Cais do Sodré to Cascais (journey 35mins).

Area by area

The heart of Lisbon was laid out by the Marquês de Pombal after the earthquake of 1755. The Rossio (as the Praça Dom Pedro IV is invariably known), with its café terraces, is linked to the stately Praça do Comércio on the waterfront by a grid of parallel streets. This area, Baixa, is still a commercial district with shops, banks and older business offices, but it is fairly dilapidated in appearance. To the north the Avenida da Liberdade is lined with hotels, airline offices and company headquarters. At the top is the Praça Marquês de Pombal, an important road junction. Beyond it lies the Parque Eduardo VII, overlooked by some of the major hotels. The modern business area has expanded north, along the Avenida da República, and west around the new Amoreiras shopping centre.

West of the Rossio lies the Chiado district, with some of the city's best shops, but the top end of the Rua da Carmo was gutted by fire in 1988. Higher up still is the Bairro Alto, an old quarter with many restaurants. Opposite, to the east of the Baixa district, is the medieval Moorish quarter of Alfama, with steep, scruffily picturesque streets around the Castelo de São Jorge.

The preferred residential districts are the Graça, near the Alfama, and to the west of the centre, around Lapa (with many embassies) and near the Parliament. There are some fine villas at Restelo, behind Belém (see *Sightseeing*). Industry is concentrated to the east (Petrogal has a refinery at Cabo Ruivo), around the port, and south of the Tagus.
The suburbs The famous, if faded, resort of Estoril (25kms/16 miles), long the haunt of exiled monarchy, and the extended fishing village of Cascais (28kms/17 miles) are now effectively suburbs of Lisbon. South of the Tagus, Cacilhas is a residential and commercial area.

Hotels

Most hotels are concentrated around the Avenida da Liberdade and the Eduardo VII park. A few big modern hotels are slightly farther out; there is virtually nowhere to stay in the old centre. Standards vary considerably, even in the top categories. The hotels given full entries all offer parking, IDD phones, air conditioning, TV with satellite, minibars, laundry service, currency exchange, and several have business centres. Advance reservations are recommended, especially in spring and autumn. Reduced rates are sometimes offered in low-season. In summer consider staying at Cascais or Estoril (see *Out of town*).

Lisboa Sheraton *E*////
Rua Latino Coelho 1, 1097
☎ 57 57 57 ⊤ 12774 fax 54 71 64
• *AE DC MC V* • *384 rooms, 16 suites, 2 restaurants, 3 bars*
This is not one of the best Sheratons, but its location (just east of Praça Marquês de Pombal) is convenient for longer-stay executives working for multinationals based on this side of town. It is a 15min drive from the airport. Public areas are very dull, but there is a splendid view from the Panorama bar. The best rooms are at the top of the Sheraton Towers. Ask for a view of the Tagus and old town. Nonsmoking rooms. Hairdresser, shops • pool, fitness centre, sauna • 2 meeting rooms (capacity up to 500).

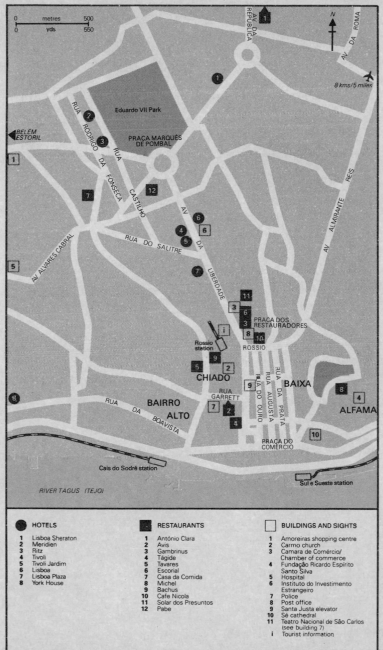

LISBON

	metres	500
0		
0	yds	550

Eduardo VII Park

PRAÇA MARQUÊS DE POMBAL

BELÉM ESTORIL

RUA RODRIGO DA FONSECA

RUA CASTILHO

RUA DO SALITRE

AV ALVARES CABRAL

AV DA REPÚBLICA

AV DA ROMA

AV ALMIRANTE REIS

8 kms/5 miles

AV DA LIBERDADE

PRAÇA DOS RESTAURADORES

Rossio station

ROSSIO

CHIADO

BAIRRO ALTO

RUA DA BOAVISTA

RUA GARRETT

BAIXA

RUA DA PRATA

RUA AUGUSTA

RUA DO OURO

ALFAMA

PRAÇA DO COMÉRCIO

Cais do Sodré station

Sul e Sueste station

RIVER TAGUS (TEJO)

HOTELS

1 Lisboa Sheraton
2 Meridien
3 Ritz
4 Tivoli
5 Tivoli Jardim
6 Lisboa
7 Lisboa Plaza
8 York House

RESTAURANTS

1 António Clara
2 Avis
3 Gambrinus
4 Tágide
5 Tavares
6 Escorial
7 Casa da Comida
8 Michel
9 Bachus
10 Cafe Nicola
11 Solar dos Presuntos
12 Pabe

BUILDINGS AND SIGHTS

1 Amoreiras shopping centre
2 Carmo church
3 Camara de Comércio/
  Chamber of commerce
4 Fundação Ricardo Espírito
  Santo Silva
5 Hospital
6 Instituto do Investimento
  Estrangeiro
7 Police
8 Post office
9 Santa Justa elevator
10 Sé cathedral
11 Teatro Nacional de São Carlos
  (see building 7)
i Tourist information

Meridien *E*////
Rua Castilho 149, 1000 ☎ *69 04 00*
⊠ *64315 fax 69 32 31* • *AE DC MC V*
• *307 rooms, 22 suites, 3 restaurants,*
1 bar
Next to the Ritz, overlooking
Eduardo VII park, the Meridien is
light, airy and modern with spacious
bedrooms in neutral colours, and
marble bathrooms. The coffee shop is
popular for buffet lunches. Medical
conferences are often held here.
Hairdresser, shops • business centre,
6 meeting rooms (capacity up to 600).

Ritz *E*////
Rua Rodrigo da Fonseca 88, 1093
☎ *69 20 20* ⊠ *12589 fax 69 17 83* •
InterContinental • *AE DC MC V* •
283 rooms, 20 suites, 2 restaurants,
1 bar
The Ritz is unquestionably the best
address in town. Its traditional style
and service contrast with its
nondescript modern exterior. The
spacious lobby and elegant lounge,
hung with striking modern tapestries,
are luxurious. Bedrooms are more
ordinary (except the suites, some with
antiques, others contemporary in
style), but all have good marble
bathrooms. The main restaurant, the
Varanda, is popular for buffet lunches
and has a summer terrace: the Grill is
more intimate, but in sober club
style. For a private working lunch
reserve the smallest function room
instead. For daytime meetings the
quiet and civilized lounge, where
afternoon tea and drinks are served,
is more pleasant than the rather
dark bar. Shops • business centre,
6 meeting rooms (capacity up to
600).

Tivoli *E*//
Av da Liberdade 185, 1200
☎ *53 01 81* ⊠ *12588 fax 57 94 61*
• *AE DC MC V* • *326 rooms, 16 suites,*
2 restaurants, 2 bars
Its central location, efficient service,
pleasant pool and fair prices attract a
continuous flow of guests to the
Tivoli, and it is wise to reserve a
room well ahead (especially on

Thursdays when TWA staff arrive *en
masse*). Europeans looking for
business contacts in Portugal often
stay here, and it is popular with the
Spanish, Brazilians and Americans.
The huge hall is a good meeting place
(the lobby bar opens at 11am). The
rooftop restaurant O Terraco, with a
small separate bar and seating area, is
very popular for business lunches,
especially in summer when the terrace
is open. Hairdresser • pool, tennis •
business centre, 4 meeting rooms
(capacity up to 200).

Tivoli Jardim *E*
Rua Júlio César Machado 7, 1200
☎ *53 99 71* ⊠ *12172 fax 55 65 66* •
AE DC MC V • *119 rooms, 1 restaurant,*
1 bar
The neighbour and sister hotel of the
Tivoli shares its pool and tennis court
and has access to its business
facilities. It is a pleasant, efficiently
run hotel, and 90% of its guests are
on business. The atmosphere here is
less bustling than in the Tivoli,
notably in the hall which is a good
quiet place for a chat. Bedrooms and
bathrooms are plain and fairly small;
rooms on the front have balconies.
There is a rather institutional
trattoria-style restaurant. Hairdresser,
newsstand.

OTHER HOTELS
Lisboa *E*// *Rua Barata Salgueiro*
15, 1100 ☎ *55 41 31* ⊠ *60228*
fax 55 41 39 • *AE DC MC V*. A new,
useful bed-and-breakfast base,
offering spotless rooms, a stylish
piano bar and good amenities.
Lisboa Plaza *E*// *Travessa do*
Salitre 7, 1200 ☎ *346 39 22* ⊠ *16402*
fax 37 16 30 • *AE DC MC V*. A chic
small family-run hotel with a very
good location and facilities. Entirely
refurbished in spring 1989. Buffet
breakfasts.
York House *E*// *Rua das Janelas*
Verdes 32, 1200 ☎ *66 24 35* ⊠ *16791*
• *AE DC MC V*. Charming small hotel
which feels like a comfortable private
home. Pleasant atmosphere and
attractive courtyard garden.

Out of town
Many visitors stay outside Lisbon to
the west, commuting on the train
from the coastal resorts, where hotels
have pools and easy access to golf and
watersports. The *Estoril Palácio*
☎ 268 04 00 at Estoril (25kms/16
miles) is a classic luxury hotel in
turn-of-the-century European resort
style, with conference facilities and its
own golf course. More fashionable
and exclusive (in both size and
clientele) is the *Albatroz* ☎ 28 28 21
at Cascais (29kms/18 miles), which
has an excellent restaurant. For an
off-duty weekend the beautiful and
quietly luxurious *Palácio dos Seteais*
☎ 923 32 00 at Sintra (30kms/19
miles west) is the perfect retreat; and

there are many smaller hotels in these
towns ideal for time off.

Clubs
The *Clube de Empresários* is a club for
business executives and professionals,
with some 400 members, based at the
António Clara (see *Restaurants*),
where members can reserve the
private rooms. Although principally a
dining club, it offers secretarial and
telex services.

> **Hotel and restaurant price guide**
> For the meanings of the hotel and
> restaurant price symbols, see
> pages 6 and 7.

Restaurants
Lisbon has a handful of restaurants well-known locally for business
entertaining, and they include those with the best food (usually fish) as
well as the most comfortable surroundings. Restaurants of the top hotels
are also suitable but in other places the menu many be more limited;
bucalhau, a dried cod dish, is ubiquitous. The restaurants recommended
serve Portuguese wines and champagne. Reservations are advisable.

António Clara *E//*
Av da República 38 ☎ *76 63 80* •
closed Sun • *AE DC MC V*
In an old house on this busy
thoroughfare, António Clara is a well-
known place for business entertaining
(see *Clubs*). The downstairs rooms are
ornate, old-fashioned salons with
well-spaced tables; upstairs there is an
additional restaurant (usually open
only at lunch) and several private
dining rooms for club members.
Service is formal but friendly, food
traditional Portuguese with some
international inspiration.

Avis *E////*
Rua Serpa Pinto 12B ☎ *32 63 91* •
closed Sat L, Sun, hols • *AE DC MC V*
• *jacket L, suit and tie D*
Senior politicians, bankers and
executives frequent the elegant dining
room of this fine old mansion in the
Chiado district. Avis represents
tradition but is still fashionable, and

the food – especially the smoked
swordfish, duck and partridge – is
very good. There is a dark club-like
bar with panelled walls and leather
upholstery adjacent to the dining
room. For extra privacy part of the
restaurant can be curtained off (this
area is ideal for a table of ten).

Gambrinus *E/////*
Rua Portas de Santo Antao 25
☎ *32 14 66* • *AE MC V*
Another well-known haunt of
politicians, bankers and the business
community, favoured for company
entertaining. It consists of two rooms,
panelled, beamed and hung with
tapestries, and a long bar where lone
lunchers sit over their newspapers.
There are no private rooms: people
who come here like to see and be
seen. Gambrinus is known for its
seafood and very professional service.
A particularly good choice for a long
lunch or late dinner.

Tágide $E///$
Largo Academia das Belas Artes 18
☎ *32 07 20 • closed Sat D, Sun •*
AE DC MC V
Tágide shows Lisbon in its best light
and is appreciated by locals and
visitors alike. There is a stupendous
view of the Tagus and the Alfama
(reserve two or three days in advance
to secure a window table), and the
cooking is excellent and appetizingly
displayed. The cool, calm and
sophisticated surroundings – 18thC
style, with pretty *azulejo* tiles – and
the attentive service set just the right
tone for a business meeting. The
superb private room, its deep red
walls hung with Old Master
paintings, has no distracting view.

OTHER RESTAURANTS
Other restaurants suitable for a
formal business meal include *Tavares*,
Rua da Misericordia 37 ☎ 32 11 12, a
famous Edwardian-style restaurant,
now somewhat faded in its glory but
with an impressive cellar. It is still
popular with older people. *Escorial*,
Rua das Portas di Santo Antao 47
☎ 36 44 29, is in the same class as its
neighbour Gambrinus for seafood,
but with slightly oppressive, though
comfortable, modern decor. *Casa da
Comida*, Travessa das Amoreiras 1
☎ 68 53 76, is worth seeking out for
its good food and attractive garden
setting. Also in the luxury class is
Michel, Largo de Santa Cruz de
Castelo 5 ☎ 86 43 38, near the
Castelo São Jorge, for cooking with a
nouvelle touch. *Bachus*, Largo da
Trindade 9 ☎ 32 28 28, has a bar
and intimate upstairs restaurant, more
suitable for dinner than a working
lunch.

Popular places for lunch in the
centre of town are the *Cafe Nicola*,
Rossio ☎ 36 05 79, where the tables
inside are more suitable if you need
to concentrate, and *Solar dos
Presuntos*, Rua Portas de Santo Antao
150–2 ☎ 32 42 53, for seafood; more
comfortable upstairs. In the Marquês
de Pombal area the authentic English
pub decor and atmosphere of *Pabe*,

Rua Duque de Palmela 27A
☎ 53 56 75, attract a high-level
business and political clientele.

The *fado* restaurants in old parts of
town like the Alfama and the Bairro
Alto are best left to tourists, but there
are some good places for a relaxed
meal. Try *O Conventual*, Praça das
Flores 45 ☎ 60 91 96, for old
monastic recipes in a quiet setting, or
the fashionable *Pap'acorda*, Rua da
Atalaia 57 ☎ 36 48 11, one of the
best in the Bairro Alto, and especially
popular for dinner. *Casanostra*,
Travessa Poco da Cidade 60, serves
good Italian *nuova cucina*. In the
Alfama area *O Faz Figura*, Rua
Paraiso 15B ☎ 86 89 81, has a terrace
with a fine view of the port, and
serves good fish.

In the Lapa district, near the
National Assembly, is the highly
regarded *Sua Excellencia*, Rua do
Conde 42 ☎ 60 36 14. Nearby *Varina
da Madragoa*, Rua da Madres 36
☎ 66 55 33, is simple and
inexpensive. The separate dining
room of the fashionable disco *Banana
Power*, Rua de Cascais ☎ 63 18 15, is
used for business entertaining but
open to members and guests only.

Out of town
Cascais has some of the best fish
restaurants in the area. The *Hotel
Albatroz* ☎ 28 28 21 has an excellent
restaurant, particularly favoured for
business entertaining. Also good are
João Padeiro ☎ 28 02 32, with
panelled dining rooms, and *Beiramar*
☎ 28 01 52, with tiled decor, next to
the fish market: at both you can
choose fish or shellfish from a display.

Bars and cafés
Cafe Nicola on the Rossio is a good
central meeting place; avoid meal
times if you only want a drink. The
lobby of the *Tivoli Hotel* is another
popular place. There are several
ornate tearooms on the Avenida da
República, but the *Ritz* is the most
suitable place for a meeting at this
hour. *Pavilhao Chines*, Rua Dom
Pedro V 89, has a quaint charm.

Entertainment

The Calouste Gulbenkian Foundation sponsors a ballet company and many concerts, ☎ 77 91 31. The *Agenda Cultural*, available in many hotels, lists the month's cultural events: otherwise buy the weekly *Sete* on Wednesdays. *What's On in Lisbon* is a useful general guide, but does not have updated details of events.
Ticket agencies ABEP, Av Liberdade 740 ☎ 32 53 60.

Opera, theatre, dance and music Grande Auditório Fundação Calouste Gulbenkian, Av de Berna ☎ 77 41 67 (concerts and ballets); *Teatro Nacional de São Carlos*, Largo de S. Carlos ☎ 36 86 64 (main opera house, season Nov–Jun). The *Teatro Nacional D. Maria II*, on Rossio Square ☎ 37 10 78 or 37 22 46, is the national theatre. The *Teatro Nacional de S. Luis*, Rua Antonio Maria Cardoso, also puts on concerts and ballets.

Cinema Recent releases are shown in the original language, with subtitles. The daily *Diário de Noticias* newspaper has the best cinema guide. *Cinemateca*, Rua Barata Salgueiro 39, shows art films.

Nightclubs and casinos Those bent on nightlife here should try a *casa de fado*, where, for the price of a drink or a meal, you can listen to melancholy romantic songs. Otherwise there are plenty of noisy, fashionable discos (*Banana Power* ☎ 63 18 15 or *Stones* ☎ 66 45 45), mostly frequented by the young, or the *Estoril Casino* ☎ 268 45 21, with floor shows and a tourist clientele.

Shopping

The traditional shopping streets are the Rua Augusta, Rua do Ouro and Rua da Prata in the Baixa district and the fashionable Rua Garrett and Rua do Carmo in the Chiado district. Newer shops are in the Avenida da Roma area. Shopping centres, like the vast new Amoreiras Centre, with many designer boutiques, are open daily until 11pm or midnight. Best purchases include leather goods, ceramics (*Fabrica Sant'Anna*, Rua do Alecrim 95, for tiles in original 17thC and 18thC designs), traditional Arraiolos rugs (*Quintao*, Rua Ivens 34, or *Almorávida*, Rua do Milagre do Santo António 10) and Agulha tapestries (*Galeria Sesimbra* at the Ritz Hotel and at Rua Castilho 77). Local ceramics can be bought at the daily market at Cascais.

Sightseeing

Alfama Medieval district of Moorish architecture and steep, labyrinthine lanes. Panoramic views from the restored Castelo São Jorge. Romanesque Sé (cathedral).
Bairro Alto Old quarter reached by Eiffel-designed elevator, with the ruins of the Gothic Carmo church.
Belém contains many sights, notably the distinctive Belém Tower, a small Manueline fortress with fine views over the Tagus, and the Jerónimos Monastery, another masterpiece of the same style. Also here are the National Coach Museum, evoking Portugal's royal past, and the Maritime Museum. Another landmark is the Monument to the Discoveries.
Pombaline Lisbon The stately streets and squares laid out by the Marquês de Pombal after the 1755 earthquake. Praça do Comércio is the most impressive.

Most museums and other sights are closed on Mondays.
Calouste Gulbenkian Museum The magnificent private art collection of the Armenian oil magnate. *Av Berna 45. Open Tue–Sun, 10–5.*
Centro de Arte Moderna Calouste Gulbenkian The Gulbenkian Foundation's modern art gallery in an attractive parkland setting. *Rua Dr Nicolau de Bettencourt. Open Tue–Sun, 10–5.*
Fundação Ricardo Espírito Santo Silva A fine museum of Portuguese silver, furniture, ceramics and rugs displayed in a 17thC palace in the Alfama area. *Largo das Portas do Sol 2. Open Mon–Sat, 10–5; Sun, 3–5.*
Madre de Deus Lovely church with a

cloister in Manueline style and a
museum of *azulejo* tiles. *Open Tue–
Sun, 10–1, 2.30–5.*

Museu Nacional de Arte Antiga The
museum of "ancient" art consists
mainly of 15th and 16thC Portuguese
primitives, plus paintings of other
European schools, and important
collections of silver. *Rua das Janelas
Verdes. Open daily, 10–5.*

Palácio Nacional da Ajuda Royal
residence with 19thC decor and
collections of sculpture and paintings.
Largo da Ajuda. Open Tue–Sun, 10–5.

Guided tours
Half-day city tours and mini-cruises
on the Tagus (and evening tours with
dinner in a *fado* restaurant) are
operated by *Cityrama* ☎ 57 55 64,
Portugal Tours ☎ 54 35 39 and RN
☎ 57 75 23.

Out of town
The most rewarding day trip from
Lisbon is to the rococo-style National
Palace at Queluz (15kms/9 miles
northwest, closed Tue), and the
romantic town of Sintra (25kms/16
miles west) where there is a great deal
to see, including the Royal Palace
(closed Wed) and 19thC Pena
Palace (closed Mon). The convent,
church and palace at Mafra
(48kms/25 miles north) are also well
worth visiting.

Spectator sports
Bullfighting There are bullrings in
Lisbon (Praça de Touros, Campo
Pequeno, Av da República) and
Cascais. The season is mainly Jul–
Sep.

Football The fortunes of the two
main clubs, the Sport Lisboa e
Benfica and Sporting Clube de
Portugal, are eagerly followed. Both
clubs have their own stadiums:
Estádio da Luz, Av Norton de Matos
☎ 72 04 56, and *Estádio José
Alvalade*, Alameda das Linhas de
Torres ☎ 79 00 75, respectively.
Tickets ABEP ☎ 37 25 94.

There is Formula 1 motor racing at
the autodrome of Estoril, also the
starting point of the annual Port
Wine Rally. Horse-racing and
show-jumping are held at the
Campo Grande hippodrome and
in Cascais.

Keeping fit
Lisbon Country Club (18kms/11 miles)
at Quinta da Aroeira, 2825 Monte de
Caparica ☎ 226 32 44, has a golf
course, tennis courts, riding and
beaches. *Lisbon Sports Club*
(25kms/16 miles) at Casal da
Carregueira, Belas, 2745 Queluz
☎ 431 00 77 or 96 00 77, offers golf,
swimming and tennis. Some
companies have their own sports
facilities and several hotels have
pools.

Fitness centres Ginasio Jardim
☎ 69 33 20 and *Health Club Soleil*
☎ 69 28 08 are both in the Amoreiras
Centre. There is another branch of
the Health Club Soleil at the Sheraton
Hotel, open to nonresidents.

Golf Estoril Golf Club (28kms/17
miles) Av da República, Estoril
☎ 268 01 76 (also pool); *Estoril-Sol
Golf* near Sintra (35kms/22 miles),
Estrada da Lagoa Azul 3, Linhó
Sintra ☎ 923 24 61; *Marinha Golf*
(30kms/19 miles) Quinta da Marinha,
Cascais ☎ 28 90 08 (also pools,
riding, tennis). The tourist office
leaflet *Golf Portugal* gives full details
of all courses.

Riding Monsanto Park, Guincho
beach. Contact Sr Nuno Veloso at
Quinta de Marinha ☎ 28 92 82.

Swimming There are pools at the
Sheraton (open to nonresidents) and
Tivoli hotels.

Tennis There are clay courts at the
Clube de Ténis do Monsanto
☎ 64 80 67. The Tivoli Hotel also
has a court. The best facilities are at
the *Clube de Ténis do Estoril*, Av
Amaral ☎ 268 16 75, *Quinta da
Marinha* (see *Golf*) ☎ 28 90 76 and
the Country Club at Cascais.

Watersports There is sailing,
waterskiing and windsurfing all along
the Lisbon coast, particularly at
Cascais and Estoril. At Cascais is the
fashionable *Clube Naval* ☎ 28 01 25.

There are windsurfing centres or schools at Estoril ☎ 268 16 65 and Cascais ☎ 28 96 94. Carcavelos is good for beginners (windsurfing school ☎ 268 01 13).

Local resources

Business services

Chambers of commerce provide meeting rooms, telex, fax, photocopying and typing services. *Business services Recursos e Servicos*, Av Engenheiro Duarte Pacheco, Torre 2, ☎ 56 30 51, and *Intess-Sociedade de Interpretes e Secretariado*, Rua São Julião 62 ☎ 87 99 47, provide secretarial, word processing and translating services.

Photocopying and printing Copipronto, Quirico Fonseca 27A ☎ 52 86 79 (including off-set printing); *Copiagrafica*, Rua Aquilas Monteverde 26 ☎ 54 62 03; *Metrone*, Rua Conde Redondo 53 ☎ 56 02 06.

Secretarial American Typing Services, Rua Castilho 38 ☎ 53 96 50; *Manpower*, Praça José Fontana 9C ☎ 53 54 54.

Translation Hospedeiras de Portugal, Borg Carneiro 63 ☎ 60 43 53 or 67 55 34; *Transtext*, Rua Pres. Arriaga 3A ☎ 67 10 30.

Communications

Local delivery Pony Express ☎ 52 23 36. The post office also has an express delivery service.

Long-distance DHL ☎ 80 85 20; *Federal Express* ☎ 89 67 97.

Post office The post office (*Correio*) at Praça dos Restaurodores is open 8am–midnight. The post office at the airport is open daily 24hrs.

Telex and fax There are public telex and fax services at Praça D. Luis 22A and Praça do Comércio (both open Mon–Fri, 9–7).

Conference/exhibition centres

The Ritz InterContinental is well-equipped for conferences (☎ 65 81 71). The *Gulbenkian Foundation*, Av de Berna 45 ☎ 76 21 46, and the *Estoril Casino* ☎ 26 01 13 are also used. Big trade fairs are held at the

Feira Internacional, Associação Indústrial Portuguesa, Praça das Indústrias 1399 ☎ 64 41 61 Ⓣⓧ 12282 *fax* 63 90 48. *Lisbon Convention Bureau* ☎ 32 55 27.

Emergencies

Bureaux de change Some banks in the centre are open Mon–Sat, 6–11pm in addition to normal banking hours (8.30–11, 1–2.45). The airport bank is open 24hrs.

Hospitals The British Hospital, Rua Saraiva de Carvalho 49 ☎ 60 37 65 or 60 20 20.

Pharmacies One pharmacy per area is open until 10pm or midnight (addresses posted on doors).

Police ☎ 36 61 41 or 347 47 30. The police station at Rua Capelo 13 has English-speaking officers.

Government offices

Ministry of Trade and Tourism, Av da República 79, 1600 ☎ 73 04 12.

Information sources

Business information Associação Comércial de Lisboa – Câmara de Comércio e Indústria Portuguesa, Rua Portas de Santo Antao 89, 1194 ☎ 32 71 79; *Camera de Comércio Portuguesa para a Comunidade Economica Europeia* (chamber of commerce), Rua Viriato 5, 1000 ☎ 57 75 62; *Associação Indústrial Portuguesa*, Praça das Indústrias, 1300 ☎ 63 90 44 (advice and information about export; see also *Conference/exhibition centres*). *Instituto do Investimento Estrangeiro*, Av da Liberdade 258, 1200 ☎ 57 06 07.

Local media The main dailies are the *Correio do Manha*, *Diário de Noticias* and *Diário Popular*.

Tourist information Tourist office, Palácio Foz, Praça dos Restauradores ☎ 36 63 07 (and airport and stations). Information in English ☎ 36 94 50 (French 36 79 27, German 36 96 43).

Thank-yous

Chocolates Godiva, Amoreiras shopping centre ☎ 37 06 94.

SPAIN

The Spanish economy experienced high rates of growth in the 1960s and early 1970s then stagnated in the face of rising oil prices and world recession. A heavy dependence on imported oil and a slowness to respond to the crisis, combined with political uncertainty, deepened Spain's recession and delayed recovery. By 1986 the economy began to pick up again, helped by a revival in world trade, a softening of world energy prices, new investment and increased competitiveness. Economic growth exceeded 5% in 1987, and Spain re-established itself as one of the most dynamic economies in Europe.

Spanish industry has gone through a period of major reorganization and restructuring, known locally as "reconversion." This process has affected many of the established industries (such as steel, shipbuilding and textiles), which had generated economic growth in the 1960s but then contracted considerably under pressure of foreign competition. Today the fastest growing sectors are electrical machinery and transport equipment. Like neighbouring Portugal, Spain has received a high level of foreign investment, particularly since becoming a member of the EC in 1986, and some of the most striking performances in manufacturing have been achieved by multinational companies, which were attracted to Spain by low unit wage costs. This is most clearly the case in the automobile industry; Spain is now a leading manufacturer of cars. Government intervention in Spanish industry has proved costly and has produced a haphazard public sector ranging across many areas but dominated by heavy industry. The public sector has performed poorly in comparison with the rest of the economy during the 1980s; most investment and improvement in productivity have been registered in the private sector. A programme of partial privatization is expected to improve the performance of some companies.

The 1980s has seen progress in other sectors of the Spanish economy. Fruit and vegetable production has expanded significantly, although the large agricultural sector as a whole remains technically backward and productivity is low by West European standards. Recent takeovers in the banking world indicate that financial modernization is underway, construction is buoyant and the country's dependence on imported oil is being reduced gradually by increased use of nuclear and hydroelectic power (although the future of the nuclear power industry is less certain than it was a few years ago). Spain has a black economy of major but unquantifiable importance.

Most of Spain's external trade is with other EC countries; France and West Germany are its most important trading partners. Its main exports are manufactured goods (including vehicles and petroleum products), which account for over 70% of the total, and foodstuffs. Spain's main imports are raw materials, semi-manufactured goods, capital goods and non-food consumer goods. Crude oil and petroleum products account for over 15% of imports, although their relative share has been declining. Spain regularly runs a visible trade deficit, although this has mounted significantly in recent years due to a rapid growth in imports (especially in capital goods) as the economy has expanded. The trade deficit is offset to a varying degree by a surplus in invisibles, particularly from tourism, transfers and remittances from migrant workers.

Rapid economic growth in the late 1980s has had a limited impact on the level of unemployment. At 19% of the active population in 1988, the level of unemployment was only slightly down on the previous year's figure, and still the highest in the EC. Per capita income is still among the lowest in Europe, while standards of social services and infrastructure also remain well below those in most other European countries. Public discontent with the government over how Spain's new-found wealth should be distributed was highlighted by the almost total support for a national one-day strike in 1988.

Geography Spain has an unusually varied landscape. The centre consists of a wide semi-arid plateau, the Meseta, traversed by a central range. It is bounded on the north and east also by mountains, including the Pyrenees, which form the frontier with France. The most important lowland areas lie in the northeast around the valley of the Ebro, on the east coast around Valencia and in the south around the valley of the Guadalquivir. The province of Almeria contains Europe's only desert.

Climate In the north the climate is temperate, with mild winters and warm summers; temperatures range from 9–18°C (48–64°F). In the centre, the climate is more extreme, with cold winters and hot, dry summers; average temperatures range from 5–24°C (41–62°F). In the south it is typically Mediterranean.

Population 38.6m; 16% are Catalan, 2% Basque.

Government Spain is a parliamentary monarchy. The king has more influence than most constitutional monarchs.

The parliament, the Cortes, has 2 chambers. Real power lies in the lower chamber, the congress of deputies. It has 350 members elected by proportional representation. The upper chamber, the senate, has 208 directly elected members and 49 regional representatives. Elections must be held at least every 4 years. The prime minister is elected by members of parliament.

Spain has 17 autonomous regions. Considerable powers were transferred from the central administration in Madrid to regional governments in the 1978 constitution. Regional affinities are very strong in some areas.

Currency The unit of currency is the peseta (Pta).

It floats freely against all foreign currencies but policy has been to maintain relative stability against the currencies of other EC countries while maintaining export competitiveness and anti-inflation policy.

Time Spain is on Central European Time, which is 1hr ahead of GMT. Summer time is in force from early Apr to the end of Sep; clocks are put forward, and Spain is then 2hrs ahead of GMT.

Dialling codes Spain's IDD code is 34. Omit the initial 9 from the city code when dialling from abroad. To make an international call from Madrid, dial 07 (for European countries) or 097, before dialling the relevant country code.

Public holidays (* some areas only) Jan 1, Jan 6, Maundy Thu*, Good Fri, Easter Mon*, May 1, May 15*, Corpus Christi, Jun 24, Jul 25, Aug 15, Oct 12*, Nov 1, Dec 6, Dec 8*, Dec 25, Dec 26*.

MADRID
City code ☎ 19

Madrid sits high on the central plateau of Spain, with wide horizons and skies famed for their clear light (but occasional smog). By European standards it is in some ways a young city: it did not become capital until the 16th century and industrialization took place only in the middle of the 20th century. Since then change has been dramatic: the population has grown from 500,000 in the mid 1950s to nearly 5m today and since the death of Franco in 1975 the city has been transformed by major urban remodelling, rapid modernization of the business world and a revolution in social values.

In part this can be attributed to the new democratic spirit and *la movida*, the cultural effervescence often mentioned by the media. More prosaically it owes much to the 25-year plan drawn up by Enrique Tierno Galvan, the socialist mayor who died in 1986, and to heavy foreign investment. The changes continue, with the emphasis on solving traffic congestion, redeveloping the southern industrialized zone, expanding office space, moving businesses to the outskirts and gearing up for 1992, when Spain's transition period of entry into the EC ends and the European single market is due to enter into force. In that year also, the country celebrates the 500th anniversary of Columbus's voyage to the New World, Barcelona hosts the Olympic Games and Seville the international exhibition (Expo 92) – both important occasions encouraging investment – and Madrid will be the Cultural Capital of Europe.

The business community is also young – many top executives, like Spain's politicians, are in their 40s – and reflects the general optimism and determination to modernize, expand and develop in industry, transport, services and the arts. Advanced technology, such as electronics, optics, pharmaceuticals and telecommunications, has overtaken the older industries (printing, textiles, cars and steel) since the industrial crisis of the late 1970s, and there has been an influx of major international investors such as AT&T which has built its first European factory here, IBM, Dow Chemical, Shell and Unilever.

Over two-thirds of the largest national companies – including petrochemical giant, Repsol, SEAT cars, Rio Tinto and Telefónica telecommunications – also have their headquarters or major offices here. Madrid remains the administrative, public service and financial centre of the country. The stock exchange, deregulated in 1989, is small but buoyant and, along with the national economy, is growing fast.

Despite the urge to make up for lost time and an extended working day, the *madrileños* value their traditions more than ever and have kept their relaxed rhythm of life – the long, late lunch, numerous fiestas, late nights and an almost complete closure in August. It is this insistence on keeping the best of the old alongside the new, as reflected in the blend of historical restoration and bold new architecture, that is turning Madrid into one of the most exciting and elegant European cities of the 1990s.

Arriving
Madrid is well served by flights world
wide, six highways (*autopistas*) and an
efficient rail network, which includes
high-speed Talgo trains to all major
Spanish cities.

Barajas Internacional airport
Spain's largest airport has two
terminals, Internacional and
Nacional, linked by a covered
corridor with travelators. Within the
Nacional terminal is a separate
check-in and handling area for the
shuttle service (*puente aéreo*) to
Barcelona (45mins). Both terminals
are spacious and there are few delays;
allow 20–30mins to clear the airport.

Facilities include bookshops,
stationers, pharmacies, banks (all
open 24hrs) and a post office in both
terminals, and a rail ticket office and
car rental companies in the
Internacional terminal. There is an
airside international VIP lounge and
press office, but no special business
facilities, although the chamber of
commerce has a desk. The Nacional
terminal has the best choice of
restaurants. Flight information
☎ 205 83 43 or airlines; general
inquiries ☎ 205 40 90; freight
inquiries ☎ 205 46 50.
Nearby hotels There are two top
hotels 5mins' drive from the airport
(free transport): *Barajas*, Av de
Logroño 305 ☎ 747 77 00 ⊠ 22255
fax 747 87 17, and *Alameda*, Av de
Logroño 100 ☎ 747 48 00 ⊠ 43809
fax 747 89 28. *Diana*, C Galeón 27
☎ 747 13 55 ⊠ 45688 fax 747 97 97
is less luxurious. All accept major
credit cards.
City link Barajas is 16kms/10 miles
east of Madrid on the Barcelona
carretera nacional (highway). The best
way into town is by taxi or by
frequent and fast buses at a sixth of
the cost.
Taxi Cabs wait outside the terminals
and are plentiful; the ride takes
25mins (longer in the rush hours) and
costs about Pta1,200.
Bus Airport buses run by EMT leave
Barajas every 15mins from 4.45am to

1.15am for Plaza Colón (journey time
30mins; fare Pta200). Inquiries
☎ 401 99 00.
Car rental The leading companies
have desks in the arrivals area of the
Internacional terminal. A car is useful
for trips outside Madrid, but not
recommended for the city.

Railway stations
Madrid has three main stations, each
with a subway station of the same
name. In each, escalators connect the
concourse with platforms below.
Porters can be hard to find, but taxis
are plentiful. Inquiries ☎ 429 05 18
or 552 05 18; reservations
☎ 429 82 28.
Estación de Atocha South of the city
centre, the new terminal which is
under construction is for suburban
arrivals from Aranjuez and
Guadalajara. (The rebuilding of the
magnificent 19thC iron and glass
station is due for completion in 1992.)
Estación de Chamartín To the north
of the city, this is the most important
station, handling services from the
northeast, east and south, including
express Talgo and InterCity services
from Barcelona, Bilbao, Seville and
Valencia as well as all international
arrivals from, or via, France. The
design and facilities are like those of a
modern airport, including banks, a
post office, information desks,
snackbars and a first-class Rail Club
lounge. Within the same complex are
cinemas, restaurants, shops and a
hotel (see *Hotels*). The journey to the
main business area and Palacio de
Congresos takes about 10mins by
taxi.
Estación del Norte For arrivals from
the north and west, including those
from Santander, Santiago de
Compostela, Avila, Salamanca and
Lisbon. This old-fashioned station
has a restaurant, bar, book and
chocolate shops, and a small taxi-
rank.

Getting around
Madrid is spread over a large area,
and the summer heat and cold in

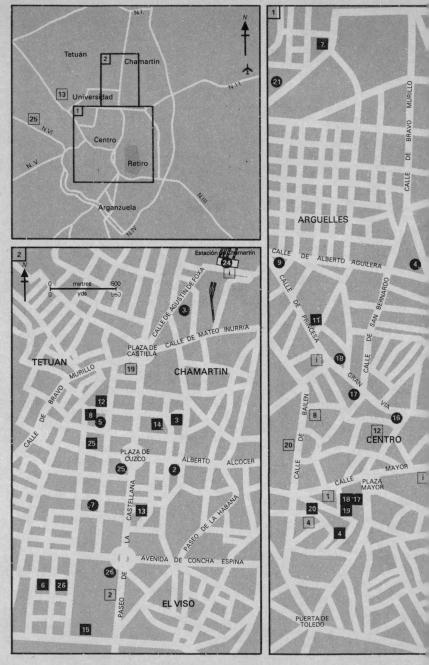

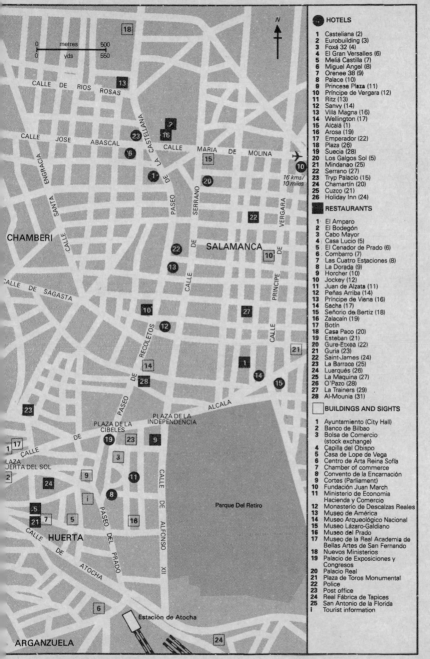

| 0 | metres | 500 |
| 0 | yds | 550 |

16 kms/
10 miles

CALLE DE RIOS ROSAS

CALLE JOSE ABASCAL

CALLE MARIA DE MOLINA

CALLE

SANTA ENGRACIA

LA CASTELLANA

PASEO DE SERRANO

PASEO DE LA CASTELLANA

CHAMBERI

CALLE DE SAGASTA

SALAMANCA

CALLE DE VERGARA

PRINCIPE DE VERGARA

CALLE

RECOLETOS

PASEO DE

ALCALA

PLAZA DE LA INDEPENDENCIA

PLAZA DE LA CIBELES

DE

PLAZA PUERTA DEL SOL

CALLE

Parque Del Retiro

CALLE DE ALFONSO XII

PASEO DEL PRADO

CALLE HUERTA

DE ATOCHA

ARGANZUELA

Estación de Atocha

HOTELS

1 Castellana (2)
2 Eurobuilding (3)
3 Foxá 32 (4)
4 El Gran Versalles (6)
5 Meliá Castilla (7)
6 Miguel Angel (8)
7 Orense 38 (9)
8 Palace (10)
9 Princesa Plaza (11)
10 Príncipe de Vergara (12)
11 Ritz (13)
12 Sanvy (14)
13 Villa Magna (16)
14 Wellington (17)
15 Alcalá (1)
16 Arosa (19)
17 Emperador (22)
18 Plaza (26)
19 Suecia (28)
20 Los Galgos Sol (5)
21 Mindanao (25)
22 Serrano (27)
23 Tryp Palacio (15)
24 Chamartín (20)
25 Cuzco (21)
26 Holiday Inn (24)

RESTAURANTS

1 El Amparo
2 El Bodegón
3 Cabo Mayor
4 Casa Lucio (5)
5 El Cenador de Prado (6)
6 Combarro (7)
7 Las Cuatro Estaciones (8)
8 La Dorada (9)
9 Horcher (10)
10 Jockey (12)
11 Juan de Alzate (11)
12 Peñas Arriba (14)
13 Príncipe de Viana (16)
14 Sacha (17)
15 Señorio de Bertiz (18)
16 Zalacaín (19)
17 Botín
18 Casa Paco (20)
19 Esteban (21)
20 Gure-Etxea (22)
21 Guria (23)
22 Saint-James (24)
23 La Barraca (25)
24 Luarqués (26)
25 La Maquina (27)
26 O'Pazo (28)
27 La Trainera (29)
28 Al-Mounia (31)

BUILDINGS AND SIGHTS

1 Ayuntamiento (City Hall)
2 Banco de Bilbao
3 Bolsa de Comercio
 (stock exchange)
4 Capilla del Obispo
5 Casa de Lope de Vega
6 Centro de Arta Reina Sofía
7 Chamber of commerce
8 Convento de la Encarnación
9 Cortes (Parliament)
10 Fundación Juan March
11 Ministerio de Economia
 Hacienda y Comercio
12 Monasterio de Descalzas Reales
13 Museo de América
14 Museo Arqueológico Nacional
15 Museo Lázaro-Galdiano
16 Museo del Prado
17 Museo de la Real Academia de
 Bellas Artes de San Fernando
18 Nuevos Ministerios
19 Palacio de Exposiciones y
 Congresos
20 Palacio Real
21 Plaza de Toros Monumental
22 Police
23 Post office
24 Real Fábrica de Tapices
25 San Antonio de la Florida
i Tourist information

winter make walking any distance uncomfortable. Within any particular district it is, however, easy enough to get around on foot; but remember that building numbers run outwards from the centre of town, Plaza Puerta del Sol. The *Guía Urbana de Madrid* with detailed maps and useful addresses is very helpful.

Taxis sport a red stripe; a sign in the nearside window, *Libre*, indicates when a cab is free. Fares are metered and a 10% tip is standard. *Radioteléfono* ☎ 247 82 00, *Tele Taxi* ☎ 445 90 08 and *Radio Taxi Assoc. Gremial* ☎ 447 51 80.

Driving Traffic is very heavy and parking, with a card bought from newsstands or tobacconists, can be almost impossible. A car is useful for trips out of town; in summer air-conditioning is essential. *Avis* ☎ 259 43 97; *Hertz* ☎ 248 58 03. *Autos O'Donnell* ☎ 274 39 89 is a reliable local company which also provides drivers.

Walking is safe at all times on main streets since the city has kept its *serenos* (night-watchmen), but beware pickpockets wherever there are crowds. As in most large cities drug dealing is a problem here.

Bus The bus system is confusing for those who don't know their way around; route charts, but not maps, are displayed. Standard services, as well as express micro-buses and a central circular service, run 5.30am–1.30am. Tickets are purchased on buses or in tens from stands in the Plaza Puerta del Sol and Plaza de la Cibeles. Inquiries ☎ 401 99 00.

Subway The Metro is clean, safe and efficient (trains run 6am–1.30am) and often a better option than a taxi during rush hours. Stations are unevenly distributed so check that short trips are worthwhile. During the day you rarely wait longer than 3mins between trains. Tickets are Pta50 within the central zone and may be bought from stations; they also come in a book (or *abono*) of 10; alternatively, there are 3- or 5-day

Metrotour passes. Inquiries ☎ 435 22 66.

Area by area

Madrid has many distinctive *barrios*, or quarters, to which the residents are greatly attached. The centre, which has grown on both sides of the long broad Paseo (P°) de la Castellana, stretches from the original Old Town up to the Manhattan-style skyline of the northern business zone. Elsewhere, the distinctions between residential and business, shopping and nightlife areas are blurred.

Centro includes the Old Town around the Palacio Real; the shopping streets around the Gran Vía and the Plaza (Pl) Puerta del Sol; and sloping down towards the Prado, the lanes of Huerta, lined with bars and restaurants which spring to life in the evenings. On the eastern edge, close to the Prado, stands the Cortes (Parliament).

The Old Town also spills over into two areas in the south that are largely working-class but have trendy enclaves and historic corners: Arganzuela, with its smart new shopping centre inside the old market at Puerto de Toledo, and Latina. To the west and north are the modern shops and apartments of Arguelles, bounded by parks and containing the University. Beyond it is the Campo de Naciones, an ambitious project to double exhibition space and provide new offices, under construction.

The three elegant 19thC midtown districts, east and north of the Old Town, traditionally make up the commercial and business centre: Retiro, which includes the museums around the Prado and the park; Salamanca, a grid of streets with smart shops, businesses and embassies; and Chamberi, less expensive and with an arty reputation. The broad Paseo de la Castellana is lined by public buildings, government offices, hotels and office blocks.

Farther north are the modern, predominantly business districts,

Tetuán and Chamartín, where the Palacio de Congresos and government ministries are dwarfed by new high-rise pedestrianized complexes of shops, hotels and banks (AZCA and Chamartín) and some startling office blocks like the Torre de Europa, the tallest on the Continent. The residential oases that remain, like El Viso, an inner-city village, and Ciudad Lineal and Hortaleza, both housing projects dating from early this century, are skyrocketing in value despite attempts to limit speculation.

The suburbs
Working-class industrial areas developed after World War II include the southern belt of Carabanchel, Usera, Villaverde and Puente de Vallecas and the northern district of La Vaguada. Notorious for bad housing, urban poverty and crime, they are now improved with major redevelopment projects. Newer dormitory towns and estates have grown up for commuters. The most desirable areas, like Pozuelo El Alarcón, Las Rozas and Milasierra to the west, extend to the cool Sierras.

Hotels

Madrid's top hotels are in three main areas: near the Old Town, in the midtown shopping area and farther north in Castellana, the modern business centre. Apart from a few luxury palaces and small new hotels or apartment blocks designed for the business traveller, they are all large and anonymous but often efficiently run. Most essential facilities, which here include air-conditioning, central heating and secure parking, are standard. Early reservations are always advisable.

Castellana P̄///
P° de la Castellana 49, 28046
☎ 410 02 00 ☒ 27686 fax 419 58 53
• InterContinental • AE DC MC V •
275 rooms, 30 suites, 1 restaurant, 1 bar
The grand Castellana is on the main boulevard of central Madrid, close to the elegant shops of Salamanca. Designed on generous lines it is popular with top ranking American executives and provides on-the-spot business facilities. The rooms are light and airy and furnished traditionally; the suites make elegant bases from which to work. The splendid round lobby in rose-coloured marble and the summer terrace are popular meeting places for those who work in the nearby banking and office districts, and the restaurant serves polished alta cocina. 24hr room service, shopping arcade, car rental • fitness room, sauna, massage • secretarial agency, 10 meeting rooms (capacity up to 500).

Eurobuilding P̄//
C Padre Damián 23, 28036

☎ 457 31 00 ☒ 22548 fax 457 97 29
• AE DC MC V • 420 rooms, 120 suites, 3 restaurants, 2 bars
The emphasis in this vast, double-lobbied hotel designed for business visitors is on smart efficiency. The suites come in various styles and there are two standards of room, differentiated mainly by size, all with large balconies. One floor, devoted entirely to convention and meeting rooms, is always busy. 24hr room service, car rental and airline reservations desks, hairdresser, shops, disco • outdoor pool, fitness rooms, saunas • business centre with multilingual secretarial services, 20 meeting rooms (capacity up to 900).

Foxá 32 P̄/
C Augustin de Foxá 32, 28036
☎ 733 10 60 ☒ 49366 fax 597 12 95
• Foxá • AE DC MC V • 161 suites, 1 restaurant, 1 bar
A modern hotel, 5mins from Estación de Chamartín and close to the Castellana business area, Foxá 32's

functional suites are either open-plan or with a separate lounge. It has a loyal Spanish business clientele. The small lobby, café-bar and grill restaurant have been redesigned in a casually elegant style. 4 meeting rooms (capacity up to 250).

El Gran Versalles *P/*
C Covarrubias 4–6, 28010
☎ *447 57 00* ⊺ˣ *49150 fax 446 39 87*
• *AE DC MC V* • *142 rooms, 3 suites, 1 restaurant, 1 bar*
This small hotel is right in the centre of fashionable Chamberi, and its friendly atmosphere and personal service have attracted a faithful Spanish clientele. The public rooms have recently had a marble and pine facelift and are attractively furnished with antiques. Bedrooms are comfortable and plain; those at the back are quieter. The bar and lounge are used for informal meetings. Parking difficult. 4 meeting rooms (capacity up to 120).

Meliá Castilla *P///*
C Capitán Haya 43, 28020
☎ *571 22 11* ⊺ˣ *23142 fax 571 22 10*
• *AE DC MC V* • *800 rooms, 20 suites, 3 restaurants, 5 bars*
Madrid's largest hotel is in the new commercial zone, north of the centre. Its sheer size allows variety in the many public areas: antiques in the lounges and bright colours in the breakfast room and the Las Vegas-style nightclub. Bedrooms are spacious and comfortable, and there are three deluxe floors with private lounges, secretarial and complementary services. The L'Albufera restaurant, used by *madrileños* businessmen at lunch time, serves excellent paella and other rice dishes. 24hr room service, shops, hairdresser, nightclub • pool, sauna, fitness room, massage • 15 meeting rooms (capacity up to 850).

Miguel Angel *P///*
C Miguel Angel 29–31, 28010
☎ *442 81 99* ⊺ˣ *44235 fax 442 53 20*
• *Hoteles Occidentales* • *AE DC MC V* •

300 rooms, 22 suites, 2 restaurants, 1 bar
Set back from the busy Paseo de la Castellana, the Miguel Angel has a welcoming, cool lobby. Antique furniture in the suites contrasts with the clear, spacious public areas, and the lounge opens in summer onto a terrace-garden. Bedrooms, decorated in restful blue, are well equipped but on the small side. 24hr room service, hairdresser, disco • pool, sauna, fitness room, massage, jacuzzi • 11 meeting rooms (capacity up to 650).

Orense 38 *P/*
C Pedro Teixera 5, 28020
☎ *571 22 19* ⊺ˣ *49939 fax 597 12 95*
• *Foxá* • *AE DC MC V* • *140 suites, 1 restaurant, 1 bar*
A beautifully designed small hotel in the smartest business area. Each of the compact suites has an office and living area, and there are small, well-equipped meeting rooms downstairs. Service is good, and the café and restaurant are popular at lunch time. Designer boutiques • fitness centre, saunas, massage, jacuzzis • 9 meeting rooms (capacity up to 10).

Palace *P///*
Pl de las Cortes 7, 28014 ☎ *429 75 51*
⊺ˣ *23903 fax 429 82 66* • *AE DC MC V* • *571 rooms, 29 suites, 2 restaurants, 2 bars*
The elegant white façade of the historic Palace looks across to the Cortes (Parliament). Built in 1912 at the instigation of Alfonso XIII for visiting crowned heads and ministers of state, the splendour of its murals and the chandeliered lobby is complemented by space and comfort in the modernized bedrooms and bathrooms. The bar, with its magnificent stained-glass, domed roof and potted palms, and a quieter side bar, are meeting points for politicians and journalists. 24hr room service, shops, designer boutique, hairdresser • business centre, 10 meeting rooms with a/v equipment (capacity up to 1,000).

Princesa Plaza P||

C de Princesa 40, 28015 ☎ *542 21 00*
TX *44378 fax 542 35 01 • AE DC MC*
V • 368 rooms, 38 suites, 2 restaurants,
2 bars

A sleek modern hotel in Arguelles,
not far from the Parque del Oeste and
surrounded by shopping streets.
Rooms are light and airy with
colourful modern paintings, and the
top floor has stunning views across
Madrid. It is usually busy with
Spanish and international conventions
in the spacious private rooms. The
informal coffeeshop, piano bar and
white, open lobby are suitable for
relaxed discussions. 24hr room
service, nonsmoking floor,
hairdresser, disco • access to Plaza
Hotel pool • 7 meeting rooms with
a/v and simultaneous translation
equipment (capacity up to 750).

Príncipe de Vergara P||

C Príncipe de Vergara 92, 28006
☎ *563 26 95* TX *27064 fax 563 72 53*
• NH • AE DC MC V • 170 rooms,
3 suites, 1 restaurant, 1 bar

The recently renovated Príncipe has
been designed throughout with clean,
contemporary lines, clear colours and
modern art. It is to the east of
Salamanca, by the exit for the airport.
Rooms have good working space, and
the staff are young, efficient and
cheerful. Facilities are tailored to
business requirements, and the sports
facilities are good. Fitness room,
sauna, squash • 8 meeting rooms with
a/v equipment (capacity up to 400).

Ritz P||||

Pl de la Lealtad 5, 28014
☎ *521 28 57* TX *43986 fax 232 87 76*
• TFH • AE DC MC V • 140 rooms,
15 suites, 1 restaurant, 1 bar

A palace overlooking the Prado, the
Ritz was opened by King Alfonso XIII
in 1910. It remains an aristocrat
among hotels. It has been restored
down to every last flourish, from the
Art Nouveau staircase to the
handwoven carpets in the suites and
lounge. The more modest bedrooms
are welcoming in their small scale and

attention to detail. The blue and
white terrace restaurant is open
through spring and summer, and the
reception rooms, with their
sculptured ceilings, marble figures
and urns, are favoured by Madrid's
high society for tea and cocktails.
Service is immaculate, although not
especially geared to business needs.
24hr room service, airport limousine
service, hairdresser • 4 meeting
rooms (capacity up to 300).

Sanvy P||

C Goya 3, 28001 ☎ *276 08 00*
TX *44994 fax 275 24 43 • NH • AE*
DC MC V • 141 rooms, 5 suites,
2 restaurants, 1 bar

Just off the Plaza Colón, the Sanvy
has a reputation as a quiet,
comfortable hotel. It has been
completely refurbished in the
uncluttered style of the 1980s. The
business centre is well-equipped with
offices and secretarial help, and the
meeting rooms are constantly busy.
The smart Belagua restaurant is one
of the most innovative in a Madrid
hotel, but it is expensive. Outdoor
pool, fitness centre • 5 meeting rooms
with a/v equipment (capacity up to
200).

Villa Magna P|||||

Pº de la Castellana 22, 28046
☎ *261 49 00* TX *22914 fax 275 95 04*
• BAS-Crest • AE DC MC V • 164 rooms,
18 suites, 1 restaurant, 1 bar

The most luxurious of the city's
modern hotels and especially popular
with English business travellers. It
was built in the 1970s, but inside all
is traditional and grand, from the
light, panelled bedrooms with antique
reproduction furniture and old prints
to the splendid function rooms with
mirrored walls and marble flooring. It
is too opulent for some tastes, but the
service is faultless. The lounge and
piano bar are smart meeting places in
diplomatic circles and among
industrialists and designers. 24hr
room service, limousine service,
hairdresser • sauna • 4 meeting
rooms (capacity up to 250).

Wellington P/
C Velázquez 8, 28001 ☎ *275 44 00*
TX *22700 fax 276 41 64* • *AE DC MC
V* • *302 rooms, 18 suites, 2 restaurants,
2 bars*
This old-fashioned, grand hotel was
built in the 19th century on one
corner of the Retiro Park. It is the
haunt of bullfighting *aficionados*
especially during the May feast of San
Isidro when the most important fights
are staged. Leisurely charm,
traditional service and conservative
decor appeal to its loyal Spanish
clients, some of whom are residents,
and to Americans in search of old
European style. Suites are luxurious,
standard rooms rather small. The bar
is popular for an after-work drink.
24hr room service, gift shops,
hairdresser • small outside pool,
sauna • 4 meeting rooms (capacity up
to 300).

OTHER HOTELS
Central Madrid
Alcalá P/ *C de Alcalá 66, 28009*
☎ *435 10 60* TX *48094 fax 435 11 05*
• *AE DC MC V*. Quiet and reliable
hotel next to the Retiro Park.
Arosa P/ *C de la Salud 21, 28013*
☎ *532 16 00* TX *43618 fax 531 31 27*
• *AE DC MC V*. Friendly, small hotel
near old Madrid.
Emperador P/ *Gran Vía 53,
28013* ☎ *247 28 00* TX *fax 247 28 17* • *AE DC MC V*.
Traditional downtown hotel with
rooftop pool.
Plaza P/ *Pl de España, 28013*
☎ *247 12 00* TX *27383 fax 248 23 89*
• *AE DC MC V*. Reliable with plenty
of services and a rooftop pool.
Suecia P *C Marqués de Casa
Riera 4, 28014* ☎ *531 69 00* TX *22313
fax 521 71 41* • *AE DC MC V*. Old
hotel near the Prado with four new
floors of club rooms; parking difficult.

Mid town
Los Galgos Sol P/ *C Claudio
Coello 139, 28006* ☎ *262 66 00*
TX *43957 fax 261 76 62* • *AE DC MC
V*. Large chain hotel in Salamanca
shopping area.

Mindanao P/// *Pº de San
Francisco de Sales 15, 28003*
☎ *549 55 00* TX *22631 fax 244 55 96*
• *AE DC MC V*. Reliable but faded
hotel in the west near the University.
Serrano P/ *C Marqués de
Villamejor 8, 28006* ☎ *435 52 00*
TX *27521 fax 564 04 97* • *HUSA* • *AE
DC MC V*. Very small and intimate,
with few facilities; reserve well ahead.
Tryp Palacio P/ *Pº de la
Castellana 57, 28036* ☎ *442 51 00*
TX *27207 fax 441 62 59* • *AE DC MC
V*. Old-fashioned and comfortable.

New north
Chamartín P/ *Estación de
Chamartín, 28016* ☎ *733 70 11*
TX *49201 fax 733 02 14* • *Entursa* •
AE DC MC V. Large modern block
above the main railway station; good
sports facilities nearby.
Cuzco P/ *Pº de la Castellana
133, 28046* ☎ *556 06 00* TX *22464
fax 456 03 72* • *AE DC MC V*.
Convention-oriented hotel near the
Palacio de Congresos.
Holiday Inn P/// *Pl Carlos Trías
Beltrán 4, 28020* ☎ *597 01 02*
TX *44709 fax 597 02 92* • *AE DC MC
V*. Part of the new *AZCA* development
near the Palacio de Congresos, with
an executive floor, pool and health
club.

Clubs
There are several private clubs to
which visitors may be invited. *Club
Financiero*, C Marqués de la Enseñada
14 ☎ 410 49 00, for men only, is the
most important for the business
community. *Club Madrid 1900*, C
Monte Esqinza 48 ☎ 410 03 14,
is for the new political and business
set. *Club Siglo XXI*, C Juan Ramón
Jiménez 8 ☎ 457 82 05, holds
seminars with the participation of top
politicians and economists.

Hotel and restaurant price guide
For the meanings of the hotel and
restaurant price symbols, see
pages 6 and 7.

Restaurants

Madrid restaurants reflect the country's fine regional cuisines, and both traditional and *nueva cocina* menus here are distinctively Spanish. International and ethnic styles of cooking are not as good. Traditional *tascas*, or taverns situated in the Old Town, provide good food in atmospheric settings.

The leisurely lunch is the main meal of the day starting at 2pm; dinner starts after 9pm. Service is always included in the price, but tipping for waiters and the cloakroom is standard. Dress rules are relaxed, but ties are preferred in smarter places. Reservations can usually be made the same day.

El Amparo P //
C Puigcerdá 8 ☎ 431 64 56 • closed Sat L, Sun, Aug • AE V
Down a quiet side street, this fashionable central restaurant has fine stylish modern cooking. The Basque-French menu evolves seasonally under the enterprising eye of Ramón Ramirez, the young chef-proprietor. Excellent unstuffy service; and clever design, combining traditional wooden beams with a split-level layout and elegant decor, gives privacy if required.

El Bodegón P //
C Pinar 15 ☎ 262 31 37 or ☎ 262 88 44 • closed Sat L, Sun, Aug • AE DC V
A smart, rather formal midtown restaurant with a predominantly business clientele, although tables are too close for confidential discussions. The broad-ranging innovative menu, known especially for its desserts, is masterminded by Pedro Subijana, one of the top Basque chefs.

Cabo Mayor P //
C Juan Hurtado Mendoza 11 ☎ 250 87 76 • closed Sun, 20 days in Aug • AE DC MC V
Hidden away (the entrance is off Calle General Gallegos), this chic restaurant is popular at lunch time with younger bankers and industrialists from the nearby business quarter. Cantabrian cuisine, with an emphasis on fish, is served in two rooms, one formal, the other more relaxed.

Casa Lucio P //
Cava Baja 35 ☎ 265 32 52 • closed Sat L, Aug • AE DC V • reservations essential
In the old streets running down from Plaza Mayor, Casa Lucio has become the smartest of Madrid's *tascas* with journalists, politicians and financiers. The regional dishes are based on superb produce, such as specially cured ham, elvers (baby eels) and oysters, and are complemented by a good choice of Riojas and the more local Valdepeñas.

El Cenador de Prado P //
C Prado 4 ☎ 429 15 61 • closed Sat L, Sun, 8 days in Aug • AE DC MC V
Famous for its designer decor – one room is a muralled, plant-filled conservatory – this is a fashionable restaurant for a smart evening out, as much a place to be seen and to see as to eat. The *nueva cocina* is inventive, the service discreet and the overall effect impressive.

Combarro P //
C Reina Mercedes 12 ☎ 254 78 15 • closed Aug • AE DC MC V
Plainly decorated, except for a colourful display of shellfish and a tank of lobsters, Combarro is close to the Palacio de Congresos and offers a range of well-chosen and superbly presented Atlantic seafood from Galicia. The cooking is reliable, and the cellar offers fine white varietal wines. Tables are well-spaced; service is efficient.

Las Cuatro Estaciones P/
C General Ibáñez Ibero 5
☎ 253 63 05 • *closed Sat, Sun,*
Aug • AE DC MC V
Friendly yet elegant, this is suitable
for a working lunch and high-
powered business entertaining in the
evenings: the sleek modern design
allows for privacy, and note pads are
left on the tables. The decor, and the
Franco-Spanish menu, changes with
the seasons.

La Dorada P////
C Orense 64–66 ☎ 270 20 04 • *closed*
Sun, Aug • AE DC V
The quality of the Andalucian fish
dishes here is famous but so is the
rushed service and the noisy main
dining room. La Dorada has recently
added a series of private rooms, and
the executives from the surrounding
business district are flocking back.
For a private room, reserve well
ahead.

Horcher P////
C Alfonso XII 6 ☎ 522 07 31 • *closed*
Sun • AE DC V • *jacket and tie* •
reservations essential
One of Madrid's classic restaurants,
near the Prado, Horcher has
maintained its reputation for *haute*
cuisine, elegant surroundings and a
fine cellar for over 40 years. The
dining room, decorated with antiques,
is quiet but offers little privacy.
Service is polite though not over
formal. The menu is largely faithful
to the luxurious old style; the goulash
is famed, and game dishes are
particularly good.

Jockey P////
C Amador de los Ríos 6 ☎ 419 24 35
• *closed Sun, Aug* • AE DC MC V •
reservations essential
In a midtown side street off the wide
Paseo de la Castellana, the elegant
Jockey has been one of the city's
most famous eating places for
decades, but there are those who
lament the recent retirement of
veteran chef Clemencio Fuentes. The
decor of the elegant dining room is

reminiscent of the 1950s. The private
rooms are often used for corporate
entertaining.

Juan de Alzate P////
C de Princesa 18 ☎ 247 00 10 • AE
DC MC V
Now considered among the city's top
half-dozen restaurants, the high
reputation of chef Inaki Izaguirre
rests on a balance of flavours,
presentation and innovation. Its
stylishness appeals to a young,
design-conscious clientele from the
media. The dining room, with well-
spaced tables, is plain but luxurious
and the service is professional.

Peñas Arriba P//
C Francisco Gervás 15 ☎ 279 29 66 •
closed Sun, Aug • DC V
A respected resturant in a prime
location in the new business area of
northern Madrid. Sober decor and a
low-key atmosphere make it popular
for lunch and dinner with politicians,
civil servants and bankers, who enjoy
the inventive fish dishes and rustic
cooking inspired by Cantabria. Bread
and desserts are homemade.

Príncipe de Viana P////
C Manuel de Falla 5 ☎ 259 48 40 •
closed Sat L, Sun, Aug • AE DC MC V
A fashionable, modern restaurant
serving stylish seasonal Basque-
Navarrese cuisine in a quiet square
near the new office blocks and tall
towers of Chamartín. Its prestigious
reputation reflects its links with
Zalacaín (see later); they are run by
son and father respectively. Very
popular, though the closely packed
tables discourage private
conversation.

Sacha P/
C Juan Hurtado de Mendoza 11
☎ 457 59 52 • *closed Sun, Aug* • AE
V • *reservations essential*
An unpretentious restaurant, in
Chamartín, that overflows into a small
garden in summer. The seasonal
menu is short, mixing Catalan with
other ideas, but the cooking is

excellent and so is the wine list, with French as well as Riojas and Penedés. Suitable for relaxed business entertaining.

Señorio de Bertiz ⓟ////
C Comandante Zorita 4 ☎ *234 45 90* •
closed Sat L, Sun, Aug • AE DC MC V
The atmosphere and decor of this midtown Basque restaurant are consistent with the menu of traditional dishes as well as new creations such as warm crayfish mousse with asparagus. Both the service and cellar, which includes Basque *txacoli*, match the food. A good choice for working meals with top executives and civil servants from the nearby ministries.

Zalacaín ⓟ////
C Alvarez de Baena 4 ☎ *261 48 40* •
closed Sat L, Sun, Aug • AE DC V
Zalacaín is in a class of its own in the city and is arguably the best in the country. Run by the formidable team of chef Urdían and restaurateur Oyarbide, the cooking is an incomparable, luxurious hybrid of traditional Spanish and modern *alta cocina*; the Spanish wines from every region are superb. Spacious rooms, elegant decor, exquisite service, and prices to match.

Bars and cafés

Bars and cafés, traditional taverns and fashionable late-night summer *terrazas* along the Paseo de la Castellana from May to September, creating traffic congestion at two in the morning, are a part of normal life. You might go out for a mid-morning coffee, an aperitif and *tapas* (small snacks) before lunch or after work, or for an after-dinner drink that stretches into the early hours.
Smart bars Some hotel bars, such as those at the *Palace, Castellana, Ritz, Villa Magna* and *Wellington*, are best for an informal business chat. Otherwise try *Hispano*, Pº de la Castellana 78, popular with yuppies, politicians and journalists; *Balmoral*, C Hermosilla 10, for the last word in

Traditional regional cooking
Madrid has many solid, unpretentious but popular small restaurants serving regional dishes.
  Traditional *madrileño* or Castilian restaurants and *tascas* abound in the Old Town; *Botín*, C Cuchilleros 17 ☎ 266 42 17, is famous but besieged by tourists. Two of the best are *Casa Paco*, Puerta Cerrada 11 ☎ 266 31 66, and *Esteban*, Cava Baja 36 ☎ 265 90 91. The Basque country is strongly represented because of its culinary reputation: *Gure-Etxea*, Pl de la Paja 12 ☎ 265 61 49, and *Guria*, C Huertas 12 ☎ 239 16 36, have plenty of atmosphere. For Valencia's rice dishes (paella is only one of many) try *Saint-James*, C Juan Bravo 26 ☎ 275 00 69 or 275 60 10, or the more rustic *La Barraca*, C Reina 29 ☎ 532 71 54. Less well-known are Asturian dishes like hake in cider or *fabada*, a bean stew, which can be sampled at *Luarqués*, C Ventura de la Vega 16 ☎ 429 61 74, and *La Maquina*, C Sor Angela de la Cruz 22 ☎ 270 61 05. Many Galician restaurants specialize in seafood, such as *O'Pazo*, C Reina Mercedes 20 ☎ 253 23 33, and *La Trainera*, C Lagasca 60 ☎ 276 80 35. Finally, *Al-Mounia*, C Recoletos 5 ☎ 275 01 73, famous for Moroccan food, has a marvellous Moorish setting as reminiscent of Andalucia as of North Africa.

cocktails or *Sportsman*, C Alcalá 65, one of the best of the many English-style bars.
Traditional Bars The *tabernas* and *mesones* of the Old Town are often packed, especially before lunch and in the early evening, but they should not be missed. Here are a few gems: *Los Gabrieles*, C Echegaray 17, and *Viva Madrid*, close by at Calle Manuel Fernández y González 7, both with old tiled interiors; *Antonio Sánchez*,

Tapas

These tantalizing little snacks, displayed in large dishes spread along the bar, come in two sizes, the smaller *pincho* and the larger *ración*, and are often eaten with an aperitif as a mid- to late-morning or early evening snack. They range from simple olives and toasted almonds through fried fish and croquettes to more elaborate *canapés*, so that you can easily construct a quick meal. There are a few places worth a special visit: *Casa Lhardy*, Ca de San Jerónimo 8, is wonderfully Edwardian, with samovars of consommé and elegant croquettes; *La Bilbaina*, C Marqués de Urquijo 27, is known for its seafood, and *Casa Paco*, Pl Humilladero 8, specializes in *madrileño* dishes, such as roast suckling pig.

C de Mesón de Paredes 13, once owned by a bullfighter and still full of his memorabilia; and the *Cerveceria Alemana*, Pl Santa Ana 6, known for its Hemingway connections as well as its beer.

Cafés The most famous of Madrid's literary cafés, *Café Gijón*, Pº de Recoletos 21, has kept its special atmosphere; *Café Universal*, C Fernando VI 13, is a favourite with politicians and intellectuals; at *Café de Oriente*, Pl de Oriente 2, which also serves food, you can watch the world go by in a historic setting. For tea it is hard to beat the *Ritz* or the *Palace*.

Entertainment

The *madrileños* are known for their *fiestas* and for their ability to stay up all night. They take great pride in and are happy to subsidize the city's cultural life. It is especially lively during San Isidro (May–June) and the mixed cultural festival in October (Festival de Otoño). Tickets are often sold only at the theatre, concert hall or other venues; ask at your hotel.

Theatre Madrid has a flourishing theatrical tradition. Tickets are cheap but can be hard to obtain. For classical drama the most prestigious theatres are the gracious *Teatro de la Comedia*, C Príncipe 14 ☎ 521 49 31, and *Teatro Español*, C Príncipe 25 ☎ 429 03 18. There is an international drama festival in March.

Opera, music and dance There are three national orchestras and two ballet companies. The main halls and theatres are: the superb new *Auditorio Nacional de Música*, C Príncipe de Vergara 136 ☎ 337 01 00; *Teatro de la Zarzuela*, C Jovellanos 4 ☎ 429 82 25, which stages opera, ballet and recitals as well as *zarzuelas* (Spanish operettas); the *Fundación Juan March*, C Castelló 77 ☎ 435 42 40, for recitals; and the *Centro Cultural de la Villa*, Pl de Colón ☎ 275 60 80. The Teatro Real will reopen as an opera house in 1992.

Jazz is increasingly popular. There are many informal club-cafés, the best of which is the *Café Central*, Pl del Angel 10 ☎ 468 08 41, and an annual festival (Oct–Nov). Details of rock concerts are given weekly in the *Guía del Ocio*.

Flamenco For the April week-long festival, Cumbre Flamenco, the best performers in Spain are engaged. The rest of the year there are the *tablaos*, or shows; try *Corral de la Pacheca*, C Juan Ramón Jiménez 26 ☎ 458 11 13, and *Café de Chinitas*, C Torija 7 ☎ 248 51 35.

Bullfighting is staged Apr–Oct in the *Plaza de Toros Las Ventas*, C Alcalá 231 ☎ 246 22 00, with the climax in May and June during San Isidro; ticket office in Calle Victoria 9, but seats are difficult to get for big fights.

Cinema Subtitled English-language films are listed under "v.o." (*versión original*) in the papers. *Filmoteca Nacional*, C de la Princesa 1 ☎ 247 16 57, and *Centro de Arte Reina Sofía*, C Santa Isabel 52 ☎ 467 50 62, show old and new, Spanish and foreign films.

Nightclubs and casino The city's nightclubs demand stamina; a night on the town may last till 6am. They are frequented by a mixture of the fashionably rich – politicians, business people and those in showbiz. *Mau Mau* in the Eurobuilding (see *Hotels*) ☎ 457 78 00 is one of the smartest. *Pachá*, C Barceló 11, *Joy Eslava*, C Arenal 11, and *Oh! Madrid* ☎ 207 86 97, a summertime favourite on the *autopista* to La Coruña, are younger and trendier. There is a free bus service from the Plaza España to the modern *Casino de Juego Gran Madrid*, 28kms/17miles northwest in Torrelodones ☎ 859 03 12. Smart dress required.

Shopping
Madrid has flourishing craft and traditional shops as well as new fashion, art and design outlets. Hours are Mon–Sat, 9–1.30, 5–8. *Mercado de Toledo*, Puerta de Toledo, is an excellent new complex of fashion, jewellery and design shops.
Fashion is concentrated in smart Salamanca, between Calle Alcalá and the Paseo de la Castellana, especially along Calle Serrano. Here the established home designers like *Sybilla*, *Purificación García* and *Adolfo Dominquez* have shops alongside the French couturiers; more avant-garde fashion is around Calle Almirante.
Department stores are open Mon–Sat, 10–8. There are four branches of *El Corte Inglés*, the most stylish department store: C Princesa 56, C Goya 76, C Raimundo Fernández Villaverde 79 and C Preciados 3 (tax refund and shipping facilities).
Gifts Fans at *Casa de Diego*, C Montera 1; the old hat shops around Plaza Mayor have wonderful sombreros; ceramics at *Antiqua Casa Talavera*, C Isabel la Católica 2; *Maty*, C Hieras 7, is for flamenco lovers; *Conde Hermanos*, C Felipe v 2, makes fine guitars. *Artespaña*, C Gran Vía 32, Pl las Cortes 3, C Hermosilla 14 and C Don Ramón de la Cruz 33, displays well designed decorative objects from silver

candlesticks to handwoven rugs.
Street markets Visit the lively *El Rastro*, the Sunday-morning flea-market around Calle Ribera de Curtidores in the Old Town: books and antiques (Plaza Camillo), cane work, wooden toys, caged birds, clothes and so on, but beware pickpockets. The stamp and coin market in Plaza Mayor, also on Sunday morning, is a more serious, orderly affair.

Sightseeing
Madrid has monumental buildings, splendid avenues and squares, outstanding art galleries and over 70 museums dating from every period since the 16th century. The *ciudad antigua*, with old *plazas*, sloping narrow streets and churches, should not be missed.
The city has more trees than any other in Europe and extensive parks. Besides the Retiro, there are three on the west of the city: *Campo del Moro*, *Parque del Oeste* and the *Casa de Campo*, once a royal hunting ground.
Banco de Bilbao An exciting modern building designed by Sainz de Oiza in 1971; a steel exterior that changes colour. *P° de la Castellana 79. Open Mon–Fri, 8.30–1; Sat, 8.30–4.30.*
Bolsa de Comercio Ornate 19thC stock exchange. *Pl de la Lealtad 1. Public gallery open Mon–Fri, 10–2.*
Capilla del Obispo Early 16thC chapel with superb wooden altarpiece and late-Gothic vaulting. *Pl de la Paja 9.*
Casa de Lope de Vega The playwright's restored 17thC home. *C Cervantes 11. Open Tue–Sun, 11–2 (Oct–May).*
Centro de Arte Reina Sofia Original 18thC hospital reopened in 1987 as a centre for contemporary art and culture, with changing exhibitions. *C Santa Isabel 52. Open Wed–Mon, 10am–9pm.*
Convento de la Encarnación Convent founded in the 17thC with a fine façade, baroque church and paintings. *Pl de la Encarnación 1. Open daily, 10–1, 4–6.*

Fundación Juan March has changing exhibitions, mainly of contemporary and abstract work. *C Castelló 77* ☎ *435 42 40.*

Monasterio de Descalzas Reales Small, sumptuous 16thC convent with a rich art collection. *Pl de las Descalzas Reales. Open Mon–Thu, 10.30–12.45, 4–5.15; Fri–Sun, 10.30–1.30.*

Museo de América A mainly Latin American collection, including pre-Columbian art and Hispano-American crafts. *Av Reyes Católicos 6* ☎ *243 94 37. Open Tue–Sun, 10–2.*

Museo Arqueológico Nacional Fine Moorish-influenced medieval and Renaissance decorative art, classical and Iberian antiquities, including the 4thC bust of the *Dama de Elche. C Serrano 13. Open daily, 9.30–1.30.*

Museo Lázaro-Galdiano A small museum containing outstanding enamels, ivories, jewellery and Old Master paintings. *C Serrano 122. Open Tue–Sun, 10–2: closed Aug.*

Museo del Prado Includes the *Casón del Buen Retiro,* C Felipe IV 13, containing 19thC Spanish art; *C Alfonxo XII 28,* with Picasso's *Guernica* (crowded); *Palacio Villahermosa,* Pl de las Cortes 6, Thyssen Collection, opening 1990. One of the world's great museums, based on 15th to 19thC royal collections including European schools and Spanish masters among whom Velázquez and Goya stand out. *Pº del Prado. Open Tue–Sat, 9–7; Sun, 9–1.45.*

Museo de la Real Academia de Bellas Artes de San Fernando Painting and sculpture, including works by Goya and El Greco. *C Alcalá 13. Open Tue–Sat, 9–7; Sun & Mon, 9–2.*

Palacio Real Superbly preserved, built in the 18thC century with a severe exterior but elaborate former royal apartments; contains tapestry, carriage, medal and music museums and the royal armoury. *C Bailén 2. Open Mon–Sat; 10–1, 4–6.15 (summer); 9.30–12.45, 3.30–5.15 (winter); Sun, 10–1.*

Parque del Retiro containing statues, fountains, exhibition galleries and a lake. Nearby the 18thC *Real Jardín Botánico* has over 30,000 species of plants.

Plaza Mayor Once the site of fiestas, bullfights, the *auto de fe* and the centre of medieval and Habsburg Madrid, now striking for its symmetry and arcades.

Real Fábrica de Tapices Workshops from the 18th century for palace furnishings, and still making tapestries of designs by artists like Goya. *C Fuentarrabía 3. Open Mon–Fri, 9.30–12.30. Closed Aug.*

San Antonio de la Florida Small domed church with frescoes by Goya of *madrileño* 18thC life which contains the artist's tomb. *Gta San Antonio de la Florida. Open Thu–Mon, 11–1.30, 3–7; Sun 11–1.30.*

Guided tours
Pullmantur ☎ 241 63 40, *Juliátours* ☎ 571 53 00 and *Trapsatur* ☎ 266 99 00 run standard city tours, and *Turismo para Todos* ☎ 266 39 00 organizes around 50 cultural trips. The *Patronato Municipal de Turismo* ☎ 266 39 00 arranges special group interest and incentive tours.

Out of town
The same companies run trips to the main sights outside town: Aranjuez (47kms/29 miles, Bourbon Palace, gardens); Avila (113kms/70 miles, city walls, cathedral, palaces, churches); El Escorial (51kms/32 miles, Philip II's monastery); Segovia (87kms/54 miles, aqueduct, fortress, cathedral); and Toledo (70kms/43 miles, cathedral, churches, El Greco's house).

Spectator sports
Basketball Spanish teams are among the best in Europe; the *Palacio de Deportes,* C Jorge Juan 99 ☎ 401 91 00, is the venue for big games.

Car and motorcycle racing *Jarama,* 27kms/16.5 miles north ☎ 447 32 00.

Horse-racing A day or evening at the

Hipódromo de la Zarzuela during Jan–Feb and Sep–Dec meetings is a social as well as a sporting event. Inquiries ☎ 207 01 40.
Soccer Real Madrid and *Atlético Madrid* command passionate support. The atmosphere at home matches is good humoured: Estadio Santiago Bernabeu, Av de Concha Espina 1 ☎ 250 06 00, and Estadio Vicente Calderón, Pº Virgen del Puerto 6 ☎ 266 47 07.

Keeping fit
Health and sports clubs have become fashionable, but most do not permit temporary members. The public facilities at C Bravo Murillo 366 and Pl del Perú are excellent; inquiries ☎ 436 90 50. Several hotels have sports facilities, notably the Príncipe de Vergara.
Fitness centres Palestra, C Bravo Murillo 5 ☎ 448 98 22, with many facilities, has a reasonable monthly membership fee. *Presidente*, C Profesor Waksman 3 ☎ 458 67 59 (men only), has a monthly fee.
Golf Federación Española de Golf, C Capitán Haya 9 ☎ 455 26 82. Players require a daily or weekly licence.
Riding Escuela Española de Equitación, Av de la Iglesia 9, Pozuelo de Alarcon. Horseback outings are organized by *Camino y Caballos*, C Duque de Liria 3 ☎ 242 31 25.
Squash The *Palestra* (see above) has squash courts.
Swimming Several hotels have pools.

Local resources
Business services
Business services in the city are excellent. For office space and/or facilities contact *Eurobusiness Centre*, C Juan Ramón Jiménez 8 ☎ 458 85 22, and *Centro Internacional de Negocios*, Pº de la Castellana 141 ☎ 572 03 60. *Resinca SA*, C Pedro Muguruza 4 ☎ 259 34 46, specializes in qualified professional staff such as economists.
Photocopying and printing
Prontaprint, C Maria de Molina 56

☎ 411 08 23; *Novaprint*, Av General Perón 23 ☎ 455 68 92. *Cavero*, Pº de la Castellana 131 ☎ 456 46 17, also offers microfiche and transparency duplication; *Fotocopias Correos*, Pº de la Castellana 131 ☎ 456 46 17 (24hrs)
Secretarial Most large hotels can arrange secretarial services. ECCO, C Eugenio Salazar 27 ☎ 415 65 49, *Cadegesa*, C Sagasta 7 ☎ 445 57 30, and *Intergrup*, C Villanueva 2 ☎ 577 36 64.
Translation Tradecom, C Nuñez de Balboa 49 ☎ 431 65 07. *Estudio Sotomayor*, C Sotomayor 7 ☎ 233 65 41, for legal and scientific work.

Communications
Local delivery Most agencies handle local, national and international deliveries: *Hora Punta* ☎ 268 20 06; ASM ☎ 413 00 11; *Mensajeros Express* ☎ 255 33 00; SEUR ☎ 416 90 11.
Long-distance delivery IBC ☎ 408 98 98; DHL ☎ 747 34 00. RENFE ☎ 314 00 00.
Post offices Central office: Palacio de Comunicaciones, Pl de Cibeles ☎ 521 81 95, is open Mon–Sat, 9am–10pm for letters, telegrams and parcels up to 2 kilos/4.4lbs and Mon–Sat, 9–2 for other postal services. The airport post office is open daily, 9am–8pm. Normal opening hours are Mon–Sat, 9–2, but stamps can be bought in any tobacco shop (*estanco*).
Telex and fax at the central post office, Mon–Sat, 8–midnight; Sun, 8–8. There are many private bureaux. *Télex 24*, C Orense 69 ☎ 571 21 88, collects and handles dictated messages.

Conference/exhibition centres
A new exhibition and conference complex is planned for 1991 as part of the Campo de Naciones development on the western edge of town. Conference organizers include SIASA *Congresos*, Pº Habana 134 ☎ 457 44 95, and *Instituto Vikingo*, Embajadoro 196 ☎ 230 59 19.
Palacio de Exposiciones y Congresos,

Pº de la Castellana 99 ☎ 455 16 00, is the largest conference centre (capacity up to 3,000) with 2 auditoriums, 9 meeting rooms (all with a/v and simultaneous translation facilities for up to 6 languages) and 3 main exhibition halls. The *Recinto Ferial*, Av de Portugal, at present the main exhibition centre, is in the Casa de Campo park and it has 4 pavilions (capacity up to 3,000), conference and concert halls, auditorium; contact IFEMA (Institución Ferial de Madrid) ☎ 470 10 14.

The *Madrid Convention Bureau*, Av de Portugal, 28011 ☎ 463 63 64, helps with conference organization.

Emergencies
Bureaux de change Banks are open Mon–Fri, 9–2; Sat, 9–1. At Barajas airport the banks are open 24hrs.
Hospitals Inquiries ☎ 098. Medical emergencies: ☎ 409 55 30; ambulance ☎ 588 44/45/46 00; *Red Cross* ☎ 233 77 77; cardiological institute ☎ 243 92 05. Hospitals: *Ciudad Sanitaria La Paz*, Pº de la Castellana 261 ☎ 734 26 00; *Ciudad Sanitaria Doce de Octubre*, Av de Córdoba ☎ 469 76 00; and *Red Cross*, Av de la Reina Victoria 24 ☎ 533 39 00.
Pharmacies A list of those on 24hr duty is posted outside all pharmacies (*farmacias de guardia*).
Police Jefatura Superior de la Policia: Puerta del Sol 7 ☎ 521 12 36; *Guardia Civil* (traffic police) ☎ 233 11 00. Emergencies ☎ 091, municipal police ☎ 092.

Government offices
Ministerio de Economia y Hacienda, Pº de la Castellana 162, 28046 ☎ 458 00 16, for information on the economy and assistance with setting up a business. *Ministerio de Industria y Energia*, Pº de la Castellana 162, 28046 ☎ 458 80 10. *Ministerio de Transportes, Turismo y Comunicaciones*, Nuevos Ministerios, Pl San Juan de la Cruz 1, 28003 ☎ 456 11 44. Visas office: C Los Madrazo 9 ☎ 521 93 50 (open Mon–Fri, 9–2).

Information sources
Business information Cámera de Comercio y Industria de Madrid (Chamber of commerce), C Huertas 13, 28012 ☎ 429 81 83; IMADE (*Instituto Madrileño de Desarollo*), C García de Paredes 92, 28010 ☎ 410 20 63, for information on the city development; *Instituto de Empresa*, C Maria de Molina 11–15, 28006 ☎ 261 83 50, for all kinds of courses; *Promadrid*, C Serrano 1, 28001 ☎ 435 90 45, coordinates public and private projects.
Local media The country's most important quality newspaper is *El País*; *Cinco Días* and *Informaciones* are financial dailies. Economics magazines like *Mercado* and *Actualidad Económica*, with international and local coverage, are widely read.
Tourist information Main office, Pl Mayor 3 ☎ 266 54 77; also at Barajas airport; Charmartín station; Torre de Madrid, Pl de España; and C Duque de Medinaceli 2. The *Patronato Municipal de Turismo*, C Señores de Luzón 10 ☎ 266 39 00, publishes a monthly newsletter in English.

Thank-yous
A bottle of duty-free bourbon or whisky will always be appreciated. *Chocolates Santa*, C Serrano 56. *Mallorca*, C Velázquez 59, open Sun am, sells cakes, cheeses and sausages as well ☎ 276 41 78.
Florists Bourgignon, C Almagro 3 ☎ 419 26 92; *Interflora*, Torrelaguna 125 ☎ 413 84 43.

BARCELONA

City code ☎ 93

Barcelona, capital of Catalonia and second city of Spain, with a population of just over 1.7m, is a business-like, cosmopolitan city bursting with energy and civic pride. It has always been more Mediterranean than Spanish in character, a reflection of its independent Catalan culture and history. The Catalans are sensitive about their culture and have a reputation for being less friendly to outsiders than other Spaniards. Since Franco's death in 1975 the region has won back an autonomous government (Generalitat) with wide-ranging powers and has restored Catalan as the co-language of education and government.

The Catalans' business acumen, the subject of many jokes in Spain, is not a myth. Traditional activities – textiles, chemicals, paper, food (Nutrexpa) and engineering (SEAT) – remain the core of the thriving manufacturing hinterland to the city and, with the port, the largest in Spain and third in the Mediterranean, account for the region's 20% share of GNP. Tourism, which brings over 15m visitors a year to Catalonia, and design in many of its applications has become important; the emphasis now is on computers, electronics and new technologies. Financial and administrative services include the Caixa de Pensions, which is Spain's largest savings bank, and the stock exchange.

A flood of foreign money has been attracted by the transport network and a strong local market. The Japanese in particular have invested heavily in Catalonia and there are over 60 multinationals with bases here including Nissan, Volkswagen and Nestlé.

Attention is now focused on preparing for the European single market and for the Olympics, both in 1992, and on converting the latter from a brief blaze of publicity to a springboard for long-term investment.

Arriving

Barcelona has excellent road and rail links with southern Europe and France as well as a small but busy international airport. A ringroad around the city is being built and the slow road to Madrid and the airport is being improved by 1992.

El Prat airport

A single terminal, 14kms/7.5 miles south of the town centre, handles over 250 scheduled and charter flights daily, with services from most European cities. Among good domestic links is the daytime 45min *puente aéreo* or (in Catalan) *pont aeri* shuttle from Madrid. Facilities include hotel reservations desk, travel agency, tourist office, a bank, bureau de change (open 24hrs), shops and restaurant. There is a chamber of commerce office upstairs (open Mon–Fri, 8–3). Airside there are Iberia VIP lounges and a small duty-free shop. Flight and freight inquiries ☎ 325 58 29.

City link Taxi or train are the best ways of reaching town.

Taxis The journey takes 20–30mins and the fare is about Pta1,500.

Car rental The major companies have desks here. A car is useful for visiting the suburbs, and central Barcelona is quite easy to negotiate.

Bus There are infrequent local day and night buses (EA and EN) that leave for Plaça d'Espanya (7.15am–3am).

Train Services run every 30mins (6am–11pm, journey time 20mins) to Central-Sants station.

Railway stations

Estació Central-Sants (Metro Sants-

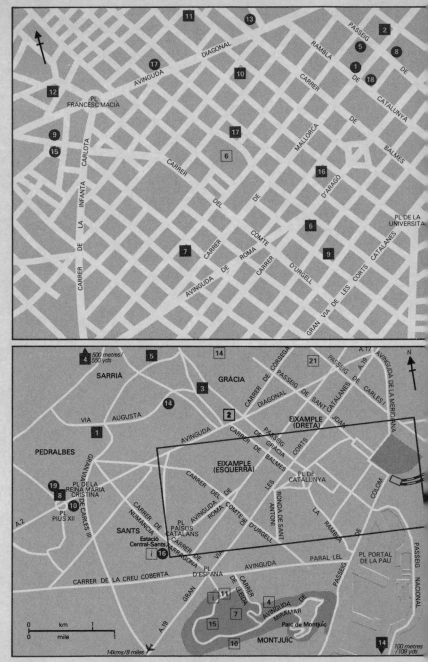

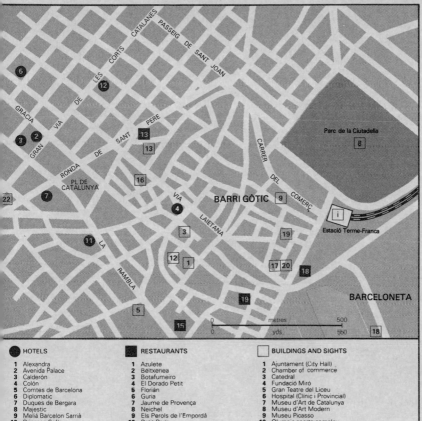

Parc de la Ciutadella ⑧

BARRI GÒTIC ⑨

Estació Terme-Franca

BARCELONETA

		metres	500
0		yds	550

HOTELS	RESTAURANTS	BUILDINGS AND SIGHTS
1 Alexandra	1 Azulete	1 Ajuntament (City Hall)
2 Avenida Palace	2 Beltxenea	2 Chamber of commerce
3 Calderón	3 Botafumeiro	3 Catedral
4 Colón	4 El Dorado Petit	4 Fundació Miró
5 Comtes de Barcelona	5 Florián	5 Gran Teatre del Liceu
6 Diplomatic	6 Guria	6 Hospital (Clinic i Provincial)
7 Duques de Bergara	7 Jaume de Provença	7 Museu d'Art de Catalunya
8 Majestic	8 Neichel	8 Museu d'Art Modern
9 Meliá Barcelon Sarrià	9 Els Perols de l'Empordà	9 Museu Picasso
10 Princess Sofia	10 Petit Paris	10 Olympic sports complex
11 Ramada Renaissance	11 Reno	11 Palau de Congressos
12 Ritz	12 Via Veneto	12 Palau de la Generalitat
13 Balmoral	13 Brasserie Flo	13 Palau de la Música
14 Cóndor	14 Can Majó	14 Park Güell
15 Derby & Gran Derby	15 Los Caracoles	15 Poble Espanyol
16 Expo	16 Chicoa	16 Police
17 Presidente	17 L'Olivé	17 Post office
18 Regente	18 Set Portes	18 Port
19 Victoria	19 El Túnel	19 Santa Maria del Mar
		20 Stock exchange: Borsa de Commerç (Casa de la Llotja)
		21 Temple Expiatori de la Sagrada Familia
		22 Universitat Central
		i Tourist information

Estació), on the west side of town, handles all Talgo (express), InterCity and international services (direct overnight sleepers from Paris and Geneva), linking trains, the airport and, with the temporary closure of Estació Terme-França, trains from France and the Costa Brava. The station is built around an enclosed ticket-only area with access to the platforms below by escalator. Facilities include cafeterias, travel agents who can reserve hotel rooms, a rail and tourist information desk, a bank, bureau de change (open Mon–Sat, 8–10; Sun, 8–2, 4–10), car rental desks, pharmacy and shops (no post office). Taxis wait outside the main entrance in the Plaça Països Catalans; the centre is 10–15mins away. Rail inquiries ☎ 322 41 42. *Estació Terme-França* has closed for building work in connection with the Olympics.

Getting around

The centre of Barcelona was designed on a generous scale with wide streets and broad avenues. There is no compact business zone, so it is rarely practicable to walk between appointments. Inquiries for all public transport at information stands in the Plaça de Catalunya; or ☎ 336 00 00. *Taxis* are plentiful and cheap with green roof-lights when they are free. A number indicates which tariff (depending on district, day of the week and time) applies. Cabs stop if hailed and wait at street junctions. During the day allow time for heavy traffic. A tip is expected. *Taxi Express* ☎ 322 22 22, *Taxi Radio Móvil* ☎ 358 11 11.
Limousines VIP *Car Service* ☎ 201 36 59.
Driving Outside the Old Town it is easy to find your way; the streets are laid out on a grid pattern. Parking permits (from automatic machines) are necessary in the clearly marked blue zone. There is plenty of secure underground parking. Do not leave valuables on the seats or even hidden; thieving is rife. The main rental

companies have offices: *Avis* ☎ 322 77 77; *Hertz* ☎ 322 97 59.
Walking In the Eixample distances are long – Avinguda Diagonal is 10kms/6 miles – and car fumes a discomfort. The Old Town can be explored on foot, but the port and old red-light district west of the Rambles should be avoided at night.
Subway The efficient Metro runs Mon–Fri, 5am–11pm; Sat, 5am–1am; Sun, 6am–1am. Changing lines can mean a long walk. Routes are identified by line number, colour and the name of the terminus. Tickets are for single or 10 trips. If you switch to the dark blue line (known as FFCC de la Generalitat) you will need a second ticket.
Bus The city's buses (operating 6am–10.30pm) are easy to use. There are single or 10-journey tickets; maps from Plaza Cibeles.

Area by area

Barcelona can be divided into four areas: the port and the Old Town and within it the Barri Gòtic, with Mount Montjuïc rising on the south; the spacious, 19thC Eixample; the residential suburbs climbing into the hills to the north and west; and the industrial and working-class urban sprawl which spreads for 50kms/31 miles both ways along the coast.

The Barri Gòtic and the Old Town are a blend of Gothic glory and street life. Away from the historic and fashionable enclaves in the Barri Gòtic, some areas have become run down (there are problems with drugs and street crime) and the Rambles have become downmarket and touristy. Close by is Barceloneta, once the preserve of fishermen, which has colourful seafood restaurants and an easy-going, village-like atmosphere. On the south, the town halts abruptly at the foot of Mount Montjuïc; preserved as a park, it contains museums, the main conference and trade fair complex and the site of the Olympics.

The Eixample is a huge 19thC grid of streets designed by engineer

Ildefons Cerdà to link the Old Town to surrounding towns. Originally residential and dignified by grand *palacetes*, it is the business and commercial district, with a mix of shops, offices, hotels, restaurants and apartments. Stamped by the modernism of Antoni Gaudí and other architects, it is divided by the grand avenue, Passeig de Gràcia, into the Esquerra (left) and Dreta (right), and cut by the great boulevards of Gran Via de les Corts Catalanes and the Diagonal, along which modern businesses and banks have crept towards the University. To the east the Olympic Village is being built in downmarket Poble Nou.

The smartest residential quarters are Sarrià and Pedralbes beyond the Eixample. Once graced with summer villas which dotted the country up into the hills, Sarrià and Pedralbes are now filled in with expensive blocks of apartments and near the Diagonal with offices. The villages farther inland on Mount Tibidabo are also commuter territory. Closer in, Gràcia, once a separate small town, has kept its 18th and 19thC character, its streets and squares, family shops and cafés behind old stone façades and is becoming chic.

Working-class housing is to the west of the Eixample, in Sants, in the adjacent town of Hospitalet and in Sant Andreu and Sant Martí. Old Factories sprawl across the Zona Franca, between the airport and Montjuïc, with a concentration of modern heavy industry including SEAT and the Motor Ibérica factory, and Vallès, with textiles, electronics and a new technology park. Finally, in the port there are over 22kms/14 miles of docks, starting at the Barceloneta, where fishing boats bring in the Mediterranean catches to the daily market, and extending southwest to the commercial docks where hundreds of cranes servicing the container ships, bulk carriers and roll-on, roll-off vehicle ferries are visible into the distance.

Hotels

Barcelona is investing heavily in a range of good hotels in preparation for the Olympics. In the meantime the Ritz is still the grandest and the renovated Ramada Renaissance the best-equipped and designed for business travellers.

Nearly all the others, both the large chain hotels and the fashionably converted Art Nouveau town houses, are in the Eixample or residential districts. Single rooms are small; prices on the larger rooms may be negotiable. Reservations should be made well ahead during fairs, in March, April and September. Facilities in common include IDD telephones, minibars and TVS with foreign-language cable channels in all rooms and secure parking facilities.

Alexandra ⟨P⟩//
C Mallorca 251, 08008 ☎ *215 30 52*
⟨TX⟩ *81107 fax 216 06 06* • *PHD Hotels*
• *AE DC MC V* • *75 rooms, 1 restaurant, 1 bar*
The outside of the Alexandra shows its architectural origins in the turn-of-the-century ironwork on the balconies. Inside, the emphasis is on black and white in the lobby and bar and in the bedroom furniture and decoration. This is a new hotel inside the shell of a renovated old building, and it has become popular with young executives as much for the service as for the *nouvelle cuisine* of the dining room. Bedrooms are rather small, but an annex nearby in Carrer Muntaner has suites. 24hr room service • access to nearby fitness club • 2 meeting rooms (capacity up to 60).

Avenida Palace P̄//
Gran Via de les Corts Catalanes 605,
08007 ☎ *301 96 00* ⊤⊠ *54734*
fax 318 12 34 • *AE DC MC V* • *212*
rooms, 16 suites, 1 restaurant, 1 bar
A central 1950s hotel, comfortably
and soberly furnished. A gilded
stairway leads down from the lobby-
lounge to meeting and banquet rooms
which have period charm. The
bedrooms on Gran Via are noisy, and
some rooms are dark. Suites are plain
but can be used as offices, and the
restaurant is popular for a working
lunch. 24hr room service, shops,
newsstand • fitness room, sauna • 4
meeting rooms (capacity up to 400).

Calderón P̄/
Rbla Catalunya 26, 08007
☎ *301 00 00* ⊤⊠ *51549 fax 317 31 57*
• *NH* • *AE DC V* • *263 rooms,*
11 suites, 1 restaurant, 1 bar
This excellent modern hotel not far
from the Plaça de Catalunya is geared
towards business travellers, athletes
(the sports facilities are the best in
central Barcelona) and those here for
the arts. The modern uncluttered
style of the lobby and lounges has
created an attractive light hotel. Its
restaurant has a reputation for Basque
alta cocina. Indoor and outdoor pools,
squash, fitness room, sauna • 12
meeting rooms (capacity up to 200).

Colón P̄
Av de la Catedral 7, 08002
☎ *301 14 04* ⊤⊠ *52654 fax 317 29 15*
• *AE DC MC V* • *180 rooms, 20 suites,*
1 restaurant, 1 bar
Guests can overlook the west front of
the Gothic cathedral from this old
hotel. Recent refurbishment shows in
the pastel colours of the bedrooms,
freshly upholstered chairs of the
lounges and glass-walled meeting
rooms. The atmosphere is
comfortable and friendly, and on
Sunday mornings you can watch
traditional *sardanas* (dances) in the
street. Good-sized single rooms. 24hr
room service, hairdresser •
multilingual secretarial service, 3
meeting rooms (capacity up to 150).

Comtes de Barcelona P̄//
Pg de Gràcia 75, 08008 ☎ *487 37 37*
⊤⊠ *51531 fax 216 08 35* • *PHD Hotels*
• *AE DC MC V* • *97 rooms, 2 suites,*
1 restaurant, 1 bar
This is a stylish hotel, from the Art
Nouveau ironwork and tiles of the
outside balconies to the galleried
atrium, split-level lobby and massive
stone ballusters of the stairway. The
clean lines of the bedrooms and
bathrooms are echoed in the small bar
and restaurant. Situated on the most
fashionable stretch of the Passeig de
Gràcia and convenient for midtown
Barcelona, this is the city's trendiest
hotel, so make reservations early.
Access to fitness club • 3 meeting
rooms (capacity up to 100).

Diplomatic P̄//
C Pau Claris 122, 08009 ☎ *317 31 00*
⊤⊠ *54701 fax 318 65 31* • *Melià* •
AE DC MC V • *203 rooms, 14 suites,*
2 restaurants, 4 bars
A busy, efficient and modern hotel
catering especially for business
travellers and politicians in midtown
Eixample. The restaurant is useful for
informal business meals. 24hr room
service, travel agents, car rental •
sun-terrace pool • secretarial service,
5 meeting rooms (capacity up to 550).

Duques de Bergara P̄/
C Bergara 11, 08002 ☎ *301 51 51*
⊤⊠ *98718 or 81257 fax 317 34 42* •
Catalonia • *AE DC MC V* • *58 rooms,*
1 suite, 1 restaurant, 1 bar
Within sight of the busy Plaça de
Catalunya and close to the Old Town,
a hotel of period character. Once a
19thC *palacete*, it has retained a
marbled entrance hall and stairway,
coffered ceilings and, in the upper
lounge, the scale and personal touches
of a private residence. Bedrooms are
light and decorated in pastels, the
bathrooms in marble (with phones).
24hr room service • 1 meeting room
(capacity up to 20).

Majestic P̄/
Pg de Gràcia 70, 08008 ☎ *215 45 12*
⊤⊠ *52211 fax 215 77 73* • *AE DC MC V* •

350 rooms, 5 suites, 1 restaurant, 1 bar
This elegant and traditional hotel in central Barcelona offers good facilities for business visitors. The large bedrooms are well equipped for working; and the executive suites, with fax, telex, video and photocopying, should be reserved well ahead. Front rooms have balconies; those at the back are quieter. Pleasant, spacious lounge. Rooftop pool • 9 meeting rooms with a/v equipment (capacity up to 600).

Meliá Barcelona Sarrià *P*////
Av de Sarrià 50, 08029 ☎ *410 60 60*
 ⊤⊠ *51033 fax 321 51 79* • *AE DC MC v* • *311 rooms, 5 suites, 2 restaurants, 1 bar*
A sleek modern block with high-tech decor and a fountain in the vast lobby. The two executive floors, with their own reception desks and secretarial services, have views towards the hills or the sea. 24hr room service, shops • fitness centre, sauna • 7 meeting rooms.

Princesa Sofía *P*////
Pl Pius XII 4, 08028 ☎ *330 71 11*
 ⊤⊠ *51683 fax 330 76 21* • *HUSA* •
AE DC MC v • *488 rooms, 22 suites, 4 restaurants, 1 bar*
This well-equipped and efficient high-rise 5-star hotel is near businesses and banks on the Diagonal (but away from the centre) and caters for conventions and exhibitions. It has good support services in a business centre and a health club. The lobby and galleried first floor are always busy but provide quiet corners for discussion. The Top City restaurant offers fine views over the nearby avenues, Ampurdán, a Catalan menu. 24hr room service, shop, hairdresser, disco • heated pool, fitness centre, sauna, massage • 20 meeting rooms (capacity up to 1,500).

Ramada Renaissance *P*//
La Rambla 111, 08002 ☎ *318 62 00*
 ⊤⊠ *54634 fax 301 77 66* • *AE DC MC v* • *203 rooms, 7 suites, 2 restaurants, 1 bar*

A 1950s hotel at the edge of the Barri Gòtic, the Renaissance (formerly named the Manila), reopened with the business executive in mind. It is luxuriously appointed, and the spacious bedrooms have large beds (and heated bathroom floors). Telex, fax, computer and printer are available. The Renaissance Club floors include a lounge, bar and dining room. The piano bar and terrace-like restaurant downstairs are popular for local business entertaining. 24hr room service • meeting rooms (capacity up to 300).

Ritz *P*////
Gran Via de les Corts Catalanes 668, 08010 ☎ *318 52 00* ⊤⊠ *52739 fax 318 01 48* • *AE DC MC v* • *167 rooms, 1 suite, 1 restaurant, 1 bar*
The Barcelona Ritz, one of the original four of that name, was opened in 1919. It is grand, exclusive and elegant, especially the pillared oval salon and the balconied restaurant. A wide staircase sweeps up from the lobby to the bedrooms, furnished with silk hangings and with marble bathrooms. Service is immaculate though facilities are not specially oriented to business needs. 24hr room service, newsstand, hairdresser • fitness centre • 7 meeting rooms (capacity up to 500).

OTHER HOTELS
Balmoral *P*/ *Via Augusta 5, 08006* ☎ *217 87 00* ⊤⊠ *54087* • *AE DC MC v*. Reliable friendly hotel with recently decorated bedrooms and a loyal Spanish business clientele.
Cóndor *P*/ *Via Augusta 127, 08006* ☎ *209 45 11* ⊤⊠ *52925 fax 202 27 13* • *AE DC MC v*. Small, elegant hotel close to pleasant surroundings in Gràcia.
Derby & Gran Derby *P*/ *C de Loreto 21 & 28, 08029* ☎ *322 32 15* ⊤⊠ *97429 fax 410 08 62* • *Best Western* • *AE DC MC v*. Refurbished hotel and a complex of excellent suites (some duplex) on a quiet street between the city centre and the Diagonal business zone.

Expo _P_/ _C Mallorca 1–23, 08014_ ☎ _325 12 12_ ⊤ₓ _54147 fax 325 11 44_ • _AE DC MC V_. Modern convention hotel close to the Estació Central-Sants, the main exhibition centre and Palau de Congressos convention halls.

Presidente _P_/ _Av Diagonal 570, 08021_ ☎ _200 21 11_ ⊤ₓ _52180 fax 200 22 66_ • _HUSA_ • _AE DC MC V_. Comfortable hotel with all standard facilities and an outdoor summer pool, not far from the modern business zone.

Regente _P_/ _Rbla de Catalunya 76, 08008_ ☎ _215 25 70_ ⊤ₓ _51939_ •

HUSA • _AE DC MC V_. Pleasant central hotel with limited public rooms but a pool and terrace.

Victoria _P_/ _Av Pedralbes 16 bis, 08034_ ☎ _204 27 54_ ⊤ₓ _98302 fax 204 27 66_ • _AE DC MC V_. Excellent roomy suites, with a smart cafeteria and a pool, in the uptown residential district of Pedralbes.

> Hotel and restaurant price guide
> For the meanings of the hotel and restaurant price symbols, see pages 6 and 7.

Restaurants

Barcelona's restaurants are varied: there are smart midtown places for business entertaining, elegant old mansions, fashionable new brasseries and unpretentious bar-cafés serving good simple food. All, except for the most expensive, draw a mixed clientele, so dress is rarely formal. Cooking styles are cosmopolitan, but Catalans are proud of their cuisine, which grafts French and Italian influences on to the regional cooking of the mountain and coast to produce robust, sunny dishes. Mealtimes are earlier than elsewhere in Spain, although dining rooms are rarely full before 2.30pm at lunch and 10pm in the evening.

Azulete _P_/ _Via Augusta 281_ ☎ _203 59 43_ • _closed Sat L, Sun, 2 weeks in Aug_ • _AE DC MC V_ Popular with young executives and the media, the Azulete has a glassed-in terrace full of plants and a period interior converted by architect Oscar Tusquet. Victoria Roque's _nueva cocina_, with French influences, is light, seasonal and imaginative. Better suited to social occasions rather than for serious business discussions.

Beltxenea _P_// _C Mallorca 275_ ☎ _215 30 24_ • _closed Sat L, Sun_ • _AE MC V_ Hidden behind a plain façade (ring the buzzer for entry) is one of the midtown's smartest restaurants. The terrace is a delight in summer. The menu combines traditional Basque dishes, like rice and clams, with

newer creations by the young chef, Miguel Ezcurra. Popular for expense-account dining at lunch; less formal in the evenings.

Botafumeiro _P_//// _C Gran de Gràcia 81_ ☎ _218 42 30_ • _closed Sun D, Mon, 2 weeks in Aug_ • _AE DC MC V_ Botafumeiro ranks among the best of Barcelona's seafood restaurants, with prices to match. Service is excellent, as are the wines – try the local Penedès whites. The long opening hours, from 1pm to 1am, draw a varied, smart crowd. Six private rooms of varying size (reserve well ahead).

El Dorado Petit _P_// _C Dolors Montserdà 51_ ☎ _204 51 53_ • _closed Sun, 2 weeks in Aug_ • _AE MC V_ This famous restaurant in an old villa in Sarrià ranks among the top dozen in Spain. The cooking is a sophisticated mix of regional and *nueva cocina*. There have been whispers about slipping standards since Luis Cruañas, the owner, departed to open a restaurant in Washington, but the elegant rooms, the terrace and the reputation still bring in the diners.

Florián [P]///
C Bertrand i Serra 20 ☎ *212 46 27* • *closed Sun, Aug* • *DC MC V*
Run by a young husband and wife, Florián has earned a reputation for its cooking, a blend of Italian and French with a distinctive style, and a large cellar of wines (largely Spanish). The menu mixes the exotic, elvers (young eels) with caviar, with the simplicity of grilled fish. Two dining rooms, decorated in cool, modern colours; attentive service.

Guria [P]
C Casanova 97–99 ☎ *253 63 25* • *closed 2 weeks in Aug* • *AE DC MC V*
The atmosphere of this Basque restaurant is both reassuring and formal with its traditional wood-panelling. Its central location is appreciated for business lunches, and tables are well spaced. The menu combines classics like *merluza* (hake) *en salsa verde* with newer dishes such as peppers with squid, and there are creamy desserts and Basque cheeses.

Jaume de Provença [P]///
C Provença 88 ☎ *230 00 29* • *closed Sun D, Mon, Aug* • *AE DC MC V*
This midtown restaurant is invariably busy because of the superb food, a combination of rustic and luxury ingredients. Try the salad made of lightly steamed shellfish, the *foie gras* with Sauternes or the *menu dégustation*. Executives flock here at lunch time, and there is a smarter room for private dining.

Neichel [P]///
Av de Pedralbes 16 bis ☎ *203 84 08* • *closed Sun, Aug* • *AE DC MC V* • *reservations essential*

In the last decade Jean-Louis Neichel has built a reputation as one of the most imaginative chefs in the city. His special gift is to fuse Spanish flavours with his own Alsacian cooking to create an unusual *nouvelle cuisine*, and the dessert trolley displays over 20 different dishes. The dining room is light and airy.

Els Perols de l'Empordà [P]/
C Villarroel 88 ☎ *323 10 33* • *closed Sun D, Mon* • *AE DC MC V*
Ampurdán, or Empordà, is a region on the northern Catalan coast famous for its rich dishes like *arròs negro* (rice coloured by squid ink) and *suquet* (fish ragoût), and this is the place in Barcelona to try them. It is a good choice for quiet conversation; the dining room has only half a dozen tables and there is a private room. The cooking, service and wine, whether local Penedès or grander Riojas, are excellent.

Petit París [P]
C París 196 ☎ *218 26 78* • *closed Sun, Jul & Aug* • *MC V*
Just off the Diagonal, this intimate restaurant has a Parisian style, though the food is a blend of Catalan and French – tartare of sea-bass, salt-cod cooked ten different ways and veal with *foie gras* – and the choice of 200 wines is varied. Popular at lunch time with people from nearby offices; more relaxed in the evening.

Reno [P]///
C Tuset 27 ☎ *200 91 29* • *AE DC MC V*
For over 30 years Reno has been serving reliable food. With its elegant decor, sober ambience and discreet service, this is the first choice for an important business occasion. The cooking is a well-prepared mixture of old and new. The cellar is extensive, with fine wines from the main Spanish regions.

Vía Veneto [P]///
C Ganduxer 10–12 ☎ *200 72 44* • *closed Sat L, Sun* • *AE DC MC V*
An excellent restaurant popular with

bankers and politicians. The menu mixes international dishes with some of Catalan origin. Service is formal but friendly, and the extensive Spanish wine list has some outstanding vintage bottles. There are several private rooms (reserve well ahead).

OTHER RESTAURANTS
For informal meals the choice is enormous and the food usually good. Many restaurants serve traditional Catalan dishes; others have adopted a style nearer *nueva cocina*. *Brasserie Flo*, C Jonqueres 10 ☎ 317 80 37, is lively, has an international menu and stays open very long hours; in Barceloneta, *Can Majó*, C Almirante Aixada 23 ☎ 319 50 96, is a family-run fish restaurant.

For Catalan atmosphere try *Los Caracoles*, C Escudellers 14 ☎ 302 31 85, in the Old Town, touristy but historic; *Chicoa*, C D'Aribau 71–73 ☎ 253 11 23, serves good Catalan cooking, especially *bacalao* (salt-cod); at *L'Olivé*, C Muntaner 171 ☎ 230 90 27, versions of home Catalan recipes are served into the early hours (very crowded); *Set Portes*, Pg Isabel II 14 ☎ 319 30 33, a large old restaurant near the port and full of atmosphere, has excellent rice dishes; and *El Túnel*, C Ample 33–35 ☎ 315 27 79, is a renowned family restaurant in a side street near the port.

Out of town
The coast north of Barcelona has several of the top restaurants in Spain. Those in Figueras and Gerona (Figures and Girona in Catalan) – notably *Ampurdán* (137kms/85 miles) ☎ (972) 50 05 62 and *Carlos Camos-Big Rock* (100kms/62 miles) ☎ (972) 81 80 12 – are a long drive (although the *autopista*, the highway, is excellent), but there are two within easy reach along the N.11: *Hispania*, in Arenys de Mar ☎ 791 03 06 (37kms/19 miles), is famed for its produce, ranging from seafood to game, cellar and setting, and *Racó*

d'en Binu in Argentona ☎ 797 01 01 (27kms/15 miles).

Bars and cafés
Catalans tend to go straight home for lunch and the evening meal unless they are part of the chic young set. Hotel bars are usually best for talking business. Otherwise try upmarket *José Luis*, Av Diagonal 520, *Gimlet*, Carrer Santaló 46, or champagne bars like *La Xampanveria*, C Provença 236.

The more traditional bars in the Barri Gòtic include the recreation of the *Els Quatre Gats*, C Montsió 5, the famous bar where Picasso met his friends, or the smart *Café de l'Opera*, La Rambla 74, open long hours. In Carrer Petritxol, there are several traditional tearooms, or *granjas*, serving caramelized Catalan custards.

Entertainment
Barcelona is a cultural capital, excelling at music and theatre, and at weekends the streets are still noisy as the nightclubbers go home when dawn breaks. Check the weekly *Guia del Ocio* or at the information office at La Rambla 99 ☎ 301 77 75. The city hosts two lively fiestas, Mercè (Sep) and El Grec (Jul & Aug), a largely open-air cultural festival.
Theatre Most performances are in Catalan. *Teatre Lliure*, C Montseny 47 ☎ 218 92 51, is known for avant-garde productions. Cabaret/music hall (racy and upmarket) is staged at *Belle Epoque*, C Muntaner 246 ☎ 209 73 85, and *El Molino*, C Vilà i Vilà 99 ☎ 241 63 83.
Music and opera Seats for the season (Nov–June) at Spain's premier opera house, *Gran Teatre del Liceu*, in Rambla dels Caputxins 65 ☎ 318 92 77, are usually sold out six months in advance. Tickets for the magnificent modernist *Palau de la Música*, C Amadeu Vives 1 ☎ 301 11 04, are sold a week before performances. Excellent concerts by the Orquestra de la Ciutat de Barcelona take place there at weekends and in Nov–Jun. The important Festival Internacional de Música de Barcelona is held here

in September and October.

There are two jazz festivals (Mar, Nov), and many good clubs, such as *La Cova del Drac*, C Tuset 30.

Flamenco Maruja Garrido at *Los Tarantos*, Plaça Reial 17 ☎ 317 80 98, provides the only good show.

Cinema Filmoteca, Trav de Gràcia 63 ☎ 201 29 06, shows subtitled English-language films.

Nightclubs and casino In general the clubs are young and trendy or arty. Many of the smarter ones, like *Regine's*, Hotel Princesa Sofía, or *Up and Down*, C Numància 179, are for members only. Others include *Universal*, C Marià Cubí 184, and *La Salsa*, Hotel Diplomatic.

The *Gran Casino*, in a 19thC palace, is 40kms/25 miles northwest at Finca Mas Soler, near Sitges.

Shopping

As befits a city that aims to rival Milan for fashion design, there are numerous designer boutiques here. The main streets for shopping and for elegant windows are Passeig de Gràcia, along the Diagonal near Plaça Francesc Marcià and the pedestrian shopping streets between the Rambles and the Cathedral.

Fashion For the creations of international and Spanish designers, and for jewellery and leather, visit Passeig de Gràcia and Rambla de Catalunya, Via Augusta and the middle of Avinguda Diagonal. The clothes of local young designers are found in the commercial galleries, *El Boulevard Rosa* (Diagonal 474 and 619 and Passeig de Gràcia 55).

Antiques Explore Carrer Palla and Carrer Banys Nous in the Old Town or the market (Thu, 9–8) in Plaça Nova. *Antiquaris*, El Bulevard dels Antiquaris, a modern market, is more expensive. *Novocento*, Pg de Gràcia 75, has Arts Nouveau and Deco.

Department stores El Corte Inglés, has excellent leather, jewellery, fashion and toy departments. The largest branches are in Plaça de Catalunya and Plaça Maria Cristina.

Markets La Boquería, the central food market at Les Rambles 91, is a feast for the eyes; *Els Encants*, in Plaça de les Glòries (Mon, Wed, Fri & Sat), is a flea-market.

Sightseeing

Many of Barcelona's monuments and museums are within easy walking distance in the Old Town, but the museums on Montjuïc and the modernist buildings of the Eixample should not be missed.

In the *Barri Gòtic* are the Catalan Gothic *Catedral* (14th–19thC), with a museum and cloisters; the *Palau de la Generalitat*, the Catalan government; the Gothic buildings (including the 16thC former royal palace) on the Plaça del Rei; and two 14thC churches, *Santa Maria del Mar* and *Santa Maria del Pì*. The whole area of small historic streets (*Carrer Montcada*) and squares (*Plaça Reial*) ends in the west with the noisy and busy *Rambles*. Be careful after dark.

Borsa de Commerç The stock exchange is in the magnificent Gothic contracting room of the Llotja. Visitors are still allowed onto the floor; jacket and tie required. *La Llotja de Mar, Plaça del Palau. Open Mon–Fri, 9–2.*

Fundació Miró Gallery and cultural foundation set up by Joan Miró, with 300 of his finest works, and other exhibitions. *Av de Miramar, Montjuïc. Open Tue–Sat, 11–8; Sun, 11–2.30.*

Monestir de Pedralbes Catalan Gothic monastery including large cloister and chapel with frescoes. *Baixada del Monestir 9. Open Tue–Fri, 9.30–2; Sun, 9.30–1.*

Montjuïc On the hill above the Old Town and site of the 17thC fort, are the pavilions and landscaped gardens from the 1929 World Fair, several museums, an amusement park, the *Poble Espanyol* (see below) and the site of the 1992 Olympics. The main stadium is being constructed inside the one built in the city's bid for the Games in 1936. There are viewing points for watching the building (*barceloneses* flock here at weekends). Take a funicular from Paral.lel Metro station or a bus from Plaça d'Espanya, then a cable car to the top.

Museu d'Art de Catalunya Outstanding collections of Romanesque and Gothic art, and later paintings. *Palau Nacional, Parc de Montjuïc. Open Mon–Fri, 9–2.*

Museu Picasso Fine collection of his work from childhood to the late period. *C Montcada 15. Open Tue–Sat, 10–8; Sun, 9–2.*

Parc de la Ciutadella Lovely 19thC park with the *Museu d'Art Modern* (open Mon, 3–7.30; Tue–Sat, 9–7.30;

Modernism

Catalan modernism was a late 19thC style of architecture using industrial materials, new building techniques and asymmetrical lines to give an organic sense of form; it reflects the close links between commerce and art that remain important today. It flowered under the patronage of the city's industrial bourgeoisie.

Antoni Gaudí is its best known architect. His most important works here are buildings in the *Park Güell*, C d'Olot, now a municipal park, the sculptural *Casa Milà* (known as *La Pedrera*), Pg de Gràcia 92, and the extraordinary unfinished church, *Temple Expiatori de la Sagrada Família*. Buildings by the movement's two other leading architects include the concert hall, *Palau de la Música*, C de Sant Pere més Alt, by Lluís Domènech i Muntaner, and *Casa Macaya*, Pg de Sant Joan 108, by Josep Puig i Cadafalch.

Less spectacular examples of the same style, from complete buildings to lamp-posts, balconies and decorative details, are everywhere in the Eixample, often inside shops, offices and hotels. The most famous are the three buildings on the Passeig de Gràcia (Nos 39–43) nicknamed the "Apple of Discord" for their rival showy façades.

Sun, 9–2) and the *Zoo. Pg de Picasso.*

Poble Espanyol A village built in a mix of Spanish regional styles; good crafts for sale. Late-night spectacles and entertainment. *Av del Marquès de Comillas. Open daily 9am–4am.*

Port To savour the atmosphere of the port explore Barceloneta on foot, swing across the harbour in the cable car from the Torre de San Sebastián or take a 45min boat trip from the pier at the end of the Rambles.

Guided tours
Juliàtours ☎ 317 64 54 and *Pullmantur* ☎ 318 51 95 offer half-day guided tours. *Terra Endins* arranges tours around special sites ☎ 232 24 13. Visits to the Olympic sites by *aomsa* ☎ 424 05 08.

Out of town
At *Montserrat*, 53kms/37m to the west, the Benedictine monastery stands against fantastic cliffs and rocks. Trains leave from the Plaça d'Espanya every 2hrs, but exploration of the buildings requires a car.

Spectator sports
Basketball at *Palau Municipal d'Esports*, Parc de Montjuïc ☎ 241 34 04.
Soccer *F.C. Barcelona*, one of the best teams in Europe, is based at Nou Camp, Av Joan XXIII ☎ 330 80 52.

Keeping fit
Barcelona is within reach of beaches (Arenys de Mar, Palamós, Blanes and Lloret) and ski-slopes (Baqueira Beret is 306kms/190 miles away and is for serious skiers). Sports clubs do not freely admit nonmembers, but the public sports complexes are excellent: *Les Corts*, Trav de les Corts ☎ 239 41 78, and *Barceloneta*, Pg Marítim ☎ 309 34 12.
Fitness centres *Sport DYR*, C Castillejos 388 ☎ 347 66 44, offers facilities, including squash, for a fee. At *Gym Aribau*, C Bon Pastor 10 ☎ 209 69 70, payment is by the class.
Golf A temporary licence is required: *Federació Catalana* ☎ 200 24 78. *Real*

Club de Golf El Prat, a top club, has two courses ☎ 379 02 78.
Sailing *Real Club Marítim de Barcelona* ☎ 315 00 07, *Real Club Náutic de Barcelona* ☎ 315 11 61.
Squash *Squash Tibidabo*, Lluis Muntadas 8 ☎ 212 46 83.
Tennis *Tenis Barcino*, Pg Forasté 23 ☎ 203 78 52.

Local resources
Business services
Lexington International Business Services, Av Diagonal 605 ☎ 410 77 50, has temporary office space, with back-up services. *Barcelona Activa*, C Llacuna 162 ☎ 401 97 00, helps new businesses.
Photocopying and printing *Novacopia* ☎ 325 80 40 and C Aragó 421 ☎ 215 30 73, *New Graphic* ☎ 209 49 23.
Secretarial *Intergrup* ☎ 215 16 24. *Ecco*, C Pau Clarìs 180 ☎ 215 87 21.
Translation *Tradutex* ☎ 317 97 42. *Dial T&T* ☎ 201 93 52; *Rosario Tauler de Canals* ☎ 301 71 81.

Communications
Local delivery *Punt a Punt* ☎ 347 57 77, *Mensajeros Express* ☎ 322 22 22.
Long-distance delivery *dhl* ☎ 321 45 61, *seur* ☎ 303 21 12 (24hrs).
Post office Central post office: Plaça Antoni López ☎ 318 38 31, open Mon–Fri, 9–10; Sat, 9–2; Sun, 10–12.
Telex and fax at the central post office Mon–Fri, 8am–9.45pm.

Conference/exhibition centres
The 1929 International Exhibition complex remains the main fair and conference centre, *Fira de Barcelona*, Av Reina Maria Cristina, 08004 ☎ 423 31 01. It has 8 large halls, including the *Palau de Congressos*. *Barcelona Convention Bureau*, Pg de Gràcia 35, 08007 ☎ 215 44 77.

Emergencies
Bureaux de change Normal bank hours are Mon–Fri, 9–2; Sat, 9–1. Exchange offices at the airport are open 24hrs, and at Central-Sants station Mon–Sat, 8.30–10; Sun,

8.30–2, 4.30–10. Several banks in the Rambles have exchange offices open Mon–Sat until mid-evening.
Hospitals Central emergency numbers Mon–Sat, 5pm–9am; Sun for 24 hrs: ☎ 230 70 00; ambulances ☎ 329 77 66 (municipal) and 300 20 20 (Red Cross). Central hospitals: *Clínic i Provincial*, C Casanova 143 ☎ 32 31 414, *Sagrat Cor*, C Vilodomat 286 ☎ 230 58 00, *Cruz Roja* (Red Cross), C Dos de Maig 301 ☎ 235 93 00, and *Santa Creu i Sant Pau*, Av Sant Antoni Maria Claret 167 ☎ 347 31 33.
Pharmacies The daily duty schedule is on display outside each pharmacy.
Police Main station: *Jefatura de Policía*, Via Laietana 43 ☎ 301 66 66.

Government offices
The *Ajuntament* (City Hall) has a Dept de Relacions Econòmiques Internacionals, at C Ciutat 4, 08002 ☎ 301 02 88.

Information sources
Cambra Oficial de Comerç, Indústria i Navegació (Chamber of commerce), Av Diagonal 452–454, 08006 ☎ 219 13 00. *Iniciatives SA*, Pg de Gràcia 2, 08007 ☎ 317 81 61, encourages projects to benefit the city. *Promoció Installacions Olyipiques*, Palau Municipal d'Esports, C Lleida 40 ☎ 423 98 68, promotes commercial use of the Olympic installations.
Local media The main quality daily newspaper is *La Vanguardia* (centre-right) and *El País* has an office here.
Tourist information at Gran Via de les Corts Catalanes 658 ☎ 301 74 43 (open Mon–Fri, 9–7; Sat, 9–2), the main railway station (open daily, 8–8) and the Palau de Congressos.

Thank-yous
Chocolates *Antoni Escribà*, Les Rambles 83 and Gran Via de les Corts Catalanes ☎ 254 73 35.
Florists at the stalls in the Rambles.
Wine *Xampany*, C Valencia 200, or *Vins i Cava La Catedral*, Plaça Ramon Berenguer El Gran 1 ☎ 319 07 29.

SWEDEN

After a period of recession and severe imbalances in the late 1970s and early 1980s, the Swedish economy has shown modest growth, helped by lower oil prices, increased exports, two devaluations of the krona and high consumer demand. Since 1984 it has enjoyed a period of rising industrial production and low unemployment, albeit at a cost of relatively high inflation. Swedes enjoy high living standards; taxes are high and public spending on social services is heavy. But the government has modified its socialist policies in recent years by announcing cuts in income tax rates and calling for more competition in the public sector.

Mining and manufacturing contribute over 25% to GDP and are based largely on exploiting local resources (timber, iron ore and hydropower). The main industries are engineering, iron and steel production, timber production and processing, chemical production and food processing. Growth in recent years has been led by vehicles and high-technology enterprises such as electronics and telecommunications. Meanwhile the long established industries, such as textiles, iron and steel production and shipbuilding, have been in decline. Sweden has a large public sector, and also has many large, industrial corporations. The government is trying to reduce the country's dependence on imported oil and phase out nuclear power by increasing the use of other energy sources.

Service industries, including financial, retail and catering services, have expanded rapidly, now accounting for over 40% of GDP. Sweden is about 80% self-sufficient in basic foods, although its highly efficient agriculture sector accounts for less than 4% of GDP.

Exports are equivalent to about 35% of GDP. The main items are machinery, wood products, pulp and paper, transport equipment (mainly vehicles), chemicals, iron and steel. The main imports are machinery, transport equipment, chemicals, mineral fuels, clothing, footwear an textiles and food products. About 50% of external trade is with EC countries, mainly West Germany, the UK and Denmark; about 20% of exports go to fellow EFTA members. Sweden generally runs a trade surplus but faces a deficit on the current account.

Geography The central lowlands, dotted with wide lakes and forests, are flanked by mountains, forests and lakes to the north, stony uplands and the major agricultural area to the very south. Fifteen per cent of the country is inside the Arctic Circle.
Climate The far north has long, cold winters and cool summers; average temperatures range -14°C (7°F) to 14°C (57°F). The south has milder weather; average temperatures range from -3°C (27°C) to 18°C (64°F).
Population 8.4m.
Government Sweden is a constitutional monarchy. The legislature, the Riksdag, has 349 members directly elected for 3 years. It elects the prime minister.
Currency Swedish krona (SKr).
Time 1hr ahead of GMT; end of Apr-end of Sep, 2hrs ahead of GMT.
Dialling codes Sweden's IDD code is 46. Omit the 0 from the city code when dialling from abroad. To make an international call from Sweden, dial 990 before dialling the relevant country code.
Public holidays Jan 1, Jan 6, Good Fri, Easter Mon, May 1

STOCKHOLM (Sverige)

City code ☎ 08

Stockholm is Sweden's largest city and its administrative, commercial and financial centre, yet many of the country's biggest manufacturers are based elsewhere in Göteborg, Linköping and Västerlås. The service sector employs 55% of the work force of the capital and industry only 20%, but even so some 20,000 companies are located here and over 1,000 foreign firms, many using Stockholm as a centre for their Scandinavian enterprises. Some of the giant Swedish companies are based in the capital, including Electrolux, Ericsson and Skandia, the large insurer. There are very large construction projects under way in or close to the city, including redevelopment around the Central station. Farther out, in the satellite town of Kista, high-tech industries are flourishing, and a major R&D complex has been opened.

Greater Stockholm has a population of over 1.5m and is the largest and most affluent market in Scandinavia for consumer goods. Foreign companies are gaining a share in this business, and some 1m visitors a year come from abroad to attend important trade exhibitions and product launches.

The capital has benefited from the revival of the Swedish economy since 1980. A sophisticated money market has been created following deregulation and liberalization in the 1980s. The Stockholm business world is small, and personal contacts are important, but most of the business community departs to rural lakeside retreats for July and August. There has been an influx of people from elsewhere in Sweden and from Eastern Europe and Third World countries, causing a housing shortage, but with its parks, clear waters and unpolluted air Stockholm is an engaging city.

Arriving

There are flights to Stockholm from numerous cities worldwide, but connections with other Scandinavian and European capitals are most frequent. A car and passenger ferry links Stockholm to Helsinki (journey time 15hrs), and there is an express train link between Copenhagen and Stockholm (journey time 8hrs 30 mins).

Arlanda airport

The international and domestic terminals are within walking distance on adjacent sites. A third runway and a new terminal are due for completion in 1990.

The airport works efficiently and provides a full range of services, all of which are usually open daily, 7am–10pm: banks, a bureau de change, restaurants and bars, accommodation office and duty-free shops (expensive). The post office is open Mon–Fri, 9–6; Sat, 9–1pm. Business facilities, ranging from telex and secretarial support to conference rooms and catering, are provided by the *Arlanda Konferens Center* ☎ 797 62 00. British Airways and SAS have first- and business-class lounges and will provide fax, telex, copying and secretarial services. Airport inquiries 24 00 00; international flights ☎ 797 30 30; domestic ☎ 797 60 90.

Nearby hotel SAS *Arlandia* ☎ (0760) 61 800 ☒ 13018 *fax* (0760) 61 970. A modern hotel, 2kms/1 mile from the airport (direct coach link), designed for business travellers: secretarial services, office and meeting room rental and extensive conference facilities. Good exercise facilities:

pool, tennis court, fitness centre, jogging track and saunas.

City link The airport is 40kms/25 miles north of the city centre. The choice is bus or cab, but a rail link is planned for the 1990s. By road the journey to the centre takes 30–45mins depending on traffic.

Taxis You may have to wait for a cab and the fare is not cheap (about Skr300).

Limousine Many people use the SAS pooled limousine service. The fare and journey time vary but Skr185 per person and 45mins to central Stockholm are typical. For a limousine from the city to the aiport ☎ 797 37 00 a day before the flight or arrange through your hotel.

Car rental All the major firms have desks in the arrivals hall.

Bus There are services at 10min intervals daily, 6.30am–10.30pm and to coincide with flights at other times, but the journey takes 60mins (fare Skr30). Passengers alight at Cityterminalen, Klarabergsviadukten, by the Central station; from there taxis take 5–10mins to reach most hotels.

Railway station
Central-stationen The station is big and busy and the hub of the local commuter and subway networks. Facilities include banks (open daily, 8am–9pm), postal and telephone services and an accommodation bureau (open Mon–Fri, 8.30–5, Oct–Apr; daily, 8am–9pm, May–Sep) in the lower hall. Taxis are generally available at the station exit. There are rapid InterCity services to all the main Swedish towns; reservations are compulsory on most express trains. Railway inquiries ☎ 22 50 60.

Getting around
Stockholm is spread out over a considerable distance. The most convenient way of getting around is usually by taxi or subway. A car is useful if you have to make frequent visits to the industrial district between the city and the airport.

Taxis Taxis can be hailed in the street or boarded at taxi-ranks, but are not always easy to obtain. Reservations can be made through a central, computerized system: in advance ☎ 15 04 00, for immediate needs ☎ 15 00 00, but delays of up to 20mins are common. Allow Skr65–85 for a cross-town journey (and 10% for a tip).

Limousines For taxi firms offering limousines ☎ 22 22 80.

Driving Most streets are one way but well signposted and the city is easy to negotiate. Congestion is rare except during rush hours, but the city's drivers can be aggressive, especially at the innumerable traffic lights. Parking is difficult, though most hotels have their own facilities. Car rental firms include: *InteRent* ☎ 21 06 50; *Avis* ☎ 44 99 80; *Budget* ☎ 33 43 83; *Europcar* ☎ 23 10 70; *Hertz* ☎ 18 13 15.

Walking is safe and pleasant in summer, but in winter the weather may be bad; rubber over-shoes are useful against the slush and ice. Road signs are in English as well as Swedish.

Bus, subway and train The city and surrounding metropolitan region has an efficient integrated subway, bus and local train network. A Stockholm Card (*Stockholmskortet*), valid for up to 3 days, can be purchased at stations; it allows unlimited travel and free admission to museums and to sightseeing trips. The subway (*Tunnelbanan*) is a useful and swift means of getting about the city. Several stations, including Centralen, at the hub of the network, are cut into rock and decorated with relief sculptures and murals.

Area by area
Stockholm consists of the tip of the Swedish mainland and a group of 14 islands linked by bridges. To the west of the city is the beautiful freshwater Lake Mälaren, separated from the Baltic Sea to the east by locks carrying major highways linking the mainland to the southern islands.

The mainland district of Norrmalm

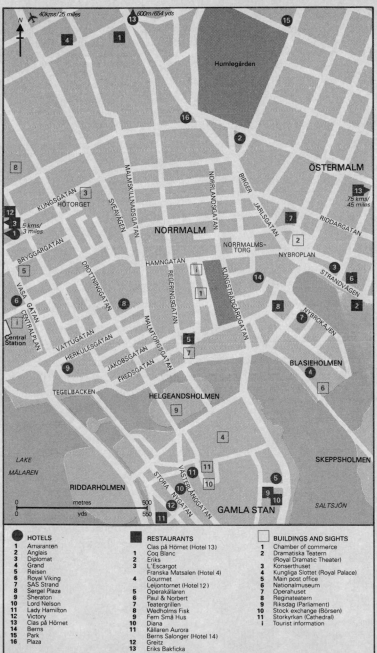

is the centre of the city and of its business activity. In area little more than 1km square, it contains the head offices of the main Swedish and overseas companies. Long-established firms have their own buildings along the waterfronts of Blasieholmen peninsula, or around Norrmalmstorg square, generally handsome turn-of-the-century blocks in neo-Gothic or Art Deco styles. Many others occupy offices in the 1960s tower blocks of Sveavägen and Drottninggatan. They are now regarded as a mistake, and the City Fathers guard more jealously the remaining historic buildings of the centre, including the Operahuset and Dramatiska Teatern, both of whose cultural performances, bars and restaurants are a focus for the city's social life. In this area, too, are most of the hotels and restaurants.

The old island city of Gamla Stan has been preserved almost intact. Little of it is visible from the mainland because it is hidden behind the bulk of the Kungliga Slottet (Royal Palace), completed in 1760. It is still used for public ceremonials, but the royal family has moved to Drottningholm Palace, a 17thC mini-Versailles, west of the city.

Behind the Royal Palace is the oldest building, the 13thC Cathedral (Storkyrkan), and, beside it, the Börsen, or stock exchange. This building is also the headquarters of the Swedish Academy which awards the annual Nobel Prize for Literature. To the east is Riddarholmen with its 18thC church, burial place of Sweden's rulers, and the Supreme Court. Numerous cobbled alleys preserving the street plan of medieval Stockholm are lined by 17thC and 18thC merchants' houses. This is tourist territory, but the cellar restaurants here are often used by executives for informal entertaining.

Between the mainland and the Old City is Helgeandsholmen dominated by the Riksdag, the parliament, and the former Bank of Sweden building, now used as ministerial offices.

Immediately west is the Stadshuset, Stockholm's City Hall and the centre of the city's administration. An extraordinary synthesis of many architectural styles completed in 1923, this building is often used as a symbol of the city.

East of the city centre is the most prestigious residential area, Östermalm, resembling parts of Paris with its wide boulevards and parks; its principal waterfront avenue, Strandvägen, is home to wealthy citizens and embassies. A short walk across the bridge is the island of Djurgården, with museums set in Skansen park, popular at weekends.

The islands to the south and west are mainly residential. Industry has been zoned north of the city, and it sprawls for miles along the airport road, the E4 Uppsalavägen highway.

Hotels

Stockholm is well-supplied with hotels. The Grand and Diplomat are traditional hotels, the Victory has outstanding service; for prestige, choose the Strand. February–May and September–November are very busy with visitors attending trade fairs and conferences. In summer (June–August), when the city is quiet, many hotels discount rates by about one-third.

Unless otherwise stated, hotels given full entries provide parking, currency exchange and rooms with IDD telephones, minibars and TVS receiving English-language satellite transmissions.

Amaranten K̄///
Kungsholmsgatan 31, S-102 20
☎ 54 10 60 ⌨ 17498 fax 52 62 48 •

Sara • AE DC MC V • *396 rooms, 14 suites, 2 restaurants, 2 bars*
This big modern hotel is part of the

state-run Sara chain (linked to the UK Trusthouse Forte group) which aims to offer competitive prices. It is as much a tourist as a business travellers' hotel, but there are executive rooms at the top of the tower, many with extensive views and with fast check-in and out and their own lounge. The location is within walking distance of the main business area. No currency exchange. Nonsmoking rooms, gift shop ● pool, sauna, fitness room ● conference centre with a/v equipment, secretarial and translation facilities, 3 meeting rooms (capacity up to 180).

Anglais *K*/

Humlegårdsgatan 23, s-102 44
☎ *24 99 00* Ⓣ *19475 fax 21 16 29* ●
AE DC MC V ● *202 rooms, 9 suites,*
1 restaurant, 1 bar
A quiet hotel, overlooking Humlegården park, with a pleasant rooftop terrace used for dining in summer. The decor is slightly old-fashioned but the bedrooms are larger than most and the service is friendly. A hotel for embassy guests, affluent tourists and business people. 10 conference rooms with a/v equipment (capacity up to 450).

Diplomat *K*/

Strandvägen 7c, s-114 56
☎ *663 58 00* Ⓣ *17119 fax 783 66 34*
● *AE DC MC V* ● *123 rooms, 7 suites,*
1 restaurant, 1 bar
The Diplomat started out in 1911 as a grandiose project on Stockholm's finest promenade and is second only to the Grand for the sumptuousness of its decor, here restrained Art Nouveau; but its atmosphere is calmer and the service more personal; the staff happily arrange to meet business needs. The single rooms are small, but the double rooms overlooking the water are spacious and elegantly furnished. Antique furniture and winter log fires in the lounges create a comforting atmosphere. The delightful teahouse room serves an excellent buffet breakfast. Parking nearby. Sauna.

Grand *K*/////

Södra Blasieholmshamnen 8, s-103 27
☎ *22 10 20* Ⓣ *19500 fax 21 86 88* ●
AE DC MC V ● *299 rooms, 20 suites,*
2 restaurants, 1 bar
The Grand is a magnificent palace built in 1874 and surrounded by the headquarters of many of Sweden's most prestigious companies. Nobel prizewinners, visiting ministers and VIPs are all accommodated here. It is at the centre of Stockholm's business life and always occupied with shareholders' meetings, conferences or receptions. The hotel has been fully restored since the Wallenbergs, Sweden's premier banking family, acquired it in 1974. The public areas are splendidly old-fashioned, with stately chandeliers, wood panelling and gilded stucco ceilings, but the bedrooms are less grand and furnished with Persian rugs and modern Swedish fabrics. Many rooms, as well as the Franska Matsalen (the "French Dining Room," see *Restaurants*), have panoramic views of the cluster of islands that make up central Stockholm and the river craft that constantly navigate between them. No hotel parking. Gift shop, hairdresser ● sauna ● secretarial and translation services and computers, 19 conference rooms and ballroom (capacity up to 1,000).

Reisen *K*/

Skeppsbron 12–14, s-111 30
☎ *22 32 60* Ⓣ *17494 fax 20 15 59* ●
Sara ● *AE DC MC V* ● *100 rooms,*
13 suites, 2 restaurants, 2 bars
The Reisen is part of the state-run Sara chain and on a prime waterfront site. The picturesque old town is a short walk away for tourists and for executives with time between appointments. Beyond the nautical antiques that crowd the lobby are some comfortable and elegantly furnished rooms and one of the better hotel restaurants in the city, the Quarter Deck. No parking. Pool, sauna ● offices for rent, 3 meeting rooms (capacity up to 50).

Royal Viking *K//*
Vasagatan 1, s-101 23 ☎ *14 10 00*
ⓣ *13900 fax 10 81 80* • *SAS* • *AE DC*
MC V • *328 rooms, 12 suites,*
3 restaurants, 2 bars
This huge modern hotel, with a
central atrium several floors high, has
business services and larger than
usual Royal Club executive rooms on
the upper floors, where the views
rival that of the hotel's Skybar. Next
to the central station, it is well sited
for the business district. The World
Trade Center complex, which will
become the base of many overseas
companies, is right next door.
Check-in and -out for SAS flights, 24hr
room service, gift shop • sauna, pool
• secretarial and translation services,
offices for rent, 8 conference rooms
(capacity up to 450).

SAS Strand *K///*
Nybrokajen 9, s-103 27 ☎ *22 29 00*
ⓣ *10504 fax 20 44 36* • *AE DC MC V*
• *137 rooms, 17 suites, 2 restaurants, 1
bar*
One of the smallest and most likeable
hotels in the SAS chain, the creeper-
covered Strand was built for the 1912
Olympics and was Ingrid Bergman's
favourite hotel. It now serves mainly
senior business travellers. There are
superb views from the windows of the
tower and waterfront rooms; all the
bedrooms are spacious and furnished
with elegant reproduction antique
furniture. The Piazza, a roofed-in
courtyard restaurant, with foliage
cascading from the upper balconies, is
both smart and attractive. Sauna •
secretarial services, offices for rent, 1
meeting room (capacity up to 20).

Sergel Plaza *K////*
Brunkebergstorg 9, s-103 27 ☎ *22 66 00*
ⓣ *16700 fax 21 50 70* • *AE DC MC V*
• *406 rooms, 12 suites, 1 restaurant, 2
bars*
Several interior designers worked on
this new hotel, opened in 1984; the
result is a quirky mixture of neo-
classical in the light and airy lobby
and an approximation to 18thC decor
elsewhere, a nod in the direction of

the hotel's namesake, the 18thC
sculptor Johan Sergel. A high level of
service has made it popular with
business travellers and won it several
awards. The rooms, despite small
windows, are large and comfortable.
Shops • sauna, solarium • secretarial
services, offices for rent, 12 meeting
rooms (capacity up to 200).

Small hotels of character
For lovers of nautical history as
well as period atmosphere and
personal service, Stockholm has
some delightful hotels:
Lord Nelson *K/*
Västerlånggatan 22, s-111 29
☎ *23 23 90* ⓣ *10434*
fax 11 11 48 • *AE DC MC V*. In
1978 Gurra and Maglis Bergtsson
bought an 18thC house in the Old
Town and converted it into this
small hotel furnished with oil
paintings and antiques from their
collection of Nelson memorabilia.
Lady Hamilton *K//*
Storkyrkobrinken 5, s-111 28
☎ *23 46 80* ⓣ *10434 fax 11 11
48* • *AE DC MC V*. This hotel and
the Lord Nelson share business
facilities with the Victory.
Victory *K///* *Lilla Nygatan 5,*
s-111 28 ☎ *14 30 90* ⓣ *14050*
fax 20 21 77 • *AE DC MC V*. The
most recently opened hotel in the
"Nelson" chain has up-to-date
business services and equipment.
The Leijontornet (Lion's Tower)
restaurant has become one of the
top places to entertain on the basis
of its wine cellar alone (see
Restaurants).
Clas på Hörnet *K/*
Surbrunnsgatan 20, s-113 48
☎ *16 51 30* ⓣ *14619 fax 33 53 15*
• *AE DC MC V*. No connection
with the Nelson chain, this is an
atmospheric conversion of an
18thC inn in the north of the city,
and furnished in traditional style.
Excellent restaurant (see
Restaurants). No parking.

Sheraton *K*⫽
Tegelbacken 6, s-101 23 ☎ *14 26 00*
ⓉⓍ *17750* • *fax 21 70 26* • *AE DC*
MC V • *444 rooms, 16 suites,*
2 restaurants, 1 bar
In a rather bleak and windswept
position near the airport terminal.
The hotel's well-insulated rooms look
over to the Old Town. The city's late
nightlife revolves around the piano
bar and casino. The Sheraton trained
many of Stockholm's hoteliers and is
now an important venue for meetings
and seminars. 24hr room service,
shops • sauna • secretarial services,
10 meeting rooms (capacity up to 400).

OTHER HOTELS
Berns *K*⫽ *Näckströmsjatan 8,*
s-111 47 ☎ *614 07 00* ⓉⓍ *12132*
fax 611 51 75 • *AE DC MC V*. Next to
the famous re-opened Berns Salonger
restaurant, this is a new hotel with

ultramodern interiors. Meeting rooms
for up to 1,000.
Park *K*⫽ *Karlavägen 43, s-102 45*
☎ *22 96 20* ⓉⓍ *10666 fax 21 62 68* •
Reso Hotels • *AE DC MC V.*
Completely renovated in 1989, in the
quiet area overlooking Humlegården
park.
Plaza *K*⫽ *Birger Jarlsgatan 29,*
s-103 95 ☎ *14 51 20* ⓉⓍ *13982*
fax 10 34 92 • *Best Western* •
AE DC MC V. Smart, new hotel in a
quiet district just off the city centre.
Some small rooms, but apartments
are available for longer visits. Sauna.

Hotel and restaurant price guide
For the meanings of the hotel and
restaurant price symbols, see
Symbols and abbreviations on pages
6 and 7.

Restaurants

Many restaurants in Stockholm have a formal dining room and a more
casual brasserie or wine bar where the menu is limited but the cuisine is
first-class and at moderate prices. The top restaurants are often full and
reservations are advisable especially during the February–May and September–November trade fair seasons. Meals start early: 12.00 for lunch,
7.00 for dinner, and an interval for resting and talking between courses is
traditional. So too is the *smörgåsbord* (buffet lunch) . Most of the dishes,
many of which are fish, are based on French or continental cuisine; gra-
vad lax, lightly cured salmon, features on most menus.

Clas på Hörnet *K*
Clas på Hörnet Hotel ☎ *16 51 30* •
AE DC MC V
This old building is a favourite with
executives, despite being a taxi ride
away from the business district. It is
noted for excellent traditional
Scandinavian food and friendly
service. Although often busy, its
atmosphere is calm. A good place for
undisturbed conversation.

Coq Blanc *K*⫽
Regeringsgatan 111 ☎ *11 61 53* •
closed Sat L, Sun, mid-Jun–mid-Aug •
AE DC MC V
The walls of the former Little
Theatre are decorated with playbills

and theatrical bygones. The main
dining room in the auditorium is
large, and the tables are well spaced;
for greater privacy reserve a table in
one of the smaller rooms "back
stage." Diners are mostly in banking
and insurance. Many dishes are based
on seafood and game, and there is a
wide choice of wines.

Eriks *K*⫽
Strandvägskajen 17 ☎ *660 60 60* •
closed Sat L, Sun • *AE DC MC V*
You dine on a boat moored in front
of the Hotel Diplomat, and tables
next to the portholes on the water
side are much in demand. A short
walk from most offices, this floating

restaurant provides a calm background for the predominantly fish dishes served in innumerable ways; there is a strong list of white wines. The bridge serves as an Oyster Bar.

L'Escargot *K*////
Scheelegatan 8 ☎ 53 05 77 • closed L, Sun, mid-Jul–mid-Aug • AE DC MC V
The atmosphere and the cuisine are distinctively Gallic in both the downstairs brasserie (for younger executives) and in the chandeliered and mirrored elegance of the upper dining room (preferred by their seniors). The *nouvelle cuisine* emphasis on seafood dishes is compromised by ultrarich desserts. Given advance warning, the chef will prepare a *menu dégustation*.

Franska Matsalen *K*/////
Grand Hotel ☎ 22 10 20 • AE DC MC V • jacket
The formal 19thC elegance of the Grand Hotel's main dining room makes it very suitable for important business entertaining, and the clientele is usually distinguished. The chefs work in full view of the guests, which means that the tables away from the kitchen, and closest to the windows overlooking the water, are preferred. Called the "French Dining Room," the emphasis has recently been on serving local and traditional cooking, with seafood and game predominant.

Gourmet *K*/
Tegnergatan 10 ☎ 31 43 98 • closed Sat L, Sun, July • AE DC MC V
Proprietor and chef, Björn Svensson and Kurt Schultes respectively, have not only established themselves as Sweden's leading wine and food writers; their restaurant is famous throughout Scandinavia and is a favourite among top Stockholm business people. The decor is relatively plain and informal. Much effort goes into the daily specials, often refined versions of traditionally rich Swedish fish and game dishes.

Fine wine list, with the emphasis on burgundies.

Leijontornet *K*
Victory Hotel ☎ 14 23 55 • closed L, Sun, July • AE DC MC V
The recently opened and busy Lion's Tower, next to the Victory Hotel in Old Stockholm, has quickly won a reputation for its inventive cuisine based on fish, game and fowl and extensive list of classic wines (sommeliers from other restaurants frequently come for tastings). The interior contains a stretch of the medieval town wall, discovered, along with a hoard of silver coins and dishes, when the basement was converted; this is a quieter and more secluded area for private business discussions.

Operakällaren *K*//
Operahuset ☎ 24 27 00 • closed July • AE DC MC V • reservations essential
This is an elegant old restaurant in Stockholm's Opera House, overlooking the water and the Royal Palace. Head chef Werner Vögeli, who is also chef to the Swedish court, puts as much imagination into the lavish and legendary lunch-time *smörgåsbord* as he does into *à la carte* dishes featuring snow grouse, hazel grouse, wild mushrooms, elk and saddle of young reindeer. The restaurant attracts politicians, diplomats, lawyers and business people, and the staff treat every guest with courteous attention. A cellar of some 300,000 wines provides ample choice, including many burgundies that are, by Stockholm's standards, reasonably priced.

Paul & Norbert *K*//
Strandvägen 9 ☎ 663 81 83 • closed Sat, Sun, July • AE DC MC V
The eponymous owners of this tiny restaurant (only nine tables) have a loyal local and international clientele. Considerable effort goes into the selection of the freshest seasonal ingredients, especially fish and wild game, and into novel sauces and

combinations. It is convenient for the city's business centre.

Teatergrillen $\boxed{K}/$
Nybrogatan 3 ☎ *10 70 44* • *closed Sat L, Sun L, July* • AE DC MC V
Late at night this candle-lit restaurant serving seafood and game at the rear of the Royal Dramatic Theatre attracts an arty crowd as well as theatregoers. By day its atmosphere is much more severe, and the tables are too closely spaced for confidential discussion. The brasserie, Riche, in the same building, is the haunt of the young, affluent and chic.

Wedholms Fisk $\boxed{K}$
Nybrokajen 17 ☎ *10 48 74* • *closed Sun, 4 weeks Jul & Aug* • AE DC MC V
This venerable establishment serves exactly what many Stockholm traditionalists like most: local fresh fish served every kind of way. The decor is plain (white walls and mirrors), and red wines are only allowed a token presence on the wine list. A safe and enjoyable venue for business entertaining.

OTHER RESTAURANTS
Many buildings in the Old Town have a cellar restaurant, and though they are popular with tourists, several are suitable for less formal business entertaining. One of the smartest is *Fem Små Hus*, Nygränd 10 ☎ 10 04 82; dishes are based on fish, meat and fruits from the wild. Nearby, *Diana*, Brunnsgränd 2 ☎ 10 73 10 (closed Sun), is decorated with nautical antiquities and can be very lively. Fresh fish and charcoal grilled meats are great attractions. *Källaren Aurora*, Munkbron 11 ☎ 21 93 59 (closed Sun), also serves salmon and meat grilled over charcoal. The restored, re-opened and well-known *Berns Salonger*, Berzelii Park ☎ 614 06 00, has four associated restaurants; Lilla Salonger ☎ 614 05 50 is a brasserie open till 3am and Röda Rumets Matsal a restaurant for gourmets ☎ 614 05 60. *Greitz*, Vasagatan 50 ☎ 23 48 20, is a fish restaurant

popular for business entertaining (closed Sat and Sun). *Eriks Bakficka*, Fredrikhovsgatan 4 ☎ 660 15 99, is a more informal version of the floating restaurant Eriks, with which it was formerly associated.

Out of town
Just 10mins by taxi from central Stockholm (5kms/3 miles north of the city on E4) is the *Ulriksdal Wärdshus*, Ulriksdals Slottspark ☎ 85 08 15, set in an 18thC inn, and overlooking the Royal Park. The *smörgåsbord* is extravagant and the seasonal fish and game dishes worth the journey. *Wärdshuset Stallmästaregården*, Norrtull ☎ 24 39 10, an old waterside inn 2 kms/1.3 miles north outside Haga Park, is popular for its atmosphere and grilled fish.

Bars and cafés
Of all the many hotel piano bars, the one at the Sheraton is the best for its music, cocktails and civilized atmosphere. The *Café Riche*, in the Royal Dramatic Theatre, Birger Jarlsgatan 4, is a popular after-work meeting place for executives. *Café Opera*, at the Opera House, is a Stockholm tradition, especially on a Friday night, and dancing begins at midnight (until 3am). Other pleasant neighbourhood bars include the English-style *Tudor Arms*, Grevgatan 31, the book-lined *Tre Backar Bar*, Tegnergatan 12-14, and the old-fashioned *Bar Cattelin* in Gamla Stan, Storkyrkobrinken 9.

Entertainment
Stockholm This Week, free at hotels and tourist information offices, details events and is published in several languages.
Theatre The 200-year-old *Dramatiska Teatern*, Nybroplan ☎ 667 06 80 (tickets), 660 68 11 (information), launched Greta Garbo, Ingrid Bergman and Max von Sydow. All the plays of the American playwright, Eugene O'Neill, were given their premiere here, and the company performs them regularly, though most

performances are in Swedish. The English-Language theatre, the *Reginateatern*, Drottninggatan 71A ☎ 20 70 00, often mounts successful shows from London and New York.
Dance and opera are performed at the *Operan* or the *Operahuset* (also known as the Royal Theatre), Gustav Adolfs Torg ☎ 24 82 40. Ingmar Bergman still directs here.
Music Leading orchestras and soloists usually perform at the *Konserthuset*, Hötorget 8 ☎ 22 18 00. This is also the home of the famous Stockholm Philharmonic Orchestra and Choir and the venue for pop and rock concerts. Jazz of a high standard is performed nightly at *Fasching*, Kungsgatan 63 ☎ 21 62 67, and *Stampen*, Stora Nygatan 5 ☎ 20 57 94.
Cinema Foreign films are shown in the original language, with subtitles. Best for new releases are *Grand 1-2-3*, Sveavägen 45 ☎ 11 24 00; *Lilla Kvarn*, Biblioteksgatan 5 ☎ 21 14 22, and *Cinema*, Birger Jarlsgatan 41 ☎ 10 13 00.
Nightclubs *Aladdin*, Barnhusgatan 12–14 ☎ 10 09 32, is a dance restaurant, with a traditional dance band. *Börsen*, Jakobsgatan 6 ☎ 10 16 00, has a cabaret every night at 10.30, often with international stars. The *Karlsson*, Kungsgatan 65, is the place where the young and dynamic go. *Valentino*, Birger Jarlsgatan 24 ☎ 14 27 80, serves French and Italian food.
Casinos At the *Sheraton Hotel* or *Bolaget*, Regeringsgatan 113 ☎ 10 20 00.

Shopping

The main streets for shopping are around Hamngatan and Drottninggatan. Most shops are open Mon–Fri, 9.30–6; Sat, 9.30–2, department stores Sat, 10–5 and Sun, 12–4 as well. Enquire about tax concessions.
Antiques Gamla Stan has many antique shops and art galleries; the greatest concentration is in the narrow alleys off Västerlånggatan.

Cameras *Hasselblads Foto*, Hamngatan 16.
China, glass and silver In Birger Jarlsgatan is exclusive *Gustavsberg* at No. 2; *Rosenthal*'s Swedish glass and chinaware is at No. 6; *Jensen*, at No. 13, stocks the Danish silversmith's own jewellery and elegant cutlery and a wide selection of glass and china.
Department store The huge NK (*Nordiska Kompaniet*), Hamngatan 18–20, sells china and crystal, furs, textiles, pewter and jewellery.
Food *Saluhall*, in Östermalmstorg, is a 100-year-old indoor market crammed with fresh produce stalls and ringed by delicatessans.
Furs *Lundgren & Peters*, Adolf Fredriks Kyrkogata 5, is one of the leading furriers; and *Sophie Ericsons*, Mäster Samuelsgatan 45, has over 5,000 furs.
Handicrafts *Svenskt Tenn*, Strandvägen 5, is excellent for pewter, handicrafts and textiles.

Sightseeing

Gamla Stan, the Old Town, should be explored on foot. The baroque-style 18thC town houses have individual eccentric gables.
Kungliga Slottet The massive 18thC Royal Palace includes the Royal Armoury, the Treasury, containing the crown jewels, and a museum of antique Roman sculpture. *Gamla Stan. Changing of the guard Mon–Fri, 12.10; Sat & Sun, 1.10. Treasury open Sep–Apr, Mon–Sat, 11–3; Sun, 12–4; May–Sep, Mon–Sat, 10–4; Sun, 12–4.*
Moderna Museet As well as works by Picasso, Matisse, Dali and Warhol, the museum of modern art mounts contemporary exhibitions, including some video art. *Skeppsholmen. Open Tue–Fri, 11–9; Sat & Sun, 11–5.*
Nationalmuseum Large collection of art, from the Renaissance to around 1900, notably by Rembrandt. *Blasieholmen. Open Tue, 10–9 (July & Aug); Wed–Sun, 10–4.*
Nordiska Museet (Nordic Museum) Swedish homes and life from the 16th century to the present, embracing the Lapland cultures, costumes, utensils

and art imaginatively displayed.
*Djurgården. Open Mon–Fri, 10–4
(Thu until 8); Sat & Sun, 12–5.*
Skansen Open-air museum devoted
to the life, work and houses of the
Swedes through the centuries.
*Djurgården. Open daily in summer to
11.30; buildings close earlier.*
Stadshuset Oriental minarets and
onion domes mix with Nordic
fortifications in the City Hall, and the
central tower, with stunning views,
dominates Stockholm's skyline. The
interior is gilded with mosaics.
*Hantverkargatan. Tours daily, 10.
Tower open daily, 10–3, May–Sep.*
Storkyrkan The Cathedral (circa
1250) where Swedish monarchs were
crowned until 1907; on special
occasions members of the royal family
still sit on their 300-year-old gilded
wooden pews. *Gamla Stan.*
Thiel Gallery Collection bought by
the state from banker Ernst Thiel;
notable works by Munch, Anders
Zorn and their contemporaries.
*Djurgården. Open Mon–Sat, 12–4;
Sun, 1–4.*
Guided tours The *Stockholm Tourist
Centre* ☎ 789 20 00 organizes tours.
Excursions by boat, which leave from
Nybroplan, include the city
waterways, the islands of Lake
Mälaren and views of the shore of the
Soviet Union from the Baltic Sea.

Out of town
About 12kms/7.5 miles west of the
city by road and and one hour by
boat is the residence of the Swedish
royal family, *Drottningholm Palace.*
Set on the island of Lovön in the
Mälaren lake, it was built in the 17th
century and is surrounded by formal
gardens. Opera and ballet
performances are held (May–Sep) in
the original Little Court Theatre.
Tickets are hard to come by. Grounds
and apartments are open Mon–Sat,
11–4.30; Sun, 12–4.30 (May–Aug);
Mon–Fri, 1–3.30; Sat & Sun, 12–3.30
(Sep). Ferries to the island leave from
the City Hall Bridge, Klara
Mälarstrand, every 30mins daily,
May–Sep.

Spectator sports
Ice hockey The national winter sport.
Important matches at the *Isstadion,*
Johanneshov ☎ 725 10 00.
Horse-racing There are flat races at
Täby Galopp ☎ 56 02 30. Trotting
takes place most afternoons at
Solvalla ☎ 28 93 60.
Soccer Big games and internationals
are played at the *Råsunda
Fotbollsstadion,* Solnavägen 55
☎ 753 09 00.

Keeping fit
Golf Within a 10–15min drive from
the centre are the *Djursholms
Golfklubb* ☎ 755 14 17 and
Drottningholms Golfklubb
☎ 759 03 11. Most clubs grant
temporary membership to members
of recognized overseas golf clubs.
Swimming is the Swedes' most
popular form of exercise. *GIH Badet,*
Drottning Sofiasväg 20 ☎ 20 13 15,
has an indoor heated pool, and
similar facilities at *Forsgrénska Badet,*
Medbargarplatsen ☎ 40 07 05, are
due to open in autumn 1990. There
are city centre beaches at
Smedsuddsbadet and *Långholmsbadet.*
Tennis *Tyresö Racketball,* with indoor
courts and facilities for squash and
badminton, is open to nonmembers
☎ 742 24 02.

Local resources
Business services
All the hotels listed can organize
secretarial services. *Sergel Office,*
Brunkebergstorg 7 ☎ 14 59 20, has
office space to rent and provides
telex, fax, copying, secretarial,
translation, telephone answering and
reception services.
Photocopying and printing at all the
listed hotels.
Secretarial *AAA Service* ☎ 14 28 25;
Teamwork ☎ 24 57 55.
Translation *David Jones*
☎ 668 36 56;
Levy Margot 83 48 63.

Communications
Local delivery *Citylink* ☎ 15 19 60;
Swedish Express ☎ 28 81 50.

Long-distance delivery DHL
☎ 92 08 50.
Post office Centralpostkontoret (main post office): Vasagatan 28–34
☎ 781 20 00, open Mon–Fri, 8–8; Sat, 9–3.
Telex and fax At all hotels listed and all city post offices.

Conference/exhibition centres
Stockholm's principal trade fair, exhibition and convention centre is *Stockholmsmässan*, Mëssvägen, s-125 80 ☎ 749 41 00, ⊠ 10660, about 8mins by train from the Central station. It has excellent facilities and hosts annual international conventions (such as the Medical Conference) and trade fairs. An extensive inner-city complex being constructed at *Norra Latin*, Drottninggatan 71 ☎ 20 09 92, is due to open in the early 1990s. The *Stockholm Convention Bureau* ☎ 23 09 90 assists with conference planning.

The *Arlandia Hotel*, POB 103, s-190 45 ☎ (0760) 61 800 ⊠ 13018, near the airport, has an auditorium (capacity up to 250), and within the airport the *Arlanda Konferens Center*, POB 67, s-190 45 ☎ 797 62 00, has 10 rooms (capacity up to 50 each) and an auditorium seating 150, with a/v equipment.

Of the city hotels used for conferences the *Grand* is the most prestigious and the *Sheraton* and *Sergel Plaza* are also used for exhibitions.

Emergencies
Bureaux de change Banks are generally open Mon–Fri, 9-3 (Thu until 5.30). The exchange office at the central station is open 8am–9pm every day and that at the airport 7–10.
Hospitals Emergencies are treated at the local district hospital. Seek hotel assistance first or call Medical Care ☎ 44 92 00. Ambulance ☎ 90 000. *City Akuten*, Holländargatan 3 ☎ 11 71 77, a private clinic (open Mon–Fri, 8am–7pm; Sat, 9–3), accepts payment by credit card. Free

emergency dental care at *St Eriks*, Fleminggatan 22 ☎ 54 05 90, open daily 8–7.
Pharmacy *(Apotek) C.W. Scheele*, Klarabergsgaten 64 ☎ 21 89 34, is open 24hrs.
Police Emergency ☎ 90 000. The main police station *(Polisstation)* is at Agnegatan 33–37 ☎ 769 30 00. Local stations are at the central station, Bryggargatan 19 and Tulegatan 4. The police lost and found office is at Tjärhovsgaten 21 ☎ 41 04 32.

Government offices
Industriförbundet (Association of Swedish Industries) POB 1133 Torsgatan 2, s-114 85 ☎ 783 80 00 ⊠ 19990. *Exportrådet* (Swedish Trade Council) POB 5513, Storgatan 19, s-114 85 ☎ 783 85 54 ⊠ 19620, is principally concerned with exports.

Information sources
Business information
Handelskammare (Stockholm Chamber of commerce), Vastra Tradgårdsgatan 9, POB 16050, s-103 22 ☎ 23 12 00. Also based in Stockholm is the British Swedish Chamber of Commerce, Grevgatan 34, POB 5512, s-114 85 ☎ 665 34 25.
Local media The most widely read Swedish-language dailies are *Svenska Dagbladat* and *Dagens Nyheter*. Foreign newspapers are available at newsstands on publication day, and hotel TVs carry 24hr international news, including half-hour business bulletins, in English.
Tourist information Stockholm Information Service, Sweden House, Kungsträdgården ☎ 789 24 17, open Mon–Fri, 9–5 ☎ 789 24 17; open Sat & Sun, 9–2; the hours are longer May–Sep.

Thank-yous
Florists Centrum Blommer ☎ 21 84 60 and MS Blomdesign ☎ 20 08 45.
Wines and spirits from state-run liquor stores *(System Bolaget)* found on nearly every city street and open Mon–Fri, 9.30–6. Wines and spirits are highly taxed and expensive.

SWITZERLAND

Switzerland has one of the highest levels of per capita income in the world. The economy has shown steady growth (except for recessions in the mid-1970s and early 1980s), with low inflation (until recently) and low unemployment. Much of the country's success is due to its neutrality and political stability, cautious economic policies and a record of industrial harmony.

Service industries, of which the most important are banking, insurance and tourism, account for over 65% of GDP. Manufacturing is highly specialized and accounts for about 25% of GDP. Traditionally, Switzerland has been strong in the machine, precision instrument (including watchmaking) and chemical industries. In recent years, these industries have been consolidated and rationalized, with a shift towards specialized high-technology products such as pharmaceuticals and medical equipment. Other traditional manufacturing industries, such as textiles, clothing and food processing have been in decline, owing to labour shortages, high unit labour costs and a lack of competitiveness on world markets. The agricultural sector is small and benefits from heavy state subsidies to farmers and guaranteed prices. Public concern for the environment has restricted the number of nuclear plants to five.

With a small domestic market, Switzerland depends on exports to generate about 35% of GDP. Its main exports are manufactures, mostly highly specialized machinery and chemical products, and precision instruments. Its main imports are energy and industrial raw materials, foods and motor vehicles. Trade with the EC now accounts for about 55% of exports and over 70% of imports. Switzerland's balance of trade is regularly in sizeable deficit. A large surplus on the balance of invisibles (namely investment income, financial services and tourism), however, keeps the balance of payments current account in surplus.

Geography Switzerland is landlocked and mountainous apart from the central plateau that runs from Lake Geneva in the southwest to Lake Constance in the northeast. The southern half of the country is covered by the Alps, dotted with glaciers, river valleys and lakes, and the source of many of Europe's great rivers, including the Rhine, Rhône and Po. To the west lie the Jura mountains.
Climate The lowlands have a temperate climate, with warm summers and cool winters. The mountains are colder.
Population 6.5m.
Government Switzerland is a federal republic consisting of 20 cantons and 6 half-cantons, each with its own government and assembly. The parlieament, the federal assembly, has a 46-member council of states and a 200-member national council, both elected for 4 years. It appoints the federal council as an executive for 4 years, and a president for 1 year.
Currency Swiss franc (SFr).
Time 1hr ahead of GMT; end Mar–end Sep, 2hrs ahead of GMT.
Dialling codes Switzerland's IDD code is 41. Omit the initial 0 from the city code when dialling from abroad. To make an international call from Switzerland, dial 00 before dialling the relevant country code.
Public holidays (* some cantons only) Jan 1, Jan 2, Good Fri, Easter Mon, Ascension Day, Whit Mon, May 1*, Aug 1*, Dec 25, Dec 26.

GENEVA (Genève)   *City code* ☎ 022

Geneva enjoys a central position in Western Europe, and it is home to 250 international organizations, the most important being the European headquarters of the United Nations. Others include the International Red Cross, ILO (International Labour Organization), WHO, UNCTAD (UN Conference on Trade and Development) and GATT. The European Organization for Nuclear Research (CERN) is based in nearby Meyrin.

The city has a prosperous and cosmopolitan atmosphere, a lakeland setting framed by the Alps and an unspoiled old centre. Nearly half of its 160,000 inhabitants are foreigners, from UN and embassy officials and multinational executives to manual workers (Italian, Spanish and Portuguese). Many Swiss working here commute from nearby cantons (*confédérés*), and some 30,000 commuters come in daily from France.

The city's economy is primarily based on services and distribution, with banking, insurance and real estate the main employers. Private banking has been Geneva's *cachet* since the 18th century, and nine private banks (such as Pictet, Lombard, Odier) still administer untold fortunes. The city is a major centre for commodity trading (grain and cotton) and for the art market, particularly in jewellery.

About 20% of the work force is employed in manufacturing, and advanced technology and telecommunications are significant. Major companies include ABB Sécheron (electrical equipment, at Pâquis), Sodeco, Charmilles (technologies), and SIP (precision instruments). Other important fields are aromatics, with Givaudan (at Vernier) and Firmenich, tobacco and the graphic arts (Caran d'Ache at Thônex). Multinationals with headquarters here include BAT, Caterpillar, Digital Equipment, Du Pont de Nemours, Hewlett Packard (at Meyrin), IBM Suisse and Union Carbide. An International Motor Show is held at Palexpo, and Fiat, Honda, Mazda and Michelin have their Swiss headquarters in Geneva.

With unemployment at under 1%, Geneva, the richest canton in rich Switzerland, has few problems. Future plans include better, faster road and rail links and shared business and housing projects with nearby Haute-Savoie and Pays de Gex in France; autoroute improvements are under way and an international business park at Annecy is projected.

Arriving

There are flights to Geneva from over 100 cities world wide and excellent links with the European rail network. From France it can be more convenient overall to take the high-speed train (TGV) from Paris or Marseille. There are also direct train services every hour from Zürich airport (less busy than Geneva). Road border points from France are congested at rush hours (the Bardonnex viaduct will relieve pressure at Perly by 1991).

Genève-Cointrin airport

Over 5.5m passengers pass through Geneva airport each year. It is used for scheduled, charter and private business flights and skiing trips. Part is on French soil (leased to the Swiss), so flights to and from French airports have domestic status. There is a single terminal on four floors.

Incoming passengers may have to wait at passport control, and the airport is crowded during major conferences and on ski-season Saturdays. Facilities in arrivals include a welcome desk (hotel reservations) open 5am–0.30am, meeting room (☎ 717 71 11), car rental desks, numerous banks (UBS and SBS agents open daily, 6am–11pm) and a post office (open Mon–Fri, 7.30–6; Sat, 7.30–11am). The French sector has a bar, boutiques and tax-free shop. Transit and departure areas are well provided with restaurants (☎ 717 76 76) and snack bars. There is a photocopier, PTT telegram and telex office (open daily, 7am–10.45pm) and VIP lounge in the departures hall. Passenger and freight inquiries ☎ 799 31 11.

Nearby hotels Penta, 75–77 ave Louis-Casaï ☎ 798 47 00 ⊤X 415571 fax 798 77 58 • AE DC MC V (a large hotel, free shuttle to airport, conference facilities). *Novotel*, route de Meyrin, CH-01210 Ferney Voltaire ☎ (023) 50 40 85 23 ⊤X 385046 fax 50 40 76 33 • AE DC MC V, is just in France; it provides a pool and tennis and an airport shuttle bus on request.
City link The airport is 5kms/3 miles west of the city centre. The taxi fare is high, so the inexpensive trolleybus is a useful alternative. The train service is quick and convenient if your destination is near the station.
Taxi A cab takes 15–20mins and costs about Swfr25.
Limousine Al Amsa International ☎ 798 44 05.
Car rental Avis ☎ 798 23 00; Al Amsa ☎ 798 44 05; Budget ☎ 798 22 53; Europcar ☎ 798 11 10; Hertz ☎ 798 22 02.
Bus The No. 10 TPG trolleybus leaves every 8–12mins (20mins after 8pm) for Cornavin station and the town centre.
Train The frequent service to Cornavin station takes 6mins. Tickets are Swfr3.40 from automatic machines.

Railway stations
The airport's Gare Cointrin is linked to the Swiss network through the Gare Cornavin. The Gare des Eaux-Vives serves arrivals from France.
Gare Cornavin Geneva's main railway station is convenient for the

best hotels and the international organizations. Services include regular InterCity trains across Switzerland, frequent EuroCity trains from Milan (4hrs 30mins) and the TGV from Paris (5 daily, 3hrs 30mins). There are frequent rail links with the airport, and buses to the Palexpo exhibition site (No.5), the UN (No.8) and Meyrin/CERN (No.15). The station is old but well-equipped: facilities include a post office (open daily, 7am–10.30pm), 4 restaurants, tourist office (hotel reservations and car rental), currency exchange and the Grand Passage shopping arcade. Inquiries and ticket reservations ☎ 731 64 50, airport check-in ☎ 732 61 00, air terminal ☎ 799 31 11.

Getting around
The business and banking areas are covered easily on foot but transport is needed to get to the United Nations area. International organizations are known by their French initials, so the UN is signposted ONU. Buses (mostly trolleybuses) run until midnight, but less frequently after 7.15pm. Parking in town is difficult.
Taxis The minimum fare is Swfr5, but no tip is required. A journey of 15kms/9 miles costs Swfr60 and fares to lakeside restaurants are expensive. Cabs wait at street junctions all over town and the suburbs. *ABC radio taxis* ☎ 794 71 11, *Ambassador cab services* ☎ 732 31 32, *Taxi-phone* ☎ 141.
Limousines Cari ☎ 732 11 12, *Executive* ☎ 732 79 77, *Globe* ☎ 731 07 50, *VIP* ☎ 731 79 25 (24hrs).
Driving A car can be useful for visitors to the UN area. Rental firms include *Alsa* ☎ 732 90 90, *Imex Trans Service* ☎ 732 73 63 (24hrs), *Léman* ☎ 732 01 43 and the major companies. In central Geneva a car is a hindrance; employees of the UN leave their cars at Cornavin when coming into the city centre.
Walking is the best way to see the Old Town. Elsewhere there is fast through traffic and it is advisable to

cross only at pedestrian lights.
Bus and tram There are clear colour-
coded routes posted at bus stops.
Tickets are bought from automatic
machines at stops, where they must
be validated. The 1hr ticket
(Swfr1.50) permits you to change
vehicles (and includes boat trips on
the *mouette*) and direction. One-day
tickets (Swfr6) are sold by TPG agents
listed at bus stops and at Cornavin
station. The only tram service is the
No.12 between Carouge and the
French border.

Area by area
The Lake of Geneva (Lac Léman)
and the River Rhône divide the city
into two distinct areas, linked by
several bridges across the river. The
rive droite includes the banking area
of Quai du Mont-Blanc, most of the
hotels, the station and the red-light
district around Rue de Berne. Beyond
are the international organizations,
Palexpo and the World Trade Center.
The whole area is known as the
rectangle d'or. Petit-Saconnex, near
the Palais des Nations, is the prime
residential area. Along the Lake are
the fine parks of La Perle du Lac and
Mon Repos.

The *quais* of the left bank, or *rive
gauche*, are lined with blocks of
offices, insurance companies and

banks. Behind them are elegant
shopping streets, the Rue du Rhône
and Rue de Rive, where a steep
ascent leads to the medieval Old
Town with its narrow cobbled lanes
and old houses, antique shops, art
galleries and bistros. To the east is
the smart residential area of Eaux-
Vives, with its lakeside parks. The
stupendous Jet d'Eau spouts in the
lake. West, towards the junction of
the Rivers Rhône and Arve, are the
commercial districts of Plainpalais
and Jonction.

The old town of Carouge, south of
the River Arve, is now a fashionable
area of restored 18thC houses.
Nearby Petit-Lancy has an old centre
and new apartment blocks.

Industry is concentrated around
Charmilles (machinery and
metallurgy), the industrial area of
Meyrin and Acacias/La Praille, but
some major firms are moving out.
The suburbs The very rich live in
lakeside districts like Cologny, or in
campagnard-style houses, with huge
balconies and gardens, towards the
French border.

Several suburbs and fringe areas
are becoming satellite towns with
lives of their own; these include
expanding, industrial Meyrin (30mins
west by bus from the centre), Grand-
Lancy and Le Lignon.

Hotels
So high are the hotel standards in Geneva that there are more rooms in
5-star hotels than in any other category. Grand, privately run hotels overlooking the lake where the service is meticulous are the most prestigious.
Hotels in lower categories are mostly modern and functional, with many
located in the station area. Several enormous new hotels are under
construction between Palexpo and the airport.

All hotels given full entries offer currency exchange, parking, a valet/
laundry service and IDD telephones, TV, video (and CNN) and minibars in
rooms.

Beau-Rivage SF //
13 quai du Mont-Blanc, CH-1201
☎ *731 02 21* TX *23362 fax 786 78 41*
• *AE DC MC V* • *109 rooms, 6 suites,
2 restaurants, 1 bar*
A recent facelift has restored the Beau

Rivage to its position as one of the
great hotels of Geneva and of Europe.
The clientele includes VIPs,
politicians, financiers and celebrities.
The grand public rooms provide a
suitable background for high-level

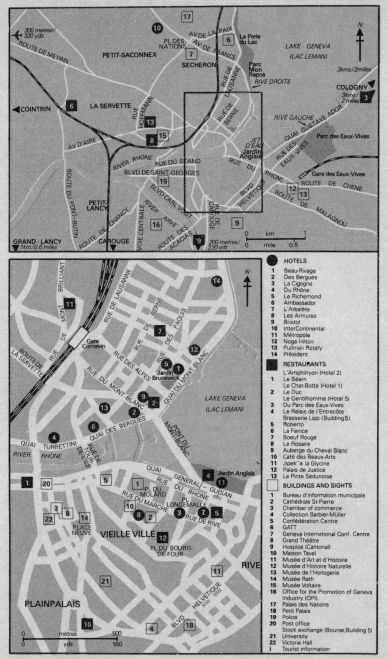

300 metres/
320 yds

ROUTE DE MEYRIN

PETIT-SACONNEX

[17]

[10]

PL DES
NATIONS

AV DE LA PAIX

AV DE FRANCE

[6] La Perle
du Lac

SECHERON

[7]

Parc Mon
Repos

RIVE DROITE

LAKE GENEVA
(LAC LEMAN)

3kms/2miles

N

◀COINTRIN

[6]

LA SERVETTE

RUE HOFFMANN

RUE DE LAUSANNE

COLOGNY
3kms/
2 miles

[3]▾

[13]

RUE DE BERNE

RIVE GAUCHE

QUAI GUSTAVE ADOR

Parc des Eaux-Vives

[8]

[15]

AV D'AIRE

RIVER RHONE

RUE DU STAND

BLVD DE SAINT-GEORGES

JET
D'EAU
Jardin
Anglais

RUE DU RHONE

QUAI DES EAUX-VIVES

Gare des Eaux-Vives

ROUTE DE CHENE

ROUTE DU PONT-BUTIN

PETIT-
LANCY

[19]

BLVD CARL VOGT

RIVER ARVE

VOIE CENTRALE

ROUTE DE CHANCY

RUE DE CAROUGE

BLVD HELVETIQUE

[12]

[13]

ROUTE DE MALAGNOU

GRAND - LANCY
1km/0.6 miles
▾

CAROUGE

[16]

ROUTE DES ACACIAS

[9]

[9]

200 metres/
220 yds

km
0   1
mile
0   0.5

BRILLIANT

RUE DE MONT

[11]

RUE DE LAUSANNE

RUE DE BERNE

RUE DES PAQUIS

[14]

N

ROUTE DE LA SERVETTE

RUE DE MONT-BLANC

Gare
Cornavin

RUE DES ALPES

[7]

[12]

RUE DU MONT-BLANC

[5] [1]
Jardin
Brunswick

QUAI DU MONT-BLANC

LAKE GENEVA
(LAC LEMAN)

[9]

[2]

[13]

[2]

QUAI DES BERGUES

PONT DU MONT-BLANC

QUAI
RIVER
TURRETTINI
RHONE

[4]

RUE DE L'ILE

Jardin Anglais

QUAI GENERAL - GUISAN

[4]

[11]

[1]

[20]

[5]

QUAI DU RHONE

RUE DU RHONE

PL DU
MOLARD

[1]

PL
LONGEMALLE

[11]

[3]

[8]

[14]

RUE DU MARCHE

[10]

[8] [2]

[3]

RUE DE RIVE

[7] [5]

[22]

PLACE
NEUVE

VIEILLE VILLE

[12]

PL DU BOURG-
DE-FOUR

RIVE

[21]

[11]

HELVETIQUE

PLAINPALAIS

[10]

[4]

BLVD
HELVETIQUE

[18]

metres   500
0
yds   550

HOTELS

● 1 Beau-Rivage
2 Des Bergues
3 La Cigogne
4 Du Rhône
5 Le Richemond
6 Ambassador
7 L'Arbalète
8 Les Armures
9 Bristol
10 InterContinental
11 Métropole
12 Noga Hilton
13 Pullman Rotary
14 Président

RESTAURANTS

■ L'Amphitryon (Hotel 2)
1 Le Béarn
Le Chat-Botté (Hotel 1)
2 Le Duc
Le Gentilhomme (Hotel 5)
3 Du Parc des Eaux-Vives
4 Le Relais de l'Entrecôte
Brasserie Lipp (Building 5)
5 Roberto
6 La Fenice
7 Boeuf Rouge
8 Le Rosaire
9 Auberge du Cheval Blanc
10 Café des Beaux-Arts
11 Jipek'a la Glycine
12 Palais de Justice
13 La Pinte Sédunoise

BUILDINGS AND SIGHTS

□ 1 Bureau d'information municipale
2 Cathédrale St-Pierre
3 Chamber of commerce
4 Collection Barbier-Müller
5 Confédération Centre
6 GATT
7 Geneva International Conf. Centre
8 Grand Théâtre
9 Hospital (Cantonal)
10 Maison Tavel
11 Musée d'Art et d'Histoire
12 Musée d'Histoire Naturelle
13 Musée de l'Horlogerie
14 Musée Rath
15 Musée Voltaire
16 Office for the Promotion of Geneva
Industry (OPI)
17 Palais des Nations
18 Petit Palais
19 Police
20 Post office
Stock exchange (Bourse; Building 5)
21 University
22 Victoria Hall
i Tourist information

conferences (for instance, of the World Economic Forum) and for glamorous auctions. Sotheby's is adjacent, and the Duchess of Windsor's jewels were sold here. After the splendour of the pillared entrance hall, and the luxury of the adjacent bar and salon, bedrooms are less imposing; ask for a renovated room; those at the back are quieter. The restaurant Quai 13 is more casual than Le Chat-Botté (see *Restaurants*). 24hr room service, limousine • secretarial and word processing facilities, 7 meeting rooms (capacity up to 450).

Des Bergues *SF* ////
33 quai des Bergues, CH-1201
☎ *731 50 50* ⊤ᴄ *23383 fax 732 19 89*
• *THF* • *AE DC MC V* • *123 rooms, 9 suites, 2 restaurants, 1 bar*
British bankers and businessmen form a high proportion of the guests in this well-known luxury hotel, and high-ranking UN officials often take the suites. French Empire-style decor and furnishings characterize the suites and public areas, including Le Pavillon, used by local bankers for quick lunches, and L'Amphitryon (see *Restaurants*). Bedrooms are traditional in style; all have brown marble bathrooms, and some have views of the Rhône. Valet parking, 24hr room service • 6 meeting rooms (capacity up to 500).

La Cigogne *SF* //
17 pl Longemalle, CH-1204 ☎ *21 42 42* ⊤ᴄ *421748 fax 21 40 65* • *AE DC MC V* •
38 rooms, 12 suites, 1 restaurant, 1 bar
La Cicogne is a new, small luxury hotel. Just off the Rue du Rhône, this medieval mansion has a welcoming country house atmosphere. Bedrooms, most with stucco walls, fireplaces and rustic or Empire-style furniture, vary in colour-scheme and layout. Although this is not a business hotel in the usual sense, you can expect personal service, and your fellow guests will probably include employees and clients of the most exclusive private banks. The panelled restaurant is frequented for lunch by people working nearby. 1 meeting room (capacity up to 25).

Du Rhône *SF* //
Quai Turrettini, CH-1211 ☎ *31 98 31* ⊤ᴄ *22213 fax 32 45 58* • *AE DC MC V*
• *281 rooms, 8 suites, 2 restaurants, 1 bar*
The Du Rhône lacks the prestige of the grand old hotels but competes well on efficiency and location. Many guests are conference attenders, and several banks favour the hotel as a base for their own employees from abroad. The public areas are modern and impersonal but the Le Neptune offers first-class cuisine and service. The latest innovation is a Bel Etage: bright bedrooms with electronic blinds, briefcase-sized safes and facilities for telex or fax machines (available from reception). 24hr room service • 10 meeting rooms (capacity up to 200).

Le Richemond *SF* ////
Jardin Brunswick, CH-1201
☎ *731 14 00* ⊤ᴄ *22598 fax 731 67 09*
• *AE DC MC V* • *69 rooms, 31 suites, 2 restaurants, 2 bars*
Run by the Armleder family since 1875, this sumptuous, chic hotel is considered by many to be the best address in Geneva. Service is smooth and scrupulous. Bedrooms are luxurious and light with king-size beds (except in the few singles); bathrooms are well-equipped, all with telephones. Suites come with various extras (many with jacuzzis), and interconnecting rooms are often taken for high protocol meetings (the Royal has a word processor, telex, fax and bullet-proof windows). The grand public salons are used for banquets and Christie's auctions, the foyer for teas and cocktails. 24hr room service • 7 meeting rooms (capacity to 250).

OTHER HOTELS
Ambassador *SF* *21 quai des Bergues, CH-1211* ☎ *731 72 00* ⊤ᴄ *412533 fax 738 90 80* • *AE DC MC V*. Traditional 4-star hotel in the banking area.

L'Arbalète *SF* // *3 rue Tour-Maîtresse, CH-1204* ☎ *28 41 55* ⊠ *427293 fax 21 96 60* • *AE DC MC V*. Small with personal service and business clientele.

Les Armures *SF* // *1 rue du Puits-St-Pierre, Vieille Ville, CH-1204* ☎ *28 91 72* ⊠ *421129 fax 28 98 46* • *AE DC MC V*. Comfortable Old Town hotel in a rustic mansion; under the same ownership as L'Arbalète.

Bristol *SF* / *8 rue du Mont-Blanc, CH-1201* ☎ *732 38 00* ⊠ *23739 fax 738 90 39* • *AE DC MC V*. Convenient and club-like business hotel. Fitness centre.

InterContinental *SF* // *7–9 Petit-Saconnex (ONU), CH-1211* ☎ *734 60 91* ⊠ *412921 fax 734 28 64* • *AE DC MC V*. Very large high-rise hotel used by UN delegates and visitors to other international organizations; good restaurant (Los Continents).

Métropole *SF* / *34 quai Général-Guisan, CH-1204* ☎ *21 13 44* ⊠ *421550 fax 21 13 50* • *AE DC MC V*. The only grand old hotel on the left bank.

Noga Hilton *SF* // *19 quai du Mont-Blanc, CH-1211* ☎ *731 98 11* ⊠ *289704 fax 738 64 32* • *AE DC*

MC V. Action-packed Hilton complex with business and fitness centres, restaurants (Le Cygne is excellent) and a disco.

Pullman Rotary *SF* / *18–20 rue du Cendrier, CH-1201* ☎ *731 52 00* ⊠ *289999 fax 731 91 69* • *AE DC MC V*. Well-equipped, comfortable and central hotel with charm.

Président *SF* // *47 quai Wilson, CH-1211* ☎ *731 10 11* ⊠ *22780 fax 731 22 06* • *AE DC MC V*. High quality hotel, completely renovated in 1988.

Out of town
La Réserve ☎ *774 17 41* at Bellevue (6kms/4 miles) has a pool, tennis courts and the notable Chinese Tse Fung restaurant. It attracts foreigners from the international organizations and wealthy Arabs, and it is popular with locals for lunch and sunbathing in summer.

> **Telephone, fax and telex numbers**
> Over the next few years all the telephone and fax numbers and many telex numbers will be changed.

Restaurants

Geneva claims to have more restaurants cited in gastronomic guides, relative to the population, than any other city in Europe. Local residents expect superb cooking and service. Two-hour lunches starting at 12.30 are quite normal, and the top restaurants invariably serve *nouvelle cuisine*. The best-known Swiss dish is *fondue*, but rich Savoyard or French cooking is more widely offered, and *filets de perche* are a classic of the lakeside restaurants. Local wines are quite good, especially the whites, and they are usually available *ouverts*. Reservations are always advisable. Main entries have been given only to the most favoured places in the centre of the town; however, in fine weather, many people will go farther afield to restaurants in the suburbs or on the lakeside (see *Out of town*).

L'Amphitryon *SF* / *Hôtel des Bergues* ☎ *732 69 56* • *closed Sat & Sun* • *AE DC MC V* • *jacket and tie* • *reservations essential* L'Amphitryon provides a spacious, light and elegant setting for a formal

business meal, and the adjacent salon is a civilized place to withdraw to for drinks. Bankers dominate the lunchtime clientele. Cooking here is classic with *nouvelle* overtones. There is a good set lunch.

Le Béarn *SF*////
4 quai de la Poste ☎ *21 00 28* • *closed*
Sat L, Sun • AE DC MC V
This small restaurant with its formal
Empire-style furnishings is patronized
chiefly by local bankers and old Swiss
families. Jean-Paul Goddard's *nouvelle
cuisine* is light and imaginative; the
excellent fish and seafood should be
accompanied by the finest Perlan
Grand Cru from his cellar. Set menus
include *le menu tradition*, an autumn
game menu and a surprise menu.
Best value is the business lunch.

Le Chat-Botté *SF*///
Hôtel Beau-Rivage ☎ *731 65 32* •
closed Sat & Sun • AE DC MC V •
jacket and tie
One of the best tables in Geneva,
under chef Richard Cressac, with a
superb wine cellar. The traditional,
panelled and beamed dining room
provides a suitable atmosphere for
business meals, and there is a very
reasonably priced *lunch d'affaire*. The
summer terrace is delightful, and
there is music in the evenings.

Le Duc *SF*//
7 quai du Mont-Blanc ☎ *731 73 30* •
closed Sun & Mon • DC MC V
A suitably serious eating place for the
nearby banking community. The
seafood here is the best in town.
Brown velvet *banquettes* and cork
walls create a comfortable if rather
sober atmosphere; avoid the more
cramped tables by the bar.

Le Gentilhomme *SF*////
*Hotel Le Richemond, 8–10 rue
Adhémar-Fabri* ☎ *731 14 00* • AE DC
MC V • *jacket and tie* • *reservations
essential*
The fine service, comfortable
surroundings and exclusive clientele
of Le Richemond extend to this very
prestigious restaurant. The business
lunch is reasonably priced, but the set
menus are expensive. In the evenings
a band serenades diners. Le Jardin is
less formal with good *fruits de mer*.
The terrace is a chic place to lunch in
the summer.

Du Parc des Eaux-Vives *SF*///
82 quai Gustave-Ador ☎ *735 41 40* •
*closed Mon, Sun D (Nov–Apr & Jan–
mid-Feb)* • AE DC MC V
An 18thC villa in its own grounds
overlooking the lake, the Parc des
Eaux-Vives is primarily geared to
high-profile functions, both business
and social, and private rooms are
available. It is also favoured for
smaller scale business entertaining,
especially on the terrace in the
summer. Classic French cuisine (with
seasonal menus) is complemented by
fabulous wine cellars. The Perret
family, owners and hosts, employs a
host of top-class staff.

OTHER RESTAURANTS
For a straightforward meal with
colleagues try: *Le Relais de
l'Entrecôte*, 49 rue du Rhône
☎ 28 05 01, a panelled Parisian-style
brasserie offering a no-choice main
course of tender *entrecôte* steak, or
Brasserie Lipp, Confédération Centre,
8 rue de la Confédération ☎ 29 31 22;
both are always packed at lunch time.
For more formal meals *Roberto*, 10
rue Pierre-Fatio ☎ 21 80 33, is an
elegant Italian restaurant, popular
with aristocratic old ladies as well as
with business people. Farther from
the centre is *La Fenice*, 78 ave de
Châtelaine ☎ 797 03 70, with friendly
service, good cooking and a paved
garden. A *rive droite* bistro, *Boeuf
Rouge*, 7 rue des Pâquis ☎ 732 75 37,
offers rich Lyonnais cooking, and
Le Rosaire, 57 rue de St-Jean
☎ 44 95 23, is known for its good
French food and excellent wines
(no credit cards). At Carouge, the
Auberge du Cheval Blanc, 15 pl de
l'Octroi ☎ 43 61 61, serves good food
and is popular at lunch.
   There are several "typical" places
for those with leisure time to spare:
Café des Beaux-Arts, 32 rue de
Carouge ☎ 29 15 02, is an old-style
bistro, famous for its intellectual
clientele. *Jipek' à la Glycine*, 21 rue
Montbrillant ☎ 733 62 85, offers
French cooking in noisy, relaxed
surroundings. The *Palais de*

Justice, 8 pl du Bourg-de-Four ☎ 20 42 54, is a rustic tavern with solid French and Swiss cuisine (good fondues and dried meat from the Grisons), frequented by lawyers and students. Near the Palais des Nations *La Pinte Sédunoise*, 18 rue Hoffmann ☎ 734 09 98, which serves Swiss cooking, is popular with journalists.

Out of town
The *Auberge du Lion d'Or*, 5 pl Pierre-Gautier ☎ 736 44 32 (closed Sat & Sun), in rural surroundings at Cologny (3.5kms/2 miles east), is pleasant for lunch and has wonderful views of the city and lake (request a table on the terrace). *Le Marignac*, 32 ave Eugène-Lance ☎ 794 04 24 (closed Sun & Mon), is a detached house in its own garden at Grand-Lancy, about 3kms/2 miles south; both are expensive. At Petit-Lancy the *Hostellerie de la Vendée*, 28 chemin de la Vendée ☎ 792 04 11, is a top-class restaurant which serves excellent French cuisine.

Convenient for the airport and Palexpo is *Le Cerf Volant*, 7 chemin des Sapins, Cointrin ☎ 798 07 57, a small restaurant featuring light Italian cooking and good service.

The many good restaurants in the countryside near the lake include, at Bellevue (6kms/3.5 miles), *Le Lacustre*, 347 route de Lausanne ☎ 774 10 02, known for its *filets de perche* served on the lakeside terrace, and *La Réserve*, 301 route de Lausanne ☎ 774 17 36, a Chinese restaurant (see *Hotels*). In Chambésy (5kms/3 miles), the *Auberge de la Cascade*, 2 chemin des Chataigniers ☎ 758 18 28, is rustic but expensive. The *Hotel du Lac*, 1296 Grand-Rue ☎ 776 15 21, in Coppet (12kms/7.5 miles), has an elegant countrified dining room with a fine terrace overlooking the lake.

For a gastronomic pilgrimage, famous *Girardet* ☎ (021) 634 05 05 in Crissier is only 30mins' drive away; but you need to reserve months ahead.

Bars and cafés
Hotel bars are the best for a business meeting; choose from the drawing-room atmosphere of the Beau Rivage, Le Richemond or the more anonymous Du Rhône, Noga Hilton or InterContinental. The Métropole is a good *rive gauche* meeting point. There are few appealing street bars and cafés in the city centre: *Harry's Bar* is a convenient but a rather ordinary wine bar in the Confédération Centre, and the *Café du Centre*, on Place Molard, is a popular brasserie.

Entertainment
Culturally, Geneva is a French-speaking city. *This Week in Geneva*, *What's on in Geneva* and a monthly *List of Events* are useful. There is a ticket agency in the *Grand Passage* department store, rue du Rhône ☎ 20 66 11.
Opera, theatre and dance The *Grand Théâtre*, pl Neuve ☎ 21 23 11, is the main venue for opera (Sep–Jun) and ballet. It can be difficult to get tickets. Other theatres (plays in French except for visiting companies) include *La Comédie*, 6 blvd des Philosophes ☎ 20 50 01 (classical plays), and *Nouveau Théâtre de Poche*, 7 rue du Cheval-Blanc ☎ 28 37 59 (contemporary).
Music The Orchestre de la Suisse Romande plays at the *Victoria Hall*, rue Hornung ☎ 28 35 73. Concerts are held in the lobby of the *Grand Théâtre*. Jazz can be heard at *Halles de l'Ile*, 1 pl de l'Ile ☎ 21 52 21.
Cinema New films are often in the original languages with subtitles.
Nightclubs and casinos The smartest nightclub is members-only *Griffin's*, 36 blvd Helvétique ☎ 735 12 18; restaurant and good café. The *Richemond* Hotel has a dance floor, the *Hilton* two nightspots.

The *Grand Casino*, 19 quai du Mont-Blanc ☎ 732 00 00, is as much a venue for galas, variety shows, concerts and plays as a place to gamble. The *Divonne Casino* is the largest in France, 15mins by car.

Shopping

Top quality and multilingual service
make Geneva one of Europe's best
cities for shopping. Most of the great
watchmakers, jewellers and top
fashion designers have shops in the
rue du Rhône. The Confédération
Centre is a convenient shopping
arcade with some chic boutiques. If
you like browsing in antique shops
and art galleries, head for the Old
Town.

Department stores Bon Génie in rue
du Marché is the classiest; *Grand
Passage* in rue du Rhône is a standard
department store.

Gifts Swiss army knives from
Fontaine, rue de la Confédération, or
Rasora, 4 rue du Port; traditional
embroidered linens from *Au Chalet
Suisse*, 18 quai Général-Guisan.

Jewellery *Benoît de Gorski*, 86 rue du
Rhône, or *Gilbert Albert*, 24 rue de la
Corraterie, for modern designs,
Gübelin, 60 rue du Rhône, for
traditional pieces. Watchmakers often
also sell jewellery.

Tobacco The original *Davidoff* is at
2 rue de Rive.

Watches *Patek Philippe*, 22 quai
Général-Guisan and 41 rue du Rhône,
Piaget, 40 and 78 rue du Rhône, and
Vacheron & Constantin, 1 rue des
Moulins, are among the top Swiss
manufacturers. For a selection of
makers visit *Les Ambassadeurs*, 39 rue
du Rhône (Audemars-Piguet) or
Bucherer, 23 rue du Rhône.

Sightseeing

Visit the lake shores in summer and
take time to wander in the
picturesque Old Town and in
Carouge. Museum information
☎ 21 43 88.

Cathédrale St-Pierre Focal point of
the Vieille Ville, constructed in the
12th and 13th centuries, where Calvin
used to preach. *Cour St-Pierre. Open
Mon–Sat, 9–12, 2–5; Jun–Sep, 9–7.
Archeological site closed Mon.*

Collection Barbier-Müller Primitive
art from Africa and the South Sea
islands. *4 rue de L'Ecole-de-Chimie.
Open Tue–Sat, 2.30–5.30.*

Maison Tavel The oldest private
house in Geneva; now contains a
museum of the city. *6 rue du
Puits-St-Pierre. Open Tue–Sun, 2–5.*

Musée d'Art et d'Histoire Archeology
and the arts, including a good
collection of Swiss and French
paintings. Konrad Witz's altarpiece of
the *Miraculous Draught of Fishes*
(1444) is usually cited as the first
landscape painting in European art
and it shows Lake Geneva. *2 rue
Charles-Galland. Open Tue–Sun,
10–5.*

Musée d'Histoire Naturelle One of
the most modern natural history
museums in Europe. *1 route de
Malagnou. Open Tue–Sat, 10–5.*

Musée de l'Horlogerie Beautiful
enamelled and jewelled timepieces
among many illustrating the history
of time measurement. *15 route de
Malagnou. Open Tue–Sat, 10–12, 2–6;
Mon, 2–6.*

Musée Rath Temporary exhibitions
of painting and sculpture. *Pl Neuve.
Open Tue–Sun, 10–12, 2–6 (Wed, also
8–11pm).*

Musée Voltaire Memorabilia of the
French philosopher and writer who
lived here 1755–65. *25 rue des Délices.
Open Mon–Fri, 2–5.*

Petit Palais European painting, from
Impressionist to avant-garde.
*2 terrasse St-Victor. Open Tue–Sun,
10–12, 2–6; Mon, 2–6.*

Guided tours

For a general view of the town by
bus, try *Key Tours* ☎ 731 41 40. The
Geneva tourist office ☎ 738 52 00
organizes walking tours of the Old
Town and Carouge (2hrs). For guided
visits to the Palais des Nations
☎ 731 02 11 ext 4539. *Mouettes
Genèvoises Navigation* ☎ 732 29 44,
Compagnie Générale de Navigation
☎ 21 25 21 and *Key Tours* organize
various lake and Rhône boat trips.
Air-Glaciers ☎ 798 92 76 offers scenic
flights.

Out of town

The romantic medieval *Château de
Chillon* (about 80kms/50 miles) and

the picturesque village of Gruyères, at the opposite end of the lake (day trips by Key Tours), are well worth visiting. Mont Salève, 6kms/3.5 miles from Geneva, offers spectacular views of the city, lake and mountains (ascent by cable-car; take passport). The *Château de Coppet* (12kms/7.5 miles) ☎ 776 10 28, was once the home of Madame de Staël.

Spectator sports

Summer regattas are held on the lake and tennis tournaments at the exclusive Club des Eaux-Vives. *Servette* is the local soccer team. The *Centre Sportif des Vernets*, 4 rue H. Wilsdorf ☎ 43 88 50, is an important venue for spectator sports.

Keeping fit

Geneva has good facilities for just about everything. Association Genèvoise des Sports ☎ 35 49 49. *Vivre a Genève*, a free guide, lists clubs and associations.
Fitness centres John Valentine, 12 rue Gautier ☎ 732 80 50, and at the *Bristol* and *Noga Hilton* hotels.
Golf Golf Club de Genève, 70 route de La Capite, Cologny ☎ 35 75 40; *Club de Bonmont*, 1261 Cheserex ☎ 69 23 45. Both accept players with handicaps.
Hang-gliding Ecole de Volta ☎ 96 33 02 provides lessons and equipment at Mont Salève (6kms/3.5 miles).
Skiing Chamonix and Megève in France are the nearest resorts (1hr); Crans-Montana, Verbier and Zermatt are within 2hrs.
Squash Squash Club de Genève ☎ 758 22 06 is at Chemin du Joli Bois, Chambésy, the *Club du Bois Carré*, 204 route de Veyrier ☎ 784 30 06, at Carouge.
Swimming Centre Sportif des Vernets (see *Spectator sports*) has an olympic pool. Other public pools include Genève-Plage (in Cologny). At Bellevue (6kms/4miles north) you can swim at the *New Sporting Club* ☎ 774 15 14 (indoor pool) or at *La Réserve* (see *Hotels*).

Tennis Tennis des Petites Fontaines, 53 chemin Grand Voiret ☎ 794 94 88; welcomes nonmembers for a fee, who may also play at off-peak hours at *Tennis du Bois Carré*, 204 route de Veyrier ☎ 784 30 06.
Walking Touring Club Suisse, 9 rue Pierre-Fatio ☎ 737 12 12, sells maps of marked routes in the canton.
Watersports Société Nautique de Genève ☎ 736 17 00 (sailing); *Ski Nautique Club de Genève* at La Perle du Lac ☎ 732 35 13 (waterskiing). Equipment rental from *Tropical Corner*, 2 rue des Barques ☎ 786 14 22, or *Louage Léman*, 44 quai Gustave Ador ☎ 35 22 63, but only in good weather.

Local resources

Business services

Offices, multilingual secretarial and translation services, and legal advice: *Answer Back* ☎ 732 62 00; *Executive Business Services* ☎ 732 08 95; *Genesis* ☎ 732 51 74; *International Business Center* ☎ 798 69 65 (near airport); *Support Services* ☎ 731 55 53.
Photocopying and printing At *Grand Passage* department store, rue du Rhône, or *Copy-Quick*, 70 rue de Carouge ☎ 29 28 27; off-set printing (and mailing) *Sro Kundig* ☎ 796 57 77 (at Châtelaine); printing at *Atar*, 11 rue de la Dole ☎ 44 64 00, and *Sprint*, 6 rue de la Colline ☎ 20 25 55.
Secretarial ABC Assistance ☎ 793 55 58; *Dactyl Bastions* ☎ 20 26 72; *Dactyl Express* ☎ 28 78 61; *Manpower* ☎ 731 68 00.
Translation Contact *Association d'Interprètes et traducteurs*, 1bis pl du Cirque ☎ 21 07 95.

Communications

Local delivery Citylink ☎ 43 33 10; GBS ☎ 41 03 41; *Intercity IC SA* ☎ 798 85 71; *Jet Service* ☎ 43 57 20 (and international) or taxi ☎ 141.
Long-distance delivery
DHL ☎ 44 44 05; *World Courrier* ☎ 42 28 70; *XP Express Parcel* ☎ 798 32 20 (at airport) and TNT *Ipec/Skypak* ☎ 798 65 44.

Post offices Poste du Stand, pl de la Poste, and Poste du Mont-Blanc, rue du Mont-Blanc, are open Mon–Fri, 7.30–6; Sat, 7.30–11am. Poste du Mont-Blanc is closed 12–1.45. *Telex and fax* at Gare Cornavin (open daily, 7am–10.30pm), the airport (open daily, 7am–10.45pm) and main post offices.

Conference/exhibition centres

The *Palexpo* exhibition halls, Case Postale 112, CH-1218, Grand-Saconnex ☎ 798 11 11 ⊺ⅹ 422784 fax 798 01 00, provide conference facilities for up to 2,400, *Geneva International Conference Centre*, 3 rue de Varembé CH-1202 ☎ 791 91 11, for up to 1,800 (mainly governmental conferences). Conventions organized by Orgexpo ☎ 798 11 11 ⊺ⅹ 422784 fax 798 01 00. The *Interprofessional Centre* (capacity up to 300), *UNI II* (capacity up to 640) and the *Thônex Centre* (capacity up to 900) are among other venues. Hotels providing facilities include the Beau-Rivage, Noga Hilton, InterContinental and Warwick (☎ 31 62 50). The tourist office has a conference and hotel reservations department ☎ 28 72 33. *Intercongress* ☎ 743 51 79 is the best conference management agency.

Emergencies

Bureaux de change Change Cendrier, 18 rue du Cendrier ☎ 732 66 67 (open Mon–Fri, 9–1, 2–7; Sat, 9–12). Useful branches of the main banks include *Crédit Suisse*, Grand Casino, 19 quai de Mont-Blanc ☎ 732 69 40 (open Mon–Fri, 7–8; Sat, 8–6), and at 1 rue de la Monnaie ☎ 22 27 54; *SBS*, Hôtel des Bergues ☎ 732 23 00 (open Mon–Sat, 8–8; Sun, 8–12.30), and 10 Place Cornavin ☎ 731 33 50 (open Mon–Fri, 7.30–7.30; Sat, 8–6) and *UBS*, 19 rue du Mont-Blanc ☎ 732 54 90 (open Mon–Fri, 7am–9pm), and at the airport ☎ 798 21 80 (open daily 6am–11pm). *Hospitals Hôpital Cantonal*, 24 rue Micheli-du-Crest ☎ 22 63 13; *Clinique la Tour*, 3 ave J-D Maillard, Meyrin ☎ 82 55 44, is an American-run private hospital. Out-patient clinics: *Permanences* ☎ 33 98 00, right bank; ☎ 46 64 44, left bank; both 7.30am–8pm, offer 24hr medical facilities. Ambulance ☎ 144 or 20 10 01. Emergency ☎ 20 25 11 (Association des Medecins) or for emergency visits ☎ 48 49 50. Dental emergencies ☎ 21 60 22 (day) ☎ 96 30 90 (night).

Pharmacies Pharmacies are open in rotation and are listed in *This Week in Geneva*, and in newspapers and posted at other pharmacies. After 11pm ☎ 20 25 11 or (emergency only) 111.

Police Emergencies ☎ 117. Commissariat de Police et Gendarmerie, 17–19 blvd Carl-Vogt ☎ 27 51 11.

Information sources

Business information Chambre de Commerce et de l'Industrie de Genève, 4 blvd du Théâtre ☎ 21 53 33; *Office pour la Promotion de l'Industrie Genèvoise (OPI)*, 9 rue Boissonnas, CH-1227 Carouge ☎ 42 42 44; *Port Franc de Genève*, 6 route du Grand-Lancy, CH-1227 Carouge ☎ 43 00 00; *World Trade Center*, 108–110 ave Louis-Casaï, CH-1215 Genève-Cointrin ☎ 798 99 89.

Local media La Suisse (mornings) and *Tribune de Genève* (afternoons) each have daily circulations of around 70,000. *Journal de Genève* is important for finance. Foreign newspapers are available by 11am on weekdays. BBC radio and the Voice of America can be heard 24hrs.

Tourist information Tourist board, 1 Tour-de-l'Ile ☎ 28 72 33; information, Gare de Cornavin ☎ 738 52 00. *Bureau d'information municipale*, 4 pl du Molard ☎ 29 99 70.

Thank-yous

Chocolates Auer, 4 rue de Rive ☎ 21 42 86; *Jenny*, 8 rue Kléberg, and *La Bonbonnière*, 11 rue de Rive. *Florist Le Breuil*, 10 quai Général-Guisan ☎ 28 50 05 (send flowers in advance).

ZÜRICH
City code ☎ 01

Financially and economically Zürich is the most important city in Switzerland. The whole metropolitan area has a population of some 840,000, but that of the city centre has steadily declined recently to around 348,000.

The Bahnhofstrasse is not exactly paved with gold, but the vaults beneath it are stocked solid. Zürich is the home of the powerful UBS, Union de Banques Suisses (largest bank in the country) and of Crédit Suisse (third largest). Also here are the Zürcher Cantonalbank, Bank Leu (both in the top six) and over 300 other banks, including half the foreign banks based in the country. Trading in currency, gold and precious metals is Zürich's chief strength. Insurance, especially reinsurance (the top three in the country, headed by Swiss Reinsurance), is an important financial service. Rentenanstalt (Swiss Life) is Europe's largest mutual life insurance company with almost 30% of the market. Zürich's stock exchange is the biggest in the country and accounts for over half of the turnover in securities in Switzerland. The city is being promoted as a centre for conventions and trade fairs, and most foreign chambers of commerce are based here, rather than in the capital. Zürich is also a focus for the international art market, with sales in May and November.

All this economic activity stems from the 19thC industrial revolution. The canton (population 1.1m) is still the biggest conglomeration of manufacturing industries in the country, although it accounts for a mere 15% of Swiss output. Zürich has been famous for textiles, especially silk and cotton, since the 18th century. This led to skills in manufacturing equipment, and metals and mechanical engineering are still important; Alusuisse (aluminium) and the diversified Oerlikon-Bührle Group, one of the biggest employers, are here. Most of the textile machinery – Zürich is still a top world producer – is made at nearby Ruti by Sulzer and at Winterthur by Rieter. The other important industrial centre in the canton is Regensdorf, notable for electronics. Dow Chemical has its European base at Horgen, just south of the city. Among the major Swiss companies based in Zürich is Swissair, with its headquarters at Kloten where around 16,000 people are employed at the airport.

Zürich has a picture-postcard Old Town and lovely lake-front setting framed by mountains. It has been a cultural centre since the Reformation and has a thriving university and theatres. The visitor will find most Züricher helpful and many as happy to speak English as French. The Protestant work ethic, preached by Huldreich Zwingli, originated here and although this is a supremely wealthy city the people mistrust showiness. Zürich has none of the frenetic pace of life of other world financial capitals; trading markets often close over lunch on a Friday afternoon.

Arriving
Zürich is roughly in the middle of Switzerland, is a major junction of the Swiss and European rail and road networks and has an airport of international importance.

Kloten airport
Kloten is an important junction (almost 30% of passengers are in

transit) and serves parts of West
Germany and Austria as well as most
of eastern Switzerland. There are two
terminals: Terminal A is for flights
from West Germany, Austria and
Eastern Europe, plus charters (busiest
in the skiing season); Terminal B
handles domestic, other European
and intercontinental flights. Facilities
include shops (open daily, 8–8),
banks and bureaux de change (open
daily, 6.30am–10.30pm), hotel
reservation and information desk,
post office (open Mon–Fri, 7–8;
Sat, 7–noon) and restaurants (in the
departure hall). The airport functions
with Swiss efficiency, but long walks
are usual. Inquiries ☎ 816 12 12;
airport information ☎ 812 71 11;
Swissair ☎ 251 34 34.

Nearby hotels There are several
useful hotels in the Glattbrugg area:
Airport, Oberhausstr 30, CH-8152
☎ 810 44 44 ⊠ 825416 fax 810 97 08
• ZuricHôtels • AE DC MC V, with a
good Japanese restaurant, meeting
rooms and airport and city bus
service; *Hilton International*,
Hohenbühlstr, CH-8158 ☎ 810 31 31
⊠ 825428 fax 810 93 66 • AE DC MC V;
Mövenpick, W. Mittelholzerstr 8,
CH-8152 ☎ 810 11 11 ⊠ 828781 fax
810 40 38 • AE DC MC V; *Novotel*,
Talackerstr 21, CH-8152 ☎ 810 31 11
⊠ 828770 fax 810 81 85 • AE DC MC V,
with business services and 8 meeting
rooms.
City link Kloten airport is 11kms/7
miles north of the city. The quickest
way into town is by train, although
you will then need a taxi from the
station. Trains leave from below
ground level; baggage trolleys can be
taken on the escalator. Some hotels
offer a minibus service.
Taxis wait outside both terminals. A
cab to the centre costs Swfr35–40 and
takes about 15mins.
Limousine Top hotels will organize
limousine pick-ups for about Swfr40;
or get in touch with the "Welcome"
information desk.
Car rental offices are on floor 5 of car
parking B. Avis ☎ 813 00 84; Budget
☎ 828 92 11; Europcar ☎ 813 20 44;

Hertz ☎ 814 05 11; InterRent
☎ 814 00 55.
Bus Buses run to the Hauptbahnhof
every 15mins. For other destinations,
and hotel minibuses, see the
timetables outside car parking B.
Train The regular service to Zürich
Hauptbahnhof takes 10–12mins and
runs every 10–20mins.

Railway stations
Work will begin in 1991 on the new
Hauptbahnhof-Südwest to extend and
replace the main station.
Zürich Hauptbahnhof has direct
EuroCity links with Munich,
Stuttgart and Vienna, and Intercity
and regional trains connect with
towns all over Switzerland (Geneva
3hrs). The present station, which is
in the heart of the city, is being
modernized and, while most
amenities are available (including the
main tourist information office),
reconstruction means that the station
will be uncharacteristically dirty and
chaotic until 1991 when building will
start on the new extension. Swissair
check-in desk; inquiries ☎ 211 50 10.
Enge, southeast of the centre, is a
useful station for commuter trains
from lakeside suburbs and convenient
for some offices and hotels. Inquiries
☎ 462 70 01.

Getting around
Most people (top executives included)
walk or take trams in the centre of
Zürich. Taxis are expensive. Tram,
trolleybus and bus tickets for single
journeys or for 24hrs (Swfr5) can be
bought from machines at stops where
they must then be validated. A
subway system is at present under
construction.
Taxis A minimum fare of Swfr5 and
traffic restrictions, particularly in the
Old Town, are deterrents for short
journeys. Cabs wait at ranks or call
Taxi Zentral Zürich ☎ 272 44 44, 44
11 22 or *Züritaxiphon* ☎ 271 11 11.
No tips are required.
Limousines Fretz ☎ 471 15 53.
Driving Cars can be left in
multistoried parking in the city centre

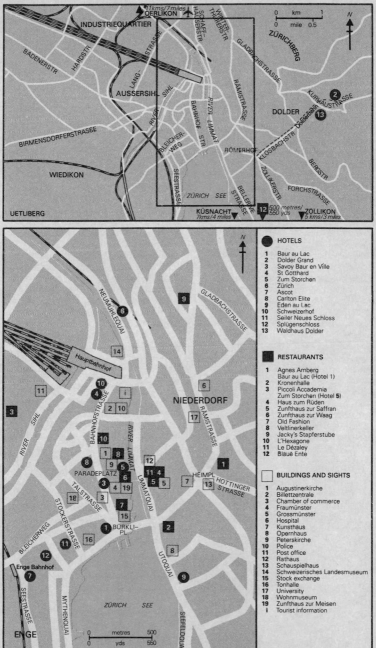

INDUSTRIEQUARTIER

11 kms/7 miles

OERLIKON

ZÜRICHBERG

BADENERSTR

HARDSTR

LANG-STRASSE

SCHAFF-HAUSERSTR

WINTER-THURERSTR

GLADBACHSTRASSE

KURHAUSSTRASSE

AUSSERSIHL

SIHL

BAHNHOFSTR

RIVER LIMMAT

RÄMISTRASSE

DOLDER

Dolderbahn

BIRMENSDORFERSTRASSE

BLEICHER-WEG

STR

RÖMERHOF

KLOSBACHSTR

BERGSTR

WIEDIKON

SEESTRASSE

ZÜRICH SEE

BELLERIVE STRASSE

ZOLLIKERSTR

FORCHSTRASSE

UETLIBERG

KÜSNACHT
7kms/4 miles

500 metres/
550 yds

ZOLLIKON
5 kms/3 miles

km 1

mile 0.5

N

NIEDERDORF

GLADBACHSTRASSE

NEUMÜHLEQUAI

Hauptbahnhof

BAHNHOFSTRASSE

RIVER LIMMAT

RÄMISTRASSE

SIHL

PARADEPLATZ

TALSTRASSE

STOCKERSTRASSE

BLEICHERWEG

LIMMATQUAI

BÜRKLI-PL

HEIMPL

HOTTINGER STRASSE

UTOQUAI

Enge Bahnhof

SEESTRASSE

MYTHENQUAI

ZÜRICH SEE

SEEFELDQUAI

ENGE

metres 500

yds 550

N

HOTELS

1 Baur au Lac
2 Dolder Grand
3 Savoy Baur en Ville
4 St Gotthard
5 Zum Storchen
6 Zürich
7 Ascot
8 Carlton Elite
9 Eden au Lac
10 Schweizerhof
11 Seiler Neues Schloss
12 Splügenschloss
13 Waldhaus Dolder

RESTAURANTS

1 Agnes Amberg
  Baur au Lac (Hotel 1)
2 Kronenhalle
3 Piccoli Accademia
  Zum Storchen (Hotel 5)
4 Haus zum Rüden
5 Zunfthaus zur Saffran
6 Zunfthaus zur Waag
7 Old Fashion
8 Veltlinerkeller
9 Jacky's Stapferstube
10 L'Hexagone
11 Le Dézaley
12 Blaue Ente

BUILDINGS AND SIGHTS

1 Augustinerkirche
2 Billettzentrale
3 Chamber of commerce
4 Fraumünster
5 Grossmünster
6 Hospital
7 Kunsthaus
8 Opernhaus
9 Peterskirche
10 Police
11 Post office
12 Rathaus
13 Schauspielhaus
14 Schweizerisches Landesmuseum
15 Stock exchange
16 Tonhalle
17 University
18 Wohnmuseum
19 Zunfthaus zur Meisen
i Tourist information

365

or at cheaper parking sites with access to public transport in the suburbs. Traffic and parking are only likely to be a problem on Thursday afternoons (late-night shopping).

Walking The River Limmat and the Bahnhofstrasse make for easy orientation, although the crooked alleys of the old part between these two landmarks can be confusing. The central park area just north of the Hauptbahnhof is notorious for drug dealing.

Tram and trolleybus The tram and trolleybus (vbz) system is comprehensive and well indicated (by numbers and colour codes) at stops and on maps. Most routes pass through Paradeplatz and/or by the Hauptbahnhof where the vbz information offices supply useful route plans. The tram system extends to many suburban railway stations and runs from 5.30am until midnight with trams every 6mins during rush hours.

Bus City and regional buses run to the suburbs, mostly from tram terminals all over town.

Train There are frequent trains, mainly from the Hauptbahnhof to the suburbs (*S-Bahn*). Also useful for some visitors is the *Dolderbahn*, a funicular railway which operates every 10–15mins from 6.20am to 11.30pm, to the Dolder Grand and past the Waldhaus Dolder (see *Hotels*) from Römerhofplatz.

Area by area

The centre of Zürich lies on both sides of the River Limmat north of the point where it flows out of the Zürichsee. The main business and banking activity is in and around elegant Bahnhofstrasse, which runs south–north from the lake to the station. Between this main thoroughfare and the river are the quaint, cobbled streets of the Old Town, where fine buildings house restaurants and boutiques. The opposite (right) bank, connected by several bridges, is also picturesque, with several old guildhalls and well-preserved streets. Behind Limmatquai is the bohemian district of Niederdorf (Dörfli), with student taverns, sleazy nightspots and streetwalkers.

The western lakefront, along and behind Mythenquai, has been nicknamed "Insurance Riviera" because of the number of insurance offices in the district (Enge). West is Wiedikon, another convenient residential and business district. The area west of the River Sihl (a tributary of the Limmat), including the Industriequartier, is mainly commercial, with banking back-up offices and computer departments, plus some industry. Aussersihl, the district to the west of the Hauptbahnhof, has a reputation as a red-light area.

The suburbs

Many Zürcher choose to live in the suburbs, either up in the hills or on the lake shore; they can be at their desks within half an hour of leaving home. The most desirable suburbs are Zollikon and Küsnacht to the east, the lakeside villages of the "Gold Coast," so called because of the wealth of the inhabitants. Nearby Forch, up in the hills, is also popular.

The main industrial suburbs are to the east, towards Regensdorf, and to the north, notably at Oerlikon, which is also the site of the zuspa trade fair and exhibition halls.

Hotels

There are two prestige hotels in Zürich, the Dolder Grand and the Baur au Lac. Otherwise, there are various conveniently situated, traditional establishments. Modern international chain hotels are less central (the Hilton at the airport, the Swissair-owned International at Oerlikon, the Nova Park near the soccer ground and the Atlantis Sheraton near the Uetliberg). All hotels are geared to the needs of business travellers, and the tourist offices at the airport and station will make reservations for a small fee.

All hotels with a main entry have IDD telephones in rooms, currency exchange, parking, concierge, laundry services, limousine service to the airport and newsstand.

Baur au Lac *SF* ////
Talstr 1, CH-8022 ☎ *221 16 50*
TX *8131567 fax 211 81 39 • AE DC MC V • 139 rooms, 16 suites, 2 restaurants, 1 bar*
One of the world's best hotels, the Baur au Lac combines superlative personal service with elegant, restful surroundings and a lovely lakeside location. It has been family-owned and run with personal style for nearly 150 years. Most bedrooms are spacious and light, with immaculate bathrooms; the loveliest are the lakeside suites. There are no singles overlooking the lake, and rooms on the canal are the quietest. Female executives are usually put in the floral suites. The ratio of staff to guests is very high, and the powers of Albert, the chief concierge, are formidable. The Hall is an elegant meeting place, and the Grill and the Pavillion (summer only) cater for all occasions (see *Restaurants*). The formal public rooms are used for Sotheby's auctions. Across the canal is the Villa Rosau, with Zürich's best nightclub (see *Entertainment*) and the Baur au Lac Club (see *Clubs*). Diagonal Club disco, hairdresser • 4 meeting rooms (capacity up to 200).

Dolder Grand *SF* //
Kurhausstr 65, CH-8032 ☎ *251 62 31*
TX *816416 fax 251 88 29 • AE DC MC V • 185 rooms, 30 suites, 1 restaurant, 1 bar*
For top executives and wealthy tourists who prefer a quiet location in rural surroundings the resolutely traditional Dolder is the answer. This fairy-tale castle 610 metres/2,000ft up in the woods has been modernized inside but is more impersonal than the rival Baur au Lac. The town centre is a 10min taxi or funicular

ride away – part of the price you pay for having superb views and a nearby golf course and swimming pool (at the Waldhaus Dolder). Bedrooms vary from luxurious tower suites to old-fashioned singles; the bedrooms in the new wing are better lit. Most guests prefer the lake view, but the forest side is cooler in summer, and less expensive. La Rotonde, the hotel's formal French restaurant, is still a prestigious venue. 8 meeting rooms (capacity up to 200).

Savoy Baur en Ville *SF* ////
Am Paradepl, CH-8022 ☎ *211 53 60*
TX *812845 fax 221 14 67 • AE DC MC V • 100 rooms, 14 suites, 3 restaurants, 1 bar*
No longer related to the Baur au Lac, the Savoy places its emphasis on being the best central hotel for the business visitor. Security is tight and service efficient, if sometimes disdainful. The meeting rooms, especially the panelled Zunftzimmer, are ideal for formal private lunches or signing agreements (absolute confidentiality is guaranteed as there is no public access on the same level). Bedrooms are comfortable, with no frills but with the usual facilities. The formal French restaurant and the Orsini (serving Italian food) are the main restaurants, but the bar also serves light meals. Shops, hairdresser • 7 meeting rooms (capacity up to 150).

St Gotthard *SF* /
Bahnhofstr 87, CH-8023 ☎ *211 55 00*
TX *812420 fax 211 24 19 • AE DC MC V • 135 rooms, 7 suites, 4 restaurants, 2 bars*
A well-situated hotel near the station, family-run for a century, with a solid reputation and constant business

clientele. The Bouillabaisse restaurant is frequented by fish-loving locals and Japanese business guests, and the Hummerbar is popular for oysters at lunch time. There have recently been reports of rather obsequious service. 3 meeting rooms (capacity up to 45).

Zum Storchen *SF* /
Am Weinpl 2, CH-8001 ☎ *211 55 10* ⊤ₓ *813354 fax 211 64 51* •
ZuricHôtels • *AE DC MC V* • *77 rooms, 1 restaurant, 2 bars*
Zum Storchen is popular with those who appreciate its welcoming atmosphere, reasonable prices, its location, at the heart of the Old Town, and river views, especially from the terrace of the Rôtisserie (see *Restaurants*). But the hotel adapts well to a business clientele; the staff are efficient, and bedrooms and bathrooms are well-equipped (a fax machine can be installed and bathroom cabinets are full of luxury emergency toiletries). Guests can even go jogging with the manager in the mornings. Zum Storchen is often used by companies giving presentations, particularly in the magnificently restored Café Litteraire upstairs, and the restaurant and intimate bar are popular in their own right. Locals frequent the crowded *buvette* café. No parking. Shops, hairdresser • 3 meeting rooms (capacity up to 45).

Zürich *SF* /
Neumühlequai 42, CH-8001 ☎ *363 63 63* ⊤ₓ *817587 fax 363 60 15* • *ZuricHôtels* • *AE DC MC V* • *211 rooms, 10 suites, 2 restaurants, 2 bars*
This convenient and comfortable, high-rise hotel overlooking the Limmat, about a 10min walk from Bahnhofstrasse, is often used for conferences. A whole new wing, with another restaurant, large rooms and more suites and function rooms, opens in Spring 1990. Shops • health club with pool, fitness centre, sauna • 8 meeting rooms with word processing and translation facilities (capacity up to 400).

OTHER HOTELS
Ascot *SF* / *Tessinerpl 9, CH-8002* ☎ *201 18 00* ⊤ₓ *815454 fax 202 72 10* • *ZuricHôtels* • *AE DC MC V*. Renovated downtown hotel opposite Bahnhof Enge, with well-equipped bedrooms.
Carlton Elite *SF* / *Bahnhofstr 41, CH-8001* ☎ *211 65 60* ⊤ₓ *812781 fax 211 30 19* • *AE DC MC V*. A good, quiet central hotel owned by UBS. Duplex apartments have terraces. Parking difficult.
Eden au Lac *SF* / *Utoquai 45, CH-8023* ☎ *261 94 04* ⊤ₓ *816339 fax 261 94 09* • *AE DC MC V*. A very conservative lakeside establishment with a good, formal restaurant (*hors-d'oeuvre chauds* are particularly recommended).
Schweizerhof *SF* / *Bahnhofpl 7, CH-8023* ☎ *211 86 40* ⊤ₓ *813754 fax 211 35 05* • *AE DC MC V*. Hotel near the station with refurbished, soundproofed rooms.
Seiler Neues Schloss *SF* / *Stockerstr 17, CH-8022* ☎ *201 65 50* ⊤ₓ *815560 fax 201 64 18* • *AE DC MC V*. Small hotel with calm, welcoming atmosphere and fresh decor. Le Jardin (☎ *201 65 77*) is popular for business lunches.
Splügenschloss *SF* / *Splügenstr 2, CH-8002* ☎ *201 08 00* ⊤ₓ *815553 fax 201 42 86* • *AE DC MC V*. Comfortable hotel in a quiet residential and business area. A modest member of the Relais et Châteaux group.
Waldhaus Dolder *SF* / *Kurhausstr 20, CH-8030* ☎ *251 93 60* ⊤ₓ *816460 fax 251 00 29* • *AE DC MC V*. Modern high-rise annex to the Dolder Grand, with indoor pool and sauna.

Out of town
The *Ermitage* ☎ *910 52 22* at Küsnacht (7kms/4 miles), is a small

---

Hotel and restaurant price guide
For the meanings of the hotel and restaurant price symbols, see pages 6 and 7.

---

country hotel with an excellent restaurant. At Schaffhausen is *Fischerzunft* ☎ (053) 25 32 81, a

charming small hotel on the banks of the Rhine about a 40min drive north of central Zürich.

Restaurants

Zürich executives usually take a two-hour lunch break, and it is normal to reserve a table for noon. The top restaurants are in the southeastern lakeside suburbs of Zollikon and Küsnacht, but the swankier establishments are often full of Japanese bankers, and most Zürcher discuss day-to-day business in less pretentious surroundings, perhaps in one of the guildhall restaurants. For a working lunch with top executives the best hotels provide a suitably formal setting (with service to match), but there is always a risk of encountering your competitors.

Most restaurants offer a daily special and/or a fixed-price lunch menu, although you may need to arrive early for these. Eating at the top restaurants is much more expensive in the evenings. *Kalbfleisch* or *Züricher Geschnetzelts*, chopped veal in a creamy sauce, served with *Rösti* (potato pancake), is Zürich's best-known dish and usually very good. It is always advisable to make reservations a few days in advance for the most exclusive restaurants.

Agnes Amberg *SF*/////
Hottingerstr 5 ☎ *251 26 26* • *closed Sat L, Mon L, Sun, 3 weeks Jul–Aug* • *AE DC MC V*
The doyenne of Zürich's famous cooking school also runs this chic, expensive restaurant. It is as suitable for business entertaining as it is for a pre-theatre meal. Stars of stage, screen and ski-slopes are among the regulars in the sophisticated grey-green salon, but at lunch there is a mainly business clientele, attracted by the *nouvelle cuisine*, the inexpensive set-price menu and the much more expensive "slim-line gourmet" menu. If you need more privacy for discussions, ask for a table near the entrance.

Baur au Lac *SF*////
Hôtel Baur au Lac ☎ *221 16 50* • *AE DC MC V* • *reservations essential*
The Baur au Lac is the classic venue for top-level business entertaining. Choose the elegant, candlelit Restaurant Français (open winter only) for formal or celebratory meals and the panelled, institutional Grill Room (with its own bar) for a quicker working lunch; the fixed-price lunch

and the *petit menu du gourmet* (three times as expensive) are popular here. In summer, take an aperitif on the terrace, looking out on the extensive park, then lunch or dine in the airy Pavillion. There is always someone from each of the "Big Three" banks lunching at the Baur au Lac, so it is not the place for a confidential banking deal.

Kronenhalle *SF*
Rämistr 4 ☎ *251 02 56* • *AE DC MC V* • *reservations essential*
A famous dining hall whose walls are lined with original works of art by 20thC European artists including Joan Miró, Picasso and Chagall. Ask for a table in the panelled main room (preferably not by the door where tourists are seated); the upstairs rooms are superficially smarter but less atmospheric. Veal sausage or *Züricher Geschnetzelts* with *Rösti* are a must, and the house wine is a good burgundy. For dessert choose the chocolate mousse *panache*. Expect motherly waitress service. The bar is frequented by Zürich's arty crowd, especially in the evenings, and by celebrities.

Piccoli Accademia *SF/*
Rotwandstr 48 ☎ *241 42 02* • *closed Sat, Sun, July* • AE DC MC V • *reservations essential*
The Piccoli Accademia has been a favourite with the local banking community for 60 years now, despite its not very appealing location, bland decor and uncomfortably close tables. Regulars come here for the bustling atmosphere, the cheerful service and the best Italian cooking in Zürich. The owner is a keen shot and game is recommended in season. The two or three daily dishes are wheeled around on the *carrello*.

Zum Storchen *SF/*
Hotel Zum Storchen ☎ *211 55 10* • AE DC MC V • *reservations essential*
The guildhall atmosphere and views overlooking the river make the Storchen a sensible choice for a not-too-formal meal with colleagues. It is popular with people in the watch, jewellery and precision instruments trades. The food is good rather than brilliant, but a terrace table in summer is a delightful place from which to see the river boats, and the hotel bar is comfortable.

OTHER RESTAURANTS

The panelled *Old Fashion*, Fraumünsterstr 15 ☎ 211 10 52, is a sound choice for a discreet meeting (it has two exits and used to be a haunt for spies); it is popular today with foreign exchange dealers.
Veltlinerkeller, Schlüsselgasse 8 ☎ 221 32 28, offers rich French and Swiss cooking with superb, straightforward service in ornate surroundings.
Jacky's Stapferstube, Culmannstr 45 ☎ 361 37 48, is small but not cramped and is known for its top-class meat. A relative newcomer to the culinary scene is *L'Hexagone*, Kuttelgasse 15 ☎ 211 94 11, where the conservatory, seasonal French cuisine and fine wines have attracted a chic crowd.

For an informal evening, try *Le Dézaley*, Römergasse 7 ☎ 251 61 29, a simple restaurant near the Grossmünster with a little summer courtyard serving Swiss food from the Vaud region, or the *Blaue Ente*, Seefeldstr 223 ☎ 55 77 06, located in the machinery room of an old mill.

Out of town

In the suburbs, but only a 10–15min taxi ride from the town centre, are two of Switzerland's best restaurants. *Chez Max*, Seestr 53, Zollikon ☎ 391 88 77, is phenomenally expensive, but the sober decor concentrates the mind on the daily *nouvelle* creations of chef Max Kehl (closed Sun & Mon). *Petermann's Kunststube*, Seestr 160 ☎ 910 07 15 at Küsnacht, is excellent and reasonable

> ### Guildhall restaurants
> Most of Zürich's former guildhalls, with medieval or baroque interiors, have taken on a new lease of life as restaurants. Inevitably they attract a tourist clientele, but they are also popular with locals. The following are among the best; and they take all the major credit cards.
> The small *Haus zum Rüden*, Limmatquai 42 ☎ 261 95 66, once used for assemblies of nobility, is now known for its French cuisine and Gothic interior. *Zunfthaus zur Saffran*, Limmatquai 54 ☎ 261 65 65 (the Spice Traders' and Bankers' Guild), which goes back to 1740 has attractive dining rooms overlooking the Limmat, but less good food. *Zunfthaus zur Waag*, Münsterhof 8 ☎ 211 07 30, a pretty 17thC house opposite the Fraumünster on the left bank, once the meeting place of the Hatters' Guild, is also useful for meetings.

> ### Changes in telephone numbers
> The 6-digit telephone numbers are in the process of changing to 7 digits.

value if you opt for the set lunch (closed Sat L, Mon).

More informal meals can be enjoyed at the *Ermitage* ☎ 910 52 22 also at Küsnacht, *Flühgasse* ☎ 53 12 15, 2kms/1 mile towards Zollikon in a half-timbered house (closed Sat & Sun), *Zum Rössli* ☎ 391 89 70 at Zollikon and *Buech* ☎ 915 10 10 at Herrliberg (3kms/ 2 miles), with tables on a terrace overlooking vineyards.

Clubs

The *Baur au Lac* club, in Villa Rosau (across the canal from the hotel), is an exclusive meeting place. There are about 500 members, mostly Swiss bankers and lawyers. It is chiefly used for business lunches, meetings and private parties (women admitted after 5pm). The *Savoy Club* at the Savoy Baur en Ville Hotel consists only of a bar/meeting room and is less prestigious. Hotel guests do not have automatic access to these clubs, but enquire about reciprocal memberships with clubs in various countries abroad.

Bars and cafés

The bars of the *Kronenhalle* and the *Old Fashion* (see *Restaurants*) are popular business rendezvous. Of the hotel bars the most frequented are the *Savoy* and the congenial *Zum Storchen*. The bar at the *Carlton Elite* attracts the expatriate British community.

The best cafés are *Sprüngli*, on Paradeplatz, and the tiny *Schober* in Napfgasse, on the right bank.

Entertainment

The free *Zürich News* has a regularly updated section on current events (and has advertisements for some of Zürich's naughtier nightspots). The central ticket office (*Billettzentrale*) is at Werdmühleplatz ☎ 221 22 83 open Mon–Fri, 10–6.30, Sat, 10–2.

Music There are regular concerts at the *Tonhalle*, Gotthardstr 5 ☎ 201 15 80 (excellent acoustics), and in churches.

Opera and dance Opernhaus, Falkenstr 1 ☎ 251 69 22/23, whose performances were once the envy of Wagner; recently refurbished.

Theatre Schauspielhaus, Rämistr 34 ☎ 251 11 11 is the main theatre which shows the German classics. *Theater am Neumarkt*, Neumarkt 5 ☎ 251 44 88 (contemporary and avant-garde), and the *Theater am Hechtplatz*, Hechtpl 7 ☎ 252 32 34 (cabarets and musicals), are among several other flourishing venues.

Cinema Films are usually shown with original soundtracks and subtitled. For programme information ☎ 122 or 123.

Nightclubs The smartest nightclub in town is *Diagonal* in the Villa Rosau, Baur au Lac Hotel. Hotel guests have automatic membership; temporary membership may be granted at the discretion of the management on less busy evenings (telephone first). Less exclusive are *Roxy*, Beatengasse 11 ☎ 211 54 57, a disco and restaurant for the young and fashionable, and the *Birdwatcher's Club*, Hotel Simplon, Schützengasse 16 ☎ 211 50 58, with a more middle-aged clientele. The entrance floor bar of the *Hotel Zürich* is a respectable late-night rendezvous, and there is sometimes good jazz at the bar at the *Nova Park*, Badenerstr 240. The *Limmatbar*, at Limmatquai 82, is popular with the "in" crowd.

Shopping

Bahnhofstrasse is one of Europe's most elegant shopping streets, and it has enticing shopfronts. The streets of the Old Town have many high-fashion boutiques and small antique or gift shops. Quality and prices in the most exclusive Zürich streets are very high, and purchases can usually be beautifully gift-wrapped. There are many specialist bookshops devoted to art, film, English and travel books. Last-minute shopping can be done at the airport for classic gifts: chocolates, Swiss army knives and watches. There is also a shopping centre at Oerlikon. Most shops are

open until 9pm on Thursdays.
Antiques are found in Neumarkt,
Kirchgasse and Rindermarkt.
Department stores Jelmoli in
Bahnhofstrasse (and at Oerlikon) is
the best traditional department store
in Switzerland and has a food
department worth seeing.
Fashion Furs, sportswear, hats and
silks are especially good. *Löw, Walter
Gross* and *Grieder* are among the big
names on Bahnhofstrasse. *Fogal* has
several branches. There are numerous
chic boutiques in the Old Town; try
Storchengasse.
Jewellery Gübelin, Bahnhofstr 36
(classic); *Gilbert Albert*, Bahnhofstr 10
(modern).
Leather goods Locher, Münsterhof
18–19 and Bahnhofstr 91; *Mädler*,
Bahnhofstr 26.
Silver Meister Silber, Bahnhofstr 28A.
Street market There is a flea-market
on Bürkliplatz (Saturdays, May–Oct).
Swiss army knives from *Dolmetsch* at
the station and elsewhere.
Toys There are two excellent shops:
Franz Carl Weber, Bahnhofstr 62,
claims to be the largest toyshop in
Europe; *Pastorini*, Weinpl 7, sells
toys in traditional materials.
Watches Türler, at Paradeplatz,
Storchengasse and the airport.

Sightseeing

In fine weather visitors should view
the city and mountains from
Felsenegg or Uetliberg or take a boat
trip on the lake.
Altstadt A stroll around the quaint
streets of the Old Town should
include seeing the *Augustinerkirche*,
Peterskirche (the oldest parish church
in the city, with the largest clockface
in Europe), the *Fraumünster* (windows
by Marc Chagall), and the baroque
guildhall *Zur Meisen* (see below). On
the right bank are the other
guildhalls, many now converted into
restaurants, and the fine baroque
Rathaus. The twin-towered
Grossmünster is a mighty landmark
with a fine if austere interior.
Kunsthaus Fine arts museum
specializing in 19th and 20thC art,

mainly but not exclusively Swiss
(notable sculptures by Alberto
Giacometti and paintings by Picasso
and Munch). Good temporary
exhibitions. *Heimpl 1. Open Mon 2–5;
Tue–Fri, 10–9; Sat & Sun 10–5.*
Schweizerisches Landesmuseum The
national museum of Swiss culture and
history, illustrated by artifacts,
sculpture, glass, furniture, ceramics,
weapons and gold and silver.
Museumstr 2. Open Tue–Sun, 2–5.
Wohnmuseum Museum of domestic
art in a pair of Zürich's fine mansions
from the 17th and 18th centuries.
*Bärengasse 22. Open Tue–Sun, 10–12,
2–5 (Sat until 6).*
Zunfthaus zur Meisen A collection of
18thC Zürich porcelain displayed in a
fine riverside baroque guildhall.
*Münsterhof 20. Open Tue–Sun, 10–12,
2–5 (Sat until 6).*

Less central, but well worth
visiting are the *E.G.Bührle Collection*,
Zollikerstr 172 (19th and 20thC
French and Old Master paintings,
open Tue & Fri, 2–5; first Fri in
month until 9pm) and the *Museum
Rietberg*, Gablerstr 15 (non-European
art from Africa and eastern Asia,
open Tue–Sun, 2–5; Wed until 9pm).

Guided tours

City tours by coach or by an
"electromobile" last about 2hrs and
are organized by the tourist office
☎ 211 40 00. Other guided visits are
from May or Jun to Sep or Oct only.
These include tours of Zürich and the
vicinity (2hrs 30mins) with a cablecar
ascent of the Felsenegg (792
metres/2,650ft; allow half a day) or a
boat trip on the lake, and walking
tours of the Old Town (about 2hrs
30mins).

Out of town

For fine views of the city and
mountains from the west the *Uetliberg*
(884 metres/2,900ft) can be reached
by railway from Zürich-Selnau
station. The baroque Benedictine
monastery at *Einsiedeln* (38kms/23.5
miles) is an hour's drive or train ride
south. Within comfortable day-trip

range are *Mount Rigi*, *Lucerne* and *Mount Säntis* (the highest mountain in eastern Switzerland, 1hr 30mins' drive). These and many other excursions are also available as guided tours. *Airtours* offers panoramic Alpine flights ☎ 814 26 20.

At *Winterthur* (25kms/15.5 miles north; 20mins by train) are the *Oskar Reinhart Collection* (famous collection of Old Masters and French Impressionists) and the *Oskar Reinhart Foundation* (Swiss, German and Austrian artists, 18th–20th centuries).

Spectator sports

Major sports events are held at the *Hallenstadion*, Wallisenstr 45 ☎ 311 30 30 (bicycle marathon in November). The main soccer teams – *Zürich* and *Hardturm* football club – play at the Hardturm (Hardturmstr 321 ☎ 272 33 88) and Letzigrund (Herdernstr 47 ☎ 491 23 33) stadiums. American football (the Zürich Renegades v. the Zürich Bay Bandits) also has a following.

Keeping fit

Health has been a preoccupation with the Swiss at least since the famous spa of Baden (24kms/15 miles northwest), the oldest in the country, was opened in 1847. Outdoor opportunities for keeping fit are abundant; for further information contact *Sportamt der Stadt Zürich* ☎ 491 23 33.

Fitness centres The *Atmos Club* at Hotel Zürich is open to nonresidents for a daily fee. *John Valentine*, Blaufahnenstr 3 ☎ 262 42 00. *Luxor*, Glärnischstr 35 ☎ 202 38 38 (monthly membership), for fitness equipment and squash.

Golf Dolder Golf Club, Kurhausstr 66 ☎ 47 50 45; *Golf and Country Club Zürich*, Zumikon ☎ 918 00 51.

Sailing Dinghies (and motor and rowing boats) can be rented along the Seefeldquai, Utoquai, Limmatquai and the Stadthuisquai.

Skiing The nearest skiing is at Flums (40mins) and Hoch-Ybrig. Flims or

Lachs (both about 1hr 30mins) offer more variety. Engelberg (1hr 15mins) is popular for glacier skiing.
St Moritz and Saas Fee are about 4hrs 30mins by car, longer by train. For cross-country skiing contact *Langlaufschule Albis* ☎ 710 86 97.

Squash Airgate Sports Center, Thurgauerstr 40 ☎ 302 40 50.

Swimming The *Waldhaus Dolder* and *Zürich* Hotels have pools. *Hallenbad City*, Sihlstr 71 ☎ 211 38 44 has an indoor pool. There are 17 public outdoor pools (at Enge, for instance, and along the lake).

Walking The hills around Zürich, notably the Hönggerberg and Zürichberg, provide splendid walking with marked *wanderweg* routes. The best views of the city and surroundings are from the top of the Rigi.

Local resources

Business services

International Office, Rennweg 32 ☎ 214 61 11, or *Executive Business Services*, Usteristr 23 ☎ 219 81 11, for offices and conference rooms, translation and secretarial services and advice on company formation.

Photocopying and printing OK *Kolb* ☎ 211 92 42. Photocopying can also be done in department stores and at the Hauptbahnhof.

Secretarial International Escorts Service ☎ 211 02 00; *Manpower* ☎ 241 25 25.

Translation Consultra ☎ 562 22 40; *Interserv* ☎ 463 49 00; *Jean-Paul Rochat* ☎ 910 58 41 (expensive). E.V.B. *Metropol* ☎ 221 32 14 (especially legal work).

Communications

Local delivery Kurier ☎ 252 66 66. The *PTT*'s own service is also useful.

Long-distance delivery DHL ☎ 363 62 66. *Federal Express* ☎ 311 33 66. *Swissair Parcel Express Service (SPEX)* ☎ 812 62 00. *Cosmotrans* ☎ 814 36 26 (fine art).

Post offices Sihlpost, Kasernenstr 95–99 ☎ 245 41 11 (main post office), open Mon–Fri, 6.30am–11pm;

Sat, 7.30–11; Sun, 9–11pm; the
Fraumünsterpost, Kappelergasse 1
and the Hauptbahnhof post office are
open the same hours.
Telex and fax Fraumünsterpost,
Kappelergasse 1 ☎ 22 13 50 (24hrs),
and at the central station and the
airport.

Conference/exhibition centres
The convention centre of the Zürich
tourist association ☎ 211 12 56 will
help organize conferences. The most
important venue is the renovated
Kongresshaus Zürich, Gotthardstr 5,
CH-8002 ☎ 201 66 88 (capacity up to
2,200). The *ZUSPA* trade fair and
exhibition halls are at *Messegelande*,
Thurgauerstr 7, Oerlikon
☎ 311 50 55 (capacity up to 4,500).

Emergencies
Bureaux de change At
Hauptbahnhof, open daily, 6.30–
11.30pm.
Hospitals Universitätsspital, Rämistr
100 ☎ 255 11 11. First aid ☎ 144.
Medical and dental emergencies
☎ 47 47 00. Ambulance
☎ 361 61 61.
Pharmacies Bellevue, Theaterstr 14
☎ 252 44 11, is open 24hrs. For
information on nearest pharmacies
☎ 111.
Police Emergency ☎ 117. City police
☎ 216 71 11. Central police station:
Bahnhofquai 3.

Information sources
*Business information Zürcher
Handelskammer* (chamber of
commerce), Bleicherweg 5, CH-8021
☎ 221 07 42, *Börsengebäude* (stock
exchange), Postfach 4031
☎ 229 21 11. *Schweizerischer Handels-
und Industrie-Verein* (Swiss Federation
of Commerce and Industry),
Börsenstr 26, CH-8001 ☎ 221 27 07.
The *Union Bank of Switzerland*,
Bahnhofstr 45 ☎ 234 11 11, has a
business library.
Local media The influential *Neue
Zürcher Zeitung* has a good reputation
for fair reporting; *Swiss Review of
World Affairs* is a monthly selection of
articles translated into English. *Bilanz*
and *Finanz und Wirtschaft* are
business periodicals. An edition of the
International Herald Tribune is printed
here.
Tourist information Zürich Tourist
Office, Bahnhofplatz 15 ☎ 211 40 00,
with offices at the airport. PTT
operates a tourist information service
☎ 111.

Thank-yous
Confectionery Teuscher, Storchengasse
9 (champagne truffles) or *Sprüngli* on
Paradeplatz and at the station (praline
gaufrettes, or wafers, *Luxembürgli*,
coloured meringues).
Florists Marsano ☎ 211 17 32;
Manfred Lacker ☎ 251 12 77 for
inspired bouquets.

UNITED KINGDOM

In the period 1950–80, the UK economy experienced sluggish growth, owing to low manufacturing output, high inflation and structural imbalances. The newly elected Conservative government's efforts to solve the nation's problems by economic reform and a tight monetary and fiscal policy were ill-timed as the world recession deepened. In 1980–81 GDP fell, manufacturing output fell further and unemployment reached record levels. Since 1982, however, growth rates have averaged nearly 3% a year (above the rate of many competitors) and since 1986 unemployment has fallen. Even so, a rise in inflation and growing trade deficit towards the end of the 1980s threatened long-term growth.

Manufacturing accounts for about 25% of GDP. Its share of GDP fell in the 1960s and 1970s, largely due to low productivity, poor management, stormy labour relations and a decline in international competitiveness. Worst affected were the traditional industries such as shipbuilding, textiles, steel and motor vehicle manufacturing. In the 1980s industry has been going through a period of rationalization and restructuring; total capacity was cut by about a sixth in the 1980–81 recession, and several state-owned companies such as British Telecom, British Gas, British Petroleum and British Steel have been privatized. Since 1982 output has grown by nearly 4% a year, due to higher productivity and better labour relations. The main growth areas are specialized chemicals, and electrical and electronic engineering.

The service sector has expanded to become the mainstay of the economy, accounting for about 55% of GDP and employing over 60% of the work force. The main activities are banking, insurance, finance, business services and leasing, retail and catering, and utilities. Agriculture, forestry and fishing account for less than 2% of GDP and employ less than 2% of the work force. But agricultural productivity is high and output provides about two-thirds of the country's total food needs.

The UK has the largest energy resources in Europe. It is a major producer of coal. Production of natural gas and oil from the North Sea began in 1967 and 1975 respectively and they have enabled the UK to become self-sufficient in energy in net terms since 1980. Although production is declining, the UK is one of the world's largest oil producers and exports have been of enormous benefit to the economy.

About 25% of GDP is derived from external trade. About half of total trade is conducted with other EC countries, principally West Germany and France. Machinery and transport equipment account for about 40% of export trade as well as an increasing percentage of import trade (20% in 1988). Petroleum exports accounted for about 20% of exports in 1985, but now account for about 7% of the total. The UK is a net importer of food and beverages. Oil exports helped offset the growing deficit on non-oil trade until the collapse of world oil prices in 1986. Since then the UK's current account has been in growing deficit.

The benefits of the new-found prosperity have not been distributed evenly across the UK. Northern Ireland, Scotland, the north of England

and the West Midlands, which previously relied on heavy industry for employment, have experienced high levels of unemployment. The south, which relies heavily on services and where much of the new industry is based, has continued to prosper. Towards the end of the 1980s there were signs of the beginning of a regeneration in the north but politically the country remains divided between the Conservative south and the Labour north.

Geography The UK consists of a large island and many small islands, forming Great Britain, and the northern part of the island of Ireland. It has a varied landscape. Scotland and Wales are mostly upland. England has uplands in the north and centre, which also contain the heavily industrialized areas. The most important lowland area is in the southeast, which contains intensively farmed areas and the highest density of population. Northern Ireland is mostly lowland. The long, indented coastline is dotted with major ports. A tunnel under the English Channel, due for completion in 1993, will provide the first rail link between the UK and mainland Europe.

Climate Britain has a mild and variable climate. Monthly average temperatures rise to 15°C (60°F) in summer and fall to 5°C (40°F) in winter. Winters tend to be harsher in Scotland, northern England, Scotland and Northern Ireland. Rainfall throughout the year.

Population 56.6m.

Government Britain is a parliamentary monarchy. There is no written constitution. The monarch's power is now largely advisory and ceremonial. Supreme legislative authority resides in Parliament.

Parliament is divided into 2 houses: the House of Commons has 650 members elected for 5 years from single-member constituencies; the much less powerful House of Lords, consists of hereditary and appointed life peers plus senior bishops of the Church of England.

Executive power lies with the prime minister, who is usually the leader of the majority party in the Commons. The prime minister chooses and presides over a Cabinet drawn mainly from the Commons.

The Conservatives won the general election in 1979 and Mrs Thatcher, the party leader, became the UK's first woman prime minister. Since then she and her party have dominated the political scene, winning re-election in 1983 and 1987.

The UK consists of England, Wales, Scotland and Northern Ireland. The last three countries have separate departments within government to deal with their affairs. The UK is highly centralized and local authorities have limited powers.

Currency The unit of currency is the pound sterling (£), which is divided into 100 pence.

The pound is allowed to float against other currencies. Increased trade with the EC has led to speculation that the UK may join the European Monetary System (EMS).

Time The UK is on Greenwich Mean Time (GMT). British Summer Time (BST) is in force from the end of Mar to the end of Sep; clocks are put forward, and the UK is then 1hr ahead of GMT.

Dialling codes The UK's IDD code is 44. Omit the initial 0 from the city code when dialling from abroad. To make an international call from the UK, dial 010 before dialling the relevant country code.

Public holidays Jan 1, Jan 2 (Scotland only), Good Fri, Easter Mon (not Scotland), first and last Mon in May, first Mon in Aug (Scotland only), last Mon in Aug (not Scotland), Dec 25, Dec 26.

LONDON

London has been a hub of world trade since the Industrial Revolution. It remains so, despite Britain's decline as a manufacturing nation. Every year 9m visitors arrive in the capital from overseas, around 3m of them on business. Not only is it the seat of government, but all major English financial institutions have their headquarters there and most large international corporations are represented as well. It is also the centre for the national media, and related businesses such as advertising and design. Companies based in other British cities find it essential to conduct much of their business in London. Close to 10m people live in the Metropolitan area.

As heavy industry has declined in the northern and western parts of the country, the southeast, with London at its heart, has become by far the most prosperous region in the UK – making the cost of commercial and residential property, as of much else, disproportionately high. London itself was once a manufacturing centre, but much of its prosperity now derives from the City, where millions of pounds a day change hands in the trading of stocks, currencies and commodities, as well as in merchant banking and insurance. The local authority for the City of London is a Corporation, dominated by business interests.

As international finance has grown more complex, the clubby, almost amateurish style of business that once prevailed in the City has given way to a high level of professional know-how. The capital's business environment has become more overtly competitive, and its inhabitants more single-minded and often more ruthless than their predecessors or their counterparts in other British cities. Time is money, and relaxed three-hour lunches have been replaced by the brisker working lunch and, increasingly, working breakfast.

In the last few years London has seen some other major changes. The Docklands area east of the City – once the commercial lifeline of the capital – has been redeveloped with Government backing and now houses some 2,000 businesses – including some light industry. It is also becoming an upmarket residential and leisure area, and has an airport and integrated public transport. The M25 motorway now circles the city; it is primarily a by-pass, but has created as many traffic problems as it has resolved. The Greater London Council has been abolished and some of its functions taken over by the borough councils which will set the new community charge or "poll tax" from April 1990.

Although London is Europe's largest capital, it avoids some of the excesses that make life so frenetic in other cities. Traffic is no longer any less chaotic, but voices are less often raised, and, despite recent changes, many of London's traditional virtues remain intact: the sense of solid permanence that derives from a 2,000-year history; the grandeur of historic areas such as Westminster and St James's; the parks, immaculate oases amid the urban maelstrom; the royal pageantry; the thriving live theatre. As a place to combine business with pleasure, few of the world's capitals can rival it.

Arriving

Most scheduled international and domestic flights arrive at Heathrow, 15 miles/24kms west of the capital. Some land at London's second airport, Gatwick, which deals mainly with holiday charter traffic, or at the new London City Airport, which opened in 1987. Journey times to the centre from both airports are similar. London also has excellent rail connections with other British cities.

Heathrow Airport

The world's busiest international airport has been undergoing redevelopment to try to cope with overcrowding. Changes to Terminal 3 were completed in late 1989.

Most European and intercontinental services, other than those of British Airways (BA), use Terminals 2 and 3 respectively. Both get extremely congested. Terminal 1 is used by domestic, UK–Ireland and some BA European flights, and crowds are much less of a problem. Terminal 4 is used by BA intercontinental flights, including Concorde, its Paris and Amsterdam services, and by Air Malta, NLM and KLM. Passengers with connecting flights find its location, away from the other three terminals, rather inconvenient. Free inter-terminal buses run every ten minutes or so; Terminals 1–3 are also connected to each other by moving walkways, and to Terminal 4 by London's subway system, the Underground.

Because of the volume of traffic, it is wise to allow for landing delays. Be prepared for a long walk from the landing bay to immigration control (only the most distant gates have moving walkways); no trolleys are available until the baggage reclaim. EC passport holders should clear immigration quickly, but other visitors, especially those on long-haul flights, can experience long delays. Only those with goods to declare or who are stopped will spend much time clearing customs. If all goes well and you have only hand baggage, you can be out of the airport in less than 30mins; but it is best to reckon on 45–60mins. The exit from customs into the main concourse of each terminal is the most convenient meeting place, but can be chaotically crowded.

If transferring to Gatwick Airport, there are several bus services. Speedlink buses depart from all terminals from 6.20am to 10.40pm, leaving every 15mins during the main part of the day, and every 30–60mins at other times. The journey takes about an hour. The cheaper, slightly slower Jetlink service leaves from the central bus station (linked by walkways to Terminals 1–3) every 30mins from 4.30am to 10.30pm, then at 12.30am and 2.30am.

Facilities Heathrow's duty-free and other shops offer a particularly wide range of goods. There are restaurants, bars, 24hr buffets, telephones and information desks in all terminals. Many airlines have private lounges. There is a business centre ☎ 759 2434 in Terminal 2 which offers a range of office and secretarial facilities; meeting rooms can be rented by the hour (there are also BT fax centres airside in Terminals 3 and 4). There are banks in each terminal, open daily, from around 6.30–7am to around 11–11.30pm; the Barclays branch in Terminal 3 arrivals is open 24 hours. The post office in Terminal 2 is open Mon–Sat, 8.30–6, Sun and hols, 9–1. Each terminal has a left luggage office, open around 5–6.45am to around 11–11.30pm. There is a lost property office ☎ 745 7727 in car park 2, opposite Terminal 2. There are expensive short-term multistoried parking areas opposite each terminal; long-term parking areas on the north side of the airport (worth using even if you are returning that day) are linked to each terminal by free buses.

Airline telephone numbers for flight inquiries are listed in the telephone directory under BAA. Air freight inquiries ☎ 745 7897.

Nearby hotels Excelsior, Bath Rd, West Drayton, Mddx UB7 0DU

☎ 759 6611 ☒ 24525 fax 759 3421 •
THF • AE DC MC V. *Holiday Inn*,
Stockley Rd, West Drayton, Mddx
UB7 9NA ☎ (0895) 445555
☒ 934518 fax 445 122 • AE DC MC V.
Post House, Sipson Rd, West
Drayton, Mddx UB7 0JU
☎ 759 2323 ☒ 934280 fax 897 8659
• THF • AE DC MC V. *Sheraton Skyline*,
Bath Rd, Hayes, Mddx UB3 5BP
☎ 759 2535 fax 750 9150 • AE DC MC
V.

City link The London Underground
is usually the quickest as well as the
cheapest way to get into the centre.
Cabs are best avoided if you can cope
with your baggage, particularly at
rush hour when the M4 motorway
into London gets very congested.
Subway There are two Piccadilly Line
stations, one at Terminal 4, the other
linked to Terminals 1–3 by moving
walkways. Trains leave every
3–7mins, 5am–11.30pm approx
(about 45mins to central London).
Baggage storage is inconvenient.
Taxi There is a rank for licensed
black cabs outside each terminal. For
all destinations within the
Metropolitan Police district (which
covers central London and most of
Greater London), the fare is metered
and, unless you are going further
than 20 miles/32kms, the driver is
legally obliged to take you. For
destinations outside the Metropolitan
Police district, you must agree the
fare in advance. A taxi ride into
central London will cost upwards of
£20, and take about an hour.
Bus Two express services into central
London (to Victoria and Euston
stations, with other stops en route)
stop at Airbus pick-up points at each
terminal, every 20–30mins,
6am–3pm, then every 30–60mins
until around 10pm. Allow at least
1hr.
Car rental Driving and parking in
London are fraught with problems,
and so car rental is sensible only if
you have to go outside the Greater
London area. Four rental firms have
desks in each terminal: Avis ☎ 897
9321, Budget ☎ 759 2216, Europcar

☎ 897 0811 and Hertz ☎ 897 3347.
Chauffeur-driven cars available.

Gatwick Airport
There can be advantages in arriving
at Gatwick: procedures take less time
and the rail link to Victoria is quicker
than the Underground from
Heathrow. But be prepared for some
congestion from package holiday
flights, particularly on Fridays and at
weekends in summer. Allow at least
15–20mins from disembarkation to
clear immigration and customs;
non-EC passport holders may take
longer. Some airlines including BA,
Air France and Lufthansa use the
North Terminal. There are meeting
points in both arrivals concourses.

If transferring to Heathrow, there
are two bus services, Speedlink
(6am–10pm) and Jetlink
(12.05am–11.05pm); departures at
same intervals as listed for Heathrow.
Facilities Landside facilities in both
terminals include 24hr restaurants,
bars, coffee shops, information desks
and shops (most open 7–10pm). The
main, 24hr duty-free shops sell an
extensive range of goods. There are
24hr banking facilities and post
offices, open Mon–Fri, 9–5.30, Sat,
9–1 in the South Terminal. The 24hr
left luggage office is on the arrivals
concourse. The lost property office
☎ (0293) 503162 is open 8.30–6.
Inquiries ☎ (0293) 28822.
*Nearby hotels Gatwick Hilton
International*, Gatwick Airport, West
Sussex RH6 0LL ☎ (0293) 518080
☒ 877021 fax 28980 • AE DC MC V.
linked to airport by covered walkway.
Gatwick Penta, Povey Cross Rd,
Horley, Surrey RH6 0BE
☎ (0293) 820169 ☒ 87440
fax 820 259 • AE DC MC V. *Post House*,
Povey Cross Rd, Horley, Surrey RH6
0BA ☎ (0293) 771621 ☒ 877351
fax 771 054 • THF • AE DC MC V.
City link The quickest way into
central London is by train. Taxis,
which are very expensive, and express
bus services can get caught up in
heavy traffic and are not
recommended.

Train The station is within the airport. Express trains to Victoria station – journey time 30mins – depart every 15mins from 6.20am to 10.50pm, hourly through the night. Trains also run to London Bridge station half-hourly until 11.50pm; journey time 30mins. Other services connect with the Midlands and the northwest.

Car rental If your business is in London, this is generally inadvisable. Avis ☎ (0293) 29721, Europcar ☎ (0293) 31062, Hertz ☎ (0293) 30555 and Kenning ☎ (0293) 514822 all have desks; reservation is recommended.

London City Airport

London City Airport offers regular daily flights to Paris, Brussels and Amsterdam. It is primarily designed for business travellers and has fast check-in and immigration procedures. Facilities include a bureau de change, restaurant, post office, newsstand and duty-free shop. There is a very efficient business and conference centre. Inquiries ☎ 474 5555.

City Link The airport is 6 miles/9.6kms from the city. Taxis are available (and can be reserved on incoming aircraft). Alternatively take the airport river bus (hourly departures) stopping at Swan Lane Pier (London Bridge Station) and Charing Cross Pier (Embankment Station) – journey time 35mins.

Railway stations

London's eight main termini circle the central area. All are on the London Underground, and several are linked by the Circle line. All have restaurants, snack stalls, bars, newsstands, bookshops, information desks and public telephones. King's Cross and Euston have Pullman lounges. Allow extra time to buy your ticket, particularly at rush hours. Do not rely on broadcast announcements of train departures and arrivals, which are unpredictable and sometimes inaudible; the information board is generally reliable. All stations have a taxi rank, though demand for cabs may exceed supply at rush hours.

Charing Cross ☎ 928 5100 Southern region terminus, serving southeastern suburbs and Kent. On Bakerloo, Jubilee and Northern subway lines; and nearby Embankment station is on Circle and District subway lines.

Euston ☎ 387 7070 London Midland region terminus (Birmingham, Liverpool, Manchester, Glasgow). On Northern and Victoria subway lines; and nearby Euston Square station is on Circle and Metropolitan lines.

King's Cross ☎ 278 2477 Eastern region terminus for long-distance trains from the north (Edinburgh, Newcastle, Leeds, Aberdeen). On Circle, Metropolitan, Northern, Piccadilly and Victoria subway lines.

Liverpool Street ☎ 928 5100 Awkwardly organized terminus of Eastern region for trains from East Anglia. On Central, Circle and Metropolitan subway lines.

Paddington ☎ 262 6767 Chief terminus of Western region. On Bakerloo, Circle, District and Metropolitan subway lines.

St Pancras ☎ 387 7070 London Midland terminus for services from northern suburbs and Midland cities including Sheffield. Shares subway links with King's Cross.

Victoria ☎ 928 5100 Main West End terminus of Southern region (Channel port services). On Circle, District and Victoria subway lines.

Waterloo ☎ 928 5100 Chief terminus of Southern region for trains from southwest. On Bakerloo and Northern subway lines.

Getting around

Within central London and during the working day, the best way to get around is to take the Underground or "tube," as the subway system is known, or, if the distance is short, to walk. Taxis are more comfortable and convenient, but they are relatively expensive and journey times are difficult to calculate because of heavy traffic. Driving yourself around

London is not recommended; congested roads, parking problems and a complicated street layout make it both tiring and time-consuming. A street guide is useful and sometimes essential; *London A to Z* can be bought from most newsstands.

Subway The nine interconnecting lines of the London Underground cover most parts of the centre and immediate suburbs, though services to the south and southeast of the Thames are more patchy. The Docklands Light Railway is connected to the underground. A free map of the system is available from ticket offices. Stations, identified by the Underground symbol (a red circle bisected by a blue horizontal line), are usually within a 10min walk in central London. Trains run every day, from around 5.30am (7.30am Sun) to around midnight. Frequency varies between a few minutes during rush hours on busy main lines to as much as 20mins on branch lines or at off-peak times. Trains and stations are usually fairly clean though, in rush hours, they tend to be unpleasantly overcrowded. Smoking is forbidden in all carriages and stations. Pick-pocketing is on the increase but in general the Underground is safe to use.

Tickets must be bought at the start of a journey, from the station ticket office or from automatic machines that take coins (some also take £5 notes). Always retain your ticket, which must be surrendered at your destination. Return tickets save time but not money. If making several journeys a day, consider buying a special daily (or weekly) pass.

Walking Most of central London is very safe. But if you are on your own after dark, it is sensible to stick to busy, well-lit roads and to avoid pedestrian subways and parks.

Taxis London's taxi drivers are licensed only after they have passed "the knowledge," a fairly stringent test of their familiarity with the city. They are generally helpful and friendly. Licensed black cabs can be hailed on the street, but do not rely on being able to find one immediately, particularly in rush hours, bad weather or late at night. The rail stations all have taxi ranks; or telephone *Dial-a-Cab* ☎ 253 5000, *Computer Cab* ☎ 286 0286 or *Mountview* ☎ 272 3030. A taxi is available if its yellow "for hire" sign is lit. If it stops to accept your fare, it will usually agree to take you (and is legally obliged to do so unless your destination is more than 6 miles/9.6kms away). Fares within the Metropolitan Police district (most of Greater London, including Heathrow) are metered; otherwise, agree the price in advance. There is a minimum fare, and small extra charges are made for each additional passenger, for baggage stowed separately, and for journeys between midnight and 6am. When paying, add a tip of around 10%. There is a taxi lost property office (personal callers only) at 15 Penton St, NW1.

As well as licensed black cabs, there are many firms offering a telephone reservation service for unlicensed mini-cabs. It is inadvisable to use one without recommendation, as many are unreliable. Good mini-cab firms can be useful for journeys late at night or outside the centre. Always get a quote when you call the firm and allow plenty of time.

Limousines Top London hotels use *Camelot Barthropp* ☎ 235 0234, *Renown* ☎ 262 5428 and *Guy Salmon* ☎ 408 1255.

Bus Maps of the complicated bus system are available from Underground stations. Bus stops indicate the identifying numbers of buses that stop there, and many carry a timetable (not to be relied on) which also indicates the main stops along each route. In rush hours buses get full and you may have to wait some time.

River Bus An express riverbus service between Chelsea Harbour and West India Pier (with 4 intermediate stops) operates at 20min intervals. It is fun but of limited convenience.

Area by area

Modern central London has three
focal points: the West End, with its
fine shops and restaurants and nearly
all the major hotels; the financial area
known as the City (site of the original
Roman settlement) with its extension,
Docklands; and between them
Westminster, headquarters of the
government. To the immediate west
of the centre, Kensington, Chelsea
and Bayswater are thriving residential
and commercial areas; to the north,
strung along the busy Euston and
Marylebone roads, are several of
London's main railway stations as
well as large office developments. All
these are north of the Thames;
although riverside commercial
development is accelerating, there is
still comparatively little south of the
Thames to attract the attention of
most business visitors.

The City (map 1)

The square mile where London
began, known simply as the City, has
always set itself apart from the rest of
the Metropolitan area – even the

police wear slightly different
uniforms. It has remained the heart
of the nation's commerce despite
rapid changes in both its appearance
and the way its business is done.

Dominated by the Stock Exchange
and the Bank of England, the City is
the province of international bankers,
accountants, stock, commodity and
insurance brokers, commercial
lawyers and subsidiary members of
the financial community. All the
English clearing banks have their
headquarters here, but they are
outnumbered by hundreds of overseas
bank branches.

During working hours the narrow,
winding streets, tracing the plan of
the medieval town, bustle with dark-
suited businessmen (business women
are noticeably in a minority) and
couriers. The warrens of dark
Victorian buildings are gradually
making way for modern office towers
wired for today's technology.

Appropriately, the hub of the City
is the Bank of England, or more
precisely the busy Underground
station called Bank. It is at a

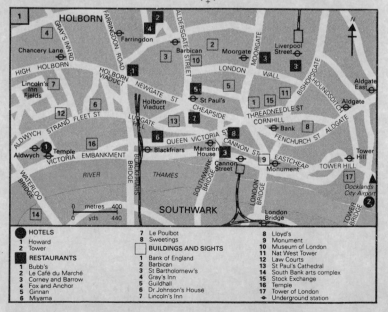

HOTELS		RESTAURANTS	BUILDINGS AND SIGHTS
1 Howard	7 Le Poulbot	1 Bubb's	1 Bank of England
2 Tower	8 Sweetings	2 Le Café du Marché	2 Barbican

HOTELS
1 Howard
2 Tower

RESTAURANTS
1 Bubb's
2 Le Café du Marché
3 Corney and Barrow
4 Fox and Anchor
5 Ginnan
6 Miyama
7 Le Poulbot
8 Sweetings

BUILDINGS AND SIGHTS
1 Bank of England
2 Barbican
3 St Bartholomew's
4 Gray's Inn
5 Guildhall
6 Dr Johnson's House
7 Lincoln's Inn
8 Lloyd's
9 Monument
10 Museum of London
11 Nat West Tower
12 Law Courts
13 St Paul's Cathedral
14 South Bank arts complex
15 Stock Exchange
16 Temple
17 Tower of London
⊖ Underground station

confusing junction of seven streets, dominated on its north side by the Bank's forbidding wall, on its east by the colonnaded Victorian Royal Exchange (now to be redeveloped) and on the south by the Corinthian pillars of the 18thC Mansion House. This is the traditional home of London's Lord Mayor, head of the Corporation of London – the City's powerful administering authority based at Guildhall.

The Stock Exchange, rebuilt in the 1960s, is along Threadneedle Street. A little further on, the National Westminster tower, London's tallest building and headquarters of the banking group, has become the focal point for redevelopment around Liverpool Street Station, the terminus for eastern England. The City's most controversial modern building, Richard Rogers' headquarters for the Lloyd's insurance group, is on Lime Street.

At evenings and weekends the centre of the City is eerily deserted. Hardly anyone lives there. The restaurants catering to business lunchers are not open for dinner and most of the pubs have closed by 8pm. The sole residential section within the square mile is the Barbican, near fragments of the northern stretch of the Roman wall. This extensive 1960s development includes a concert hall, a theatre (home of the Royal Shakespeare Company) and a conference centre.

West of the Bank stands St Paul's Cathedral, its splendid dome now partly obscured by tall buildings. Down Ludgate Hill from the Cathedral is the Old Bailey, at the end of which stands London's main criminal court. The neo-Gothic civil law courts are on the Strand, just outside the City boundary. Across the road are Inner and Middle Temple, self-contained clusters of law offices around two charming greens. St Bride's Church, tucked away off Fleet Street, is one of Sir Christopher Wren's finest.

Fleet Street, once the home of the national newspaper industry, has been deserted in favour of modern publishing centres, many in the abandoned dockyards downstream from Tower Bridge. The move began in 1986, when four titles moved to Wapping, just east of one of the capital's main tourist attractions, the Tower of London. Hard by is St Katharine's Dock, now a marina and leisure area. Beyond is the Isle of Dogs, with the Canary wharf financial centre. Once tough and unsalubrious, *Docklands* is becoming an expensive residential district, its old warehouses now converted into luxury apartments.

Around the edges of the City are the remains of enclaves once devoted to distinctive types of commerce. North of the Tower, Aldgate and Whitechapel were centres of the clothing trade, with a mainly Jewish population. With Stepney, they constitute the *East End*, traditionally the most impoverished area of London. Today, they accommodate many Asian merchants. Clerkenwell has many small printing companies and typesetters, while Hatton Garden is the centre of the capital's jewellery trade. Smithfield, known for its wholesale meat market, lies alongside St Bartholomew's, the City's oldest, most charming church.

The West End (*maps 2 and 3*)
The postal district W1, the heart of the West End, embraces the best addresses in London, including the finest hotels, the most prestigious offices and the most expensive apartments. Park Lane sets the tone. Running from Marble Arch to Hyde Park Corner, along the eastern edge of the park, its grand hotels are interspersed with the offices of financial institutions that prefer this plush, discreet atmosphere to the more frenetic, enclosed world of the City. Chauffeur-driven limousines are commonplace, and this area attracts many of London's wealthiest visitors.

The aura of wealth is sustained as you move east of Park Lane into the narrow streets of *Mayfair*, where high property values have forced the conversion of many opulent houses into offices for concerns that require a distinguished profile, such as public relations consultancies, financial services, lawyers, embassies and consulates. The United States Embassy occupies a squat, forbidding building on the west side of Grosvenor Square.

Mayfair is enclosed on its other sides by three of the capital's most famous streets: Piccadilly, Regent Street and Oxford Street. Piccadilly's reputation as London's liveliest thoroughfare is no longer deserved. East from Hyde Park Corner, it starts with a series of undistinguished buildings overlooking Green Park. Then come one of London's grandest hotels, the Ritz, and the vestiges of the capital's most exclusive shopping district, of which Fortnum & Mason's is an increasingly isolated survivor amid airline offices and national tourist bureaux. Behind Fortnum's, Jermyn Street contains small shops specializing in men's shirts and shoes.

Bond Street, connecting Piccadilly with Regent Street, is a good choice for serious shopping, especially for women's fashion, jewellery, art and antiques. In nearby Savile Row, several bespoke tailors, their number diminished by steep rents, uphold the traditions that have made the street synonymous with the finest in men's tailoring. Larger men's stores are on Regent Street, a wide, curving thoroughfare linking Piccadilly Circus and Oxford Circus. Here, as in Piccadilly, the travel industry is much in evidence. West to Marble Arch, Oxford Street is lined with London's best-known department and chain stores.

North of Oxford Circus, on Langham Place, is the Art Deco headquarters of the British Broadcasting Corporation. To its east, a cramped garment manufacturing district supplies many Oxford Street stores and keeps the streets choked all day with delivery vehicles. Further

east, Charlotte Street is the home of Channel 4 television and a number of advertising agencies. Tottenham Court Road, parallel with it, is lined with electronics shops selling video and audio equipment, computers and their components. Nearby *Soho* is an area of narrow streets and alleys where for years some of London's best restaurants have cohabited with the gaudiest aspects of its sex industry. Strip clubs, peep shows and "encounter" bars set traps for the gullible, but recently the area's reputation has enjoyed a revival with the opening of several bars and restaurants attracting a fashion-conscious, mainly young clientele, many of them from the media world.

Wardour Street, running south from Oxford Street, is the headquarters of the film production and distribution industry. In the surrounding warren of streets a colony of small independent television production houses has been established, along with video and sound recording studios. Artists' agents and others that feed off the entertainment industry have moved in with them. Wardour Street stretches south into *Chinatown*: fanning out from Gerrard Street, this colourful and aromatic neighbourhood has taken over the southeastern part of Soho.

The live theatre district is split in two. One part is centred on Shaftesbury Avenue, northeast of Piccadilly Circus, and extends south into Haymarket – also the home of the Design Centre and the main London office of American Express. The other is at the eastern end of the Strand, near its junction with Aldwych. The National Theatre and the rest of the *South Bank* entertainment complex, stark in grey concrete, is across Waterloo Bridge. To its east, the Shell Centre, the skyscraper headquarters of the international oil company, faces Waterloo station.

Back across the river at the other end of the Strand is Charing Cross

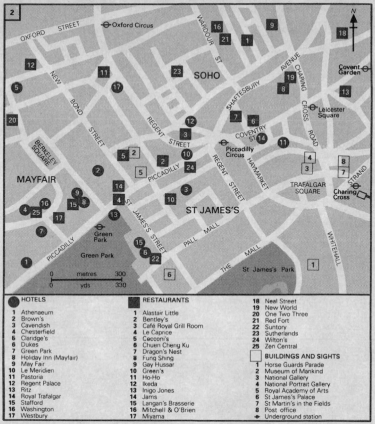

N

2

OXFORD STREET — Oxford Circus

WARDOUR ST.

16
21 1
9
18

12
11
23
SOHO

5
17

SHAFTESBURY AVENUE
CHARING CROSS ROAD

19
8

Covent Garden

20

NEW BOND STREET
REGENT STREET
BERKELEY SQUARE

7 6
COVENTRY ST
14
11

13

Leicester Square

12
3
10
Piccadilly Circus

MAYFAIR

5 2
2
5
PICCADILLY
24

HAYMARKET
REGENT STREET

4
3
8
7

14
3
10
TRAFALGAR SQUARE

Charing Cross

9
16
15 8
4
ST JAMES'S STREET

4
25
17
13
ST JAMES'S

7
Green Park

15

PICCADILLY
Green Park
PALL MALL

6
22

WHITEHALL

6

THE MALL
St James's Park
1

0 metres 300
0 yds 330

HOTELS		RESTAURANTS		18	Neal Street
1	Athenaeum	1	Alastair Little	19	New World
2	Brown's	2	Bentley's	20	One Two Three
3	Cavendish	3	Café Royal Grill Room	21	Red Fort
4	Chesterfield	4	Le Caprice	22	Suntory
5	Claridge's	5	Cecconi's	23	Sutherlands
6	Dukes	6	Chuen Cheng Ku	24	Wilton's
7	Green Park	7	Dragon's Nest	25	Zen Central
8	Holiday Inn (Mayfair)	8	Fung Shing		
9	May Fair	9	Gay Hussar		**BUILDINGS AND SIGHTS**
10	Le Meridien	10	Green's	1	Horse Guards Parade
11	Pastoria	11	Ho-Ho	2	Museum of Mankind
12	Regent Palace	12	Ikeda	3	National Gallery
13	Ritz	13	Inigo Jones	4	National Portrait Gallery
14	Royal Trafalgar	14	Jams	5	Royal Academy of Arts
15	Stafford	15	Langan's Brasserie	6	St James's Palace
16	Washington	16	Mitchell & O'Brien	7	St Martin's in the Fields
17	Westbury	17	Miyama	8	Post office
				—	Underground station

Station. To its north, the shell of the former *Covent Garden* wholesale vegetable market (now housed south of the river, at Vauxhall) has been converted into a pleasing precinct of restaurants, shops and museums, justly popular with tourists. At the centre is Inigo Jones' handsome St Paul's Church. A number of book publishers, design houses and the ubiquitous advertising agents have established themselves here since the market moved. The largest concentration of publishers is around Bedford Square in *Bloomsbury*, near the British Museum, but, as more are absorbed into conglomerates, they leave their atmospheric offices in these traditional areas and move to more efficient premises. As for bookshops, Charing Cross Road still boasts a substantial number, though fewer than in the past.

Westminster and Victoria *(map 3)*
The neo-Gothic Parliament buildings at Westminster are surrounded by extensive offices housing the great departments of state. Nearby St James's Park is a popular place for a lunchtime stroll. Civil service mandarins are more likely to be found at their clubs in and around Pall Mall. An invitation to one of these is a prized indication of acceptance into the highest circles. (See also *Clubs*.)

Trafalgar Square is an incoherent

public space dominated by traffic and the 170ft Nelson's Column. It is linked to Westminster by Whitehall, which contains Inigo Jones' stately Banqueting House and government offices. In Victoria Street, running west from Westminster Abbey, modern blocks house the Department of Trade, and ministries, and the Queen Elizabeth II conference centre. At the far end, Victoria Station is the rail terminus for the south coast. Between Victoria and Knightsbridge is Belgravia, almost equal to Mayfair as a centre of luxury homes and embassies.

Facing Green Park and St James's Park is the Queen's London home, Buckingham Palace, where the daily changing of the guard is a popular spectacle with visitors. The Mall, paved in red and fringed with green verges, provides a regal approach to the palace. Northeast of it, the older *St James's Palace* gives its name to an appropriately stylish, elegant neighbourhood.

North London *(map 3)*

Euston Road and its western extension Marylebone Road form the northern boundary of Central London. Constantly jammed with through traffic fed from the Oxford motorway, as well as vehicles making for the main-line railway stations, this is an unattractive stretch of road, redeemed only by the proximity of Regent's Park and the splendid early-18thC terraces, designed by Nash, adjacent to it.

King's Cross, St Pancras and Euston stations, grouped within a few hundred paces of one another, together handle main-line trains between London and the Midlands, the North of England and Scotland. Consequently dozens of small, cheap hotels, some poorly maintained, were established in the surrounding streets. St Pancras, the least used of the three stations, is the most striking architecturally, a red-brick neo-Gothic extravaganza designed by Sir Gilbert Scott. Further west, in Marylebone

Road, are two smaller stations, Marylebone and Baker Street, used by commuters to the northwestern suburbs. Paddington, the terminus for Wales and the West Country, is further on again, beyond bustling Edgware Road.

No doubt because of its proximity to main-line stations, Marylebone Road has been selected for corporate headquarters by a number of companies with business interests across the country. British Rail and the British Waterways Board have their head offices there, as do the chain stores Woolworth's and British Home Stores. Marks & Spencer's buying and administrative office is nearby, on Baker Street, famous as the fictional home of the great detective, Sherlock Holmes. At the top end of Baker Street, across Marylebone Road, the London Business School occupies an imposing site on the edge of Regent's Park. To the north of the park runs Regent's Canal, once an important commercial link with the north but now used for pleasure.

Further east, past Madame Tussaud's waxworks and the Royal Academy of Music, Harley Street and Devonshire Place run into Marylebone Road from the south. These attractive Queen Anne terraces, and those in Wimpole Street (the southern extension of Devonshire Place), house scores of Britain's leading medical specialists and private clinics.

East again, and the quiet, ordered atmosphere quickly changes at Great Portland Street – once a centre of the retail motor trade and still containing a few showrooms for high-priced sports cars, limousines and imported models. Euston Road begins here, with, on its north side, the Euston Centre, a modern office development containing the headquarters of Thames Television and Capital Radio, commercial stations serving the London area. Just south of here and west of Tottenham Court Road, some independent television production

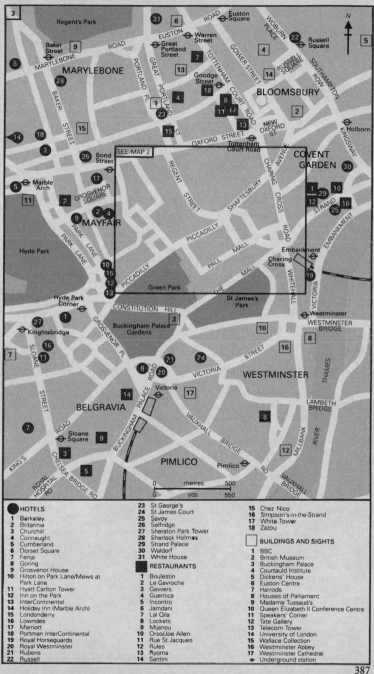

N

3
Regent's Park

ROAD   Euston   **31** **6**
EUSTON   Square
Baker   **9**   Warren
Street   Great   Street
MARYLEBONE   Portland   **7**
ROAD   Street   **13**
MARYLEBONE   Goodge
6   **28**   Street   **18**
Great Portland St

22 Russell
Square   **5**

4

14   BLOOMSBURY   **2**

4

8 Holborn

14 **18**   **15**   **15**   **5**   **46**   **23**   **11**   **7/**   NEW OXFORD ST
3   **26** Bond   OXFORD STREET   **13**   **73**
Street   Tottenham
SEE MAP 2   Court Road
COVENT
GARDEN   **30**

Marble   **17**
5 Arch   **1** **29** **10**
11   GROSVENOR   **12**   **16**
2   SQUARE   **25**
9 MAYFAIR   **2** **4**

Hyde Park   PARK LANE

10
15
12
13
PICCADILLY   Green Park   Embankment
Charing
Cross
19
Hyde Park   St James's
Corner   **1**   Park   Westminster
27   **3**   WESTMINSTER
Knightsbridge   Buckingham Palace   BRIDGE
Gardens   **10**   **8**
16

7   **16**
11   **21** **24**   **16**   WESTMINSTER

8 **20**   VICTORIA   **8**
BELGRAVIA   **14** Victoria   **17**   LAMBETH
BRIDGE
Sloane   **8**
7   Square   **9**
3   **12**
5   PIMLICO   Pimlico   **12**

metres   500
yds   550

companies have spread north from Soho, in the shadow of the tall Telecom Tower (formerly Post Office Tower), a key element in the nation's telecommunications network.

On the other side of Tottenham Court Road, behind the smart furniture store, Heal's, is the University of London complex – a confusing patchwork of grey, severe buildings of uncompromisingly institutional appearance. Close by is University College hospital, one of several medical centres in this area.

Chelsea, Kensington, Bayswater (map 4)

Chelsea was once raffish and Bohemian. Artists lived around Cheyne Walk for the river views, and were joined by poets and writers. The enterprising Royal Court Theatre, on Sloane Square, is a vigorous but isolated reminder of the literary tradition. In the 1960s, the King's Road, running west from Sloane Square, became the heart of "swinging London." Fashion boutiques, trendy restaurants and wine bars sprang up all along it, side by side with the antique shops. A few of the low Victorian shops and houses have been pulled down to make way for office buildings – generally for new and enterprising companies that hope, once established, to move to more prestigious addresses in the West End. But the King's Road is still a lively focus of fashion. Today Chelsea is an expensive address, the traditional habitat of the "Sloane Ranger." The new Chelsea Harbour development (with riverbus services to the city) has once again shifted attention to the river. The Chelsea Flower Show, an annual social and horticultural event is held at the Royal Hospital between Sloane Square and the river in late May.

North of the King's Road are the southern reaches of *Kensington*, an extensive jumble of terraced houses, mansion flats and hotels covering the architectural styles of the last 150 years. Kensington High Street is a useful alternative to Oxford Street for shopping, with branches of many of the same chain stores and one department store, as well as the inevitable office buildings.

Knightsbridge, the eastern extension of the High Street, remains one of London's most fashionable addresses, both commercial and residential, partly because of its proximity to the renowned department store, Harrods, in the adjoining Brompton Road. Shoppers crowd the main streets by day, and later the area is kept busy by its variety of restaurants, hotels and nightclubs. North of the green expanse of Kensington Gardens is *Bayswater*, where the flats and hotels, shops and offices are generally a notch or two less smart than in Kensington. It is London's most cosmopolitan area, teeming with young people from overseas on English language courses or working in the hotel and catering industries. Queensway, Bayswater's central street, is by night a lively and colourful spot.

To the west, *Notting Hill* and *Holland Park* were among the first inner-city areas to be "gentrified." Run-down rooming houses were bought by middle-class couples and refurbished to become family homes. Although Notting Hill still stages a Caribbean carnival every August, many immigrants have been priced out of the area. Much the same is happening in *Earl's Court*, to the south, the site of the capital's largest exhibition centre.

The suburbs

Fast train services mean that London's dormitory areas stretch 60 miles/95kms and more from the centre, taking in towns such as Cambridge to the east, Eastbourne to the south, Oxford to the west and Rugby to the north. In the intervening hinterland are suburbs whose convenience and desirability vary according to no easily definable pattern.

The residential districts close to

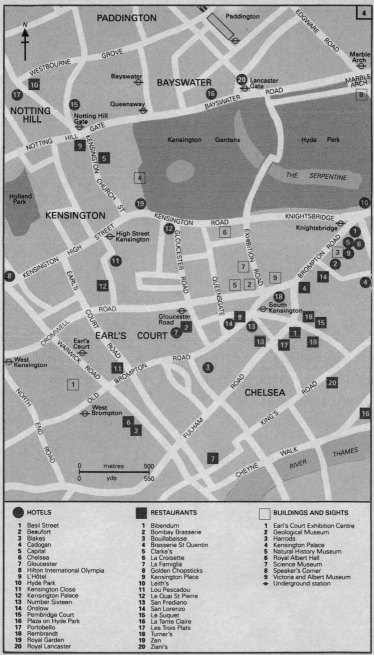

Map labels

PADDINGTON
Paddington
EDGWARE ROAD
Marble Arch
WESTBOURNE GROVE
Bayswater
BAYSWATER
Lancaster Gate
MARBLE ARCH
NOTTING HILL
Queensway
BAYSWATER ROAD
Notting Hill Gate
NOTTING HILL GATE
KENSINGTON CHURCH ST
Kensington Gardens
Hyde Park
Holland Park
KENSINGTON
THE SERPENTINE
High Street Kensington
KENSINGTON ROAD
KNIGHTSBRIDGE
Knightsbridge
GLOUCESTER ROAD
EXHIBITION ROAD
BROMPTON ROAD
KENSINGTON HIGH STREET
EARL'S
QUEENSGATE
South Kensington
CROMWELL ROAD
Gloucester Road
EARL'S COURT
WARWICK ROAD
West Kensington
BROMPTON ROAD
CHELSEA
OLD BROMPTON ROAD
West Brompton
FULHAM ROAD
KING'S ROAD
NORTH END ROAD
CHEYNE WALK
RIVER THAMES

0 metres 500
0 yds 550

HOTELS

1 Basil Street
2 Beaufort
3 Blakes
4 Cadogan
5 Capital
6 Chelsea
7 Gloucester
8 Hilton International Olympia
9 L'Hôtel
10 Hyde Park
11 Kensington Close
12 Kensington Palace
13 Number Sixteen
14 Onslow
15 Pembridge Court
16 Plaza on Hyde Park
17 Portobello
18 Rembrandt
19 Royal Garden
20 Royal Lancaster

RESTAURANTS

1 Bibendum
2 Bombay Brasserie
3 Bouillabaisse
4 Brasserie St Quentin
5 Clarke's
6 La Croisette
7 La Famiglia
8 Golden Chopsticks
9 Kensington Place
10 Leith's
11 Lou Pescadou
12 Le Quai St Pierre
13 San Frediano
14 San Lorenzo
15 Le Suquet
16 La Tante Claire
17 Les Trois Plats
18 Turner's
19 Zen
20 Ziani's

BUILDINGS AND SIGHTS

1 Earl's Court Exhibition Centre
2 Geological Museum
3 Harrods
4 Kensington Palace
5 Natural History Museum
6 Royal Albert Hall
7 Science Museum
8 Speaker's Corner
9 Victoria and Albert Museum
⬥ Underground station

central London are prone to quite rapid changes of character. *Islington*, north of the City, had become run down until the 1950s, when it was one of the first inner areas to be reclaimed by the wealthy professional class. Yet *Hackney* and *Holloway*, alongside, have yet to undergo that transformation.

Postal districts give a clue to social status. As a general principle, any which has a W in it (W, NW, SW, WC) is likely to be preferable to one with an E (E, NE, SE) – but there are notable exceptions. *Dulwich* (SE21), where Mrs Thatcher has bought a home, is one of the most desirable and bucolic of the suburbs close to London – certainly several steps up the scale from nearby *Brixton* (SW9); and the old riverside houses and converted warehouses of *Limehouse* (E1) are inhabited by a select crowd including politicians, film producers and actors. Across the river, *Greenwich* and *Blackheath* are attractive inner suburbs.

Ethnic groups have established communities in many districts, without dominating them as completely as in American cities. The Jews that settled in the East End at the end of the 19thC moved northwest as they grew more successful, to parts of *Hampstead*, *Golders Green*, *Hendon* and *Finchley*, and later still further out to *Edgware* and *Watford*. But these areas contain large numbers of non-Jews as well.

Hampstead, with its neighbour Highgate, has long had a reputation as the habitat of artists, writers and the intelligentsia generally. The equivalent parts of southwest London are *Barnes*, *Richmond* and *Twickenham*, by the river, which are favoured by workers in television because of their comparative proximity to the BBC Television Centre at Shepherd's Bush.

Further out, the "stockbroker belt" is the collective name given to a number of disparate areas some 25 miles/40kms from London, mainly to the south and west. Here, the urban sprawl has been forced to give way to the countryside because of planning regulations imposing a "green belt" beyond the inner suburbs. The high earners live with their families in rambling houses standing in their own grounds with two cars in the garage and sometimes even a pony in the paddock. Areas (and their main settlements) that fall within this category include, to the south, the North Downs in Surrey (Esher, Leatherhead, Guildford); to the west, the Thames Valley (Windsor, Henley, Virginia Water, Ascot); and, to the northwest, the Chilterns (Chesham, the Chalfonts, High Wycombe).

Few of the green-belt suburbs to the east of London, such as those in Essex, near Epping Forest, and in northern Kent (Beckenham, Bexleyheath, Dartford), have anything like the same cachet as those to the west. Their inhabitants are likely to be skilled artisans – workers in the printing industry, for example – or middle-rank white collar workers. The wealthy and successful prefer to head west at the end of the day. But these are only general rules, with many exceptions. It is unsafe to draw too many conclusions about people from their home address.

What remains of London's light industry is scattered in pockets around the perimeter, often on small industrial estates: the breweries; timber and furniture construction near Epping Forest; manufacturing and service industries to the west, with a concentration near Heathrow and Gatwick airports; and some light engineering east of the city on both sides of the river.

Telephone numbers
London's single area code, 01, is due to be replaced in April 1990 by two new codes, 071 and 081, for central and outer areas respectively.

Hotels

The hotels which make London special are those whose pedigree stretches back for decades, sometimes even a century or more. At these – the Connaught, Claridge's, the Savoy – traditional decor and standards of personal service are allied to modern comforts and facilities. Such places cost no more than the top modern hotels in London, but their formality may not be to everyone's taste. Among the choice of newer hotels, there are of course one or two fine examples; and, for seasoned international travellers weary of large hotels, London has a good crop of small, luxury places to stay.

London hotels do not have all the facilities which some international travellers may expect. Air conditioning is by no means standard; swimming pools, health and business centres, even private hotel parking areas are all rarities. Facilities which can be taken for granted (unless otherwise stated) are: IDD telephones, televisions and minibars in all bedrooms, and 24hr room service.

Almost all of London's best hotels are in the West End, Chelsea, Kensington and Knightsbridge (see maps 2, 3 and 4). Few are close to the City – the capital's financial district. Prices remain buoyant owing to a shortage of hotel beds, making reservation advisable, particularly in summer. Many business hotels offer drastically reduced rates at weekends throughout the year. If arriving without reserved accommodation, you may be able to find a room through the London Tourist Board, which has offices at Heathrow Airport and Victoria Station. Alternatively, try the British Tourist Authority offices in Lower Regent Street or one of the many commercial agencies at stations and airports.

Athenaeum *£/////*
116 Piccadilly, W1V OBJ (map 2)
☎ 499 3464 TX 261589 fax 493 1860
• *Rank* • AE DC MC V • *90 rooms, 22 suites, 33 apartments, 1 restaurant, 1 bar*
Though a modern (1970s) hotel, the Athenaeum has a pleasantly clubby air. Bedrooms and public rooms are furnished in sober good taste, and the service is discreet but lavish: even jogging suits are provided (Green Park lies opposite). Guests are mainly business executives, particularly from banking and insurance, leavened by the occasional celebrity. Women travelling alone are made to feel particularly welcome. Many guests opt for one of the hotel's Down Street apartments which include a sitting room (with dining table) large enough for an informal meeting. Parking • 3 meeting rooms (capacity up to 50).

Basil Street *£///*
8 Basil St, SW3 1AH (map 4)
☎ 581 3311 TX 28379 fax 581 3693 •
AE DC MC V • *95 rooms, 1 suite, 2 restaurants, 2 bars*
Not a conventionally smart hotel but one with great character and an excellent Knightsbridge location, just a 2min walk from Harrods. The atmosphere is relaxed, and the spacious first-floor lounge and dining room retain a certain Edwardian elegance. Bedrooms vary; the best are spacious and equipped with huge pine-panelled bathrooms. 3 meeting rooms (capacity up to 55).

Berkeley *£/////*
Wilton Pl, SW1X 7RL (map 3)
☎ 235 6000 TX 919252 fax 235 4300
• *Savoy Group* • AE DC MC V • *133 rooms, 27 suites, 2 restaurants, 1 bar*
A thoroughbred hotel, stylish and

smoothly run, which prides itself on attentive personal service (organized separately on each floor). The Berkeley's transition in 1972 from its century-old site in Mayfair to an imposing modern residence in a quiet location close to Hyde Park Corner was superbly executed. It gained modern amenities – rooftop pool, gym, cinema, private underground parking area, air conditioning – while losing very little of its identity. A devoted clientele of both business people and private travellers appreciate the service, the dignified, unfussy public rooms and the spacious, individually designed bedrooms. 5 meeting rooms (capacity up to 150), banqueting hall.

Britannia £////
Grosvenor Sq, W1A 3AN (map 3)
☎ 629 9400 ⊺⊼ 23941 fax 629 7736 •
InterContinental • AE DC MC V • *340 rooms, 14 suites, 2 restaurants, 2 bars*
Close to the American Embassy on prestigious Grosvenor Square (but with the main entrance at the back), the Britannia has a large transatlantic clientele. The busy classical-style hall is a good meeting place and both the fairly formal café and the restaurant are suitable for business meals. Standard bedrooms are fairly spacious, in quiet neutral colour-schemes, and not conspicuously luxurious; the 90 de luxe rooms have sitting areas, separate desk and extra telephones. Georgian shopping arcade, hairdresser, barber, florist, newsstand • secretarial service, 3 meeting rooms (capacity up to 120).

Brown's £////
Albemarle St and Dover St, W1A 4SW (map 2) ☎ 493 6020 ⊺⊼ 28686
fax 493 9381 • THF • AE DC MC V •
120 rooms, 13 suites, 1 restaurant, 1 bar
Many distinguished people have stayed at Brown's since its opening in 1837, including Rudyard Kipling and several Roosevelts. Americans still flock here, attracted by the palpable Englishness of the place. Downstairs the historic charm holds true, and

upstairs bedrooms are mostly spacious but old-fashioned: some singles are small. The best rooms are those, like the reasonably priced studio suites on the fifth floor, which have been unpretentiously modernized. Barber • 7 meeting rooms (capacity up to 70).

Capital £/////
22 Basil St, SW3 1AT (map 4)
☎ 589 5171 ⊺⊼ 919042 fax 225 0011
• AE DC MC V • *40 bedrooms, 8 suites, 2 restaurants, 1 bar*
The antithesis of an impersonal business hotel, the Capital is small, friendly and luxurious. Beyond the tiny but highly efficient reception area lies an intimate bar and one of the most sophisticated restaurants in London (see *Restaurants*). Reserve a table when you reserve your room. The comfortable bedrooms have been redecorated and furnished in English country-house taste; some in dark colours and paisley prints, others lighter and floral. *L'Hôtel* (see *Other hotels*) is a classy bed and breakfast establishment under the same management. Limited hotel parking • 2 meeting rooms (capacity up to 24).

Chesterfield £////
35 Charles St, W1X 8LX (map 2)
☎ 491 2622 ⊺⊼ 269394 fax 491 4793
• AE DC MC V • *131 rooms, 6 suites, 1 restaurant, 1 bar*
In a quiet position off Berkeley Square in Mayfair, the Chesterfield could be taken for a private club with its leather armchairs, panelled library and first-class service. Buffet lunch and supper are served in an attractive glass-roofed internal courtyard while Butler's restaurant provides more formal dining. Bedrooms are small but brightly decorated. 2 meeting rooms (capacity up to 70).

Hotel price guide
For the meanings of the hotel price symbols, see *Symbols and abbreviations* on pages 6 and 7.

Churchill £////
30 Portman Sq, W1A 4ZX (map 3)
☎ 486 5800 ⊤X 264831 fax 935 0431
• AE DC MC V • *443 rooms, 45 suites,*
3 restaurants, 1 bar
Large, luxurious and located within a
3min walk from Oxford Street, the
Churchill caters almost exclusively to
the business traveller. Bedrooms are
exceptionally spacious and
comfortable and the splendid lobby
and thickly carpeted public rooms are
suitably impressive. As well as a
French restaurant, there is a coffee
shop serving light meals until 1am.
Service throughout is excellent.
Hairdresser, gift shop, pharmacy,
parking area under hotel • business
centre with many meeting rooms
(capacity up to 200), secretarial
service.

Claridge's £/////
Brook St, W1A 2JQ (map 2)
☎ 629 8860 ⊤X 21872 fax 499 2210 •
Savoy Group • AE DC MC V • *135*
rooms, 5 suites, 2 restaurants
Like a true aristocrat, Claridge's
impresses by understatement rather
than by gaudy display. Inside this
unassuming Victorian building on a
quiet Mayfair thoroughfare, the
marble tiled lobby and traditional
sitting room are perfectly preserved.
Service is respectful and old-
fashioned: drinks are served by
liveried footmen; the press of a bell
will instantly summon a maid or
valet. Bedrooms are very large by
modern standards, often with a
separate dressing room, log fire or
marvellous Art Deco fittings. Much
favoured by royalty and visiting heads
of state, Claridge's is a place where
politicians become statesmen and
even ordinary mortals are made to
feel very special. Hairdresser, florist •
4 meeting rooms (capacity up to 200).

Connaught £////
16 Carlos Pl, W1Y 6AL (map 3)
☎ 499 7070 ⊤X 296376 fax 495 3262
• *Savoy Group* • MC • *66 rooms, 24*
suites, 2 restaurants, 1 bar

No special concessions are made to
the business visitor at the Connaught,
a hotel dedicated to serving its loyal
clientele. Securing a room is
genuinely difficult, unless you have a
recommendation from a regular guest.
Reservations are made even a year
ahead for high points of the British
social calendar such as Ascot and
Wimbledon. The foundations of the
hotel's worldwide reputation are
impeccable service and attention to
detail. The Restaurant and Grill have
also maintained their status (see
Restaurants). The decor throughout is
that of a comfortable English country
house, with antiques, oil paintings
and vases of fresh flowers. Rooms are
large, comfortable and individually
furnished in cheerful colours.

Dukes £/////
35 St James's Pl, SW1A 1NY (map 2)
☎ 491 4840 ⊤X 28283 fax 493 1264 •
AE DC MC V • *36 rooms, 26 suites,*
2 restaurants, 1 bar
A luxury hotel hidden away in a gaslit
courtyard in St James's, close to
Piccadilly, Dukes has the character of
an Edwardian town house, but with
ample modern amenities. Recent
refurbishment has left the whole hotel
spick and span and all the bedrooms
are now a good size. Some people,
however, may find the tiny lounge,
bar and restaurant somewhat
oppressive. 1 meeting room (capacity
30).

Goring £//
15 Beeston Pl, SW1W OJW (map 3)
☎ 834 8211 ⊤X 919166 fax 834 4393
• AE DC MC V • *84 rooms, 5 suites,*
1 restaurant, 1 bar
Owned by the Goring family since it
was built in 1910, this hotel is old-
fashioned in the best sense. The
polite friendliness of the staff, the
unpretentious country house comfort
of the public areas and the traditional
fare in the restaurant are appreciated
by visiting dowagers and Belgravia
businessmen alike. The bar, sitting
room and back bedrooms overlook a
quiet garden (no access). Front rooms

are double-glazed against the noise of Beeston Place. Some rooms have been refurbished to a high standard, and include whirlpool baths and air conditioning. Limited parking • 5 meeting rooms (capacity up to 55).

Grosvenor House £//////
Park La, W1A 3AA (map 3)
☎ 499 6363 ☒ 24871 fax 493 3341 •
THF • *AE DC MC V* • *380 rooms, 74 suites, 4 restaurants, 1 bar*
It may lack the style and character of some of its rivals, but as a prime business hotel the Grosvenor House does its job efficiently and Ninety Park Lane is a good restaurant (see *Restaurants*). Its Great Room hosts many of London's big award ceremonies, fairs and conventions. Public areas and bedrooms are comfortable but unremarkable; service is efficient though detached. The higher-priced 'Crown Club" executive floor offers extras such as its own lounge and check-in desk and butler service. The hotel has a well-known basement health club (see *Keeping fit*). Hairdresser, gift shop, florist, parking • pool, gym • business centre with many meeting rooms (capacity up to 1,750), secretarial service.

Hilton on Park Lane £//////
22 Park La, W1A 2HH (map 3)
☎ 493 8000 ☒ 24873 fax 493 4957 •
AE DC MC V • *446 rooms, 54 suites, 3 restaurants, 4 bars*
This 28-floor London landmark has wonderful views over the city. The ground floor bustles like a busy airport; there is a separate check-in for the four executive floors at the top of the hotel. Bedrooms and suites throughout are smart and modern, with luxury suites at the very top and a whole floor (the 13th) reserved for nonsmokers. The Hilton has three very different restaurants; the Roof (see *Restaurants*) at the top, the new continental-style Brasserie, off the lobby and Trader Vic's, at the bottom. Parking • sauna, solarium • Business centre, 5 meeting rooms.

Howard £//////
Temple Pl, WC2R 2PR (map 1)
☎ 836 3555 ☒ 268047 fax 379 4547
• *Barclays Hotels* • *AE DC MC V* • *117 rooms, 24 suites, 1 restaurant, 1 bar*
Overlooking the Thames next to the Temple, on the very edge of the City, the Howard is one of London's newer luxury hotels, well-equipped for the senior corporate traveller. The public areas are very grand; adjacent to the lobby are the restaurant and bar whose luxury is slightly relieved by views of a small patio garden. Bedrooms are very relaxing and furnished with reproduction antiques. Service is appropriately smooth. Parking • 4 meeting rooms (capacity up to 250).

Hyatt Carlton Tower £//////
2 Cadogan Pl, SW1X 9PY (map 3)
☎ 235 5411 ☒ 21944 fax 235 9129 •
AE DC MC V • *163 rooms, 61 suites, 4 restaurants, 2 bars*
After major refurbishment in 1987 the Hyatt Carlton Tower can vie for the position of best business hotel in London. All bedrooms have been refitted to high standards and decorated in attractive pastel shades; executive suites have luxuries like whirlpool baths and compact disc players. Fine views over Belgravia, Knightsbridge and Chelsea can be had from upper floors. The food, too, in the Chelsea Room and the Rib Room, is of a high standard (see *Restaurants*); light meals are served in the elegant Chinoiserie lounge on the ground floor. Jewellers, hairdresser, florist, parking • health club with exercise equipment • business centre, 3 meeting rooms (capacity up to 300).

Hyde Park £//////
66 Knightsbridge, SW1Y 7LA (map 4)
☎ 235 2000 ☒ 262057 fax 235 4552
• *THF* • *AE DC MC V* • *161 rooms, 19 suites, 3 restaurants, 1 bar*
One of London's grandest old hotels, the Hyde Park was at one time much patronized by Europe's crowned heads. After a spell in the doldrums, it has been fully restored to its former

glory, although nowadays it is mainly senior foreign executives who step into the splendid lobby – a pure Edwardian extravaganza of marble inlaid with marble, ornate gilt mirrors and a vast chandelier. The restaurant, too, looking out onto Hyde Park, is palatial. Some rooms face the park; those at the front look straight down at the grinding traffic of Knightsbridge, and others give onto internal courtyards with no views and little natural light. All rooms are spacious, air-conditioned and furnished with antiques or good reproductions. Hairdresser, florist • 6 meeting rooms (capacity up to 250).

Inn on the Park £//////
Hamilton Pl, Park La, W1A 1AZ (map 3) ☎ *499 0888* ☒ *22771 fax 493 1895 • Four Seasons • AE DC MC V • 201 rooms, 27 suites, 2 restaurants, 2 bars*
The only Four Seasons hotel in Europe, the Inn on the Park attracts a large clientele from North America. It is reckoned by many to be the best-run modern hotel in London, with an air of elegant and luxurious calm and more style and individuality than its close neighbours, the Hilton and the Inter-Continental. Both the hotel's restaurants are well-regarded: Lanes' fixed-price lunch menus attract the Mayfair business community, while the Four Seasons is as well suited to serious business discussions as to entertaining in style. Bedrooms combine comfort and charm with the efficiency of an office; the 12 conservatory rooms have light and luxurious sitting areas. An excellent choice for senior executives travelling with their spouses, and popular with a wide cross-section of celebrities. Gift, jewellery and china shops, florist, parking • 5 meeting rooms (capacity up to 400).

InterContinental £//////
1 Hamilton Pl, W1V OQY (map 3) ☎ *409 3131* ☒ *25853 fax 493 3476 • AE DC MC V • 416 rooms, 75 suites, 4 restaurants, 1 bar*

A hotel geared to the busy corporate traveller. Though it lacks the finesse of the greatest London hotels, its business facilities are enviable: satellite video conferencing can be arranged; there is a desk in the lobby for sending telex and fax; the air-conditioned bedrooms each have dual sockets and two telephones, with a third in the bathroom. The hotel's restaurant, Le Soufflé (see *Restaurants*), is a good choice for formal entertaining. Hairdresser, shops • health centre with gym, sauna, plunge pool • meeting rooms (capacity up to 1,000).

Marriott £//////
10 Grosvenor Sq, W1A 4AW (map 3) ☎ *493 1232* ☒ *268101 fax 491 3201 • AE DC MC V • 205 rooms, 18 suites, 2 restaurants, 1 bar*
Centrally located in the same square as the American embassy, the Marriott is much favoured by transatlantic business visitors. It is a smoothly operated if predictable modern hotel, with stylish public areas and a well-equipped business centre (including a Federal Express Dropbox for urgent packages). Since standard bedrooms are fairly anodyne, it is worth upgrading to the more spacious and imaginative "Executive Kings" rooms. Gift shop • business centre, 3 meeting rooms (capacity up to 375).

Le Meridien £//////
Piccadilly, W1V OBH (map 2) ☎ *734 8000* ☒ *25795 • AE DC MC V • 253 rooms, 31 suites, 4 restaurants, 3 bars*
Massively refurbished by Gleneagles Hotels in 1985, and bought by the Air France Meridien chain in 1986, the old Piccadilly is now a showpiece business hotel. Visitors admire the Edwardian splendour of the beautifully restored Oak Room (see *Restaurants*) and the conservatory-style brasserie created by glazing the roof terrace overlooking teeming Piccadilly. There is a magnificent basement health club (see *Keeping fit*), reserved for members and hotel

guests, as well as a lounge and quiet library in which to work. The bedrooms are less scintillating but well-equipped. Hairdresser • health centre with pool, gym, squash, saunas, solarium • 10 meeting rooms (capacity up to 250).

Ritz   £////
Piccadilly, W1V 9DG (map 2)
☎ 493 8181 ⊤ₓ 267200 fax 493 2687
• Cunard • AE DC MC V • 114 rooms, 14 suites, 1 restaurant, 1 bar
Sparkling once more after several years of decline. Bedrooms have been totally modernized and the ground floor restored to its former glory: a ravishing confection of pink, adorned with statues and chandeliers and crowned by a wonderful *trompe l'oeil* ceiling in the restaurant. While lunch at the Ritz may attract more businessmen than *beau monde* these days, this famous hotel still has glamour. But don't expect the aristocratic restraint of some of London's other great hotels: there is Big Band dancing in the Palm Court on Friday and Saturday nights as well as that daily highlight, afternoon tea – plenty of occasions to enjoy "putting on the Ritz." Hairdresser, barber, florist • 3 meeting rooms (capacity up to 50).

St James Court   £////
51 Buckingham Gate, SW1E 6AF (map 3) ☎ 834 6655 ⊤ₓ 938075 fax 630 7587 • Taj International • AE DC MC V • 373 rooms, 17 suites, 3 restaurants, 1 bar
Convenient for Westminster, the St James Court is also the nearest hotel to the new Queen Elizabeth II centre and is much used by conference delegates. The large business centre in the hotel provides full secretarial back-up and is itself used for small conferences. Another strength of this hotel is gastronomy – the Auberge de Provence (see *Restaurants*) and the Inn of Happiness providing contrasting cuisines. There are also good keep-fit facilities. But the bedrooms and public areas, decorated

in traditional style, are dull. Ninety apartments in an annexe nearby have the use of hotel facilities. Health club • business centre with 15 meeting rooms (capacity up to 120).

Savoy   £////
The Strand, WC2R OEU (map 3)
☎ 836 4343 ⊤ₓ 24234 fax 240 6040
• AE DC MC V • 152 rooms, 48 suites, 2 restaurants, 2 bars
Founded by Richard D'Oyly Carte with the profits of Gilbert and Sullivan's operettas, the Savoy continues to marry showbusiness and big business. The hotel's theatrical decor appeals to visiting stars of stage and screen; business travellers appreciate its proximity to the City and its many private dining rooms and function rooms. Both the severe yew-panelled Savoy Grill (see *Restaurants*) and the River restaurant are popular for business entertaining. Bedrooms vary in size and quality; the best are huge and decorated with antiques or original Art Deco fittings. Some have fine views of the Thames. Most of the bathrooms have retained fittings of epic grandeur. Hairdresser, florist, gift shop, parking, airport office • 13 meeting rooms (capacity up to 450).

Sheraton Park Tower   £////
101 Knightsbridge, SW1X 7RN (map 4) ☎ 235 8050 ⊤ₓ 917222
fax 235 8231 • AE DC MC V • 295 rooms, 29 suites, 1 restaurant, 1 bar
The smart buildings of Knightsbridge are abruptly punctuated – some say blighted – by the Sheraton's 17-floor cylindrical tower. It was designed so that every bedroom faces outwards; all are spacious and thoroughly comfortable in an anonymous modern style (those on the executive floor offer plusher fittings at a higher price). The panelled lobby and bar are pleasingly uncluttered; the conservatory-style restaurant, opening onto Knightsbridge, has a good reputation. Hairdresser, parking • 5 meeting rooms (capacity up to 250).

Stafford £///
16–18 St James's Pl, SW1A 1NJ
(map 2) ☎ *493 0111* ⊤ₓ *28602*
fax 493 7121 • *AE DC MC V* • *Cunard*
• *62 rooms, 5 suites, 1 restaurant, 1 bar*
Discreetly tucked away in
gentlemanly St James's, this calm and
dignified hotel largely caters to
business travellers. Afternoon tea is
served in a charming sitting-room
decorated with ornate Adam-style
plasterwork, while sporting pennants
and leather seats create a more clubby
ambience in the American Bar. The
dining room boasts wines from the
famous 300-year-old cellars. Upstairs
the corridors are narrow and
labyrinthine but the adequately-sized
bedrooms have a pleasant, country
house charm. Limited hotel parking •
5 meeting rooms (capacity up to 30).

Credit card abbreviations	
AE	American Express
DC	Diners Club
MC	Access/MasterCard
V	Visa

OTHER HOTELS
In addition to the hotels described in
the previous pages, business travellers
to London can choose from a number
of good chain hotels. Though they
may have less character or cachet, they
provide a reasonable standard of
accommodation and service, often –
though not invariably – at a slightly
lower price.

Hilton
International Kensington *179–199*
Holland Park Ave W11 4UL (map 4)
☎ *603 3355* ⊤ₓ *919763 fax 602 9397*
• *AE DC MC V* • **International**
Olympia *380 Kensington High St W14*
8NL (map 4) ☎ *603 3333* ⊤ₓ *22229*
fax 603 4686 • *AE DC MC V.* In
addition to the above Hiltons, the
chain operates the club-like **Mews at**
Park Lane *Stanhope Row, Park Lane*
W1Y 7HE (map 3) ☎ *493 7222* ⊤ₓ
24665 fax 629 9423, and the more
modest **Plaza on Hyde Park** *Lancaster*

Gate W2 3NA (map 4) ☎ *262 5022*
⊤ₓ *8954372 fax 724 8666* and
Sherlock Holmes *Baker St W1M*
1LB (map 3) ☎ *486 6161* ⊤ₓ *8954837*
fax 486 0884.

Holiday Inns
Marble Arch *134 George St, W1H*
6DN (map 3) ☎ *723 1277* ⊤ₓ *27983*
fax 402 0666 • *AE DC MC V* •
Mayfair *3 Berkeley St, W1X 6NE*
(map 2) ☎ *493 8282* ⊤ₓ *24561*
fax 629 2827 • *AE DC MC V.* The
Mayfair is a near-top hotel with a
prime location; Marble Arch is a little
lower in price and standard. Both
hotels have pools.

InterContinental
May Fair *Stratton St, W1A 2AN*
(map 2) ☎ *629 7777* ⊤ₓ *262526*
fax 629 1459 • **Portman**
InterContinental *22 Portman Sq,*
W1H 9FL (map 3) ☎ *486 5844* ⊤ₓ
261526 fax 935 0537 • *AE DC MC V.*
In addition to the InterContinental
and the Britannia (see main entries),
there are two other London members
of the group. The showy May Fair is
arguably the most luxurious; the
Portman InterContinental, near
Marble Arch, is the most modern,
competent and comfortable.

Rank
Gloucester *4 Harrington Gdns, SW7*
4LH (map 4) ☎ *373 6030* ⊤ₓ *917505*
fax 373 0409 • *AE DC MC V* • **Royal**
Garden *Kensington High St, W8 4PT*
(map 4) ☎ *937 8000* ⊤ₓ *263151*
fax 938 4532 • *AE DC MC V* • **Royal**
Lancaster *Lancaster Ter, W2 2TY*
(map 4) ☎ *262 6737* ⊤ₓ *24822*
fax 724 3191 • *AE DC MC V* • **White**
House *Albany St, NW1 3UP (map 3)*
☎ *387 1200* ⊤ₓ *24111 fax 388 0091* •
AE DC MC V. Rank's most central
London hotel is the Athenaeum (see
main entries). The Gloucester, Royal
Garden and Royal Lancaster are all
large, modern luxury hotels on the
western side of the city centre. The
cheaper White House is north of the
centre, near Euston Station and
Regent's Park.

Sarova

Chelsea *17 Sloane St, SW1X 9NU (map 4)* ☎ *235 4377* ⊠ *919111 fax 235 3705* • *AE DC MC V* • **Green Park** *Half Moon St, W1Y 8BP (map 2)* ☎ *629 7522* ⊠ *28856 fax 491 8971* • *AE DC MC V* • **Pastoria** *St Martin's St, WC2H 7HL (map 2)* ☎ *930 8641* ⊠ *25538 fax 925 0551* • *AE DC MC V* • **Rembrandt** *11 Thurloe Pl, SW7 2RS (map 4)* ☎ *589 8100* ⊠ *295828 fax 225 3363* • *AE DC MC V* • **Rubens** *Buckingham Palace Rd, SW1W OPS (map 3)* ☎ *834 6600* ⊠ *916577 fax 828 5401* • *AE DC MC V* • **Washington** *Curzon St, W1Y 8DT (map 2)* ☎ *499 7000* ⊠ *24540 fax 495 6172* • *AE DC MC V*. A range of well-run hotels with good conference facilities. The Washington was re-opened after total refurbishment in May 1989 as the flagship of this group; the recently acquired Chelsea has been up-graded and offers contemporary decor and a good restaurant. The Green Park, modestly priced for Mayfair, has also been redecorated. The Rubens and the Rembrandt (with the biggest function rooms in the group) are traditional hotels in good locations. The Pastoria, just off Leicester Square, is the smallest in the group.

Thistle

Cadogan *75 Sloane St, SW1X 9SG (map 4)* ☎ *235 7141* ⊠ *267893 fax 245 0994* • *AE DC MC V* • **Kensington Palace** *De Vere Gdns, W8 5AF (map 4)* ☎ *937 8121* ⊠ *262422 fax 937 2816* • *AE DC MC V* • **Lowndes** *21 Lowndes St SW1X 9ES (map 3)* ☎ *235 6020* ⊠ *919065 fax 235 1154* • *AE DC MC V* • **Royal Horseguards** *2 Whitehall Ct, SW1A 2EJ (map 3)* ☎ *839 3400* ⊠ *917096 fax 925 2149* • *AE DC MC V* • **Royal Trafalgar** *Whitcomb St, WC2H 7HG (map 2)* ☎ *930 4477* ⊠ *298564 fax 925 2149* • *AE DC MC V* • **Royal Westminster** *49 Buckingham Palace Rd, SW1W OQT (map 3)* ☎ *834 1821* ⊠ *916821 fax 931 7542* • *AE DC MC V* • **Selfridge** *400 Orchard St, W1H OJS (map 3)* ☎ *408 2080* ⊠ *22361 fax 629 8849* • *AE DC MC V* • **Tower** *St Katharine's Way, E1 9LD (map 1)* ☎ *481 2575* ⊠ *885934 fax 488 4106* • *AE DC MC V*. Generally reliable executive hotels in some useful locations. The Tower Thistle, overlooking the Tower of London and St Katharine's Dock, is one of the largest hotels in the capital (826 bedrooms). Thistle's most luxurious London properties are the Selfridge, off Oxford Street, the Royal Westminster, near Buckingham Palace, and two small hotels in Chelsea, the Lowndes and the Cadogan. The other three are slightly cheaper.

Trusthouse Forte

Cavendish *Jermyn St, SW1Y 6JF (map 2)* ☎ *930 2111* ⊠ *263187 fax 839 2125* • *AE DC MC V* • **Cumberland** *Marble Arch, W1A 4RF (map 3)* ☎ *262 1234* ⊠ *22215 fax 724 4621* • *AE DC MC V* • **Kensington Close** *Wright's La, W8 5SP (map 4)* ☎ *937 8170* ⊠ *23914 fax 937 8289* • *AE DC MC V* • **Londonderry** *Park La, W1Y 8AP (map 3)* ☎ *493 7292* ⊠ *263292 fax 495 1395* • *AE DC MC V* **Onslow** *109–113 Queen's Gate, SW7 5LR (map 4)* ☎ *589 6300* ⊠ *262180 fax 589 6300* • *AE DC MC V* • **Regent Palace** *Sherwood St, W1A 4BZ (map 2)* ☎ *734 7000* ⊠ *23740 fax 734 6435* • *AE DC MC V* • **Russell** *Russell Square, WC1B 5BE (map 3)* ☎ *837 6470* ⊠ *24615 fax 837 2857* • *AE DC MC V* • **St George's** *Langham Pl, W1N 8QS (map 3)* ☎ *580 0111* ⊠ *27274 fax 436 7997* • *AE DC MC V* • **Strand Palace** *369 The Strand, WC2R OJJ (map 3)* ☎ *836 8080* ⊠ *24208 fax 836 2077* • *AE DC MC V* • **Waldorf** *Aldwych, WC2B 4DD (map 3)* ☎ *836 2400* ⊠ *24574 fax 836 7244* • *AE DC MC V* • **Westbury** *Conduit St, W1A 4UH (map 2)* ☎ *629 7755* ⊠ *24378 fax 495 1163* • *AE DC MC V*. Apart from Brown's, the Grosvenor House and the Hyde Park (see main entries), THF's other de luxe London properties are the Waldorf, on the edge of fashionable Covent

Garden, the Westbury, in Mayfair, and the Londonderry, on Park Lane. The remainder are reputable middle-market establishments: the Cavendish in decorous Jermyn Street; the 900-room Cumberland, at Marble Arch; the large, modern Kensington Close (see *Keeping fit*); the Onslow, consisting of several terrace houses in South Kensington; the good-value Regent Palace in Soho; the elderly Russell in literary Bloomsbury; St George's, occupying the upper floors of a tower block near the BBC's Broadcasting House, with splendid views from its top-floor cocktail lounge; and the huge Strand Palace.

Small hotels of quality and character

The following hotels, all with less than 40 bedrooms, are more personal in atmosphere than the hotels described above, and mostly less expensive. They offer bed and breakfast only, except where indicated. Room service is usually limited and drinks may be offered on an honesty bar basis. The Beaufort, Dorset Square and Fenja provide secretarial services.

Beaufort *£///* *33 Beaufort Gdns, SW3 1PP (map 4)* ☎ *584 5252* TX *929200 fax 589 2834* • *AE DC MC V.* Expensive small hotel in a cul-de-sac near Harrods. Pretty, light decor with personal touches. Guests are given their own front door key.
Blakes *£////* *33 Roland Gdns, SW7 3PF (map 4)* ☎ *370 6701* TX *8813500 fax 373 0442* • *AE DC MC V.* Small hotel in South Kensington, much used by media and advertising people, who enjoy the individuality of its decor and the quality of its small restaurant.
Dorset Square *£///* *39–40 Dorset Sq, NW1 6QN (map 3)* ☎ *723 7874* TX *263964 fax 724 3328* • *AE MC V.* One of London's original and grandest "country house" hotels, decorated and run with flair. The conservatory-style restaurant is popular for business lunches. 24hr room service, chauffeured car available to guests.
Fenja *£////* *69 Cadogan Gdns, SW3 2RB (map 3)* ☎ *589 7333* TX *934272 fax 581 4958* • *AE DC*

MC V. More home than hotel, the Fenja (with just 14 tastefully decorated bedrooms) is for those who want a very comfortable and tranquil base in Chelsea. Meeting rooms and small sitting room available.
L'Hôtel *£////* *28 Basil St, SW3 1AT (map 4)* ☎ *589 6286* TX *919042 fax 225 0011* • *AE V.* Under the same management as the Capital (see above), this is a classy bed and breakfast establishment, with 12 spacious, prettily furnished rooms. Breakfast is served in the chic Metro bistro (see *Bars*). No room service.
Number Sixteen *£////* *16 Sumner Pl, SW3 3EG (map 4)* ☎ *589 5232* TX *266638 fax 584 8615* • *AE DC MC V.* A popular hotel created in a handsome South Kensington terrace, with a pretty garden.
Pembridge Court *£///* *34 Pembridge Gdns, W2 4DX (map 4)* ☎ *229 9977* TX *298363 fax 727 4982* • *AE DC MC V.* A carefully modernized 19thC house close to Notting Hill Gate, favoured by budget-conscious media people. Cap's, with a separate entrance, is a popular local bistro.
Portobello *£//* *22 Stanley Gdns, W11 2NG (map 4)* ☎ *727 2777* TX *21879* • *AE DC MC V.* An eccentric little hotel much frequented by those in the antiques and record businesses. Rooms range from exotic suites to cabin-sized singles. Bar and restaurant.

Clubs

Historically, the club is the Englishman's refuge from his wife, his children and the stresses of his occupation – a congenial place to recline in a leather armchair, "blackball" (the club term for veto) unsuitable club candidates and drink good vintage wine at bargain prices. In recent years, though, attitudes have changed. Women are now allowed into all of London's 60 clubs save three (the Beefsteak, Pratt's and White's). Members can also use their clubs to entertain business colleagues, as long as discussions are conducted discreetly: in these gentlemanly sanctums, eyebrows would be raised at the flourishing of balance sheets and company reports.

The following clubs are the most prominent.

The Athenaeum, 107 Pall Mall, SW1. The definitive club of the Establishment: judges, ambassadors and bishops.

The Beefsteak, 9 Irving St. WC2. Peers who can read and write and journalists who have learned table manners is how the Earl of Kintore describes the members. They eat at a long communal table and address the waiters and stewards as "Charles."

Brooks's, 61 St James's Street, SW1. Originally set up in the 18thC as an antidote to White's. Continues to have an eclectic, liberal membership with strong St James's wine trade representation.

Buck's, 18 Clifford St, W1. Favoured by English and American businessmen, also by women for its unfusty atmosphere.

The Carlton, 69 St James's St, SW1. The club of the Conservatives, it once served the function of the party's Central Office. Now better known for its *cordon bleu* than its conspiracies.

The Cavalry and Guards, 127 Piccadilly, W1. Members are retired or serving officers in the army's grander regiments. Their consumption of champagne is higher than in any other club in London.

The City of London, 19 Old Broad St, EC2. The oldest of the four City clubs, and reserved for partners or directors. Usually open only for lunch.

The Garrick, 15 Garrick St, WC2. Frequented by publishers, barristers, journalists and actors – conversation is rarely dull. Prince Charles is a member.

Mark's, 46 Charles St, W1. The most stylish lunch and dinner club in London, created by Mark Birley, founder of the enduringly successful nightclub, Annabel's (see *Entertainment*). Predictably popular with the jet set.

The RAC, 89–91 Pall Mall, SW1. Favoured by the physically active it has a large swimming pool, squash court, gymnasium and Turkish bath. The past chairman described it as "a businessman's leisure centre."

The Reform, 104 Pall Mall, SW1. Largely the club of the thinking left: Whitehall mandarins, BBC apparatchiks, liberal politicians and "wet" economists.

The St James's Club, 7 Park Pl, SW1. London's flashiest club, created by the high-profile millionaire, Peter de Savary. Its wealthy members are mostly fun, fast and foreign.

The Turf, 5 Carlton House Ter, SW1. The robust and sporting upper classes set the tone for this amusing club. On the whole, the members are less riotous than in earlier days when one noble lord would habitually relieve himself in the fireplace.

White's, 37 St James's St, SW1. London's most famous club, where members are either very rich or very grand and usually both; they include the Dukes of Edinburgh and Kent.

Other noted clubs are the *Army and Navy*, the *Naval and Military* and the *RAF*, for serving and retired officers; the *Gresham Club*, for executives in the City of London; the *Groucho* and *Moscow* clubs, for the media; and *Boodle's*, for country squires.

Restaurants

The best of London's restaurants can compete with those of any other European capital. The range in all price-brackets expands year by year, and covers most of the world's great cuisines. It is still true, however, that the safest bets for business meals tend to be those serving French or Anglo-French cooking, whether classical or modern. Almost all of the so-called "ethnic" restaurants are better suited to more casual dining.

Over the last few years, the traditional romance between British restaurants and all culinary things French has become more frequently formalized in consultancy "marriages' between highly Michelin-starred chefs from across the Channel and ambitious London kitchens with their own permanent staffs. The Frenchman lends his name on the basis of a monthly (or less frequent) visit during which his input may range from teaching new dishes or redesigning the whole menu to merely keeping an eye on things. At their most successful – as, for example, at the Oak Room – these arrangements mean that the home team receives regular injections of stimulating ideas. At their worst, the British chef resents the intrusion and the visitor seems to care for little more than his fee.

At lunch time, the smartest restaurants are arenas for high-powered business entertaining with prices generally pitched at expense-account level, although some offer good-value fixed-price menus (see below). The three-hour lunch, beginning with aperitifs and ending with brandy and cigars, has largely disappeared; 90 minutes is more common, and abstaining from alcohol is perfectly acceptable, although a knowledge and appreciation of wine is seen as a mark of sophistication. Meal times tend to be fairly rigid by European standards – about 1pm for lunch and 8–8.30pm for dinner. Reserve as far ahead as possible (a contact telephone number will often be requested) and you may be asked to reconfirm the day before the meal; if there is no table at the time you prefer and you are determined to eat at a particular restaurant, try asking for before 12.30pm or 7.30pm. Spare tables are particularly hard to find in December, when many restaurants are hosting pre-Christmas parties.

However full a restaurant's register may be, the high rate of "no shows" means that it is worth trying for a table at even the best places at the last minute on the actual day. Some restaurants run waiting lists and will contact you in the event of a cancellation. Common courtesy, of course, demands that reserved customers changing their minds should inform the restaurant, so that their table may be liberated. Those who do not may be faced with legal action, as the industry has shown itself increasingly willing to take positive steps to recoup lost revenue.

Best for high-powered entertaining
Bibendum • Boulestin • Connaught Restaurant • Connaught Grill Room • Le Gavroche • Inigo Jones • Ninety Park Lane • Oak Room • Le Soufflé • La Tante Claire.

Best for top-value fixed-price lunches
Auberge de Provence • Boulestin • Capital • Chez Nico • Clarke's • Le Gavroche • Gay Hussar • Inigo Jones • Mijanou • Oak Room • Rue St Jacques • La Tante Claire.

Alastair Little £///
49 Frith Street, W1 (map 2)
☎ *734 5183* • *closed Sat L* • *no credit cards*
A fashionable place for informal entertaining by young media people. Little's inventive, highly personal menu, which changes twice a day – or more often – according to his shopping, features simply cooked fish and meat with vivid sauces. Short, original wine list.

Auberge de Provence £////
St James's Court Hotel (map 3)
☎ *821 1899* • AE DC MC V
Part of a luxuriously renovated hotel and apartment complex, this unpretentious yet sophisticated restaurant is under the consultancy of Michelin three-star chef Jean-André Charial from L'Oustau de Baumière. The menu offers gutsy southern French fare, refined for metropolitan palates, with especially good fish dishes. Service is generally excellent, and there is a good-value fixed-price lunch menu. The wine list includes appropriate southern-French bargains as well as pricier Bordeaux vintages.

Bibendum £////
Michelin House, 81 Fulham Rd, SW3 (map 4) ☎ *581 5817* • MC V
Chef Simon Hopkinson has created London's most fashionable restaurant of recent years in the Conran-ized old Michelin building in South Kensington. The decor is cool and modern with nods to the Gauloise-packet view of France commonly associated with the Conran style. The food is an intelligent fusion of hearty French rustic with deft, idiosyncratic touches. Service can be very slow. The wine list inhabits a monied world of its own, where few ordinary mortals may follow. If you are unable to get a table, check out Hopkinson's old place, **Hilaire**, 68 Old Brompton Road, SW7 ☎ 584 8993, which upholds excellent standards and equally elevated prices.

City restaurants
While it is no longer necessary to be invited into directors' dining rooms to eat comparatively well in this part of London, there is no restaurant in these parts to compete – for prestige or good food – with the best in the West End. The nearest to an exception is *Le Poulbot* (see under *Le Gavroche* in main entries). Otherwise, the young, flash, late-1980s' idea of power-lunching has prompted the creation of a new style of establishment typified by two of *Corney & Barrow's* three main addresses: 44 Cannon St, EC4 (map 1) ☎ 248 1700 – a striking pink and grey dining area with a modern international menu; 118 Moorgate, EC2 (map 1) ☎ 628 2898, with its sometimes frenzied atmosphere, showy decor and more *nouvelle*-influenced menu; and 109 Old Broad Street, EC2 (map 1)

☎ 638 9308 or 920 9560, where the atmosphere is more sober. Old City stalwarts that have registered the revolution include *Sweetings*, 39 Queen Victoria St, EC4 (map 1) ☎ 248 3062, with its Victorian character, refectory tables, Dickensian crush and good solid fish; and *Bubb's*, 329 Central Market, EC1 (map 1) ☎ 236 2435, a provincial-French Smithfield spot. The latter seems gradually to be losing popularity to *Le Café du Marché*, 22 Charterhouse Sq, EC1 (map 1) ☎ 608 1609, with its expansive country air and well-handled Gallic menu. Close by is the market pub with the most famous cholesterol-sodden breakfasts in the area: the *Fox & Anchor*, 115 Charterhouse St, EC1 (map 1) ☎ 253 4838.
See also Miyama (under *Japanese restaurants*).

Boulestin £////
1A Henrietta St, WC2 (map 3)
☎ 836 7061 • closed Sat L, Sun, 1
week Christmas, 3 weeks Aug • AE DC
MC V • jackets; no pipes
This well-upholstered dining room
with its impressive oil paintings,
widely spaced tables and discreet
service is that rare phenomenon: a
restaurant for grown-ups. The food is
rich, classical French with nouvelle-ish
airs – at its best memorable, at worst
prettily correct. Vegetarians are
catered for on the main menu.
Excellent cheeses. Classy wine list
includes rarities. Reserve well ahead
for lunch, when there is a good-value
fixed-price menu.

Capital Hotel £////
Basil St, SW3 (map 4) ☎ 589 5171 •
AE DC MC V
The dining room of one of London's
most comfortable and personally run
small hotels provides a quietly
opulent setting for some assured,
middle-of-the-road modern cooking.
Talented young chef Philip Britten
originally gained a Michelin star when
he took over the former Battersea
premises of mentor Nico Ladenis.
The Capital, under proprietor David
Levin, has been something of a
launching pad for British chefs over
the last decade or so: Shaun Hill of
Gidleigh Park on Dartmoor, Richard
Shepherd and Brian Turner (of
Langan's Brasserie and Turner's – see
Fashionable informality) have all been
through its kitchens. Service is
friendly and efficient. The wine list is
entirely French with some very grand
bottles at less than exorbitant prices.
Good-value fixed price lunch.

Chez Nico £////
35 Great Portland St, W1 (map 3)
☎ 436 8846 • closed Sat & Sun • DC
MC V •jacket and tie D; no pipes.
The highest promise of controversial
chef Nico Ladenis's previous London
addresses is finally fulfilled in this
elegant L-shaped room (opened
Spring 1989). Everything jells, from
the debonair Parisian reference of the

stained-glass mock cupola and
waiters' floor-length aprons to food
which salutes the Mediterranean and
farther afield while remaining
immediately recognizable as the
product of a very individual genius.
Correspondingly high standards of
service, and an excellent wine
list. The restaurant of its time and
place.

Clarke's £///
124 Kensington Church St, W8 (map 4)
☎ 221 9225 • closed Sat & Sun • MC
V • pipes and cigars discouraged while
others are eating
After a stint at Michael's in Santa
Monica, Sally Clarke was among the
first to bring a touch of the new
California cuisine to London at her
pretty two-floor restaurant. Prime
ingredients appear in original, fresh-
tasting juxtaposition; char-grilling,
fresh herbs and fine oils are
hallmarks. Popular with well-heeled

Japanese restaurants
Although it has recently become
quite fashionable, Japanese food is
still considered rather esoteric by
most Britons, as well as relatively
expensive. As a result, London's
couple of dozen Japanese
restaurants – particularly those at
the top end of the price range –
are patronized predominantly by
the Japanese community. Most
prestigious (and therefore most
expensive) is Suntory, 72 St
James's St, SW1 (map 2)
☎ 409 0201. Fine restaurants in
descending grades from this are:
Miyama, 38 Clarges St, W1 (map
2) ☎ 409 0750, and 17 Godliman
St, EC4 (map 1) ☎ 489 1937; One
Two Three, 27 Davies St, W1
(map 2) ☎ 409 0750; Ikeda, 30
Brook St, W1 (map 2) ☎ 499
7145; Ryoma, 14 Hanway St, W1
(map 3) ☎ 637 7720; and Ginnan,
5 Cathedral Pl, EC4 (map 1)
☎ 236 4120/5150.

locals for no-choice dinners, tailing off after 10pm into suppers with no main course. Useful for business lunches in the area, when it is quieter and the good-value fixed-price menu offers a limited choice. Fashionable wine list with serious US presence.

Connaught, Restaurant *£/////*
Carlos Pl, W1 (map 3) ☎ *491 0668* •
MC • *jacket and tie; no pipes*
Gleaming panelling, starched linen, well-spaced tables and generally polished service enhance the reputation of what may well be the last of London's great, traditional hotel restaurants. Even when less than perfect, it is the safest bet for a top-drawer business meal with older clients. Michel Bourdin presides over a finely-tuned kitchen offering a long menu (changed in part every day) in a distinguished style that injects the Anglo-French *haute cuisine* with considered innovation. Fish, game and roasts are highlights; the bread-and-butter pudding is the best in town. Old-school, expensive wine list, strongest on Bordeaux. Reserve well ahead.

Connaught, Grill Room *£/////*
Carlos Pl, W1 (map 3) ☎ *499 7070* •
closed Sat & Sun • *MC* • *jacket and tie; no pipes*
Smaller than the restaurant (see above), and painted rather than panelled, the quietly refined grill is aristocratic London's refuge. The menu emphasizes the simpler, English strain of Bourdin's cooking – from roast lamb to braised oxtail.

Le Gavroche *£/////*
43 Upper Brook St, W1 (map 3)
☎ *408 0881* • *closed Sat & Sun* • *AE*
DC MC V • *jacket and tie; no pipes*
The first restaurant in London to earn three stars from Michelin; French, of course, and a favourite with the *corps diplomatique*. This ostentatiously comfortable Mayfair basement is the most obvious choice

Chinese restaurants
With a few notable exceptions, London's Chinese restaurants fall into the "off-duty" category; decor is often simple, if not downright scruffy, and service uncomprehending or offhand. The food, though, can be superb, and is usually excellent value. Some of the best is to be found in Soho's Chinatown, close to the main theatre district. *Fung Shing*, 15 Lisle St, WC2 (map 2) ☎ 437 1539 – highly rated by Cantonophiles – is one of the more comfortable. *Chuen Cheng Ku*, 17 Wardour St, W1 ☎ 437 1398, and *New World*, Gerrard Pl, W1 ☎ 734 0677 (both map 2), offer the best dim sum (served until about 5.30pm). Closer to Regent Street, *Ho-Ho*, 29 Maddox St, W1 (map 2) ☎ 493 1228, has dishes from all the main regions of China. More upmarket still are *Golden Chopsticks*, 1 Harrington Rd, SW7 (map 4) ☎ 584 0855, and *Dragon's Nest*, 58–60 Shaftesbury Ave, W1 (map 2) ☎ 437 3119. But most sophisticated of all – in terms of decor, clientele, food and service – is *Zen Central*, 20–22 Queen St, Mayfair, W1 (map 2) ☎ 629 8103, the stylish sister of the original, still thriving, *Zen*, Chelsea Cloisters, Sloane Ave, SW3 (map 4) ☎ 589 1781.

for high-powered entertaining, particularly at lunch time when the fixed-price menu is a relative bargain. The inspired and inspirational Albert Roux – rare among his peers in remaining at his stove despite fame and wealth – creates dishes that are modern and rich with their roots in regional France. Service is urbane, impeccable but far from intimidating; the sommelier is a considerate guide through the complex wine list. **Le Poulbot**, 45 Cheapside, EC2 (map 1) ☎ 236 4379, under Roux auspices, offers arguably the City's most

Sacred cows
A number of old-style establishments manage to retain their lofty position and popularity despite, or perhaps because of, their refusal to adapt to new styles of cooking and presentation. Most are known more for their grandeur or historical associations than for the quality of their food. The clearest exception is the *White Tower*, 1 Percy St, W1 (map 3) ☎ 636 8141, a grand old Greek with some remarkably good cooking. Less gastronomically remarkable are: *Simpson's-in-the-Strand*, 100 The Strand, WC2 (map 3) ☎ 836 9112 – a last bastion of the mammoth roast in male chauvinist surroundings; *Rules*, 35 Maiden La, WC2 (map 3) ☎ 836 5314 – for "English" food and theatrical decor; *Lockets*, Marsham Ct, Marsham St, SW1 (map 3) ☎ 834 9552 – a parliamentary favourite, complete with Division Bell; *Bentley's*, 11–15 Swallow St, W1 (map 2) ☎ 734 4756; and the *Café Royal Grill Room*, 68 Regent St, W1 (map 2) ☎ 437 9090, where Oscar Wilde entertained the previous *fin de siècle*, under the same glorious ceiling.
　Also see Savoy Grill and Ritz (under *Hotel restaurants*).

distinguished food. **Gavvers**, 61–63 Lower Sloane St, SW1 (map 3) ☎ 730 5983, in the original home of Le Gavroche, offers less ambitious dinners to a lively young set at a reasonable all-inclusive price that includes an aperitif and wine. A similar formula is now also available at **Les Trois Plats**, 4 Sydney St, SW3 (map 4) ☎ 352 3433.

Gay Hussar　*£//*
2 Greek St, W1 (map 2) ☎ *437 0973* • *closed Sun* • *no credit cards*
The most famous political restaurant

in town – a long-time favourite of literate old socialists whose books line the walls, and who get to eat downstairs. Although no longer owned by Hungarian-trained Victor Sassie, standards seem to be holding up. The long menu features weighty variations on the themes of carp, beetroot, hare, dumplings and goose. The set lunch is particularly good value, as are the wines which include some notable Hungarians and decent Bordeaux.

Inigo Jones　*£/////*
14 Garrick St, WC2 (map 2) ☎ *836 6456/3223* • *closed Sat L, Sun* • *AE DC MC V* • *jacket and tie preferred*
Paul Gayler's neat, attractively lit restaurant with bare-brick walls and large windows offers some of the purest *nouvelle cuisine* in Britain. Polished service (like the best young American service except that these waiters are French) and the generally good value of the fixed-price menu make it an excellent choice for business lunches. There are also vegetarian and fixed-price pre-theatre menus. Interesting, expensive list of 250 wines, many unobtainable elsewhere.

South of the river
Two of the best restaurants in the capital make the unlikely areas of Wandsworth and Battersea *au courant* gastronomic destinations. Chef-proprietor Marco Pierre White of *Harvey's*, 2 Bellevue Rd, SW17 ☎ 672 0114, is widely tipped to make a rapid ascent through the Michelin echelons. *L'Arlequin*, 123 Queenstown Rd, SW8 ☎ 622 0555, offers supremely assured modern interpretations of French provisional cooking. If you are unable to get into either of these, settle for the modern British bias of *Cavaliers*, 129 Queenstown Rd, SW8 ☎ 720 6960.

Hotel restaurants

The whiff of snobbery that hangs around London's more traditional hotels leads many potential customers of their restaurants to expect pompous service, over-elaborate menus and an altogether intimidating grandness. Times change, and now some of the best food in London is to be found in hotels, several of which are described in the main entries (notably Le Soufflé in the InterContinental, Ninety Park Lane in the Grosvenor House, the Oak Room of Le Meridien and the two Connaught restaurants). In other places the gulf between standards of food and decor remains enormous. The most tragic example is in the fabulous rococo main dining room of the *Ritz*, Piccadilly, W1 (map 2) ☎ 493 8181. Another relic of the capital's lost grandeur is that panelled and clubby erstwhile haunt of Fleet Street editors, the Grill Room of the *Savoy*, The Strand, WC2 (map 3) ☎ 836 4343. With views out over the treetops of Cadogan Place, the food is better in the well-padded Chelsea Room of the *Hyatt Carlton Tower*, 2 Cadogan Pl, SW1 (map 3) ☎ 235 5411, where chef Bernard Gaume makes full use of luxury ingredients in highly wrought modern French dishes. Downstairs is the more relaxed Rib Room with the best American-style roast beef in London and a good range of seafood. Chef David Dorricott also has a following for the sometimes magnificent food at Truffles Restaurant, *Portman InterContinental*, 22 Portman Sq, W1 (map 3) ☎ 486 5844. It will be interesting to see how chef David Nicholls – well-respected during his time at the Britannia (see *Hotels*) – develops the kitchen's reputation at his present posting, the *Royal Garden*, Kensington High St, W8 (map 4) ☎ 937 8000.

Indian restaurants

Britain's most extravagant experience of eating from the sub-continent is to be had at the *Bombay Brasserie*, Bailey's Hotel, Courtfield Close, SW7 (map 4) ☎ 370 4040. The surroundings include tent-like canopies and a leafy conservatory with pool; the food ranges from Bombay beach snacks to a Parsi wedding breakfast. Drawbacks are inattentive service and some cramped tables. The service is hardly better at the only other address with completely distinguished food: *Jamdani*, 34 Charlotte St, W1 (map 3) ☎ 631 0417 or 636 1178. Slightly simpler but still cosmopolitan places are: *Red Fort*, 77 Dean St, W1 (map 2) ☎ 437 2525, and *Lal Qila*, 117 Tottenham Court Rd, W1 (map 3) ☎ 387 4570.

Leith's £////

92 Kensington Park Rd, W11 (map 4) ☎ *299 4481 • closed L, Christmas and Boxing days, Aug bank hol • AE DC MC V • no pipes*

Prue Leith's curiously old-fashioned restaurant, on the ground floor of a large Victorian house, remains popular for intimate business dinners. It can often accept reservations at short notice, and is open at weekends. Fine, pricey wines.

Mijanou £///

143 Ebury St, SW1 (map 3) ☎ *730 4099 • closed Sat & Sun • AE DC MC*

An intimate little restaurant, popular with the gourmets of Belgravia in the evening and a more businessy set at lunch time. Sonia Blech's inventive food makes use of ingredients such as bourbon, wild rice, pecans and pickled aubergines. Nonsmokers can opt for clean air, though disappointing decor, in the basement room. Long, well-composed wine list.

Neal Street £///
26 Neal St, WC2 (map 2) ☎ *836 8368*
• *closed Sat, Sun, Christmas to New
Year* • *AE DC MC V*
The smartest place in the northern
reaches of Covent Garden and one of
London's few remaining "manager's
restaurants." The guiding hand here
is TV-cook and author, Antonio
Carluccio. The menu is elegant
modern Italian with a strong hand in
wild fungi, which are Carluccio's
obsession.

Ninety Park Lane £////
Grosvenor House Hotel (map 3)
☎ *499 6363* • *closed Sat L, Sun* • *AE
DC MC V* • *jacket and tie*
This most sybaritic restaurant – fitted
out like a country mansion – provides
some of the best food on Park Lane.
It owes its quality and elaborate style
to Michelin three-star consultant chef
Louis Outhier, formerly of La
Napoule. His food deals in vivid
flavours, whether the intensity of
black truffle or the pungency of green
coriander. The original permanent
chef, Stephen Goodlad, has now
moved on, to be replaced by Jean
Fouillet, whose pedigree includes
running two Michelin-starred
restaurants in France. Voluminous
wine list with many tempting half-
bottles.

Oak Room £////
Le Meridien Hotel (map 2)
☎ *734 8000* • *closed Sat L, Sun*
• *AE DC MC V*
After the Ritz, this is the prettiest
grand hotel dining room in town.
Service is excellent. The kitchens are
under the joint influence of full-time
English head chef David Chambers
and consultant Michel Lorain, who
has his own Michelin three-starred
restaurant in Burgundy. The success
of the marriage is that the join
doesn't show. Both partners bring
their own stylish modern ideas to a
menu which has featured lightly
smoked seabass on a bed of shredded,
crisply fried vegetables and a pretty
plate of assorted apple desserts

including caramelized slices and a
pure, clean Granny Smith sorbet.
Fixed-price lunches offer some of the
best value in town for this style of
establishment.

Rue St Jaques £////
5 Charlotte St, W1 (map 3) ☎ *637
0222* • *closed Sat L, Sun, nat hols* •
AE DC MC V • *jacket and tie; no pipes*
This attractively irregular series of
dining rooms on two floors is
especially popular with advertising
and media executives at lunch time,
rather quieter at night. The fashion-
conscious food does not always live
up to its undeniably glamorous
appearance. Competitively priced set
lunch. The wine list offers few
bargains.

Italian restaurants
Most of London's top Italian
restaurants are known less for
their food – most rate a poor
second or third after the better
French and Chinese places – than
for their chic style and fashionable
clientele. In this mould, *San
Lorenzo*, 22 Beauchamp Pl, SW3
(map 4) ☎ 584 1074, has the best
food and most film stars.
Cecconi's, 5A Burlington Gdns,
W1 (map 2) ☎ 434 1509, is the
most expensive. *Santini*, 29 Ebury
St, SW1 (map 3) ☎ 730 4094/
8275, and its relation *L'Incontro*,
87 Pimlico Rd, SW1 (map 3)
☎ 730 6327, are modern,
sophisticated and pricey. A trio of
useful Italians in the Covent
Garden area are the rather clubby
Giovanni's, 10 Goodwins Court,
WC2 ☎ 240 2877, the elegant
Luigi's, 15 Tavistock St, WC2
☎ 240 1795, and *Piccolo Mondo*,
31 Catherine St, WC2 ☎ 836
3609. Other relaxed, friendly,
reliable addresses include *La
Famiglia*, 7 Langton St, SW1
(map 4) ☎ 351 0761, and *San
Frediano*, 62–64 Fulham Rd, SW3
(map 4) ☎ 584 8375.

Fashionable informality
The more established "in-crowd" still prefers *Le Caprice*, Arlington House, Arlington St, SW1 (map 2) ☎ 629 2239, and *Langan's Brasserie*, Stratton St, W1 (map 2) ☎ 493 6437, for casual eating. Younger venues include: *Very Simply Nico*, 48A Rochester Row, SW1 (map 3) ☎ 630 8061 – serving the best no-nonsense brasserie food in town, this is Chez Nico's second string; *Kensington Place*, 201 Kensington Church St, W8 (map 4) ☎ 727 3184 – futuristic brasserie; *Fifty-One Fifty-One*, Chelsea Cloisters, Sloane Ave, SW3 (map 4) ☎ 730 5151 – the country's best Cajun/Creole food; *Guernica*, 21A Foley St, W1 (map 3) ☎ 580 0623 – cool, intimate joint with Basque-influenced menu; *Brasserie St Quentin*, 243 Brompton Rd, SW3 (map 4) ☎ 581 5131 or 589 8005 – smart-ish Gallic diner; *Mitchell & O'Brien*, 2 St Anne's Court, W1 (map 2) ☎ 434 9941 – a hi-tech version of a New York bar and deli;

River Café, Thames Wharf, Rainville Rd, W6 ☎ 385 3344 – cult Italian canteen; and *Ziani's*, 45 Radnor Walk, SW3 (map 4) ☎ 352 2698 – to experience trendy Chelsea *en fête* (poor wine list). Two individual chefs with their own supporters are soi-disant "parfumier of taste" Garry Hollihead at *Sutherlands*, 45 Lexington St, W1 (map 2) ☎ 434 3401, and bluff Yorkshireman Brian Turner at *Turner's*, 87–89 Walton St, SW3 (map 4) ☎ 584 6711. Of the New York clone establishments, *Jams*, 42 Albemarle St, W1 (map 2) ☎ 499 8293, has not been hugged as tightly to fashionable London's bosom as *Orso*, 27 Wellington St, WC2 (map 3) ☎ 240 5269, a cool grey basement offering a short menu of simple, stylish Italian dishes. Round the corner at 13 Exeter St (map 3) ☎ 836 0651 is the more upbeat parent restaurant, *Joe Allen*, still filling many a halfway famous face till the small hours with fast American food.

Le Soufflé £|////
InterContinental Hotel (map 3)
☎ 409 3131 • *closed Sat L* • AE DC MC V • *jacket and tie*
Another good choice for top-flight business entertaining, if not quite in the Connaught class of *belle époque* luxury. The food consistently rises above the relentlessly "international" level of the rest of the hotel. Peter Kromberg's kitchens treat fine ingredients with respect: the soufflés are indeed very good, but there is much else besides, in the most accomplished modern manner. Set lunches offer good value. Service can be slow. Impressive wine list, mostly in double and triple figures.

La Tante Claire £|////
68–69 Royal Hospital Rd, SW3 (map 4) ☎ 352 6045 • *closed Sat, Sun, nat hols, 10 days Easter & Christmas, 3 weeks Aug/Sep* • AE DC

MC V • *jacket and tie D; no pipes or cigars*
Pierre Koffman's stylishly restrained restaurant is a place of pilgrimage for serious gastronomes. His assured interpretation of French regional cooking sets the standard for other top-flight establishments. Performance is as faultless front of house as it is in the kitchen. Reserve well ahead, especially for lunch when the *carte* is supplemented by the best-value fixed-price lunch in London. The French wine list has appropriate great names at immense prices and some more modest *vins de pays*.

Telephone numbers
London's single area code, 01, is due to be replaced in April 1990 by two new codes, 071 and 081, for central and outer areas.

Bars

London has plenty of pubs and wine bars, but the overall standard is poor and the few good places desperately crowded. Generally, they are used for off-duty lunches and after-work drinks; those in the City usually close by 8pm and at weekends. Pubs are often rather scruffy, though some have real character; wine bars tend to be smarter; and there are a handful of chic cocktail and champagne bars.

Wine bars Partly because there are so few decent restaurants in the area, many of the City's business community head for a wine bar at lunchtime. The most exclusive, and the tiniest, is the *Greenhouse*, 16 Royal Exchange, EC3 which serves champagne and top-quality seafood. Wine merchants *Corney & Barrow* run several smart bars attached to classy restaurants (see *City restaurants*) at 109 Broad St, EC2, 118 Moorgate, EC2 and 44 Cannon St, EC4. The *Pavilion*, Finsbury Circus Gdns, Finsbury Circus, EC2 and *Bow Wine Vaults* in Bow Lane are old city favourites. The *Colony* wine bars at 48 Aldgate High St, EC3; 9 Cutler St E1 and 33 Broadgate St EC2 have excellent food. Rather more casual in style – sawdust on the floor, candles on the tables – are the 30 or so bars owned by *Davys of London* and the rapidly improving *Balls Bros* bars (all listed in the phone book).

Elsewhere in London, wine bars attract a more mixed clientele. Close to Harrods, is the smart *Le Métro*, 28 Basil St, SW3; reservations ☎ 589 6286: light food, excellent French wines. In Soho, the ground-floor bar of *L'Escargot Brasserie*, 48 Greek St, W1, which has interesting food and distinguished wines but slow service, is still popular with local media executives, though many have deserted it for two nearby members-only clubs, Groucho's and the Moscow. In Victoria/Belgravia, the *Ebury*, 139 Ebury St, SW1 attracts an affluent crowd of local residents and antique dealers: fine wines, also

bistro-type food; reservations ☎ 730 5447. Handy for the high-rise offices lining Victoria Street, SW1, *Methuselah's* (at number 29) – also with comfortable restaurant ☎ 222 0424 – is one of three related bars known for their outstanding wines and imaginative food; the others are the *Cork and Bottle*, 44 Cranbourn St, WC2, near Leicester Square, and *Shampers*, 4 Kingly St, W1, behind Regent Street.

Cocktail and champagne bars
London's traditional grand hotels are a safe bet if meeting for a drink; the piano bar at the *Dorchester*, Park La, W1 (see *Hotels*) is particularly comfortable and elegant, and serves excellent cocktails and good snacks. For a bit more flash and dash, *Kettners* in Soho, 29 Romilly St, W1 has a cool champagne bar. Moving upmarket and into a smarter district, *Green's Champagne Bar* in St James's, 36 Duke St, SW1 is a small, clubby establishment which serves smoked salmon, crab and the best oysters in town; sit at the bar, or if you want more privacy reserve an alcove table ☎ 930 4566.

Pubs For a view of the Thames, a touch of history and well-kept beer, try the *Angel*, Bermondsey Wall East, SE16 or the *Mayflower*, 117 Rotherhithe St, SE16. Inland, a short walk from the Angel, is London's only surviving galleried coaching inn, the *George*, 77 Borough High St, SE1. On the other side of London, there's the *Dove* at Hammersmith, Upper Mall, W6. Other, more central old-fashioned inns include the claustrophobic *Lamb & Flag*, near Covent Garden, Rose St, WC2; *Ye Olde Cheshire Cheese*, 145 Fleet St, EC4, haunt of generations of lawyers and journalists (though now outnumbered by tourists); and, handy for the City, the *Black Friar*, 174 Queen Victoria St, EC4, a splendidly preserved example of Art Nouveau. By way of contrast, *Henry J Bean*, 197 King's Rd, SW3 is an exuberantly Americanized Chelsea pub with garden.

Entertainment

London is not a 24-hour city – pub and restaurant closing hours and the lack of late-night transport make sure of that – but the range of evening entertainment on offer is huge. Theatre and all kinds of music are London's particular strengths. The best weekly magazines devoted to events in London are *Time Out* and *City Limits*. Both carry full listings, reviews, news and opinions, and have an alternative/leftish stance. The evening newspaper, the *Standard*, has adequate cinema and West End theatre listings, but little on other entertainment.

Ticket agencies Tickets for most events are available in advance from box offices or West End ticket agencies; *Keith Prowse* ☎ 741 9999 is the largest general agency. Many venues take credit card reservations by telephone, and most hotels will make reservations for you. Seats for popular shows, particularly successful musicals and major National Theatre productions, may need to be reserved months ahead. There is also a ticket kiosk in Leicester Square which sells West End theatre tickets at half price plus commission for same-day performances (open from 12 noon for matinées, 2pm for evening shows).

Theatre The main theatre district is the West End, around Covent Garden and Soho, and the prestigious "establishment" theatres are not far away. Just across the river on the South Bank, the *National Theatre*, SE1 ☎ 928 2252 is three theatres in one building: the *Olivier*, an amphitheatre; the *Lyttleton*, which has a proscenium stage; and the *Cottesloe*, a studio theatre. All present modern and classic drama. There are always a few tickets available on the day to personal callers (from 10am). The London home of the Royal Shakespeare Company is the *Barbican* theatre, EC2 ☎ 628 8795 and its associated studio, the *Pit*. Performances include first-run and standard works as well as those of Shakespeare.

London has a big and thriving Fringe scene, with independent, mainly young companies performing plays, revues and cabaret in pubs and art centres as well as theatres. Venues include London's most established anti-establishment theatre, the *Royal Court*, Sloane Sq, SW1 ☎ 730 1745; the *Young Vic*, The Cut, SE1 ☎ 928 6363; and the *Shaw Theatre*, Euston Rd, NW1 ☎ 388 1394.

Music London has a number of famous symphony orchestras, among them the London Philharmonic, the Philharmonia, the Royal Philharmonic, the BBC Symphony, the London Symphony and the London Sinfonietta. The South Bank complex has three auditoria: the 3,000-seater *Royal Festival Hall*, which presents symphony orchestras and has excellent acoustics; the *Queen Elizabeth Hall*, which seats 1,100 and specializes in chamber music; and the *Purcell Room*, which seats 372 and presents solo recitals. All three also put on occasional non-classical events, and share a common ticket office ☎ 928 3002 (information) ☎ 928 8800 (reservations). The *Royal Albert Hall*, Kensington Gore, SW7 ☎ 589 3203 (information) ☎ 589 8212 (reservations) is a fine Victorian building. Its acoustically imperfect circular auditorium is best known for its "Proms" concert season of classical music, lasting from July to September, when the middle of the hall is cleared of seats, allowing the audience to stand or wander while listening to the music. The *Barbican Centre*, EC2 ☎ 638 4141 (information) ☎ 638 8891 (reservations) is the home of the London Symphony Orchestra.

Rock and pop venues tend to be as evanescent as the music. Major tours have their London dates at *Earl's Court Centre*, SW7 ☎ 385 1200, *Wembley Arena*, Lakeside Way, Wembley ☎ 902 1234 or *Hammersmith Odeon*, Queen Caroline St, W6 ☎ 748 4081. Most gigs in the capital are in pubs and clubs. Among the more long-lasting, featuring US visitors and up-and-coming British acts, are the *Marquee*, Charing Cross Rd, W1 ☎ 437 6603; *Dingwalls*, Camden Lock, NW1 ☎ 267 4967; and the *Camden Palace*, Camden High St, NW1 ☎ 387 0428. Jazz is often to be found in pubs. The big names appear at the well-known jazz club, *Ronnie Scott's*, Frith St, W1 ☎ 439 0747; and there is jazz every evening except Monday in the basement of the *Pizza Express*, Dean St, W1 ☎ 437 9595. The *Bass Clef*, Coronet St, N1 ☎ 729 2476 features jazz, Latin and African music seven nights a week.

Opera London supports two opera companies. The Royal Opera Company (ROC) is in residence at the *Royal Opera House*, Bow St, WC2 ☎ 240 1066. It is essential to reserve seats well in advance for major productions. Over 60 rear amphitheatre seats – dizzyingly high in this theatre – are available at 10am on the day of the performance, but overnight queues may form for these. English National Opera (ENO) is based at the *London Coliseum*, St Martin's La, WC2 ☎ 836 3161 (information) ☎ 240 5258 (reservations). Its productions, usually sung in English, are as popular as those of the ROC and as difficult to get into. Balcony seats are available from 10am on the day of performance. The *Queen Elizabeth Hall* and the *Royal Festival Hall* (see above) sometimes produce operas, and visiting companies appear at *Sadler's Wells* (see below).

Dance The Royal Ballet Company shares the *Royal Opera House* with the ROC, and the London Festival Ballet shares the *London Coliseum* with the ENO. *Sadler's Wells*, Rosebery Ave, EC1 ☎ 278 8916 was the original home of the Royal Ballet and the ENO and now features visiting companies in programmes of opera, ballet and contemporary dance. Contemporary and modern dance troupes perform all over the city in theatres, arts centres, colleges, warehouses and art galleries.

Cinema There are more cinemas than films to be found in London. The West End cinemas feature first-run and revival films, mostly American or British. Foreign language films are generally run with subtitles in English; dubbing is unusual. Art house films can be seen at various independent cinemas such as the two *Curzon* cinemas, in Curzon St, W1 ☎ 499 3737 and Shaftesbury Ave, W1 ☎ 439 4805; the *Gate*, Notting Hill Gate, W11 ☎ 727 4043; the *Camden Plaza*, Camden High St, NW1 ☎ 485 2443; the *Chelsea*, King's Rd, SW3 ☎ 351 3742; the *Screen on the Green*, Islington Green, N1 ☎ 226 3520; and the *Minema*, Knightsbridge, SW1 ☎ 235 4225. There are also various cinema clubs with daily changes of programme. Membership is available to the visitor on a cheap daily or weekly basis. Prime among these is the *National Film Theatre*, South Bank, SE1 ☎ 928 3232.

Nightclubs and casinos Nightclubs are as fleetingly fashionable as rock venues, but *Annabel's*, Berkeley Sq, W1 ☎ 629 3558 is here to stay; discreet and of high quality, an introduction from a member is almost essential. Similar strictures apply to *Raffles*, King's Rd, SW3 ☎ 352 1091, *Stocks*, King's Rd, SW3 ☎ 351 3461, *Tokyo Joe's*, Clarges St, W1 ☎ 409 1832 and *Tramp*, Jermyn St, SW1 ☎ 734 3174. Glamour and noise are to be found at clubs such as the *Limelight*, Shaftesbury Ave, W1 ☎ 434 0572 and *Stringfellows*, Upper St Martin's La, WC2 ☎ 240 5534; no membership, but the doorman must like your looks. If he doesn't, you can head for the vast *Hippodrome*, Cranbourn St, WC2 ☎ 437 4311, also owned by nightclub king Peter Stringfellow.

Casinos are strictly controlled. To visit one you must join, which takes 48 hours, or be introduced by a member. The elegant *Aspinall's*, Curzon St, W1 ☎ 629 4400, and the civilized *Crockford's*, Curzon St, W1 ☎ 493 7771 are the classiest.

Shopping

Many visitors to London put shopping high on their list of things to do during their stay, and with reason: the range of goods is superb and prices often compare very favourably with those back home, particularly for high-quality items. The West End, which has the greatest concentration of shops, divides into quite distinct shopping areas, usually referred to by the name of the main street. The capital's best department stores are ideal for one-stop shopping if time is short. Most London shops are open Mon–Sat, 9 or 9.30 to 5.30 or 6, staying open later on one evening, to 7 or later (see the area details below).

Tax refunds Most of the large department stores and some smaller shops operate a retail export scheme which often allows overseas visitors to claim refunds of the value added tax (VAT) included in the price of many purchases.

Main shopping areas

Knightsbridge The smartest shopping area, dominated by *Harrods*, the world's most famous store; you will find almost anything there, and the Food Halls are well worth a look even if you are not buying. *Harvey Nichols* is smaller and more select, offering an excellent range of top-quality clothing. The range of shops is otherwise similar to those in New Bond Street (see below), with branches of *Saint Laurent*, *Charles Jourdan* and *Bally* alongside *Mappin & Webb*, *The Scotch House* and *Austin Reed*. Ultra-chic Beauchamp Place is particularly good for top British fashion (Bruce Oldfield). Late opening: Wed, 7pm.

Oxford Street Branches of Britain's top retailing chains and large department stores like *Selfridges*, *Marks & Spencer* and *John Lewis* offer an excellent choice of medium-price and quality clothing, accessories and household goods; chic boutiques in nearby St Christopher's Place. Very busy in summer and at Christmas.

Late opening: Thu, 7.30–8pm.

Bond Street Exclusive, expensive and stylish. Best visited on a weekday as some of the shops close for all or part of Saturday. Old Bond Street, which runs off Piccadilly, has top art dealers (*Agnew*, *Colnaghi*, *Leger*) and smart clothes and accessories shops (*Chanel*, *Gucci*). Its extension, glamorous New Bond Street, has *Saint Laurent*, *Ralph Lauren* and other international names as well as some uniquely English shops like *Asprey* and *The White House* (lingerie and children's clothes). Several high-quality shoe shops include *Bruno Magli*, *Pinet* and *Fratelli Rossetti*. The fine art auctioneers, *Sotheby's*, are based here; for modern art, visit the nearby Cork Street galleries. Running up off Brook Street to Bond Street Underground station (actually on Oxford Street) is South Molton Street, with top fashion houses *Browns* and *Joseph*. At the Piccadilly end of Bond Street is the charming early-19thC Burlington Arcade, a good place to buy cashmere.

Piccadilly Scattered along this busy road are a handful of the city's best known stores. Try *Simpson's* for tailored clothes and accessories, *Fortnum & Mason* for its food and fashion departments and *Hatchards* for books. Facing Piccadilly Circus, *Lillywhites* has the best selection of sportswear in London. In Haymarket, *Burberrys* is renowned for its rainwear; and the *Design Centre* provides a showcase for modern British design. For top-quality men's shirts, ties and shoes (particularly made to measure), head for Jermyn Street (which has other interesting specialist shops) and St James's Street. For tailors, you have to cross Piccadilly for Sackville Street and Savile Row.

Regent Street More attractive and upmarket than Oxford Street, Regent Street offers a good mixture of specialist shops and department stores. *Liberty's*, known for its distinctive fabrics and furnishings, is a good place to find attractive gifts and *Dickens and Jones* is excellent for fashion. Good clothes shops include *Jaeger*, *Burberrys*, *Aquascutum*, *Scotch House*, *Laura Ashley* and *Austin Reed*. Other shops worth a visit include the six floors of *Hamleys* toyshop; two famous jewellers, *Garrard* (the Queen's jeweller) and *Mappin & Webb*; and *Wedgwood* (on the corner of Oxford Street). Late opening: Thu, 7.30pm.

Covent Garden The converted market buildings now house speciality shops selling trendy clothes and shoes, books, decorative goods both classy and offbeat, kitchen equipment, fine chocolates, wholefoods and other natural products including toiletries. Market stalls sell a range of hand-crafted gifts and clothes, except on Mondays when antiques take over. Some shops and stalls are open on Sundays. More of the same, together with several galleries, can be found in nearby narrow streets such as Neal Street and Floral Street.

King's Road More for sightseeing than for shopping, the King's Road still attracts the young and exhibitionist. The classier clothes and gift shops are at the Sloane Square end, with the department store *Peter Jones* and, at the bottom of Sloane Street, the more exclusive *General Trading Company*. Further down the King's Road, numerous boutiques vie for space with antique dealers. Late opening: Wed, 8pm.

High Street, Kensington This more compact version of Oxford Street has branches of chain stores alongside more individualistic shops and an antiques Hypermarket. Kensington Church Street, opposite the department store, *House of Fraser*, is known for antiques. Late opening: Wed, 7pm. Many shops in High Street, Kensington, stay open to 8pm on Thursdays.

Leading department stores
Harrods Brompton Rd ☎ 730 1234, open Mon–Sat, 9–6 (9.30–7, Wed). Facilities include bank/bureau de change, export bureau, tourist information, fulfilment of telephone orders backed by credit card.

Harvey Nichols Knightsbridge ☎ 235 5000, open Mon–Fri, 10–5.30; Sat, 10–6. Facilities include export documentation and shipping (account customers only; retail export scheme not operated), fulfilment of telephone orders backed by credit card.

John Lewis Oxford St ☎ 629 7711, open Mon–Sat, 9–5.30 (9.30–8, Thu). Retail export scheme operated. No credit cards. Telephone orders and despatch for account customers only.

Liberty's Regent St ☎ 734 1234, open Mon–Sat, 9.30–6 (9.30–7.30, Thu). Retail export scheme operated.

Marks & Spencer 458 Oxford St ☎ 935 7954, open Mon and Tue, 9–7; Sat, 9–6. M & S credit card only.

Peter Jones Sloane Sq ☎ 730 3434, open Mon–Sat, 9–5.30 (9.30–7, Wed). Retail export scheme operated. No credit cards. Telephone orders and despatch for account customers only.

Selfridges Oxford St ☎ 629 1234, open Mon–Sat, 9.30–6 (9.30–8, Thu). Retail export scheme operated.

Street markets
London has a large number of street markets, most selling food but some specializing in antiques and bric-à-brac. The best known is the Saturday morning market in *Portobello Road*, W11 – don't expect to find bargains. The Sunday market in *Petticoat Lane*, Middlesex St, E1 and nearby Brick Lane starts in the early hours. On Fridays, antique buyers including dealers head for the *Bermondsey Street* market, SE1 – again, get there at dawn or earlier to beat the competition. *Camden Lock* market, NW1, open at weekends, has a range of arts and crafts, period clothes.

Sightseeing

London's greatest attractions are its historic buildings and an enormous variety of museums and galleries containing treasures from all over the world, the legacy of centuries of trade, exploration and imperial power. For those with limited spare time, there are small areas rich in interest such as Westminster, Bloomsbury, South Kensington and Greenwich. The most crowded time is Easter to October, but there is no real off-season, and the top attractions – the big museums, the Tower, St Paul's and Westminster Abbey – are always busy. Some places are closed on national holidays; ring to check. Sightseeing is not expensive although charges have been introduced, with some controversy, at several galleries and churches that could previously be visited free. The London Tourist Board ☎ 730 3488 gives general advice.

British Museum Vast and wide-ranging collection with archeological bias. Relics of Greece, Rome, Egypt and Mesopotamia; oriental art and Chinese ceramics. *Great Russell St, WC1 (map 3). Open Mon–Sat, 10–5; Sun, 2.30–6.*

Buckingham Palace Official residence of monarch since 1837. Dull 20thC façade hides Nash's earlier palace from crowds at the railings. The *Queen's Gallery* ☎ 930 4832 houses annually changing exhibitions of items from royal collections of fine art, jewellery, photographs. *Buckingham Gate, SW1 (map 3). Open (gallery only) Tue–Sat, 10.30–5; Sun, 2–5.* The *Royal Mews* displays royal carriages and harness. *Buckingham Palace Rd, SW1 (map 3). Open Wed & Thu, 2–4.*

Changing of the Guard The Palace guard is changed with due ceremony at 11.30. This daily pageant (alternate days in winter) always attracts a crowd. *Buckingham Palace, SW1 (map 3).*

Courtauld Institute Galleries Major collection of Impressionist and Post-Impressionist painting and Old Masters. *Woburn Sq, WC1 (map 3) until end 1989. Re-opening Somerset Ho, Strand WC2 in May 1990. Open Mon–Sat, 10–5; Sun, 2–5.*

Covent Garden Once the home of London's fruit and vegetable market, the handsome iron and glass buildings of the Piazza now house shops, restaurants and a craft market. Street entertainers perform in front of the Tuscan portico of Inigo Jones's *St Paul's Church* (entrance through peaceful courtyard garden). The *London Transport Museum* (open daily, 10–6) in the Flower Market has models, memorabilia and complete vehicles. *Covent Garden, WC2 (map 3).*

Dickens' House Tall, narrow terraced house packed with pictures, letters, furniture, manuscripts and memorabilia of England's most famous novelist. *Doughty St, WC1 (map 3). Open Mon–Sat, 10–5.*

Geological Museum Makes the most of unpromising material. Exhibitions of gemstones, mineralogy and story of the Earth; good audio-visual presentations. *Exhibition Rd, SW7 (map 4). Open Mon–Sat, 10–6; Sun, 1–6.*

Greenwich Attractive old Thames-side district with astronomical and sea-faring associations. Tea clipper *Cutty Sark* is in dry dock at the waterside. *Open Mon–Sat, 10–6; Sun, 12–6.* The baroque *Royal Naval College* has a painted Hall and Chapel. *Open Fri–Wed, 2.30–4.30.* Behind the College is the *National Maritime Museum*, largest of its kind in the world; above it, in the Park, is Wren's *Royal Observatory*, site of the GMT meridian line. *Both open Mon–Sat, 10–6; Sun, 2–5.30.*

Hayward Gallery Concrete building surmounted by a neon sculpture in the South Bank complex, home of Arts Council exhibitions. *South Bank, SE1 (map 1) ☎ 928 3144. Open Mon–Wed, 10–8; Thu–Sat, 10–6; Sun, 12–6.*

Horse Guards Parade A chance to be photographed next to a resplendently uniformed and mounted member of the Household Cavalry. Behind, bounded by state buildings, is the parade ground. The guard is changed at 11am (10am on Sun). *Whitehall, SW1 (map 2)*.

Houses of Parliament 19thC extravaganza, best seen from the river or Westminster Bridge. Northern clock tower houses the famous bell, Big Ben. Westminster Hall, only remnant of the medieval palace, has a majestic timber roof. During sittings, the public are admitted to visitors' galleries in both Commons and Lords. *Parliament Sq, SW1 (map 3)* ☎ *219 4272 (Commons)* ☎ *219 3107 (Lords). Opening times vary*.

Imperial War Museum 20thC warfare, at home and abroad; art, photographs, films, models, weaponry, aircraft enlarged space; new "Blitz Experience." *Lambeth Rd, SE11. Open Mon–Sat, 10–6; Sun, 2–6*.

Dr Johnson's House Terraced house in which Johnson lived and worked on his dictionary from 1748 to 1759. Pictures and memorabilia of 18thC London literati. *Gough St, EC4 (map 1). Open Mon–Sat, 11–5.30 (to 5pm, Oct–Apr)*.

Madame Tussaud's Wax images of the famous and infamous. Always crowded, full of children. *Marylebone Rd, NW1 (map 3). Open daily, 10–5.30*. Next door is the *Planetarium*, with shows every 30min. *Open daily, 11–4.30*.

Museum of London Two millenia of London's history in very informative and well laid out museum. Models and archeological finds; displays on 18th–20thC include whole interiors, shop fronts and the Lord Mayor's coach. Compact, but rarely crowded. *London Wall, EC2 (map 1). Open Tue–Sat, 10–6; Sun, 2–6*.

Museum of Mankind Several well mounted, long-running exhibitions from the ethnographic collections of the British Museum. Permanent displays include Benin bronzes, Aztec mosaics, Amerindian carvings. *Burlington Gdns, W1 (map 2). Open Mon–Sat, 10–5; Sun, 2.30–6*.

Parks and gardens
Inner London is surprisingly green. *Hyde Park* and *Kensington Gardens* (both map 4), separated by the Serpentine, form the largest area of parkland; the latter contain *Kensington Palace*, home of the Prince and Princess of Wales (*State apartments open Mon–Sat, 9–4.45; Sun, 1–4.45). St James's Park* (map 3) has a lake full of wildfowl and fine views of Whitehall and Buckingham Palace. *Regent's Park* (map 3), surrounded by wonderful stuccoed classical terraces, has fine gardens as well as the Zoo (see main entries). Further out, *Kew Gardens* is a botanical paradise; *Hampstead Heath* is high and hilly, dotted with ponds and woods; and *Richmond Park* provides miles of parkland and heath with roaming deer.

Museum of the Moving Image
MOMI is a new film museum with visitor participation and visual tricks. *South Bank SE1 (map 1). Open Tue–Sat, 10–8, Sun, 10–6*.

National Gallery A large, world-class collection of paintings, all well-lit and well-labelled, with particularly fine Italian, Dutch and Flemish works. *Trafalgar Sq, WC2 (map 2). Open Mon–Sat, 10–6; Sun, 2–6*.

National Portrait Gallery Paintings, photographs, drawings and caricatures of the famous arranged chronologically from Middle Ages to today. *St Martin's Pl, WC2 (map 2). Open Mon–Fri, 10–5; Sat, 10–6; Sun, 2–6*.

Natural History Museum Handsome Victorian building, housing millions of specimens. Dinosaur skeletons and life-size whale models vie for space with lively self-contained exhibitions on evolution and human biology aimed at the many younger visitors. *Cromwell Rd, SW7 (map 4). Open Mon–Sat, 10–6; Sun, 2.30–6*.

Royal Academy of Arts Home of the painting establishment since 1768.

Major temporary exhibitions; *Madonna and Child* relief by Michelangelo the star of the permanent exhibition. *Piccadilly, W1 (map 2)* ☎ *734 3471. Open daily, 10–6.*

St Bartholomew the Great A massive Romanesque priory church in the shadow of Barts teaching hospital. 15thC gate-house, excellent monuments and oldest peal of bells in England. *West Smithfield, EC1 (map 1).*

St James's Palace Low battlemented Tudor building in red brick, royal residence 1698–1837. Round the back, in Stable Yard Rd, is Clarence House, home of the Queen Mother. *Pall Mall, SW1 (map 2).*

St Martin's in the Fields Classical church in northwest corner of Trafalgar Square. Tower and spire unusually placed over portico. Interior light and spacious with fine moulded ceiling. Free lunchtime chamber music concerts. *Trafalgar Sq, WC2 (map 2).*

St Paul's Cathedral London's principal church, built by Sir Christopher Wren at end of 17thC. Exterior of finely carved Portland stone dominated by 365ft central dome. Inside heavily decorated, sometimes gaudy, with excellent wood carving and wrought ironwork. Crypt contains tombs of Wellington, Nelson and Wren among many others. Fine views, inside and out, from galleries in the dome. *EC4 (map 1). Open daily, 7.30–6. Crypt and dome open Mon–Fri, 10–4; Sat, 11–4 (to 3pm, Oct–Mar).*

Science Museum Museum of technology – steam and electricity, space and undersea exploration – chemistry, physics, medicine, photography and cinematography; displays of engines and vehicles. *Exhibition Rd, SW7 (map 4). Open Mon–Sat, 10–6; Sun, 11–6.*

Speakers' Corner Northwest tip of Hyde Park set aside since 1872 as a public forum and a magnet for extroverts and eccentrics. Weekends only – Sundays are best. Nearby is

Marble Arch, once the gateway to Buckingham Palace, now surrounded by traffic. *Marble Arch, W2 (map 3).*

Tate Gallery. British and modern painting. Constable, Blake, Pre-Raphaelites and, especially, Turner well-represented; modern collection large, but has gaps. Temporary exhibitions. *Millbank, SW1 (map 3)* ☎ *821 1313. Open Mon–Sat, 10–6; Sun, 2–6.*

Thames Barrier Visitors' Centre The barrier, completed in 1984, has removed the threat of flooding from London. Exhibition and film, also 20min boat trips around the barrier. *Unity Way, SE18. Open Mon–Fri, 10.30–5; Sat & Sun, 10.30–5.30.*

Tower of London One-time royal residence, fortress and prison, dating from the 11thC. Now houses extensive collections of arms and armour and the Crown Jewels, watched over by Yeoman Warders in their Tudor uniforms. Very popular; arrive early to avoid the worst crowds. *EC3 (map 1). Open Mar–Oct, Mon–Sat, 9.30–5.45; Sun, 2–5.45; Nov–Feb, Mon–Sat, 9.30–5.* Nearby is *Tower Bridge*, built in the late 19thC when the Pool of London was a busy port. Lift in N Tower leads to exhibition and the upper walkways; views up and down the river. *Open daily, 10–6.30 (to 4.45pm, Nov–Mar).*

Legal London

The *Law Courts* in the Strand (map 1), a cross between a castle and a cathedral, and the *Central Criminal Court* in Old Bailey have public galleries for the viewing of trials. South of the Strand is the *Temple*, with its round church, gardens and courtyard, the heart of legal London. Most barristers have offices here or in the other Inns of Court, *Gray's Inn* and *Lincoln's Inn*, both of which have tranquil gardens and good houses; Lincoln's Inn also has *Sir John Soane's Museum*, a delightfully eccentric collection of pictures and antiquities (*open Tue–Sat, 10–5*).

Upstream on the south bank is moored *HMS Belfast*, the World War II cruiser. *Morgans La, SE1. Open Apr–Oct, 10–6; Nov–Mar, 10–4.30.* Just downstream from the Bridge, masked by the ugly bulk of the World Trade Centre, is *St Katharine's Dock*, developed as a marina with shops, restaurants and exhibitions.

Victoria and Albert Museum
Rambling treasure house specializing in art and design, commonly known as the V&A. Sculpture, clothing, chinoiserie, musical instruments, Persian carpets, furniture; drawings and paintings by Constable, Raphael cartoons. *Cromwell Rd, SW7 (map 4). Open Mon–Sat, 10–6; Sun, 2.30–6.*

Wallace Collection Private 19thC art collection in grand house. Largely French rococo in taste, some Flemish and Dutch. Paintings, furniture, arms and armour, pottery and porcelain.

Manchester Sq, W1 (map 3). Open Mon–Sat, 10–5; Sun, 2–5.
Westminster Abbey Mainly 12th–14thC collegiate church. Aisles packed with memorials, shrine of Edward the Confessor, the coronation throne. To the south, quietly dignified cloisters, octagonal chapter house. Museum in undercroft. *Broad Sanctuary, SW1 (map 3).*

Westminster Cathedral England's principal Catholic church, an early-20thC Byzantine-style basilica in red brick. Marble-decorated interior, cool, dark and fragrant. *Ashley Pl, SW1 (map 3).*

Zoological Gardens Oldest zoo in the world. Important and extensive collection of animals, many in new houses designed to give them more freedom. Penguin pool and Snowdon Aviary are architectural landmarks. *Regent's Park, NW1. Open Apr–Oct, Mon–Sat, 9–6; Sun, 9–7; Nov–Mar, daily, 10–4.*

Guided tours
The quickest general introduction to London can be gained from a bus or coach tour. Several operators run on a circular route (1hr 30mins–2hrs): *London Sightseeing Tours* ☎ 622 7783, *London Coaches* ☎ 227 3456 and *London Pride* ☎ 629 4999. The *Harrods* tour ☎ 581 3603 – the most expensive and luxurious – has taped commentary in eight languages, as does the *Cityrama* tour ☎ 720 6663. *Evan Evans* ☎ 839 6415 and *Frames Rickards* ☎ 837 3111 both run daily luxury coach tours: half-days in the West End (am) or City (pm) and full-day tours of both. It's worth paying the extra for the *Harrods* all-day tour (Thu only) which includes lunch at Lockets (see *Restaurants*).
River trips Boats run frequent daily trips from Charing Cross and Westminster piers to the Tower and

Greenwich. From Easter to October they go downstream to the Barrier or upstream (Westminster only) to Kew (1hr 30mins each way) or Hampton Court (a 3hr trip each way). Recorded information ☎ 730 4812.
Walking tours Most are in the afternoon, start at a subway station and last two hours. Themed walks include Royal London, Dickens' London and Haunted London. Programmes change daily; ring first. *City Walks* ☎ 937 4281, *City Sights* ☎ 739 2372, *London Walks* ☎ 441 8906, *Streets of London* ☎ 882 3414. *Cockney Walks* ☎ 504 9159 focus on the history of working people in the East End.
Private tours To rent a car complete with driver/guide to fulfil your own itinerary, ask at your hotel or call direct: *British Tours* ☎ 629 5267, *Take a Guide* ☎ 221 5475.

Spectator sports

Cricket London has two main cricket grounds which host major inter-county and international test matches: *Lord's*, St John's Wood Rd, NW8 ☎ 289 1611, home of the sport's ruling body, the Marylebone Cricket Club (MCC), and of the Middlesex county side; and the *Oval*, Kennington Oval, SE11 ☎ 582 6660, home of the Surrey county side. Season: Apr–Sep.

Horse-racing There are several courses on the fringes of London including *Epsom*, *Kempton Park* and *Sandown Park*. For information ☎ (0372) 69523. Season: all year; Flat racing summer; steeplechasing winter.

Polo Matches are played on most weekends and some weekdays in summer at *Smiths Lawn*, Windsor Great Park, Berkshire, home of the Guards' Club; in *Richmond Park* (near Roehampton Gate); and at *Cowdray Park*, Midhurst, W. Sussex. Information from the Hurlingham Polo Association ☎ (079 85) 277 or 254. Season: May–Sep.

Rugby union The London teams are London Welsh, London Irish, London Scottish, Wasps, Richmond, Rosslyn Park and Saracens. Important matches, including a series of internationals (Oct–Feb), are played at *Twickenham*, Whitton Rd, Middx ☎ 891 5969 home of the sports controlling body, the Rugby Football Union. Season: mainly Sep–Apr.

Soccer London's main professional teams are Arsenal, Charlton Athletic, Chelsea, Crystal Palace, Fulham, Millwall, Orient, Queen's Park Rangers, Tottenham Hotspur ("Spurs"), West Ham United and Wimbledon. Matches are held at the teams' home grounds with the finals at *Wembley*. Information about matches from the Football Association ☎ 262 4542 and Football League (0253) 729421. Season: Aug–Apr. Amateur matches are played in many London parks at weekends througout the season.

Top social events

Many of the major sporting events that take place in and around London are also social events. As most of them take place in June and July, they are a marvellous excuse for a grand picnic, with hampers of fine food and wine. These occasions are a much-prized opportunity for big business to woo important clients and consolidate high-level personal contacts. *Universal Events* ☎ 622 8677 for tickets.

Horse-racing Royal Ascot, in June; the Derby, at *Epsom*, also in June and the more relaxed "Glorious" *Goodwood*, Chichester, W. Sussex, in late July.

Polo Cartier International, at *Smiths Lawn*, in July; British Open, at *Cowdray Park*, in July.

Rowing Royal Regatta, at Henley-on-Thames, Oxfordshire, in July; Oxford and Cambridge Boat Race, from Putney to Mortlake on the Thames, in March or April.

Tennis Wimbledon, in late June–early July.

Keeping fit

Londoners may not be as demonstrative in their pursuit of fitness as their New York counterparts, but the US fashion for physical exercise caught on several years ago. Unfortunately for the visitor, the best public facilities are located in residential areas some distance from the main hotel and business districts, and tend to be very crowded. If you want regular, easy access to a pool or gym, your best bet is to stay in a hotel with an in-house health club or to take out temporary membership of a good private sports or health club.

Three of the listed hotels have exceptional facilities. The spacious Champneys club in the Meridien includes a well-designed pool, Nautilus and conventional gyms and two squash courts. The club at the Grosvenor House Hotel is smaller but offers informed instruction as well as a pleasant if not large pool and a well-planned gym. The Kensington Close (see *Other hotels*) has a pool, squash court, gym and sauna. Other hotels with more limited facilities are the Hilton, the Hyatt Carlton Tower, the InterContinental (see main entries) and the Holiday Inns (see *Other hotels*).

Fitness centres Temporary membership is available at two good private health clubs: *Holmes Place*, 188A Fulham Rd, SW10 ☎ 352 9452, which has a pool, mixed and women-only gyms, exercise classes, massage and beauty treatments; and *The Hogarth*, 1A Airedale Ave, Chiswick, W4 ☎ 995 4600, which has squash and tennis courts, a gym, a pool, exercise classes and massage. In Covent Garden, *The Fitness Centre*, 11–12 Floral St, WC2 ☎ 836 6544, has a wide choice of dance and exercise classes, as well as an excellent gym and various beauty treatments. Next door, the *Sanctuary* ☎ 240 9635 is for women only: exotic leisure pool, steam room, sauna, various treatments. *Pineapple*, 7 Langley St, WC2 ☎ 836 4004 is one of London's best-known dance and aerobics studios; there are other Pineapples in Harrington Rd, SW7 ☎ 581 0466 and Paddington St, W1 ☎ 487 3444.

Golf The best courses are some way out of town. Most require a letter of introduction; one notable exception is the *Wentworth*, Virginia Water, Surrey ☎ (099 04) 2201, which allows non-members to play for a green fee on weekdays. Closer to central London, the *Hampstead Golf Club*, Winnington Rd, N2 ☎ 455 0203 has a very good nine-hole course, also open to non-members for a green fee on weekdays, and at some weekends.

Riding *Ross Nye*, Bathurst Mews, W2 ☎ 262 3791, offers rides around Hyde Park as well as tuition.

Squash *North Kensington Squash Club*, Barlby Rd W10 ☎ 969 6678, and at fitness and sports centres and hotels.

Swimming Some health clubs and hotels (see above) have pools; otherwise, the best central public pools are at *Dolphin Square*, Grosvenor Rd, SW1 ☎ 798 8686 (also squash and tennis) and in the *Queen Mother Sports Centre*, Vauxhall Bridge Rd, SW1 ☎ 798 2125 (also squash and other sports).

Tennis There are pleasant public courts in *Regent's Park* (12 hard courts and changing rooms) and *Hyde Park* (2 hard courts); reservations (in person only) essential. The best tennis clubs are strictly members only but any spare courts at the *London Indoor Tennis Club*, Alfred Rd, W2 ☎ 286 1985, can be used by non-members if reserved 24 hours ahead.

Local resources
London has a bewildering number of firms offering all the kinds of facility or service you might need, and more. Many of them pay to be listed in British Telecom's *Yellow Pages* area directories, but entry is no indication of quality and the listings are not comprehensive. Your London business contacts may be able to make personal recommendations (though larger companies often have in-house services); and many of the top hotels can cater for the business needs of their guests as well as providing general information.

Business services
There are several companies offering fully serviced office accommodation including receptionist, telephonist, telex and secretarial staff on a daily or weekly basis. *Association of Business Centres* ☎ 439 0623 has offices in the City and West End. British Telecom's *Network 9* ☎ 629 9999 has offices just off Oxford Street. *Management Business Services* ☎ 408 1611 are off Regent Street and *International Office Centre* ☎ 603 4500 is in Kensington. *Angela Pike Associates*, 9 Curzon St, W1 ☎ 491 1616, and in Le Meridien Hotel ☎ 434 4425 offers secretarial and staffing services, word processing, translations and photocopying.

Photocopying and printing There are copy shops everywhere, and many stationers and public libraries also have photocopying facilities. Several chains have branches throughout London, usually open Mon–Fri, 9–5.30. Contact head office for nearest branch: *Kall-Kwik* ☎ (089 56) 32700; *Pip* ☎ 965 0700; *Prontaprint* ☎ 930 1571; *Xerox* ☎ 100 and ask for Freefone Xerox Copy Centre. *Sackville Photocopy*, 12 Heddon St, W1 ☎ 734 1948, is open until 9pm.

Secretarial For general temporary staff: *Kelly Girl* ☎ 100 and ask for Freefone Kelly Girl; *Alfred Marks* ☎ 437 7855. For bilingual permanent and temporary office staff: *International Secretaries* ☎ 491 7100; *Multilingual Services* ☎ 836 3794; *Polyglot Agency* ☎ 247 5242. For typing and word processing, collected and delivered, *Central London Typing Services* ☎ 437 1067. For legal work, *Law Temps* ☎ 734 1164.

Translation Interlingua TTI ☎ 240 5361; *Tek Translation* ☎ 749 3211; *Transtelex* ☎ 381 0967. For simultaneous interpreters, *Amherst Conference Services* ☎ 998 3103.

Communications

International couriers DHL ☎ 890 9000; *Federal Express* ☎ 0800 123800 (toll-free); *IML* ☎ 890 8888; *Securicor Express International* (Europe only) ☎ 770 7000; *Transworld Couriers* ☎ 240 2626.

Local messenger services A–Z Couriers ☎ 251 2615; *Delta* ☎ 453 1111; *Mercury Express* ☎ 272 4858; *Vanguard Messengers* ☎ 258 1818; *West 1* ☎ 631 1131.

Post offices The *Trafalgar Square* branch, William IV St, WC2, is open Mon–Sat, 9–8.

Telex and fax Both facilities are widely available. The Post Office's *Intelpost* system ☎ (0268) 44044 is a fax transmission network linking 114 post offices in Great Britain, 11 of them in London, with post offices in over 30 other countries. Messenger collection and delivery can be

arranged. There is a *fax and telex service, including translation,* Mon–Fri, 8–7.30, at *BTI Bureau Services*, Electra House, Temple P1, Victoria Embankment, WC2 ☎ 836 6432, and at *Westminster Communications Centre*, 1A Broadway, SW1 ☎ 222 4444, Mon–Sat, 9–7 (no telexes Sat). Fax is also available at *BT Business Centre*, Canary Wharf, West India Dock, E14 ☎ 515 1234. To send telex and fax messages by telephone or courier, contact *Dictators* ☎ 318 1235, open Mon–Fri, 8.30–8.30, Sat, 8.30–5, Sun, 8.30–1; *British Monomarks* ☎ 405 4442, open Mon–Fri, 8–11, Sat & Sun, 9–1; or *Fax Services* ☎ 671 7321, open Mon–Fri, 8–8, Sat, 9–1.

Conference/exhibition centres

Earl's Court, Warwick Rd, SW5 ☎ 385 1200: the oldest and largest exhibition centre in London, expanding to 100,000 sq metres of floor space; conference/banqueting facilities. *Olympia*, Kensington, W14 ☎ 385 1200: three two-floor exhibition halls that together have 30,000 sq metres of floor space, self-contained Victorian Pillar Hall (seats up to 600) and new conference centre. *Wembley Conference Centre*, Wembley ☎ 902 8833: the first purpose-built conference centre in London. The Grand Hall seats 2,700, suites a further 900, and there are several smaller rooms. Full technical facilities, including closed circuit television and simultaneous translation. Three exhibition suites with 6,000 sq metres. In the same complex: *Wembley Exhibition Hall*, with 5,000 sq metres of space, and *Wembley Arena*, better known for sports and entertainments events. The new *London Arena*, Limeharbour E1 ☎ 538 8800, is also multipurpose and can accommodate over 12,000 delegates. *Barbican Centre*, Barbican, EC2 ☎ 638 4141: doubles as an arts and conference centre. The hall seats 2,000 and the three cinemas 150–280; also several smaller rooms. Full technical facilities, simultaneous interpretation. *Queen Elizabeth II Conference Centre*, Broad Sanctuary, SW1 ☎ 222 5000: the most modern in central London, with a 750-seat auditorium, several conference rooms and dozens of smaller rooms. Two floors reserved for government use. Simultaneous interpretation, closed circuit television, telex and office services, high security. *Alexandra Palace*, Wood Green, N22 ☎ 883 6477, has a Great Hall with 6,670 sq metres of exhibition space. *Central Hall*, Westminster, SW1 ☎ 222 8010: an older venue, recently rehabilitated; Great Hall and eight other rooms can seat more than 5,000.

Emergencies

Bureaux de change Your hotel can usually change money or traveller's cheques, though you will get a better rate at a bank. Most London banks have standard opening hours (Mon–Fri, 9.30–3.30) but some branches now open on Sat. These include branches of *Lloyds* at 399 Oxford St, W1 and at Selfridges store, Oxford St (both 10–4); *Barclays* branches at 140–142 King's Rd, SW3 and 74 Kensington High St, W8 open 9.30–12; and *National Westminster* branches at 466 Oxford St, W1 and 250 Regent St, W1, open 9.30–12.30. If stuck, there are bureaux de change at the main railway stations and several subway stations, as well as in the West End; some branches of *Chequepoint* are open 24hrs.
Hospitals 24hr casualty departments: *Charing Cross*, Fulham Palace Rd, W6 ☎ 846 1234; *Guy's*, St Thomas St, SE1 ☎ 955 5000; *London*, Whitechapel Rd, E1 ☎ 377 7000; *Royal Free*, Pond St, NW3 ☎ 794 0500; *St Bartholomew's* (Bart's), West Smithfield, EC1 ☎ 601 8888; *St Thomas's*, Lambeth Palace Rd, SE1 ☎ 928 9292; *University College*, Gower St, WC1 ☎ 387 9300.

Emergency dental treatment: *Eastman Dental Hospital*, 256 Gray's Inn Rd, WC1 ☎ 837 3646 (Mon–Fri, 9–4.30); *Guy's*, St Thomas St, SE1

☎ 955 5000 (Mon–Fri, 9–3.30); *London*, Turner St, E1 ☎ 377 7000 (Mon–Fri, 8.30–11.30, 12.30–3), *University College Dental Hospital*, Mortimer Mkt, WC1 ☎ 387 9300 (Mon–Fri, 9–2.30). Private dentists offering treatment outside these hours can be found in the *Yellow Pages* telephone directory, under "Dental Surgeons."
Pharmacies There are no 24hr pharmacies in London. Most branches of *Boots* are open Mon–Sat, 8–7; branches in Queensway until 10pm. Branches of *Bliss Chemist* are open every day: Marble Arch, W1 (9am–12pm), Sloane Sq SW1 (Mon–Fri 8.30–8.30, Sat 9–8.30, Sun 10–5), Edgware Rd (Mon–Sat 9–9, Sun 10–9); and *Warman-Freed*, Golders Green Rd is open daily, 8am–12pm.
Police The *City Police* ☎ 601 2222 cover the City, which includes most of the EC postal districts. The rest of London is covered by the *Metropolitan Police* whose headquarters are *New Scotland Yard* ☎ 230 1212. There are more than 100 local stations in Greater London; the central London stations share a common switchboard ☎ 434 5212.

Government offices

British Overseas Trade Board (*BOTB*), 1 Victoria St, SW1H 0ET ☎ 215 7877: for inquiries about exporting from the UK, trade missions to the UK. *Central Office of Information*, Hercules Rd, SE1 7DU ☎ 928 2345: responsible for disseminating official information about government policies and activities. *Central Statistical Office*, Cabinet Office, Great George St, SW1P 3AQ ☎ 270 6363: statistical information from all other government departments. *Customs and Excise*, New King's Beam House, Upper Grnd, SE1 9PJ ☎ 620 1313: for general inquiries about import duties and value added tax. *Department of Employment*, Caxton House, Tothill St, SW1H 9NA ☎ 273 3000: for inquiries about work permits, training services, earnings, employment legislation, trade unions. *Department of Trade and Industry*, 1 Victoria St, SW1H OET ☏ 215 7877: for inquiries about consumer protection and safety, patents, companies legislation, insolvency, trade marks and copyright, manufacturing standards, promotion of research and development, financial aid and technical services to industry. *Home Office*, 50 Queen Anne's Gate, SW1H 9AT ☏ 273 3000: for inquiries about data protection, charities, shop hours, gambling. Immigration inquiries to Lunar House, 40 Wellesley Rd, Croydon, Surrey CR9 2BY ☏ 686 0688. *Inland Revenue*, Somerset House, Strand, WC2R 1LB ☏ 438 6622, for general inquiries about direct taxes.

Information sources
Business information The *National Economic Development Office*, 21 Millbank, SW1P 4QX ☏ 217 4000, is an independent research body which publishes useful free industry sector reports. The London *Chamber of Commerce and Industry*, 69 Cannon St, EC4N 5AB ☏ 248 4444, has a wide range of information services including sources of supply and distribution. The *Association of British Chambers of Commerce*, 212 Shaftesbury Ave, WC2H 8EW ☏ 240 5831, co-ordinates and represents all of the UK's 86 incorporated chambers of commerce. Market information and introductions throughout UK, contacts for joint ventures or setting up of local subsidiaries. The *City Business Library*, 106 Fenchurch St EC3 M5JB ☏ 638 8215, is open Mon–Fri, 9.30–5.
Local media The *Standard*, an evening paper, concentrates on fairly lightweight news coverage and features but also carries market prices, basic business news and a useful listing of West End theatre and cinema programmes. The national newspapers and journals are allLondon-based and London-oriented. Two local radio stations

which broadcast up-to-date rush-hour travel reports are *LBC*, a 24hr news station on 261m 1152kHz, 97.3 VHF, and *BBC Radio London*, mainly a music station, on 206m 1458kHz, 94.9 VHF.
Tourist information The *London Tourist Board*, 26 Grosvenor Gdns, SW1 ODUW ☏ 730 3488, has an Information Centre at Victoria station, SW1, open daily, 9–8.30 (Nov–Mar, Mon–Sat, 9–7 and 9–5pm) which also runs a hotel reservations service. There are smaller centres at *Harrods*, Knightsbridge, SW1, and *Selfridges*, Oxford St, W1, open during shop hours, and at Heathrow airport. Public transport information: *London Transport*, 55 Broadway, SW1 ☏ 222 1234. See also *Entertainment*.

Thank-yous
Florists The following high-class florists all take credit card orders and deliver in the London area, Mon–Fri: *Edward Goodyear*, 45 Brook St, W1 ☏ 629 1508; *Pulbrook and Gould*, 181 Sloane St, SW1 ☏ 235 3186; and *Moyses Stevens*, 6 Bruton St, W1 ☏ 493 8171. Many London florists are part of the Interflora network and will take telephone credit card orders.
Confectioners High-quality hand-made chocolates can be ordered by telephone and delivered by courier, Mon–Sat, from *Charbonnel et Walker*, 28 Old Bond St, W1 ☏ 491 0939, or *Rococo*, 321 King's Rd, SW3 ☏ 352 5857.
Hampers Fortnum & Mason ☏ 734 8040 and *Harrods* ☏ 730 1234 (see *Shopping*) will deliver a wide range of fine food hampers.
Wine merchants Specialist merchants who will take credit card orders and advise on selection include *Berry Bros*, 3 St James's St SW1 ☏ 839 9033 (delivery charge for less than a case, or to addresses outside London); *La Vigneronne*, 105 Old Brompton Rd ☏ 589 6113 (delivery free within central London); and branches of *H. Allen Smith* ☏ 405 3106 (delivery charge on most orders).

BIRMINGHAM
City code ☎ 021

Britain's second biggest city is in the centre of the industrial West Midlands. Historically, Birmingham was known as the city of a thousand trades. Today its main industries are vehicle manufacture, metallurgy, electrical and mechanical engineering and, increasingly, computer technology; high-tech companies are attracted to the Science Parks next to the city's two universities, Birmingham and Aston. Financial and business services are also expanding.

In the 1970s, increased competition from abroad and the recession hit Birmingham hard, but the picture now looks rosier for "Brum," as the city is nicknamed. In 1987 the city embarked on a £460m investment programme, intended to create 30,000 new jobs by 1991. A million sq feet of office space is under construction.

Birmingham's central location in Britain led to the decision to build the National Exhibition Centre on its outskirts rather than in London. The NEC has been a great success and the city is confident that the new £122m International Convention Centre, scheduled to open in 1991, will be just as successful.

Arriving
New Street Station is at the centre of the nation's InterCity rail network and Birmingham is close to the M1, M5, M6 and M42 motorways. There are scheduled air services from European and domestic airports.

Birmingham International Airport Facilities are good for an airport of this size and more are planned. Airport information ☎ 767 7145; freight inquiries ☎ 767 5511.
City link It is a 2min ride on the MAGLEV elevated shuttle system to *Birmingham International* station, from where there are frequent train services into the city. The journey should take no more than about 20mins, roughly the same as by taxi and half the time by bus. Renting a car makes sense only if you have appointments away from the centre.
Taxi The rank outside the terminal building usually has plenty of cabs waiting. Reservations ☎ 782 3744.
Car rental Avis, Hertz and Europcar have desks.

Railway station
New Street is one of Britain's busiest stations. There are InterCity services from London Euston every 30mins during the day, and connections with other parts of the country are good. The station is within walking distance of anywhere in the centre; there are always plenty of taxis at the rank outside. *Europcar* desk ☎ 643 0614. Timetable inquiries ☎ 643 0614.

Getting around
Within the compact city centre the quickest way to get around is to walk. The one-way system makes driving difficult, and few city-centre hotels have their own parking space. Be cautious about walking about on your own at night, particularly through the underpasses. A car or a taxi is the best way to get around the city's sprawling suburbs, and there are useful rail links between the centre and the NEC and nearby cities such as Coventry and Wolverhampton.
Taxis are London-style black cabs, with meters. There is a prompt radio taxi service ☎ 427 8888, and there are several ranks in the centre, including one outside New Street station. Don't rely on finding a cab on the street.
Driving A map showing the one-way system and where you can park in the

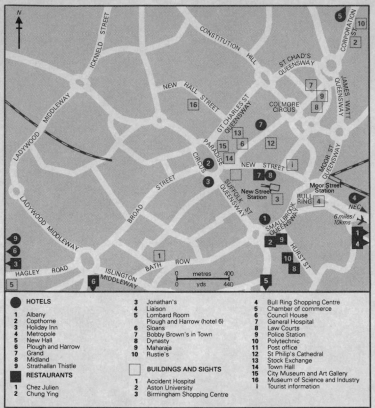

N

ICKNIELD STREET

CONSTITUTION HILL

ST CHAD'S QUEENSWAY

CORPORATION ST

5

10

2

LADYWOOD MIDDLEWAY

NEW HALL STREET

16

GT CHARLES ST QUEENSWAY

COLMORE CIRCUS

JAMES WATT QUEENSWAY

7

9

8

13

7

PARADISE

15

6

12

14

CIRCUS

2

NEW STREET

i

MOOR ST QUEENSWAY

3

SUFFOLK ST QUEENSWAY

7

8

New Street Station

Moor Street Station

LADYWOOD MIDDLEWAY

BROAD STREET

3

New Street Station

3

BULL RING

4

NEC

4

6 miles/ 10kms

1

SMALLBROOK QUEENSWAY

HURST ST

1

4

9

6

3

HAGLEY ROAD

1

BATH ROW

ISLINGTON MIDDLEWAY

2

9

10

8

0 metres 400

0 yds 440

5

6

5

5

	HOTELS	3	Jonathan's	4	Bull Ring Shopping Centre
1	Albany	4	Liaison	5	Chamber of commerce
2	Copthorne	5	Lombard Room	6	Council House
3	Holiday Inn		Plough and Harrow (hotel 6)	7	General Hospital
4	Metropole	6	Sloans	8	Law Courts
5	New Hall	7	Bobby Brown's in Town	9	Police Station
6	Plough and Harrow	8	Dynasty	10	Polytechnic
7	Grand	9	Maharaja	11	Post office
8	Midland	10	Rustie's	12	St Philip's Cathedral
9	Strathallan Thistle			13	Stock Exchange
	RESTAURANTS		BUILDINGS AND SIGHTS	14	Town Hall
1	Chez Julien			15	City Museum and Art Gallery
2	Chung Ying	1	Accident Hospital	16	Museum of Science and Industry
		2	Aston University	i	Tourist information
		3	Birmingham Shopping Centre		

city centre is available from the Birmingham Convention and Visitor Bureau at the NEC. If renting a car, all the major firms have offices; and a smaller firm, *Guy Salmon* ☎ 643 4052, offers a 24hr free delivery and collection service.
Limousines Silverline ☎ 705 5555, *County Travel* ☎ 236 7221, *Beaufort Cars* ☎ 784 4444.

Area by area
The overwhelming impression of the city centre is one of characterless concrete buildings of the 1960s onwards, undistinguished shopping streets and, despite some pedestrianized roads either side of Corporation Street, a city dominated by traffic. Older buildings, mainly

legacies of Victorian civic pride and prosperity such as the Council House overlooking Victoria Square, cannot compete.

The centre divides along a northeast–southwest line. On one side, the main shopping area stretches between New Street station and Colmore Circus. Colmore Row – in effect, bankers' row – forms the boundary of the office area, with the main municipal buildings to the south, the law courts to the north, and quiet side streets in between where many law and accountancy firms are to be found.
The suburbs To the southwest of the centre, the busy Hagley Road (together with Harborne Road) is both a business area popular with

architects' and design practices, also insurance and accountancy firms and the main hotel district outside the centre. To its south, Edgbaston and, to a lesser extent, Harborne are Birmingham's most sought-after residential areas, with many large Georgian houses, exclusive golf and tennis clubs and private schools. Farther out, Sutton Coldfield and Tamworth (to the northeast) and Solihull (to the southeast) are also desirable places to live. By contrast, Birmingham has a number of run-down suburbs suffering from poor housing, high unemployment among the young, racial tension and drug abuse.

Birmingham has attractive countryside around it in all directions, and the good road links make it possible to commute into the city from some distance.

Hotels

The major hotels are concentrated in the city centre, where parking space is at a premium. Along the busy Hagley Road to the west is a string of lower-priced hotels as well as the city's most prestigious central hotel, the Plough and Harrow. The early 1990s will see the opening of the luxurious Regency Hyatt in the new convention centre complex. For help with reservations, contact the Birmingham Convention and Visitor Bureau ☎ 780 4321.

Albany *£//*
Smallbrook Queensway, B5 4EW
☎ *643 8171* ⊠ *337031 fax 631 2523*
• *THF* • *AE DC MC V* • *254 rooms,*
1 suite, 2 restaurants, 2 bars
The Albany, despite its unprepossessing modern exterior, is one of Birmingham's best central business hotels. Bedrooms are practical and comfortable and the main restaurant is good for business entertaining. There is a well-equipped health and sports club. 24hr room service • pool, saunas, sunbeds, squash courts, gym, snooker • business centre, 10 meeting rooms (capacity up to 630).

Copthorne *£//*
Paradise Circus, B3 3HJ ☎ *200 2727*
⊠ *339026 fax 200 1197* • *Copthorne* •
AE DC MC V • *215 rooms, 8 suites,*
1 restaurant, 1 bar
The city centre's newest hotel has 23 floors and an impressive range of facilities, aimed primarily at the business traveller. Nonsmoking rooms, 24hr room service, garage parking • pool, jacuzzi, sauna, gym • business centre, 16 meeting rooms (capacity up to 184).

Holiday Inn *£//*
Holliday St, B1 1HH ☎ *631 2000*
⊠ *337272 fax 643 9018* • *AE DC MC*
V • *290 rooms, 5 suites, 1 restaurant,*
2 bars
The Holiday Inn is located on the edge of the city centre. Bedrooms are spacious and well-equipped; some are reserved for nonsmokers. Guests on the club floor enjoy extra services such as secretarial help. The Terrace bar is popular with the after-work business crowd, and the pool bar with Birmingham's younger set. 24hr room service • small indoor pool, solarium, fitness area • 5 meeting rooms (capacity up to 150).

Metropole *£//*
National Exhibition Centre, B40 1PP
☎ *780 4242* ⊠ *336129 fax 780 3923*
• *AE DC MC V* • *666 rooms, 12 suites,*
2 restaurants, 4 bars
Owned by the multinational company Lonhro and just a short walk from the NEC exhibition halls, the Metropole is accustomed to handling the needs of business travellers, and hosts many conferences and local functions. The public areas are comfortable and spacious, and

bedrooms are well-equipped. The Terrace restaurant overlooking the lake is good for important business entertaining; on Fridays and Saturdays there is a dinner dance. The hotel offers a movie channel as well as a cinema. 24hr room service, newsstand/gift shop, hairdresser, cinema • squash courts, sauna, sunbed • 35 meeting rooms (capacity up to 1,800).

New Hall *£///*
Walmley Rd, Sutton Coldfield, B75 7UU ☎ *378 2442* ⊤ₓ *333580 fax 378 4637* • *Thistle* • *AE DC MC V* • *59 rooms, 6 suites, 1 restaurant, 1 bar*
This old moated house, complete with battlements and drawbridge, has recently been painstakingly transformed into a luxury hotel. The surroundings are rural but the NEC and M42 and M6 motorways are within a few minutes' drive. The suites are in the 16thC part with moat views and are individually furnished; 50 rooms are in a modern wing. Great stress is laid on service and the restaurant has quickly established a high reputation. 24hr room service • croquet, putting, fishing • 2 meeting rooms (capacity up to 50).

Plough and Harrow *£///*
Hagley Rd, Edgbaston, B16 8LS ☎ *454 4111* ⊤ₓ *338074 fax 454 1868* • *AE DC MC V* • *41 rooms, 3 suites, 1 restaurant, 2 bars*
The Plough and Harrow has long been the place in Birmingham for senior executives to stay, and the emphasis is on personal service and high standards. The original building, which contains the ornate restaurant (see *Restaurants*) and elegant lounge bar, dates from the 16th century. Most of the well-equipped bedrooms are in a modern extension to the rear, but are furnished in traditional style, with button-back leather chairs and dark wood. One room has a jacuzzi. 24hr room service • jogging track • 2 meeting rooms (capacity up to 60).

OTHER HOTELS
Grand *£///* *Colmore Row, B3 2DA* ☎ *236 7951* ⊤ₓ *338174 fax 233 1465* • *Queen's Moat* • *AE DC MC V*. Competently run central hotel with grand ballroom.
Midland *£///* *New St, B2 4JT* ☎ *643 2601* ⊤ₓ *338419 fax 643 5075* • *Inter Hotel* • *AE DC MC V*. Refurbished central hotel with five bars and two excellent restaurants.
Strathallan Thistle *£//* *Hagley Rd, Edgbaston, B16 9RY* ☎ *455 9777* ⊤ₓ *336680 fax 454 9432* • *AE DC MC V*. Well-run circular modern hotel not far from the centre; single rooms are small but well-equipped. Solarium and meeting rooms.

Hagley Road is a good area to look for accommodation, including the *Cobden* ☎ *454 6061* at No. 257. Farther out, there is a *THF Post House* ☎ *357 7444* near junction 7 of the M6.

Out of town
Sutton Coldfield, Solihull and Meriden are all pleasant areas within 10 miles/16kms from the city centre. Well served by motorways, they are very convenient for the NEC. Two traditional hotels at Sutton Coldfield are *Penns Hall* (Embassy) ☎ *351 3111* and the *Belfry* (De Vere) ☎ *(0675) 70301*, which has a championship golf course. Also worth considering are the *George* (Embassy) ☎ *704 1241* in Solihull and the *Forest of Arden* (Country Club Hotels) ☎ *(0676) 22118*, a new golf and country club hotel in Meriden with its own pool. But the most stylish out-of-town hotel is *Grafton Manor* ☎ *(0527) 31525* at Bromsgrove, 13 miles/21kms southwest, a luxurious Elizabethan house with a fine restaurant.

Credit card abbreviations	
AE	American Express
DC	Diners Club
MC	Access/MasterCard
V	Visa

Restaurants

With few exceptions, Birmingham's restaurants cannot match their sophisticated London counterparts. Several of the better places are on the edge of the city centre, in the Hagley Road area or, farther out but handier for the NEC, around Solihull or Sutton Coldfield.

Chez Julien *£//*
1036 Stratford Rd, Monkpath, Shirley
☎ *744 7232 • closed Sat L, Sun • AE DC MC V • jacket and tie preferred*
Owner Julien Graffin's compatriot Jean-François Berville does the cooking in this relaxed French restaurant just outside Solihull. The menu concentrates on classic French dishes, with a wide choice of fish, and service is attentive. Good value fixed-price lunch and fine French wines.

Chung Ying *£*
17 Thorpe St, ☎ *666 6622 • AE DC MC V*
This huge brick warehouse, not far from the Hippodrome, has become one of the city's best places to eat. The menu stretches from *dim sum* to vegetarian dishes, but set menus simplify the choice.

Jonathan's *£//*
16 Wolverhampton Rd ☎ *429 3757 • AE DC MC V*
Jonathan's concentrates on recreating a Victorian atmosphere and Victorian cooking, and is best suited to celebrating rather than making deals. The wine list is wide-ranging, with a selection of champagnes and plenty of half-bottles.

Liaison *£//*
761 Old Lode Lane, Solihull
☎ *743 3993 • closed L, Sun, Mon, Aug and 2 weeks Dec. • AE DC MC V*
Solihull's best restaurant is also one of the best in Birmingham. One of the owners, Patricia Plunkett, is responsible for the adventurous menu which changes with the seasons; the other, Ann van der Tuin, ensures that service is calmly efficient. The room is stylish and restrained and there is a good list of mostly French wines.

Lombard Room *£///*
180 Lifford Lane, Kings Norton
☎ *459 9111 • closed Mon, Sat L, Sun D • AE DC MC V*
The cuisine is *nouvelle* in style but portions are generous at this attractive restaurant in a converted old mill, a 15min drive from the city centre. The *vitesse* menu is good value and guarantees that business customers can have lunch in an hour. Long and interesting wine list.

Plough and Harrow *£///*
135 Hagley Rd ☎ *454 4111 • AE DC MC V • smart dress; jacket and tie D*
This elegant restaurant is in a class of its own, in style and price if not cooking. The food is mainly French, a mixture of simple, classic dishes and a more ambitious *sélection gastronomique* created by the chef, Tonio Andreas. There are cheaper, fixed-price set meals, including a three-course English lunch menu (Mon–Thu) and a four-course no-choice *dîner gourmand* (Fri & Sat). The wine list is long, expensive and mainly French, with mostly fine Bordeaux wines.

Sloans *£///*
2729 Chad Sq, Hawthorne Rd, Edgbaston ☎ *455 6697 • closed Sat L, Sun D, Christmas • AE DC MC V*
The setting, in an ordinary suburban shopping parade, is not immediately impressive, but the interior of Sloans is smooth and comfortable. The food is French, a skilful mixture of traditional and modern styles by chef-patron Roger Narbett, previously with the Roux brothers in London and under his father at the Bell Inn at Belbroughton, just outside Birmingham. At lunchtime there is a good-value *menu rapide*.

OTHER RESTAURANTS

Among the ubiquitous Bobby Brown's chain of informal, popular restaurants in the Birmingham area, one of the most central is *Bobby Brown's in Town*, Burlington Passage, New St ☎ 643 4464, a friendly bistro in a large cellar, down a passage close to the station.

South of the centre around the Hippodrome, there is a good selection of ethnic restaurants in Hurst Street, particularly Indian and Chinese. Reliable ones include *Dynasty* ☎ 622 1410, for Cantonese and Pekinese food, and *Maharaja* ☎ 622 2641, for Indian. *Rustie's* ☎ 622 4137 is a jolly Caribbean restaurant owned by the television personality, Rustie Lee.

Bars

The bars of the major hotels are popular meeting places suitable for a discussion over a drink. Close to the law courts on the northeast fringe of the centre, *Hawkins*, 205 Corporation St ☎ 236 2001, is a light and attractive bustling split-level cáfe-bar. *Horts*, Five Ways, Harborne Rd ☎ 454 4672, is a more relaxed, comfortable wine bar, handy for the area's many offices.

Birmingham's most characterful pub is the *Bartons Arms*, north of the centre in Aston High Street (which is the A34) – a grand, lively Edwardian gin-palace. The *Old Contemptibles*, 176 Edmund St, is a central Edwardian pub which does a thriving trade in bar lunches.

Entertainment

Although London's nightlife is a potent attraction despite the journey involved, Birmingham has a reasonable choice of entertainment, particularly theatre and music, and Stratford-upon-Avon is only about a 45min drive away. The NEC Information Bureau will make reservations, and has a ticket outlet in City Arcade, off Corporation Street. For listings, see the free local magazine, *What's On*.

Theatre and ballet The *Hippodrome*, Hurst St ☎ 622 7486, is the new base of Sadler's Wells Royal Ballet. Welsh National Opera and the London Contemporary Dance Theatre visit regularly. It also hosts a wide range of other top-class performances. The *Repertory Theatre*, Broad St ☎ 236 4455, stages contemporary drama; *Alexandra Theatre* (The Alex), Station St ☎ 643 1231 offers lighter fare.

Music Under the conductor Simon Rattle the City of Birmingham Symphony Orchestra has earned international acclaim; concerts by the CBSO and visiting orchestras are given in the *Town Hall*, Victoria Sq ☎ 236 1555. The local Chamber Music Society promotes recitals by international ensembles at the *Adrian Boult Hall*, Paradise Pl ☎ 331 5908. The *NEC Arena* hosts shows by pop and rock megastars; more intimate rock shows take place at the *Odeon*, New St ☎ 643 6101.

Nightclubs proliferate but generally pull in a young local crowd. *Liberty's*, 184 Hagley Rd (closed Sun & Mon), is the most stylish.

Shopping

Birmingham is not a good place to look for classy clothes, though branches of Britain's top retailing chains as well as department stores line New Street, Corporation Street and the High Street. *Rackhams* is the best department store and many of the best individual shops are to be found nearby. Also worth browsing around is the attractive new *Pavilions* shopping mall.

Jewellery-making is still a local craft, and there are several antique markets: in Edgbaston St (Mon am), Bromsgrove St (Thu) and off Broad St (Thu & Sun am).

Sightseeing

There is little of great interest to see in Birmingham but there is plenty in the surrounding towns and countryside.

Aston Hall Fine brick-built Jacobean

mansion standing amid parkland just north of the centre; notable panelled Long Gallery. *Trinity Rd, Aston. Open mid-Mar–Oct, daily 2–5.*

City Museum and Art Gallery Major archeological, natural history and art displays, including a famous collection of Pre-Raphaelite paintings. *Chamberlain Sq. Open Mon–Sat, 9.30–5; Sun, 2–5.*

Museum of Science and Industry A wide-ranging collection, with a particularly impressive Engineering Hall – turbines, locomotives, arms. *Newhall St. Open Mon–Sat, 9.30–5; Sun, 2–5.*

Patrick Collection Motor museum with vintage to modern racing cars displayed in Victorian mill buildings. *Lifford Lane, Kings Norton. Open mid-Mar–Nov, 11–5.30; Jan–mid-Mar, Sun only.*

Out of town
Visitors may have Stratford-upon-Avon high on their agenda; be warned that the sights it offers are not in themselves spectacular. But there is much around Birmingham that is spectacular: dramatic castles at Kenilworth (ruined) and Warwick (one of Britain's best preserved); ancient cathedrals at Lichfield and Worcester and a modern one at Coventry; and the historic houses of Ragley Hall (at Alcester) and Hagley Hall (near Stourbridge).

Spectator sports
Cricket Warwickshire county and international Test matches are played at *Edgbaston County Ground* ☎ 440 4292.

Racing There are regular meetings at *Wolverhampton* ☎ (0902) 24481, *Stratford-upon-Avon* ☎ (0789) 67949 and *Warwick* ☎ (0926) 491553; and the famous course at *Cheltenham* ☎ (0242) 513014 is easily reached by the M5.

Rugby The major clubs in the area are Birmingham, who play at *Wythall* ☎ (0564) 822955, and Moseley, who play at *The Reddings* ☎ 449 2149.

Soccer Aston Villa play at *Villa Park*

☎ 327 6604; Birmingham City at *St Andrews* ☎ 772 0101. Other well-known clubs nearby are Coventry City ☎ (0203) 258879 and West Bromwich Albion ☎ 525 8888.

Motor-racing An annual "Super Prix" is run through the streets of the city centre on August Bank Holiday.

Keeping fit
Several hotels have fitness centres. The best municipal sports and fitness centre is at *Aston Villa* ☎ 328 8330, a joint development with the football club.

Golf The best known local course is the championship course at the *Belfry Hotel*, ☎ (0675) 70301, at Sutton Coldfield.

Squash There are six courts at the Aston Villa Sports Centre, and both the Albany and Metropole hotels have courts.

Swimming The Albany, Copthorne and Holiday Inn hotels have pools.

Tennis There are public courts in most of the larger parks. Those at *Handsworth Leisure Centre* ☎ 454 0564 are floodlit.

Local resources
Business services
If your hotel cannot help, companies which provide a wide range of business services are *Copy + Type + Print* ☎ 236 7531 and *Solihull Secretarial and Printing Services* ☎ 705 1967.

Photocopying and printing Kall-Kwik ☎ 632 5015, *Print Media* ☎ 643 2114, *Prontaprint* ☎ 236 2255.

Secretarial Gem ☎ 236 1995, *Warwick Executive Services* ☎ 632 5444.

Translation Berlitz ☎ 643 4334, *Interlingua TTI* ☎ 236 3524.

Communications
International delivery DHL ☎ (0675) 65712, *IML* ☎ 773 5949, *TNT Skypak* ☎ 782 2345.

Local delivery DR Express ☎ 454 2479, *Expressway* ☎ 454 0813.

Post office Main office: Victoria Sq ☎ 644 8653.

Telex and fax Commercial Communications ☎ 643 8060 ⊡ 337045, *Telex Service Agency* ☎ 523 7126 ⊡ 336520.

Conference/exhibition centres

The *National Exhibition Centre* (NEC) ☎ 780 4141, which opened in 1976, is about 10 miles/16kms from Birmingham. It is the biggest exhibition centre in Britain and the tenth largest in Western Europe, and attracts 3m visitors a year. Some 45 trade fairs and 10 public exhibitions are staged there each year.

Plans for the £122m *International Convention Centre* (ICC) in Broad Street, opening in 1991, include a conference hall for 1,500, a concert hall and nine other exhibition halls.

Numerous hotels have facilities for conferences; the *Birmingham Metropole* has the largest capacity (1,800). Other venues include the *Town Hall* ☎ 235 3942, the *Botanical Gardens* ☎ 456 2244 and the *Patrick Collection* ☎ 459 9111.

Emergencies

Bureaux de change Late opening: *American Express*, Martineau Sq, Mon–Fri, 9–5, at the airport, daily, 6.30am–9.30pm (10.30 in summer); *Lloyds* in Lewis's store, Bull St, Mon–Sat, 9.30–5; *Thomas Cook*, 99 New St, Mon–Sat, 9–5.

Hospitals 24hr casualty departments: *Accident Hospital*, Bath Row ☎ 643 7041; *General Hospital*, Steelhouse Lane ☎ 236 8611. Emergency dental treatment: *General Hospital*, Mon–Fri, 9–11, 2–3.

Pharmacies Late opening: *Boots*, 16 New St ☎ 631 2322, open Mon–Fri until 9pm, Sat until 6pm, Sun, 10–2. *Police* Main station: Steelhouse Lane ☎ 200 1111.

Government offices

The *Government Services Centre* at the NEC ☎ 780 2721 stocks useful leaflets. There is also an office of HM Customs and Excise ☎ 780 2310. The city council's *Economic Development Unit*, which can provide financial assistance as well as information for incoming or expanding firms, is at Baskerville House, Broad St, B1 2NA ☎ 235 2222 *fax* 233 1942. The regional office of the *Department of Trade and Industry* is at Ladywood House, Stephenson St, B2 4DT ☎ 632 4111.

Information sources

Business information Birmingham *Chamber of Industry and Commerce*, 75 Harborne Rd, B15 3DH ☎ 454 6171; *West Midlands Industrial Development Association*, Chantry House, High St, Coleshill, Warwickshire, B46 3BP ☎ (0675) 62577.

Local media The local morning paper is the *Birmingham Post*, a middle-of-the-road tabloid with substantial business coverage (national and local). The *Evening Mail*, from the same publisher, is a more boisterous tabloid which faces competition from the *Express & Star*, published in neighbouring Wolverhampton, and the free *Daily News* (Tue–Fri).

Tourist information Information centres: City Arcade ☎ 643 2514; Piazza, National Exhibition Centre ☎ 780 4141.

Thank-yous

Florists Prestons ☎ 707 7070, *Russells* ☎ 455 0951.

Wine merchants Threshers ☎ 784 5945, *Peter Dominic* ☎ 236 6733. *Chocolates Sweet Indulgence* ☎ 236 4274.

EDINBURGH
City code ☎ 031

A walk along Edinburgh's George Street, with views of the Castle and medieval Old Town on one side and the Fife hills on the other, will quickly confirm the Scottish capital's reputation as one of the most beautiful of cities. What is much less obvious to the casual visitor is that George Street is also at the centre of a finance industry which has made this relatively small city (population 460,000) the second largest investment centre in Europe.

Edinburgh is a city dominated by the professions and has been so since the Act of Union in 1707 removed the Scots parliament from the city, but safeguarded the separate and distinctive identities of the Scottish church and legal system. The Edinburgh establishment of lawyers and ministers, as well as the academics who taught them in Edinburgh's 16thC university, were joined over the years by doctors, bankers, accountants, financiers and, with the large-scale devolution of administrative responsibility for Scotland in the 1930s, civil servants. These groups have modelled the city in their own image: steadfastly unexuberant (though this changes briefly each August when the International Festival brings noise and colour to the generally subdued streets), but civilized and successful. While the decline in heavy manufacturing industries has brought stagnation to so much of Scotland over the past 30 years, Edinburgh, with its predominantly service-sector economy, has continued to prosper.

Arriving

Edinburgh enjoys good air and rail links with other British cities. Its only fast road links, however, are with Glasgow to the west via the M8 and with Perth to the north on the A90. Motorists approaching from the south will find themselves on slower roads.

Edinburgh Airport (Turnhouse)
Edinburgh's small airport is 7 miles/11kms west of the city centre, just off the road to Glasgow. It handles direct scheduled flights from four European cities (Amsterdam, Dublin, Düsseldorf, Paris), but traffic is mainly domestic, with links to all the major UK airports. There are some 23 flights a day (10 shuttle) from London (Heathrow, Gatwick and Stansted), journey time approx 1hr 10mins.

The relatively modern terminal building has a good range of facilities for an airport of this size, including two business lounges, an accommodation desk and a well-stocked duty-free shop. The bureau de change closes at 7pm Mon–Fri, 2.30pm Sat, 5pm Sun. Airport information ☎ 344 3136, freight inquiries ☎ 344 3107.

Nearby hotels Royal Scot, 111 Glasgow Rd, EH12 8NF ☎ 334 9191 ⊠ 727197 fax 316 4507 ● AE DC MC V. Unpromising exterior but recently refurbished interior; pool.

City link The fastest way to get into the city is by car or taxi; journey time around 20mins but allow an extra 15mins during rush hours.

Taxis are always available and the service is efficient.

Car rental Recommended if your hotel or appointments lie outside the compact city centre. Avis, Europcar, Hertz and Swan National have desks.

Railway station
Edinburgh Waverley Located in the heart of the city. It has good rail connections with all major British cities including an hourly InterCity service from London King's Cross

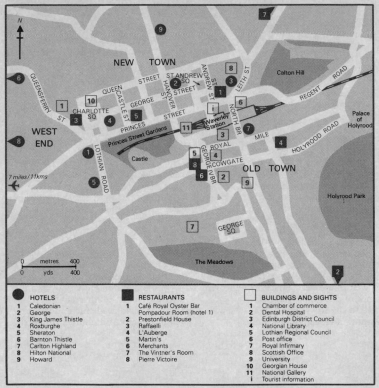

Calton Hill

WEST END

7 miles/11kms

Castle

Princes Street Gardens

Waverley Station

ROYAL MILE

OLD TOWN

Palace of Holyrood

Holyrood Park

GEORGE SQ.

The Meadows

| | 0 | metres | 400 | |
| | 0 | yds | 400 | |

HOTELS
1 Caledonian
2 George
3 King James Thistle
4 Roxburghe
5 Sheraton
6 Barnton Thistle
7 Carlton Highland
8 Hilton National
9 Howard

RESTAURANTS
1 Café Royal Oyster Bar
   Pompadour Room (hotel 1)
2 Prestonfield House
3 Raffaelli
4 L'Auberge
5 Martin's
6 Merchants
7 The Vintner's Room
8 Pierre Victoire

BUILDINGS AND SIGHTS
1 Chamber of commerce
2 Dental Hospital
3 Edinburgh District Council
4 National Library
5 Lothian Regional Council
6 Post office
7 Royal Infirmary
8 Scottish Office
9 University
10 Georgian House
11 National Gallery
i Tourist information

(journey time approx 4hrs 40mins) and a half-hourly service from Glasgow Queen Street (journey time 45mins). Sleeper services operate nightly from London, Bristol, Inverness, Poole and Plymouth. The station taxi rank is the city's largest, but demand can exceed supply. Passenger inquiries ☎ 556 2451, sleeper reservations ☎ 556 5633.

Getting around
Edinburgh has a good public transport system, but the traveller with business in and around the small city centre will probably find the combination of walking and taxi rides most convenient.
Walking is often the most pleasant as well as the quickest way of getting around the city centre, despite its hilliness. Edinburgh has a remarkably low level of street crime.
Taxis The licensed radio-linked black cabs are reliable and reasonably priced, and can usually be hailed easily in the street. Telephone reservations: *Radiocabs* ☎ 225 9000, *City Cabs* ☎ 228 1211.
Limousines Edinburgh Fly Drive ☎ 556 5418.
Driving The main drawback is traffic congestion. Parking is relatively easy, but Edinburgh has a large number of traffic wardens. All the major car rental chains have offices in the city centre.

Area by area
The commercial and residential heart of Edinburgh lies to the north of Princes Street Gardens in an area laid out in the 18th century and since then known as the New Town. The

cramped centre it supplanted, known as the Old Town, is now the focus of Edinburgh's tourist trade.

First New Town
The centre of business activity in Edinburgh is a rectangle less than 1 mile/1.6kms long and five streets deep, bounded by Charlotte Square and St Andrew Square to the west and east and by Princes Street and Queen Street to the south and north. The area retains its Georgian street layout. Around Charlotte Square – designed by Robert Adam, Edinburgh's most famous architectural son – are grouped the investment houses, such as Baillie Gifford and Ivory & Sime. St Andrew Square is dominated by the headquarters of the great life insurance companies including Standard Life, the largest in Europe, as well as the head office of the Royal Bank of Scotland. Immediately behind the Royal Bank looms New St Andrew's House, housing the principal sections of the Scottish Office. Elsewhere in this area are to be found leading Edinburgh stockbrokers, such as Wood Mackenzie; the city's few merchant bankers, including Noble Grossart; large lawyers' practices such as Dundas & Wilson; and some of Edinburgh's smartest shops.

The residential New Town
There is a fair chance that the Edinburgh lawyer or banker whom the business traveller meets in a Queen Street office has come to work from a spacious Georgian home just a few minutes' walk away. Edinburgh, uniquely among British cities, has retained a substantial residential core. North of Queen Street is the largest remaining area of Georgian housing in the world. The small talk of the Edinburgh establishment often seems to revolve around architectural niceties, and an admiring reference to the quality of a host's ornate plasterwork ceiling has broken the ice at many a New Town party.

Outer New Town and Leith
Many of the most sought-after properties in Edinburgh are on the outskirts of the New Town, whether at the West End – which also has the city's largest concentration of advertising and design agencies and architects' offices – or to the north in Stockbridge (particularly Ann Street) and Inverleith, or to the east on Calton Hill. Farther to the north are the fashionable Victorian suburbs of Trinity and Edinburgh's port of Leith, where Charles I played golf. Since 1981 Leith, which had fallen on hard times, has been the subject of a major revitalization project spearheaded by the Scottish Development Agency.

Old Town and South Side
The Old Town, built on either side of the "Royal Mile" which runs from the Castle down to Holyrood, is the heart of tourist Edinburgh. South of it lies the main academic and medical area of the city. Edinburgh University is centred on George Square; the Royal Infirmary is immediately to the west. The University Science Departments are located at King's Buildings, 2 miles/3.2kms south. The main campus of Heriot Watt, the city's second, technology-based university, is at Riccarton, southwest of the city.

The suburbs
Edinburgh's western suburbs contain some commercial buildings but are predominantly residential. The smartest areas are Murrayfield, Ravelston, Corstorphine and Barnton. Some executives take advantage of Edinburgh's fine rural surroundings and commute from Fife, West Lothian or East Lothian.

Credit card abbreviations	
AE	American Express
DC	Diners Club
MC	Access/MasterCard
V	Visa

Hotels

Edinburgh's major city-centre hotels are grouped at either end of Princes Street. At the east end, the North British, long regarded as rival to the Caledonian, is closed until 1990 for refurbishment. In summer, particularly during the Festival, rooms in the centre of town are in short supply, but there are a number of comfortable hotels in the suburbs as well as farther out in the lovely Lothian countryside (see *Out of town*). All hotels listed have 24hr room service, currency exchange and parking (unless otherwise stated), and rooms have IDD telephones.

Caledonian £///
Princes St, EH1 2AB ☎ *225 2433*
TX *72179 fax 225 6632* • *AE DC MC V*
• *237 rooms, 24 suites, 2 restaurants, 3 bars*

Few would dispute that this grand Edwardian building houses the best hotel in town. The rooms and suites on the main façade with their magnificent views of the Castle Rock and Princes Street are often monopolized in summer by Edinburgh's wealthier tourists, but the business traveller may prefer the equally generous and rather quieter rooms on Rutland Street or overlooking the hotel's small central garden. Throughout much of the year the Caledonian maintains the atmosphere of an exclusive business rather than a tourist hotel. The quiet and spacious lounge and Gazebo Restaurant are useful for business discussions, and the Pompadour (see *Restaurants*) remains the city's most prestigious traditional restaurant. Service is friendly and efficient, with attention to detail. Gift shop, hairdresser • 6 meeting rooms (capacity up to 300).

George £///
George St, EH2 2PB ☎ *225 1251*
TX *72570 fax 226 5644* • *AE DC MC V*
• *195 rooms, 10 suites, 2 restaurants, 1 bar*

Located at the heart of the capital's business area, the George was created in 1950 out of three Georgian terraced houses. In 1967 a seven-floor extension allowed this hitherto select establishment to enter the world of package tours. "Staying at the George" is still a fine boast and, though it has lost its hushed tones, the hotel's decoration and furnishing is first-class. The Carvery, once the business hall of a prominent Edinburgh company, is highly rated among local business executives for both lunch and dinner entertaining. Bedrooms range widely between poky single rooms and grandly elegant suites, one including a jacuzzi. Gift shop, hairdresser • 4 meeting rooms (capacity up to 320).

King James Thistle £///
Leith St, EH1 3SW ☎ *556 0111*
TX *727200 fax 557 5333* • *AE DC MC V* • *142 rooms, 5 suites, 1 restaurant, 2 bars*

Although the obtrusive 1970s shopping centre, of which the King James Thistle is a part, is hardly the ideal setting for a hotel with first-class aspirations, the management aims high. Ample-sized rooms (some nonsmoking) are well-equipped. Pleasant extras include bathrobes, fresh flowers and toiletries. Executive Club guests have access to a small, private "honesty" bar and an annex for private discussions. The brasserie is well suited to relaxed business entertaining and is popular for breakfast meetings. Newsstand • 3 meeting rooms (capacity up to 250).

Hotel price guide
For the meanings of the hotel price symbols, see *Symbols and abbreviations* on pages 6 and 7.

Roxburghe £//
Charlotte Sq, EH2 4RG ☎ *225 3921*
TX *727054 fax 220 2518* •
AE DC MC V • *75 rooms, 1 suite,*
2 restaurants, 2 bars
Civilized, conservative, a little self-
satisfied, the Roxburghe is the most
Edinburgh of hotels. The lift may be
in need of a touch of paint and the
restaurants may lack distinction, but
the patrician style – one of Adam
chimneypieces and 18thC prints – is
unmistakably authentic. Bedrooms
are comfortable, spacious and well
decorated, and Charlotte Square is
both attractive and very convenient.
The hotel's clubby atmosphere echoes
that of many affluent lawyers' offices
and finance houses nearby, whose
executives make good use of the
Roxburghe's quiet, attractive cocktail
bar. No parking. 2 meeting rooms
(capacity up to 100).

Sheraton £//
1 Festival Sq, EH3 9SR ☎ *229 9131*
TX *72398 fax 228 4510* • *AE DC MC V*
• *235 rooms, 28 suites, 1 restaurant,*
2 bars
The Sheraton, opened in 1984, is
central Edinburgh's newest
international-style hotel. Bedrooms
are spacious and well laid out; studio
rooms, which have a seating area,
cost considerably less than a suite.
The light and airy Beaufort
Restaurant is a popular lunching
place for many local, and particularly
female, executives. Gift shop,
hairdresser • pool, fitness room,
solarium • 2 meeting rooms (capacity
up to 485).

OTHER HOTELS
Barnton Thistle £// *Queensferry*
Rd, EH4 6AS ☎ *339 1144*
TX *727928 fax 339 5521* • *AE DC*
MC V. Reliable suburban hotel within
a 10min drive of the airport. Relaxed
atmosphere, bedrooms small but well-
equipped.
Carlton Highland £// *North*
Bridge, EH1 1SD ☎ *556 7277*
TX *727001 fax 556 2691* • *AE DC MC*
V. Guests have free use of the

Carlton's own excellent leisure club,
with pool, solarium, sauna, Turkish
bath, gym, squash and snooker.
Bedrooms are comfortable; public
areas decorated in a mix of styles.
Hilton National £// *69 Belford*
Rd, EH4 3DG ☎ *332 2545*
TX *727979 fax 332 3805* • *AE DC MC*
V. The former Ladbroke Dragonara
has an attractive waterside setting. A
15min walk from city centre.
Howard £// *32–36 Great King St,*
EH3 6QH ☎ *557 3500* TX *727887*
fax 557 6515 • *AE DC MC V*.
Intimate, hospitable hotel in three
Georgian houses, a 5min walk from
the centre. Lively bar, the Claret Jug,
popular with local executives.

Out of town
The countryside around
Edinburgh has a number of hotels
and restaurants used by the
business community. To the east,
Gullane – home of the Honourable
Company of Edinburgh Golfers –
boasts the stylish *Greywalls Hotel*
☎ (0620) 842144, designed by
Edwin Lutyens, and *La Potinière*
☎ (0620) 843214, one of
Scotland's finest small restaurants
(reservations need to be made
months ahead); and the attractive
neighbouring village of Dirleton
has the *Open Arms Hotel and
Restaurant* ☎ (062 085) 241. To
the west of the city, and
conveniently located for the
airport, is the 17thC *Houstoun
House Hotel*, Uphall ☎ (0506)
853831, popular for its original
fixed-price menu and an
outstanding wine list.

Clubs
Behind an anonymous modern
doorway on Princes Street is
Edinburgh's only really smart
gentlemen's club, the *New Club*.
Though built in the 1960s, it
inherited much of the original
panelling, fittings and furniture of the
old club it replaced, as well as the

loyalty of the Edinburgh establishment, seen here in its most concentrated form: a guest at the New Club will be surrounded by senior civil servants, academics, bankers and lawyers.

Restaurants

The range and standards of Edinburgh's restaurants have improved immensely over the past 15 years. Currently the most prestigious places for business entertaining are the Pompadour Room and Prestonfield House.

Café Royal Oyster Bar £//
17 West Register St ☎ *556 4124* • *MC V*

The wise visitor sticks to simple dishes in the Oyster Bar. What people come for is the splendid Victorian setting: large stained-glass windows depicting sportsmen; ornate plasterwork ceilings, decorative ceramic tiles. The Oyster Bar is a favourite lunching place for Royal Bank executives, the rear of whose St Andrew Square headquarters it overlooks.

Pompadour Room £////
Caledonian Hotel ☎ *225 2433* • *closed Sat, Sun L* • *AE DC MC V* • *jacket and tie*

Edinburgh's most exclusive restaurant is where the financiers and lawyers from nearby Charlotte Square will be found with their top clients. Attentive service is matched by a fine *nouvelle cuisine* presentation of the best local meat, game, fish and vegetables. The fixed-price set lunch menu features Scottish dishes.

Prestonfield House £////
Priestfield Rd ☎ *668 3346* • *AE DC MC V* • *jacket and tie*

This handsome 17thC mansion, standing in extensive grounds less than a 10min drive from the city centre, is where local business people take American colleagues they want to impress; distinguished guests of the past have included Benjamin Franklin. The picture-lined dining rooms have fine views over Holyrood Park and Arthur's Seat. The food, a rich combination of French and Scottish cuisines, is less memorable.

Raffaelli £//
10–11 Randolph Pl ☎ *225 6060* • *closed Sat L, Sun, end Dec–early Jan* • *AE DC MC V*

Raffaelli provides a first-class venue for business lunches: a convenient location just behind Charlotte Square; a good selection of Italian wines; smart, bright, traditional decor; long afternoon opening hours. It is, as a result, extremely popular in the middle of the day and service can be slow.

OTHER RESTAURANTS
L'Auberge, 56 St Mary's St ☎ 556 5888, *Martin's*, 72 Rose St, North Lane ☎ 225 3106, and *Merchants*, 17 Merchant St ☎ 225 4009, all provide reliable and good-value meals in the city centre. L'Auberge has the additional attraction of a business lunch menu at weekends. *The Vintner's Room*, 87 Giles St ☎ 554 6767, offers elegant candle-lit dining beneath 18thC plasterwork off the beaten track in Leith. *Pierre Victoire*, 10 Victoria St ☎ 225 1721, is a friendly, informal French restaurant in the Old Town.

> **Restaurant price guide**
> For the meanings of the restaurant price symbols, see *Symbols and abbreviations* on pages 6 and 7.

Bars

For business discussions over drinks, the hotel bars are a safe bet, particularly that of the Roxburghe. By tradition, Rose Street was

Edinburgh's great drinking area.
Nowadays, however, only the
Abbotsford, 3 Rose St, reaches the
exacting standard demanded by
connoisseurs of real ale, atmosphere
and architecture. Elsewhere in the
city it is matched by *Bennets*, 8 Leven
St (just beside the Kings Theatre).
Good wine bars include the
Waterfront, 1c Dock Pl, where in fine
weather an artistic clientele spills out
onto the Leith dockside; the *Doric*, 15
Market St, a favourite with *Scotsman*
journalists; and *Whighams*, 13 Hope
St, which at lunchtime is crowded
with business people.

Entertainment

For a city of its character and
influence, Edinburgh's cultural life is
surprisingly low key outside the
Festival. The best guide to what's on
is *The List*, published fortnightly.
What's On in Edinburgh is available
free in most hotels or from the
Tourist Information Centre.
Theatre, ballet, opera Edinburgh's
three mainstream theatres, the
Lyceum, Grindlay St ☎ 229 9697, the
Kings, Leven St ☎ 229 1201, and the
Playhouse, Greenside Pl ☎ 557 2590,
stage generally rather unadventurous
productions for most of the year,
enlivened by seasonal visits from the
Glasgow-based Scottish Opera and
Scottish Ballet. The *Traverse*,
Grassmarket ☎ 226 2633, puts on
high-quality alternative theatre.
Music For large orchestral
productions Edinburgh relies on the
Glasgow-based Scottish National
Orchestra, which provides a concert
each Friday in winter and spring at
the *Usher Hall*, Lothian Rd ☎ 228
1155. First-rate chamber music is
performed by two Edinburgh-based
companies, the Scottish Baroque
Ensemble and the Scottish Chamber
Orchestra, in the attractive *Queen's
Hall*, Clerk St ☎ 668 3456.

Shopping

The main shopping areas are George
Street, Princes Street and, for
Scottish goods, the Royal Mile, which

The Edinburgh Festival
The great strength of Edinburgh's
Festival is that it is at least six
festivals in one. Quite apart from
the main International Festival,
there is the huge Fringe
encompassing everything from
poetry readings in bars to street
theatre, the nightly Military
Tattoo at the Castle, the Film
Festival, the Jazz Festival and
last, but by no means least in
business terms, the Television
Festival where many a media deal
has been sewn up behind the
scenes.

The business traveller prepared
to brave the crowds in Edinburgh
in August will enjoy a marvellous
atmosphere and a host of cultural
delights. Details of the
International Festival programme
are available from the Festival
Office, Market St, from April
onwards; reservations are
advisable for main events.

---

includes the High Street.
Antiques and art The Grassmarket,
Victoria Street, St Stephen's Street
and Thistle Street areas contain
Edinburgh's largest range of antique
shops.
Clothing Finest quality tartan and
woollens, including cashmere, are
available from *Kinloch Anderson*, 46
High St, and *Jenners*, 48 Princes St,
which is the city's classiest
department store.
Food The most famous producer of
haggis, an acquired taste, is *Charles
McSween*, 130 Bruntsfield Pl; but
more approachable Scottish food,
including smoked salmon, can be
found at the *Salmon Pool*, at the
airport.
Whisky *The Whisky Shop*, Waverley
Market (adjoining the station), offers
a wide range of malts. The real
connoisseur, however, will persuade a
member of the *Scotch Malt Whisky
Society*, 87 Giles St, to part with a
bottle.

Sightseeing

Edinburgh is one of the six most popular tourist cities in Britain. In addition to the famous and, in summer, crowded sights of the Castle, the Palace of Holyrood and the linking Royal Mile, the considerably quieter Georgian streets and squares of the New Town are well worth a look.

Royal Mile Running through the centre of medieval Edinburgh, the Royal Mile is a single street which starts as Lawnmarket, becomes the High Street and ends up as the Canongate. At the top stands the *Castle*, a great complex of buildings including the 12thC St Margaret's Chapel and the State Apartments housing Scotland's Crown Jewels (*open Mon–Sat, 9.30–4.30; Sun, 12.30–3.30*).

Interesting buildings along the Royal Mile include *Gladstone's Land*, a 17thC merchant's house; *The High Kirk of St Giles*, Edinburgh's principal church; *John Knox House*, the supposed home of the 16thC reformer; and *Huntly House*, the city museum which has superb collections of Edinburgh silver and ceramics.

At the bottom stands the *Palace of Holyrood*, the Queen's residence in Scotland, notable for its royal connections, which date back to Mary Queen of Scots and beyond, and its fine 17thC architecture and interiors. *Open Mon–Sat, 9.30–5.15; Sun, 10.30–4.30 (except when in official use – generally Jul 14–Aug 4).*

Georgian House 18thC interior, lavishly recreated by the National Trust for Scotland in one of Robert Adam's fine houses. *7 Charlotte Sq. Open Mon–Sat, 10–5; Sun, 2–5.*

National Gallery of Scotland Well laid out gallery of small rooms packed with masterpieces including major works by Raphael, Titian, El Greco, Velasquez, Rembrandt and the French Impressionists, and the unequalled Sutherland Poussins. *The Mound. Open Mon–Sat, 10–5; Sun, 2–5.*

Spectator sports

Rugby union The city's *Murrayfield* ground ☎ 337 2346 hosts international rugby matches and, in the preceding week, the business bars and luncheon places will be buzzing with talk of Scotland's chances on the coming Saturday.

Soccer Edinburgh's two major teams are *Heart of Midlothian* (Hearts) ☎ 337 6132 and *Hibernian Football Club* (Hibs) ☎ 661 2159.

Keeping fit

Health and sports centres The Carlton Highland's club (see *Hotels*) is open to nonresidents.

Golf As befits the original home of the game, Edinburgh has a superb selection of golf courses. There are no fewer than 28 within the city boundary and, just outside, the two oldest golf clubs in the world: the socially more prestigious Honourable Company of Edinburgh Golfers at *Muirfield*, Gullane, East Lothian ☎ (0620) 842123, and The Royal Burgess Golfing Society at Whitehouse Road, Barnton ☎ 339 2075. These clubs play a very important part in the business and social life of the capital. The sight of a group of bankers and lawyers on a green at Muirfield has confirmed many a visitor's suspicions about the tight-knit nature of the Edinburgh establishment.

Scotland's most famous course, *St Andrew's* ☎ (0334) 73393, is just over a 1hr drive from the city and, like Edinburgh's clubs, is open to visitors.

Squash Visitors can take out a weekly membership at the *Edinburgh Club*, 7 Hillside Pl ☎ 556 8845.

Swimming The best public pool is the olympic-sized *Royal Commonwealth Pool*, Dalkeith Rd ☎ 667 7211, which also has a sauna.

Local resources

Business services

Alva Business Centre, 82 Great King St ☎ 557 2222, offers offices, secretarial services, telex, fax and electronic mail. *Berlitz Translation*

Services, 24–26 Fredrick St ☎ 226 7198 and *Edinburgh Translations*, 14 Stafford St ☎ 225 8965 both provide translation services.
Photocopying and printing PDC ☎ 226 4231, *Kall Kwik* ☎ 226 6268 or 556 6222, *Prontaprint* ☎ 557 3670.
Secretarial *Typerite* ☎ 226 5855.

Communications
International delivery *Federal Express* ☎ 440 2555, TNT ☎ 339 7277 (airport office).
Local delivery QED *Couriers* ☎ 557 3877, *Eagle Couriers* ☎ 557 1219.
Post office Main office: Waterloo Pl tel 550 8246.
Telex and fax *Alva Business Centre* ☎ 557 2222 *fax* 557 2861.

Conference/exhibition centres
There are no exhibition centres within Edinburgh itself, but the *Royal Highland and Agricultural Showground*, Ingliston ☎ 333 2843, just beside the airport, is the venue for several annual trade fairs.

Emergencies
Bureaux de change *Exchange International*, 23 Princes St, is open daily, 8–10. The *Trustee Savings Bank* at Cameron Toll Shopping Centre, Dalkeith Rd, is open Mon–Sat, 9.30–5; Sun, 12 noon–4.
Hospitals 24hr casualty department: the *Royal Infirmary*, 1 Lauriston Pl ☎ 229 2477. Emergency dental treatment is available, in normal working hours, at the *Edinburgh Dental Hospital*, 31 Chambers St ☎ 225 9511; or from the *Western General Hospital*, Crewe Rd South ☎ 332 2525, Mon–Fri, 7.30pm–10pm; Sat and Sun, 10am–noon.

Pharmacies *Boots the Chemist*, 48 Shandwick Pl ☎ 225 6757, open Mon–Sat, 8.45–9; Sun, 11–4.30.
Police Lothian and Borders Police Headquarters: Fettes Ave ☎ 311 3131.

Government offices
The local government offices are *Edinburgh District Council*, City Chambers, High St, EH1 1YJ ☎ 225 2424, and *Lothian Regional Council*, George IV Bridge, EH1 1UQ ☎ 229 9292. The central information office at the *Scottish Office*, New St Andrew's House, St James Centre, EH1 3TB ☎ 556 8400, is a useful starting point for inquiries.

Information sources
Business information *Edinburgh Chamber of Commerce and Industry*, 3 Randolph Cres, EH3 7UD ☎ 225 5851, will provide information about the products and services of member companies. The *National Library of Scotland*, George IV Bridge (open Mon–Fri, 9.30–8.30; Sat, 9.30–1), is Scotland's copyright library, and so holds all UK publications.
Local media *The Scotsman*, Edinburgh's daily newspaper, has good coverage of the Scottish political scene and an adequate business section. The best Edinburgh-based business magazine is the monthly *Scottish Business Insider*.
Tourist information *Tourist Information and Accommodation Centre*, Waverley Market ☎ 557 2727.

Thank-yous
Florist *Jenners* ☎ 225 2442; also for chocolates.
Wine merchant *Justerini & Brooks* ☎ 226 4202.

GLASGOW
City code ☎ 041

The most loyal of Glaswegians could not deny that Scotland's largest city (population 750,000) has suffered from a bad image. The almost rural university and cathedral town was transformed by the opening up of 18thC trade routes across the Atlantic into a wealthy commercial city and the business centre for heavy manufacturing industries based in the city suburbs and outlying towns: the coal mines of Hamilton fired the steel mills of Motherwell which provided the materials for the shipyards of Govan and Clydebank. Industrialization brought its attendant social problems and the economic decline which followed has exacerbated them. The name Glasgow became synonymous with slums, alcoholism, gang warfare, sectarianism (the city's 19thC prosperity attracted massive Catholic Irish immigration) and soccer violence.

Glasgow still has daunting social and economic problems, evident in the empty shipyards of the Clyde and grim outlying housing estates such as Easterhouse and Castlemilk. But recent times have seen a real change for the better, and central Glasgow nowadays has an air of relative prosperity. An imaginative City Council has encouraged private investment, seized opportunities for central government aid mostly directed through the Glasgow-based Scottish Development Agency in recent years and also contributed heavily itself to Glasgow's future as a business centre. Milestones in this development have included the opening of the Burrell Collection in 1983 and of the Scottish Exhibition Centre in 1985 and the 1988 Garden Festival. Glasgow remains an important financial centre, albeit on a smaller scale than Edinburgh. Significant institutions include Britoil (now part of BP) and the Scottish Development Agency.

Whatever the economic fate of west Central Scotland – and many are waiting to see what reality there is behind the hype of Silicon Glen – the area's chief city, at least, has regained its self-confidence. Glaswegians can contrast their lot with that of some of the once great industrial cities of northern England and perhaps indulge themselves in what they would usually deride as an Edinburgh vice: a touch of smugness.

Arriving
Glasgow has the best air, rail and road connections of any Scottish city.

Glasgow Airport
Scotland's major airport, 8 miles/13kms west of the city, handles direct flights from throughout western Europe, all the main British cities, including 26 daily from London (Stansted, Heathrow and Gatwick), and numerous local Scottish airports. The bureau de change is open daily in summer, 8–11; winter, Sat, 8–10; Sun, 8–5. There are two VIP lounges.

Airport information ☎ 887 1111.
Nearby hotels Excelsior, Abbotsinch, Paisley ☎ 887 1212 TX 777733 ●
AE DC MC V. Next to the terminal building.
City link The airport is linked to the city by the M8 motorway which continues eastwards to Edinburgh. Access to central Glasgow is fast (15–20mins) except in rush hours when traffic jams can add up to 15mins to the journey. It is worth renting a car if you have business in Glasgow's outlying suburbs or towns; otherwise, take a taxi.

Taxi The taxi service to the city centre is convenient and reasonably priced.

Car rental Avis, Hertz, Europcar and Swan National have offices at the terminal.

Railway stations

Glasgow Central Glasgow's fine Victorian terminus handles all rail traffic from the south and west including about five trains every day from London Euston (journey time approx 6hrs). There are also fast direct connections from the Midlands and northwest England. Sleeper services operate nightly from London, Bristol and Inverness. There is a Pullman lounge, and a large taxi rank. Passenger inquiries ☎ 204 2844; sleeper reservations ☎ 221 2305.

Queen Street Handles all train services from the north and east including those from Edinburgh and Aberdeen. Inquiries ☎ 204 2844. Taxis are always available from the taxi rank on the east side of the station.

Getting around

The city centre is marginally less compact than that of Edinburgh but it is still easy to get around Glasgow, using a combination of walking with subway and taxi for longer distances within the city and car or train for visits to surrounding towns.

Walking The quickest way to travel between appointments in the city centre north of the Clyde and east of the M8 motorway is to walk. Once you get used to the street grid, finding your way around is relatively easy. Despite its reputation, Glasgow is a relatively safe city in which to walk.

Taxis Glasgow's licensed radio-linked black cabs, hailed easily on the street, are convenient and reasonably priced. Cabbies are generally very helpful. Telephone reservations: *Radio Taxis* ☎ 332 7070.

Subway Glasgow's "tube" with its tiny orange trains has a single circle line which is particularly useful for visitors with business in the West End or University areas of the city. Stations and trains are clean and the service frequent and fast.

Driving Once the visitor gets used to central Glasgow's one-way system and the urban motorway with its numerous entrances and exits, the city is a relatively easy one in which to drive. The centre is less congested than Edinburgh and easier to park in. If renting a car, *Budget* ☎ 226 4141 and *Europcar* ☎ 221 5257 have central offices.

Trains ScotRail's TransClyde trains operate an extensive service to Glasgow's suburbs and outlying towns from lower level stations at both Queen Street and Central. Services are fast, regular and convenient but many trains and stations are poorly maintained. Details of services and maps of the network are available from both Queen Street and Central. Inquiries ☎ 204 2844.

Area by area

Central Glasgow extends westwards along the north bank of the river Clyde from the High Street, the old heart of the city, as far as the river Kelvin and the University area. In the eastern end of this district are the magnificent Victorian City Chambers in George Street, still the City Council's headquarters; the Scottish Stock Exchange, in St George's Place; and Glasgow's second university, Strathclyde, with its strong technology and engineering departments.

To the west, around St Vincent Street, is the city's main commercial district with magnificent Victorian buildings recently restored and cleaned. It looks remarkably like many late-19thC North American east coast cities, with its regular street grid and massive stone buildings. At its western end are to be found the modern offices of several newer business organizations including the Scottish Development Agency as well as the Albany and Holiday Inn hotels.

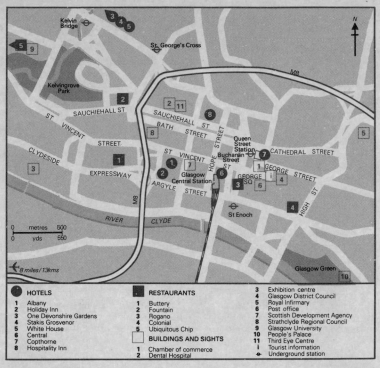

HOTELS	RESTAURANTS	3 Exhibition centre
1 Albany	1 Buttery	4 Glasgow District Council
2 Holiday Inn	2 Fountain	5 Royal Infirmary
3 One Devonshire Gardens	3 Rogano	6 Post office
4 Stakis Grosvenor	4 Colonial	7 Scottish Development Agency
5 White House	5 Ubiquitous Chip	8 Strathclyde Regional Council
6 Central		9 Glasgow University
7 Copthorne	BUILDINGS AND SIGHTS	10 People's Palace
8 Hospitality Inn		11 Third Eye Centre
	1 Chamber of commerce	i Tourist information
	2 Dental Hospital	Underground station

Across the motorway, the attractive mixed business and residential areas of Kelvinside and Woodside are overlooked by the neo-Gothic buildings of the 15thC Glasgow University, Scotland's second oldest. Beyond the University are the Byres and Western Roads areas, among the smartest of the city's residential districts. South of the Clyde, the once notorious slums of the Gorbals have been replaced by tower blocks set in green but rather empty spaces. Farther south are the prosperous suburbs of Queens Park and Pollokshaws.

Industrial hinterland

Glasgow's 19thC prosperity was built on the factories of its outlying communities. Today the formerly great shipbuilding towns of Port Glasgow and Greenock and the textile town of Paisley struggle to maintain their economies. To the north, on the opposite bank of the Clyde, another once great shipbuilding community, Clydebank, has, with considerable government aid, bravely set about developing a substantial business park. Government aid has also begun to bring new economic life to the engineering and mining towns – Wishaw, Motherwell, Hamilton – to the east of Glasgow.

Residential suburbs

Glasgow lies within easy reach of the lovely countryside of the Highland foothills and this has prompted many executives to settle in the northern suburbs of Bearsden and Milngavie as well as in the rural areas such as Blanefield just beyond. Those who prefer the attractions of the Clyde coast with its fine sailing commute into the city from towns to the west such as Helensburgh.

Hotels

At one time the now rather faded Central was the smart hotel in Glasgow. Nowadays the business traveller wishing to stay in the centre has the choice of a number of very adequate, if somewhat uninspiring, modern hotels. The exceptions are One Devonshire Gardens and the White House, both slightly to the west of the city centre, which offer more individual service.

Albany £///
Bothwell St, G2 7EN ☎ 248 2656 ⊤ₓ 77440 fax 221 8986 • AE DC MC V • 254 rooms, 3 suites, 2 restaurants, 3 bars

Well located near the city centre and the Scottish Exhibition Centre, the Albany is regarded by the business community as one of Glasgow's leading hotels. Built in 1973 it now faces competition from more recent arrivals like the neighbouring Holiday Inn, and its prices, once the highest in the city, have been moderated accordingly. In the holiday season, the lobby and reception areas may be congested with tour groups. However, the ground-floor public areas and bedrooms are spacious and luxurious, and attentive staff are always on hand. Business lunches as well as evening meals are competitively priced. 24hr room service, express check-out • 4 meeting rooms (capacity up to 15) and conference facilities for up to 800.

Holiday Inn £///
Anderston, Argyle St, G3 8RR ☎ 226 5577 ⊤ₓ 776355 fax 221 9202 • AE DC MC V • 298 rooms, 6 suites, 4 restaurants, 2 bars

The atmosphere of this popular hotel, with its plush modern decor and foyer complete with fountain and views of the swimming pool, seems to capture the optimistic exuberance of "the new Glasgow." Centrally located within a short walk of Central Station and easy access of Glasgow airport, near the Scottish Exhibition Centre and Anderston Centre, the Holiday Inn has won a well-deserved reputation as one of the best conference venues in town. Club Europe members get the exclusivity of the 12th floor, extras in the bedrooms like plants and bathrobes, free secretarial services, newspapers and express check-out. 24hr room service • pool, jacuzzi, gym, squash, saunas, solarium • 13 meeting rooms (capacity up to 800).

One Devonshire Gardens £///
Devonshire Gdns, G12 OUX ☎ 339 2001 fax 337 1663 • AE DC MC V • 8 rooms, 1 restaurant

Glasgow's most elegant hotel is situated in a Victorian terraced house in the quiet and fashionable West End of the city. Its interiors have been beautifully restored, and its restaurant, featuring often novel treatments of traditional dishes, is the best hotel restaurant in the city. The hotel's virtues reflect its small size: a sense of personal care and attention to detail. Room service: 7am–midnight.

Stakis Grosvenor £///
Grosvenor Ter, Great Western Rd, G12 OTA ☎ 339 8811 ⊤ₓ 776247 fax 334 0710 • AE DC MC V • 92 rooms, 3 suites, 3 restaurants, 3 bars

The Grosvenor is Reo Stakis's flagship hotel in his native city. Its gorgeous period appearance is only skin-deep; little of the fine Victorian facade of the West End's Grosvenor Terrace survived a devastating fire some years ago, and the entire frontage was eventually reconstructed. The plush public areas are furnished with reproduction antiques. Bedrooms are adequate, well-equipped and comfortable, staff pleasant and helpful. 24hr room service, express check-out • 5 meeting rooms (capacity up to 450).

White House £//
12 Cleveden Cres, G12 OPA
☎ *339 9375* TX *777582 fax 337 1430*
• *AE DC MC V* • *32 rooms*
The privately-owned White House has the atmosphere of a country house but is only 20mins from the centre. It attracts clients from multinational companies, many of them on lengthy stays, and is also used as a discreet haven for smaller conferences. The hotel has absorbed four houses in a quiet elegant Victorian terrace. There are no bars or public rooms, but each of the exceptionally spacious suites is equipped with a kitchen, dining area, bedroom and bathroom; and there are six mews houses with a high degree of privacy and plenty of space. All accommodation is backed up by a room service which includes meals; guests wishing to eat out are offered courtesy cars to three of Glasgow's best restaurants. Throughout the hotel, decor is of a high standard, with fine Victorian and Edwardian features lovingly retained. Room service 7am–10pm, express check-out

• conference suite with meeting rooms (capacity up to 25).

OTHER HOTELS
Central £/ *Gordon St, G1 3SF*
☎ *221 9680* TX *777771 fax 226 3948*
• *AE DC MC V.* This magnificent Victorian pile overlooking the railway station has a melancholy atmosphere of faded glory, but it retains its loyal followers among business visitors who appreciate its competitive prices and spacious bedrooms.
Copthorne £// *George Sq, G2 1DS* ☎ *332 6711* TX *778147 fax 332 4264* • *AE DC MC V.*
Hospitality Inn £// *36 Cambridge St, G2 3HN* ☎ *332 3311* TX *777334 fax 332 4050* • *Mount Charlotte* • *AE DC MC V.*

Clubs
The Glasgow business community has a fairly democratic image of itself, preferring to meet in the city's lively restaurants rather than in exclusive private clubs. The one club of any note in the centre, the *RAC* in Blythswood Square, is rather dowdy.

Restaurants
Glasgow has relatively few good restaurants for a city of its size, and so business entertaining is largely confined to a handful which as a result become crowded at peak times.

Buttery £//
652 Argyle St ☎ *221 8188* • *closed Sat L, Sun* • *AE DC MC V*
Although hidden away in the sole surviving 19thC building in an area just to the west of the urban motorway, the Buttery has won wide recognition for its imaginative food – mainly Scottish with a strong *nouvelle cuisine* influence. The restaurant occupies a converted Victorian pub with fine stained glass, but the smart waitresses and general ambience make it suitable for more formal dining.

Fountain £//
2 Woodside Cres ☎ *332 6396* • *closed Sat L, Sun* • *AE DC MC V*
The Fountain may lack the

individuality of some other Glasgow restaurants but its attractive and spacious dining room, peaceful atmosphere, subdued lights and good French food make it an excellent place for business dining. It is well used by the numerous architectural, design, advertising and other offices in the neighbourhood.

Rogano £//
11 Exchange Pl ☎ *248 4055* • *closed Sun* • *AE DC MC V*
Rogano's fine Art Deco interior dates back to its completion in the same year as the *Queen Mary* was being fitted out down the Clyde. Recent sympathetic renovation has confirmed its place as a favourite central

Glasgow restaurant and it is consequently filled at lunchtime with executives from the businesses and financial institutions in and around St Vincent Street. The Oyster Bar is an excellent place for a less formal lunch.

OTHER RESTAURANTS
It takes a courageous restaurateur to offer an adventurous and fairly pricey line in *nouvelle cuisine* in the still rather seedy surroundings of Glasgow's High Street; unfortunately the *Colonial*, 25 High St ☎ 552 1923, handicaps itself by serving its fine food in a single, rather stark room with sparse mock-Tudorish furnishings – not really the right ambience for business entertaining.

A superb wine (and whisky) list, attractive conservatory-like interior and adventurous if unpredictable cooking are the main features of the relaxed *Ubiquitous Chip*, 12 Ashton La ☎ 334 5007, which attracts a fair number of academics and media people.

Bars
Glasgow has, sadly, lost nearly all its fine, traditional pubs. However, in recent years a number of reasonable wine bars have opened. Of the many around George Square, two of the best are *Cafe Gandolfi*, 64 Albion St ☎ 552 6813, and *Babbity Bowster*, 16 Blackfriars St ☎ 552 5055. The *Belfry*, 654 Argyle St, the quiet downstairs bar of the Buttery (see *Restaurants*), provides good, simple food and a relaxed atmosphere. *De Quinceys*, 71 Renfield St, an attractively converted dairy, is a favourite central lunching place for young executives.

Entertainment
Glasgow, nominated European City of Culture for 1990, is the home of Scotland's major orchestral, opera, ballet and theatre companies. The annual Mayfest provides a popularist, Glaswegian version of Edinburgh's International Festival, while year-

round the Third Eye Centre (see *Sightseeing*) provides drama and music as well as art shows.

The best guide to what's on is *The List*, published fortnightly. Greater Glasgow Tourist Board produces a monthly guide, *Arrival*, available free in most hotels or from the Board's office (see *Local resources*).
Theatre, ballet, opera The home of the widely acclaimed Scottish Opera as well as Scottish Ballet is the *Kings Theatre*, Bath St ☎ 552 5961. The main opera productions are in the autumn and spring. The *Citizens*, Gorbals St ☎ 429 0022, Glasgow's innovative repertory theatre, enjoys a national reputation.
Music The impressive *City Hall*, Candleriggs provides a weekly venue for the Glasgow-based Scottish National Orchestra.

Shopping
Buchanan Street is Glasgow's main shopping area, and its shops include the city's leading department store *Frasers*.
Scottish goods The *Scotch House*, 87 Buchanan St, is the best place for clothing. *The Ubiquitous Chip's Wine Shop*, Ashton La, carries a wide range of malt whiskies.
Antiques and art The best place to look is in and around West Regent Street between Renfield Street and Blythswood Square. Among the outstanding galleries in the area are the *Fine Art Society*, 134 Blythswood St, and *T. & R. Annan*, 130 W Campbell St.

Sightseeing
At one time the visitor to Glasgow in search of sights was all too often directed to the Edinburgh train. The opening of the Burrell Collection has changed all this, not only shifting visitors' perceptions of the city but also encouraging Glaswegians to promote their city's other attractions more energetically.
Burrell Collection Assembled in the first half of this century by a Glasgow shipping magnate, Sir William

Burrell, this superb collection was opened by the Queen in 1983. It is housed in an award-winning purpose-built museum which takes full advantage of its attractive parkland setting. Apart from some good Impressionist drawings and paintings, almost everything is pre-18thC, and the range is vast: exquisite Oriental rugs and ceramics, 17thC European tapestries and furniture, medieval stone and stained glass, statuary and mosaics from Rome and Egypt. Few other collections in Britain have treasures of such quality. *Pollok Park. Open Mon–Sat, 10–5; Sun, 2–5.* Also in the Park, within a 10min walk of the Burrell, is *Pollok House*, a mid-18thC mansion with a exceptional collection of Spanish Old Masters. *Open Mon–Sat, 10–5; Sun, 2–5.*

City Chambers Visitors wishing to gain some idea of Glasgow's 19thC mercantile wealth and pride should take one of the guided tours around the sumptuous Victorian City Chambers. The marbled entrance hall and the Faience Corridor constructed entirely of ceramic tiles are of particular note. *George Sq. Open Mon–Thu, 10.30–2.30 (subject to functions).*

Hunterian Museum and Art Gallery Glasgow University's Hunterian Museum, established in the 18thC through the bequest of a former student, William Hunter, contains a particularly fine archaeological and geological collection including Hunter's own very interesting coin cabinets. The nearby art gallery has a collection which includes a good group of paintings by James McNeill Whistler. *Glasgow University. Open Mon–Fri, 9.30–5; Sat, 9.30–1.*

People's Palace Extensive and charming collection of material relating to the history of Glasgow. *Glasgow Green. Open Mon–Sat, 10–5; Sun, 2–5.*

Charles Rennie Mackintosh Society The former Queens Cross Church, designed by Mackintosh in 1897, now serves as an information centre for those interested in Glasgow's great Art Nouveau architect. *870 Garscube Rd. Open Tue, Thu, Fri, 12 noon–5; Sun, 2.30–5.*

Third Eye Centre One of Scotland's leading venues for modern art exhibitions. The Centre also has a good drama, film and music programme. *350 Sauchiehall St. Open Tue–Sat, 10–5.30; Sun, 2–5.30.*

Guided tours The best way to see the city is by one of the reasonably priced taxi tours operated by *Radio Taxis* ☎ 331 2424.

Out of town

Glasgow lies within sight of the Highland hills and a drive of less than an hour takes the visitor well into the beautiful countryside of the Trossachs and Loch Lomond-side. Those with more time to spare are recommended to take the 2hr scenic route to Inveraray, a picturesque 18thC village which boasts the castle home of the Dukes of Argyll, open to the public, on the shore of Loch Fyne.

Spectator sports
Soccer Glasgow is the home of Scottish football. The national ground is located at *Hampden Park* ☎ 632 1275. Local football is dominated by the Old Firm" of Celtic and Rangers (by tradition Catholic and Protestant respectively), but in different parts of the city and in the outlying areas there are equally strong allegiances to such local teams as Partick Thistle, Airdrie and Motherwell. Matches are generally good-natured if slightly rowdy affairs and are safe for spectators.

Keeping fit
Like their counterparts in other Scottish cities, Glasgow executives tend to view keeping fit in terms of a round of golf, but the younger generation of Glaswegians are becoming more interested in newer forms of exercise.

Sports and health clubs Of the various private clubs in the city centre, *Ritchies Health and Fitness*

Club, 11 Oswald St ☎ 248 5455, which has a gym, sauna, jacuzzi and solarium, is open to business visitors.
Golf The smart club, and home of the Glasgow Open, is *Haggs Castle* golf course, Dembreck Rd ☎ 427 0480.
Jogging Glasgow's numerous public parks, which include Pollok, Kelvingrove and the Botanic Garden, are good places for jogging. The walkway along the river Kelvin in Kelvingrove Park is also popular.

Local resources
Business services
The major hotels can provide or organize basic services. *Executive Services*, 11 Bothwell St ☎ 221 7867, and *Lexus*, 181 Pitt St ☎ 221 5266, both provide technical translations, photocopying, telex, fax, secretarial and word processing services. *Executive Services* can also provide short-term office accommodation.
Photocopying and printing *Prontaprint* ☎ 221 3615, *Kallkwik* ☎ 552 1597.

Communications
International delivery DHL ☎ 889 4242.
Local delivery QED ☎ 248 2440
Post office Main office: George Sq.
Telex and fax See *Business services*.

Conference/exhibition centres
The *Scottish Exhibition and Conference Centre* ☎ 248 3000, opened in 1985, occupies a 64-acre riverside site 1 mile/1.6kms to the west of the city centre. Its facilities include five linked halls ranging in size from 8,370 sq feet/775 sq metres to 108,000 sq feet/10,000 sq metres, a 2,000-seat auditorium and a 230-seat seminar suite. The Centre has become the established location for a number of Scotland's main trade shows, including those of the motor, travel, printing and building trades. Road access is from the adjacent Clyde Expressway, and there is ample parking space. There is also a frequent TransClyde rail link from

Central Station to Finnieston. Details of other conference facilities in Glasgow are available from the Greater Glasgow Tourist Board, 39 St Vincent Pl, G1 2ER ☎ 227 4885.

Emergencies
Bureaux de change The bureau de change at Central Station is open daily, 8.30–9.30.
Hospitals 24hr casualty department: *Glasgow Royal Infirmary*, 86 Castle St ☎ 552 3535. Emergency dental treatment: *Dental Hospital*, 378 Sauchiehall St ☎ 332 7020, Mon–Fri, 9–3.30; Sun, 10.30–12noon.
Pharmacies T. S. McNee, 382 Springburn Rd ☎ 558 5209, Mon–Fri, 9–9; Sat, 9.30–5.30; Sun, 12–5.
Police Main station: Stewart St ☎ 332 1113.

Government offices
Glasgow District Council, City Chambers, G2 1DU ☎ 221 9600, and *Strathclyde Regional Council*, 20 India St, G2 4PF ☎ 204 2900, are the two local government authorities. The *Scottish Development Agency*, 120 Bothwell St, G2 7JP ☎ 248 2700, provides aid for businesses wishing to establish branches in Scotland as well as contacts with a wide variety of Scottish firms.

Information sources
Business information Glasgow *Chamber of Commerce*, 30 George Sq, G1 1EU ☎ 204 2121, can provide information about members' products and services.
Local media The daily *Glasgow Herald* provides a good coverage of business activities in the city.
Tourist information Greater Glasgow Tourist Board, 35–39 St Vincent Pl ☎ 227 4880. See *Entertainment* for guides to what's on in the city.

Thank-yous
Confectionery Frasers, Buchanan St. ☎ 221 6401. (see *Shopping*).
Florist Stems ☎ 339 8070.
Wine Merchants Ubiquitous Chip Wine Shop ☎ 334 7109.